FEMINIST
FRAMEWORKS

FEMINIST FRAMEWORKS

Alternative
Theoretical Accounts
of the
Relations between
Women and Men

THIRD EDITION

Alison M. Jaggar
University of Colorado at Boulder

Paula S. Rothenberg
The William Paterson College of New Jersey

Boston, Massachusetts   Burr Ridge, Illinois
Dubuque, Iowa   Madison, Wisconsin   New York, New York
San Francisco, California   St. Louis, Missouri

McGraw-Hill

A Division of The McGraw-Hill Companies

This book is printed on acid-free paper.

FEMINIST FRAMEWORKS
Alternative Theoretical Accounts of the Relations between Women and Men

9 10 11 12 13 14 BKMBKM 9 9 8 7

ISBN 0-07-032253-8

This book was set in Times Roman by The Clarinda Company.
The editors were Cynthia Ward and Tom Holton;
the production supervisor was Al Rihner.
The cover was designed by Nicholas Krenitsky and Karen K. Quigley.

Library of Congress Cataloging-in-Publication Data

Feminist frameworks: alternative theoretical accounts of the
   relations between women and men / [edited by] Alison M. Jaggar,
   Paula S. Rothenberg.—3rd ed.
      p.   cm.
   Includes bibliographical references and index.
   ISBN 0-07-032253-8
   1. Feminism—United States.   2. Sexism.   3. Social institutions.
   4. Women's rights.   5. Social change.   I. Jaggar, Alison M.
   II. Rothenburg, Paula S., (date).
   HQ1426.F47   1993
   305.42'0973—dc20   92-30611

About the Authors

Alison M. Jaggar is Professor of Philosophy and Women's Studies at the University of Colorado at Boulder. She has also taught at the University of Illinois at Chicago, the University of California at Los Angeles, and Rutgers University, where she held the Laurie New Jersey Chair in Women's Studies. Her books include *Feminist Politics and Human Nature* and *Gender/Body/Knowledge: Feminist Reconstruction of Being and Knowing*, coedited with Susan R. Bordo. Currently she is working on two books, *Living with Contradictions: Moral Controversies in Feminism*, and *Toward a Feminist Conception of Practical Reason*. Jaggar was a founder member of the Society for Women in Philosophy and is past chair of the American Philosophical Association Committee on the Status of Women. She works with local feminist organizations and sees feminist scholarship as inseparable from feminist activism.

Paula S. Rothenberg is Director of The New Jersey Project: Integrating the Scholarship on Gender, a statewide curriculum transformation project, and is Professor of Philosophy and Women's Studies at The William Paterson College of New Jersey where she has taught since 1969. She serves on the Advisory Board of the New Jersey Multicultural Studies Project and is a former Regional Coordinator of the National Women's Studies Association Mid-Atlantic Region. Rothenberg is the coeditor of *Philosophy Now* and *Ethics in Perspective* and the author of *Race, Class, and Gender in the United States*. Her articles and essays appear in journals and anthologies in philosophy, women's studies, education, and African-American Studies. She has also lectured and consulted on multicultural and gender curriculum transformation at colleges and universities across the country.

Contents

PART 2
WHY THEORY?

PART 3
THEORIES OF WOMEN'S SUBORDINATION

PART 4
PRACTICE: CONTEMPORARY ISSUES THROUGH THE LENSES

Introduction

NEW VOICES, NEW FEMINISMS

The world in general and U.S. society in particular have changed a great deal since the early 1980s when we began preparing a much revised second edition of this book. The differences are even greater if we look back to the mid-1970s when we first met and started work on what would become the first edition of *Feminist Frameworks.* Yet, against a background of enormous change, we find remarkable and disturbing similarities in the condition of women in this society and all over the globe. Although many young women and men entering college today harbor the belief that the situation of women in the United States improved markedly twenty years ago as a result of the movements for women's liberation and civil rights, one need only look at the increasing restrictions on women's rights to abortion, the ever-increasing number of women and children living in poverty, the escalating violence against women, and the persistent and shocking absence of women in significant numbers and diversity from the U.S. Congress and other legislative and policy-making bodies around the world to realize that things have not changed very much for most women. While some women indeed are fortunate enough to enjoy much greater life opportunities than their mothers, the life situations of most women may even have deteriorated.

The first edition of *Feminist Frameworks* was conceived in a period of intense excitement and controversy as millions of women in Western Europe and North America came to see themselves as oppressed and moved into action against that oppression. The new feminists of the late 1960s and early 1970s exposed every modern institution to critical scrutiny. Like their predecessors of the late nineteenth and early twentieth centuries, these feminists criticized male dominance in education, religion, government, and the economy. What especially distinguished them from earlier feminists, however, was their challenge to the organization of so-called personal life: marriage, family, and sexuality.

The first edition of *Feminist Frameworks* reflected these concerns and placed them within the dominant debates of the day: on the one hand, the debate within the left concerning the relationship between women's subordination and capitalism; on the other hand, the debate within feminism concerning the relationship between women's subordination and normative heterosexuality or, conversely, between women's liberation and lesbianism. Although a few articles by or about women of color were included in the first edition of *Feminist Frameworks,* the issue of race was treated in an extremely perfunctory manner. This reflected the fact that, in spite of the purportedly comprehensive nature of its social critique, the feminism of that period often was embarrassingly narrow. While claiming to represent the interests of all women, it was in fact a feminism whose most prominent spokespeople were white, middle-class, and often oblivious to the ways in which race, ethnicity, and class impacted on women's lives to inform their possibilities and create their personhood. It is ironic, of course, that a political and intellectual movement that had begun by criticizing traditional institutions and scholarship for leaving out women's concerns and perspectives should itself define "women" and "feminism" in ways that excluded the experience and perspectives of large numbers of women of color—though it did address to some extent the concerns of poor and working-class women.

By the time the second edition of *Feminist Frameworks* was in preparation, feminist theory was beginning to come to terms with what amounted to its racist bias. Our second edition responded to this shift by adding a new section of writings by and about women of color under the heading "Feminism and Women of Color." While we did not think these writings were intended as another comprehensive feminist framework in the sense of offering a radically alternative analysis of women's subordination, it was clear to us that they offered a distinctive perspecvtive on social reality, one that could not be subsumed under any of the existing frameworks.

Our inclusion of "Feminism and Women of Color" appeared at the time as a significant expansion and redefinition of feminist theory. In retrospect, however, it is clear that we still marginalized those voices. Perhaps this was unavoidable. Many women of color writing at that time were concerned primarily with pointing out the deficiencies and distortions of writings generated by white middle-class women in the name of all women; they were only beginning the process of elaborating the alternative perspectives that would soon become the basis for their radical overhaul of feminist theory. Much of the writing by women of color included in the second edition of *Feminist Frameworks* thus reflects a kind of dialogue between women of color and feminism; indeed, the very topic heading we chose implied a separation between the two. It is interesting to remember that virtually none of the pieces we selected at that time by women of color had been published originally in academic women's studies publications. Instead, they had appeared originally in the popular press, including *Essence* and *Ms.,* and in black studies periodicals, such as *The Black Scholar,* or were excerpted from full-length books by thinkers such as bell hooks and Angela Davis.

Unquestionably the biggest change in feminism since the publication of the last edition of *Feminist Frameworks* is the way in which issues of race and ethnicity have now been recognized as integral to a feminist perspective. Unfortunately, this does not mean that the voices of women from every racial or ethnic group even within North America can yet claim a full and fair hearing. Writings of African-American women and Latina women have so far achieved the broadest distribution, while the voices of Asian-American women, Native Americans, Pacific Islanders, and others have had considerably less success being heard. Nontheless, feminist theory for the most part has come to recognize the ways in which race and ethnicity, class, sexuality, and a host of other variables are indissolubly linked in the construction of women's experience. While feminist theory acknowledges no single orthodoxy and continues to be characterized by vigorous debate, many feminists are no longer willing to apply the term "feminist" to any perspective not thoroughly multicultural and inclusive in its starting point.

This shift in feminist theoretical perspectives is reflected in the third edition of *Feminist Frameworks* by the elimination of the old section "Feminism and Women of Color" and the addition of two new frameworks, "Multicultural Feminism" and "Global Feminism." No longer presented merely as voices of women of color in dialogue with feminism, our addition of these two frameworks recognizes issues of race and ethnicity as essential to defining feminist discourse.

Whereas "Multicultural Feminism" addresses issues of race and ethnicity primarily as they emerge in North America, "Global Feminism" looks at the situation of women in other parts of the world. Although the second edition of *Feminist Frameworks* included several articles with an international focus, the addition of "Global Feminism" as a distinct framework reflects our belief that feminists must understand and address women's subordination in a world perspective. As the world economic system becomes increasingly integrated and both the privileges and the exploitation of women in Western Europe and North America are tied increasingly tightly to the privileges and exploitation of women around the globe, it becomes ever more important for feminism to think and act globally as well as locally.

STRUCTURAL CHANGES IN THE THIRD EDITION OF *FEMINIST FRAMEWORKS*

This third edition differs from previous editions of *Feminist Frameworks* not simply in the addition of new selections or even entirely new frameworks. It is also structually different from the previous editions, most evidently in that it now comprises four rather than three parts. The new part is Part Two, and it is entitled "Why Theory?"

"Why Theory?" is a response to the second major development that occurred in academic feminism during the decade of the 1980s. Partly as a result of the justified complaints by women of color that previous feminist theory had excluded them, feminists in the 1980s expressed a new skepticism about the desirability and even the possibility of theory that aimed to produce broad generalizations and comprehensive social analyses. While this skepticism was partly rooted in the perceived inadequacies of previous feminist theories, it also reflected a shift in the larger intellectual environment, particularly North Americans' increasing acceptance of European postmodern insights. Feminists of the 1980s thus confronted new questions about the social construction of knowledge, the positioning of the knower, the possibility of large-scale generalizations, and even the viability of the category "woman." The selections in Part Two, "Why Theory?," address these questions in various ways, reflecting on what constitutes "theory" and about the value and consequences of privileging theory in the first place.

Influenced by these and other feminist reflections on the nature of theory, we have to some extent modified our previous understandings of feminist frameworks. Although we have retained the title *Feminist Frameworks,* the positions we present vary not only in their commitment to feminism and in their degree of comprehensiveness, but even in their theoretical aspirations. The newer frameworks, unlike some of the older ones, do not pretend to provide final or authoritative accounts of women's subordination. Later in this introduction, as well as in the introduction to Part Three, we shall discuss the significance of this change.

As in previous editions, the framework we identify as conservatism is far from feminist insofar as it rationalizes rather than opposes women's subordination. As on previous occasions, we seriously debated the inclusion of this framework but decided in the end that, because biological determinism remains so influential, some of the classic biodeterminist rationales for the subordination of women still held an interest that went beyond the merely historical. An innovation of this edition, however, is our inclusion of an incisive feminist critique of biological determinism in the section on conservatism. We think this innovation is justified on pedagogical grounds, but it is, of course, a departure from the principles of organization used in structuring previous editions of *Feminist Frameworks.* The remainder of Part Three, "Theories of Women's Subordination," conforms to the general structure of previous editions, although it adds the two new frameworks described above.

Part Four represents a last and major departure from our original principles of organization. Here we have abandoned our earlier system of organizing the selections according to the various frameworks they represent. When we first began work on *Feminist Frameworks,* it was relatively easy to look at essays and articles presenting some perspective on feminist practice or everyday life and recognize them as aspects of one or another theoretical framework. Feminists have learned from each other over the past two decades, however, and recent feminist discussions of practical issues are often much less simplistic than earlier ones. Even as we were preparing the second edition of *Feminist Frameworks,* we were beginning to be uneasy with grouping some articles according to frameworks because it seemed increasingly that we were in danger of oversimplifying or distorting the author's position. This problem is compounded, now that we have added two more frameworks, by the difficulty of reproducing the sheer quantity of material necessary to represent *seven* different frameworks. In consequence, we have finally decided to abandon the original structure that grouped the selections according to framework. We felt that continuing to do this would devote too much space to material whose interest is now primarily historical and would leave too little space for the more recent and theoretically sophisticated discussions of which we want to include as many as possible.

This does not mean that it is no longer useful to read feminist writing in light of the old categories or frameworks. Quite the contrary. We believe that the ability to evaluate the various feminist recommendations for practice continues to require that we identify the theoretical underpinnings or assumptions of those recommendations. The challenge for the reader now is to discover the ways in which many of the more practical writings contained in Part Four incorporate theoretical assumptions that are derived simultaneously from several of the frameworks. Identifying the various strands of theorizing incorporated into any given essay is crucial to determining its coherence and comprehensiveness and to evaluating different approaches to conceptualizing and solving social problems.

FRAMEWORKS, LENSES AND CHANGING CONCEPTIONS OF THEORY

Readers familiar with the previous two editions of *Feminist Frameworks* will notice that this volume introduces the metaphor of "lenses" to identify the multiple perspectives incorporated in the various feminist frameworks. Our adoption of this metaphor signals something of a change in our conception of feminist frameworks.

As we presented them in our earlier editions, feminist frameworks were integrated theories of women's place both in our present society and in the new society that feminists were struggling to build. We saw feminist frameworks as including descriptive, explanatory, and normative elements, offering both comprehensive analyses of the nature and causes of women's subordination and correlated sets of proposals for ending it. Thus, we assumed that the main task of feminist theory was to develop a framework that would do all of the following: It would accurately describe the social realities of women's subordination; it would provide a deep explanation of how those realities came to be; and it would offer recommendations for transforming those realities that would reflect feminist values, provide a guide in most situations, and be efficacious in ending women's subordination.

Obviously, we expected a lot of our theorists—but in the 1970s things were moving so rapidly that our expectations did not seem unreasonable. As we noted at the beginning of this introduction, contemporary feminist theory emerged in a period of intense political activity—and it generated intellectual activity that was equally intense. Many women were moved to action by feminism's revelations of, for instance, the widespread extent of discrimination, harassment, rape, and domestic violence. They—we—were also excited by the boldness and incisiveness of feminism's theoretical moves—that gender was analytically separable from sex, that the personal was political, that rape was about violence rather than sexuality, that sexual harassment was a form of discrimination, that women's "choices" in fact were coerced. On top of all this, we were inspired by the new moral and political visions offered by feminism: visions of a world of freedom and justice, not to mention physical and economic security, for women, a world without gender and without class. Feminist theory was providing answers to questions that often we had barely recognized, and we were exhilarated by its descriptive, explanatory, and moral power.

The sorts of high expectations held by feminists in the 1970s are common in the early stages of any theoretical development. In these early stages, conceptual boundaries are challenged, paradigms are shifted, and theorists, using broad brush strokes, paint entirely new pictures of reality. As new paradigms are established in any field, however, their limitations become apparent, early formulations are revised, and extravagant hopes that the new theories will answer all significant questions must be reduced to something more realistic. What Thomas Kuhn[1] calls "normal science" replaces "revolutionary science." Twenty-five years of disciplinary and interdisciplinary research have demonstrated that much early feminist theory was not only enormously visionary and fruitful but also embarrassingly simplistic. This quarter-century of scholarly work, coupled with contemporary postmodern challenges to the possibility of complete and comprehensive ("totalizing") social analyses (described in our introduction to Part Two), has made many feminists skeptical that any single framework will be adequate for all situations. We share this skepticism.

Our suspicion of theoretical frameworks that purport to be entirely complete, comprehensive, and final does not mean that we reject all large-scale social theorizing. As we describe in our introduction to Part Three, however, the maturing of feminist scholarship inevitably has resulted in a shift away from general foundational issues to more specific and detailed analyses. Formulating the category of gender and separating it from sex was a tremendous theoretical breakthrough because it made visible a system of male domination that until then had seemed to be an unchangeable fact of nature. What feminists have now come to realize, however, is that there is no generic woman; every woman has some specific class, race, age, marital status, etc. Consequently, our theoretical as well as our political interests have moved away from considering women in general, what we used to call questions of "women as women," toward exploring the ways in which gender is necessarily shaped in conjunction with other systems of domination.

In its effort to conceptualize the multiplicity of systems of domination to which many women are subjected, earlier feminist theory often adopted a kind of "add-on" approach. For example, in a classic 1970 essay, "Double Jeopardy," Francis Beale[2] argued that black women suffered from double (sex and race) or triple (and poverty) oppression. By contrast, "Multiple Jeopardy," a essay published twenty years later by Deborah King and excerpted in Part Three, argues for understanding the specific oppression of black women in terms of multiplication rather than addition. King denies that racism, sexism, and classism are simply independent systems that all happen to impinge in black women who therefore confront racism *plus* sexism *plus* classism. Instead, King argues, these various systems modify and intensify each other so that black women's oppression is qualitatively as well as quantitatively different from that of other women. Black women confront racism *times* sexism *times* classism. King's work clearly builds on Beale's, even to the extent of echoing Beale's title, but her metaphor of multiplication seems to do a better job of conveying the ways in which various systems of domination may interact with and transform each other.

Our metaphor of lenses expresses a similar point. In this book, lenses represent the categories feminists use to organize our understandings of social reality. Even though, as we explain in our introduction to Part Three, feminists often used to insist that one or another category had more explanatory power than all the rest, feminists nowadays generally acknowledge that women's subordination can be understood adequately only in terms of several categories. The metaphor of lenses, which may be superimposed on each other, is intended in part to convey how our perceptions are enriched and transformed when we interpret the subordination of women simultaneously in terms of several categories—or view it simultaneously through several lenses.

The lens metaphor has additional significance in context of the fact that few feminists any longer insist on unswerving loyalty to a single theoretical framework. Instead, feminists increasingly recognize that different theoretical approaches are likely to be useful in different circumstances and for different purposes. People typically employ different lenses depending on what they are studying, their location with respect to the object of study, the condition of their eyes, and the purposes of their investigation. The metaphor of lenses expresses the recognition that feminist theories ultimately are tools designed for a practical purpose—the purpose of understanding women's subordination in order to end it. The metaphor also suggests the flexibility of feminist conceptual tools and the openness and contingency of our theoretical choices.

We do not think it possible to stipulate in advance which lenses will be appropriate to any given situation. We find it almost unimaginable that a feminist investigation, dedicated by definition to understanding women's subordination, could ever dispense with the lens of gender; but we also recognize that using the lens of gender alone is likely to result in some specific group being taken to represent all women and consequently in distorted perceptions. Even though we know that several lenses are generally necessary to avoid monovision, however, we cannot say in advance of any particular investigation precisely what lenses those shoud be. Clearly, different lenses will make visible different features of situations, but which features most deserve emphasis on any given occasion depends on a variety of factors and will be partially a value judgment, even, in a broad sense, a political judgment.

As we stated at the end of our general introduction to each of the previous editions of *Feminist Frameworks,* feminist theories are designed for a practical purpose: They are tools for improving women's condition. But which tools are best adapted for that purpose? What account of women's situation is most illuminating? Which proposals for social change are most conducive to human well-being and fulfillment? Now, more than ever, we believe that these questions can be answered only in the context of the feminist stuggle. We believe that the adequacy of each of the frameworks presented is to be measured ultimately by its usefulness for building a better society. We have never viewed the feminist frameworks as setting up blueprints for the position of women in future utopias. Instead, we have found it more helpful to view feminist theorizing as a search for the conditions under which women will be able to exercise significantly free choice about our own future position in society. In our view, as we have stated in previous editions, liberation is not a clearly defined end state but rather a continual process. To look at feminist theories in this pragmatic, even political, way helps to avoid abstract speculations about the ultimate nature of liberation and encourages us to focus instead on the specific institutions that limit our choices. We may then evaluate feminist frameworks according to their success in identifying the conditions that prevent us from freely choosing which our potentialities we wish to fulfill.

We believe that every position presented in this book has contributed valuable insights to feminist theory; we also believe that each of these positions has blind spots and limitations. By presenting the major feminist frameworks in a way that demonstrates both the continuities and the contrasts between them, we intend to inspire critical evaluation of each theory's contributions and flaws, strengths and weaknesses. In this way, we hope that our book will contribute to developing even better understandings of women's subordination—and move us toward a world no longer structured by dominance and subordination.

IN ACKNOWLEDGMENT

As with previous editions, many people have contributed to this book. First among them, as always, are the authors whose writing is included; we are extremely grateful to them for allowing us to reprint their work. In addition many people, including our students, have given us comments on the two previous editions of this book and on this manuscript. Although we cannot thank each one by name, we would like them to know how much we appreciated all their suggestions. We are especially grateful to the following people for their help: Risa Anderson, Alison Bailey, Harry Brod, Lori Gruen, Wendy Kolmar, Marcia Lind, Carol Sheffield, Pamela Vose, and the anonymous McGraw-Hill reviewers. Paula thanks Martina Nowak and Judy Baker Fronfield and Alison thanks Irene Diehl, Norma Nungester, Martha Leahy, and Amy Wagner for their help with various aspects of manuscript preparation. We are also grateful to all the people at McGraw-Hill who worked on our book, especially Tom Holton and our patient and ever optimistic editor, Cynthia Ward. Finally, Paula would like to thank her family for their continuing goodwill, patience and humor, and Alison is grateful for the continuing support of her family, especially David's willingness to resolve computer glitches.

Alison M. Jaggar
Paula S. Rothenberg

NOTES

1. Thomas Kuhn: *The Structure of Scientific Revolutions,* University of Chicago Press, 1962.
2. Frances Beale: "Double Jeopardy: To Be Black and Female," Toni Cade (ed.), in *The Black Woman,* Signet, New York, 1970.

PART 1

Continuing Problems

What is the situation of women and men in the world today? Ask that question of diverse populations and you will find enormous differences in the way women and men of different classes, different racial and ethnic groups, different nationalities, and different sexual orientations respond. Where some believe that we have come close to establishing a society, if not yet a world, of relative equality and justice, others maintain that vast inequalities of opportunity, treatment, and condition continue to separate us—holding deadly implications for many in the United States and the majority of those on the planet. Still others believe that the pendulum has swung too far in the other direction, tipping the balance of power and privilege in favor of those previously disenfranchised. In Part 1 of this book we examine some of the problems that confront women and men at the close of the twentieth century, problems ranging from immediate and seemingly "personal" issues that women and men address in their relations with each other every day to issues of violence and systemic exploitation that literally span the globe and shape relations not only between individuals but between entire nations and populations.

Currently, women make up a little more than half the world's population. Most women are not of European descent, although white women still dominate numerically as well as in other ways in the United States. Of every 100 women in the United States today, 13 are African American, 8 are Hispanic/Latina, 84 are white, and 3 are of other racial/ethnic groups. Projections suggest that by the middle of the twenty-first century, of 100 women, 16 will be African American, 17 will be Hispanic/Latina/Chicana, 75 will be white, and 9 will be of other racial/ethnic groups.[1] In spite of considerable media hype to the contrary, and even in light of the very real economic and social gains made by some groups of women, current statistics continue to paint a disturbing

1

picture of the ways in which differences among people impact on opportunity and achievement.

On the surface, the lives of young women today often appear to some to be very different from those of their mothers. The majority of women today either work or are looking for work outside the home. Entering the work force early, they continue to work outside the home even after having children, and the gap between male and female earnings, at least among college-educated workers between the ages of eighteen and twenty-four, has decreased considerably.[2] Women are marrying later, and more women are choosing not to marry. The number of out-of-wedlock births has increased steadily over the past several decades, with the greatest increases in such births occurring among white women. Interestingly, while white women are more likely to keep their babies than in the past, they are twice as likely to give them up if they are girls. More women divorce than ever before, and more head single-parent families. More women are receiving higher education, and more manage to enter professions traditionally regarded as exclusively male.[3] On the other hand, though women make up the majority of those in college and on average get better grades, men are still more likely to graduate, and women with four years of college earn just about the same salary as men who have only a high school diploma.[4] According to U.S. Census Bureau figures for 1989, the earnings for people twenty-five and older with four or more years of college showed white men averaging $41,090 a year and black men $31,380, while white women earned $27,440 and black women averaged $29,730.[5] And statistics indicate that the pay gap between full-time working men and women grows wider as they get older.[6] The work force continues to reflect gender and race segregation, with the majority of women, especially women of color, continuing to work in low-paying, dead-end jobs traditionally defined as "women's work."[7]

It is not surprising, then, to find that in families where children stay with the mother after the parents separate, income drops an average of 37 percent in four months.[8] After divorce, women and children experience a 73 percent decline in their standard of living, while the man's standard of living actually increases by 42 percent.[9] While 16.2 percent of all families live in poverty, 46 percent of all mother-child families live in poverty, with 60.7 percent of mother-child Hispanic/Latina families, 59.5 percent of mother-child African-American families, and 38.7 percent of white mother-child families living at or below the poverty level.[10] One out of eight children in America under the age of twelve misses meals because there is no money to buy food.[11] An infant is born into poverty every thirty-five seconds in the United States, and women and their children constitute the majority of those in poverty in this country. White households in the United States have ten times the median wealth of black households and eight times that of Hispanics.[12]

One of the more disturbing things about these patterns is how little attention they receive. As suggested by the excerpt from Ruth Sidel's study *On Her Own: Growing Up in the Shadow of the American Dream,* which opens Part 1, the expectations many women have for their lives are shaped more by media representations of the good life and media stereotypes of "superwomen" having it all than by a realistic understanding of the economic realities women face in society today. The increase in women's labor force participation we have witnessed over the past two decades has not been accompanied by a proportionate decrease in women's family or household responsibilities. As Sidel and others suggest, changes in the socially acceptable roles currently available to women have come largely through adding on new responsibilities and possibilities to those already assigned to them rather than through structural changes in social institutions or interpersonal relationships.

The persistence of labor force segregation combined with the lack of comprehensive, high-quality health care and child care continues to be a major obstacle to a decent quality of life for most women and children in the U.S. today. Women enter a work force where occupational segregation is increasing, with nearly 80 percent of working women holding jobs as secretaries, administrative support workers, and salesclerks. "Women represent less than one half of one percent of top corporate managers, less than 6% of law partners, less than 8% of federal and state judges and a mere 10% of tenured faculty at 4 year institutions and 3 or 4 percent at ivy league colleges."[13] Even apart from occupational segregation, men generally earn more than women even in the same occupation. The gap between earnings of full-time women and men workers, which widens as we grow older, reflects not only labor force segregation but also the existence of what many refer to as a "glass ceiling" which functions effectively to prevent women of all colors and men of color from advancing beyond a certain point within the company hierarchy.

Once employed, women face the task of obtaining safe and affordable quality day care for their infants and preschool children and before- and after-school care for children of school age. Even when acceptable child care arrangements can be made, a rarity for the majority of women in the United States today, parents, most often mothers, must find a way to arrange care for children who are too ill to attend school or day care and locate and pay for health care services for their families. Further, women who have traditionally borne the burden of child care within the family now increasingly find themselves assuming the burden of parental care in a society which has succeeded in extending the life span of some portions of the population without taking any steps to ensure the quality of that increased longevity. As reported in "Trading Places," an article included in Part 1, "More than half the women who care for elderly relatives also work outside the home and nearly 40 percent are still raising children of their own."

Once in the workplace, whether it be factory, office, boardroom, or classroom, women frequently find themselves the object of sexual harassment, with pay increases, promotions, and even continued employment often contingent upon sexual favors for male supervisors. Women students and workers often face the difficult choice of risking loss of reputation, credentials, references, or employment by reporting the harassment versus living with the humiliation and fear that result from allowing harassing behavior to go unchallenged.

Women continue to find themselves caught in a double bind by a society that insists women should make themselves feminine and attractive and then blames them for provoking unwanted sexual attention. While many young women today report feeling much less constrained by social images of femininity and female beauty than their mothers' generation, many social commentators report a renewed emphasis on the importance of a woman's appearance, and popular culture is once again conveying the message that success for women is directly related to conforming to prevailing ideals of feminine attractiveness. Where in the past models used to be 8 percent thinner than the average woman, today models are a whopping 23 percent thinner and the horrific rise in anorexia and bulimia indicates that we are internalizing society's messages about what constitutes at least one aspect of female beauty with alarming consequences.[14]

The issue of who will control our bodies has long been of central importance in women's lives. While all Africans brought to this country as slaves were forced to live and work under conditions of extreme cruelty, brutality, and exploitation, African-American women under slavery faced the additional horror of rape or forced mating at the hands of their white masters, who claimed the right to use their bodies for breeding, pleasure, or both. Later generations of Latina, African-American, and poor white women have found their bodies the objects of equally racist social and economic policies which have imposed forced sterilization on many. For centuries women have fought for the right to bear children by choice and with dignity and have struggled to claim or protect their bodies from the demands of fathers, brothers, uncles, husbands, mentors, employers, and the state. Although *Roe v. Wade* guaranteed the legal right to abortion in 1973, a series of Supreme Court decisions since that time has permitted states to constrain abortions in many ways, making it difficult or impossible for many women to exercise that right. Two of the selections in this section draw attention to the ever-increasing state restrictions on women's right to choose.

Partly as a result of the women's movement and changes in women's roles, men too are questioning the economic and social responsibilities assigned to them by gender, race, and class stereotyping, and many books and workshops now encourage men to think about becoming "the new man." While some men's organizations are genuinely pro-feminist, the ones that get media attention are often quite misogynist, blaming women rather than social/political and economic forces for men's alienation or discontent. Men of all racial and social groups find themselves constrained by a series of myths about masculinity that deprive them of genuinely intimate relationships with women as well as other men and often keep them emotionally and physically removed from their children. Yet, these same men are often reluctant to examine the effects of male privilege on their lives, let alone relinquish that privilege in order to construct new and different images of self and new forms of relationships.

When we shift our focus from industrialized nations such as the United States, we find that centuries of focusing on the lives of elite women in the West have left us extraordinarily ignorant about the lives of women and men in the majority of countries in the world. As Jessie Bernard has written, "Since the global female world even at the local level is only now in the process of becoming visible, writing about it must of necessity be tentative."[15] However, we do know that while our condition varies widely, "overall two-thirds of the world's illiterates are women and the vast majority of the poor, the starving, the least educated . . . are women. Women and children make up 90 percent of all refugee populations."[16] Part 1 of *Feminist Frameworks* includes several articles that offer a glimpse of some of the most basic issues of survival faced by women throughout the world. Along with the selections that focus on women and men in the United States, they provide a suggestive rather than an exhaustive or complete picture of the world in which we live and of the problems we confront as we prepare to enter the twenty-first century.

NOTES

1 Cynthia Taeuber: *Statistical Handbook on Women in America,* Oryx Press, Phoenix, Ariz., 1991, p. 1.
2 *Newark Star Ledger,* Nov. 14, 1991, p. 9.
3 *Statistical Handbook on Women in America,* preface.
4 *Newark Star Ledger,* Nov. 14, 1991, p. 9.
5 *Black Issues in Higher Education,* vol. 8, no. 127, Oct. 24, 1991, p. 4.
6 *Newark Star Ledger,* Nov. 14, 1991, p. 9.
7 Ruth Sidel: *Women and Children Last,* Penguin Books, New York, 1992, p. 168.
8 *The Washington Post,* Mar. 7, 1991, p. A21.
9 Marianne Takas: "Divorce Law and Policy: The Rising Backlash," in Paula Rothenberg (ed.), *Racism and Sexism: An Integrated Study,* St. Martin's Press, New York, 1988, p. 159.
10 *Statistical Handbook on Women in America,* p. 194, B8-1.
11 *The New York Times,* Mar. 27, 1991, p. A18.
12 *The Washington Post,* Jan. 11, 1991, p. A3.
13 Sidel, p. 168.
14 Elayne Rapping: "Good News, Bad News," *The Women's Review of Books,* October 1991, pp. 1–3.
15 Jessie Bernard: *The Female World From a Global Perspective,* Indiana University Press, Bloomington, 1987, p. xi.
16 *Newark Star Ledger,* Mar. 2, 1992, p. 2.

Mixed Messages

Ruth Sidel

Love the mansion. But do I really want to be mayor?

Woman speaking on the telephone
in a Diane Von Furstenberg
advertisement

She comes out every evening in a different sexy dress—some with ruffles, some strapless, some with sequins or lace, some short, some long, provocative yet somehow sweet, but all ultrafeminine, the old-fashioned way. And she's always smiling, smiling and clapping. Not applauding—clapping. She's Vanna White, recognizable by millions of Americans. She walks, she pirouettes, she models jewelry and furs, and she turns letters. She is the "girl" of the fifties, the Barbie doll come alive on our television screens six times a week—in some cities twice a day, six times a week.

And then there is Bonnie Blair. Lean and determined, she skated into our consciousness in her peach-and-gray body suit, which was neither masculine nor feminine but was made to help her do the job. When she realized she had set a world-record time of 39.10 seconds and had won the gold medal in the 500-meter speed-skating race at the 1988 Winter Olympic games, she threw her arms up and her head back in a thrilling moment of accomplishment and exultation.

Two images of women: the woman who is and the woman who does; the woman who is exhibited and exhibits herself as a commodity and the woman who because of skill and hard work is valued for her accomplishments. This duality of images of woman is all around us: on the one hand, the women lawyers and M.B.A.s in their suits, carrying briefcases, the perfect wife/mother/professional of the television sitcoms, the oh-so-successful women jumping, leaping, running in action shots about the pages of fashion magazines; and on the other hand, the women featured in the *Sports Illustrated* "swimsuit issue," the socialites on the women's pages in the latest designer clothes, and the nude women provocatively displayed in the pages of *Playboy* and *Penthouse*.

What are our young women to fathom from these disparate images? What are the messages we send them in our popular culture with every advertisement, every song, every film, and every sitcom? What are we telling them about our expectations of their future roles in society?

There is no doubt that woman as success story has been a major theme of the 1980s: women in law, women in medicine, women in banking, even women on Wall Street—but also women employees who have a clever idea for the firm and are promoted to vice-president, and homemakers who have a clever idea and become successful entrepreneurs. Above all, there is the image of the professional woman who, combining hard work and commitment, "makes it" in the world of work.

In magazines, in the "style" sections of newspapers, and on television she is often portrayed—this prototype, this model of how to do it all, be it all, and have it all—as outgoing, attractive, personable, bright, and "assertive" but surely not too "aggressive." She is likely to be in her thirties; she exercises, has a snappy executive wardrobe, flies all over the country or the world with relative ease, is comfortable eating alone in upscale restaurants, and, while never pushy, certainly does not allow the maître d' to give her a table in front of the kitchen.

If she is married, her husband is comradely, egalitarian, "supportive," and "does his share" at home. If there are children, they are smiling and happy and she is involved with them, too. Despite her often hectic schedule, she makes time for their plays and recitals, and the family gets away for companionable weekends together—often skiing. Above all, she is confident, fulfilled—and she can even whip up a quick, elegant dinner for eight when necessary. She's a woman for our time.

But despite the number of women in the work force and the number who are the primary breadwinners and caretakers of their families, the role of sex object is by no means obsolete. The objectification of women is still all around us. Beauty pageants remain a booming business for the sponsors, the participants, and the media. The onlookers are in a real sense participants as well. While some of us may scoff and mock this archaic vestige of another era, an estimated 55 million Americans—75 percent of them women—tune in each year to watch the Miss America Pageant. Many yearn, sometimes against their will, to look just like the contestants, and feel any deviation must be due to personal failure. "If only I dieted enough and exercised enough," the fantasy goes, "I could [should] look like that, too." If we doubt that these women are models for how millions of Americans would like to look, we need only examine the statistics on diseases such as anorexia nervosa and bulimia ("women's diseases," virtually unknown in the male population but particularly prevalent among women in their late teens and early twenties) to realize that women are tyrannized by the desire to be thin. A recent study reported in the journal *Pediatrics* found that by the age of seven girls come to believe that thin is beautiful. By adolescence most girls think they are fatter than they really are; according to the physician who conducted the study, "One young girl broke into tears when her mother asked her to go for a swim. The girl said she'd look too fat in a swimsuit, when in fact her weight was normal for her height."

And, of course, it is not just the Miss America Pageant but the Miss Universe, Miss USA, Miss Teen USA, and all the state and local pageants that feed into the grand finales. That amounts to a lot of young women in bathing suits walking up and down a lot of runways and being judged, for the most part, on how they look. In 1987, for example, some eighty thousand women vied for the title of Miss America in local and state contests. No matter how well they juggle or sing or play "Malagüeña" on the accordion, we all know that it is their measurements and pretty faces and how well they turn that are really being judged. And the message is not lost on the young women who are watching and trying to figure out who they are, what they want to be, and how they will get there. According to clinical psychologist Dr. Susan Schenkel, the Miss America competition is "the contemporary embodiment of the traditional fairy tale: it's like magic elevating you to success. Because most of us are exposed to these images at a very young age, they remain a visceral part of us, no matter how much we may resist them intellectually." Dr. Rita Freedman, author of *Beauty Bound,* a book about images of women's beauty, states, "Physical attractiveness is still a major source of women's power and they tune into these shows to find out what an attractive female is supposed to look like. They want to know how to package themselves."

To "win," it may even be necessary to transform not only one's body but also one's ethnic image. The 1988 Miss California, Marlise Ricardos, tried three times to win the title. It was only after she changed her hair color from brunet to blond and wore blue contact lenses when she competed that she became entitled to represent California in the 1988 Miss America contest in Atlantic City. As journalist Anne Taylor Fleming has observed, "She's the ultimate self-made competitor, a chemically 'sun-streaked' miss who rid herself of both pounds and ethnic identity to please pageant judges."

Women are also told in a variety of ways that although many of them may be executives on the way up, they must also still be warm, expressive, and frivolous, perhaps more concerned about what they wear than about the next corporate merger. An excellent example of this double message is an engaging Smirnoff vodka advertisement that shows three young, upwardly mobile women having drinks (all with vodka, presumably) while laughing, gesturing in typically feminine ways, and admiring a pair of red, sling-back, spike-heel shoes. The message the ad seems to be giving is, "You're working women now, you're out for a drink without a man, you're 'liberated,' but we know that underneath all that you're still into feelings and fashion."

This ad at least presumes by their clothes that these are working women out for a relaxing, good time. A far more disturbing example of advertising that seems to be urging a retreat from feminism is the Diane Von Furstenberg ad in the *New York Times* special section *Fashions of the Times* in February 1988. A woman is sitting on a chair talking on the telephone, one shoe kicked off, her fashionably short skirt halfway up her thigh. She says, "Love the mansion. But do I really want to be mayor?" The next page shows her with a tall stack of packages wrapped in a way that indicates they are from fashionable shops, and gives the answer: "No, there are better ways of having it all—and for a lot less!" What are the implications of this incredible ad? That the only reason women are interested in being mayor is to live in the mansion? That they are not really interested in power and substance and hard work? How is our woman in the advertisement going to get the "mansion" and all those consumer goods? There is certainly no indication that she plans to go into law, banking, or medicine instead of politics. Is the implication really that she is going to get them through a man, that she would rather marry the mayor than be one? In 1988? What is going on?

Recent fashion trends have surely indicated that there has been substantial backlash in reaction to the women's movement and to the changing nature of women's roles over the past twenty-five years. In 1987, just about the time that women's wages reached the all-time pinnacle of 65 percent of men's wages, fashion took an abrupt turn—many would say backwards. The stylish look moved from relatively simple clothes with shoulder pads, a modified dress-for-success look, to plunging necklines, bare shoulders, "waistlines snugly fitted, and skirts . . . rounded in an egg shape, tightly draped, or flared and poufed with myriad petticoats." Tops are "translucent if not transparent," dresses often "look like lingerie, with slip tops and lacy edges." And everywhere the short skirt. Skirts two, three, and four inches above the knee in the board room, the courtroom, and the operating room? Skirts above the knee to sell insurance and real estate or to do the taxes of a Fortune 500 company? Are women really going to get pay equity or run for the House of Representatives in a plunging neckline and a draped skirt? Why did we see "the most seductive, feminine-looking clothes since the days of Napoleon I's Empire" in the late 1980s? Did we try to go too far too fast? Is this the backlash to all those career women of the past decade? One designer said that women in his clothes will look "like little dolls"; one analyst has termed it "bimbo chic." These clothes, which hark back to the fifties but are far more provocative, are clearly not for the aspiring CEO or the nurse's aide. To their credit, millions of American women rejected these extreme styles and simply stopped buying for the period of time when that was all that was available. While the shortest skirts have all but disappeared, many clothes still end an inch or two above the knee, giving women a little-girl look hardly compatible with positions of power and respect in a society in which the dark blue suit is the ultimate badge of authority.

There is, moreover, the stereotypic look of the prostitute about some of the clothes and poses in many contemporary advertisements: black net stockings; see-through black lace; women draped over chairs, waiting to be used. The most flagrant advertisements showing woman-as-erotic-object and man-as-powerful-manipulator are those for Guess jeans. These ads, which appear in a variety of women's and general-interest magazines, are frequently several pages long, as though they are telling a story. The man is older, perhaps in his fifties, sinister looking, with dark glasses; the women are young, intense, and often partially nude. In one picture a woman nude above the waist, her skirt pulled up to show black net stockings, sits on the man's lap. There is a table nearby indicating that they have had dinner and possibly a good deal of wine. In another picture in the series, a young woman is leaning over him as though she is about to mount him. He has a faint smile, almost a sneer, on his face. He is calling the shots; she is there to amuse him, to service him. The final picture shows a young woman, in her late teens or early twenties, dressed only in what looks to be a black leotard and a jean jacket (jean jackets can be worn anywhere!), kneeling at his feet. We know he is rich, because the door to the room is in dark-grained wood with a handsome brass handle. She looks up at him inquiringly, obediently. Is she about to perform fellatio? Is he going to beat her, whip her? There is certainly a sadomasochistic tone to this series of advertisements. At the very least, we are seeing the "ritualization of subordination," as sociologist Erving Goffman has termed it, which is often manifested by "lowering oneself physically in some form . . . of prostration." There is no doubt in these ads who is in charge.

Yet another series of advertisements for Guess jeans is centered on the toreador theme. The women are again young, in provocative clothes, and are either waiting for the great man to appear or swooning, almost literally, against a poster of the handsome bullfighter. On the opposite page the toreador is shown in action: on a horse, the adoring multitudes all around, fighting the bull, and finally walking off in glory to resounding cheers. It is no accident that Guess jeans uses the most macho of all male images—the bullfighter—and pictures women as flimsily dressed, yearning, passive, carried away by desire. These advertisements seem targeted to the adolescent young woman. Is it the ad agencies' view that adolescents are "turned on" by pictures of submissive women and dominant men, by implied sadomasochism? There is certainly evidence that sadomasochism sells in the culture at large; much of the content in sex shops and sex magazines and the incredible amount of violence in films and on television attest to the pervasiveness of the themes of cruelty and pain. Sociologist Lynn Chancer has, in fact, suggested that sadomasochistic relationships are deeply imbedded in many aspects of American culture, particularly those that involve male-female interaction.

These are not the only ads in which women are portrayed as being "carried away," either literally or figuratively. In magazine after magazine, in image after image, women are literally being carried by men, leaning on men, being helped down from a height of two feet, or figuratively being carried away by emotion. When men and women are portrayed together, men are invariably solid citizens, responsible, dependable, in charge, busy; women are emoting, leaning, giddy, carried away—clearly not the persons you would choose to perform your neurosurgery, to handle your money, or even to care for your child.

While many designers have retreated from the extreme clothes of 1987, in part because women refused to buy what one observer called "a new boffo outrage each season," women are still often portrayed as little girls, seductive, passive, dependent, and, above all, beautiful and thin, with knock-'em-dead figures. After twenty-five years of the women's movement, is it how we look that is really important after all?

Women's magazines are key transmitters of values, attitudes, information, and the latest consensus about appropriate behavior. They help to socialize young women into their adult roles and enable more mature women to stay *au courant* with norms, expectations, and style. In a period of rapidly changing expectations, they have played a crucial role in molding women's attitudes toward work, toward family life, and toward themselves.

In an effort to understand the messages young women are receiving, fourteen women's magazines for March 1988 were systematically examined for content, for the ways in which women were portrayed, and for the values and norms that were both subtly and directly communicated. The magazines, chosen for their appeal to a broad spectrum of women by age, class, and interest, were *Seventeen, Mademoiselle, Glamour, Cosmopolitan, Harper's Bazaar, Vogue, Ladies' Home Journal, Working Mother, New Women, Self, Working Woman, Savvy, Ms.,* and *Essence.* All of the magazines focused, in varying degrees, on beauty tips, hair, fashion, fitness, health, food (both nutrition and recipes), and work. Virtually everyone pictured is clearly middle class; several magazines (*Vogue, Savvy,* and *Harper's Bazaar*) are upper middle class in tone, with an emphasis on upper-class life-style. A few of the magazines openly disparage the lower middle and working classes: a comic strip in *Seventeen* indicates that any high-school student foolish enough to invite a guy who works in an auto muffler shop to the school prom will find that he is no better than a prehuman ape, and *Mademoiselle* cautions women who want to move up the career ladder not to "leave the ratty little sweater on the chair just like the secretary does." Among the hundreds of features, viewpoints, articles, occasional fiction, advice, and how-to columns, there was not one instance of members of the working class being depicted in a positive light.

The overall message, transmitted both explicitly and implicitly, is "You can be all you want to be." You can be fit, thin, and trim; you can have a good job, be upwardly mobile, and invest your money wisely; you can wear stunning suits in your march toward success or slinky, sexy, almost childlike clothes, if you prefer; you can have an attractive, no-fuss hairstyle and blend just the right, ever-flattering makeup; you can have great (albeit safe) sex and know just what to do when *he* cannot perform; and, above all, you really *can* have it all—a warm, close family life and lucrative, pleasurable work. You really *can* have both love and success. It may mean starting your own business at home, but there are all those success stories to serve as models: Mrs. Fields, who has made millions on her chocolate-chip cookies and looks gorgeous too; the woman from Virginia who does $1 million worth of business annually making flags and is about to license national franchises; or the woman from Scottsdale, Arizona, who delivers teddy bears as special-occasion gifts the way FTD sells flowers and currently owns two stores, twenty-three franchises, and has annual sales of $1.5 million. What could be easier? And all that is involved are skills that women already have! Women are being told that they can use traditional female skills and make a fortune without ever leaving the kitchen or the sewing machine. The implication is that the fulfillment of the American Dream can be simply one clever idea or marketing strategy away. . . .

Are women's magazines the Horatio Alger novels of our time? Part of their mission is to help women cope with a rapidly changing society. From the "tips" on hair, fashion, and makeup to the reviews of books, films, and drama and the longer, often thoughtful, articles on health, sexual mores, or work options, they put women in touch with current attitudes, norms, and expectations. And at the same time they reaffirm the American Dream: by telling women repeatedly that they can, if they work hard enough, exercise long enough, eat correctly, and dress fashionably, achieve their dreams, these powerful agents of socialization are reinforcing the ideology that in America the individual can indeed make of herself whatever she chooses. Since there is rarely a suggestion that opportunity is related to economic, political, or social factors beyond the control of the individual, if a woman does not succeed after all these how-tos, perhaps she has no one to blame but herself. Moreover, the constant emphasis on celebrities, on stars, on those who have succeeded beyond most people's wildest dreams serves to reinforce the message.

Some of the magazines deal explicitly with the American Dream and extend it beyond the individual to the family unit. With the March 1988 issue, *Ms.* began a new series entitled "Tracking the Dream." . . .

That same month, March 1988, *Ladies' Home Journal* also ran an article on the American Dream. The lives and finances of four families, each with two children, were described: a black family with an annual income of $28,600, and three white families, one with an income of $43,000, another with an income of $60,000, and the last with an income of $150,000. Each of the families has two parents, and in all but one both parents work. (In the remaining family, the wife plans to return to work within the year, when the younger child enters school full-time.) All of the families own their own homes and various luxury consumer goods—VCRs, stereos, a cabin cruiser, central air conditioning—and one has taken an anniversary trip to Hawaii. The family earning $28,600 says that life is a constant struggle but stresses that they have come a long way from the near-poverty days early in their marriage. The family earning $150,000 is striving for an income of $250,000; the husband states, "Success is being able to work a four-day week and still get what you want." The *Ladies' Home Journal* summarizes, "The American Dream of the good life for all is still very much with us."

In all these magazines, scattered among the hairstyles, the fashion layouts, and the endless advertisements is perhaps the central message: the American Dream is alive and well. If you work hard, believe in yourself, and consume relentlessly, you too can be a success in America.

One of the most appealing twists on the "having it all" theme was pictured on the cover and inside the December 1987 *Harper's Bazaar* in an extensive and lavish layout. Amid the holiday glitter, the "festive fantasy" of "blazing gold sequins," "paillettes," and "huge faux gems," actresses Shelley Long and Phylicia Rashad and model Christie Brinkley were pictured in sumptuous designer gowns and jewels while holding their own young children, also dressed in lavish outfits. *Bazaar*'s Christmas issue is not only celebrating gorgeous women who are performers and mothers ("The most popular mom on television, 'The Cosby Show's Phylicia Rashad does an equally good job of parenting in reality" and "Nothing expresses the true meaning of this season more clearly than the special glow between mother and child") but is also celebrating the family ("For even in this age of high-tech and high finance, the primal bonds of family—no matter how stretched or strained—remain squarely at the heart of Christmas"). Nothing is sacred in the selling of consumerism—especially at Christmas time. The message is clear: these women truly have it all—money, beauty, fabulous careers, husbands, and beautiful babies. Should the rest of us expect anything less?

Yet another example of the having-it-all-including-baby theme is a Donna Karan advertisement in the August 1988 issue of *Vogue*. The "mother" is lying half on the bed and half on the floor, dressed in a black, scoop-backed bodysuit. She is presumably a professional woman, since she is reading papers concerning shareholders. Strewn around the bedroom are clothes, pocketbooks, shoes, and scads of jewelry. A baby is sitting on the bed, presumably a girl, also "working" with pen and paper, an open notebook nearby. The child is wearing nothing more than a diaper and a necklace—a Donna Karan necklace, one assumes. The message again is clear: it *is* possible to have it all—and, by the way, it is never too early to teach a girl to want pretty things! . . .

What, then, is popular culture telling young women? The messages are clearly conflicting. The fundamental message seems to be that while women's lives have changed dramatically because so many of them are in the work force, supporting or at the very least helping to support themselves and their families, many other aspects of their lives have changed very little. The message is that women can be successful in the workplace and look the part as well but had better not forget how to be provocative, sexy, dependent; that women are to be in charge of their own lives yet "carried away" either by their own feelings or by men; that women can be it all, have it all, and do it all, but while ability and hard work are important, looks are still crucial. With the right clothes and the right look—in other words, the right packaging—women can market themselves the way any other commodity is marketed and achieve their dreams in both the public and the private sphere.

The messages of television and films are more complex. On the one hand, women can be anything they wish, but on the other, their personal lives, not their work lives, are nearly always predominant. You may be a lawyer, but your private life is what is really important. In much of popular culture the women may wear suits and carry briefcases, but their new roles often seem grafted onto the traditional ones of the past—the sex object, the "caring" person more involved with private than with public concerns, or the individual in search of fulfillment through love. Because American society has not truly accepted the implications of women's new roles and therefore not adapted to those profound changes, most popular culture has not really integrated these changes, either. It is often as though a veneer of pseudofeminism is lightly brushed over the story line but underneath that veneer is the same old message. Issues such as dominance and subservience, autonomy and dependence, and how to truly, realistically mesh career and caring are rarely explored seriously. When they are, conflicts are often resolved through traditional solutions.

Moreover, television's need for a wrap-up of the problem each week (or occasionally after two or more episodes) requires simplistic solutions that are invariably within the control of the individual. Seldom are problems depicted as larger than the individual's or the family unit's capacity for coping; rarely are problems depicted as systemic, originating in the very structure of society. The individual generally finds a solution, a formula for working out the problem or conflict, thereby further strengthening the ideology of individualism, an ideology that states, week after week, that we are indeed in charge of our lives and can make of them what we wish. Women may find it harder to regulate their lives because of their presumed greater need for love and approval or because of their again presumed greater conflicts around doing and caring, but in the long run the illusion of self-determination is generally preserved.

But the message of popular culture is above all that everyone is middle and upper middle class. Women are portrayed as doctors, lawyers, and television stars, rarely as salespeople, secretaries, nurse's aides. And when they are playing working-class roles, they are nearly always objects of derision, of sympathy, or of humor. For young women growing up today, the options as reflected by much of popular culture are upper-middle-class options. You need to have a job with status, dress stunningly, and live well if not magnificently. Other measures of success are rarely portrayed. While little in popular culture tells you how to get there, the implication is that the American Dream is there for those who want to make it a reality. . . .

By defining success almost solely in terms of status, wealth, and power, we are presenting few realistic options for the vast majority of American women and men. Popular culture, by focusing almost entirely on the lives of the top fifth of the population, reinforces the ideology of the American Dream but implicitly devalues all those who will never achieve it. And when young women describe their dreams for the future—their hopes of affluence, their images of themselves as successful professionals, their conflicts around doing and caring, their belief that they must be able to take care of themselves and solve their problems on an individual basis, or, in some cases, when they speak flatly of their inability to imagine a future at all—we know they have been listening to the mixed messages of much of American popular culture.

Being a Boy

Julius Lester

As boys go, I wasn't much. I mean, I tried to be a boy and spent many childhood hours pummeling my hardly formed ego with failure at cowboys and Indians, baseball, football, lying, and sneaking out of the house. When our neighborhood gang raided a neighbor's pear tree, I was the only one who got sick from the purloined fruit. I also failed at setting fire to our garage, an art at which any five-year-old boy should be adept. I was, however, the neighborhood champion at getting beat up. "That Julius can take it, man," the boys used to say, almost in admiration, after I emerged from another battle, tears brimming in my eyes but refusing to fall.

My efforts at being a boy earned me a pair of scarred knees that are a record of a childhood spent falling from bicycles, trees, the tops of fences, and porch steps; of tripping as I ran (generally from a fight), walked, or simply tried to remain upright on windy days.

I tried to believe my parents when they told me I was a boy, but I could find no objective proof for such an assertion. Each morning during the summer, as I cuddled up in the quiet of a corner with a book, my mother would push me out the back door and into the yard. And throughout the day as my blood was let as if I were a patient of 17th-century medicine, I thought of the girls sitting in the shade of porches, playing with their dolls, toy refrigerators and stoves.

There was the life, I thought! No constant pressure to prove oneself. No necessity always to be competing. While I humiliated myself on football and baseball fields, the girls stood on the sidelines laughing at me, because they didn't have to do anything except be girls. The rising of each sun brought me to the starting line of yet another day's Olympic decathlon, with no hope of ever winning even a bronze medal.

Through no fault of my own I reached adolescence. While the pressure to prove myself on the athletic field lessened, the overall situation got worse—because now I had to prove myself with girls. Just how I was supposed to go about doing this was beyond me, especially because, at the age of 14, I was four foot nine and weighed 78 pounds. (I think there may have been one 10-year-old girl in the neighborhood smaller than I.) Nonetheless, duty called, and with my ninth-grade gym-class jockstrap flapping between my legs, off I went.

To get a girlfriend, though, a boy had to have some asset beyond the fact that he was alive. I wasn't handsome like Bill McCord, who had girls after him like a cop-killer has policemen. I wasn't ugly like Romeo Jones, but at least the girls noticed him: "That ol' ugly boy better stay 'way from me!" I was just there, like a vase your grandmother gives you at Christmas that you don't like or dislike, can't get rid of, and don't know what to do with. More than ever I wished I were a girl. Boys were the ones who had to take the initiative and all the responsibility. (I hate responsibility so much that if my heart didn't beat of itself, I would now be a dim memory.)

It was the boy who had to ask the girl for a date, a frightening enough prospect until it occurred to me that she might say no! That meant risking my ego, which was about as substantial as a toilet-paper raincoat in the African rainy season. But I had to thrust that ego forward to be judged, accepted, or rejected by some girl. It wasn't fair! Who was she to sit back like a queen with the power to create joy by her consent or destruction by her denial? It wasn't fair—but that's the way it was.

But if (God forbid!) she should say Yes, then my problem would begin in earnest, because I was the one who said where we would go (and waited in terror for her approval of my choice). I was the one who picked her up at her house where I was inspected by her parents as if I were a possible carrier of syphilis (which I didn't think one could get from masturbating, but then again, Jesus was born of a virgin, so what did I know?). Once we were on our way, it was I who had to pay the bus fare, the price of the movie tickets, and whatever she decided to stuff her stomach with afterward. (And the smallest girls are all stomach.) Finally, the girl was taken home where once again I was inspected (the father looking covertly at my fly and the mother examining the girl's hair). The evening was over and the girl had done nothing except honor me with her presence. All the work had been mine.

Imagining this procedure over and over was more than enough: I was a sophomore in college before I had my first date.

I wasn't a total failure in high school, though, for occasionally I would go to a party, determined to salvage my self-esteem. The parties usually took place in somebody's darkened basement. There was generally a surreptitious wine bottle or two being passed furtively among the boys, and a record player with an insatiable appetite for Johnny Mathis records. Boys gathered on one side of the room and girls on the other. There were always a few boys and girls who'd come to the party for the sole purpose of grinding away their sexual frustrations to Johnny Mathis's falsetto, and they would begin dancing to their own music before the record player was plugged in. It took a little longer for others to get started, but no one matched my talent for standing by the punch bowl. For hours, I would try to make my legs do what they had been doing without effort since I was nine months old, but for some reason they would show all the symptoms of paralysis on those evenings.

After several hours of wondering whether I was going to die ("Julius Lester, a sixteen-year-old, died at a party last night, a half-eaten Ritz cracker in one hand and a potato chip dipped in pimiento-cheese spread in the other. Cause of death: failure to be a boy"), I would push my way to the other side of the room where the girls sat like a hanging jury. I would pass by the girl I wanted to dance with. If I was going to be refused, let it be by someone I didn't particularly like. Unfortunately, there weren't many in that category. I had more crushes than I had pimples.

Finally, through what surely could only have been the direct intervention of the Almighty, I would find myself on the dance floor with a girl. And none of my prior agony could compare to the thought of actually dancing. But there I was and I had to dance with her. Social custom decreed that I was supposed to lead, because I was the boy. Why? I'd wonder. Let her lead. Girls were better dancers anyway. It didn't matter. She stood there waiting for me to take charge. She wouldn't have been worse off if she'd waited for me to turn white.

But, reciting "Invictus" to myself, I placed my arms around her, being careful to keep my armpits closed because, somehow, I had managed to overwhelm a half jar of deodorant and a good-size bottle of cologne. With sweaty armpits, "Invictus," and legs afflicted again with polio, I took her in my arms, careful not to hold her so far away that she would think I didn't like her, but equally careful not to hold her so close that she could feel the catastrophe which had befallen me the instant I touched her hand. My penis, totally disobeying the lecture I'd given it before we left home, was as rigid as Governor Wallace's jaw would be if I asked for his daughter's hand in marriage.

God, how I envied girls at that moment. Wherever *it* was on them, it didn't dangle between their legs like an elephant's trunk. No wonder boys talked about nothing but sex. That thing was always there. Every time we went to the john, there *it* was, twitching around like a fat little worm on a fishing hook. When we took baths, it floated in the water like a lazy fish and God forbid we should touch it! It sprang to life like lightning leaping from a cloud. I wished I could cut it off, or at least keep it tucked between my legs, as if it were a tail that had been mistakenly attached to the wrong end. But I was helpless. It was there, with a life and mind of its own, having no other function than to embarrass me.

Fortunately, the girls I danced with were discreet and pretended that they felt nothing unusual rubbing against them as we danced. But I was always convinced that the next day they were all calling up their friends to exclaim: "Guess what, girl? Julius Lester got one! I ain't lyin'!"

Now, of course, I know that it was as difficult being a girl as it was a boy, if not more so. While I stood paralyzed at one end of a dance floor trying to find the courage to ask a girl for a dance, most of the girls waited in terror at the other, afraid that no one, not even I, would ask them. And while I resented having to ask a girl for a date, wasn't it also horrible to be the one who waited for the phone to ring? And how many of those girls who laughed at me making a fool of myself on the baseball diamond would have gladly given up their places on the sidelines for mine on the field?

No, it wasn't easy for any of us, girls and boys, as we forced our beautiful, free-flowing child-selves into those narrow, constricting cubicles labeled *female* and *male*. I tried, but I wasn't good at being a boy. Now, I'm glad, knowing that a man is nothing but the figment of a penis's imagination, and any man should want to be something more than that.

Feminism's Personal Questions—for Men

William H. Becker

The ratio of males to females in my "Masculinity and Femininity" course remains only 1 to 5, despite the fact that the course gives equal attention to each gender. Males encouraged to enroll often respond, "I don't need another semester of male-bashing"—not realizing that this course is not only pro-feminist but also strongly male-affirmative.

These students, like most other American males, usually know about only one side of feminism, the social-political side. They know that feminism raises fundamental social and political questions, questions about justice and equality and power for women—which necessarily involve criticism of male dominance, of male attitudes, of men. They hear these questions being asked regularly now, even in the mass media, in movies such as *Working Girl* and *The Accused,* in TV shows like *Roseanne* and *Murphy Brown.*

Yet for the most part they—again, in company with most males—have not yet begun to hear the second set of questions posed by feminism, the personal-psychological-spiritual ones that call for an honest probing of men's needs and aspirations, as well as women's, and imply empathy and compassion for both. Some of these questions are: Why do you define manhood as being tough, in control, in charge, superior to what is non-male, detached—even from your own feelings? If that's what it means, do you really want to be a man? Why are your most intimate male-male conversations limited to work and sports, weather and whether (i.e., sex)? Is that really all you want from and for your male friends? How have you gotten trapped in patterns of noncommunication and withdrawal from your father, and from your sons—all the while yearning for some real connection? Why do you so often flee from personal intimacy to impersonal work?

Some American men have heard and begun to struggle with these questions and they, like feminists who earlier worked to raise the consciousness of women, are beginning to raise these questions with other men. This minority is creating a pro-feminist men's liberation movement in this country. The 14th national Men and Masculinity conference, sponsored by the National Organization for Changing Men (NOCM), was held last June in Pittsburgh, with about 350 men and perhaps 20 women in attendance. Most of the conference time was spent in small-group workshops on topics such as: "Lies Men Tell Themselves," "My Father, My Self," "Connecting with Our Children," "Men Against Pornography," "Coming Out: A Process for All of Us—Gay, Straight, and Bisexual" and "Men's Spirituality"—all of which are unusually personal and risky topics for men.

These titles, by themselves, suggest two major reasons why few men have so far "heard" the personal questions feminism poses of them: pain and fear. These workshops are occasions for the honest examination of men's lives as they actually are, not to be confused with the way men (and women) are conditioned to think they should be. Such self-examination involves the uncovering of pain: the places where men hurt; where we hide our vulnerability, neediness and failure; where we yearn for nurture, acceptance, connection rather than detachment. More than once, in the midst of these workshops, the image came to my mind: "years of tears, waiting to be shed."

But it is not easy for men, who have been taught that it is not manly to cry, to acknowledge even today's share of tears, let alone to confess this dammed-up accumulation from the past. There are men who find it easier and more acceptable (in the eyes of the impassive god "manhood") to beat their wives and children than to cry. Such violence must be exposed, resisted, and punished, as the women's movement insists (NOCM has a task force on "Ending Men's Violence," which sponsors peer-counseling groups for men who batter); but we can also have compassion for brothers conditioned to batter their wives as a substitute for crying in their arms, even as we do for sisters socialized to accept such abuse as their due.

Besides this unacknowledged pain there is unconscious fear, namely profound homophobia, which is simply the other side of our socially constructed ideal of masculinity. The man is tough, controlling, detached, businesslike. The gay man is, like the woman, a non-man: weak, passive, open in display of affection and emotion, playful. Because the distinguishing mark of the gay male is attraction to and association with other males, there is little wonder that our male homophobia makes us fearful of any invitation to sit together with other men to share our real feelings and concerns. "Was there a lot of touchy-feely?"—that was the first question I was asked by a male faculty colleague when I mentioned that I had just gotten back from the Pittsburgh conference.

However, it is not only men clinging to a traditional image of masculinity who find it hard to hear these profoundly personal gender questions; nor is it only traditional women. By far the most intense and determined resistance to these issues I have encountered in my own experience came from a group of "liberal" colleagues at Bucknell, both women and men, who argued against the proposal to give some attention to such questions—men's studies, if you will—along with women's studies, which is already an established part of our curriculum. Here we go again, they argued; women finally get funding for women's studies and now men, who always know a good thing when they see it, want to come in and take it over for their own male-centered purposes. If it isn't focused on men, men don't consider it important.

It is not that I do not understand this argument, nor that I am unable to empathize with the anger and self-assertion that lie behind it. I simply believe the argument is mistaken. For in this case, the "good thing" in question is something feminism wants men to see and know: namely, those new insights into being a man in our society that have been brought to light largely by feminist analysis. And the fact is that most males are not yet aware that this good thing even exists, let alone how desperately they need it. The proper role of feminism, surely, is not to reject or resist the "new masculinity" to which it has given birth, but rather to encourage its growth, maturation, and self-criticism. It is important that males become pro-feminist by supporting the social-political demand for women's equality, but the more profound meaning of male pro-feminism is, finally, personal and spiritual: that we males commit ourselves to discovering, exploring and teaching our sons and daughters a new understanding of masculinity.

To be a man is to care, to love, to be able to give oneself generously as husband, father, son, friend, colleague, mentor, citizen, fellow creature. To be a "big" man is to need and accept love, without counting this as a weakness; to give love, without counting the cost; to be open to new and even threatening questions and perspectives; to be loyal to the true and the good, though that may well mean coming in second, or even finishing last.

The Politics of Housework

Pat Mainardi

Though women do not complain of the power of husbands, each complains of her own husband, or of the husbands of her friends. It is the same in all other cases of servitude; at least in the commencement of the emancipatory movement. The serfs did not at first complain of the power of the lords, but only of their tyranny.

John Stuart Mill
On the Subjection of Women

Liberated women—very different from women's liberation! The first signals all kinds of goodies, to warm the hearts (not to mention other parts) of the most radical men. The other signals—*housework.* The first brings sex without marriage, sex before marriage, cozy housekeeping arrangements ("You see, I'm living with this chick") and the self-content of knowing that you're not the kind of man who wants a doormat instead of a woman. That will come later. After all, who wants that old commodity anymore, the Standard American Housewife, all husband, home and kids. The New Commodity, the Liberated Woman, has sex a lot and has a Career, preferably something that can be fitted in with the household chores—like dancing, pottery, or painting.

On the other hand is women's liberation—and housework. What? You say this is all trivial? Wonderful! That's what I thought. It seemed perfectly reasonable. We both had careers, both had to work a couple of days a week to earn enough to live on, so why shouldn't we share the housework? So I suggested it to my mate and he agreed—most men are too hip to turn you down flat. "You're right," he said. "It's only fair."

Then an interesting thing happened. I can only explain it by stating that we women have been brainwashed more than even we can imagine. Probably too many years of seeing television women in ecstasy over their shiny waxed floors or breaking down over their dirty shirt collars. Men have no such conditioning. They recognize the essential fact of housework right from the very beginning. Which is that it stinks. Here's my list of dirty chores: buying groceries, carting them home and putting them away; cooking meals and washing dishes and pots; doing the laundry; digging out the place when things get out of control; washing floors. The list could go on but the sheer necessities are bad enough. All of us have to do these things, or get some one else to do them for us. The longer my husband contemplated these chores, the more repulsed he became, and so proceeded the change from the normally sweet considerate Dr. Jekyll into the crafty Mr. Hyde who would stop at nothing to avoid the horrors of—*housework.* As he felt himself backed into a corner laden with dirty dishes, brooms, mops, and reeking garbage his front teeth grew longer and pointier, his fingernails haggled and his eyes grew wild. Housework trivial? Not on your life! Just try to share the burden.

So ensued a dialogue that's been going on for several years. Here are some of the high points:

"I don't mind sharing the housework, but I don't do it very well. We should each do the things we're best at."

Meaning: Unfortunately I'm no good at things like washing dishes or cooking. What I do best is a little light carpentry, changing light bulbs, moving furniture *(how often do you move furniture?)*.

Also meaning: Historically the lower classes (black men and us) have had hundreds of years experience doing menial jobs. It would be a waste of manpower to train someone else to do them now.

Also meaning: I don't like the dull stupid boring jobs, so you should do them.

"I don't mind sharing the work, but you'll have to show me how to do it."

Meaning: I ask a lot of questions and you'll have to show me everything everytime I do it because I don't remember so good. Also don't try to sit down and read while I'm doing my jobs because I'm going to annoy hell out of you until it's easier to do them yourself.

"We used to be so happy!" (Said whenever it was his turn to do something.)

Meaning: I used to be so happy.

Meaning: Life without housework is bliss. *(No quarrel here. Perfect agreement.)*

"We have different standards, and why should I have to work to your standards. That's unfair."

Meaning: If I begin to get bugged by the dirt and crap I will say "This place sure is a sty" or "How can anyone live like this?" and wait for your reaction. I know that all women have a sore called "Guilt over a messy house" or "Household work is ultimately my responsibility." I know that men have caused that sore—if anyone visits and the place *is* a sty, they're not going to leave and say, "He sure is a lousy housekeeper." You'll take the rap in any case. I can outwait you.

Also meaning: I can provoke innumerable scenes over the housework issue. Eventually doing all the housework yourself will be less painful to you than trying to get me to do half. Or I'll suggest we get a maid. She will do my share of the work. You will do yours. It's women's work.

"I've got nothing against sharing the housework, but you can't make me do it on your schedule."

Meaning: Passive resistance. I'll do it when I damned well please, if at all. If my job is doing dishes, it's easier to do them once a week. If taking out laundry, once a month. If washing the floors, once a year. If you don't like it, do it yourself oftener, and then I won't do it at all.

"I *hate* it more than you. You don't mind it so much."

Meaning: Housework is garbage work. It's the worst crap I've ever done. It's degrading and humiliating for someone of *my* intelligence to do it. But for someone of *your* intelligence . . .

"Housework is too trivial to even talk about."

Meaning: It's even more trivial to do. Housework is beneath my status. My purpose in life is to deal with matters of significance. Yours is to deal with matters of insignificance. You should do the housework.

"This problem of housework is not a man-woman problem! In any relationship between two people one is going to have a stronger personality and dominate."

Meaning: That stronger personality had better be *me.*

"In animal societies, wolves, for example, the top animal is usually a male even where he is not chosen for brute strength but on the basis of cunning and intelligence. Isn't that interesting?"

Meaning: I have historical, psychological, anthropological, and biological justification for keeping you down. How can you ask the top wolf to be equal?

"Women's liberation isn't really a political movement."

Meaning: The Revolution is coming too close to home.

Also meaning: I am only interested in how I am oppressed, not how I oppress others. Therefore the war, the draft, and the university are political. Women's liberation is not.

"Man's accomplishments have always depended on getting help from other people, mostly women. What great man would have accomplished what he did if he had to do his own housework?"

Meaning: Oppression is built into the System and I, as the white American male, receive the benefits of this System. I don't want to give them up.

POSTSCRIPT

Participatory democracy begins at home. If you are planning to implement your politics, there are certain things to remember.

1 He *is* feeling it more than you. He's losing some leisure and you're gaining it. The measure of your oppression is his resistance.

2 A great many American men are not accustomed to doing monotonous repetitive work which never ushers in any lasting let alone important achievement. This is why they would rather repair a cabinet than wash dishes. If human endeavors are like a pyramid with man's highest achievements at the top, then keeping oneself alive is at the bottom. Men have always had servants (us) to take care of this bottom strata of life while they have confined their efforts to the rarefied upper regions. It is thus ironic when they ask of women—where are your great painters, statesmen, etc? Mme. Matisse ran a millinery shop so he could paint. Mrs. Martin Luther King kept his house and raised his babies.

3 It is a traumatizing experience for someone who has always thought of himself as being against any oppression or exploitation of one human being by another to realize that in his daily life he has been accepting and implementing (and benefiting from) this exploitation; that his rationalization is little different from that of the racist who says "Black people don't feel pain" (women don't mind doing the shitwork); and that the oldest form of oppression in history has been the oppression of 50 percent of the population by the other 50 percent.

4 Arm yourself with some knowledge of the psychology of oppressed peoples everywhere, and a few facts about the animal kingdom. I admit playing top wolf or who runs the gorillas is silly but as a last resort men bring it up all the time. Talk about bees. If you feel really hostile bring up the sex life of spiders. They have sex. She bites off his head.

The psychology of oppressed people is not silly. Jews, immigrants, black men, and all women have employed the same psychological mechanisms to survive: admiring the oppressor, glorifying the oppressor, wanting to be like the oppressor, wanting the oppressor to like them, mostly because the oppressor held all the power.

5 In a sense, all men everywhere are slightly schizoid—divorced from the reality of maintaining life. This makes it easier for them to play games with it. It is almost a cliché that women feel greater grief at sending a son off to war or losing him to that war because they bore him, suckled him, and raised him. The men who foment those wars did none of those things and have a more superficial estimate of the worth of human life. One hour a day is a low estimate of the amount of time one has to spend "keeping" oneself. By foisting this off on others, man gains seven hours a week—one working day more to play with his mind and not his human needs. Over the course of generations it is easy to see whence evolved the horrifying abstractions of modern life.

6 With the death of each form of oppression, life changes and new forms evolve. English aristocrats at the turn of the century were horrified at the idea of enfranchising working men—were sure that it signaled the death of civilization and a return to barbarism. Some working men were even deceived by this line. Similarly with the minimum wage, abolition of slavery, and female suffrage. Life changes but it goes on. Don't fall for any line about the death of everything if men take a turn at the dishes. They will imply that you are holding back the Revolution (their Revolution). But you are advancing it (your Revolution).

7 Keep checking up. Periodically consider who's actually *doing* the jobs. These things have a way of backsliding so that a year later once again the woman is doing everything. After a year make a list of jobs the man has rarely if ever done. You will find cleaning pots, toilets, refrigerators and ovens high on the list. Use time sheets if necessary. He will accuse you of being petty. He is above that sort of thing—(housework). Bear in mind what the worst jobs are, namely the ones that have to be done every day or several times a day. Also the ones that are dirty—it's more pleasant to pick up books, newspapers, etc. than to wash dishes. Alternate the bad jobs. It's the daily grind that gets you down. Also make sure that you don't have the responsibility for the housework with occasional help from him. "I'll cook dinner for you tonight" implies it's really your job and isn't he a nice guy to do some of it for you.

8 Most men had a rich and rewarding bachelor life during which they did not starve or become encrusted with crud or buried under the litter. There is a taboo that says that women mustn't strain themselves in the presence of men: we haul around 50 pounds of groceries if we have to but aren't allowed to open a jar if there is someone around to do it for us. The reverse side of the coin is that men aren't supposed to be able to take care of themselves without a woman. Both are excuses for making women do the housework.

9 Beware of the double whammy. He won't do the little things he always did because you're now a "Liberated Woman," right? Of course he won't do anything else either . . .

I was just finishing this when my husband came in and asked what I was doing. Writing a paper on housework. Housework? he said. *Housework?* Oh my god how trivial can you get. A paper on housework.

LITTLE POLITICS OF HOUSEWORK QUIZ

The lowest job in the army, used as punishment is: (a) working 9–5; (b) kitchen duty (K.P.).

When a man lives with his family, his: (a) father (b) mother does his housework.

When he lives with a woman, (a) he (b) she does the housework.

(A) his son (b) his daughter learns in preschool how much fun it is to iron daddy's handkerchief.

From the *New York Times,* 9/21/69: "Former Greek Official George Mylonas pays the penalty for differing with the ruling junta in Athens by performing household chores on the island of Amorgos where he lives in forced exile" (with hilarious photo of a miserable Mylonas carrying his own water). What the *Times* means is that he ought to have (a) indoor plumbing (b) a maid.

Dr. Spock said (*Redbook* 3/69): "Biologically and temperamentally I believe, women were made to be concerned first and foremost with child care, husband care, and home care." Think about: (a) *who* made us (b) why? (c) what is the effect on their lives (d) what is the effect on our lives?

From *Time* 1/5/70, "Like their American counterparts, many housing project housewives are said to suffer from neurosis. And for the first time in Japanese history, many young husbands today complain of being henpecked. Their wives are beginning to demand detailed explanations when they don't come home straight from work and some Japanese males nowadays are even compelled to do housework." According to *Time,* women become neurotic: (a) when they are forced to do the maintenance work for the male caste all day every day of their lives or (b) when they no longer want to do the maintenance work for the male caste all day every day of their lives.

Calling All Working Fathers

Mary Kay Blakely

"Hello, Tony? This is Ryan's mom. Is your father there?" It's 7:30 on a Wednesday evening, I am sitting at my desk, my son's class list of 22 names and telephone numbers in front of me. I am only on the D's. "Nobody kept answering," as Holden Caulfield once said.

"He's watching TV," Tony replied.

"Great," I said, making a check mark next to his name. "Tell him I want to talk to him."

While Tony notifies his dad, I scan the list and look up at the clock. I still have work to do this evening, on a deadline that should have been mailed Express two hours ago. That afternoon, I'd called the editor waiting on the other end, who wasn't surprised to receive the message, "I'm running late."

She's a mother, too, so she knows the chagrin of uttering that phrase to colleagues, and she is kind. She gives me another day. By doing so, she has just made her own job harder—at 5:00, she has to step into her boss's office and report, "We're running late." My motherhood has just changed from "I" to "we," becoming plural again, thanks to another woman.

Tony's dad is taking his time. I try to recall what programs are on the air at 7:30 P.M., but the last one I remember watching was "Marcus Welby, M.D." Leisure time has disappeared from my life, which is how I became a Room Mother in the first place. I couldn't volunteer to be a Field Trip Mother or a Cafeteria Mother, because those required daytime hours, but Room Mothers can make their phone calls at night.

I still try to do my share of PTA-type tasks, because I don't want to fuel the current flames between mothers who work at home and mothers who work outside. Mrs. Laura L. Luteri, of Mt. Prospect, Illinois, just fired a tiny grenade into my camp, in a letter to the editor of *Better Homes and Gardens*. She wrote that she was sick of hearing the excuse, "I can't, I work," from women like me.

Mrs. Luteri resents me for depending on women like her to fill in. In fact, I am depending on school administrations to recognize that Room Mother and Cafeteria Mother and Field Trip Mother should all become paid positions.

"Hello?" A male voice interrupts my thoughts with a touch of boredom. The voice doesn't sound as if it's dressed in a suit and tie; it has a sweatshirt and jeans on, but it manages to talk down to me nevertheless. Perhaps I have been referred to as "Ryan's mom," and so I sit up a little straighter and introduce myself.

"Hello, Mr. D., this is Mary Kay Blakely. I'm the Room Mother for Mr. Baldino's sixth-grade class," I begin in my most professional voice.

"Hold on," he interrupts, "I'll get my wife." The professional disguise fails. "Room Mother" gives me away—he recognizes this as a woman's call.

"No, wait," I reply instantly, keeping him attached to the receiver. "I've already spoken to your wife several times this year. . . ."

A mental image of Mrs. D. flashes into my mind—like all the mothers of the children in Mr. Baldino's class, she is making dinner. I call during dinner to save myself time dialing repeats—working mothers are usually home at dinnertime. "Oh, God," they sigh when I mention my name, "let me get a pencil." Four times this year, I have made requests on their time and heard their fatigue. The cumulative guilt of 22 sighs repeated four times made me revise the message I'm sending out. I've only changed one word.

"We're asking the sixth-grade fathers . . ." I begin, and falter slightly. It is an editorial "we," but in fact I have no authority behind me. The other Room Mothers are not asking for fathers tonight. It is a "we" to make me bigger than "I," a "we" representing the plurality of motherhood, a "we" to give some power to the request I'm about to make.

"We're asking the fathers," I repeat, "to make brownies for the class party next Wednesday. Will you send a dozen to school with Tony?" I stop, to let the request sink in. I imagine Mr. D.'s eyebrows rising up on his forehead.

"Me?" he asks incredulously. After 12 years of fatherhood, Mr. D. has apparently never been asked to make brownies, never been a Room Mother. Perhaps he is a father who spends "quality time" with his children on weekends and evenings, but he did not sound like a man who knew his way around the kitchen. That's where mothers generally conduct their "quality time," helping children with homework while making dinner and taking phone calls.

"Oh, I don't know, I've never made brownies." Mr. D. chuckles, as if I were teasing him. But I'm not.

"It's easy. All you have to do is read the box." I'm prepared to give him detailed instructions, over the phone, on how to make brownies. Fudge brownies, brownies with nuts, blondie brownies . . . suddenly, Mr. D. has 12 years of knowing nothing about brownies to make up for with me. I realize I'm getting worked up. I pretend that I'm late on my deadline because I've been making brownies all day.

Be patient, I caution myself—if he's never been asked to help out, how can I expect him to know? He could know from watching Mrs. D.'s fatigue, by observing the diminishing "quality" of her time in the kitchen. He does not see her exhaustion, perhaps, because "exhausted" is the way women in kitchens have always looked. Maybe he thinks "exhausted" is a normal state for us. The mothers in Mr. Baldino's class have been forgiving fathers on "how could he know" grounds for 12 years. Mr. D.'s "learning" time has just expired.

"I'll see what I can do," he says, taking me for a fool. "I'll see" is not the same as "I will." Those two words and their lack of commitment are why "working father" is still unfamiliar to the culture; why men and their newspapers fill up the early morning commuter trains, in time for "power breakfasts," while women catch the later ones, after junior high carpools; why executive mothers are telling the press they are leaving their jobs because they "can't do both," while their executive husbands are never even interviewed. "I'll see" is just inches above "I won't"—the phrase given up, with reluctance, in the seventies.

"We need a commitment tonight," I insist, keeping him on the phone. I am speaking to Mr. D., but I am thinking of the man in the study next to mine, the one I argued with last night, the one who's also working under a crushing deadline. He hates these arguments, as do I, because we both "understand" the pressures of work and family. We both understand, but I am the one who meets them. His deadline meant a month of 60-hour weeks at his office, a month of brief appearances at home. "I have no *choice*," he would say, apologetically, listing the emergencies, "I have to work."

"Tell that to Laura L. Luteri," I reply, although he'd never recognize the *Better Homes and Gardens* reader, or have any inkling of why she hates me.

"You *see* no choice," I amend, naming others. He could quit his job, I suggested last night, but didn't mean it. I couldn't argue persuasively for that choice, since my salary wasn't close to meeting our expenses. He made more money, and making more bread is partly why men are exempted from making the brownies.

Or he could quit the family, I offered as a second alternative, although I didn't mean that either. They were the kinds of statements that get blown out heatedly during arguments, born of injury or jealousy. But he *had* temporarily quit the family, and by empathizing with his deadlines I lost ground on my own. What good did it do us to "think" equality if we didn't get to live it?

Or finally, he could introduce his boss to the term "working father" and the phrase "I'm running late." That's the "choice" I campaigned for heavily. It would diminish his considerable esteem at work, and wouldn't be easily accepted. There is no plurality of working fathers, and he would undoubtedly have to run late alone. But in a month of 60-hour workweeks, the subject of home responsibilities had never come up at his office. How could his boss know he needs time for his family if he didn't ask? His boss could know, of course, if he chose to "see" the family portrait on his desk and consider for a moment how such pictures are developed. Faces of affection don't just happen, he would have to conclude. They take time and care.

"You have to ask to change your hours," I pressed. "Our lives have to catch up with our heads."

"I'll see," he said.

"Mr. D., we need to know tonight," I repeat, asking for brownies but wishing for a revolution in the priorities of men. "If you can't bake them yourself, Sara Lee offers a good alternative." While I wait for his answer, I think about opening a new business, a consulting firm to help fathers "see," to discuss the many options to "I can't, I work."

"Okay," he says, recognizing the only answer that will return him to his TV program. "A dozen brownies, next Wednesday."

I then dial the number for Mr. F., repeating my message, then Misters L. and M. I am thrilled to raise the eyebrows of the fathers in Mr. Baldino's class. I imagine I am healing some tensions among women, between the mothers at home and outside it.

I have begun with brownies, but I plan to ask for day care and field trips next. I want fathers to absorb some of the home pressures they leave to mothers. When working fathers have the same needs as working mothers, corporations will begin to "see" the need for day care, flextime, sick days for family. The truth: when working fathers need the same benefits as working mothers, we will have them.

My deadline is still ahead of me when I finish the last call. But I feel successful, having pledges for 144 brownies, all from fathers. I can't be certain Mr. D. or Mr. F. did not immediately delegate the responsibility to their wives: "Tony needs a dozen brownies." Or that their wives did not reply, "I don't do brownies." But I realize, this evening, that I was through excusing fathers who "understood," but "had no choice." Understanding is fine, but now I want fathers to put their brownies where their mouths are.

The Politics of Talking in Couples:
Conversus Interruptus and Other Disorders

Barbara Ehrenreich

Not too long ago, this magazine carried an article on how to talk to a man in bed.[1] My only disappointment was that it was not followed up by a series of articles on how to talk to a man in other settings and on other items of furniture: "Talking in Living Rooms," for example, "Talking in Dinettes," and "Talking on Straight-Backed Chairs." For it is my conviction, based on years of what sociologists call participant observation, that far more male-female relationships die in the dining room than in the bedroom. And the problem is not the cuisine, it's the conversation.

The fact is that we are going through a profound Crisis in Intersex Conversation, and that this crisis has been the subject of a vast systematic cover-up. I am not referring to the well-known difficulty of maintaining equity in public discourse—meetings, cocktail parties, seminars, and the like—a problem amply documented by our feminist foresisters in the late sixties. I am referring to the much more insidious problem of intimate conversation between consenting adults of different sexes. Television evangelists alert us daily to new threats to the family, ranging from sex education to secular humanism. No one, however, mentions the crisis in conversation, which is far more serious. It threatens not only the family, but also the casual affair, the illicit liaison, and possibly the entire institution of heterosexuality.

I can understand that there are solid artistic and commercial reasons for the cover-up. If art were forced to conform to conversational reality, "A Man and a Woman" would have been done as a silent film, and the Broadway hit *The Lunch Hour* would have been condensed, quite adequately, into *The Coffee Break*. Imagine, for example, what would happen if the current spate of Gothic novels were required to meet truth-in-conversation standards:

She: Now that we are alone there is so much to talk about! I am filled with such confusion, for I have never told you the secret of my origins. . . .
He: Hmmm.
She: The truth about my identity and my true relationship to the Earl of D'Arcy, not to mention the real reason why the uppermost room in the far turret of Weathermore Manor has been sealed for thirty years!

---

[1] See "Talking in Bed—Now That We Know What We Want, How Do We Say It?" by Lonnie Barbach and Linda Levine (January, 1981).

He: Uh-huh.
She: You know the room at the top of the spiral staircase over the stables? Well, there's something so terrifying, so abominable, so *evil* . . .
He: Hey, will you look at that? It stopped raining.

Nevertheless, the truth about male-female conversations has been leaking out. In her book, *On Loving Men* (Dial Press), Jane Lazarre recounts a particularly disastrous conversational attempt with one of the objects of her love. Jane has just spent a long phone call consoling her recently widowed mother-in-law, who is hysterical with grief. She tells her husband about the call (after all, it was *his* mother), "after which we both lie there quietly." But she is still—understandably—shaken, and begins to fantasize losing her own husband:

> Crying by now, due to the reality of my fantasy as well as the full comprehension of my mother-in-law's pain, I turn to James, then intrude upon his perpetual silence and ask, "What are you thinking?" hoping for once to be answered from some vulnerable depth. . . . And he admitted (it was an admission because he was incredulous himself at the fact): "I was thinking about the Knicks. Wondering if they were going to trade Frazier."

Jane Lazarre attributes her husband's talent for aborting conversations to some "quality of character" peculiar to him and, in the book, goes off in search of more verbose companionship. Thousands of other women have also concluded that theirs was an individual problem: "*He* just doesn't listen to me," "I just can't talk to him," and so forth. This, however, is a mistake. We are not dealing with individual problems— unfortunate conversational mismatches—but with a crisis of genderwide proportions.

Much of the credit for uncovering the crisis must go to a few stealthy sociologists who have devoted themselves to listening in on male-female conversations. Pamela Fishman planted tape recorders in the homes of three couples and recorded (with their permission) more than 50 hours of real-life chitchat. The picture that emerges from Fishman's work is that of women engaged in a more or less solitary battle to keep the conversational ball rolling. Women nurture infant conversations—throwing out little hookers like "you know?" in order to enlist some help from their companions. Meanwhile, the men are often working at cross-purposes, dousing conversations with "ummms," non sequiturs, and unaccountable pauses. And, in case you're wondering, the subjects that Fishman's women nourished and men killed were neither boringly trivial nor threateningly intimate: they were frequently about current events, articles read, work in progress. Furthermore, the subjects of Fishman's research were couples who described themselves as "liberated" from sex roles. One can only wonder what she might have found by leaving her tape recorder in the average Levittown breakfast nook.

The problem is not that men are so taken with the strong, silent look that they *can't* talk. Sociologists Candace West and Donald Zimmerman did some extensive eavesdropping at various sites around the University of California campus at Santa Barbara and found that men interrupt women much more often than they interrupt other men and that they do so more often than women interrupt either men or other women. In analyzing her tapes of men and women who live together, Pamela Fishman found that topics introduced by men "succeeded" conversationally 96 percent of the time, while those introduced by women succeeded only 36 percent of the time and fell flat the rest of the time. Men can and will talk—if they can set the terms.

There are all kinds of explanations for the conversational mismatch between the sexes, none of which require more than a rudimentary feminist analysis. First, there's the fact that men are more powerful as a class of people, and expect to dominate in day-to-day interactions, verbal or otherwise. Take any intersex gathering and—unless a determined countereffort is undertaken—the basses and tenors quickly overpower the altos and sopranos.

For most men, public discourse is a competitive sport, in which points are scored with decisive finger jabs and conclusive table poundings, while adversaries are blocked with shoulder thrusts or tackled with sudden interruptions. This style does not, of course, carry over well to the conversational private sector. As one male informant admitted to me, albeit under mild duress, "If you're just with a woman there's no real competition. What's the point of talking?"

Male dominance is not the only problem. There's also male insecurity. When men have talked honestly about talking (or about not talking), either under psychiatric pressure or the lure of royalties, they tell us they are *afraid* to talk to women. Marc Feigen Fasteau confessed in *The Male Machine* (McGraw-Hill) that a "familiar blankness" overcame him in conversations with his wife, resulting from an "imagined fear that spontaneous talk will reveal unacceptable feelings—almost anything that would show vulnerability or indicate that the speaker doesn't 'measure up' to the masculine ideal."

Given the cultural barriers to intersex conversation, the amazing thing is that we would even expect women and men to have anything to say to each other for more than 10 minutes at a stretch. The barriers are ancient—perhaps rooted, as some up-and-coming paleontologist may soon discover, in the contrast between the occasional guttural utterances exchanged in male hunting bands and the extended discussions characteristic of female food-gathering groups. History does offer a scattering of successful mixed-sex conversational duos—Voltaire and Madame Du Châtelet, Marie and Pierre Curie—but the mass expectation that ordinary men and women should engage in conversation as a *routine* activity probably dates back no further than the 1950s and the era of "togetherness." Until then, male-female conversation had served principally as an element of courtship, sustained by sexual tension and easily abandoned after the nuptials. After suburbanization threw millions of couples alone together in tiny tract houses for whole weekends at a stretch, however, media pundits decided that conversation was not only a healthy but a necessary marital activity, even if the topic never rose above the level of septic tanks and aluminum siding. While I have no direct evidence, the success of these early mixed-sex conversational endeavors may perhaps be gauged by the mass influx of women into the work force and the explosive spread of feminism in the 1960s and 1970s.

It was feminism, of course, that raised women's conversational expectations. In consciousness-raising groups and National Organization for Women chapters, women's centers and caucuses, women discovered (or rediscovered) the possibilities of conversation as an act of collective creativity: the intimate sharing of personal experience, the weaving of the personal into the general and political, the adventure of freewheeling speculation unrestrained by academic rules or boundaries.

As men became aware of the heightened demands being placed upon them, their intellectual spokesmen quickly displaced the problem into the realm of sexuality. Thus Christopher Lasch, in discussing men's response to feminism, never even touches upon the conversational crisis, but tells us that "women's sexual demands terrify men," evoking images of "the vagina which threatens to eat them alive." But we could just as well invert this florid Freudiana and conclude that it is women's verbal demands that terrify men and that the dread *vagina dentata* (devouring, toothed vagina) of male fantasy is in fact a *mouth* symbol, all set to voice some conversational overture such as "Don't you think it's interesting that . . . ?"

Now that the crisis is out in the open, what do we do about it? Is there any way to teach a grown man, or short of that, a little one, how to converse in a manner that is stimulating, interesting, and satisfying to women? One approach might be to work through the educational system, introducing required mixed-gender courses in English Conversation. Or we might take a clinical approach, setting up therapeutic centers to treat Male Conversational Dysfunction. Various diagnostic categories leap to mind: "Conversational Impotence" (total inability to get a subject off the ground); "Premature Ejaculation" (having the answer to everything, before anybody else gets a chance to utter a sentence); "Conversus Interruptus"; and so forth. It may even be necessary, in extreme cases, to provide specially trained female Conversational Surrogates.

My own intuition is that the conversational crisis will be solved only when women and men—not just women—together realize their common need for both social and personal change. After all, women have discovered each other and the joy of cooperative discourse through a common political project—the feminist movement. So struck was I with this possibility that I tried it out loud on a male companion: "Can you imagine women and men together in a movement that demands both social and personal transformation?" There was a long, and I hoped pregnant, pause. Then he said, "Hmmmmm."

Trading Places

Melinda Beck et al.

Like many daughters of aging parents, Sandy Berman didn't recognize at first how far her mother and father had slipped. "You are so used to your parents being mentally competent that you don't realize what you're dealing with for a long time," says the Northridge, Calif., schoolteacher, 47. Her parents had been living with trash piling up in their home for almost a year when Berman finally convinced them to move closer. But the move only hastened their decline. Berman's father, 83, became forgetful and overdosed on his insulin. Her mother, 74, couldn't find her way from the bedroom to the bathroom. For months, Berman called every morning before going to work, and stopped by every afternoon. "I was going to make everything right, and better and perfect," she says. "But everything I did turned into mush."

While her mother was sweet and cooperative, Berman says, age turned her father mean. He called at all hours of the night and thought his daughter was stealing his money. He hired a detective and changed the locks on the door. Berman was haunted by anxiety attacks. Her job teaching third grade was her only refuge. "When the bell rang at the end of the day, my stomach started to clench," she says. She worried that she was neglecting her husband and son, and longed to be mothered herself again. She lost 30 pounds and had fantasies of running away: *"San Fernando Valley schoolteacher disappears. No one knows why she didn't come home for dinner. . . ."*

In February 1989, Berman snapped. "I was nurturing at home, at school and at my parents', and getting nothing back," she says. She quit work and stopped seeing her parents for two months, all the while making decisions for them with the help of a geriatric counselor and a lawyer. Diagnosed with Alzheimer's disease and paranoia, her father went from one nursing facility to another, and died in May 1989. Berman found a board-and-care home for her mother and enrolled her in an adult day-care center to keep her mind stimulated. These days, Berman visits her twice a month, and calls once a week, though her mother doesn't seem to know if she has called or not. Berman has returned to work, but she still wonders—and always will—"Did I do the right thing?"

Anguish, frustration, devotion and love. A fierce tangle of emotions comes with parenting one's aged parents, and there isn't time to sort out the feelings, let alone make dinner, fold the laundry and get to work. More than 6 million elderly Americans need help with such basics as getting out of bed and going to the bathroom; millions more can't manage meals, money or transportation. Most are cared for by family members, at home, for free—and most families wouldn't have it any other way. There are myriad variations: "children" in their 60s looking after parents in their 80s; spouses spending their golden years tending ailing mates; empty-nesters who had paid the last tuition check only to have an aged relative move in. Increasingly, men are shouldering such responsibilities. Still, three fourths of those caring for the elderly are women, as it has always been. "Until the last couple of decades, women were home," explains Diane Piktialis of Work/Family Directions, a Boston consulting firm. "Caregiving was their job."

But today they have other jobs as well. More than half the women who care for elderly relatives also work outside the home; nearly 40 percent are still raising children of their own. In fact, just when many women on the "Mommy Track" thought they could get back to their careers, some are finding themselves on an even longer "Daughter Track," with their parents, or their husband's parents, growing frail. The average American woman will spend 17 years raising children and 18 years helping aged parents, according to a 1988 U.S. House of Representatives report. As the population ages and chronic, disabling conditions become more common, many more families will care for aged relatives. And because they delayed childbirth, more couples will find themselves "sandwiched" between child care and elder care. The oldest baby boomers are now in their mid-40s; their parents are mostly in their late 60s and early 70s, when disabilities tend to begin. In the next few years, predicts Dana Friedman of the Families and Work Institute, there will be a "groundswell of baby boomers experiencing these problems."

The strains on women, long evident in their personal lives, are now showing up in the workplace. In recent years, about 14 percent of caregivers to the elderly have switched from full- to part-time jobs and 12 percent have left the work force, according to the American Association of Retired Persons. Another 28 percent have considered quitting their jobs, other studies have found. That's just what's aboveboard. Many employees are afraid to let on that they spent that "sick day" taking Mom to the doctor, visiting nursing homes or applying for Medicare. Many women shop, cook and clean for their parents before work, after work and on lunch hours, stealing time to confer on the phone during the day. "Caring for a dependent adult has become, for many, a second full-time job," says Bernard M. Kilbourn, a former regional director of the U.S. Health and Human Services Department, now with a consulting group, Caregivers Guidance Systems, Inc.

To date, only about 3 percent of U.S. companies have policies that assist employees caring for the elderly. But Friedman predicts that such programs will become "the new, pioneering benefit of the 1990s." Businesses may have no choice. With the baby bust sharply reducing the number of young workers entering the job market, the U.S. Bureau of Labor Statistics warns that 60 percent of the growth in the labor force this decade will be women, virtually all aged 35 to 54. "This is the age group that's feeling the brunt of child-care responsibilities," says the BLS's Jesse Benjamin. "This is also the age group where elder care hits. It's a double whammy."

Congress is encouraging more family-friendly work policies—at least, it has tried. After five years of debate, lawmakers recently passed the Family and Medical Leave Act, requiring companies with more than 50 employees to grant them up to 12 weeks' unpaid leave to care for newborn or adopted children or relatives who are seriously ill. But President George Bush vetoed the bill, on the ground that government should not dictate corporate benefits.

American society is just waking up to the needs of an aging population. Even the words "elder care" and "caregiver" are new to the lexicon. Now, "there's a name and a description, and people are beginning to say, 'I fit into that,'" says Louise Fradkin, cofounder of the support group Children of Aging Parents (CAPS), which has more than 100 chapters nationwide. For years, Fradkin says, caring for aged relatives was a hidden responsibility, one that most women assumed in silence. Even the major feminist groups have been slow to make it a cause. The National Organization for Women, for example, has been more concerned with abortion rights and advancement for women in the workplace than with family roles. "The problem today's midlife woman faces is that the rhetoric of the '70s and the realities of the '90s are somewhat discordant," says Michael Creedon of the National Council on the Aging.

Only the Older Women's League (OWL), a Washington advocacy group, has made elder care a pressing issue. "No matter what else we talk about, our members always come back to caregiving—it has a big impact on all their other roles," says OWL executive director Joan Kuriansky. "We get letters from women who are taking care of their children, and their parents and possibly *their* parents. They are running from place to place. How do we expect them to do that and stay employed?"

That is the dilemma of the Daughter Track. While women have become a major force in the American workplace, their roles as caregivers remain entrenched in the expectations of society and individual families. "Often it's the woman's own sense of what's required of her," says Kuriansky. "Some of it is emotional. Some of it is economic—she may feel that she cannot contribute financially as much as a man does." And just as with child care, says CAPS's Fradkin, "women feel they have to be super-women and do it all themselves."

Those who do ask for help at home are often frustrated. Many husbands are unable—or unwilling—to confront the emotional demands of elder care, even when the aged parents are their own. Two years ago, Pamela Resnick of Coral Springs, Fla., quit her job and moved her ailing father-in-law in. While he was in and out of hospitals, she says, "he always wanted to see me—not even my husband. My husband doesn't deal very well with that type of scene." Joan Segal, 49, who quit her job to care for her mother, threatened to leave her husband unless he helped her mother more. Since then, Segal says, "he's so protective you'd think she was his own mother."

Grandchildren may also be swept into the changing family dynamics, and that adds to the guilt many women feel. Krissteen Davis, 43, a divorced accounting supervisor, has cut down her work hours since her 63-year-old mother, an Alzheimer's victim, came to live with her in Kansas City. Still, Davis's 13-year-old daughter must be home by 3:30 each day when her grandmother returns from an adult day-care center. "It's been hard on all of us," says Davis. Yet she says her mother "did for me when I was young. What's a couple of years out of my life?" . . .

Responsibility for an elderly relative usually falls to the woman who is nearest. And sometimes no one is close. Roughly one third of caregivers manage care for their aged parents long distance, assessing changing needs over the phone and with reports from neighbors. Even though her mother and father lived in a residential community that provided housekeeping and meals, Saretta Berlin, 60, flew from Philadelphia to Ft. Lauderdale, Fla., every 10 days during much of 1989, when her parents were failing. "I would tell myself that if I just made it to the plane, I would be OK," she says. "Then perfect strangers would ask me how I was doing, and the floodgates would open." Even now, with her father dead and her mother in a retirement home, Berlin calls daily and visits every three weeks or so.

As Berlin found, even when families put a parent in a nursing home, their responsibilities don't end. Many grown children rearrange their lives to visit as often as possible, and field lonely phone calls, night and day. Only about 10 percent of the disabled elderly are in such facilities—and the decision can haunt their families long afterward. Linda Hunt still feels guilty about putting her mother in a home three years ago—even though she was blind and Hunt was holding down two full-time jobs. "You think you should be able to do it all, but you can't," she says. "First you care for your children, then your mother. Pretty soon you just give your whole self to other people." . . .

Unlike child care, the responsibilities of elder care often come suddenly. A stroke or broken hip can mean the difference between a parent living independently and needing round-the-clock care. And while a child's needs can be planned for, an older person's requirements are often difficult to assess. Can Dad still manage in his own home? Will he need care for a few months—or many years? What's more, says

Kilbourn, "in dealing with your parents, you do not have total control. Any decision . . . can be met with resistance if not total refusal to cooperate."

Reversing roles is one of the hardest aspects of caring for an aged parent. Krissteen Davis says her mother was "a really sharp lady—and one of my best friends" before Alzheimer's set in. Now, Davis says, "sometimes she just sits there like a little lump that used to be a person." Elderly people find it even harder to relinquish their old parental roles. Many are desperately afraid of burdening their busy children, yet desperately afraid of being alone.

Dot von Gerbig's mother and father moved in to help her in 1969, when she was a widow raising small children. Today, they still share her Honey Brook, Pa., home, along with her second husband and their 15-year-old son. Von Gerbig's father, 92, is confined to a wheelchair; her mother, 84, is mentally confused, and both are legally blind. Before leaving for work at 7 a.m. von Gerbig arranges every aspect of their lives, laying out clothes and organizing food in the refrigerator, so they can manage by themselves until she returns. "So far, we're making it," says von Gerbig, 52. But she lives in fear that something will go wrong and make her break her vow to keep them out of a nursing home. What troubles her even more, she says, is how terribly cruel the aging process is. "It makes me angry and it makes me fearful," she says. "It's an awful thing that a person does a good job all his life and this is his reward."

Most caregivers lament that they can't do more for their parents. Some of the toughest constraints are financial. Medicare does not cover the costs of long-term care, anywhere. Medicaid will pay for nursing homes, and home care in some states, but only after a patient has depleted his assets nearly to the poverty level. Thus, many elderly people exhaust their life savings paying for care, and families dig deep into their own pockets to help them.

Many married women, particularly those in low-paying jobs, find it cheaper to quit work and care for aging relatives themselves than to hire home health care. Professional women are less inclined to quit and more apt to hire help. Many are torn between the parents they cherish and the work they love. Just when many have gotten a long-awaited promotion, they find their parents in need of care. . . .

What can employers do to make that easier? One of the most helpful things is to acknowledge the situation. "Corporate America needs to create an environment where employees can say, 'I have a problem with an elder who needs care,'" says OWL president Lou Glasse. The Travelers Companies was one of the first to do so; after a 1985 survey found that 28 percent of its workers over 30 cared for an aged parent, on an average of 10 hours a week, Travelers started a series of support programs. Today's leader may be The Stride Rite Corp., which this year opened the nation's first on-site intergenerational day-care center.

Other forward-looking firms have devised a wide range of programs and benefits. One of the most common, and least costly, is simply to educate employees about social services available in their communities. Some firms hold lunchtime seminars or "Caregiver Fairs," where local agencies describe their programs. Some publish detailed handbooks for employees, covering everything from how to select a nursing home to how to locate and pay for respite care. Growing numbers of companies also contract with private consulting firms that can help employees manage care even for relatives in distant cities. Work/Family Directions has developed programs for 21 national firms, linking their clients' employees with 175 agencies across the country. It also provides an 800 number for support and advice. In a few cities, government agencies provide similar services. Employees "don't want a way out of their caregiving responsibilities—they just want some help in coping," says Barbara Lepis, director of Partnership for Eldercare, a New York City program working with American Express, Philip Morris and J.P. Morgan.

The same Employee Assistance Programs (EAPs) that assist workers with drug and alcohol problems can often help with strains on the home front. In fact, EAP counselors frequently find that caregiving duties are at the root of employees' financial, marital or job-performance difficulties. Teresa Freeman, EAP manager at Travelers, says one employee was referred to her office because she was crying at work; another had been put on warning because she was unable to learn new skills. Both, it turned out, were caring for elderly parents and were cracking under the strain. Freeman formed a support group of caregiving employees. But other firms have found that support groups don't work well in situations where bosses and their subordinates may be reluctant to share intimate problems. Lepis says the chemistry works better when such sessions are called "caregiver exchanges" that deal with a specific topic, such as filling out a medical form. "Then we are able to get a cross-strata of the work force to commiserate together about this stupid form," she says.

Some firms are training supervisors to be compassionate about the demands workers face at home. Managers must also be reminded that the Mommy Track, and the Daughter Track, should not be slower roads to advancement. Otherwise, warned OWL in its 1989 Mother's Day report, "only orphans with no children could be placed on the fast track to professional success." . . .

In the end, there is only so much the business world can do to help America's caregivers. Many liberal lawmakers and more than 100 special-interest groups are pressing the federal government to do more. In March, the U.S. Bipartisan Commission on Comprehensive Health Care proposed a giant new long-term care program that would guarantee home health care and three free months in a nursing home to all severely disabled Americans who need it, regardless of age or income. But the price tag—an estimated $42 billion a year—virtually assures that no legislative action will be taken any time soon.

Even without creating a massive new entitlement program, the federal government could do more to help the elderly and those who care for them. Federal funding for the network of social-service programs serving the elderly is a paltry $710 million a year; services are sparse and fragmented in many areas. Most offices are open only 9 to 5, forcing caregivers to deal with them during work hours. OWL is pressing the Social Security Administration to rewrite rules that penalize workers who take time out to care for children or aged dependents. Upon retirement, a worker's monthly benefit is determined by averaging his or her earnings over the past 35 years. A zero is entered for any year not worked, no matter what the reason. Caregiving, says OWL executive director Kuriansky, "is a wonderful dimension of woman as nurturer—and it's something we don't want to undermine. But in playing that role, we want to make sure she is rewarded, not penalized."

Most women on the Daughter Track do not want to give up their family responsibilities—no matter what personal or professional sacrifices it entails. Many see their efforts as a chance to repay the time and care their parents gave them—a chance to say, again, *I love you,* before it's too late. What they would like is more understanding at work, more support from the men in their lives, more community services to help them—and a little applause from a world that often turns too fast to take time out for love.

Native American Women Today

Shirley Hill Witt

The stereotypes concerning Native Americans popular among the descendants of the European pioneers—whether in legend or on television—nonetheless depict *male* Natives. A different set of stereotypes materializes when one says "an Indian woman" or, so demeaningly, a "squaw." In fact, it takes some effort to conjure up an impression of that invisible Native woman.

On a time line of New World history, one might locate Malinche of Aztec Mexico, Pocahontas of Virginia, and Sacajawea of the Northwest. They are probably the only female "personalities" that come to mind out of the great faceless sea of all the Native women who were born, lived, and died in this hemisphere.

And ironically, these three Native women are not now Native heroines, if they ever were. In Mexico, the term "malinchismo" refers to selling out one's people to the enemy. Malinche, Pocahontas, and Sacajawea aided—perhaps unwittingly—in the downfall of their own people.

Another stereotype, the personality-less squaw, is regarded as a brown lump of a drudge, chewing buffalo hide, putting that tipi up and down again and again, carrying heavy burdens along with the dogs while the tribe moves ever onward, away from the pursuing cavalry.

The term "squaw" began as a perfectly acceptable Algonkian term meaning "woman." In time, it became synonymous with "drudge" and, in some areas, "prostitute." The ugliest epithet a frontiersman could receive was to be called a "squaw-man"—the lowliest of the low.

Very much rarer is the image of a bronze nubile naked "princess," a child of nature or beloved concoction of Hollywood producers. This version is often compounded with the Pocahontas legend. As the story goes, she dies in self-sacrifice, saving the life of the white man for whom she bears an unrequited love, so that he may live happily ever after with a voluptuous but high-buttoned blonde.

Since all stereotypes are unsatisfactory and do not replicate real people, the myths of Native women of the past ought also to be retired to the graveyard of stereotypes. But what about stereotypes of modern Native women—are there any to be laid to rest? Present stereotypes are also male, are they not? The drunken Indian, the Cadillac Indian, Lonesome Polecat—facelessness still characterizes Native American women.

In this third quarter of the century, Native Americans yet remain the faceless minority despite a few "uprisings" such as Alcatraz, the Trail of Broken Treaties, and the Second Wounded Knee. That these "uprisings" were of definitive importance to the Indian world only underscores its basic invisibility to most Americans, many of whom pass off those protests as trivial and, naturally, futile—much ado about nothing.

And if a million Native Americans reside below national consciousness, certainly that fifty-or-so percent of them that are female are all the more nonentities.

BEFORE COLUMBUS

As many as 280 distinct aboriginal societies existed in North America prior to Columbus. In several, the roles of Native women stand in stark contrast to those of Europeans. These societies were matriarchal, matrilineal, and matrilocal—which is to say that women largely controlled family matters, inheritance passed through the female line, and upon marriage the bride usually brought her groom into her mother's household.

In a matrilocal society all the women were blood relatives and all the males were outsiders. This sort of residence pattern was frequently seen among agricultural societies in which women bore the responsibility for farming. It guaranteed a close-knit working force of women who had grown up with each other and the land.

Somewhat similar was the style of acquiring a spouse called "bride service" or "suitor service." In this case, the prospective husband went to live and work in his future bride's home for a period of time, proving his ability to manage a family of his own. This essentially resulted in temporary matrilocal residence. After the birth of the first child, the husband usually took his new family with him to live among his own kin.

In matrilineal, matrilocal society, a woman forever remained part of her original household, her family of orientation. All the women she grew up with stayed nearby, although she "lost" her brothers to other households. All the husbands were outsiders brought into the family at the time of marriage.

In such societies, usually agricultural, the economy was maintained largely by females. The fields and harvests were the property of women. Daughters inherited rights to fields and the like through their mothers—fields which they had worked in all their lives in one capacity or another, from chasing away the crows as a child to tilling the soil as an adult.

Women working together certainly characterized aboriginal economy. This lifestyle was roughly similar in such widespread groups as the Iroquois, the Mandan, the Hopi and Zuni, and various Eastern Pueblos. Among the Hopi and the Zuni the husband joined the bride's household upon marriage. The fields were owned by the women, as were their products, the house, and related implements. However, the men labored in the gardens and were (with the unmarried brothers) responsible for much or most of the work.

The strong and influential position of women in Navajo society extended beyond social and economic life. Navajo women also controlled a large share of the political and religious life of the people, called the Dinè. Hogans, herds, and equipment were passed down through the female line, from mother to daughters. Like the Iroquois, women were integral to the religious cycle. The Navajo female puberty ceremony ranked among the most important of Dinè activities.

Although the lives of Native American women differed greatly from tribe to tribe, their life-styles exhibited a great deal more independence and security than those of the European women who came to these shores. Indian women had individual freedom within tribal life that women in more "advanced" societies were not to experience for several generations. Furthermore—and in contrast—Native women increased in value in the estimation of their society as they grew older. Their cumulative wisdom was considered one of society's most valuable resources.

TODAY

What do we know about Native American women today? Inclusive statements such as the following refer to both sexes:

• Only 13.4 percent of the U.S. Indian population had completed eight years of school by 1970.

• The average educational level of all Indians under federal supervision is five school years.

• Dropout rates for Indians are twice the national average.

• Only 18 percent of the students in federal Indian schools go to college; the national average is 50 percent.

• Only 3 percent of the Indian students who enroll in college graduate; the national average is 32 percent.

• Indians suffer from unemployment and underemployment—up to 90 percent unemployment on some reservations in winter months.

• Indians have a high birth rate, a high infant mortality rate, and a short life expectancy.

But there are differences in how these facts relate to Native American women as opposed to men. There has not been equal treatment of Native males and females any more than there has been equal treatment of the two sexes among non-Natives. We can look at this by considering a few major institutions affecting all our lives—education, employment, and health.

Education

For over a century the federal government has assumed the responsibility for educating Native Americans to the standards of the general population. Nearly every treaty contained provisions for education—a teacher, a school, etc.—as partial payment for lands and rights surrendered.

Until recent years, the U.S. Bureau of Indian Affairs educational system relied upon the boarding school as the cornerstone of Native education, the foundation for indoctrination. Generation after generation of Native children were processed through boarding schools, from the time they were five or six years old until departure or graduation, whichever came first. They lived away from their homes from four to twelve years except during summer (and in some cases, even then). They became divorced from their cultures in line with the government's master plan for the ultimate solution to the "Indian Problem": assimilation.

And so generation after generation of Native women have been processed through a system clearly goal-oriented. That is to say, the government's master plan for women has been to generate an endless stream of domestics and, to a lesser extent, secretaries. The vocational choices for Native children in boarding schools have always been exceedingly narrow and sexist. Boys do woodworking, car repair, house painting, or farm work, while girls do domestic or secretarial work.

Writing about Stewart Indian School in their book *To Live on This Earth,* Estelle Fuchs and Robert J. Havighurst report:

> The girls may choose from only two fields: general and home service (domestic work) or "hospital ward attendant" training, which the girls consider a degrading farce, a euphemism (they say) for more domestic work.

Thus young women are even more suppressed in working toward their aspirations than are boys. Furthermore, just as the males will more than likely find they must move away from their communities to practice their crafts, females cannot exercise their learned domestic crafts in the reservation setting either. A woman cannot even play out the role of a domestic, or the average American housewife and mother (as portrayed by the BIA), in the reservation atmosphere. As one author explains the Navajo woman's dilemma:

> Reservation life . . . cannot support the picture of the average American homemaker. The starched and relatively expensive advertised clothes are out of place and unobtainable. The polished floors and picture windows which generated her envious school dreams are so removed from the hogan or log cabin as to become unreal. The many convenient appliances are too expensive and would not run without electricity. The clean and smiling children require more water than the Navajo family can afford the time to haul. Parent Teacher Association meetings, of which she may have read, are the product of tax-supported schools with the parent in the ultimate role of employer. On the reservation the government-appointed teacher is viewed more as an authority figure than a public servant.

Off-reservation, given the prevalence of Indian poverty, the all-American home-maker role still is thwarted, although hiring out as a domestic servant is possible.

Statistics about the educational attainment of Indians, Eskimos, and Aleuts are not hard to come by, but it is very difficult to obtain figures by sex. The exhaustive Havighurst report does not provide separate tabulations by sex in its summary volu ne *To Live on This Earth.* A U.S. Civil Rights Commission staff report found that 5.8 percent of the Indian males and 6.2 percent of the Indian females in a recent Southwest study had completed eight years of school. (The rate for all U.S. Indians in 1970 was 13.4 percent.)

The impression left from scanning available surveys is that in recent years females attain more years of formal education than do males, although some fifty years ago probably the reverse was true. This impression sits uneasily with study after study indicating that Native women are dramatically less acculturated than males.

Much data suggests that the BIA educational system is less effective for females than it is for males in creating successful mainstream prototypes—although young males have an alarming suicide rate that is far higher than that of females.

An investigation by Harry W. Martin, *et al.,* showed that of 411 Indian women at two Oklahoma Public Health Service medical out-patient clinics, 59.4 percent were classified as mildly or severely neurotic, compared to 50 percent of the males.

For the severely neurotic category alone, 31.7 percent of the Indian females were found to be severely impaired. This was almost one third more than the males, who rated 23.7 percent. No clear relationship seemed to exist between the ages of the women and the incidence of impairment. (Men, on the other hand, tended to show neurotic symptoms more often in the fifty to fifty-nine age bracket.)

When scores and level of education were correlated, it appeared that males with less education suffered more psychiatric problems than high school graduates, although the rates rose again with post–high school attainment. For females, a similar set of rates prevailed, but—as with suicide—their rate was not as acute as the male rate.

Such evidence suggests that amid the general failure of the federal system to educate Native Americans in school curricula, the system also acculturates native females to a lesser degree than males. It cannot even transform women from native homemakers into mainstream homemakers. The neurotic response seems to tell us of widespread female disorganization and unhappiness.

The suicide statistics for young males who rate as more acculturated than females simply point up the shallowness of the assimilationist mentality of the BIA educational system. Is it not ironic that after more than a century of perfecting a federal indoctrination system, their best product—the more acculturated males—so often seek self-destruction, while nearly one third of the females abide in a state of neuroticism?

Employment

Employment of Native women is as one might expect, considering the level and quality of their educational background. Most employed women are domestics, whether in private homes, in janitorial positions, or in hospitals. The *Navajo Times* newspaper regularly carries want ads such as:

> WANTED strong young woman for live-in babysitter and mother's helper. No smoking or drinking. Call collect: San Diego, California.

As one young woman commented, "They must have run out of black maids." Perhaps the economic reality is that blacks are no longer at the bottom of the pile. Indians who have or will go to the cities are taking their place.

Federal employment for Native Americans essentially means employment in the BIA or the Indian Health Service. Native women in the BIA provide a veritable army of clerks and secretaries. They are concentrated, of course, in lower GS ratings, powerless and vulnerable. The U.S. Civil Rights Commission's *Southwest Indian Report* disclosed that in Arizona, Indians comprised 81.2 percent of all the personnel in grades 1 (lowest) through 5, but white personnel constituted only 7.3 percent of employees in these grades.

The figure for Natives includes both male and female employees, but it might not be unreasonable to suggest that females outnumber males among Natives employed as GS white collar employees. And although men most likely outnumber women in the blue collar jobs, the large numbers of native women in BIA and IHS domestic jobs (for example, hospital ward attendant) should not be overlooked. In general, the *Southwest Indian Report* concluded that although Indians constitute the majority of BIA employees in Arizona and New Mexico, they are disproportionately concentrated in the lower wage, nonprofessional jobs.

In the Commission report, Ms. Julia Porter, a retired Indian nurse who also testified about Indian employment in the IHS, noted that "most of the supervisors are Anglos. You never see an Indian head nurse or a supervisor. You see a lot of janitors. You see a lot of low-grade employees over there." Ms. Ella Rumley, of the Tucson Indian Center, reported that Indians who have jobs in that area are employed only in menial positions. There are no Indian retail clerks, tellers, or secretaries, to her knowledge. The Arizona State Employment Service reported that domestic employment placement averaged out to "approximately 34 percent of the job placements available for Indians in the years 1969 and 1970."

Moreover, given the wage disparity between the sexes in salary in the general population, it comes as no surprise that Native women in clerical and domestic work far often receive only pittances for their labor. The reasons for absenteeism and short-term employment which may to some degree characterize Native as well as Anglo female employment are similar: responsibility for the survival of home and family. Outside employment and familial duties conflict for all women. In addition, discrimination and prejudice produce low employee morale, inhibiting commitment to a job. Native women and men are passed over in promotions, as shown in the congressional staff report *No Room at the Top*—meaning "no Natives need apply."

Sadly, even in the brief but brilliant days of the BIA New Team under former Commissioner Louis R. Bruce, an Iroquois-Sioux, Native females in the upper echelons were scarce. One doesn't need to be an Anglo to be a male chauvinist! The common complaint is, of course, that no "qualified" Native women are available. This brings to mind the statement of U.S. Civil Rights Commissioner Frankie M. Freeman.

> I have been on this Commission . . . for about 8½ years. And I remember back in February of 1965 when the Commission held hearings in Jackson, Mississippi (and was told) "We can't find any qualified . . . blacks." . . . And then in December of 1968 we went to San Antonio, Texas (and, we were told) they could not find any "qualified" Mexican Americans or Chicanos! And in February of this year we were in New York, and they couldn't find any "qualified" Puerto Ricans! And today you can't find any "qualified" Indians! What disturbs me is that the word "qualified" only gets put in front of a member of a minority or an ethnic. The assumption seems to be that all whites are qualified. You never hear about anybody looking for a "qualified white person." . . . It seems that the word "qualified" sort of dangles as an excuse for discriminating against minorities. In this sense, clearly *all* women must be included as minority members, but to be a woman *and* a minority member can be all the more difficult.

Health

President Johnson observed that "the health level of the American Indian is the lowest of any major population group in the United States." The situation has not improved, as the *Southwest Indian Report* demonstrates. It is inexplicable that the federal government provides the best health service anywhere in the world to its astronauts, military, and veterans, while its service to Native Americans is hopelessly inadequate. The obligation of the federal government to provide health services to Native Americans derives also from treaty obligations, and appears to be administered in as incompetent a fashion as are the educational services.

The symptom-oriented practice of the IHS makes preventive medicine a secondary effort. Social as well as biologic pathologies are not being attacked at their source, but rather at the stage of acute disability.

Not long ago, Dr. Sophie D. Aberle, a Ph.D. anthropologist and an M.D., advised against following her two-degree pattern:

> No [she said], don't go after the M.D. now that you have your Ph.D. in anthropology, for two reasons: one, because you wouldn't want to spend the rest of your life interacting with doctors—they're so shallow! And two, as a doctor I can cure gross symptoms perhaps, but I have to send [people] back into the environment in which they got sick in the first place. Cure the social ills and we're a long way down the road to curing the symptoms.

As it relates to women, the major "preventive" effort has been in the area of birth control and family planning. One gets the impression that it is the sole program concerned with before-the-fact care. But Native Americans on the whole reject the concept of birth control. In an impoverished environment, whether rural or city slum, infant mortality is extremely high. As Robert L. Kane and Rosalie A. Kane describe the rationale for unimpeded reproduction in their book *Federal Health Care (with Reservations!):*

> In earlier years, population growth was crucial to survival of the tribe and its people. In many agrarian societies, children are a form of economic protection. They guarantee a pool of manpower for maintaining and enlarging one's holdings; they are a source of protection and support when the parents can no longer work. With high rates of infant mortality, large numbers of offspring are needed to ensure that several will survive to adulthood.

When the standard of living is raised above the subsistence level, Third World nations usually experience a diminution of the birth rate. The Native American population so far does not seem to have taken a downward swing. In fact, birth rates for some Native groups may be the highest ever recorded anywhere.

Birth control is a topic laden with tension for many groups, particularly for non-whites in this country. Federal birth control programs began with nonwhites: Puerto Ricans, Navajos, and blacks. It is not too difficult to understand how some may view this first effort as an attempt to pinch off nonwhite birth production. It is hard not to draw such a conclusion.

Among Native Americans, the memory of genocide and tribal extinction is a raw unhealing wound. Fear persists that the desire for the "ultimate solution to the Indian Problem"—the extinguishment of Native Americans—still lives. Kane and Kane say of birth control:

> It is associated with extinction as a people, [with] genocide. The tension runs close to the surface when Navajos discuss this issue. Many interpret efforts along the family planning line as an attempt to breed the race into oblivion. Other Indian tribes have virtually disap-

peared because of declining birth rates in the face of captivity and inhospitable government reservations.

Native intractability can be sensed in the statement made at a community discussion with IHS officials about family planning. A Navajo woman concluded "As long as there are big Navajos, there will be little Navajos." And then the meeting broke up.

An exceedingly interesting set of investigations by two Egyptian female scientists, Laila Hamamsy and Hind Khattah, seems to cast in a new light the accelerating birth rates among some Navajo groups. Their thesis suggests that white American males are the cause, and in a wholly unexpected way.

First, Navajos are traditionally matriarchal, matrilineal, and matrilocal. From such a position of strength, Navajo women performed a wide array of roles necessary for the survival and success of the extended family.

However, as the thesis goes, white Anglo males from a rigidly paternalistic, male-dominated society refused to recognize and deal with the fact of Navajo matriarchy. Instead, they dealt only with Navajo males on all matters where the two cultures touched. As a result, more and more of the women's roles were supplanted by male actors and then male takeover.

There seems to be a statistical correlation between the period in which Anglo ascendancy impinged on female roles, and the onset and acceleration of the birth rate around the peripheral Navajo communities where most cultural interaction takes place. Anglo culture as practiced by white males brought about the loss of nearly all Navajo women's roles save that of childbearer. When producing offspring is one's only vehicle for gaining prestige and ego satisfaction, then we can expect the birth rate to ascend.

To what extent this thesis can apply to other minority groups—and also to middle-class white American females who are now the biggest producers of offspring—is not yet answerable. But the thesis is appealing, in any event.

Other preventive programs are virtually nonexistent. Among some of the Northern Pueblo groups and elsewhere, prenatal care clinics are held sporadically and with a minimum of success. This is the fault of both lack of funds and lack of commitment on the part of the IHS and the general lack of information available to potential users about such programs.

That preventive programs can and do succeed where there is commitment is seen in the fine example set by Dr. Annie Wauneka. She received the National Peace Medal for bringing to her Navajo people information and procedures they could use to combat tuberculosis ravaging on the reservation at that time.

Charges that Native Americans are locked into superstition and therefore hostile to modern medicine just are not factual. Preventive programs properly couched would no doubt be welcome. But, as the Citizen's Advocate Center reports in *Our Brother's Keeper:*

> The Public Health Service has no outreach system or delivery system, no systematic preventive care program, no early detection system. Thus . . . (it) is not structured to cope at the right point and on the proper scale with the underlying causes of poor health.

SOME COMMENTS

In the briefest way, this article has touched upon a few of the major institutions of life—education, employment, and health—as they are experienced by Native American women.

The next step in understanding among women and between peoples is mutual identification of needs. Many of life's difficulties for Native women are no different than those of other minority women—blacks, Chicanas, or the Appalachian poor. And then when the commonalities between minority and majority women are recognized—if not on a socioeconomic level, at least on a philosophic level—we may expect to witness a national movement for the equality of peoples and sexes.

When the Boss Wants Sex

Yla Eason

Florine Mitchell watched the lights blink through each number as the elevator sped to the top floor. She and her boss were on their way to get her desk supplies. "Have you ever made love to a white man?" her boss asked casually. Florine wrinkled her brow and stared at him in disbelief. "Would you slap my face if I made a pass at you?" he inquired in the same tone. Florine shook her head quickly in astonishment and searched the elevator walls for something on which to focus. Suddenly the doors opened and she broke her silence with a sigh. Florine looked at her watch. She had been on this new job one hour.

Florine was exposed to something just then dawning on the American consciousness and rising in the courts. In 1976, no one was sure what to call it. Today that something is clearly defined as sexual harassment. Unfortunately for Florine Mitchell (not her real name), that precise definition did not come soon enough.

Later, as she stepped into the storage room, her boss told his new assistant manager how attractive she was and leaned forward to kiss her. Blocking his move, Florine announced, "I don't go for that, and I wish you wouldn't try it again. As long as I've worked, I've never gotten involved with anybody on the job, especially my *boss*." He apologized.

At lunch he talked about the sad sexual relationship he shared with his wife. "We sleep in separate bedrooms," he confessed. Florine was edgy, and she told him that she felt awkward listening to him discuss his personal life. Again, he apologized.

"I like you," her boss declared three days later. "Don't like me," Florine snapped, trying not to bruise his ego. "I have a boyfriend I'm in love with, and I have no intentions of cutting out on him." This time her boss didn't apologize. Instead he said, "Think about it." Florine was thoroughly confused. It puzzled her that a man in his position was coming on to her this way.

When she discovered in her desk a lewd cartoon, which her superior laughingly admitted placing there, she threatened to tell *his* superior. "Go ahead," he mockingly advised. "He's my best friend."

"You're gonna make love to me," he insisted a few days later. He then explained the details of an out-of-town trip he was arranging to the branch office. After the meeting, he continued, she would spend the night with him at a hotel. This offer frightened her, and she thought quickly about the mortgage note she had to make next month, her two sons, her separation from her husband and her family several hundred miles away. If she'd had this job longer, she could collect unemployment. Florine decided she couldn't quit now. She would reason with him. She would go on the trip "strictly for the job" and come back that night. He repeated his request. "No way in hell," she stressed. "Think about it," he said.

Had sexual harassment been a more publicized issue, Florine would have known what her options were. She also would have known that hers was not an isolated case. Statistics say 50 to 80 percent of all women in the work place have been subject to verbal or physical harassment. Of the four and a half million Black women who work, only a few escape the hazard. . . .

Less than two months later, Florine Mitchell was fired. Shortly afterward she filed a suit alleging sexual harassment, saying she was fired because she refused to sleep with him. He denied all her charges and claimed he never propositioned her. She lost her case and is now raising money to appeal the decision. Florine believes the court ruled in her boss' favor because neither the judge nor the jury understood what sexual harassment was, nor could they believe a Black woman would be so naively vulnerable.

No one bothered to point out to the court then, or most recently, that Black women have been in the forefront of the movement against sexual harassment. Black women have filed the cases that have resulted in (1) a legal definition of sexual harassment, (2) the identification of sexual advances on the job as sex discrimination, (3) the prohibition against sexual harassment under Title VII of the Civil Rights Act of 1964, and (4) the determination that employers can be liable for sexual harassment.

Munford v. *J. T. Barnes* was the first harassment case granted a jury trial. *Williams* v. *Saxbe* established that dismissal because of refusing sexual advances was sex discrimination. *Barnes* v. *the EPA* (Environmental Protection Agency) defined sexual harassment and declared it illegal under Title VII. *Miller* v. *Bank of America* confirmed that an employer is liable for the sexual harassment acts of its supervisors, and *Alexander* v. *Yale University* argued that the university is responsible for acknowledging and acting on the sexual harassment complaints of students against faculty.

These cases, all brought by Black women, helped shape the new employer guidelines on sexual harassment issued by the Equal Employment Opportunity Commission (EEOC) in September 1980. EEOC, the agency charged with enforcing the antidiscrimination laws, Title VII of the Civil Rights Act of 1964, defines sexual harassment as an unwanted and unwelcome sexual advance, request for sexual favors, or any other verbal or physical conduct of a sexual nature that occurs on the job. Although sexual harassment usually takes place between a superior and a subordinate, the EEOC's new rules cover harassment of employees by other employees and by customers. And though all court cases to date involve the harassment of a female by a male, men are equally protected from harassment in the policy.

The EEOC specifically states that sexual harassment is an illegal act when one of three conditions is met. *One,* when submission is made a condition of employment;

two, when it unreasonably interferes with one's work performance; or *three,* when it creates an intimidating, hostile or offensive working environment.

If 50 to 80 percent of working women have been sexually harassed, 50 percent of those harassed fail to report it, according to Working Women's Institute, a sexual harassment counseling service in New York. Susan Meyer, the institute's executive director, adds, "Very often we ignore our feelings about it. There is a lot of ambivalence among women because society blames us for men coming on to us." Susan Meyer, who is white, credits Black women with taking the lead in this movement before many white women considered it serious.

One speculation as to why we have so aggressively pursued this issue is that as the last hired and first fired, we have the least to lose. History shows that the most oppressed people tend to be in the forefront of civil uprisings. Moreover, we are sensitized to discriminatory acts on the job and thus more aware of and less conditioned to abiding by them.

Paulette Barnes, herself a victim of sexual harassment *(Barnes* v. *Train),* offers another theory. "White women tend to go along with a problem on the job because they have been brought up by white men to feel like 'you have to do what you have to do to get where you're going.'" She adds, however, that Black women are the ones "stigmatized as being involved in sex (on the job)." Unfortunately, too, because some women are willing to exchange sexual encounters for promotions and raises on the job, other women are expected to do the same.

"Women who say yes have set a norm," declares Paulette Barnes, who assumed the position of administrative assistant to a man who, ironically, was an equal-opportunity director. Two months after she started there, he told her, "I remember the first day I saw you. You had on a little yellow dress, and I said, golly, that's my type of woman. I could help you further your career." Then he crudely described what type of sexual pleasure he imagined her having with him. Paulette "cussed him out in a nice way" and continued her work. A week later he timidly approached her to see whether they were still friends. Reassured, he invited her to the annual backyard barbecue for employees at his home. Paulette attended with her two children, the man she was dating and his son. The next day at work, her boss was furious. "Why you brought that man to my house, I don't know," he said in a rage. "If you want to throw your men in my face, you're gonna have to get another job." "I'm not going nowhere," a defiant Paulette responded. Two months later she had to go—he abolished her job.

In 1972, when she brought her case to the court, there was no name for sexual harassment and she was told to bring a charge of racial discrimination instead (a white man was later hired at a higher salary for her position).

The woman who preceded Paulette as administrative assistant testified on Paulette's behalf that the director had expected sexual compliance from his subordinates. The woman, who was white, had slept with her supervisor because she knew it was necessary to get the job and to keep moving up in her position. However, she had also documented everything. She showed Christmas and Valentine's cards, receipts for gifts and the dates of their sexual meetings. Paulette lost and took her case to appeals court, where the judge ruled that her boss' request for sexual favors was sex discrimination and therefore against the law. She received a cash settlement.

For most women who fight a sexual harassment case, it is an emotionally draining battle that causes depression and periods of self-doubt and loss of self-esteem. They report not feeling good about themselves, mainly because their private life is an open book during the trial process. Often their love relationships suffer, their subsequent work performance is less confident, they are shunned by other workers and employers as troublemakers. In addition, the experience is often handled by the courts as if it were a rape case, which causes more women to be reluctant about disclosing its existence. "My lawyer asked me if I could handle the court's bringing up the fact that I had two children but didn't marry their father," recounts Paulette Barnes. "I told her, 'I faced it then, and I can deal with it again.'"

Then there are those few women who are flattered by their boss' attention until it jeopardizes their job or gets out of hand and they have difficulty explaining why they endured the treatment before. Also, there are those who do not want to cause trouble and thus say nothing and start looking for a new place to work. But it is the humiliation of realizing they have been victimized that gnaws at most women's self-concept after these experiences—explaining it to themselves is the hardest part.

And justification is not easy, because studies show age, dress, position, looks, education, romance and love have nothing to do with whom a man will choose to harass. Any woman can have sex appeal—and beauty, as the cliche goes, is in the eye of the beholder. One woman seeking counseling after an incident threw her hands up totally perplexed. "Look at me," she explained, "I'm 50 years old!"

Dr. Cynthia D. Barnes, a respected New York–based psychiatrist, says one reason we women are so unraveled by the experience is that we never thought it could happen. "You never think a man is going to do this. Even when there have been many things that actually led up to it, women are shocked, embarrassed, distraught." This reaction occurs, she adds, because of the way women are raised to think about men. "Women are also taught that men are there to take care of them. It's hard to think that a man who is there to protect you is also assaulting you."

Florine Mitchell bears out that analysis. She says that at first "I wondered why he acted that way, and I thought he was silly, but harmless. It took me a while to figure out he was hitting on me." When it dawned on her what she had endured as his employee, "I became withdrawn and ashamed of myself. I blamed myself and tried to figure out what I did wrong." She broke up with her boyfriend because she had trouble relating to men afterward. During a discussion with a man, he attempted a harmless joke, and she cut him off, cracked on him and tried to belittle him. She accepted a job at lower pay with no raise for three years because she had a female boss and she refused to look for better employment because she was afraid she would have to work for a man. She was unable to keep a relationship going with a man, spent a lot of time alone at home crying, sought counseling and reports that it took her four years to start feeling good about herself and to realize that all men aren't deceptive. But she adds today, "It [sexual harassment] is the greatest pain anyone can experience at any one time." She says that when she realized she was not at fault for what happened to her, she could accept herself again.

Suffering continues for the victims, Cynthia Barnes says, because "for many women, it's hard to blame the man. They learn from their parents that relationships with men represent a dual-edged sword—men may exploit you as well as guard you. So when it happens, women don't want to believe it. They think maybe this is a caring statement rather than sexual harassment." Susan Meyer adds that there is no rationale for the treatment. "Sexual harassment is a power play. In many ways it's a game where men play out their economic power over women." Women testify to this, saying that what surprised them most when it happened was its spontaneity and the man's lack of guilt. One woman, an executive with a New York hair-care company, reports how she was standing in her office when the president of the division walked in, dropped down on his knees and ran his hand up and down her leg. The experience so shocked her that she just stood and stared at him. When she asked him why, he simply replied, "I looked and I had to touch. I couldn't help it." She was outraged, first because he felt that free to invade her privacy and second because he was white. . . .

Fighting a court case is a costly and exhausting process and requires a good lawyer, a lot of time—digging up details and recalling events—and stamina. First, legal fees can average $100 an hour. It doesn't take long to run up a big bill if the lawyer spends 20 hours on your case. Second, one must present evidence that proves one's claim: witnesses to events, memos, letters, details of conversations, people who have had similar experiences, personnel files, statistics on hiring procedures and practices, employment records. Third, a person needs patience, determination, a sense of purpose and strength to endure the questioning and what some call the "debilitating lies" that arise during the process. Also, courts are often hostile and unsympathetic toward Black women, especially if the case is against a white male with some authority or social position.

Barbara Sims (not her real name), who brought the first student-initiated case of sexual harassment to court, claims she lost her case because the judge, a white female, refused to allow much of her supporting evidence in court.

When Barbara was a college sophomore, she alleges, a professor asked her, "How bad do you want an A in this course?" She shunned his bait, saying, "I would like an A, but it's not an insane desire of mine." "I would really hate to give you a C," he repeated until it sounded threatening. He then asked, "Will you make love to me?" Barbara quickly answered no. He commented on her body and she asked to leave. She was almost at her dorm before she realized her refusal meant she would get a C on her paper. "I was shocked, then I got angry," she says. For this to happen in an academic environment, she says, creates "an assumption of my inferiority as a Black person as well as my lack of seriousness as a woman." He denied her charges.

In court the judge did not permit students who had experienced harassment under the professor to testify, because they had graduated. Although Barbara told her dean immediately after the incident, and the dean said there was nothing that could be done, that conversation was not allowed to be presented as testimony. Also, she had given a written statement regarding the incident to a Black professor, but neither his testimony nor that statement was allowed. "It was all incredibly racist," asserts Barbara. Her lawyer, a white woman, says she was "shocked by the callousness" of the court. She adds that the case was lost because "the judge didn't want to believe us." They were "procedurally restricted," she says, from mentioning any other cases that related to Barbara's charge.

After Barbara's case, the college instituted a policy whereby women who had been harassed could initiate a formal complaint; none existed at the time Barbara complained. Today companies and organizations, warned by EEOC that they have an obligation to create a working environment free of harassment, are issuing rules of behavior to employees. American Telephone and Telegraph, with more than 85,000 Black women employees in its Bell system nationwide, recently issued a statement saying, "An employee who has been found guilty of sexually harassing another employee can get fired for it."

As more women are made aware of the rules against sexual harassment and how it operates, fewer incidences will be allowed to continue. However, the price associated with confronting the issue remains high. Of particular concern to most women is how their spouses respond. Neither Florine Mitchell nor Paulette Barnes told their male companions about the incident when it occurred. They cited fear of his "causing a scene" and their not wanting to hurt him by telling him about another man's abusive behavior. Both women said they were "protecting" their man against possibly reacting physically against their boss. "Women don't tell because they are embarrassed it happened, and they know they are bringing themselves up for scrutiny as to whether or not they were provocative and encouraged it," psychiatrist Cynthia Barnes explains. In order to combat the problem more effectively, she believes, "women have to stop being so trusting. Women like to be nice, but we must be aware that there's a potential attraction, and to most men there's not much difference between a working woman and a woman who exists for his sexual gratification."

Susan Meyer (of Working Women's Institute) adds, "As women, we need to be clear about our role as workers. We need to take ourselves seriously and be aware of our rights on the job. When we are harassed, we can't say, 'I'm imagining it.' Chances are you aren't the only one he has harassed." Florine Mitchell agrees that a woman who has been harassed should talk about it with other women at work. "People knew it was happening on my job, but it was kept very hush-hush. I thought I could ignore the man. My way to handle it was to leave him alone—show him no encouragement and he would get tired. I thought as long as I'm doing a good job, he can't fire me."

Although Florine Mitchell is still fighting her battle, she has assumed a new position as a manager for another concern. Her former boss continues to deny having harassed her, and she occasionally must talk with him in her new position. Barbara Sims is now a law student at the University of California in Berkeley and says she might appeal her decision; Diane Williams is finishing her last year of law school as well. Paulette Barnes is an instructor of air traffic controllers in Oklahoma City, Okla. The sexual harassment events profoundly changed their lives, but none regrets her decision to fight. Paulette says she spoke up because "I was a mother who was working, and I had kids to support. Suppose I didn't take a stand there and ten or 15 years from now my daughter comes along and it's still happening." Diane Williams concurs. "So many of us have to work; therefore the situation has to be corrected. I have too much confidence in myself as a person and as a professional to subject myself to that treatment."

Abortion—Every Woman's Right

Proclamation of the New York Pro-Choice Coalition at St. Patrick's Cathedral, April 2, 1989

On behalf of the women of New York City and their sisters throughout this country and out of love for truth and the desire to bring it to light

We stand here today to affirm the following to Cardinal John J. O'Connor, who has blessed, praised and housed the anti-abortion fanatics of "Operation Rescue":

That you have consistently turned a deaf ear and a cold heart to women by repeatedly ignoring urgent requests to meet with us about the terror and violence towards women that "Operation Rescue" represents.

That you have added to the atmosphere of fear, terror and anxiety that women must face when attempting to exercise their constitutional right to abortion.

That you have encouraged the fanaticism and women hating that feeds the politics of "Operation Rescue."

Now, therefore, we stand here, not as beggars at your gate, but as people of conscience to affirm that:

I. Women are full moral agents with the right and ability to choose when and whether or not they will be mothers.

II. Abortion is a choice made by each individual for profound personal reasons that no man or state should judge.

III. The right to make reproductive choices is women's legacy throughout history and belongs to every woman regardless of age, class, race, religion or sexual preference.

IV. Abortion is a life-affirming act chosen within the context of women's lives and women's sexuality.

V. Abortion is often the most moral choice in a world that frequently denies health-care, housing, education and economic survival.

Aborting Choice

Randy Albelda

In the wake of a growing number of restrictions on abortion services around the country, a woman's ability to get an abortion increasingly depends on how much money she has and where she lives. Women with money or access to money will continue to be able to get abortions, while poor women will suffer the most from recent assaults on abortion rights.

Since last year's *Webster v. Reproductive Health Services* Supreme Court decision, several states have passed laws restricting abortion services. As the supply of abortion services diminishes, the demand for abortions will remain strong, and the price of abortions will rise. Like all market transactions, the effects of price increases are not neutral. Having lost most federal funding of abortions several years ago, poor women will be hurt the most while all women will be forced to pay more.

WHO GETS ABORTIONS

Close to two-thirds of all women have at least one unintended pregnancy in their lives, according to a report on abortion and women's health by the Alan Guttmacher Institute, a private, nonprofit organization that researches family planning. Of women who get pregnant unintentionally, close to half terminate their pregnancy by abortion, 13% have miscarriages, and 40% have their babies.

In a 1987 survey, the most common reason for having an abortion (76% of respondents) was that the woman was not ready for how a baby would change her life—specifically, a baby would interfere with employment, school, or other responsibilities. About 68% said they could not afford a baby because they were single, unemployed, or a student. Just over half the sample said they were seeking an abortion because they did not want to raise a child alone.

Women who have abortions are more likely to be young, poor, non-white, and unmarried than the average of all women of child-bearing age. About 60% of all women who get abortions are under the age of 25. One-third of all women who have abortions have family incomes below $11,000, while in the population as a whole, 15% of all women between 15 and 44 years of age live in families with incomes below that amount. Fewer than one out of every five women getting an abortion is married, despite the fact that almost one out of every two women of child-bearing age is married. Compared to other women, black women and Latinas are more likely to get abortions, while Catholics are more likely to have an abortion than are Jewish or Protestant women.

LEGAL PATCHWORK

Since the 1989 *Webster* ruling, an uneven pattern of abortion statutes across the states has been emerging, similar to the patchwork of laws that existed during the eight years prior to the 1973 *Roe v. Wade* decision that legalized abortion. As states impose more restrictions, a woman's access to legal abortions will depend on where she lives and how much money she has.

The *Webster* decision upheld a Missouri law that was among the most restrictive in the nation, opening the way for other states to curb abortion services. Since then, several states have approved laws obstructing abortion services, ranging from parental consent laws to stricter stipulations on who can provide abortions. These developments increase the cost of abortions, either directly through changing where a woman can get an abortion or indirectly through limiting the supply of abortions.

Many of the new laws hurt low-income women the most. The Missouri statute bans abortions in public hospitals (even if no public funds are used) and prohibits public employees from participating in abortions except to save a woman's life. Only 13% of all abortions were performed in hospitals around the country in 1985. However, low-income women and women of color are much more likely to have their abortions in a hospital than white middle-class women.

At the same time, several states have enacted requirements that abortions, especially in the second trimester, be performed in hospitals instead of outpatient clinics. Because a hospital abortion typically costs two to three times as much as a clinic abortion, this mandate once again hits poor women the hardest.

Faced with higher priced abortions and a lack of public funding, poor women need more time to raise the necessary funds. Delaying the procedure until later in the pregnancy increases both the costs and the health risks. Abortions performed in the eleventh or twelfth week of pregnancy are three times more dangerous than abortions performed in the eighth week, and the risks increase as the pregnancy progresses. The average fee for an abortion performed in a clinic within the first 12 weeks of pregnancy was $247 last year, while the average price soared to $697 for an abortion at 20 weeks of pregnancy.

In addition to price increases for the abortion procedure itself, women will have to pick up other costs of limited access to abortion services. Women who cannot get an abortion near their homes will also have to pay transportation and possibly accommodation costs.

THE BUCK STOPS HERE

Few women are able to turn to public funding to cover these increased costs. Congress has restricted or prohibited the use of federal Medicaid funds for abortions since 1976, when the Hyde Amendment was passed. Federal funds are currently available for abortions only when the life of the woman is endangered by pregnancy. The federal government paid for just 322 abortions in 1987, and that included some services following miscarriages. Only 13 states use their own revenues to provide medically necessary abortions for low-income women, the Guttmacher Institute reported earlier this year.

Of women who would obtain a publicly funded abortion if they could, up to 80% raise the money to pay for an abortion themselves. To pay for the procedure, many buy less food or clothing or let other bills go unpaid; a majority report that the abortion was a serious financial hardship. A small percentage of women who are unable to get public funding attempt self-induced abortions, or seek an abortion from an unregulated, illegal provider.

The ultimate cost of limiting the supply of abortions is death. A conservative estimate of the number of deaths attributed to abortions was 193 in 1965, when abortion was illegal in every state except when the pregnancy threatened the mother's life. Over half of these deaths were women of color. The number of deaths declined after 1970, when 15 states liberalized abortion laws, and continued to fall after the 1973 *Roe v. Wade* decision. In 1985, from the 1.6 million legal abortions performed, six women are known to have died.

UNWANTED CHILDREN

Restrictions on the supply of abortion services, combined with earlier bans on public funding, will cause more women to bear more unwanted children and to struggle with the accompanying financial costs. As a result of public funding bans in the late 1970s, 20% of women who would have received a Medicaid-funded abortion in 1980 carried their unwanted pregnancy to term.

In purely economic terms, being a mother involves heavy financial burdens. Besides the obvious costs attached to rearing children (such as adequate health care, clothing, and food), a major cost is lost wages. Because women still do most childcare, they must often quit a job or school to care for young children.

Women who leave the labor force temporarily or interrupt their education also lose work experience and skills. Women with discontinuous work experience obtain smaller salary bases and fewer raises than workers who never left the labor force. And although schooling for women does not pay off as much as for men, women with more education make more than women with less than education.

Women who must work while also caring for children, including many single mothers, face additional constraints. First, childcare responsibilities reduce the time available to work. Second, women on the average earn less than men. The combination of limited time and low wages can be devastating, as is suggested by the fact that poverty rates for single mothers are six times that of married couples.

WHAT'S WRONG WITH THIS PICTURE

Even if every state outlawed abortions, women would still have them. Limiting abortion services will never eliminate the demand for these services. Only by reducing the number of unintended pregnancies and the cost of having children will there be less demand for abortions.

Women in the United States have a higher rate of unintended pregnancies than women in Canada and almost all Western European countries, despite similar birthrates. Compared to these countries, the United States has a relatively low use of contraceptives. It's no wonder U.S. women are more likely to seek an abortion than are their European and Canadian sisters. Safer contraceptive devices and increased educational services would help reduce the demand for abortions.

But while birth control reduces the likelihood of pregnancy, it does not eliminate it. In 1987, 43% of all women with unintended pregnancies were using some form of birth control. More widespread use of contraceptives will not eliminate unintended pregnancies.

Neither recent developments in the battle over abortion nor the tactics of abortion opponents have eliminated women's need for safe, cheap abortions. While abortion opponents want to restrict the supply of abortions, they also condemn birth control and fail to promote policies that would reduce the demand for abortions by easing the financial burden of parenting. As long as women need abortions, limiting the supply of abortions penalizes women in general, and poor women the most.

RESOURCES: The Alan Guttmacher Institute, *Abortion and Women's Health: A Turning Point for America?,* 1990; Rachel Benson Gold and Sandra Guardado, "Public Funding of Family Planning, Sterilization and Abortion Services, 1987" *Family Planning Perspectives,* September/October 1988.

The Impact of Sexism, Racism and Classism on HIV-Infected Women

Bo Keppel

Laura is back in the hospital. Every few months I call, and when she answers I relax. Laura is my touchstone. She is many people's touchstone—those with AIDS, those who are sick, but have no symptoms, and all who have worked with her at the AIDS Center. Once again she has pneumonia, not pneumocystis, but a serious bacterial kind. She says I'm not to worry; she'll go home tomorrow. Yes, once again she'll lick it. Laura's a fighter. She's had this disease for ten years. She'll be fine—for now.

Laura is a woman with AIDS, one of the more than 15,000 that had been diagnosed in the United States as of November 30, 1990 (Centers for Disease Control, 1990). Laura is 34, white, and traces her infection to sharing a needle with a junkie in 1980. She was poor, depressed without her kids, and tried drugs. Laura is not typical of HIV-infected women in the 1990s. Today most HIV-infected women are women of color, black or Latina, and have contracted the virus from having sex with a partner who used drugs, but just like Laura most HIV-infected women are poor.

Fifteen thousand American women have AIDS. Another 100,000 are thought to have the virus. Many of those are very sick, but according to the Centers for Disease Control they don't have AIDS. The official CDC definition does not include the gynecological infections and conditions so many HIV-infected women contract before getting some of the diseases which are included in the definition. HIV-infected women get vaginal candidiasis so severe and persistent it cannot be controlled by medications which successfully cure it in non-HIV-infected women. Cervical and uterine tumors grow with speeds far beyond those in women without HIV disease. Yet, none of these conditions qualify HIV-infected women for an AIDS diagnosis. The CDC argues that only conditions which do not occur in people who are not infected with HIV are included in the AIDS definition. However, oral thrush, more common to men in the early stages, is included in the CDC definition and is found in people other than those with HIV.

Why is it important for poor women with the virus to be diagnosed with AIDS? Without that label, women are not eligible for social security disability and other services which may make the difference between life with dignity or death in poverty.

Poverty is common among women of color (Wilkerson & Gresham, 1989) and the AIDS epidemic has only brought into focus the racism, sexism and classism that poor women of color suffer. Since 1987, when the rapid increase of HIV infection in women was recognized, they have been treated by the medical community and the press as the infectors of men and children (Wofsy, 1987; Where are the women? 1988). Government money was spent on counting the number of infected prostitutes (Leads from the MMR, 1987), yet no one tested their johns. A government researcher with the CDC wrote in 1987, "We must be committed to preventing HIV infection in women. Until we succeed, we will be only partially successful in preventing AIDS in newborns" (Guinan, 1987). Why weren't women worth protecting for themselves?

The medical community knows little about AIDS in women, because so few HIV-infected women have been studied. It also isn't known how such AIDS drugs as AZT, pentamidine, and bactrim affect women, because women have never been included in drug trials in this country. Except for people in prison, women have been the only group of adults specifically excluded from drug trials. This has supposedly been to protect the well-being of any future children they may have (Swennson, 1989). Although not specifically excluded, minorities have not been well represented in drug trials either (Swennson, 1989). The ACLU challenged this practice in 1988 (Hapern, 1989), but neither the drug companies, the CDC, nor the National Institutes for Health changed their practices. In March 1990 the National Institute of Allergy and Infectious Disease admitted that "large groups of individuals, notably women, minorities and intravenous drug users were only modestly represented" in studies on the use of AZT on asymptomatic HIV-infected people, suggesting it really didn't matter as "there is no reason to believe these recommendations are not equally applicable to these populations" (Recommendations for Zidovudine: early infection, 1990).

However, research presented at the NIH's first conference devoted to women and HIV infection held in December 1990, a full ten years after the epidemic began, indicates AZT causes malignant uterine tumors in female mice and rats when the dosages are high (Ayers, 1990). What constitutes high dosage in women is not known because AZT has not been tested on women, although many infected women are now using it. And AZT and other drugs won't be tested on women until drug companies and the government seek them out and make it possible for them to see a doctor by providing transportation and childcare.

Seeing a doctor is not an option for many poor women. In many minority neighborhoods, people have no access to healthcare. The effects of this are clear: blacks suffer higher incidences of cancer and cardiovascular disease and higher infant mortality; greater numbers of black women than white die of influenza and pneumonia (Lee,

1989); the gap in life expectancy between whites and people of color continues to grow (Lee, 1989; Hilts, 1989). Minorities with AIDS die faster than whites with the disease (Bolton, 1988), and a black woman is nine times more likely to die of AIDS-related causes than is a white woman (Forrester, 1990).

There are few medical services for poor women with AIDS living in urban areas. Three hundred urban hospitals closed in 1989 alone (Naimond, 1990), and those public hospitals that remain open are so overtaxed and underfunded that many cannot even provide pentamidine, the common treatment to prevent PCP, the pneumonia that kills so many people with AIDS (Hornung, 1989).

Healthcare is also nonexistent for the growing numbers of HIV-infected homeless women. Increasing numbers of the homeless are black or Latina women and children (First, Roth, Arewa, 1989). Nearly 30 percent of homeless people are estimated to be HIV infected (Rosenthal, 1990). Living on the street can only worsen a weakened immune system, and living in a shelter exposes that immune system to tuberculosis (and other organisms) it can't fight off. Tuberculosis is often fatal to people with AIDS.

Like my friend Laura, many women with the virus got it from sharing needles to shoot drugs. But few drug treatment programs exist: in New York City there are spots for 42,000 of the estimated 500,000 addicts (Lee, 1990). Few of these spots are available to women and even fewer to pregnant women or women with children. In 1989 the entire state of Massachusetts had only 16 places in drug programs for addicted mothers (Engle, 1989). Crack addiction is rampant among poor urban women, and is associated with HIV infection when addicts resort to selling their bodies for a vial of crack. The National Institute on Drug Abuse estimates 10 of every 100 pregnant women have used or are using cocaine in some form (Lee, 1990). Yet a survey conducted in 1990 in New York City found that 87 percent of the drug programs would not accept crack-addicted pregnant women on Medicaid (Lewin, 1990).

Even if a woman is lucky enough to find a treatment program that will accept her, and to have family or friends to care for her children while she is there, she may come out worse than she went in. Most drug programs were developed for men and use confrontational approaches (Reed, 1987) that can be destructive to addicted women who suffer even lower self-esteem, higher degrees of depression and greater anxiety than addicted men (Sherrod, 1990). Yet as of 1990 only four programs in the whole United States had therapeutic programs designed specifically to meet the needs of addicted women (Cohen, 1989). Women in male-oriented programs are seen as sicker, less motivated, and having no morals (Reed, 1987). If a woman in treatment is a lesbian or a prostitute, imagine the disdain she suffers. If she is also HIV infected, the chances she'll find an environment in which she can get off drugs are slim.

Six months pregnant for her second child, my friend Laura found out she had AIDS when her dying three year old was diagnosed. Both babies died. Women like Laura who bear HIV-infected children are looked on as villains. Their children are called "innocent victims," as if their mothers were somehow "guilty" and deserved their infection. Many, like Laura, do not find out they are infected until they are pregnant. Those who know their HIV status find themselves in a Catch-22. They are advised not to get pregnant, yet if they are poor, they must buy contraceptives with their limited funds, as neither Medicaid nor food stamps will cover their cost (Cochran & Mays, 1989). If they refuse their partner's appeal for sex, or if they tell him he must use a condom, they may find themselves abandoned, beaten, or worse (Norwood, 1987). Pregnant HIV-positive women are routinely advised to have an abortion in order not to bear an HIV-infected child. The chances of bearing a child with the virus are only 20 to 30 percent, or conversely, the chances of bearing a healthy child are 80 to 70 percent (Bardeguez, 1990), pretty good odds. Why then are these women urged to abort?

Abortion frequently is not an option for poor women. Lack of access to medical services often prevents poor pregnant women of color from finding prenatal care until well after the first trimester, when the procedure can't legally be done. ["The crack dealer is on the corner, the liquor store is down the block, but the pre-natal clinic may be two buses and five hours away" (Schmidt, 1990).] Nor is abortion readily available to poor women. Only fourteen states and the District of Columbia fund abortions (Mitchell, 1988). Ironically, even if HIV-infected women can pay, an abortion may still not be available. A study by the Human Rights Commission of New York City found that abortions which had been scheduled were cancelled by the clinics once investigators making the appointments identified themselves as HIV infected (Taravella, 1989).

Even though contraception is expensive and abortions are hard to get, HIV-infected women can be taken to court for bearing an HIV-infected child on the grounds that ". . . where the infection (of the child) was unavoidable, the child should not have been conceived or born" (Dickens, 1988). The 1989 conviction of a black woman in Florida for delivering a cocaine-addicted child, and the jailing of alcoholic Native American women who are pregnant, to prevent the birth of infants with fetal alcohol syndrome (Engle, 1989), indicate that such use of the law against HIV-infected women is not far off.

What then is being done to protect women from HIV infection? Very little. One company is experimenting with a "female condom" which they say will allow women to protect themselves from the virus, but since the device protrudes from the vagina, cooperation of the male in its use is still required. The government is not involved in developing methods for women to control the means of their own protection.

Neither is the government interested in protecting lesbians from infection. The CDC's refusal to track the spread of the virus via woman-to-woman sex has put lesbian women at risk. Believing they were safe, many did not protect themselves from infection. The number of infected lesbians is not known, because the CDC still does not count them. That lesbians "do not count" was clear at the National Institute for Health's 1990 Women and HIV Conference where not one of the thirty-three workshops nor one of the twenty-two keynote speakers mentioned HIV and lesbians. Lesbians, however, have begun to protect themselves, publicizing the use of Glad Wrap for oral sex.

Adolescent girls are not being protected either. Meaningful sex education in the schools has declined as a result of vocal opposition by the right-wing minority, although poll after poll shows that the majority of parents want effective sex education for their school children (Gordon, 1990). While 11 percent of all infected adults are women, 19 percent of all infected teens are girls (Fair, 1990). State-mandated AIDS education in the schools is woefully ineffective in changing behavior. A study of teenaged girls showed that while three-quarters knew that abstinence and condoms could prevent HIV, 85 percent were sexually active and only 10 percent had *ever* used a condom (Rickert, Jay, Gottlieb, Bridges, 1989).

Sexism, racism and classism have taken their toll on women for centuries the world over. AIDS is only one more in a series of abuses all women, but especially women of color and poor women, have had to endure. What do women want? To be given the information and the means to protect ourselves from HIV infection. To be free to refuse sex or to have it safely. To be free from blame for our skin color, our poverty, our sexual orientation, our HIV infection. To be free to choose to have a child or to abort a fetus. To be given the chance to get off drugs. To be free from accusations of causing HIV in our children and lovers. To be part of drug treatment trials. To have our gynecological HIV symptoms taken seriously. To be given the medical treatment we need. To be provided with household and childcare help when we are too sick to tend to them ourselves. To be allowed to live our lives with meaning and to die with dignity.

Laura is back facilitating the HIV-positive women's support group. "This last bout took off about twenty pounds, but I'll gain it back," she tells the women. "I just think positively, live one day at a time. I'll be around a long time. After all, I have a lot of kids to talk to about AIDS. Girls have got to know they're at risk. They've got to take care of themselves." She pauses. "No one else will."

Laura Lee Cantrell
of Bethlehem, Pennsylvania, died at 34 years of age on
May 24, 1991.

REFERENCES

Ayers, K. (1990, December 13). Paper presented at National Conference on Women and HIV Infection, Washington D.C.

Bardeguez, A. (1990, June 17). Paper presented at New Jersey Women and AIDS Second Annual Symposium, Elizabeth, N.J.

Bolton, L. (1988). AIDS: the development of social policy. *Journal of National Black Nurses,* 2(2), 10–14.

Centers for Disease Control (1990, December). *HIV/AIDS Surveillance Report,* p. 10.

Cochran, S., Mays, V. (1989). Women and AIDS-related concerns: roles for psychologists in helping the worried well. *American Psychologist, 44*(3), 529–535.

Cohen, J. B., Hauer, L. B., Wofsy, C. B. (1989). Women and IV drugs: parental and heterosexual transmission of human immunodeficiency virus. *Journal of Drug Issues, 19*(1), 39–56.

Dickens, B. (1988). Legal rights and duties in the AIDS epidemic. *Science, 239*(541), 573–622.

Engle, J. (1989, August 24). *Morning Edition.* Washington, National Public Radio.

Fair, J. (1990). HIV infection among adolescents. *ARCS News, 5*(1), 1–2.

First, R. J., Roth, D., Arewa, B. D. (1989, March–April). Homelessness: understanding the dimensions of the problem for minorities. *Social Work,* pp. 120–124.

Forrester, C. (1990, September 17). Paper presented at the New Jersey Women and AIDS Network Second Annual Symposium, Elizabeth, N.J.

Gordon, S. (1990). Editorial. *Health Education,* (21:1) 4–5.

Guinan, M., Hardy, A. (1987). Epidemiology of AIDS in women in the US. *JAMA, 257*(15), 2039–2042.

Halpern, S. (1989, May 5). AIDS: rethinking the risk. *MS,* pp. 80, 84–85, 87.

Hilts, P. (1989, October 9). Growing gap in life expectancies of blacks and whites is emerging. *New York Times,* p. A8.

Hornung, R. (1989, June 20). Drug of no choice; most city hospitals don't have pentamidine. *Village Voice,* p. 16.

Leads from the MMWR: Antibody to HIV in female prostitutes (1987). *JAMA, 257*(15), 2011–2013.

Lee, F. (1989, July 21). Black doctors urge study of factors in risk of AIDS. *New York Times,* p. B7.

Lee, F. (1990, December 17). Pregnant drug abusers find hope in program. *New York Times,* Sec. B, p. 3, Col. 1.

Lewin, T. (1990, February 5). Drug use in pregnancy: new issue for the courts. *New York Times,* p. A14.

Mitchell, J. (1988). What about the mothers of HIV infected babies? *NAN Multi-cultural Notes on AIDS Education and Service, 1*(10) 1–2.

Naimond, P. (1990, March 27). *All Things Considered.* Washington, National Public Radio.

Norwood, C. (1987). *Advice for life: a women's guide to AIDS risks and prevention.* New York: Pantheon Books.

Recommendations for zidovudine: early infection (1990). *JAMA, 263*(12), 1606–1609.

Reed, B. G. (1987). Developing women-sensitive drug dependence treatment services: why so difficult? *Journal of Psychoactive Drugs, 19*(2), 151–164.

Ricket, V. I., Jay, M. S., Gottlieb, A., Bridges, C. (1989). Adolescents and AIDS: female's attitudes toward condom use. *Journal of Adolescent Health Care, 10*(4), 313–316.

Rosenthal, E. (1990, February 22). Health care for the homeless: treating the by-products of life on the street. *New York Times,* p. B9.

Schmidt, M. T. (1990, Fall). Taking charge of our life. *Pep Talk,* p. 2.

Sherrod, J. (1990, September 17). Paper presented at New Jersey Women and AIDS Second Annual Symposium, Elizabeth, N.J.

Svensson, C. K. (1989). Representation of American blacks in clinical trials of new drugs. *JAMA, 261*(2), 263–265.

Taravella, S. (1989). Women with AIDS find abortions hard to get in New York. *Modern Healthcare, 19*(33), 16.

Where are the women? (1988, November/December). *The Network News,* p. 6.

Wilkerson, M. B., Gresham, J. H. (1989, July 24/31). Sexual politics of welfare: the racialization of poverty. *The Nation,* pp. 126–128.

Wofsy, C. B. (1987). Editorial: Human immunodeficiency virus infection in women. *JAMA, 257*(15), 2074–2076.

Hate Violence Against Women

Suzanne Pharr

Women and men in Canada, the U.S., and worldwide were stunned and appalled by the massacre of 14 women in the University of Montreal engineering school. There has been outrage, grief and intense questioning in the aftermath of this murder. People have wanted to know what could be the motivation for such an outrageous act, and there has been some relief drawn from the suicide note that many read as a statement of a deranged mind, suggesting that these killings were an isolated incident.

However, those of us who who are longtime workers in the women's anti-violence movement know that these killings, while seeming to contain elements of madness, are simply one more piece of the more routine, less sensational hate murders of women that we deal with every day. According to the FBI, there are several thousand women killed by their husbands and boyfriends each year. This number does not include the great numbers of women killed by rapists on the street and in their homes. Almost all of these are women who die horrible deaths of brutality and terror with no public outcry and outrage for the waste of their lives.

There is media and public response when the murder is sensational either in numbers, in the esteemed worth of the victim, or when it is cross-race and the perpetrator is a man of color. Hence, the extensive coverage of the Montreal massacre, the rape of the white female investment banker in Central Park, and the Republicans' use of Willie Horton as the rapist most to be feared. Otherwise, when murders and rapes of women are briefly reported daily in our papers and on television, the public, accustomed to the ordinariness of rape and murder of women and desensitized to it, simply see it as one more trivial incident in the expected way of life for women. It's just one more woman violated or dead; turn the page; flip the channel.

To see how staggering these numbers are, let's look just at one state, the small (pop. 2.3 million), mostly rural state of Arkansas. At the Women's Project, for almost a year now we've been monitoring hate violence in Arkansas, and unlike other monitoring groups, we include sexist violence along with racist, anti-Semitic and homophobic violence. During the first six months of the year, we were putting the project in place and quite possibly missed some of the murders of women; nevertheless, our records show 37 women and girls murdered in 1989. Their killers were husbands, boyfriends, acquaintances, strangers. Most of the women were killed in their homes and all were murders in which robbery was not the motive. Their ages ranged from 5 years old to 88. Some were raped and killed; all were brutal murders. Some were urban, some rural; some rich, some poor; some white, some women of color.

A few examples will be enough to show the level of hatred and violence that was present in all the murders. A 67 year old woman was shot twice with a crossbow and dumped into a farm pond, her head covered with plastic and her body weighted down with six concrete blocks; a 22 year old woman was abducted from her home by three armed men while her small children watched, taken to an abandoned house, raped, sodomized and killed; a 30 year old teacher was slashed and stabbed dozens of times; a 19 year old woman was beaten to death and buried in a shallow grave; a 5 year old girl was raped, strangled and stuffed into a tree; a 32 year old paraplegic was killed, a 35 lb. weight tied to her, and dropped into the Ouachita River; an 86 year old woman was suffocated in her home.

Added to these brutal murders are the statistics from Arkansas Children and Family Services that indicate 1353 girls were sexually assaulted in 1988, and from the Arkansas Crime Information Center that 656 rapes were reported in 1988. In November the Arkansas *Gazette* reported that in the first six months of 1989, Little Rock had more rapes—119—than Washington, D.C.—90—a city three times its size. When we understand that only about 10% of all rapes are reported, these numbers become significantly larger. All in all, when the numbers of murders, rapes, and sexual assaults of girls are put together there emerges a grim picture of the brutal hate violence launched against women and girls.

I don't believe Arkansas is an exception in this violence. From battered women's programs, from rape crisis programs, from crime statistics, we know that women are beaten, raped and killed in every state of this country, every day. Because so many women are viciously beaten and their lives placed in jeopardy, this country has over 1100 battered women's programs, all filled to overflowing, and more being developed every day.

Wherever we live in the U.S., women live in a war zone where we may be attacked, terrorized, or abducted at any moment. Women are not safe in the home, on the street, or at the workplace. Or, as in Montreal, in a school setting on the eve of final exams for 14 women about to enter engineering jobs that only recently became accessible to them in a world that considers engineering "men's work." There is no safe place, no "proper" kind of woman whose behavior exempts her, no fully protected woman.

While we recognize the absence of safety in all women's lives, no matter what class or race, we also are aware that women of color have even less safety than white women. Women of color are the targets of the combined hatred of racism and sexism, and as such, they experience both racist and sexist violence against their lives from white people as well as sexist violence from men of color, and often racist responses and services when they seek help.

Recently, the writers of a hate crime bill that went before Congress could not agree to put women alongside people of color, Jews, gay men and lesbians as targets of hate crimes. This seems to me a critical error in moral and political judgment, one reminiscent of the immoral decision the white women of the 19th century women's movement made when they decided to turn their backs on black women in order to secure the participation of white Southern women. There is never a "more politically appropriate" time to bring in a group of people—in this case, 52% of the population—that is this country's largest target of hate crimes. When hate crimes are limited to anti-Semitic, racist, and homophobic violence, there is inherent confusion: when Jewish women are killed, when women of color are killed, when lesbians are raped or killed, it is often impossible to determine if they were attacked because of their religion, race, sexual identity, or their *gender*.

The U.S. Justice Department's guidelines to determine bias motivation for a crime include common sense (i.e., crossburning or offensive graffiti), language used by the assailant, the severity of the attack, a lack of provocation, previous history of similar incidents in the same area, and an absence of any other apparent motive. Under this definition, rape would be an apparent hate crime, often severe—including armed assault, beating and killing—often repeated in the same neighborhood or area, no other apparent motive, and almost always abusive woman-hating language.

The same would be true with our monitored cases of battering that ends in murder. In the majority of the cases, the woman was beaten (sometimes there was a long history of battering) and then killed. Rather than crossburnings or offensive graffiti, the hate material is pornography. Most telling is the absence of any other apparent motive. And then there are the countless beatings and acts of terrorism that don't end in murder but do lasting physical and psychological damage to women. An example from Arkansas:

> (A woman) reported battery and terroristic threatening. She said her neighbor/ex-boyfriend threatened her with a handgun, and beat her, knocking her down a flight of stairs where she landed on a rock terrace.
>
> (She) sustained permanent damage to her eardrum, two black eyes and extensive bruises and lacerations. She stated her assailant was not intoxicated; that he bragged of having been a Golden Gloves boxer; and he allegedly told her he could not be arrested for beating her since he struck her with his hands open. (Washington County *Observer* 8/17/89)

Men beat, rape and kill women because they *can;* that is, because they live in a society that gives permission to the hatred of women.

This country minimizes hate violence against women because women's lives are not valued, because the violence is so commonplace that people become numb to it, because people do not want to look at the institutions and systems that support it, and because people do not want to recognize how widespread the hatred is and how many perpetrators there are among us on every level of society.

It is only when women's lives are valued that this violence will be ended. If 37 African Americans were killed by whites in Arkansas, our organization would be leading the organizing to investigate and end the murders; or if 37 Jews were killed by gentiles; or if 37 gay men or lesbians were murdered by heterosexuals—for all of these other groups we monitor violence against, we would be in the forefront of organizing on their behalf. But why not on behalf of women? We talk about violence against women and help develop organizations that provide safety and support for victims, but even we sometimes get numbed to its immensity, to its everydayness, to the loss of freedom it brings with it.

All of us must stop minimizing this violence against women. We must bring it to the forefront of our social consciousness and name it for what it is: not the gentler, less descriptive words such as family violence, or domestic violence, or wife or spouse abuse, or sexual assault, but *hate violence against women.* It does not erupt naturally or by chance from the domesticity of our lives; it comes from a climate of woman hating.

For too long when women have named this violence as what it is, we have been called man-haters by people who want the truth kept quiet. "Man-hater" is a common expression but "woman-hater" is not, despite the brutal evidence of woman-hating that surrounds us: murder, rape, battering, incest. The common use of the word "man-hater" is a diversionary tactic that keeps us from looking at the hard reality of the source of violence in our lives. The threat of the label "man-hater" threatens women with loss of privilege and controls our behavior, but more importantly, it keeps us from working honestly and forcefully on our own behalf to end the violence that destroys us.

Social change occurs when those who experience injustice organize to improve or save their lives. Women must overcome the fear of organizing on behalf of women, no matter what the threat. We must organize together to eliminate the root causes of violence against us.

We must make sure that hate violence against women is monitored and documented separate from general homicides so that we can be clear about the extent of it, the tactics, the institutions and systems that allow it to continue. We must hold our institutions accountable. In December 1989, the Arkansas *Gazette* ran a series of articles about local hospitals "dumping" rape victims, that is, refusing to give rape examinations because they did not want to get involved in legal cases. Such inhumane practices are dehumanizing to women and lead to public indifference to rape and its terrible consequences.

We must create a society that does not give men permission to rape and kill women. We all must believe that women's lives are as important as the lives of men. If we created a memorial to the women dead from this war against them—just over the past decade—our memorial would rest next to the Vietnam Memorial in Washington in numbers and human loss to this nation. The massacre must end.

The Global War Against Women

Lori Heise

Violence against women—including assault, mutilation, murder, infanticide, rape, and cruel neglect—is perhaps the most pervasive yet least recognized human rights issue in the world. It is also a profound health problem sapping women's physical and emotional vitality and undermining their confidence—both of which are vital to achieving important social goals, especially in the Third World. Despite its invisibility, the dimensions of this problem are vast. In Bangkok, Thailand, a reported 50 percent of married women are beaten regularly by their husbands. In the barrios of Quito, Ecuador, 80 percent of women are said to have been physically abused. And in Nicaragua, 44 percent of men admit to beating their wives or girlfriends. Equally shocking statistics can be found in the industrial world. Then there are the less recognized forms of violence. In Nepal, female babies die from neglect because parents value sons over daughters; in Sudan, girls' genitals are mutilated to ensure virginity until marriage; and in India, young brides are murdered by their husbands when parents fail to provide enough dowry. This is not random violence. In all these instances, women are targets of violence because of their sex. The risk factor is being female.

Most of these abuses have been reported in one or another country, at one or another time. But it is only when you begin to amass statistics and reports from around the world that the horrifying dimensions of this global war on women come into focus. For me the revelation came only recently after talking with scores of women throughout the world. I never intended to investigate violence; I was researching maternal and child health issues overseas. But I would commonly begin my interviews with a simple question: What is your biggest problem? With unnerving frequency, the answer came back: "My husband beats me."

These are women who daily have to walk four hours to gather enough wood for the evening meal, whose children commonly die of treatable illnesses, whose security can be wiped out with one failed rain. Yet when defining their own concerns, they see violence as their greatest dilemma. Those dedicated to helping Third World women would do well to listen.

More than simply a "women's issue," violence thwarts other widely held goals for human progress in the Third World. Study after study has shown that educating mothers is the single most effective way to reduce child mortality—not because it imparts new knowledge or skills related to health, but because it erodes fatalism, improves self-confidence, and changes the power balance within the family.

In effect, these studies say that a woman's sense of self is critical to reducing infant mortality. Yet acts of violence and society's tacit acceptance of these acts stand as constant reminders to women of their low worth in society. Where women's status is critical to achieving a social goal—such as controlling population growth and improving child survival—violence will remain a powerful obstacle to progress.

Measured by its human costs alone, female-focused violence is worthy of international attention and action. But it has seldom been raised at that level, much less addressed. Millions of dollars are spent each year to protect the human rights of fetuses. It is time to stand up for the human rights of women.

The Indian subcontinent is home to one of the most pernicious forms of wife abuse, known locally as "bride-burning" or "dowry death." Decades ago the term dowry referred to the gifts a woman received from her parents upon marriage. Now dowry has become an important part of premarital negotiations in India and refers to the wealth that the bride's parents must pay the groom as part of the marriage settlement.

Once a gesture of love, the ever-escalating dowry now represents a real financial burden to the parents of daughters. Increasingly, dowry is being seen by prospective husbands as a "get rich quick" scheme, with young brides suffering severe abuse if promised money or goods do not materialize. In its most severe form, dowry harassment ends in suicide or murder, freeing the husband to pursue a more lucrative arrangement.

Dowry deaths are notoriously undercounted, largely because the husband and his relatives frequently try to disguise the murder as a suicide or an accident, and the police are loathe to get involved. A frequent scam is to set the woman alight with kerosene, and then claim she died in a kitchen accident—hence the term bride-burning. In 1987 the police officially recorded 1,786 dowry deaths in all of India, but the Ahmedabad Women's Action Group estimates that 1,000 women may have been burned alive that year in Gujurat state alone.

A quick look at mortality data from India reveals the reasonableness of this claim. In both urban Maharashtra and greater Bombay, 19 percent of all deaths among women 15 to 44 years old are due to "accidental burns." In other Third World countries, such as Guatemala, Ecuador, and Chile, the same statistic is less than 1 percent.

Elsewhere in the world, this marriage transaction is reversed, with prospective husbands paying "bridewealth" to secure a woman's hand in marriage. In many cultures—especially in Africa—the exchange has become so commercialized that inflated costs of bridewealth leave the man with the distinct impression that he has "purchased" his wife.

The notion that bridewealth confers ownership was clearly depicted during recent parliamentary debates in Papua New Guinea over whether wife-beating should be made illegal. Transcripts show that most ministers were violently against the idea of parliament interfering in "traditional family life." Minister William Wi of North Waghi argued that wife-beating "is an accepted custom and we are wasting our time debating the issue." Another parliamentarian added: "I paid for my wife, so she should not overrule my decisions, because I am the head of the family."

It is this unequal balance of power—institutionalized in the structure of the patriarchal family—that is at the root of wife-beating. As Cheryl Bernard, director of Austria's Ludwig Boltzmann Institute of Politics, notes: "Violence against women in the family takes place because the perpetrators feel, and their environment encourages them to feel, that this is an acceptable exercise of male prerogative, a legitimate and appropriate way to relieve their own tension in conditions of stress, to sanction female behavior . . . or just to enjoy a feeling of supremacy."

While stress and alcohol may increase the likelihood of violence, they do not "cause" it. Rather, it is the belief that violence is an acceptable way to resolve conflict, and that women are "appropriate" and "safe" targets for abuse, that leads to battering.

Most cultures around the world today have strong historical, religious, and legal legacies that reinforce the legitimacy of wife-beating. Under English common law, for example, a husband had the legal right to discipline his wife—subject to a "rule of thumb" that barred him from using a stick broader than his thumb. Judicial decisions in England and the United States upheld this right until well into the 19th century. In April, a New York judge let off with only five years probation a Chinese immigrant who admitted bludgeoning his wife to death. The judge justified the light sentence partly by reference to traditional Chinese attitudes toward female adultery.

While less overt, the preference for male offspring in many cultures can be as damaging and potentially fatal to females as rape or assault. The same sentiment that once motivated infanticide is now expressed in the systematic neglect of daughters—a neglect so severe in some countries that girls aged 2 to 4 die at nearly twice the rate of boys.

"Let it be late, but let it be a son," goes a saying in Nepal, a country that shares its strong preference for male children with the rest of the Indian subcontinent, as well as China, South Korea, and Taiwan. In these cultures and others, sons are highly valued because only they can perpetuate the family line and perform certain religious rituals. Even more important, sons represent an economic asset to the family and a source of security for parents in their old age.

Studies confirm that where the preference for sons is strong, girls receive inferior medical care and education, and less food. In Punjab, India, for example, parents spend more than twice as much on medical care for boy infants as for girls.

In fact, the pressure to bear sons is so great in India and China that women have begun using amniocentesis as a sex identification test to selectively abort female fetuses. Until protests forced them to stop, Indian sex detection clinics boldly advertised it was better to spend $38 now on terminating a girl than $3,800 later on her dowry. Of 8,000 fetuses examined at six abortion clinics in Bombay, 7,999 were found to be female.

In parts of Africa and the Middle East, young girls suffer another form of violence, euphemistically known as female circumcision. More accurately, this operation—which removes all or part of the external female genitalia, including the clitoris—is a life-threatening form of mutilation. According to the World Health Organization, more than 80 million women have undergone this surgery in Africa alone.

While female circumcision has its origin in the male desire to control female sexuality, today a host of other superstitions and beliefs sustains the practice. Some Moslem groups mistakenly believe that it is demanded by the Islamic faith, although it has no basis in the Koran. Others believe the operation will increase fertility, affirm femininity, or prevent still births. Yet ultimately what drives the tradition is that men will not marry uncircumcised women, believing them to be promiscuous, unclean, and sexually untrustworthy.

The medical complications of circumcision are severe. Immediate risks include hemorrhage, tetanus and blood poisoning from unsterile and often primitive cutting implements (knife, razor blade, or broken glass), and shock from the pain of the operation, which is carried out without anesthesia. It is not uncommon for these complications to result in death.

The long-term effects, in addition to loss of all sexual feeling, include chronic urinary tract infections, pelvic infections that can lead to infertility, painful intercourse, and severe scarring that can cause tearing of tissue and hemorrhage during childbirth. In fact, women who are infibulated—the most severe form of circumcision—must be cut open on their wedding night to make intercourse possible, and more cuts are necessary for delivery of a child.

Despite these horrific health effects, many people still oppose the eradication of this practice. As late as June 1988, Muslim religious scholars in Somalia argued that milder forms of circumcision should be maintained to temper female sexuality. Others defend circumcision as an "important African tradition." But as the Kenyan women's magazine *Viva* observes: "There is nothing 'African' about injustice or violence, whether it takes the form of mistreated wives and mothers, or slums or circumcision. Often the very men who . . . excuse injustice to women with the phrase 'it is African' are wearing three-piece pin-striped suits and shiny shoes."

Fortunately, women have not sat idle in the face of such abuse. Around the world they are organizing shelters, lobbying for legal reform, and fighting the sexism that underlies violence.

Most industrial countries and at least a dozen developing nations now have shelter movements to provide refuge for abused women and their children. Brazil has established almost 30 all-female police stations for victims of rape, battering, and incest.

And in Africa women are organizing education campaigns to combat sexual surgery. Elsewhere women have organized in their own defense. In San Juan de Miraflores, a shantytown of Lima, women carry whistles that they use to summon other women in case of attack.

Yet it will take more than the dedicated action of a few women to end crimes of gender. Most important is for women worldwide to recognize their common oppression. Violence against women cuts across all cultures and all socioeconomic groups. Indeed, we in America live in our own glass house: In the United States a woman is beaten every 15 seconds, and each day four women are killed by their batterers.

Such statistics are as important as they are shocking. Violence persists in part because it is hidden. If governments and women's groups can expose violence through surveys and better documentation, then ignorance will no longer be an excuse for inaction.

Also critical is challenging the legal framework that undergirds male violence, such as unequal inheritance statutes, discriminatory family laws, and a husband's right to chastise. Especially important are the social inequities and cultural beliefs that leave women economically dependent on men. As long as women must marry to survive, they will do whatever they must to secure a husband—including tolerating abuse and submitting themselves and their daughters to sexual surgery.

Action against violence, however, must come from the international community as well as from the grass roots. Where governments tacitly condone violence through their silence, or worse yet, legitimize it through discriminatory laws and customs, international pressure can be an important impetus for reform. Putting violence against women high on the international agenda is not appeasing a "special interest" group. It is restoring the birthright of half of humanity.

Hungry at Debt's Door

Jon Steinberg

The Third World debt crisis is usually discussed in financial terms—billions of dollars owed, looming defaults, unbelievable interest rates. Ultimately, of course, it matters because it affects people—in today's economy, all of us. The worst dangers for Americans are potential, but for hundreds of millions of people in the Third World, the crash has already happened, with particularly devastating consequences for women—homemakers and factory workers, peasants and prostitutes.

Women in the Third World have never had it easy. Peasant women, the overwhelming majority, cook and clean; walk hours every day to fetch water and firewood; tend the children and the elderly; grow most of the food for household consumption; and sell fruits and vegetables, crafts, and livestock on market days. Because no money is paid for this wearing, never-ending labor, it has always been invisible in economic statistics.

"In Latin America and parts of Asia where there are large plantations, a man is hired to be Juan Valdez picking the coffee," relates Joyce Yu, former director of the Ms. Foundation for Women and a UN program consultant. "Mom and the kids are following behind, but the bags are Juan's, and he decides how the money he gets is spent. He'll probably share some of it with the family, spend some on transportation, some on hanging out—he's not being profligate; we're not talking about thousands of dollars." Even a small increase in smoking of machine-rolled cigarettes in India, for example, "has been linked to a significant reduction in the nutritional intake of wives and children."

Entire Asian families make sophisticated products such as umbrellas or steering wheels in their rural huts, but the husband who gets the money is the only one officially employed. A World Bank project in Malawi labeled men the managers of farms even though they were away doing migrant labor and their wives did all the work.

More and more wives began doing all the work in the 1970s, when borrowed money flowed into the largest Third World cities. Nairobi, Bombay, and Mexico City sprawled as land-poor peasants flocked to find jobs in modern factories and backyard machine shops, or to provide services for those lucky enough to get steady employment. Some of these internal migrants went home for holidays with money and perhaps a transistor radio for the women and children they had left behind. Millions stopped sending money and never went back.

The feminization of rural society was so complete in some areas that entire villages had virtually no able-bodied men. By the early 1980s, women were cultivating half the land in the Third World, although they owned perhaps less than one percent of it.

Food supplies did increase worldwide in the 1970s, and enough money from international loans trickled down for clinics, schools, and other services. Infant mortality rates declined dramatically and more children received at least some education. Times couldn't be called good, but they could get a lot worse. When growing debt increased the pressure to develop exports, and cash crop cultivation was added to traditional women's burdens, households that had been on the edge began to slide into the abyss.

On August 12, 1982, Jesus Silva Herzog, then Mexico's minister of finance, called the chairman of the U.S. Federal Reserve Bank, the U.S. Treasury secretary, and the head of the International Monetary Fund to tell them that there was no way Mexico could come up with the more than $11 billion interest due on its debt within the year. "The world was different after that," he said later of these conversations and the ensuing cascade of events. This was an understatement.

A few small countries already had defaulted in all but name, but this was Mexico, whose $80 billion debt included loans from the nine largest U.S. banks equal to nearly half their stockholders equity. The Mexican finance minister didn't have to remind them that default could pull the banks under, and the world economy might follow.

When Mexico and other Third World nations started accumulating heavy debts in the 1970s, it was as easy as running up a bill on a new charge card. Banks awash in surplus cash sent representatives into every Third World city with an airport to drum up government and private business.

"Chocolate prices are high," the international financial community told governments in the tropics. "Plant more cacao trees; we'll lend you the money; you can pay us back out of the money you earn from the crop." And Third World countries did expand production in cacao and copper and shoes and sugar for export.

"And why not borrow more," the bankers urged, "so you can buy those imported cars or buses you want—or the tanks?" Lenders did not stop making loans at interest rates far below the rate of inflation when Venezuelan borrowings made a "quick trip," returning to private accounts at banks in New York or Geneva. Nor did they demand cuts in Philippine military spending as a condition for new funds.

"Banks don't lend money to get it back," notes Christine Bindert of Shearson Lehman. "If they did they'd be out of business. The best thing for them is if you keep paying your 18 or 20 percent interest. The problem comes when you can't even do that."

That started to happen in 1981 when the Federal Reserve Bank pushed international interest rates sky-high. The industrialized nations sank into their worst postwar recession and cut imports of everything from Algerian wine to Zairean cobalt.

As an oil exporter, Mexico was more fortunate than most, but it had borrowed heavily assuming that oil revenues would be there to pay off the debt. When the price of oil dropped once again, the Mexican government scrambled for additional loans to meet payments on its existing mountain of foreign debt—in 1982 already equal to $1,000 for every Mexican man, woman, and child.

Like other countries running a deficit, Mexico had gone to the International Monetary Fund, a lending institution controlled and largely funded by the U.S. and its major industrialized allies. Aside from granting loans, the IMF, in effect, certifies credit-worthiness. Without its imprimatur, it's hard to find private banks willing to lend, particularly at interest rates anywhere near the market rate.

When finance minister Silva Herzog called the IMF, he knew any new funds would be contingent upon even stricter than usual adherence to the IMF and World Bank "structural adjustment" program: encourage exports; reduce government subsidies for food and state-owned companies; allow foreign investment; devalue the currency to improve the balance of trade.

This regimen has side effects, however. Devaluation raised the price of imports, causing inflation. The IMF-inspired austerity measures bankrupted hundreds of Mexican companies and threw tens of thousands of people out of work. The government slashed imports so drastically that Mexico ran a trade surplus for the year. But it was still billions short of what it needed to service the debt. It was like trying to run up a high-speed down escalator.

In the days that followed, Mexican policymakers seemed prepared to resist IMF terms. President José Lopez Portillo called the crisis a "financial plague" in his term's final "State of the State" address. "As in medieval times, it is scourging country after country. It is transmitted by rats and its consequences are unemployment and poverty, industrial bankruptcy and speculative enrichment." But Lopez Portillo had to make a quick decision: accept the terms or take the uncharted, radical course of debt repudiation.

For the conservative elite, this wasn't much of a choice. Disengagement from the United States would be about as easy for Mexico as it would be for Minnesota. Echoes of populist phrases were still ringing, but so was the IMF phone—with word that Mexico would accept its conditions.

But the IMF wanted to be sure it wasn't giving Mexicans billions of dollars just so it could pay off bank loans. In an unprecedented move, the IMF managing director demanded that the private lenders kick in another $5 billion for development in addition to agreeing to postpone payments on the existing loans—or else the IMF would walk away and leave them buried in bad papers. The banks came up with the $5 billion. Since then, similar packages have been arranged for dozens of countries. And each new agreement entails tightening the economic screws further.

Horrifying statistics can indicate some of the suffering that followed: Argentina's inflation was 114 percent a month in June 1989; per capita income is down 40 percent in Mexico since 1982. But such numbers show only the collapsing financial house. The cruelest devastation is inside the home.

Most Mexican peasants may not even have heard about their government's 1982 agreement with the IMF, but they were soon all too aware that prices of shoes and cooking oil were climbing while the price they got for their corn stayed about the same. To raise output, they had to buy fertilizer, and they couldn't borrow to pay for it because government funding was going for export crops. These peasants are wearing their clothes until the cloth is so thin a needle and thread tears more holes than it can fix. When bus fares double they walk to the market to sell the chickens they can no longer afford to eat themselves. They return home without the cans of tomato paste they had always bought at the government store because the price has doubled and doubled again.

Mothers share their food among the young ones until they are dizzy with hunger themselves. But babies grow thinner and sicker. And all a mother can do is watch and pray—and take a little more from the girls to put on the boys' plates. In the Third World, malnutrition is four times as prevalent among girls as boys. Clinics have closed in budget cutbacks. After years of decline, the infant mortality rate has begun creeping up in the Third World. The psychological impact on a woman of witnessing these effects on their families is "largely overlooked by male policymakers and planners," according to Peggy Antrobus, a Jamaican social scientist.

The toll is great for fathers as well, but they often respond by leaving when conditions start to deteriorate. Most Mexicans who have slipped across the border to the U.S. are men desperate to feed their families.

When men go, the household remains. But women are virtually the definition of the household—the keepers of social bonds, unspoken and invisible, that make life secure and predictable. To leave their ancestral village, they have to be hard-pressed. To leave it as thousands do for agribusiness work—where they confront low pay and sprays that sometimes kill the young ones they must take along to the fields—these women have to believe that the only alternative is watching their children starve.

The growing preponderance of women on Mexican agribusiness farms is part of a global phenomenon. The flowers you buy in Philadelphia may come from Colombian plantations where 70 percent of the work force is women. Some 90 percent of Honduran tobacco workers are women.

For many teenage girls in Mexico and throughout the Third World, urban life begins in a brothel. Thailand, with a population of 50 million, has 300,000 prostitutes. They help service billions in foreign debt.

"Tourism is the second largest source of foreign exchange there and it's literally off the backs of women," says Joyce Yu. "The government turns a blind eye and promotes the 'Land of Smiles' tourist image. The prostitution is very highly organized. Tourists are met by a representative of a very bona fide tour agency and whisked to a plush, Western-style hotel where women are brought to them in their rooms. Or they go to a room with a one-way mirror to look and say, 'I want number 48.' "

Over the past two decades millions of slightly older Third World women have found work assembling computer chips or toys in cities or in "free trade zones" with reduced customs duties. New jobs are always opening up because eye deterioration, bans on married women, low pay, and constant stress push most of these workers out by the time they're 30. Yet young women vie for these jobs. "I would certainly not be well received if I suggested to women that those assembly jobs are terrible and they shouldn't do them," says Barbara Adams, formerly of the American Friends Service Committee's UN office. "They'd say to me, 'What do you suggest? Can I come and do *your* job?' "

Measures taken to increase exports tend to narrow even the meager choice available. In assembly and manufacturing plants, the adjustment programs demanded by the IMF have squeezed out small labor-intensive companies and accelerated the pace of work in factories that remain. "In the 1980s women's work has become more menial, less transferable to another job," notes feminist researcher Caren Grown. When retraining programs do exist, they are usually limited to skilled laborers—men.

For those who manage to keep their jobs, real wages have fallen by 20, 30, even 50 percent in many countries. In Peru, it took 17 minutes working at the minimum wage to pay for a kilo of rice in 1980; four years later it took over two hours.

"Chicken is going for two to three U.S. dollars a pound in Jamaica and the average weekly wage is twelve dollars for those lucky enough to have a job," reports Jamaican economist Marjorie Williams. "These prices and the elimination of social services force mothers to find work in the informal sector—this includes prostitution, which has increased dramatically."

Each week thousands of families migrate to Mexico City, often to join earlier migrants from their village in a shantytown. "Town" is a misnomer for these agglomerations with populations of up to two and a half million. In fact they are known as "lost cities" in Mexico's capital. The population of the entire metropolis has swelled to 18 million and is expected to reach 30 million by the year 2000.

When a peasant family arrives in one of these massive Third World cities, every member capable of earning anything must immediately seek employment. The miserable incomes, long hours, and dispersed locations of whatever work they manage to find quickly reduce the family to a marginal enterprise subsidized by maternal love.

"The street is almost always the child's workplace," notes Zuleica Lopes Cavalcanti de Oliveira, a Brazilian sociologist, "mainly the boy's, while the girl remains at home substituting for the mother in domestic tasks and caring for younger siblings." The mother may be out on the street selling home-prepared foods, with her evenings spent doing whatever chores she can before collapsing from exhaustion. Or if the daughter is lucky she finds work as a live-in maid with a middle-class family, whose scraps are heartier than meals at her own home. But jobs as maids are harder and harder to find. Throughout the Third World, women who were until recently comfortably middle class are discovering the life of the urban poor at first hand.

For the already poor, the decline in living standards has stripped away not only their traditional life, but whatever possessions families have saved for over decades. Beginning with "appliances that don't work or are considered expendable," write Brazilian researchers Teresita de Barbieri and Orlandina de Oliveira, "little by little almost anything can go: chairs, tables, the stove, the gas tanks, the beds, clothes, shoes, electricity, water."

Unbearable as it seems now, this suffering is steadily growing. Few Third World countries have been able to reduce their debt. On the contrary.

Between 1982 and the end of 1988 Mexico paid $50 billion to creditors, but in that time its $80 billion debt grew to $110 billion. In country after country the story is the same. Every indicator of economic, social, physical, and mental health is dropping, and the only growth industry is prostitution, or, in a few countries, drugs.

The U.S. has also paid a price for the austerity demanded by the IMF. The decrease in Third World purchasing power reduces the market for U.S. products, costing us 1.6 million jobs in 1986, according to the Joint Economic Committee of Congress.

"Frankly," says Shearson Lehman's Christine Bindert, "I've been very surprised that the multinationals have not been able to put more pressure on Washington to find solutions." Shortly before his appointment as managing director of the IMF, Michel Camdessus noted in an article that every debt crisis over the past 2500 years has ended in inflation, bankruptcy, or war.

The Reagan administration promised more public and private loans to countries that sold off government-owned corporations and opened up their economy to foreign investment. These countries, the argument went, could then grow rapidly enough to pay off their debts.

In a more sophisticated form, this strategy included promoting structural change to improve the conditions of women. "You get out of debt by shifting to more profitable lines of production," noted Barbara Herz, head of the World Bank's two-year-old Division of Women and Development. "If you give women these opportunities—education, health care, credits—it will pay off for the efficiency of the economy, for their children, and for the environment."

But such payoffs take years, and drastic measures were necessary. Within two months of taking office, President Bush's Treasury Secretary Nicholas F. Brady put the U.S. on the side of debt reduction for the first time. The Brady Plan calls for private lenders to choose between writing off part of their debt, lowering their interest rates, or loaning additional funds. They would get backing for their remaining debt from the World Bank and the IMF—which get a lot of their money from U.S. taxpayers—and Japan.

Of course, with world debt at $1.2 trillion and growing, not everyone can get U.S. guarantees. Once again Mexico seemed the prime candidate. Mexican President Carlos Salinas de Gortari, a strong advocate of privatization of the economy and closer ties to the U.S., faced impossible debt payments. Even so, it took months before the Mexican and U.S. governments and negotiators for some 500 private banks finally signed an accord in July.

Mexico receives favored treatment and has oil to export, so if the Brady Plan can't work across the Rio Grande, it has little hope of providing a global solution. At this point the prognosis isn't good.

Even though its interest payments will be lower, Mexico will have a hard time meeting them. The economy is still a disaster. As in other countries, cuts in state expenditures hurt Mexican-owned private firms and discourage foreign investors. In 1986, multinational corporations invested only half as much as they took out of the country in profits. Almost all the new foreign investment is to expand existing tourist and assembly businesses—hardly the basis for a strong, balanced economy.

President Salinas will have to show better results soon. If the votes in last year's election had been counted fairly, the winner might well have been Cuauhtemoc Cárdenas, a leftist nationalist who calls for a debt moratorium and redistribution of national wealth.

At this point, even a moratorium is considered too moderate by many. They call for outright repudiation. "I didn't borrow the money, I didn't benefit, I don't want to pay it back," Dominga Valasquez of the Federation of Shantytown Housewives in La Paz, Bolivia, declared, expressing sentiments shared by millions of Latin Americans. Nonetheless, Velasquez and others are well aware that their poverty did not begin with the debt crisis, and ending the crisis won't eliminate it.

"Poor people in Third World countries can only benefit from economic growth or debt relief if their governments care enough," points out political economist Cheryl Payer, "if the people use their power."

It is a safe bet that a lot of people will use their power to avert the destruction of their cultures and their lives. What forms their defense takes will be determined in part by how the rest of us respond to their plight.

Suggestions for Further Reading: Part 1

The literature on various aspects of feminism is now so extensive that we have made no attempt to provide exhaustive bibliographies. Instead, we have suggested just a few books that provide accessible introductions to various topics or have become classics in the field.

Best, Raphaela: *We've All Got Scars: What Boys and Girls Learn in Elementary School,* Indiana University Press, Bloomington, 1983.

Brod, Harry: *The Making of Masculinities: The New Men's Studies,* Unwin Hyman, Boston, 1987.

Brown, Lester, et al.: *The State of the World,* Norton, New York (annual).

Chesler, Phyllis: *Women and Madness,* Doubleday, New York, 1972.

Ehrenreich, Barbara, and Deidre English: *For Her Own Good: 150 Years of the Experts' Advice to Women,* Anchor, New York, 1979.

Essed, Philomena: *Everyday Racism,* Hunter House, Claremont, Calif., 1990.

Faludi, Susan: *Backlash: The Undeclared War Against American Women,* Crown, New York, 1991.

Freedman, Estelle B.: *Odd Girls and Twilight Lovers: A History of Lesbian Life in Twentieth-Century America,* Columbia University Press, New York, 1991.

Friedan, Betty: *The Feminine Mystique,* Dell, New York, 1970.

Gornick, Vivian, and Barbara K. Moran (eds.): *Women in Sexist Society,* Signet, New York, 1972.

Kimmel, Michael, and Michael Messner: *Men's Lives,* Collier Macmillan, London, 1989.

Lerner, Gerda (ed.): *Black Women in White America: A Documentary History,* Vintage, New York, 1973.

Millett, Kate: *Sexual Politics,* Avon, New York, 1971.

Morgan, Robin (ed.): *Sisterhood Is Powerful,* Vintage, New York, 1970.

Shaaban, Bouthaina: *Both Right and Left Handed: Arab Women Talk About Their Lives,* Indiana University Press, Bloomington, 1991.

Sidel, Ruth: *Women and Children Last,* Penguin, New York, 1992.

Tannen, Deborah: *You Just Don't Understand: Women and Men in Conversation,* Ballantine, New York, 1990.

Thompson, Karen, and Julie Andrzejewski: *Why Can't Sharon Thompson Come Home?* San Francisco, Spinster/Aunt Lute, 1988.

Wolf, Naomi: *The Beauty Myth: How Images of Beauty Are Used Against Women,* William Morrow, New York, 1991.

The American Woman: A Status Report, Norton, New York (annual).

PART 2

Why Theory?

A theory, in the broadest sense, offers a general account of how a range of phenomena are systematically interconnected; by placing individual items in a larger context, it increases our understanding both of the whole and of the parts constituting that whole. Because people always want to make sense of their worlds, for the sake of intellectual satisfaction as well as practical control, every human society develops theories designed to organize reality in ways that make it intelligible.

Feminism is incipiently theoretical just to the extent that it understands the plights of individual women as connected with each other, as instances of systematic subordination rather than the results of coincidental misfortune. Some Western feminists have sought to develop this basic insight into a comprehensive account of the subordination of women, including its supposed essence and origin, because they believe that constructing a theory in this more elaborate and ambitious sense is a necessary prerequisite for developing effective strategies to liberate women. Without a fully developed theory, they fear, feminist strategies to oppose women's subordination may address only its symbols and symptoms rather than attacking its underlying causes.

The earliest attempts by Western feminists to theorize the subordination of women often utilized ideals and concepts initially developed to account for systems of domination and inequality not perceived as gendered. In the mid-nineteenth century, for instance, John Stuart Mill and Harriet Taylor challenged women's subordination in terms borrowed from liberal critiques of hereditary caste societies; other nineteenth-century feminists explained the subordination of women in terms of Marxist theory, describing bourgeois women in the household as a kind of domestic proletariat and linking the origin of women's subordination with the origin of class society. Similarly, some North American writers in both the nineteenth and twentieth centuries have attempted to legitimate feminist concerns by comparing the situation of women with the situation of African Americans, appropriating variously the rhetoric of abolitionism, civil rights, black nationalism, or black power.

Inspired by the late 1960s resurgence of feminism in Western Europe and North America, the first (1978) edition of *Feminist Frameworks* was structured around the debates between feminists who clung to traditional theoretical models of women's subordination, both liberal and Marxist, and those radical and socialist feminists who proposed new and more distinctively feminist models. The second edition of *Feminist Frameworks,* published in 1984, included challenges raised by feminists of color to both old and new theoretical models but continued to focus on the question of which theoretical framework accounted best for the subordination of women. The organization of both the first two editions of *Feminist Frameworks* around the question of which was the most adequate feminist theory clearly suggested that a systematic and comprehensive account of women's subordination was not only possible but also desirable. During the 1980s, however, these assumptions came under sustained attack: The very project of constructing a theory of women's subordination, at least as theory had been understood traditionally, became discredited among many feminists who charged theory itself with being "elitist," "totalizing," "arrogant," and even "terroristic."

The contemporary feminist distrust of theory has several sources, at least some of which lie in the shortcomings of past feminist theories. Many groups of women, including women of color, lesbians, disabled women, colonized and immigrant women, as well as other groups, have complained, usually with justice, that the generalizations made by feminist theorists often fail to account for their experiences. It is of course obvious that feminist theories whose generalizations about all women are based on the experience of a limited group are biased and invalid. What is less obvious is that promoting such theories may constitute an injury as well as an insult to the members of the groups ignored. Excluding some groups from the normative category "woman" encourages feminist neglect of their needs and interests; even recognizing the needs of these groups as "special interests" is a way of delegitimating them.

Theories involving false generalizations about women are sometimes criticized as "essentialist," meaning that they assume some unique "essence" of womanhood common to all women everywhere; for instance, such theories may be said to assume that all women are sexually victimized, or mothers, or restricted to the domestic sphere. That many feminists now challenge theoretical projects in terms like "essentialist" indicates that the current feminist suspicion of theory is influenced not only by complaints of exclusion made by specific groups of women but also by the contemporary poststructuralist and postmodern attacks on all supposedly comprehensive "grand theories."

This is obviously not the place to attempt a full exposition of such complex and amorphous intellectual and cultural phenomena as poststructuralism and postmodernism, but we can note that they are characterized by, among other things, a rejection of such modernist assumptions as that reality has an inherent order or structure objectively discernible through scientific inquiry. Rejecting European Enlightenment ideals of universal value and transcendent reason, postmodernists

emphasize that what becomes culturally legitimated as knowledge
specific exercises of social power. Thus "reason," according to post
merely a set of variable cultural conventions licensing certain infere
no more than an effect of the rules of a given "discourse"; and object
what is agreed by those in power, a rhetorical form that masks their s
interests.

Feminists have given postmodernism a mixed reception. On the one hand, we have
appreciated its insistence that experience, like written texts, is open to a multitude of
possible interpretations; its interest in the local and the daily; its recognition of
diversity and consequent opposition to the false universalizations of "totalizing"
theory; and its recognition of the complex interconnections between knowledge and
power. On the other hand, postmodernism's challenge to traditional conceptions of
subjectivity and truth has surfaced at precisely that moment in history when women
are asserting ourselves as subjects and claiming to establish new truths.
Epistemological relativism is not conducive to social activism, and for this reason
some feminists have concluded that postmodernism is actually dangerous to feminist
political projects.

Despite its dangers and limitations, we believe that postmodernism has made some
significant contributions to feminism. In this volume, however, we have not
emphasized postmodern approaches. One reason is that much postmodern work
focuses more on the analysis of written texts than on direct social analysis. In addition,
we find that postmodern scholarship is even more likely than other scholarship to be
written in arcane language inaccessible to the uninitiated, thus reinforcing the
perception of many activists that academic feminism no longer has much to do with
the daily struggles of real-life women. It is ironic that postmodern approaches to
theory, which began by criticizing the elitism of traditional feminist theory, should
now themselves often appear as exercises in privilege.

In Part 2, "Why Theory?" we therefore examine some of the other kinds of
questions that have been raised by feminists about the project of understanding
women's situation in theoretical terms. This new part is made necessary by the fact
that theory itself has now become problematized and we can no longer assume, as we
did in previous editions of *Feminist Frameworks,* that while feminists disagree over
which theory best accounts for women's subordination, we generally agree on what
counts as theoretical adequacy.

The reader may find it interesting to reflect on the extent to which differences
among the authors reflect their grounding in different disciplines within both the
humanities and social sciences. The first article is written by Jane Flax, who is both a
political theorist and a psychoanalyst; the second by Bettina Aptheker, a historian; the
third by sociologist Pat Hill Collins; and the final piece by Marilyn Frye, whose
training is in philosophy. Taken together, these articles offer several different
conceptions of the nature of feminist theory and reflect part of the debate currently
going on among feminists over both the form and content such theory might assume.

The article by Jane Flax begins by noting that women's relation to theory has been
rendered problematic by a male-dominated culture that has given men responsibility
for intellectual labor and made women responsible for emotional life, treating reason

and emotion as antithetical. In this article, written in 1979 for an activist rather than an academic audience, Flax defines theory as systematic and analytical and notes that these characteristics make many women afraid of it, since they have internalized the cultural prescription that women are unable to think abstractly. Flax asserts, however, that thinking theoretically is not inherently different from everyday thinking, and she regards it as essential for feminists to engage in theory, both to remedy the biases and omissions of nonfeminist social theories and in order to figure out what kinds of changes are needed to end the subordination of women. While the details of Flax's own social analysis were always controversial, her understanding of the nature and tasks of feminist theory was widely shared during the first decade of contemporary feminism.

Bettina Aptheker's contribution, published in 1989, may be seen as a response to charges that the prefabricated and rigid categories of much social theory often obscure rather than reveal the reality of many women's lives. Aptheker recommends what might be called a bottom-up rather than top-down approach, a search for the meanings that can be found in the daily activities of ordinary women. Discovering and connecting these meanings, she contends, will help feminists develop what she calls a "map" of women's reality from women's point of view, a view that she refers to as "women's standpoint." Aptheker's conception of feminist theory is different from Flax's in that it does not mention a need for comprehensive categories or deep structural analyses. In this respect Aptheker, who is white, shares the belief held by many feminist theorists of color that feminist theory must remain close to the everyday experiences of ordinary women.

Because so much previous feminist theory has rendered the experiences of women of color and of poor women of all colors invisible, Aptheker and others argue that the very project of doing theory may well privilege the lives of some. Their emphasis on listening to the voices of many women reflects their belief that such attention is a prerequisite for doing any theory that is genuinely inclusive. Some have even suggested shifting the emphasis from "theory" which is both passive and narrowly academic to the project of "theorizing" which is immediately active and more broadly inclusive.

The third piece included in Part 2 is an extract from Patricia Hill Collins' 1990 book *Black Feminist Thought*. In this chapter, Collins is concerned with questions of epistemology; that is, questions about the nature of knowledge and justification. Challenging some central assumptions of the conventionally accepted epistemology of positivism, Collins denies that knowledge claims are ever entirely value-neutral and asserts that even the accepted process for evaluating such claims is itself biased so as to favor the claims made by white men. She proposes that the claims made by African-American women should be assessed in terms of an alternative epistemology that is both Afrocentric, insofar as it draws on African traditions, and feminist, insofar as it draws on ways of knowing that the West has associated historically with women.

As a sociologist's view, Collins' conception of the task of black feminist theory might be seen as a revalidation or reaffirmation of the kind of theorizing undertaken by the white feminists of the 1960s and 1970s which later fell out of favor. While her focus on African-American women makes it clear that she has no pretensions to generalizing about the experience of all women everywhere, Collins is interested in constructing a systematic account of the social mechanisms through which this large group of women has been subordinated, as well as identifying the means by which African-American women have resisted their subordination.

Because African-American women would be central rather than peripheral to this account and because their real interests would be accurately represented in it, Collins believes that such an account would reflect the standpoint of black women, while also illuminating the experience of other women. Although both Collins and Aptheker attribute their concept of "standpoint" to the work of Nancy Hartsock, they seem to use the term in somewhat different senses: for Aptheker, who does not aspire to go beyond women's own perceptions of their situations, a standpoint is indistinguishable from a perspective; for Collins, by contrast, it is distinguished by drawing on, but ultimately transcending, the perceptions of African-American women. Collins' work tests the possibility of constructing feminist theories whose scope is less than universal but more than microscopic, theories which analyze as well as describe and which draw explicit implications for political action.

In the last piece in this section, Marilyn Frye reflects on "the possibility of feminist theory." Like most feminists currently reflecting on this question, she is concerned with two (related) dilemmas. One is the dilemma of how to generalize about women while recognizing the inexhaustible differences among them; the other is the dilemma of how to assert the truth of one's claims while recognizing that intelligent women may disagree. Frye suggests that the first dilemma disappears if feminist theory is regarded as naming patterns of male dominance, patterns giving meaning not only to events that conform to the pattern but also to the inevitable exceptions that fail to conform. She suggests that the solution to the second dilemma lies in communicating with others who can help identify both the limits of the pattern and its relationship to other patterns. This suggestion is especially interesting because it implies that the task of constructing feminist theory must be a collective rather than an individual project— and a project not restricted to those with academic credentials. Frye concludes that, in virtue of our common, though not homogeneous, oppression, women are constituted as an epistemic community with a shared interest in understanding—and changing— our social reality.

Women Do Theory

Jane Flax

I begin with an overview of feminist theory and a discussion of the activity of theorizing. I then present a theoretical framework that I've developed after trying various theories and finding none of them sufficient to explain the range of things I think a feminist theorist needs to explain.

Let me say a little about how I ended up doing feminist theory. I have been interested in philosophy and political theory for a long time. I am also interested in psychoanalysis, and have practiced as a feminist therapist. So, partly, I've been trying to put together more traditional ideas of theory with those I've learned as a therapist, especially from psychoanalysis.

Very early I began to connect theory with political activity. I chose political science because I thought there I would learn about politics—which was a mistake. Some political scientists seem to consider theory to be something done 3,000 years ago by Aristotle and Plato, unrelated to the present world. And yet, one of my attractions to theory was that through it, I could learn to systematize my experience. Political science was not much help.

Over time, however, I have found traditional theory to be very helpful in recognizing other people's mental processes as they try to understand the structure of the world systematically. That is, much traditional theory is a kind of internal discourse among thinkers—like a 3,000-year conversation in which people take up each others' ideas and reapply them. I'm interested in many parts of that discourse: what can politics do; what is the ideal political system; what are just relationships; what does "equality" mean?

These issues have been dealt with in the women's movement, but not always in the context of theory. For instance, what it would mean to have a really liberated society is a question of equality and justice that has been debated since the first political theory was attempted. But feminists don't often think of our questions as part of that ongoing political discourse.

In traditional political theory, however, the relationships between men and women, and the status of women, are rarely discussed. They are certainly not generally seen as problems. Some traditional political theorists talk about the family and the role it plays for the state of course; and some have argued for the liberation of women. Plato, for instance, argued that women *could* be philosopher kings since these should be chosen on merit and no inherent proof existed that women were any less intellectually capable than men.[1] Other political theorists, however, have argued that woman cannot think abstractly and has a less developed moral sense. Thus, part of the problem feminist theorists face is taking the general "grammar" and concepts of traditional theory and applying them to women and the issues that affect us.

This brings me to the questions, "what is feminist theory?" and, more generally, "what is theory?" The most important characteristic of theory is that it is a *systematic, analytic* approach to everyday experience. This everybody does unconsciously. To theorize, then, is to bring this unconscious process to a conscious level so it can be developed and refined. All of us operate on theories, though most of them are implicit. We screen out certain things; we allow others to affect us; we make choices and we don't always understand why. Theory, in other words, makes those choices conscious, and enables us to use them more efficiently.

For example, implicit in my choices about the work I could do is an understanding of where power lies, what I'm likely to be able to do, where I'm likely to meet the most frustration, and when I'm likely to be most effective. I might not think through those things consciously, but I make choices on these bases. If you push that explanation, you'll find a series of assumptions about the way the world works, what's available (to me), and what isn't. That's implicit theory-making. The problem is to make it explicit.

BLOCKS TO EXPLICIT THEORY

One of the problems with theory is that women aren't supposed to be able to do it; women aren't supposed to be able to think abstractly. So when you say to a woman, "Okay, now let's read theory," she's likely to panic.

In addition, theoretical writing is often so full of jargon that it seems divorced from ordinary experience. Unfortunately, many theorists have an entrepreneurial interest, a territorial mentality, and they encourage everyone else to believe that their work is impossibly complex. This discourages women—and men—from engaging in theory because it seems hostile and unintelligible. I don't think that the issues *are* inherently so difficult or so far removed from ordinary understanding. I think theorists build turfs and *make* it difficult for others to understand that turf—just like any other professional.

FEMINIST THEORY

Feminist theory is based on a series of assumptions. First, it assumes that men and women have different experiences; that the world is not the same for men and women. Some women think the experiences of women should be identical to the experiences of men. Others would like to transform the world so that there are no such dichotomous experiences. Proponents of both views, however, assume that women's experiences differ from men's, and that one task of feminist theory is to explain that difference.

Secondly, feminist theory assumes that women's oppression is not a subset of some other social relationship. Some argue that if the class system were destroyed, then women would not be oppressed—I don't classify that as feminist theory. Feminist theory assumes that women's oppression is a unique constellation of social problems and has to be understood in itself, and not as a subset of class or any other structure.

It also assumes that women's oppression is not merely a case of what the Chinese call "bad attitudes." I have problems with the word "sexism," because the term implies that women's oppression will disappear when men become more enlightened. On the contrary, I think feminist theory assumes that the oppression of women is part of the way the structure of the world is organized, and that one task of feminist theory is to explain how and why this structure evolved.

Feminist theory names this structure "patriarchy," and assumes that it is a historical force that has a material and psychological base. What I mean by "patriarchy" is the system in which men have more power than women, and have more access to whatever society esteems. What society esteems obviously varies from culture to culture; but if you look at the spheres of power, you'll find that all who have it are male. This is a long-term historical fact rooted in real things. It's not a question of bad attitudes; it's not a historical accident—there are real advantages to men in retaining control over women. Feminist theorists want to explain why that's so.

Patriarchy works backwards as well. It affects the way men and women feel about themselves, and is so deeply internalized that we can't imagine a world without gender. As much as we talk about androgyny, or some situation in which gender isn't so significant, I don't think any of us could imagine a world in which gender would not bring with it many special meanings. *We* may still want to attach special meanings to gender, but a feminist theory would argue that the power attached to gender should disappear; it should not determine whether a person is excluded or included in whatever is esteemed by society.

GOALS OF FEMINIST THEORY

Feminist theory has several purposes. The first is to understand the power differential between men and women. How did it come into being? Why does it exist now? What maintains it? How do the power relations between men and women affect other power relations—for instance, race and class—and how does patriarchy reinforce other oppressive power structures?

Secondly, the purpose is to understand women's oppression—how it evolved, how it changes over time, how it's related to other forms of oppression, and finally, how to change our oppression.

In feminist theory, one issue that emerges consistently is the necessity to understand the family, because it is one of the central mediating structures between all other structures of oppression. The family is where we're internally formed, where we learn about gender, where we experience class and race systems in personal and intimate ways. Therefore, understanding the functions of the family should be one of the crucial goals of feminist theory; yet it remains an area that is particularly undeveloped.

A third purpose of feminist theory is to overcome oppression. Feminist theory is the foundation of action and there is no pretense that theory can be neutral. Within feminist theory is a commitment to change oppressive structures and to connect abstract ideas with concrete problems for political action. It is senseless to study the situation of women without a concomitant commitment to do something about it. The theorist has to draw out the consequences of the theory and use life experience as a part of her basis for understanding, for feeding into the development of theory.

Traditional political theory has always been attached to action. Plato wrote *The Republic* partly because he thought that Athenian democracy was degenerating and he wanted to understand why, and how. It's only contemporary social science theory that claims to be objective, neutral, value-free. I don't think any form of knowledge is neutral, but certainly feminist theory cannot claim neutrality. I think that's one of the problems of women's studies programs. They are too often developed as though they are mere intellectual exercises; some may be, but the study of women is not.

THE EVOLVING THEORETICAL FRAMEWORK

I assume that feminist theory must point to a clear and real base for the oppression of women—feminist theory has to be rooted in human experience. I also assume that there are three basic realms of human activity.

The first is production—we need to produce food, clothing and shelter for our survival. (Obviously, different cultures will produce in different ways. Even people who live on tropical islands have to organize the gathering and preparation of coconuts.) Marx called this the material substructure of human life, and I call it the realm of production.

People also need to reproduce. Not only must we produce the next generation biologically, but we also need to reproduce good citizens for the society. We need to inculcate the values, attitudes, and beliefs appropriate to that culture. A good American citizen will have ideas and expectations very different from a good Mesopotamian citizen living 3,000 years ago. But no matter which society, somehow the unformed person must be trained in its values. In our society, acculturation is conducted by a variety of organizations, including the family and later the school, and the state is involved in setting out certain policies which translate into procedures for acculturating individuals.

The third realm of human activity is the individual's internal life. This is what Freud called "the unconscious," and what I call "psychodynamics." The psychodynamic sphere is where our biological and our mental lives meet, and must be organized. One of the most important aspects of this sphere is sexuality. One of the questions feminists must ask is how a basically "polymorphous species"[2] ends up, in most cultures, a genitally-oriented, heterosexual and monogamous species. Though all cultures allow varying degrees and varieties of sexual pleasure, every civilization channels its citizens' eroticism into practices acceptable to the society.

When we talk about the situation of women, we must examine how all three spheres cooperate to produce our oppression. The elimination of an oppressive structure in one sphere only is inadequate because the other spheres will re-emerge as even more oppressive.

For instance, in the Soviet Union, where the class system is supposedly abolished, men *still* retain the power. The upper structure of the Communist Party is almost entirely male. And while women may move into occupations (as in the United States), those occupations lose their prestige when they do.[3]

Why didn't the oppression of women disappear? For one thing, the structure of the family was not altered—no efforts were made to change the reproductive spheres.[4] So, even though one structure of oppression may have been dealt with, the other two remain intact. Hence, we cannot expect women to be fully participating persons, nor that the full range of women's experience will be expressed in social values. This is a material view of women in that it locates oppression within our material lives. And yet it also teaches us to look at each of the three spheres of human activity, to see how each one particularly impinges upon women.

THE INTERSECTION OF SPHERES

One of the most important characteristics of the family is that all three spheres inter-sect here. In our society, the family is the structure in which we learn to repress and channel our sexuality—where homosexuality is forbidden and where heterosexuality is promoted. It's also the place in which, obviously, external authority is transmitted by and translated in our parents' teachings. It's in the family that the standards of acceptable social behavior are first taught.

Even though most production is no longer done within the family, this is still the structure in which we are taught behaviors appropriate to our class. Lillian Rubin, in *Worlds of Pain,* shows that working-class people become acculturated in the proper expectations of their class and that these expectations are perpetuated from generation to generation. So, the class system impinges upon the family, not only in the obvious ways (such as the kinds of housing or childcare you can afford), but also in more sub-tle ways.

Other structures influence and are perpetuated by these three spheres. The state, for example, structures and benefits from the ways reproduction and psychodynamics interact in class divisions and modes of production. It also benefits from the lingering effects of the psychodynamic sphere on political and personal action.

Reproduction is obviously segregated on the basis of sex. Women are nurturers, men are authority figures—a very important distinction in terms of the developing per-son. This means that both acculturation and reproduction are sex-segregated.

Thus, as feminism teaches us, the class system is not the same for men and women. It's a mistake to take traditional class analysis and impose it upon the experience of women when it is clear that women's work is sex-segregated and class-segregated (80% of women work in jobs where more than half the jobs are held by women).

And finally, the psychodynamic sphere so thoroughly remembers that we're either a *male* or a *female* person, that gender becomes part of who we are. Thus, though we succeed in developing an analysis of patriarchy and capitalism, we still find ourselves repeating old, self-defeating patterns. We can't explain how this happens. Rationally, we've got it all worked out, and yet something refuses to change. That's partly because a great deal happens unconsciously, as we act out old patterns that are accessi-ble neither to reason nor to control since the psychodynamic sphere *is* unconscious. It's the realm of dreams and associations. It's the world of sexuality; it's your internal life. But also it's hard for us to grasp because feminists haven't done much work on it.

CONCLUSION

My assumptions are, then, that these three spheres of life are crucial for everybody, that they're experienced differently by men and women, and that both the experience and the oppression of women are rooted in all three. I believe we must examine each sphere to see how women's and men's experience are different, and how it contributes to that difference. If we would end the oppression of women, we must transform all three spheres; change in one sphere alone will not liberate women.

The psychodynamic sphere can be changed by completely transforming the rearing of children. Dorothy Dinnerstein's book, *The Mermaid and the Minotaur,* is a good reference on the transformation of childrearing. Dinnerstein maintains that both males and females have to be present in the child's life from infancy. It's important that children not be raised by one female person, or a group of female persons. The child also needs peers. In fact, it makes day care and childrearing not something that enables women to work, but locates both right in the center of feminist demands. A feminist revolution must deal with the way children are reared. To create liberated persons requires a transformation in childrearing.

It also means that homosexuality is not just a nicety we support to appease our lesbian sisters. We must recognize that heterosexuality is also part of the structure of the oppression of women. Sexual repression is one of the ways in which women are oppressed and one of the ways in which patriarchy is maintained. On another level, restraining sexuality is a very powerful way of controlling people—as Wilhelm Reich understood in his analysis of the Nazis. Therefore, to fight for a variety of expressions of sexuality has to be part of feminism. It shouldn't be incorporated because lesbians insist, "What about us?" It's absolutely central to feminism. These are two concrete conclusions which grow out of an analysis of the psychodynamic sphere.

NOTES

1 An interesting sidelight is that the head of Plato's academy was a woman who was stoned by the Christians—one of the first of the Christians' many acts against women playing an intellectual, active role.

2 Polymorphous means that we can derive erotic pleasure from a wide variety of experiences; not only from experiences between ourselves and other persons, but also between ourselves and all sorts of physical objects.

3 Seventy-five percent of physicians in the Soviet Union are women, but a physician there is like a social worker here.

4 It's not permissible to be a homosexual or to engage in sexual relations with many different persons of either gender in the Soviet Union, China or Cuba.

Tapestries of Life

Bettina Aptheker

Women's everyday lives are often fragmented and dispersed, caught up short between a job, dinner, and the laundry. They are often episodic. That is, they are often determined by events outside of women's control, such as the opening or closing of a factory in which most of them and/or their husbands are employed. Likewise, women are frequently required to move from city to city or country to country, uprooting family and community, because their husbands' corporate, professional, or military assignments are relocated. Women are continually interrupted. Projects, especially their own, are put aside to be completed on another day or in another year. In the course of a day, a week, women carry the threads of many tasks in their hands at the same time.

Poet Deena Metzger once wrote: "Each day is a tapestry, threads of broccoli, promotion, couches, children, politics, shopping, building, planting, thinking interweave in intimate connection with insistent cycles of birth, existence, and death."[1] Some of these things also happen to men, but not all of them, and they don't happen in the same ways because most men in the United States are not ultimately responsible for maintaining personal relationships and networks. They are not primarily responsible for emotional work. They are not primarily responsible for the children, the elders, the relatives, the holidays, the cooking, the cleaning, the shopping, the mending, the laundry. Their position as men, even as working-class men and men of color, gives them access to more resources and status relative to the women and families of their communities because the society institutionalizes a system of male domination.

By the dailiness of women's lives I mean the patterns women create and the meanings women invent each day and over time as a result of their labors and in the context of their subordinated status to men. The point is not to describe every aspect of daily life or to represent a schedule of priorities in which some activities are more important or accorded more status than others. The point is to suggest a way of knowing from the meanings women give to their labors. The search for dailiness is a method of work that allows us to take the patterns women create and the meanings women invent and learn from them. If we map what we learn, connecting one meaning or invention to another, we begin to lay out a different way of seeing reality. This way of seeing is what I refer to as women's standpoint.[2] And this standpoint pivots, of course, depending upon the class, cultural, or racial locations of its subjects, and upon their age, sexual preference, physical abilities, the nature of their work and personal relationships. What is proposed is a mapping of that which has been traditionally erased or hidden.

To find a starting point for this map we may turn back to our mothers, as Susan Griffin suggested we do in her book *Woman and Nature.* We turn back to our mothers for clarity, Griffin said. We turn back to them not only personally, to see what their individual lives were like, but also to them collectively for the shared memories of women. Griffin wrote:

> We listened for the stories of their lives. We heard old stories retold. . . . We heard again the story of the clean house, we heard the story of the kitchen, the story of mending, the story of the soiled clothes. . . . of the cries of birthing, the story of waking at night, the story of the shut door, the story of the voice raging. . . .[3]

In this turning we see that many of our mothers sacrificed, worked hard, nurtured, did the best they could to "make do," to improve the quality of our daily lives. We also know that some of our mothers died before we were grown. We see that others of our mothers were alcoholic, abusive, emotionally distant. We see that some of our mothers abandoned us as children. We see that some of our mothers were materially privileged but spiritually impoverished. From all of these stories we learn about the reality of women's lives, about the suffering, the failure, the struggle to nurture well. We learn about how other women took care of children who were not their own—grandmothers and aunts, friends and older sisters—women who just took over the child care and did the best they could to raise us. In the conflict between mothers and daughters we learn about the ways in which women are divided from each other, about how we are taught to compete with each other. All of this speaks to women's social condition, to women's social reality enforced by class, by race, by the prescription of gendered roles, inscribed in the dailiness of women's lives.

Many of women's stories have never been written. They form an oral tradition, passed on from one generation to the next. Sometimes they are just seen as anecdotes about family "characters" and their antics. Sometimes they are teaching stories. They are about having respect, about having decent values, about how to live properly, about how to survive.

Cultures shape stories in different ways, and stories pass on women's consciousness as it has been shaped by specific cultural, racial, and class experience. Central to women's consciousness, of course, is an understanding of the ways of men. Sometimes we have heard these stories so often we don't think they are important. Then a situation arises, and we need help, and we remember a story because the help we need is embedded in it. We hear the voice of the teller again, and we remember the details. The story is useful.

Some of the stories I remember from my childhood were not told, they were enacted. And it was only when I was older and learned other things that I could interpret how my mother acted. For example, my mother had a very good friend whose name was Helen West Heller. She was an artist. She was a very elderly woman when I was a child. I can remember going with my mother to visit this woman. She lived in an apartment in lower Manhattan. It was in a very poor neighborhood. She lived, I think, in what were called cold-water flats. I remember that the apartment was relatively dark except for the focused light of special lamps. I remember the smell of oil paints, canvases stacked everywhere, heavy bags of sand which the artist could still lift. I remember that two of her oil paintings hung in our living room, that there were many women shown working in the paintings, and animals too, like cows and monkeys, and that the overriding colors of those paintings were oranges and browns. I remember the artist preparing tea for Mother and me, and serving it in small, rose-petaled tea cups. What I remember most, though, is that Mother never visited Helen West Heller without bringing her bags of groceries.

Some of us cannot remember women's stories. We think we must have heard stories from our mothers, grandmothers, or aunts. But when we think about it we can't remember anything or we can remember family jokes, or the repetition of stories about hurt feelings, or feuds. These do not feel like teaching stories, although sometimes later we realize that we have learned from them. Sometimes we better remember stories by our fathers, grandfathers, and uncles. And sometimes, too, in those stories, women are made to seem incoherent or unreasonable or frivolous. The fact that some of us cannot remember the women's stories—the fact that some women may never have told stories to their children—is a symptom of our oppression as women.

The "thealogian" Carol Christ, in her book *Diving Deep and Surfacing,* wrote of the importance of stories as a way of knowing:

> Without stories there is no articulation of experience. Without stories a woman is lost when she comes to make the important decisions in her life. She does not learn to value her struggles, to celebrate her strengths, to comprehend her pain. Without stories she cannot under-

stand herself. Without stories she is alienated from the deeper experiences of self and world that have been called spiritual or religious.[4]

In the context of her book, Christ was writing especially about women's need to create stories now from our own experiences so we can pass these on.

Leslie Marmon Silko, storyteller and poet of the Laguna pueblo in New Mexico, wrote down stories she could remember from her childhood, many of them told to her by a woman she knew as Aunt Susie—Susie Marmon—who was her father's aunt:

> Around 1896
> when she was a young woman
> she had been sent away to Carlisle Indian school
> in Pennsylvania.
> After she finished at the Indian School
> she attended Dickinson College in Carlisle.
>
> When she returned to Laguna
> she continued her studies
> particularly of history
>
> . . . .
> From the time that I can remember her
> she worked at her kitchen table
> with her books and papers spread over the oil cloth.
> She wrote beautiful long hand script
> but her eyesight was not good
> and so she wrote very slowly.[5]

She was, Silko continued, "a brilliant woman, a scholar of her own making who cherished the Laguna stories all her life."

From Silko, as she was taught by Susie Marmon and others in her family and pueblo, we begin to understand the importance of stories in a more systematic and coherent way, of the connection between oral tradition, storytelling, the invention of meaning, and the preservation of cultural identity:

> She was of a generation
> the last generation here at Laguna
> that passed down an entire culture
> by word of mouth
> an entire history
> an entire vision of the world
> which depended upon memory
> and retelling by subsequent generations.[6]

In the context of the history of the physical and cultural destruction of American Indian peoples brought about by the European and Euro-American conquest, storytelling became central to the struggle for cultural integrity and physical survival. Near the end of her book, Silko tells "The Storyteller's Escape." She begins with these words:

> the storyteller keeps the stories
>   all the escape stories

> She says "with these stories of ours
> we can escape almost anything.
> With these stories we will survive."[7]

Women's stories serve a purpose that is analogous to those of tribal peoples. And many tribal stories are also, of course, specifically women's stories. They serve an analogous purpose because in male-dominated society women's ways of seeing, women's culture both in an artistic sense and in the sense of beliefs and values, are systematically erased, denied, invalidated, trivialized. In some cases, as in Europe between the thirteenth and seventeenth centuries during the witch trials, as in the United States during slavery, the physical survival of many thousands of women has been very tenuous. Women's stories locate women's cultures, women's ways of seeing; they designate meaning, make women's consciousness visible to us. Stories transform our experiences into ways of knowing—about ourselves as women and about ourselves as women looking at the world. . . .

Stories are one of the ways in which women give meaning to the things that happen in a lifetime, and the dailiness of life also structures the telling, the ordering of thought, the significance allocated to different pieces of the story. In studying a "theory of form in feminist autobiography," the literary critic Suzanne Juhasz suggested that "the concept of dailiness [is] a structuring principle in women's lives":

> When you ask a woman, "what happened?" you often get an answer in style that [is] . . . circumstantial, complex, and contextual. You hear a series of "he saids" and "she saids"; you are told what they were wearing, where they were sitting, what they were eating; and slowly the story unrolls. The woman is omitting no detail that she can remember, because all details have to do with her sense of the nature of "what happened." A man, on the other hand, will characteristically summarize: give you the gist, the result, the *point* of the event. . . . In their form, women's lives tend to be like the stories that they tell: they show less a pattern of linear development towards some clear goal than one repetitive, cumulative, cyclical structure. One thinks of housework or childcare: of domestic life in general. . . . Dailiness matters to most women; dailiness is by definition never a conclusion, always a process.[8]

Probably all of us have heard stories told in this way, although it is also important to recognize that cultures shape the way stories are told as much as their content. Juhasz's description is only one of several possible modes, but her general points are important: dailiness is a process rather than a conclusion; it structures thought. Women's stories are different from men's in content and form.

Women use stories in their everyday lives, and especially as a way of doing emotional work. Discussing the significance of talk among women friends, sociologists Fern Johnson and Elizabeth Aries showed the ways in which stories are shared. Disputing the dominant culture's trivialization of women's talk, Johnson and Aries described the intimacy among women friends and the compelling, therapeutic, tactical, and emotional support women provide for each other. As one woman put it, a close friend "makes you feel like a worthwhile human being—that you are capable of loving and sharing."[9]

Some of the stories I use in this chapter (and in this book) are part of women's oral histories; some have been stitched into quilts or planted in gardens or painted or sculpted or written in letters and journals. Some are stories from my own life; others have been published by women in the United States at different times. Some are from academic sources, which I have read as though they were stories but in a different form—stories about the women who wrote them and about the women who were the subject of their study. Women's stories evoke distinct meanings, distinct spacial and temporal arrangements. They have been crafted in or out of the artifacts of daily life, beckoning us to see. These stories reveal that women have not been exclusively or primarily victims, crushed by circumstances, but survivors and creators, their artifacts of beauty arising as it were from nothing.

The act of knowing from our own experience "is so simple," Alice Walker tells us, "that many of us have spent years discovering it. We have constantly looked high, when we should have looked high—and low." She continues:

> For example; in the Smithsonian Institution in Washington, D.C., there hangs a quilt unlike any other in the world. In fanciful, inspired, and simple and identifiable figures, it portrays the story of the crucifixion. It is considered rare beyond price. Though it follows no known pattern of quiltmaking and though it is made of bits and pieces of worthless rags, it is obviously the work of a person of powerful imagination and deep spiritual feeling. Below this quilt I saw a note that says it was made by an anonymous Black woman from Alabama a hundred years ago.
>
> If we could locate this anonymous Black woman from Alabama, she would turn out to be one of our grandmothers—an artist who left her mark in the only materials she could afford and in the only medium her position in society allowed her to use.[10]

The dailiness of women's lives pervades our literature, and our history, and our art. It was deposited for us in the course of living done by ordinary women, our grandmothers, and great-great grandmothers. Alice Walker learned a way of knowing from the quilt she saw at the Smithsonian. Describing Walker's method of writing, literary critic Gloria Wade-Gayles observed that she pieces "bits and pieces of used material rescued from oblivion into a profound and terrifying picture of black suffering in the South."[11] Moreover, in remembering her mother's garden as she had seen it in childhood, Walker also saw her mother's artistry and presented its meaning to us. The garden was an act of renewal, a way to transcend the limits of poverty, to nurture children and neighbors, to make life aesthetically bearable. Walker recalls:

> My mother adorned with flowers whatever shabby house we were forced to live in. And not just your typical straggly country strand of zinnias either. She planted ambitious gardens— and still does—with over fifty different varieties of plants that bloom profusely from early March until late November. . . . Because of her creativity with flowers even my memories of poverty are seen through a screen of blooms—sunflowers, petunias, roses, dahlias, forsythia, spirea, delphiniums, verbena . . . and on and on.[12]

From this search for her mother's garden, Walker saw many of women's everyday labors in a new light. She learned to think in new ways. The quilt gave her a new way of seeing. . . .

The need for beauty, for art, is everywhere in the dailiness of women's lives: in plants and gardens, in the textile arts, in the linen tablecloths and ritual dinners prepared with elaborate care, sometimes for days in advance, sometimes collectively, the pieces of it eventually brought together—Thanksgiving, Christmas, the Chinese New Year, the Jewish Passover. Carrying the feelings of what she had learned about life and growth in her garden, Bernice Mennis describes the preparation for a Passover *tsimmes*[*] in her mother's kitchen. The dailiness of women's labors is given new meaning:

We worked together   my mother and I
in her kitchen of forty-five years
where the water drips cold
and the hot water never gets
really hot   where the oven
must be watched and the refrigerator strapped closed.
I was to grate 20 carrots.
And I   the jogger basketball athlete
invested in my woman's body strength
grated 6 carrots with great
difficulty   my arm exhausted
my fingers grated
And you   my 4' 11"
74 year old mother
grated 14 carrots
without stopping
evenly
not easily or quickly
but calmly
silently
providing again
the dark coarse uneven ground.[13]

In a similar way, Paule Marshall described the poets in the kitchen of her childhood, her mother and her mother's friends who taught her about language as art. They worked as domestic servants in the Flatbush section of Brooklyn by day, and in the early evening gathered together to talk before going home to cook dinner for their husbands and children:

The basement kitchen of the brownstone house where my family lived was the usual gathering place. Once inside the warm safety of its walls the women threw off the drab coats and hats, seated themselves at the large center table, drank their cups of tea or cocoa, and talked. While my sister and I sat at a smaller table over in a corner doing our homework, they talked—endlessly, passionately, poetically, and with impressive range. No subject was beyond them.[14]

In a vein similar to Alice Walker's thoughts about art and creativity in women's lives, Marshall tells of these women who made of language an art form that "in keep-

---

[*]Literally the Yiddish word *tsimmes* means "to make a big deal over something" that shouldn't warrant it. The idea of carrot *tsimmes* is a big fuss over making carrots, a simple vegetable made into an astonishingly wonderful treat.

ing with the African tradition in which art and life are one—was an integral part of their lives." Language was the resource they had available to them, and they used it to express the many subtleties of life they observed. For example, Marshall said that nothing, no matter how beautiful, was ever described as simply beautiful: "It was always 'beautiful-ugly': the beautiful-ugly dress, the beautiful-ugly house. . . ." Pondering this paradox in the linking of opposites, Marshall concluded: "My mother and her friends were expressing what they believed to be a fundamental dualism in life: the idea that a thing is at the same time its opposite, and that these opposites, these contradictions make up the whole. . . . Using everyday speech, the simple, common-place words—but always with imagination and skill—they gave voice to the most complex ideas."[15] . . .

From these stories set in basements, in kitchens, we can see that although these are places of hard work—some have called it drudgery—they are also places of conversation, art, learning, light, warmth, and comfort. In many homes the kitchen is the hub of social intercourse while the "living room" is a misnomer because either it is too formal for such a purpose, or it is the "men's room" in which television, football, and beer prevail. A women's standpoint emerges from these scenes and stories suggesting ideas, feelings, and sensibilities about the nature of beauty, about personal and social change, about the conditions necessary for life and growth, about the importance of interpersonal communication and friendship. These ideas, and certainly the feeling of dailiness from which they emanate, contrast sharply with those of the dominant culture. . . .

NOTES

1 Deena Metzger, "In Her Own Image," *Heresies* 1 (May 1977): 7.

2 The concept of a women's standpoint is elaborated theoretically in an essay by Nancy Hartsock, "The Feminist Standpoint: Developing the Ground for a Specifically Feminist Historical Materialism," in *Discovering Reality: Feminist Perspectives on Epistemology, Metaphysics, Methodology, and Philosophy of Science,* ed. Sandra Harding and Merrill B. Hintikka (Dordrecht and Boston: D. Reidel, 1983). Hartsock's essay, which I originally read in manuscript in 1980, significantly influenced my ideas in the shaping of this book.

3 Susan Griffin, *Woman and Nature: The Roaring Inside Her* (New York: Harper and Row, 1978), p. 201.

4 Carol Christ, *Diving Deep and Surfacing: Women Writers on Spiritual Quest* (Boston: Beacon Press, 1980), p. 1. In a later book, Christ refers to herself as a *thealogian* in an effort to feminize the tradition. See *Reflections on a Journey to the Goddess* (San Francisco: Harper and Row, 1987), especially, "Introduction: Finding the Voices of Feminist Thealogy."

5 Leslie Marmon Silko, *Storyteller* (New York: Seaver Books, 1981), pp. 3–4.

6 Ibid., pp. 4–5.

7 Ibid., p. 247.

8 Susanne Juhasz, "Towards a Theory of Form in Feminist Autobiography: Kate Millett's *Flying* and *Sita;* Maxine Hong Kingston's *The Woman Warrior,*" in *Women's Autobiography: Essays in Criticism,* ed. Estelle C. Jelinek (Bloomington: Indiana University Press, 1980), pp. 223–24.

9 Fern L. Johnson and Elizabeth J. Aries, "The Talk of Women Friends," *Women's Studies International Forum* 6:4 (1983): 358.

10 Alice Walker, "In Search of Our Mothers' Gardens," in her book *In Search of Our Mothers' Gardens: Womanist Prose* (San Diego: Harcourt Brace Jovanovich, 1983), p. 239.

11 Gloria Wade-Gayles, *No Crystal Stair: Visions of Race and Sex in Black Women's Fiction* (New York: Pilgrim Press, 1984), p. 102. Wade-Gayles was referring specifically to Alice Walker's novel *The Third Life of Grange Copeland.*

12 Walker, "In Search of Our Mothers' Gardens," p. 241.

13 Bernice Mennis, "The Miracle," *Sinister Wisdom,* no. 29/30 (1986): 175. This was a special issue of *Sinister Wisdom* entitled *The Tribe of Dina: A Jewish Women's Anthology,* with guest editors Melanie Kaye/Kantrowitz and Irena Klepfisz.

14 Paule Marshall, "The Making of a Writer from the Poets in the Kitchen," *New York Times Book Review,* January 9, 1983, p. 3.

15 Ibid., p. 34.

Toward an Afrocentric Feminist Epistemology

Patricia Hill Collins

. . . One key epistemological concern facing Black women intellectuals is the question of what constitutes adequate justifications that a given knowledge claim, such as a fact or theory, is true. In producing the specialized knowledge of Black feminist thought, Black women intellectuals often encounter two distinct epistemologies: one representing elite white male interests and the other expressing Afrocentric feminist concerns. Epistemological choices about who to trust, what to believe, and why something is true are not benign academic issues. Instead, these concerns tap the fundamental question of which versions of truth will prevail and shape thought and action.

THE EUROCENTRIC, MASCULINIST KNOWLEDGE VALIDATION PROCESS

Institutions, paradigms, and other elements of the knowledge validation procedure controlled by elite white men constitute the Eurocentric masculinist knowledge validation process. The purpose of this process is to represent a white male standpoint. Although it reflects powerful white males interest, various dimensions of the process are not necessarily managed by white men themselves. Scholars, publishers, and other experts represent specific interests and credentialing processes, and their knowledge claims must satisfy the political and epistemological criteria of the contexts in which they reside (Kuhn 1962; Mulkay 1979).

Two political criteria influence the knowledge validation process. First, knowledge claims are evaluated by a community of experts whose members represent the standpoints of the groups from which they originate. Within the Eurocentric masculinist process this means that a scholar making a knowledge claim must convince a scholarly community controlled by white men that a given claim is justified. Second, each community of experts must maintain its credibility as defined by the larger group in which it is situated and from which it draws its basic, taken-for-granted knowledge. This means that scholarly communities that challenge basic beliefs held in the culture at large will be deemed less credible than those which support popular perspectives.

When white men control the knowledge validation process, both political criteria can work to suppress Black feminist thought. Given that the general culture shaping the taken-for-granted knowledge of the community of experts is permeated by widespread notions of Black and female inferiority, new knowledge claims that seem to violate these fundamental assumptions are likely to be viewed as anomalies (Kuhn 1962). Moreover, specialized thought challenging notions of Black and female inferiority is unlikely to be generated from within a white-male-controlled academic community because both the kinds of questions that could be asked and the explanations that would be found satisfying would necessarily reflect a basic lack of familiarity with Black women's reality.

The experiences of African-American women scholars illustrate how individuals who wish to rearticulate a Black women's standpoint through Black feminist thought can be suppressed by a white-male-controlled knowledge validation process. Exclusion from basic literacy, quality educational experiences, and faculty and administrative positions has limited Black women's access to influential academic positions (Zinn et al. 1986). While Black women can produce knowledge claims that contest those advanced by the white male community, this community does not grant that Black women scholars have competing knowledge claims based in another knowledge validation process. As a consequence, any credentials controlled by white male academicians can be denied to Black women producing Black feminist thought on the grounds that it is not credible research. . . .

African-American women academicians who persist in trying to rearticulate a Black women's standpoint also face potential rejection of our knowledge claims on epistemological grounds. Just as the material realities of the powerful and the dominated produce separate standpoints, each group may also have distinctive epistemologies or theories of knowledge. Black women scholars may know that something is true but be unwilling or unable to legitimate our claims using Eurocentric, masculinist criteria for consistency with substantiated knowledge and criteria for methodological adequacy. For any body of knowledge, new knowledge claims must be consistent with an existing body of knowledge that the group controlling the interpretive context accepts as true. The methods used to validate knowledge claims must also be acceptable to the group controlling the knowledge validation process.

The criteria for the methodological adequacy of positivism illustrate the epistemological standards that Black women scholars would have to satisfy in legitimating Black feminist thought using a Eurocentric masculinist epistemology. . . .

Positivist approaches aim to create scientific descriptions of reality by producing objective generalizations. Because researchers have widely differing values, experiences, and emotions, genuine science is thought to be unattainable unless all human characteristics except rationality are eliminated from the research process. By following strict methodological rules, scientists aim to distance themselves from the values, vested interests, and emotions generated by their class, race, sex, or unique situation. By decontextualizing themselves, they allegedly become detached observers and manipulators of nature (Jaggar 1983; Harding 1986). Moreover, this researcher decontextualization is paralleled by comparable efforts to remove the objects of study from their contexts. The result of this entire process is often the separation of information from meaning (Fausto-Sterling 1989).

Several requirements typify positivist methodological approaches. First, research methods generally require a distancing of the researcher from her or his "object" of study by defining the researcher as a "subject" with full human subjectivity and by objectifying the "object" of study (Keller 1985; Asante 1987; Hooks 1989). A second requirement is the absence of emotions from the research process (Hochschild 1975; Jaggar 1983). Third, ethics and values are deemed inappropriate in the research process, either as the reason for scientific inquiry or as part of the research process itself (Richards 1980; Haan et al. 1983). Finally, adversarial debates, whether written or oral, become the preferred method of ascertaining truth: the arguments that can withstand the greatest assault and survive intact become the strongest truths (Moulton 1983).

Such criteria ask African-American women to objectify ourselves, devalue our emotional life, displace our motivations for furthering knowledge about Black women, and confront in an adversarial relationship those with more social, economic and professional power. It therefore seems unlikely that Black women would use a positivist epistemological stance in rearticulating a Black women's standpoint. Black women are more likely to choose an alternative epistemology for assessing knowledge claims, one using different standards that are consistent with Black women's criteria for substantiated knowledge and with our criteria for methodological adequacy. If such an epistemology exists, what are its contours? Moreover, what is its role in the production of Black feminist thought?

THE CONTOURS OF AN AFROCENTRIC FEMINIST EPISTEMOLOGY

Africanist analyses of the Black experience generally agree on the fundamental elements of an Afrocentric standpoint (Okanlawon 1972). Despite varying histories, Black societies reflect elements of a core African value system that existed prior to and independently of racial oppression (Jahn 1961; Mbiti 1969; Diop 1974; Zahan 1979; Sobel 1979; Richards 1980, 1990; Asante 1987; Myers 1988). Moreover, as a result of colonialism, imperialism, slavery, apartheid, and other systems of racial domination, Black people share a common experience of oppression. These two factors foster shared Afrocentric values that permeate the family structure, religious institutions, culture, and community life of Blacks in varying parts of Africa, the Caribbean, South America, and North America (Walton 1971; Gayle 1971; Smitherman 1977; Shimkin et al. 1978; Walker 1980; Sudarkasa 1981b; Thompson 1983; Mitchell and Lewter 1986; Asante 1987; Brown 1989). This Afrocentric consciousness permeates the shared history of people of African descent through the framework of a distinctive Afrocentric epistemology (Turner 1984).

Feminist scholars advance a similar argument by asserting that women share a history of gender oppression, primarily through sex/gender hierarchies (Eisenstein 1983; Hartsock 1983b; Andersen 1988). These experiences transcend divisions among women created by race, social class, religion, sexual orientation, and ethnicity and form the basis of a women's standpoint with a corresponding feminist consciousness and epistemology (Rosaldo 1974; D. Smith 1987; Hartsock 1983a; Jaggar 1983).

Because Black women have access to both the Afrocentric and the feminist standpoints, an alternative epistemology used to rearticulate a Black women's standpoint should reflect elements of both traditions. The search for the distinguishing features of an alternative epistemology used by African-American women reveals that values and ideas Africanist scholars identify as characteristically "Black" often bear remarkable resemblance to similar ideas claimed by feminist scholars as characteristically "female."[1] This similarity suggests that the material conditions of race, class, and gender oppression can vary dramatically and yet generate some uniformity in the epistemologies of subordinate groups. Thus the significance of an Afrocentric feminist epistemology may lie in how such an epistemology enriches our understanding of how subordinate groups create knowledge that fosters resistance. . . .

Like a Black women's standpoint, an Afrocentric feminist epistemology is rooted in the everyday experiences of African-American women. In spite of diversity that exists among women, what are the dimensions of an Afrocentric feminist epistemology?

CONCRETE EXPERIENCE AS A CRITERION OF MEANING

"My aunt used to say, 'A heap see, but a few know,'" remembers Carolyn Chase, a 31-year-old inner-city Black woman (Gwaltney 1980, 83). This saying depicts two types of knowing—knowledge and wisdom—and taps the first dimension of an Afrocentric feminist epistemology. Living life as Black women requires wisdom because knowledge about the dynamics of race, gender, and class oppression has been essential to Black women's survival. African-American women give such wisdom high credence in assessing knowledge.

Allusions to these two types of knowing pervade the words of a range of African-American women. Zilpha Elaw, a preacher of the mid-1800s, explains the tenacity of racism: "The pride of a white skin is a bauble of great value with many in some parts of the United States, who readily sacrifice their intelligence to their prejudices, and possess more knowledge than wisdom" (Andrews 1986, 85). In describing differences separating African-American and white women, Nancy White invokes a similar rule: "When you come right down to it, white women just *think* they are free. Black women *know* they ain't free" (Gwaltney 1980, 147). Geneva Smitherman, a college professor specializing in African-American linguistics, suggests that "from a black perspective, written documents are limited in what they can teach about life and survival in the world. Blacks are quick to ridicule 'educated fools,'. . . they have 'book learning' but no 'mother wit,' knowledge, but not wisdom" (Smitherman 1977, 76). Mabel Lincoln eloquently summarizes the distinction between knowledge and wisdom: "To black people like me, a fool is funny—you know, people who love to break bad, people you can't tell anything to, folks that would take a shotgun to a roach" (Gwaltney 1980, 68).

African-American women need wisdom to know how to deal with the "educated fools" who would "take a shotgun to a roach." As members of a subordinate group, Black women cannot afford to be fools of any type, for our objectification as the Other denies us the protections that white skin, maleness, and wealth confer. This distinction between knowledge and wisdom, and the use of experience as the cutting edge dividing them, has been key to Black women's survival. In the context of race, gender, and class oppression, the distinction is essential. Knowledge without wisdom is adequate for the powerful, but wisdom is essential to the survival of the subordinate. . . .

Experience as a criterion of meaning with practical images as its symbolic vehicles is a fundamental epistemological tenet in African-American thought systems (Mitchell and Lewter 1986). "Look at my arm!" Sojourner Truth proclaimed: "I have ploughed, and planted, and gathered into barns, and no man could head me! And ain't I a woman?" (Loewenberg and Bogin 1976, 235). By invoking concrete practical images from her own life to symbolize new meanings, Truth deconstructed the prevailing notions of woman. Stories, narratives, and Bible principles are selected for their applicability to the lived experiences of African-Americans and become symbolic representations of a whole wealth of experience. Bible tales are often told for the wisdom they express about everyday life, so their interpretation involves no need for scientific historical verification. The narrative method requires that the story be told, not torn apart in analysis, and trusted as core belief, not "admired as science" (Mitchell and Lewter 1986, 8). . . .

Some feminist scholars offer a similar claim that women as a group are more likely than men to use concrete knowledge in assessing knowledge claims. For example, a substantial number of the 135 women in a study of women's cognitive development were "connected knowers" and were drawn to the sort of knowledge that emerges from first-hand observation (Belenky et al. 1986). Such women felt that because knowledge comes from experience, the best way of understanding another person's ideas was to develop empathy and share the experiences that led the person to form those ideas.

In valuing the concrete, African-American women invoke not only an Afrocentric tradition but a women's tradition as well. Some feminist theorists suggest that women are socialized in complex relational nexuses where contextual rules versus abstract principles govern behavior (Chodorow 1978; Gilligan 1982). This socialization process is thought to stimulate characteristic ways of knowing (Hartsock 1983a; Belenky et al. 1986). These theorists suggest that women are more likely to experience two modes of knowing: one located in the body and the space it occupies and the other passing beyond it. Through their child-rearing and nurturing activities, women mediate these two modes and use the concrete experiences of their daily lives to assess more abstract knowledge claims (D. Smith 1987).

Although valuing the concrete may be more representative of women than men, social class differences among women may generate differential expression of this women's value. One study of working-class women's ways of knowing found that both white and African-American women rely on common sense and intuition (Luttrell 1989). These forms of knowledge allow for subjectivity between the knower and the known, rest in the women themselves (not in higher authorities), and are experienced directly in the world (not through abstractions). . . .

In traditional African-American communities Black women find considerable institutional support for valuing concrete experience. Black women's centrality in families, churches, and other community organizations allows us to share our concrete knowledge of what it takes to be self-defined Black women with younger, less experienced sisters. "Sisterhood is not new to Black women," asserts Bonnie Thornton Dill, but "while Black women have fostered and encouraged sisterhood, we have not used it as the anvil to forge our political identities" (1983, 134). Though not expressed in explicitly political terms, this relationship of sisterhood among Black women can be seen as a model for a whole series of relationships African-American women have with one another (Gilkes 1985; Giddings 1988).

Given that Black churches and families are both woman-centered, Afrocentric institutions, African-American women traditionally have found considerable institutional support for this dimension of an Afrocentric feminist epistemology. While white women may value the concrete, it is questionable whether white families—particularly middle-class nuclear ones—and white community institutions provide comparable types of support. Similarly, while Black men are supported by Afrocentric institutions, they cannot participate in Black women's sisterhood. In terms of Black women's relationships with one another, African-American women may find it easier than others to recognize connectedness as a primary way of knowing, simply because we are encouraged to do so by a Black women's tradition of sisterhood.

THE USE OF DIALOGUE IN ASSESSING KNOWLEDGE CLAIMS

"Dialogue implies talk between two subjects, not the speech of subject and object. It is a humanizing speech, one that challenges and resists domination," asserts Bell Hooks (1989, 131). For Black women new knowledge claims are rarely worked out in isolation from other individuals and are usually developed through dialogues with other members of a community. A primary epistemological assumption underlying the use of dialogue in assessing knowledge claims is that connectedness rather than separation is an essential component of the knowledge validation process (Belenky et al. 1986, 18).

This belief in connectedness and the use of dialogue as one of its criteria for methodological adequacy has Afrocentric roots. In contrast to Western, either/or dichotomous thought, the traditional African worldview is holistic and seeks harmony. "One must understand that to become human, to realize the promise of becoming human, is the only important task of the person," posits Molefi Asante (1987, 185). People become more human and empowered only in the context of a community, and only when they "become seekers of the type of connections, interactions, and meetings that lead to harmony" (p. 185). The power of the word generally (Jahn 1961), and dialogues specifically, allows this to happen.

Not to be confused with adversarial debate, the use of dialogue has deep roots in an African-based oral tradition and in African-American culture (Sidran 1971; Smitherman 1977; Kochman 1981; Stanback 1985). . . .

The widespread use of the call-and-response discourse mode among African-Americans illustrates the importance placed on dialogue. Composed of spontaneous verbal and nonverbal interaction between speaker and listener in which all of the speaker's statements, or "calls," are punctuated by expressions, or "responses," from the listener, this Black discourse mode pervades African-American culture. The fundamental requirement of this interactive network is active participation of all individuals (Smitherman 1977, 108). For ideas to be tested and validated, everyone in the group must participate. To refuse to join in, especially if one really disagrees with what has been said, is seen as "cheating" (Kochman 1981, 28). . . .

Black women's centrality in families and community organizations provides African-American women with a high degree of support for invoking dialogue as a dimension of an Afrocentric feminist epistemology. However, when African-American women use dialogues in assessing knowledge claims, we might be invoking a particularly female way of knowing as well. Feminist scholars contend that men and women are socialized to seek different types of autonomy—the former based on separation, the latter seeking connectedness—and that this variation in types of autonomy parallels the characteristic differences between male and female ways of knowing (Chodorow 1978; Keller 1983; Belenky et al. 1986). For instance, in contrast to the visual metaphors (such as equating knowledge with illumination, knowing with seeing, and truth with light) that scientists and philosophers typically use, women tend to ground their epistemological premises in metaphors suggesting finding a voice, speaking, and listening (Belenky et al. 1986). The words of the Black woman who struggled for her education at Medgar Evers College resonate with the importance placed on voice: "I was basically a shy and reserved person prior to the struggle at Medgar, but I found my voice—and I used it! Now, I will never lose my voice again!" (Nicola-McLaughlin and Chandler 1988, 195).

While significant differences exist between Black women's family experiences and those of middle-class white women, African-American women clearly are affected by general cultural norms prescribing certain familial roles for women. Thus in terms of the role of dialogue in an Afrocentric feminist epistemology, Black women may again experience a convergence of the values of the African-American community and women's experiences.

THE ETHIC OF CARING

"Ole white preachers used to talk wid dey tongues widdout sayin' nothin', but Jesus told us slaves to talk wid our hearts" (Webber 1978, 127). These words of an ex-slave suggest that ideas cannot be divorced from the individuals who create and share them. This theme of talking with the heart taps the ethic of caring, another dimension of an alternative epistemology used by African-American women. Just as the ex-slave used the wisdom in his heart to reject the ideas of the preachers who talked "wid dey tongues widdout sayin' nothin'," the ethic of caring suggests that personal expressiveness, emotions, and empathy are central to the knowledge validation process.

One of three interrelated components comprising the ethic of caring is the emphasis placed on individual uniqueness. Rooted in a tradition of African humanism, each individual is thought to be a unique expression of a common spirit, power, or energy inherent in all life.[2] When Alice Walker "never doubted her powers of judgment because her mother assumed they were sound," she invokes the sense of individual uniqueness taught to her by her mother (Washington 1984, 145). The polyrhythms in African-American music, in which no one main beat subordinates the others, is paralleled by the theme of individual expression in Black women's quilting. Black women quilters place strong color and patterns next to one another and see the individual differences not as detracting from each piece but as enriching the whole quilt (Brown 1989). This belief in individual uniqueness is illustrated by the value placed on personal expressiveness in African-American communities (Smitherman 1977; Kochman 1981; Mitchell and Lewter 1986). Johnetta Ray, an inner-city resident, describes this Afrocentric emphasis on individual uniqueness: "No matter how hard we try, I don't think black people will ever develop much of a herd instinct. We are profound individualists with a passion for self-expression" (Gwaltney 1980, 228).

A second component of the ethic of caring concerns the appropriateness of emotions in dialogues. Emotion indicates that a speaker believes in the validity of an argument. Consider Ntozake Shange's description of one of the goals of her work: "Our [Western] society allows people to be absolutely neurotic and totally out of touch with their feelings and everyone else's feelings, and yet be very respectable. This, to me, is a travesty. . . . I'm trying to change the idea of seeing emotions and intellect as distinct faculties" (Tate 1983, 156). The Black women's blues tradition's history of personal expressiveness heals this either/or dichotomous rift separating emotion and intellect. For example, in her rendition of "Strange Fruit," Billie Holiday's lyrics blend seamlessly with the emotion of her delivery to render a trenchant social commentary on southern lynching. Without emotion, Aretha Franklin's (1967) cry for "respect" would be virtually meaningless.

A third component of the ethic of caring involves developing the capacity for empathy. Harriet Jones, a 16-year-old Black woman, explains to her interviewer why she chose to open up to him: "Some things in my life are so hard for me to bear, and it makes me feel better to know that you feel sorry about those things and would change them if you could" (Gwaltney 1980, 11). Without her belief in his empathy, she found it difficult to talk. Black women writers often explore the growth of empathy as part of an ethic of caring. For example, the growing respect that the Black slave woman Dessa and the white woman Rufel gain for one another in Sherley Anne Williams's *Dessa Rose* stems from their increased understanding of each other's positions. After watching Rufel fight off the advances of a white man, Dessa lay awake thinking: "The white woman was subject to the same ravisment as me; this the thought that kept me awake. I hadn't knowed white mens could use a white woman like that, just take her by force same as they could with us" (1986, 220). As a result of her new-found empathy, Dessa observed, "it was like we had a secret between us" (p. 220). . . .

There is growing evidence that the ethic of caring may be part of women's experience as well (Noddings 1984). Certain dimensions of women's ways of knowing bear striking resemblance to Afrocentric expressions of the ethic of caring. Belenky et al. (1986) point out that two contrasting epistemological orientations characterize knowing: one an epistemology of separation based on impersonal procedures for establishing truth and the other, an epistemology of connection in which truth emerges through care. While these ways of knowing are not gender specific, disproportionate numbers of women rely on connected knowing.

The emphasis placed on expressiveness and emotion in African-American communities bears marked resemblance to feminist perspectives on the importance of personality in connected knowing. Separate knowers try to subtract the personality of an individual from his or her ideas because they see personality as biasing those ideas. In contrast, connected knowers see personality as adding to an individual's ideas and feel that the personality of each group member enriches a group's understanding. The significance of individual uniqueness, personal expressiveness, and empathy in African-American communities thus resembles the importance that some feminist analyses place on women's "inner voice" (Belenky et al. 1986).

The convergence of Afrocentric and feminist values in the ethic of caring seems particularly acute. White women may have access to a women's tradition valuing emotion and expressiveness, but few Eurocentric institutions except the family validate this way of knowing. In contrast, Black women have long had the support of the Black church, an institution with deep roots in the African past and a philosophy that accepts and encourages expressiveness and an ethic of caring. Black men share in this Afrocentric tradition. But they must resolve the contradictions that confront them in searching for Afrocentric models of masculinity in the face of abstract, unemotional notions of masculinity imposed on them (Hoch 1979). The differences among race/gender groups thus hinge on differences in their access to institutional supports valuing one type of knowing over another. Although Black women may be denigrated within white-male-controlled academic institutions, other institutions, such as Black families and churches, which encourage the expression of Black female power seem to do so, in part, by way of their support for an Afrocentric feminist epistemology.

THE ETHIC OF PERSONAL ACCOUNTABILITY

An ethic of personal accountability is the final dimension of an alternative epistemology. Not only must individuals develop their knowledge claims through dialogue and present them in a style proving their concern for their ideas, but people are expected to be accountable for their knowledge claims. Zilpha Elaw's description of slavery reflects this notion that every idea has an owner and that the owner's identity matters: "Oh, the abominations of slavery! . . . Every case of slavery, however lenient its inflictions and mitigated its atrocities, indicates an oppressor, the oppressed, and oppression" (Andrews 1986, 98). For Elaw abstract definitions of slavery mesh with the concrete identities of its perpetrators and its victims. African-Americans consider it essential for individuals to have personal positions on issues and assume full responsibility for arguing their validity (Kochman 1981).

Assessments of an individual's knowledge claims simultaneously evaluate an individual's character, values, and ethics. African-Americans reject the Eurocentric, masculinist belief that probing into an individual's personal viewpoint is outside the boundaries of discussion. Rather, all views expressed and actions taken are thought to derive from a central set of core beliefs that cannot be other than personal (Kochman 1981, 23). "Does Aretha really *believe* that Black women should get 'respect,' or is she just mouthing the words?" is a valid question in an Afrocentric feminist epistemology. Knowledge claims made by individuals respected for their moral and ethical connections to their ideas will carry more weight than those offered by less respected figures. . . .

The ethic of personal accountability is clearly an Afrocentric value, but is it feminist as well? While limited by its attention to middle-class, white women, Carol Gilligan's (1982) work suggests that there is a female model for moral development whereby women are more inclined to link morality to responsibility, relationships, and the ability to maintain social ties. If this is the case, then African-American women again experience a convergence of values from Afrocentric and female institutions.

The use of an Afrocentric feminist epistemology in traditional Black church services illustrates the interactive nature of all four dimensions and also serves as a metaphor for the distinguishing features of an Afrocentric feminist way of knowing. The services represent more than dialogues between the rationality used in examining biblical texts and stories and the emotion inherent in the use of reason for this purpose. The rationale for such dialogues involves the task of examining concrete experiences for the presence of an ethic of caring. Neither emotion nor ethics is subordinated to reason. Instead, emotion, ethics, and reason are used as interconnected, essential components in assessing knowledge claims. In an Afrocentric feminist epistemology, values lie at the heart of the knowledge validation process such that inquiry always has an ethical aim.

Alternative knowledge claims in and of themselves are rarely threatening to conventional knowledge. Such claims are routinely ignored, discredited, or simply absorbed and marginalized in existing paradigms. Much more threatening is the challenge that alternative epistemologies offer to the basic process used by the powerful to legitimate their knowledge claims. If the epistemology used to validate knowledge comes into question, then all prior knowledge claims validated under the dominant model become suspect. An alternative epistemology challenges all certified knowledge and opens up the question of whether what has been taken to be true can stand the test of alternative ways of validating truth. The existence of a self-defined Black women's standpoint using an Afrocentric feminist epistemology calls into question the content of what currently passes as truth and simultaneously challenges the process of arriving at that truth.

NOTES

1 In critiques of the Eurocentric, masculinist knowledge validation process, what Africanist scholars label "white" and "Eurocentric" feminist scholars describe as "male-dominated" and "masculinist." Although he does not emphasize its patriarchal and racist features, Morris Berman's *The Reenchantment of the World* (1981) provides an important discussion of Western thought. Afrocentric analyses of this same process can be found in Asante (1987) and Richards (1980, 1990). For feminist analyses see Hartsock (1983a, 1983b) and Harding (1986), especially Chapter Seven, "Other 'Others' and Fractured Identities: Issues for Epistemologists," pp. 163–96.

2 In discussing the West African Sacred Cosmos, Mechal Sobel notes that *Nyam,* a root word in many West African languages, connotes an enduring spirit, power, or energy possessed by all

life. Despite the pervasiveness of this important concept in African humanism (see Jahn 1961, for example), its definition remains elusive. Sobel observes, "every individual analyzing the various Sacred Cosmos of West Africans has recognized the reality of this force, but no one has yet adequately translated this concept into Western terms" (1979, 13). For a comprehensive discussion of African spirituality, see Richards (1990).

The Possibility of Feminist Theory

Marilyn Frye[*]

Imagine that a single individual had written up an exhaustive description of a sedated elephant as observed from one spot for one hour and then, with delighted self-satisfaction, had heralded that achievement as a complete, accurate, and profound account of The Elephant. The androcentrism of the accumulated philosophy and science of the Western world is like that. A few, a few men, have with a like satisfaction told the story of the world and human experience—have created what pretends to be progressively a more and more complete, accurate, and profound account of what they call "Man and His World." The Man whose (incomplete) story this is turns out to be a species of males to which there is awkwardly, problematically, and paradoxically appended a subspecies or alterspecies of individuals of which men are born but which are not men. It is a story that does not fit women and that women do not fit.

In the light of what is generally considered common knowledge (the official story of "Man and His World") a great deal of most women's experience appears anomalous, discrepant, idiosyncratic, chaotic, "crazy."[1] In that dim light our lives are to a great extent either unintelligible or intelligible only as pathological or degenerate. As long as each woman thinks that her experience alone is thus discrepant, she tends to trust the received wisdom and distrust her own senses and judgment. For instance, she will believe that her "inexplicable" pain is imaginary, a phantasm. In consciousness-raising conversations among themselves (however intentionally or unintentionally joined) women discover that similar "anomalies" occur in most of their lives and that those "anomalies" taken together form a pattern, or many patterns. The fragments that were each woman's singular oddities (often previously perceived as her own faults or defects) are collectively perceived to fit together into a coherent whole. The happy side of this is that we learn we are not sick or monstrous, and we learn to trust our perception. The unhappy side is that the coherent whole we discover is a pattern of oppression. Women's lives are full to overflowing with the evidence of the imbalanced distribution of woes and wealth between the women and the men of each class, race,

[*]An earlier version of this work was delivered as an invited paper on the program of the Central Division of the American Philosophical Association, May 1, 1987, and the earliest work on it was supported by the Center for the Study of Women in Society at the University of Oregon. I am indebted at many points to conversations with Carolyn Shafer and to comments made by many women on the various occasions over the last five years when I have given talks in which I was working out various aspects of these thoughts.

and circumstance. In consciousness-raising the data coalesce into knowledge: knowledge of the oppression of women by men.

When women's experience is made intelligible in the communications of consciousness-raising we can recognize that it is in the structures of men's stories of the world that women do not make sense—that our own experience, collectively and jointly appreciated, can generate a picture of ourselves and the world within which we are intelligible. The consciousness-raising process reveals us to ourselves as authoritative perceivers which are neither men nor the fantastical, impossible feminine beings which populate the men's world story. Our existence is not inherently paradoxical or problematic. Our existence *is* an indigestible mass of discrepant data for the patriarchal world story. From the point of view of the discrepant data, that story appears appallingly partial and distorted—it seems a childish, and fantastic, albeit dangerous fiction. Assuming our perceptual authority, we have undertaken, as we must, to rewrite the world. The project of feminist theory is to write a new encyclopedia. Its title: *The World, According to Women.*[2]

The historically dominant Western man-made world story claims universality and objectivity but, from the point of view of feminists, conspicuously lacks both. Thinking to improve upon that story, we assumed ours should be both. By adding voices to the conversation, we expected to achieve a broader consensus in the intersubjective agreement that justifies the claim to objectivity and thus also a grounding for legitimate universalization.[3]

As many introductory philosophy textbooks will tell you, the Western tradition of philosophy presupposes the intelligibility of the universe—the doctrine that *it* and *we* (human beings) are such that it can be understood by us. The human knower, in principle any human knower, can, in principle, understand the universe.[4] This presupposes a fundamental uniformity of human knowers such that in principle any knower is interchangeable with any other knower. In practice it means that as you add to the group whose intersubjective agreement will count as objectivity, you are adding pieces of a single and coherent cosmic jigsaw puzzle. You may not know where the pieces fit, but you presume it is not possible that any of them do not fit. Noncongruence of observers' observations is either merely apparent or due to observers' mistakes or errors which are themselves ultimately explainable, ultimately congruent with the rest of the world picture. If one accepts this body of doctrine, one thinks all knowers are essentially alike, that is, are essentially like oneself; one thinks then that one can speak not just as oneself, but as a human being.

For feminist thinkers of the present era the first and most fundamental act of our own emancipation was granting ourselves authority as perceivers, and we accomplished that act by discovering agreement in the experiences and perceptions of women. It makes sense that when the feminist thinker assumes her authority as a knower, she claims her equal perceptual rights in the pseudodemocracy of the interchangeable knowers of the intelligible universe. It makes sense that she would carry over the assumption that all knowers are essentially alike into the supposition that all humans similarly positioned (in this case, as women in patriarchy) have in principle, as knowers, the same knowledge. She would think she could speak not just as herself but as a woman.

The new world writers had first to overcome the deceptions and distortions that made us unknown to ourselves. We have made remarkable progress: many, many of us have rewritten many chapters of our own lives and are living lives neither we nor our mothers would have imagined possible—or even imagined at all. We have deconstructed canons, reperiodized history, revised language, dissolved disciplines, added a huge cast of characters, and broken most of the rules of logic and good taste. But we have also discovered our own vast ignorance of other women of our own time. We have repeatedly discovered that we have overlooked or misunderstood the truths of the experience of some groups of women and that we have been overlooked or misunderstood by some other segment or school of feminist thought. We have had great difficulty coming to terms with the fact of differences among women—differences associated with race, class, ethnicity, religion, nationality, sexuality, age, physical ability, and even such variety among women as is associated just with peculiarities of individual history.

What we want to do is to speak of and to and from the circumstances, experience, and perception of those who are historically, materially, and culturally constructed by or through the concept *woman.* But the differences among women across cultures, locales, and generations make it clear that although all female humans may live lives shaped by concepts of Woman, they are not all shaped by the same concept of Woman. Even in any one narrowly circumscribed community and time, no female individual is a rubber-stamped replica of the prevailing concept of Woman. (The concept of Woman that prevails in my neighborhood is internally contradictory; nobody *could* fit it.) Furthermore, Woman is not the only concept or social category any of us lives under. Each of us is a woman of some class, some color, some occupation, some ethnic or religious group. One is or is not someone's sister, wife, mother, daughter, aunt, teacher, student, boss, or employee. One is or is not alcoholic, a survivor of cancer, a survivor of the Holocaust. One is or is not able-bodied. One is fat or thin. One is lesbian or heterosexual or bisexual or off-scale. A woman of color moves in the (Western) world as both "a woman" and "of color." A white woman also moves both as "a woman" and as "white," whether or not her experience forces upon her a clear consciousness of the latter. Lesbians must reject the question: Are you more fundamentally women, or lesbians? And we insist that heterosexual women recognize that everywhere they move as women they also move as heterosexual. No one encounters the world simply as *a woman.* Nobody observes and theorizes simply as *a woman.* If there are in every locale perspectives and meanings that can properly be called women's, there is nonetheless no such thing as *a* or *the* woman's story of what is going on.

Schematically and experientially the problem of difference in feminist theory is simple: a good deal of feminist thinking has issued in statements and descriptions that pertain to "women" unmodified for distinctions among them. These are the sorts of statements their authors want to be making. But when such statements and descriptions are delivered in public they meet with critics, who are women, who report that the statements are appallingly partial, untrue, or even unintelligible when judged by their own experience and by what is common knowledge among women of their kind, class, or group. This criticism seems to be (and I have felt it to be) devastating.

Feminism (the worldview, the philosophy) rests on a most empirical base: staking your life on the trustworthiness of your own body as a source of knowledge. It rests equally fundamentally on intersubjective agreement, since some kind of agreement in perceptions and experience among women is what gives our sense data, our body data, the compelling cogency which made it possible to trust them. It is an unforgettable, irreversible, and definitive fact of feminist experience that respect for women's experience/voice/perception/knowledge, our own and others', is the ground and foundation of our emancipation—of both the necessity and the possibility of rewriting, recreating, the world. Thus it is only by a violent dishonesty that we could, or can, fail to give credence to women's voices—even when they differ wildly and conflict. When we do give them credence it soon becomes clear that, taken as a whole, "women's experience" is not uniform and coherent in the ways required to ground a structure of knowledge as that has traditionally been understood.[5]

Thus has the feminist faith in and respect for the experience and voice of every woman seemed to lead us into the valley of the shadow of humanism—wishy-washy, laissez-faire, I'm O.K.—You're O.K., relativistic humanism (or more recently into the bottomless bog of relativistic apolitical postmodernism)—where there are no Women and there is no Truth. Which is not where we want to be.

The way out, or the way back in, I think, is to clarify how the practice of feminist theory departed from the predominating modern Western epistemology even before some theorists began revising feminism into a form of postmodernism.

The world story we have rejected is written in a code whose syntax respects enumerative, statistical, and metaphysical generalization. Of these, enumerative generalization is probably kindest to particulars. But it is so weak that to be true such a generalization must do a kind of violence by remarking the unremarkable and unsaying everything that is worth saying about the individuals in question. (For example, I hardly honor my colleagues in the Michigan State University Philosophy Department by saying that they all have offices on the MSU campus, which is the most substantial thing I can think of that I know is unqualifiedly true of every one of them.) Statistical generalization may be the next kindest to particulars since it is cheerful about coexisting with (that is, ignoring) discrepant data. Metaphysical generalization, declaring this or that to be the what-it-is of a thing, threatens the annihilation of that which does not fit its prescription. For example, women are nurturant; if you are not nurturant you are not a real woman, but a monster. All generalization seems unjust to particulars, as is reflected in the aversion people so commonly have to "being labeled." Generalization subsumes particulars, reduces them to a common denominator. Nomination is domination, or so it seems.

It might seem that in response to the embarrassment of these paradoxes, we should retreat into autobiography or string suitable adjectives onto the noun *woman,* and many of us have tried both. (Speaking as an able-bodied college-educated Christian-raised middle-class middle-aged and middle-sized white Anglo lesbian living in the Midwest, I can report that these strategies both reduce one to silliness and raise serious questions about adjective ranking in English.) More moderately, we might back up to narrowing the subject of our claims to specific groups of women identified by race, class, nationality, and so forth. In some cases we have done this—at the risk, even so, of overgeneralizing or stereotyping—but what we have to say, or what we thought we had to say, is not just a compendium of claims about the circumstances and experiences of women of particular groups. Our project is theoretical, philosophical, political. You have to have some sort of genuinely general generality to have theory, philosophy, politics.

But feminism has been going at generality in another way from the start. We need to pay more attention to what we have been doing. In consciousness-raising there is a movement away from the isolation of the individual, the particular. But even in the most culturally homogeneous local consciousness-raising group, women's lives were not revealed to be as alike as two copies of the morning paper. We agreed neither in the details of our experience nor in opinions and judgments. We perceived similarities in our experiences, but we did not determine the relative statistical frequencies of the events and circumstances we found to be "common." And the question of what a woman is, far from being answered, was becoming unanswerable and perhaps unaskable. The generalizing movement of our "science" was not toward metaphysical, statistical, or universal generalization.

In consciousness-raising women engage in a communication that has aptly been called "hearing each other into speech."[6] It is speaking unspoken facts and feelings, unburying the data of our lives. But as the naming occurs, each woman's speech creating context for the other's, the data of our experience reveal patterns both within the experience of one woman and among the experiences of several women. The experiences of each woman and of the women collectively generate a new web of meaning. Our process has been one of discovering, recognizing, and creating patterns—patterns within which experience made a new kind of sense, or, in many instances, for the first time made any sense at all. Instead of bringing a phase of enquiry to closure by summing up what is known, as other ways of generalizing do, pattern recognition/construction opens fields of meaning and generates new interpretive possibilities. Instead of drawing conclusions from observations, it generates observations.

Naming patterns is not reductive or totalitarian. For instance, we realize that men interrupt women more than women interrupt men in conversation: we recognize a pattern of dominance in conversation—male dominance. We do not say that every man in every conversation with any woman always interrupts. (We do not hazard a guess, either, as to the exact statistical frequency of this phenomenon, though once someone did a study on it, and it turned out to be even higher than any of us suspected.) We do not close any questions about men's awareness of what they are doing, or women's experience of it. What we do is sketch a schema within which certain meanings are sustained. It makes sense of a woman's feeling stifled, frustrated, angry, or stupid when she is in the company of men. It makes sense of the women who lower the pitch of their voices and use the most elite vocabulary they can command when they want to be heard in a male realm. And when a man repeatedly interrupts me, I do not just dumbly suffer the battery; in knowledge of the pattern, I interpret this event, I know it as an *act*, as "dominating." Recognizing a pattern like this can also lead out along various associative axes to other discoveries. The pattern of conversational interruption readily suggests itself as a simile for the naming of other abridgements, interferences, and amputations we suffer but have not named.

   Patterns sketched in broad strokes make sense of out experiences, but it is not a single or uniform sense. They make our different experiences intelligible in different ways. Naming patterns is like charting the prevailing winds over a continent, which does not imply that every individual and item in the landscape is identically affected.[7] For instance, male violence patterns experiences as different as that of overprotective paternalism and of incest, as different as the veil and the bikini. The differences of experience and history are in fact necessary to perceiving the patterns. It is precisely in the homogeneity of isolation that one *cannot* see patterns and one remains unintelligible to oneself. What we discover when we break into connection with other women cannot possibly be uniform women's experience and perception, or we would discover nothing. It is precisely the articulation and differentiation of the experiences formulated in consciousness-raising that give rise to meaning. Pattern discovery and invention require encounters with difference, with variety. The generality of pattern is not a generality that defeats or is defeated by variety.

Our game is pattern perception. Our epistemological issues have to do with the strategies of discovering patterns and articulating them effectively, judging the strength and scope of patterns, properly locating the particulars of experience with reference to patterns, understanding the variance of experience from what we take to be a pattern. As I see it, full reflective philosophical discussion of these issues has barely begun, and I cannot write the treatise that develops them either alone or yet. But I will survey some of the territory.
   We have used a variety of strategies for discovering patterns, for making sense of what does not make sense. The main thing is to notice what does not make sense. Discovering patterns requires novel acts of attention. Consciousness-raising techniques typically promote just such unruliness by breaking the accustomed structures of conversation. Adopting practices designed to give every woman equal voice and equal audience, and to postpone judgment, defense, advocacy, and persuasion, the members of the group block the accustomed paths of thought and perception. In the consequent chaos, they slide, wander, or break into uncharted semantic space. In this wilderness one can see what does not make sense—incongruities, bizarreness, anomaly, unspeakable acts, unthinkable accusations, semantic "black holes,"[8] These things are denied, veiled, disguised, or hidden by practices and language that embody and protect privileged perceptions and opinions. But they are often, perhaps characteristically, flagged by "outlaw emotions,"[9] and a powerful strategy of discovery therefore is to legitimize an outlaw emotion. You feel something—anger, pain, despair, joy, an erotic rush—that is not what you are supposed to be feeling. Everything invites you to stifle it, decide you are imagining it or are overreacting, or declare yourself crazy or bad. The strategy of discovery, enabled by the consciousness-raising structures, is to put that feeling at the center, let it be presumed normal, appropriate, true, real, and then see how everything else falls out around it. Over and over, for instance, women's pain, taken simply as pain—real and appropriate pain—uncovers and confirms the pattern and reiterated patterns of male violence. Similarly, giving any "minority" voice centrality in the force field of meanings reveals patterns to us.[10]

Other strategies of pattern perception are all the familiar strategies of creativity and of self-defense: cultivating the ability to be astounded by ordinary things, the capacity for loving attention, confidence in one's senses, a sensitivity to smokescreens and fishy stories, and so on.

Pattern perception and processes of checking such perception also require recognition that not everything that is intelligibly located by a pattern *fits* the pattern. A great deal of what I have said over the years about women is not true of me (as critics both hostile and friendly have often pointed out), and much of it is not true of most of the women to whom I have said it. One reason this is so is that many of the patterns we discover are not so much *descriptive* and *prescriptive*—patterns of expectation, bribe, and penalty from which many individual women manage to deviate to a greater or lesser extent by rejection, resistance, or avoidance. A very significant aspect of feminist theory is an *affirmation* of the disparity between the lived reality of women and the patterns of patriarchy. In the project of making oneself intelligible, it is as useful to recognize forces to which one is *not* yielding as it is to recognize forces by which one is being shaped or immobilized. For instance, there are kinds of prudishness, "modesty," and shame that shape women's experience of sexuality (not in all cultures, but certainly not only in Western ones). For the women who are not contaminated by these diseases it is nonetheless relevant to some of the meanings of their sexual experience that many women are thus shaped, that many men expect women to be so, and that the woman who is exceptional in this respect has acquired her own shape partly in resistance to the force of that mold and/or partly by some form of insulation or obliviousness that surely has other interesting manifestations. Recognizing the pattern and "placing" herself in the range of meanings it sets up will contribute to her understanding of herself and her world even if she is not a woman restrained and distorted by sexual shame.

But in addition to the fact that individual divergence from the pattern we perceive is not generally to be understood as a disconfirmation of the alleged existence or strength of the pattern, there are limits to how much any one pattern patterns. Patterns are like metaphors. (Perhaps patterns *are* metaphors.) Just as an illuminating metaphor eventually breaks down when persistently pressed, the patterns that make experience intelligible only make so much of it intelligible at a time, and over time that range may change. In pressing a good metaphor, one finds out a great deal by exploring its limits, understanding where and why it breaks down, and one can do the same with patterns. An important part of pattern perception is exploring the range of the pattern, and a way of going wrong is misjudging scope.

An example of this sort of mistake that comes from the heart of some important feminist theorizing is in perceptions of patterns of dependence of women on men. Anyone who is oppressing another is very likely exploiting social structures that coerce the other into some kind and degree of dependence upon the oppressor (for otherwise the victim could and would extricate herself from the situation). But the middle white American pattern of coerced one-on-one economic and psychological dependence of females on males with limited but real opportunities for individual women's ad hoc escape from the trap is only a local working out of a higher order pattern. In many cultural locales dependency is more collective, not primarily economic, more or less escapable, or more or less extreme. We can err by taking one local expression of the pattern as a global pattern or by thinking that there is no such global pattern because we see that not everyone experiences the particular expression of it that has been brought to our attention (for example, assuming that since single women are not economically dependent on a husband, they are independent of men).

If the occupational hazard of pattern perceivers is misjudging scope, the remedy is communication. The strategy by which one proceeds to test pattern recognition involves many inquirers' articulating patterns they perceive and running them by as great a variety of others as possible. Others will respond by saying something like, "Yes, that makes sense, it illuminates my experience," or, "That doesn't sound like my life, you're not talking about me." Patterns emerge in the responses and signal the limits of the meaning making powers of the patterns one has articulated. A pattern is not bogus or fictitious either simply because things do not fit it (the nonfit may be as powerfully significant as any fit) or simply because there are limits to what it patterns.

One might consider requiring of the articulation of patterns that they explicitly signal the limits of their powers and applications and then criticize those that do not or that signal it wrongly. But the similarity of patterns and metaphors is salient again here. When one says that life is a stage, one does not and cannot specify in precisely what dimensions and to exactly what degree life is stagelike. One aspect of the power of metaphor is the openness of its invitation to interpretation—it casts light of a certain color, but does not determine how its object looks in that light to any particular observer. The patterns articulated by the feminist theorist similarly have the power to make lives and experiences usefully intelligible in part because they do *not* fix their own applications but provide only a frame for the making of meaning. Neither patterns nor metaphors contain specifications of their limits. They work until they stop working. You find out where that is by working them until they dissolve. Like a metaphor, a pattern has to be appreciated, put to use. You may outrun its power without realizing you have if you are not paying attention to the voices and perception of many women.

The business of telling when one is just wrong about a pattern, when one is misperceiving, is very tricky for women in our current states of community, or lack of it. We work in a climate of inquiry where a mainstream knowledge industry works constantly to undermine our confidence in our perceptions, where political exigencies tempt us to forced unity, and where everything would keep women from forming epistemic community. In such conditions we operate without clear and dependable intuitions of plausibility and without adequate benefit of the monitoring function provided by a clear sense of audience. It is very hard to know when we are getting it right and when we are off the wall. Our first urgency, therefore, built into our situation and our method, is to be engaged with the greatest possible range of perceivers, of theorizers. What we are about is remetaphoring the world. We need as many and various perceivers as possible to mix metaphors wildly enough so we will never be short of them, never have to push one beyond its limits, just for lack of another to take up where it left off.

The whole female population of the planet is neither a speaker nor an audience. It does not have a story. But communications among women—kin, friends, coworkers, writers and their readers, explorers and the audiences of their stories—have generated world stories in which the lives and fates of humans on this planet fall out along fault lines of female and male as prominently and consistently as on fault lines of wealth and of tribal, racial, or national identities. Those lines are characterized by women's doing more work and controlling less wealth than men, by men's doing far more violence to women than women do to men, and by men's world stories marginalizing, reducing, and erasing women. We have not assumed but discovered these patterns and their many ramifications. In this discovery we have also discovered the grounds of epistemic community. It is not a homogeneous community, and it does not have to be so in order to ground and validate feminist theory. In fact it *cannot* be so if it is to support the meaning making of feminist theory.

If a common (but not homogeneous) oppression is what constitutes us an epistemic community, what will happen when we free ourselves? First, I would suppose that a common history of oppression and liberation would hold us for a long time in a degree of community. Eventually, perhaps, we will fall into a happy and harmless theoretical disarray. What we are writing, *The World, According to Women,* has never been anything but an anthology, a collection of tales unified, like any yarn, only by successively overlapping threads held together by friction, not riveted by logic. There is no reason to predict or require that it must forever hold together at all. Perhaps eventually the category *woman* will be obsolete. But perhaps not.

NOTES

1 Deborah Rhode suggested that what I am saying here is simply that women's experience appears to be "different." But in the current lingo, influenced by the French, "difference" is an abstract and generic term. What I am referring to here is two quite specific things—that which is flat-out unintelligible (which is not quite what the French, following Derrida and in the shadow of Lacan, mean by "difference"), and that which is specifically and concretely "different" in that it is abnormal, in the negatively charged sense of that concept. I am talking here from the experience of women. We do not experience ourselves, under the conceptual net of patriarchal forms, as abstractly and semantically "different," but as unintelligible or abnormal. So also do men commonly experience women.

2 My use of *we, our, feminist theorists,* and *feminist theory* is and will remain problematic. I know I am not the only one engaged in the pilgrimage described here, but I could not and would not pretend to say who else this speaks for. For those who do not identify with this *we,* I think the essay can be read as a record of what *some* women who have called themselves feminists and theorists have thought and done.

3 This approach is perhaps the general tendency of which the "feminist empiricism" described by Sandra Harding is a more specific instance. See Harding, *The Science Question in Feminism* (Ithaca: Cornell University Press, 1986), 24–25.

4 This dogma has been questioned within that same tradition, but it still has power in contemporary thinking. The "postmodern" critique of this tradition's concepts of truth, reality, and knowledge is by no means universally acknowledged as sound, and furthermore the transformation of worldview that would be involved in actually abandoning those concepts is more profound than most of us can manage in less than a decade or so.

5 Cf. Maria Lugones, "Playfulness, 'World'-Travelling, and Loving Perception," Hypatia 2 (1987): 3–19.

6 This phrase was coined by Nelle Morton in a talk given at an American Academy of

Religion Workshop, December 28, 1977 (cited in Mary Daly, *Gyn/Ecology: The Meta-ethics of Radical Feminism* [Boston: Beacon, 1978], 313).

7 For some elaboration of this point see the introduction to my book *The Politics of Reality: Essays in Feminist Theory* (Trumansburg, N.Y.: Crossing, 1983), xii–xiv.

8 The term comes from Ruth Ginsberg (conversation).

9 The phrase as used in this context is due to Alison Jaggar.

10 The centering of a Black woman's voice and views as accomplished in Bell Hooks's *Feminist Theory: From Margin to Center* (Boston: South End, 1984) is a good example of this. The entire phenomenon of U.S. feminism looks very different when cast as relatively marginal to the lives and interests of Black and poor women than when cast as central to history.

Suggestions for Further Reading: Part 2

The literature on various aspects of feminism is now so extensive that we have made no attempt to provide exhaustive bibliographies. Instead, we have suggested just a few books that provide accessible introductions to various topics or have become classics in the field.

Aptheker, Bettina: *Tapestries of Life: Women's Work, Women's Consciousness and the Meaning of Daily Experience,* University of Massachusetts Press, Amherst, 1989.

Belenky, Mary Field, Blythe McVicker Clinchy, Nancy Rule Goldberger, and Jill Mattuck Tarule: *Women's Ways of Knowing: The Development of Self, Voice and Mind,* Basic Books, New York, 1986.

Bleier, Ruth (ed.): *Feminist Approaches to Science,* Pergamon, New York, 1986.

Eichler, Margrit: *Nonsexist Research Methods: A Practical Guide,* Allen & Unwin, Boston, 1988.

Fine, Michelle: *The Possibilities of Feminist Research,* University of Michigan Press, Ann Arbor, 1991.

Fausto-Sterling, Anne: *Myths of Gender,* Basic Books, New York, 1985.

Garry, Ann, and Marilyn Pearsall (eds.): *Women, Knowledge and Reality: Explorations in Feminist Philosophy,* Unwin Hyman, Boston, 1989.

Gilligan, Carol: *In a Different Voice: Psychological Theory and Women's Development,* Harvard University Press, Cambridge, Mass., 1982.

Harding, Sandra (ed.): *Feminism and Methodology: Social Science Issues,* Indiana University Press, Bloomington and Indianapolis, 1987.

Hull, Gloria T., Patricia Bell Scott, and Barbara Smith: *All the Women Are White, All the Blacks Are Men, But Some of Us Are Brave: Black Women's Studies,* The Feminist Press, Old Westbury, N.Y., 1982.

Lloyd, Genevieve: *The Man of Reason: 'Male' and 'Female' in Western Philosophy,* University of Minnesota Press, Minneapolis, 1984.

Nicholson, Linda J.: *Feminism/Postmodernism,* Routledge, New York, 1990.

Tuana, Nancy (ed.): *Feminism and Science,* Indiana University Press, Bloomington and Indianapolis, 1989.

PART 3

Theories of Women's Subordination

We have noted that one way in which this third edition of *Feminist Frameworks* differs from the previous editions is in recognizing that the notion of feminist theory itself has now become problematic. Questions that once were the undisputed starting points of feminist theory, for example, the question of the fundamental cause of women's subordination, not only are often viewed as irrelevant to contemporary social analysis but sometimes even as illegitimate.[1] Categories once assumed indispensable are challenged, including even the category "woman."[2] The traditional goals and methods of feminist theory are questioned, and some feminists now reject theory in any form.

While many criticisms of feminist "grand" theories are well taken, we have explained in our introduction to Part 2 that we do not think they discredit the entire enterprise of feminist theory, understood as an attempt to reach a comprehensive as well as detailed understanding of the subordination of women in relation to other forms of domination. Theories in any sphere are always open to challenge—but challenges have constructive as well as destructive aspects. Even as they identify flaws in existing conceptualizations, they also point, explicitly or implicitly, toward alternative ways of thinking. Recent criticisms of feminist theory have demonstrated conclusively, in our view, that universal generalizations about women are almost certain to be false; that different groups of women experience subordination in very different ways—and that some may not even be conscious of or concerned about subordination at all; that some women exercise power over others—as well as over some men; that what appear to be the most urgent issues facing feminism vary according to social perspective and historical moment; and that there is no uniquely privileged standpoint from which a final or authoritative feminist theory may be constructed. Accepting these insights, however, does not entail that feminist theory must be abandoned. It does entail that, in developing future theories, we must be sensitive not only to difference but also to dominance, self-reflective about the ways in which our perceptions are influenced by our own situations and, above all, that each of us must listen respectfully to women whose situations and perceptions are very different from our own.

In Part 3 of this volume, we present a number of feminist attempts to conceptualize and reconceptualize women's subordination. Some of them rely on "old" frameworks, uninfluenced by the kinds of criticisms mentioned above; other, more recent, frameworks are designed to counter earlier omissions and distortions by beginning from the perspectives of women marginalized by previous theories. All of them are contemporary in the sense that at least some feminists presently adhere to each, but they also follow a certain progression insofar as the later theories respond to perceived shortcomings in the earlier ones. Although they are rivals to each other in the sense of offering alternative understandings of women's subordination, they are not competitors in the simple sense of providing different answers to precisely the same questions. Instead, and like most theoretical developments, as old issues begin to appear uninteresting or unfruitful and new ones become more urgent or salient, the central questions of feminist theory have been reformulated. One example of such a reformulation is the contemporary feminist shift away from a concern with issues of primacy.

THE ROOTS OF WOMEN'S SUBORDINATION

In previous editions of *Feminist Frameworks,* the editors' introduction to the theories or frameworks began with a section entitled "The Roots of Women's Oppression." This section reflected the fact that feminist theory throughout the 1970s was preoccupied with issues of "primacy," one aspect of which was a search for the "root" of women's subordination. Some theorists wrote as though the root was the original historic (or prehistoric) cause; others interpreted the metaphor of root to mean the primary or most important cause maintaining the subordination of women today. Regardless of what they meant by "root" or what they took it to be, feminists of the 1970s generally agreed that discovering the root cause of women's subordination was one of the primary tasks confronting feminist theory. Their reasoning is implicit in their choice of metaphor: Weeds that are cut down often regrow and can be eradicated only by being uprooted. Similarly, most feminist theorists reasoned, the subordination of women could be eradicated only by abolishing or transforming the deep structures that supposedly nourished it. Determining the root of women's subordination was seen as a prerequisite for identifying political strategies to end it.

Between the late 1960s and the early 1980s, feminist theorists gave a variety of answers to the question of the root of women's subordination. Some theories identified the root as biological, residing in women's supposedly lesser physical strength (Mill), or in the dependence supposedly resulting from female incapacities related to childbearing (Firestone), or in men's supposed propensity to rape and women's to be raped (Brownmiller). Others argued that biological differences were salient only in certain social contexts and located the root of women's subordination in certain social structures or institutions: in class society (Engels), in male control of women's sexuality (Bunch and MacKinnon), or in female child rearing (Chodorow and Dinnerstein). In addition to being highly speculative, these theories were also extremely general: Not only were most of them "class-blind," but all of them were "race-blind." Inevitably they were charged with ignoring differences between women—a charge that some authors addressed with varying degrees of plausibility.

Simultaneously with debating the root cause of the subordination of women, feminists in this period also disputed "primacy" in another sense. This emerged as the question whether subordination on the basis of sex was the most urgent problem currently facing women. Marxist feminists contended that economic class constituted the most significant division in capitalist societies, arguing that the deepest interests of working-class women were those they shared with working-class men. Reviving a dispute from the turn of the century, they alleged that the reforms sought by women of the capitalist class would fail to benefit and might even injure the interests of working-class women who should therefore unite, as one slogan had it, to "Defeat Bourgeois Feminism!" A parallel disagreement divided white feminists from many feminists of color, especially black feminists. Some black women felt that their deepest interests were shared with black men rather than with white women and asserted that their primary political task was challenging racism rather than male domination. Imperialism was seen as creating yet another division between women, since metropolitan women obviously benefited from the labors of women on the periphery. Some colonized women, such as Australian aboriginals and some Native Americans, claimed that local forms of male domination were a direct consequence of colonization; others, such as Vietnamese, Palestinian, and South African women, argued that struggles against indigenous forms of male domination should be deferred until national autonomy was achieved.

Throughout the decade of the 1970s, discussion of these questions was intense and often confused, partly because of the ambiguity of the word "primary" which is open to a variety of interpretations, including "first," "most significant," and "most urgent." This ambiguity helped to obscure the conceptual distinction between the original and the maintaining cause of women's subordination—what we might call its production and its reproduction. The same ambiguity may also have encouraged some feminist theorists to confuse the earliest form of domination with the form that was causally deepest, the one that had the greatest impact on women's lives, and the one that should be attacked first. Thus some feminists inferred, for instance, that the original cause of the subordination of women must be the deepest as well as causally the most significant—and therefore also the most politically urgent.

Crucial as these debates appeared twenty or even ten years ago, today they seem not only dated but often incoherent. Feminists over the past decade have learned to conceptualize sex, gender, race, and class in more sophisticated and nuanced ways, ways that no longer permit the simple oppositions generating the earlier debates. Feminist theory today, as we shall see, addresses questions quite different from those surrounding primacy.

WOMEN'S SUBORDINATION THROUGH THE LENS OF SEX: CONSERVATISM

To the extent that it wishes to retain the status quo, conservatism obviously cannot be regarded as a framework that is feminist. Applied to issues of gender, conservatism typically offers an explanation for the subordination of women that works simultaneously as a rationalization for it. Secular versions of conservatism often account for women's subordination in terms of human biology and warn of the high cost, in terms of social inefficiency and human unhappiness, of any deviation from this supposedly biologically engendered norm. Despite the fact that conservatism is not feminist, two samples of biodeterminist conservative arguments are included here— along with a feminist rejoinder—because biological justifications of women's subordination continue to be widely circulated.

Over the past twenty years, psychoanalytic explanations of people's behavior have been superseded to a considerable extent by biopsychiatric approaches. These, as their name implies, attempt to explain many human desires, moods, and actions in terms of biological phenomena such as brain chemistry. Until about 1970, however, Freudian theory was probably the most powerful secular rationale for women's subordination, and even today it retains considerable influence. We have again reprinted extracts from Freud's famous article "Femininity," partly for its historical significance and partly as a basis for understanding recent feminist attempts to reread Freud in ways that illuminate the subordination of women without at the same time rationalizing it.

Sociobiology is the second version of conservatism presented here. Sociobiological approaches to understanding human behavior came to prominence in 1975 with the publication of entomologist Edward O. Wilson's ground-breaking work *Sociobiology: The New Synthesis.* Most of this massive tome was devoted to explaining insect behavior, but it was the last chapter, in which Wilson extended his theory to human action, that predictably aroused the most public interest and controversy. Wilson later elaborated his reflections on this topic in the popular paperback *On Human Nature* (1978), from which the present extract is taken. Like Freud, Wilson refrains from asserting that changes in traditional gender arrangements are impossible, but he argues that any fundamental changes in these arrangements are contrary to the biological predispositions of human males and females, predispositions that originally had some evolutionary advantage. Wilson claims that thwarting these predispositions will impose social and individual costs much higher than the benefits produced.

Ruth Hubbard is a Harvard biologist who, despite—or perhaps because of—her training, strongly opposes biodeterminist explanations of human action. Challenging both biological reductionism and biological holism, she argues that it is impossible in principle to separate biology's effect on human behavior from social and economic influences. Although Hubbard's piece is clearly feminist rather than gender-conservative, its inclusion in this section is designed to help students understand the ultimate incoherence of all biodeterminist explanations of human action, including but not limited to psychoanalysis and sociobiology. Looking through only the lens of sex obscures as much as it reveals about women's subordination.

WOMEN'S SUBORDINATION THROUGH THE LENS OF GENDER: LIBERALISM

Liberal feminism has its origins in the social contract theories of the sixteenth and seventeenth centuries. These theories were distinguished from previous political theories in part by their insistence that all forms of social domination or authority needed to be justified. Early liberal theorists postulated the fundamental equality of all men, based on their allegedly equal potential for reason, and promoted the social ideals of liberty and equality.

Just as the liberal conception of equality meant only that political inequalities required justification, not that men were to be equal with each other in all respects, so the liberal conception of liberty did not mean that men could do anything they liked. Instead, liberty was construed to mean that governmental authority was legitimate only if it rested on the consent of the governed and only if it were constrained within certain limits. Liberals characteristically explain the limits of governmental authority in terms of a distinction between the so-called public aspects of human life, which government may legitimately regulate, and the so-called private arena, within which government has no authority to intervene. Liberals continue to debate just where the line between the public and private spheres should be drawn, but they never doubt that the preservation of liberty necessitates the drawing of such a line.

Almost as soon as the new liberal ideals of liberty and equality were promulgated, women began to demand that they too should be free and equal. The first sustained Western feminist theory was Mary Wollstonecraft's *A Vindication of the Rights of Woman,* inspired by the French Revolution and published in 1792. Wollstonecraft pointed the direction for later liberal feminism by arguing that biological sex differences were entirely irrelevant to granting political rights. Since the possession of rationality was then considered the proper basis for the attribution of such rights, Wollstonecraft argued that women's capacity to reason was equal with that of men. She claimed that the apparent inferiority of the female intellect was due to women's inferior education and should be interpreted as the *result* of women's social inequality rather than as a *justification* for it.

Wollstonecraft's distinction between biological facts and social norms foreshadowed the distinction between sex and gender made by twentieth-century liberal feminists. Briefly put, twentieth-century liberal feminists came to distinguish conceptually between sex, which they regarded as a socially invariant biological difference between males and females, and gender, which they defined as a historically variable set of social norms and expectations prescribing appropriate behavior for men and women. Sex thus may be a property of nonhuman as well as human beings, whereas gender can be attributed only to humans. Looking through the lens of gender, liberal feminists perceive women's subordination as a consequence of gendered norms rather than biological sex. Liberal feminist activism is therefore directed toward criticizing the injustice of those norms and working toward changing them.

Liberal feminists favor gender equality in the sense of equal opportunities for men and women—a sense continuous with the classical liberal interpretation of equality, which construed equal opportunities to mean the "career open to talent" as opposed to family or rank. Liberal feminists contend that the ideal of gendered equality of opportunity remains desirable irrespective of the nature of biological sex differences. If social opportunities were equally available to men and women, positions would be filled by the very best people available, while individual liberty and probably individual happiness would be maximized. Liberal feminists regard these justifications for gendered equality of opportunity as valid even if it were to turn out that biological differences in fact enabled one sex or the other to take better advantage of certain opportunities.

The insistence that women's opportunities should be equal with men's is a distinguishing theme in liberal feminism. It is the central claim in John Stuart Mill's classic essay *On the Subjection of Women* (1869), extracted here, as well as the central moral insight of the National Organization for Women's *Bill of Rights,* first promulgated in 1967, a year after NOW's formation. Largely as a consequence of liberal feminist activism, the idea that women and men should enjoy equal opportunities has now become so generally accepted in North America that it is rarely disputed in public.

Intense public controversy has erupted, however, over exactly what counts as equality of opportunity. Does it require simply the repeal of legal discrimination against women, as John Stuart Mill sometimes seemed to assume, or must certain other conditions be fulfilled? Presumably, as Mary Wollstonecraft noted, it requires equal educational opportunities for men and women—but how should they be measured? Even feminist teachers often unintentionally give less attention to the girls than to the boys in their classes, and far less scholarship money is available for female than for male college athletes (Ref. AAUW report). Does equality of opportunity require that pregnancy and maternity leaves be available to women—or should they be parental leaves? Does it require that educational institutions and employers establish child care centers? Does it require so-called preferential treatment for women? Does it even require the right to abortion?

The NOW *Bill of Rights,* reprinted here, obviously promotes a much stronger conception of equal opportunity than that currently held by the general public—at least in the contemporary United States. Discussion of this issue constitutes a major part of liberal feminism, and much of the rest of their debate concerns the issue of privacy. Contemporary liberal feminists are committed, like other liberals, to a distinction between the public and the private spheres, and they appeal to this distinction in arguing for women's right to choose on such controversial issues as abortion, pornography, and prostitution—claims that sharply separate liberal feminists from many radical feminists. While the commitment to privacy distinguishes liberal feminism from other feminist theories, it must also be noted that liberal feminists often draw the line between public and private spheres differently from other liberals. In particular, liberal feminists are more concerned with issues such as domestic violence and the economic vulnerability of homemakers, and so they are more likely than other liberals to recommend that domestic life be subjected to a certain degree of government regulation in order to ensure women's economic security as well as their physical safety.

WOMEN'S SUBORDINATION THROUGH THE LENS OF CLASS: CLASSICAL MARXISM

In spite of recent world developments, which have called into question many traditional interpretations of Marxism, much contemporary feminist theory continues to be influenced by Marxist ways of thinking. For this reason, as well as because of Marxism's historical significance, it is important for present-day feminists to understand the main tenets of classical Marxist feminism.

Classical Marxism rejects even more decisively than liberal feminism the conservative notion of an essential and biologically determined human nature. Marx saw that human beings, throughout the course of history, have had recourse to many different techniques for feeding, sheltering, clothing, and reproducing themselves, and he argued that these various techniques have given rise to a variety of forms of social organization or "modes of production." The social relations that constitute these modes of production are, in Marx's view, the primary determinants of human nature which, rather than being a transhistorical constant, is shaped instead both by the general form of society and by an individual's specific place within that society. While reminiscent of liberal environmentalism, the Marxist view is distinct in asserting that people are capable of radically transforming their society and so ultimately of creating their own natures.

In addition to rejecting conservative biodeterminism, Marxists challenge the liberal assumption that genuine equality of opportunity is possible under capitalism, where a relatively small class of people, the capitalist class, controls the productive resources of the society and exploits the labor of the working class. In such circumstances, Marxists believe, equality of opportunity can be no more than a myth that rationalizes unequal privileges.

Because they regard human nature as resulting from specific systems of social organization rather than causing them, Marxists deny that women's subordination is rooted in male and female biology. Instead, in his 1884 classic, *The Origin of the Family: Private Property and the State,* a portion of which is reprinted here, Marx's coauthor Frederick Engels asserted that the subordination of women was a direct consequence of the introduction of private property. Engels hypothesized that, with the development of agriculture, which was a far more efficient and productive means of subsistence than the previous system of hunting and gathering, a relatively few men seized control of the main productive resources, transforming them into their own private property, and thereby established the first class society. Engels went on to speculate that women were immediately subordinated in order to guarantee the paternity of property-owning men, ensuring that those who inherited the property would be these men's own biological offspring.

Not only do classical Marxists claim that the establishment of class society was the original cause of women's subordination, but they go on to assert that it is capitalism, the contemporary form of class society, which today perpetuates the subordination of women by enforcing their economic dependence on men. Marxists argue that keeping women subordinate is functional to the capitalist system in a wide variety of ways, from getting a large amount of socially necessary work done at very low cost to providing a reserve pool of low-paid labor which exerts a continuing downward pressure on wages. While capitalism may extend hitherto male privileges to a few token women, classical Marxists believe that it cannot permit most women to be the economic and social equals of men.

If the subordination of women is ultimately maintained by the capitalist system, then, according to classical Marxist thinking, that system should be the primary target of women's political activism. Working-class women's needs can be met not by allying with women of the capitalist class, who have an interest in retaining the capitalist status quo, but rather by joining with working-class men not just to "defeat bourgeois feminism" but to establish a socialist system. This position is argued in the present volume by Evelyn Reed, whose 1970 article was written to challenge radical feminist ideas then newly emerging. Reed perceives women's subordination almost exclusively through the lens of class and, like all traditional Marxists, she believes that women's economic dependence on men can be abolished only under socialism, which would return the ownership of the main productive resources to society as a whole—including women. Only socialism can provide the material basis for true gender equality and, once this basis is established, bourgeois prejudices about women, like bourgeois stereotypes of the working class, will be shown to be entirely unfounded.

WOMEN'S SUBORDINATION THROUGH THE LENS OF SEX/GENDER AND SEXUALITY: RADICAL FEMINISM

While liberal and classical Marxist feminisms each represent a long political tradition, radical feminism dates only from the late 1960s. It emerged initially in the United States as a response by women civil rights and peace activists to the sexism they encountered first in the daily practices of their male coworkers and then in the Marxist theory by which so many activists of the time were inspired. The new radical feminists objected especially to the "class reductionism" of traditional Marxism, which they saw as a rationale for diminishing the seriousness of women's concerns as well as for endlessly deferring action on them.

One distinguishing feature of radical feminism is its insistence that the subordination of women is primary, not secondary, to other forms of domination. Part of what the early radical feminists meant by this was that women's subordination was not causally dependent on other systems of domination, such as class society, either originally or in the present; some argued, indeed, that other systems of domination should be seen as resulting from the subordination of women. In addition, radical feminists asserted that women's subordination was more widespread than other forms of domination, existing in virtually every known society, that it caused even more suffering and damage than other systems of domination, and that it was more recalcitrant to change because it was more deeply established in individual psyches and social practices. In consequence, radical feminists concluded that challenging women's subordination should be the top priority for social activists.

While radical feminists agreed on the primacy of women's subordination, they did not agree on one account of either its origins or its nature. One of the first systematic radical feminist theories, Shulamith Firestone's *The Dialectic of Sex,* which appeared in 1970, argued that women's subordination was rooted in certain universal features of human biology, features said to include weakness caused by female reproductive physiology, which supposedly necessitated women's dependence on men. In spite of the apparent biodeterminism of this account, Firestone's conclusions are feminist rather than conservative because she does not regard sex as unchangeable. Instead, she argues that advanced technology is now able to compensate for these biological inequalities by permitting extrauterine reproduction or "test-tube babies," a development that will finally end women's dependence on men and permit genuine sex equality.

Other radical feminist accounts of the subordination of women are less sanguine about the emancipatory potential of advanced technology but more positive about women's biological capacities. Some assert that women are biologically superior to men not only in their capacity to give birth but in their freedom from "testosterone poisoning." More recently, radical feminists have challenged the conceptual validity of the liberal feminist distinction between sex and gender, arguing not simply that gender norms must have been influenced by biological sex differences but that they also shaped social understandings of sex and even the way sex differences have evolved. This point is expressed forcefully by Monique Wittig who goes beyond the relatively familiar claim that feminine psychology is socially imposed to assert that even women's bodies are socially constructed. Nothing about women is "natural"; women are not born but made. In a similar vein, Catharine MacKinnon argues that the main concern for feminism is not the nature of sex differences but rather the social arrangements that take male biology as the social norm while devaluing female biology. For many radical feminists, sex and gender are ultimately inseparable, and women's subordination must be viewed through what we have called the sex/gender lens.

Women's bodies remain central even in those radical feminist analyses that refrain from addressing abstract theoretical questions about the relationship between human biology and human social arrangements. Many radical feminists see the subordination of women as rooted in the social practices through which men control women's bodies, especially women's procreative and sexual capacities. Some radical feminists target compulsory motherhood, including women's lack of control over conception, abortion, and the conditions of giving birth and rearing children; others emphasize male control of women's sexuality through institutions such as prostitution, pornography, and heterosexuality itself.

Although issues of procreation and sexuality were addressed to some extent by ancient and medieval political theorists, modern political theory has usually regarded them as lying beyond the scope of political concern, categorizing them instead as "private" or "personal." Radical feminists, by contrast, assert that procreation and sexuality are deeply political in being fundamentally organized by male power, and they argue that the relegation of these issues to the personal realm fulfills the ideological purpose of trivializing them and delegitimizing women's struggles to change those practices. Charlotte Bunch's 1975 article, reprinted below, is an early example of this radical feminist approach. It argues that normative heterosexuality is an institution dividing women from each other and concludes that lesbians are the vanguard of the feminist revolution. Bunch's capitalization of the word "lesbian" reflects her conviction that lesbianism is not merely a personal preference but a political decision made within the context of political struggle. The late 1960s slogan "The Personal is Political" neatly expresses this characteristically radical feminist conviction.

WOMEN'S SUBORDINATION THROUGH THE LENS OF SEX/GENDER, SEXUALITY, AND CLASS: SOCIALIST FEMINISM

Socialist feminism emerged in the second half of the 1970s in response to the discomfort many feminists felt with both the gender-blindness of traditional Marxism and the class-blindness of early radical feminism. These feminists believed that, while traditional understandings of Marxism indeed often functioned to obscure the seriousness of male dominance, some approximation of Marxist method was nevertheless indispensable to developing an adequate feminist theory and practice. They took up the theoretical project of revising Marxism in a way that would incorporate radical feminist insights and the practical project of devising strategies for political action that would challenge male dominance simultaneously with capitalism.

The statement from the Charlotte Perkins Gilman Chapter of the New American Movement (one of the organizations later merged into the Democratic Socialists of America) offers a clear summary of the fundamental tenets of socialist feminism, focusing primarily on its implications for political practice. The authors of this statement insist that feminism and socialism each need the other. While the history of feminist and socialist movements in the United States amply demonstrates both that feminism may be elitist and that socialism may be sexist, socialist feminists argue that the political goals of neither movement can be met in isolation from the other. Socialists must attend to the needs of the female half of the working class, and feminists must recognize that genuine sex equality is possible only under socialism. Together, the two movements generate the vision of a radically transformed society that is truly free and equal.

Socialist feminism has produced a multitude of arguments designed to demonstrate how women's subordination can be understood adequately only if it is viewed simultaneously through the lenses of sex/gender, sexuality, and class. We have reprinted a brief extract from Juliet Mitchell's classic essay "Women: The Longest Revolution," one of the earliest of such arguments, a longer version of which appeared in our first edition. Refusing to give theoretical primacy to the mode of production as traditionally understood, Mitchell argues that the subordination of women must be analyzed in terms of four interlocking social structures: production, reproduction, sexuality, and child rearing. When structuralist interpretations of Marxism were generally abandoned in the 1970s, later socialist feminists abandoned Mitchell's language of "structures," but they retained her conviction that a full understanding of women's subordination required attention to ways of organizing the satisfaction not only of such human needs as food, clothing, and shelter but also of other needs that were equally essential but neglected in traditional Marxist theory. These needs were said to include sexuality, children, and emotional nurturance.

Our final example of socialist feminist theory is an extract from Heidi Hartmann's "The Unhappy Marriage of Marxism and Feminism," a longer version of which appeared in our second edition. Early drafts of this highly influential paper, coauthored originally with Amy Bridges, were circulated widely in typescript during the 1970s. In the finally published version, Hartmann criticizes prevailing formulations of both classical Marxism and radical feminism, arguing that the sex-blind categories of traditional Marxism are inadequate to comprehend the subordination of women, while the class-blind and ahistorical categories of radical feminism, especially the category of patriarchy, are too broad to understand the variety of women's experiences. Hartmann offers a redefinition of patriarchy in terms of male control over women's labor, control that is exerted both within the home and outside it. Drawing on this definition, she examines the ways in which women's experience is shaped by the reciprocal relationship between patriarchy and capitalism, which she regards as mutually interdependent and reinforcing systems implicated equally in the subordination of women.

WOMEN'S SUBORDINATION THROUGH THE LENS OF SEX/GENDER, SEXUALITY, CLASS, AND RACE: MULTICULTURAL FEMINISM

The new section "Multicultural Feminism" succeeds the section "Feminism and Women of Color" introduced in our second edition. Our change in title, as well as in the readings, is intended to express how, in the time that has elapsed between the second and third editions of *Feminist Frameworks,* the issues raised by women of color have moved from the margin to the center of feminist concern. Women of color have moved from challenging their exclusion from (white) feminism to claiming their right, as feminists, to redefine previous understandings of feminist issues and feminist theory.

Our multicultural feminist selections are authored, respectively, by a Chicana feminist, a Chinese-American feminist, an African-American feminist, and a white Jewish feminist, the last of whom is a distinguished historian of African-American women. Writing in the first person singular, Cherrie Moraga describes her experience as the lesbian daughter of a Chicana mother and a white father. Moraga's narrative describes how class, race, gender, and sexuality operated in her life as interacting systems of subordination and illuminates how their interaction is transformative rather than simply additive. For instance, Moraga's experience of subordination is not intelligible as the experience of a "typical," i.e., heterosexual, Chicana added to that of a "typical," i.e., white, lesbian. Within the context of Chicano culture, women's sexuality acquires meanings distinct from those it is assigned in the Anglo world, so that being a lesbian Chicana is very different not only from being a heterosexual Chicana but also from being a white lesbian.

Class, race, gender, and sexuality are equally intertwined in the lives of Asian-American women. Esther Ngan-Ling Chow describes some of their intersections, noting that many Asian-American women place a higher priority on eradicating racism than sexism. Ethnic bonds between Asian-American women are so strong that they often feel they have more in common with Asian-American women of different class backgrounds than with women of different racial or ethnic identifications. Chow argues that, in order for Asian-American women to overcome the multitude of barriers that inhibit their full social participation, they must be involved in Asian-American activism and also unite with other feminists of color and white feminists.

Deborah King's influential article, "Multiple Jeopardy," challenges the invisibility of black women in critical theories of both race and sex, noting that the experience of black women cannot be assimilated with that of either black men or white women. Racism and sexism compound each other in the lives of black women, most of whom suffer also from classism and some from homophobia. King argues that these systems of domination are interactive and interdependent, so that the situation of black women becomes one that she calls "multiple jeopardy." King demonstrates how the relative significance of each system varies according to the specific social and historical phenomenon in question, and she is severely critical of what she calls "monist" ideologies, which insist on the theoretical and political primacy of just one of these systems. Monistic politics are divisive, inevitably marginalizing certain groups, and King asserts that black feminist ideology, which melds elements from race liberation, class liberation, and women's liberation, necessarily opposes such separatist forms of political organizing. Instead, black feminism fixes its focus on the self-determination of black women, whom it portrays as powerful, independent, political subjects.

Drawing on the work of women of color, Gerda Lerner reflects that the so-called issue of difference in feminism is better understood as the issue of hierarchy or dominance. While dominance is established originally by force, it is maintained only because the dominated group puts "a negative mark" on difference, creating a group perceived as "other" whose subordination is regarded as natural and just. Lerner asserts that sex, class, and race dominance not only are interrelated and inseparable in the present but were so "from the start." These systems of domination are not conceptually distinct but must be defined in relation to each other; for instance, class and race are both "genderic," expressed and institutionalized in terms that are always different for men and women, just as gender is always mediated by class and race. Lerner calls for feminists to construct a new conceptual framework that displays these interactions, a framework whose construction she envisions as a collective project drawing on feminine as well as masculine ways of knowing.

WOMEN'S SITUATION WORLDWIDE: GLOBAL FEMINISM

"Global feminism" is the second new framework introduced in this third edition of *Feminist Frameworks*. It reflects Western feminists' increasing awareness that our lives are inseparably connected with the lives of women in what is sometimes called the developing world. Although frequently unrecognized, these connections include shared histories, often histories of invasion and colonization, shared interests, including the interest in a habitable planet, and shared destinies, as our resources, our labor, our markets, and our cultures become increasingly integrated into a "new world order" dominated by transnational capital. In these rapidly changing circumstances, women's subordination can be understood only if yet another lens is added to the previous ones. This is the lens of imperialism or postcolonialism.

Our section opens with the classic 1981 article by Charlotte Bunch, who is credited with inventing the term "global feminism." Bunch is also, of course, the author of "Lesbians in Revolt," another classic article reprinted here in the section "Radical Feminism," and it is interesting to see the evolution of her views in the course of only a few years. In her "Prospects for Global Feminism," Bunch insists that feminism, rather than being a laundry list of so-called women's issues, instead is a transformational politics dedicated not simply to gender equality within existing systems of injustice but rather to implementing "new visions for how societies might exist without injustice at their core." A genuinely global feminism must address the social forces that divide women, forces such as race, class, sexuality, colonialism, poverty, religion, and nationality, recognizing that struggling against these is not additional to the struggle against male domination but rather an integral part of it. Global feminism must pay special attention to the difficult question of how to value cultural diversity and at the same time oppose domination rationalized by appeals to either tradition or modernization.

"Surviving Beyond Fear," by Ximena Bunster-Bunalto, describes women's experiences of torture and terror in Latin America, experiences so atrocious that we hesitated to include the piece. Our ultimate decision to do so was based partly on our political conviction that such abuses should receive the widest possible publicity, and partly on our belief that the article raises at least two important theoretical issues. First, it demonstrates that "women's issues" are not limited to such familiar and obviously gendered causes as equal pay and child care; apparently nongendered issues, like national liberation, military dictatorship, and democracy, in fact have implications that are deeply gendered. Second, Bunster's description of the Latin American ideology of *machismo/Marianismo* invites us to reflect on how the gender-specific forms of torture that she describes might in some sense be generated by these bipolar conceptions of men and women.

In "Bananas, Bases and Patriarchy," Cynthia Enloe explores the interrelations among several systems of domination affecting the lives of women in Central America. She suggests that European colonialism sowed the seeds of the Latin-American ideologies of *machismo* and Indian inferiority. These seeds were later cultivated by U.S. militarism and imperialism in order to inhibit union organizing and perpetuate the low wages which together sustain the kind of internationally dependent, militarized society we have come to call a "banana republic." The economies of these societies now depend heavily on women's cheap labor in such foreign-controlled industries as light assembly, data entry, and tourism—not to mention prostitution. The questions Enloe raises in this pioneering study became the basis of her 1989 book, *Bananas, Beaches and Bases,*[3] in which she explores these and other relationships in greater depth.

Andree Nicola McLaughlin's article reflects the reality that not all black women are of African descent and that their cultural heritages are extremely diverse. This reality is often obscured by the oversimplification of race implicit in the dualistic categories and language that pervade the popular culture as well as academic discourse. Like Deborah King, McLaughlin describes black women's situation in terms of "multiple jeopardy" but, because her vision extends beyond African-American women, McLaughlin recognizes additional systems of domination, including those based on religion, ethnicity, region, caste, and color. Despite the diversity of their situations, black people share a common political opposition to the imperialism, colonialism, and racism by which they all are threatened, and this common threat constitutes the basis for their identification not as a racial group but rather as an intercontinental political class. Although—or perhaps because—black women are engaged in such a wide variety of specific struggles, McLaughlin asserts that their political-class activism has a universal import, embodying opposition to all forms of oppression for all people. "Multiply-identified, Black women in various regions of the world are offering a holistic conception of the struggle for social justice and human freedom." They are creating an alternative to the "imperialist-derived secularism of Western culture that fragments the universe, . . . redefining themselves in their entirety and, hence, the men, children, Earth, and the universe."

Global feminism is not an exhaustive collection of categories or lenses capable of completely comprehending the subordination of women. Constructing such a final or "totalizing" framework is no longer considered either possible or desirable by today's feminists. Instead, the value of global feminism lies in its recognition that women's subordinations are both diverse and interconnected, so that they can be understood only in terms of a multitude of organizing categories or what we have called lenses. Different lenses are more useful or salient on different occasions, depending on each woman's situation as well as on the purposes of particular investigations. Specific questions about which lenses are appropriate on which occasions have now replaced general concerns about primacy at the center of feminist theory. The one general claim of which we can be certain is that only by superimposing multiple lenses can feminists make women's subordination fully visible in its variety as well as its sameness, its conflicts as well as its commonality.

NOTES

1 In her *Gender and History: The Limits of Social Theory in the Age of the Family* (Columbia University Press, New York, 1986), Linda Nicholson argues that the search for "the" cause of women's subordination presupposes an untenable positivist conception of social explanation.
2 Denise Riley: *"Am I That Name?: Feminism and the Category of 'Women' in History,"* University of Minnesota Press, Minneapolis, 1989.
3 Cynthia Enloe: *Bananas, Beaches and Bases: Making Feminist Sense of International Politics,* University of California Press, Berkeley, 1989.

Women's Subordination Through the Lens of Sex: Conservatism

Femininity

Sigmund Freud

. . . In conformity with its peculiar nature, psycho-analysis does not try to describe what a woman is—that would be a task it could scarcely perform—but sets about enquiring how she comes into being, how a woman develops out of a child with a bisexual disposition. . . .

. . . A little girl is as a rule less aggressive, defiant and self-sufficient; she seems to have a greater need for being shown affection and on that account to be more dependent and pliant. It is probably only as a result of this pliancy that she can be taught more easily and quicker to control her excretions: urine and faeces are the first gifts that children make to those who look after them, and controlling them is the first concession to which the instinctual life of children can be induced. One gets an impression, too, that little girls are more intelligent and livelier than boys of the same age; they go out more to meet the external world and at the same time form stronger object-cathexes. I cannot say whether this lead in development has been confirmed by exact observations, but in any case there is no question that girls cannot be described as intellectually backward. These sexual differences are not, however, of great consequence: they can be outweighed by individual variations. For our immediate purposes they can be disregarded.

Both sexes seem to pass through the early phases of libidinal development in the same manner. It might have been expected that in girls there would already have been some lag in aggressiveness in the sadistic-anal phase, but such is not the case. Analysis of children's play has shown our women analysts that the aggressive impulses of little girls leave nothing to be desired in the way of abundance and violence. With their entry into the phallic phase the differences between the sexes are completely eclipsed by their agreements. We are now obliged to recognize that the little girl is a little man. In boys, as we know, this phase is marked by the fact that they have learnt how to derive pleasurable sensations from their small penis and connect its excited state with their ideas of sexual intercourse. Little girls do the same thing with their still smaller clitoris. It seems that with them all their masturbatory acts are carried out on this penis-equivalent, and that the truly feminine vagina is still undiscovered by both sexes. It is true that there are a few isolated reports of early vaginal sensations as well, but it could not be easy to distinguish these from sensations in the anus or vestibulum; in any case they cannot play a great part. We are entitled to keep to our view that in the phallic phase of girls the clitoris is the leading erotogenic zone. But it is not, of course, going to remain so. With the change to femininity the clitoris should wholly or in part hand over its sensitivity, and at the same time its importance, to the vagina. This would be one of the two tasks which a woman has to perform in the course of her development, whereas the more fortunate man has only to continue at the time of his sexual maturity the activity that he has previously carried out at the period of the early efflorescence of his sexuality.

We shall return to the part played by the clitoris; let us now turn to the second task with which a girl's development is burdened. A boy's mother is the first object of his love, and she remains so too during the formation of his Oedipus complex and, in essence, all through his life. For a girl too her first object must be her mother (and the figures of wet-nurses and foster-mothers that merge into her). The first object-cathexes occur in attachment to the satisfaction of the major and simple vital needs, and the circumstances of the care of children are the same for both sexes. But in the Oedipus situation the girl's father has become her love-object, and we expect that in the normal course of development she will find her way from this paternal object to her final choice of an object. In the course of time, therefore, a girl has to change her erotogenic zone and her object—both of which a boy retains. The question then arises of how this happens: in particular, how does a girl pass from her mother to an attachment to her father? or, in other words, how does she pass from her masculine phase to the feminine one to which she is biologically destined? . . .

. . . All these factors—the slights, the disappointments in love, the jealousy, the seduction followed by prohibition—are, after all, also in operation in the relation of a *boy* to his mother and are yet unable to alienate him from the maternal object. Unless we can find something that is specific for girls and is not present or not in the same way present in boys, we shall not have explained the termination of the attachment of girls to their mother.

I believe we have found this specific factor, and indeed where we expected to find it, even though in a surprising form. Where we expected to find it, I say, for it lies in the castration complex. After all, the anatomical distinction [between the sexes] must express itself in psychical consequences. It was, however, a surprise to learn from analyses that girls hold their mother responsible for their lack of a penis and do not forgive her for their being thus put at a disadvantage.

As you hear, then, we ascribe a castration complex to women as well. And for good reasons, though its content cannot be the same as with boys. In the latter the castration complex arises after they have learnt from the sight of the female genitals that the organ which they value so highly need not necessarily accompany the body. At this the boy recalls to mind the threats he brought on himself by his doings with that organ, he begins to give credence to them and falls under the influence of fear of castration, which will be the most powerful motive force in his subsequent development. The castration complex of girls is also started by the sight of the genitals of the other sex. They at once notice the difference and, it must be admitted, its significance too. They feel seriously wronged, often declare that they want to "have something like it too," and fall a victim to "envy for the penis," which will leave ineradicable traces on their development and the formation of their character and which will not be surmounted in even the most favourable cases without a severe expenditure of psychical energy. The girl's recognition of the fact of her being without a penis does not by any means imply that she submits to the fact easily. On the contrary, she continues to hold on for a long time to the wish to get something like it herself and she believes in that possibility for improbably long years; and analysis can show that, at a period when knowledge of reality has long since rejected the fulfilment of the wish as unattainable, it persists in the unconscious and retains a considerable cathexis of energy. The wish to get the longed-for penis eventually in spite of everything may contribute to the motives that drive a mature woman to analysis, and what she may reasonably expect from analysis—a capacity, for instance, to carry on an intellectual profession—may often be recognized as a sublimated modification of this repressed wish.

One cannot very well doubt the importance of envy for the penis. You may take it as an instance of male injustice if I assert that envy and jealousy play an even greater part in the mental life of women than of men. It is not that I think these characteristics are absent in men or that I think they have no other roots in women than envy for the penis; but I am inclined to attribute their greater amount in women to this latter influence. . . .

The discovery that she is castrated is a turning-point in a girl's growth. Three possible lines of development start from it: one leads to sexual inhibition or to neurosis, the second to change of character in the sense of a masculinity complex, the third, finally, to normal femininity. We have learnt a fair amount, though not everything, about all three.

The essential content of the first is as follows: the little girl has hitherto lived in a masculine way, has been able to get pleasure by the excitation of her clitoris and has brought this activity into relation with her sexual wishes directed towards her mother, which are often active ones; now, owing to the influence of her penis-envy, she loses her enjoyment in her phallic sexuality. Her self-love is mortified by the comparison with the boy's far superior equipment and in consequence she renounces her masturbatory satisfaction from her clitoris, repudiates her love for her mother and at the same time not infrequently represses a good part of her sexual trends in general. No doubt her turning away from her mother does not occur all at once, for to begin with the girl regards her castration as an individual misfortune, and only gradually extends it to other females and finally to her mother as well. Her love was directed to her *phallic* mother; with the discovery that her mother is castrated it becomes possible to drop her as an object, so that the motives for hostility, which have long been accumulating, gain the upper hand. This means, therefore, that as a result of the discovery of women's lack of a penis they are debased in value for girls just as they are for boys and later perhaps for men.

You all know the immense aetiological importance attributed by our neurotic patients to their masturbation. They make it responsible for all their troubles and we have the greatest difficulty in persuading them that they are mistaken. In fact, however, we ought to admit to them that they are right, for masturbation is the executive agent of infantile sexuality, from the faulty development of which they are indeed suffering. But what neurotics mostly blame is the masturbation of the period of puberty; they have mostly forgotten that of early infancy, which is what is really in question.
. . . From the development of girls, which is what my present lecture is concerned with, I can give you the example of a child herself trying to get free from masturbating. She does not always succeed in this. If envy for the penis has provoked a powerful impulse against clitoridal masturbation but this nevertheless refuses to give way, a violent struggle for liberation ensues in which the girl, as it were, herself takes over the role of her deposed mother and gives expression to her entire dissatisfaction with her inferior clitoris in her efforts against obtaining satisfaction from it. Many years later, when her masturbatory activity has long since been suppressed, an interest still persists which we must interpret as a defence against a temptation that is still dreaded. It manifests itself in the emergence of sympathy for those to whom similar difficulties are attributed, it plays a part as a motive in contracting a marriage and, indeed, it may determine the choice of a husband or lover. Disposing of early infantile masturbation is truly no easy or indifferent business.

Along with the abandonment of clitoridal masturbation a certain amount of activity is renounced. Passivity now has the upper hand, and the girl's turning to her father is accomplished principally with the help of passive instinctual impulses. You can see that a wave of development like this, which clears the phallic activity out of the way, smooths the ground for femininity. If too much is not lost in the course of it through repression, this femininity may turn out to be normal. The wish with which the girl turns to her father is no doubt originally the wish for the penis which her mother has refused her and which she now expects from her father. The feminine situation is only established, however, if the wish for a penis is replaced by one for a baby, if, that is, a baby takes the place of a penis in accordance with an ancient symbolic equivalence. It has not escaped us that the girl has wished for a baby earlier, in the undisturbed phallic phase: that, of course, was the meaning of her playing with dolls. But that play was not in fact an expression of her femininity; it served as an identification with her mother with the intention of substituting activity for passivity. *She* was playing the part of her mother and the doll was herself: now she could do with the baby everything that her mother used to do with her. Not until the emergence of the wish for a penis does the doll-baby become a baby from the girl's father, and thereafter the aim of the most powerful feminine wish. Her happiness is great if later on this wish for a baby finds fulfilment in reality, and quite especially so if the baby is a little boy who brings the longed-for penis with him. Often enough in her combined picture of "a baby from her father" the emphasis is laid on the baby and her father left unstressed. In this way the ancient masculine wish for the possession of a penis is still faintly visible through the femininity now achieved. But perhaps we ought rather to recognize this wish for a penis as being *par excellence* a feminine one.

With the transference of the wish for a penis-baby on to her father, the girl has entered the situation of the Oedipus complex. Her hostility to her mother, which did not need to be freshly created, is now greatly intensified, for she becomes the girl's rival, who receives from her father everything that she desires from him. For a long time the girl's Oedipus complex concealed her pre-Oedipus attachment to her mother from our view, though it is nevertheless so important and leaves such lasting fixations behind it. For girls the Oedipus situation is the outcome of a long and difficult development; it is a kind of preliminary solution, a position of rest which is not soon abandoned, especially as the beginning of the latency period is not far distant. And we are now struck by a difference between the two sexes, which is probably momentous, in regard to the relation of the Oedipus complex to the castration complex. In a boy the Oedipus complex, in which he desires his mother and would like to get rid of his father as being a rival, develops naturally from the phase of his phallic sexuality. The threat of castration compels him, however, to give up that attitude. Under the impression of the danger of losing his penis, the Oedipus complex is abandoned, repressed and, in the most normal cases, entirely destroyed, and a severe super-ego is set up as its heir. What happens with a girl is almost the opposite. The castration complex prepares for the Oedipus complex instead of destroying it; the girl is driven out of her attachment to her mother through the influence of her envy for the penis and she enters the Oedipus situation as though into a haven of refuge. In the absence of fear of castration the chief motive is lacking which leads boys to surmount the Oedipus complex. Girls remain in it for an indeterminate length of time; they demolish it late and, even so, incompletely. In these circumstances the formation of the super-ego must suffer; it cannot attain the strength and independence which give it its cultural significance, and feminists are not pleased when we point out to them the effects of this factor upon the average feminine character.

To get back a little. We mentioned as the second possible reaction to the discovery of female castration the development of a powerful masculinity complex. By this we mean that the girl refuses, as it were, to recognize the unwelcome fact and, defiantly rebellious, even exaggerates her previous masculinity, clings to her clitoridal activity and takes refuge in an identification with her phallic mother or her father. What can it be that decides in favour of this outcome? We can only suppose that it is a constitutional factor, a greater amount of activity, such as is ordinarily characteristic of a male. However that may be, the essence of this process is that at this point in development the wave of passivity is avoided which opens the way to the turn towards femininity. The extreme achievement of such a masculinity complex would appear to be the influencing of the choice of an object in the sense of manifest homosexuality. Analytic experience teaches us, to be sure, that female homosexuality is seldom or never a direct continuation of infantile masculinity. Even for a girl of this kind it seems necessary that she should take her father as an object for some time and enter the Oedipus situation. But afterwards, as a result of her inevitable disappointments from her father, she is driven to regress into her early masculinity complex. The significance of these disappointments must not be exaggerated; a girl who is destined to become feminine is not spared them, though they do not have the same effect. The predominance of the constitutional factor seems indisputable; but the two phases in the development of female homosexuality are well mirrored in the practices of homosexuals, who play the parts of mother and baby with each other as often and as clearly as those of husband and wife.

What I have been telling you here may be described as the prehistory of women. It is a product of the very last few years and may have been of interest to you as an example of detailed analytic work. . . .

It is not my intention to pursue the further behavior of femininity through puberty to the period of maturity. Our knowledge, moreover, would be insufficient for the purpose. But I will bring a few features together in what follows. Taking its prehistory as a starting-point, I will only emphasize here that the development of femininity remains exposed to disturbance by the residual phenomena of the early masculine period. Regressions to the fixations of the pre-Oedipus phases very frequently occur; in the course of some women's lives there is a repeated alternation between periods in which masculinity or femininity gains the upper hand. Some portions of what we men call "the enigma of women" may perhaps be derived from this expression of bisexuality in women's lives. But another question seems to have become ripe for judgement in the course of these researches. We have called the motive force of sexual life "the libido." Sexual life is dominated by the polarity of masculine-feminine; thus the notion suggests itself of considering the relation of the libido to this antithesis. It would not be surprising if it were to turn out that each sexuality had its own special libido appropriated to it, so that one sort of libido would pursue the aims of a masculine sexual life and another sort those of a feminine one. But nothing of the kind is true. There is only one libido, which serves both the masculine and the feminine sexual functions. To it itself we cannot assign any sex; if, following the conventional equation of activity and masculinity, we are inclined to describe it as masculine, we must not forget that it also covers trends with a passive aim. Nevertheless the juxtaposition "feminine libido" is without any justification. Furthermore, it is our impression that more constraint has been applied to the libido when it is pressed into the service of the feminine function, and that—to speak teleologically—Nature takes less careful account of its [that function's] demands than in the case of masculinity. And the reason for this may lie—thinking once again teleologically—in the fact that the accomplishment of the aim of biology has been entrusted to the aggressiveness of men and has been made to some extent independent of women's consent.

The sexual frigidity of women, the frequency of which appears to confirm this disregard, is a phenomenon that is still insufficiently understood. Sometimes it is psychogenic and in that case accessible to influence; but in other cases it suggests the hypothesis of its being constitutionally determined and even of there being a contributory anatomical factor.

I have promised to tell you of a few more psychical peculiarities of mature femininity, as we come across them in analytic observation. We do not lay claim to more than an average validity for these assertions; nor is it always easy to distinguish what should be ascribed to the influence of the sexual function and what to social breeding.

Thus, we attribute a larger amount of narcissism to femininity, which also affects women's choice of object, so that to be loved is a stronger need for them than to love. The effect of penis-envy has a share, further, in the physical vanity of women, since they are bound to value their charms more highly as a late compensation for their original sexual inferiority. Shame, which is considered to be a feminine characteristic *par excellence* but is far more a matter of convention than might be supposed, has as its purpose, we believe, concealment of genital deficiency. We are not forgetting that at a later time shame takes on other functions. It seems that women have made few contributions to the discoveries and inventions in the history of civilization; there is, however, one technique which they may have invented—that of plaiting and weaving. If that is so, we should be tempted to guess the unconscious motive for the achievement. Nature herself would seem to have given the model which this achievement imitates by causing the growth at maturity of the pubic hair that conceals the genitals. The step that remained to be taken lay in making the threads adhere to one another, while on the body they stick into the skin and are only matted together. If you reject this idea as fantastic and regard my belief in the influence of lack of a penis on the configuration of femininity as an *idée fixe,* I am of course defenceless.

The determinants of women's choice of an object are often made unrecognizable by social conditions. Where the choice is able to show itself freely, it is often made in accordance with the narcissistic ideal of the man whom the girl had wished to become. If the girl has remained in her attachment to her father—that is, in the Oedipus complex—her choice is made according to the paternal type. Since, when she turned from her mother to her father, the hostility of her ambivalent relation remained with her mother, a choice of this kind should guarantee a happy marriage. But very often the outcome is of a kind that presents a general threat to such a settlement of the conflict due to ambivalence. The hostility that has been left behind follows in the train of the positive attachment and spreads over on to the new object. The woman's husband, who to begin with inherited from her father, becomes after a time her mother's heir as well. So it may easily happen that the second half of a woman's life may be filled by the struggle against her husband, just as the shorter first half was filled by her rebellion against her mother. When this reaction has been lived through, a second marriage may easily turn out very much more satisfying. Another alteration in a woman's nature, for which lovers are unprepared, may occur in a marriage after the first child is born. Under the influence of a woman's becoming a mother herself, an identification with her own mother may be revived, against which she had striven up till the time of her marriage, and this may attract all the available libido to itself, so that the compulsion to repeat reproduces an unhappy marriage between her parents. The difference in a mother's reaction to the birth of a son or a daughter shows that the old factor of lack of a penis has even now not lost its strength. A mother is only brought unlimited satisfaction by her relation to a son; this is altogether the most perfect, the most free from ambivalence of all human relations. A mother can transfer to her son the ambition which she has been obliged to suppress in herself, and she can expect from him the satisfaction of all that has been left over in her of her masculinity complex. Even a marriage is not made secure until the wife has succeeded in making her husband her child as well and in acting as a mother to him.

A woman's identification with her mother allows us to distinguish two strata: the pre-Oedipus one which rests on her affectionate attachment to her mother and takes her as a model, and the later one from the Oedipus complex which seeks to get rid of her mother and take her place with her father. We are no doubt justified in saying that much of both of them is left over for the future and that neither of them is adequately surmounted in the course of development. But the phase of the affectionate pre-Oedipus attachment is the decisive one for a woman's future: during it preparations are made for the acquisition of the characteristics with which she will later fulfil her role in the sexual function and perform her invaluable social tasks. It is in this identification too that she acquires her attractiveness to a man, whose Oedipus attachment to his mother it kindles into passion. How often it happens, however, that it is only his son who obtains what he himself aspired to! One gets an impression that a man's love and a woman's are a phase apart psychologically.

The fact that women must be regarded as having little sense of justice is no doubt related to the predominance of envy in their mental life; for the demand for justice is a modification of envy and lays down the condition subject to which one can put envy aside. We also regard women as weaker in their social interests and as having less capacity for sublimating their instincts than men. The former is no doubt derived from the dissocial quality which unquestionably characterizes all sexual relations. Lovers find sufficiency in each other, and families too resist inclusion in more comprehensive associations. The aptitude for sublimation is subject to the greatest individual variations. On the other hand I cannot help mentioning an impression that we are constantly receiving during analytic practice. A man of about thirty strikes us as a youthful, somewhat unformed individual, whom we expect to make powerful use of the possibilities for development opened up to him by analysis. A woman of the same age, however, often frightens us by her psychical rigidity and unchangeability. Her libido has taken up final positions and seems incapable of exchanging them for others. There are no paths open to further development; it is as though the whole process had already run its course and remains thenceforward insusceptible to influence—as though, indeed, the difficult development to femininity had exhausted the possibilities of the person concerned. . . .

Sex

Edward O. Wilson

Sex is central to human biology and a protean phenomenon that permeates every aspect of our existence and takes new forms through each step in the life cycle. Its complexity and ambiguity are due to the fact that sex is not designed primarily for reproduction. . . .

Why, then, has sex evolved?

The principal answer is that sex creates diversity. And diversity is the way a parent hedges its bets against an unpredictably changing environment. Imagine a case of two animal species, both of which consist entirely of individuals carrying two genes. Let us arbitrarily label one gene *A* and the other *a*. For instance, these genes might be for brown (*A*) versus blue (*a*) eye color, or right-handedness (*A*) versus left-handedness (*a*). Each individual is *Aa* because it possesses both genes. Suppose that one species reproduces without sex. Then all the offspring of every parent will be *Aa*.

The other population uses sex for reproduction; it produces sex cells, each of which contains only one of the genes, *A* or *a*. When two individuals mate they combine their sex cells, and since each adult contributes sex cells bearing either *A* or *a*, three kinds of offspring are possible: *AA, Aa,* and *aa*. So, from a starting population of *Aa* individuals, asexual parents can produce only *Aa* offspring, while sexual parents can produce *AA, Aa,* and *aa* offspring. Now let the environment change—say a hard winter, a flood, or the invasion of a dangerous predator—so that *aa* individuals are favored. In the next generation, the sexually reproducing population will have the advantage and will consist predominantly of *aa* organisms until conditions change to favor, perhaps, *AA* or *Aa* individuals.

Diversity, and thus adaptability, explains why so many kinds of organisms bother with sexual reproduction. They vastly outnumber the species that rely on the direct and simple but, in the long run, less prudent modes of sexless multiplication. . . .

The quintessential female is an individual specialized for making eggs. The large size of the egg enables it to resist drying, to survive adverse periods by consuming stored yolk, to be moved to safety by the parent, and to divide at least a few times after fertilization before needing to ingest nutrients from the outside. The male is defined as the manufacturer of the sperm, the little gamete. A sperm is a minimum cellular unit, stripped down to a head packed with DNA and powered by a tail containing just enough stored energy to carry the vehicle to the egg.

When the two gametes unite in fertilization they create an instant mixture of genes surrounded by the durable housing of the egg. By cooperating to create zygotes, the female and male make it more likely that at least some of their offspring will survive in the event of a changing environment. A fertilized egg differs from an asexually reproducing cell in one fundamental respect: it contains a newly assembled mixture of genes.

The anatomical difference between the two kinds of sex cell is often extreme. In particular, the human egg is eighty-five thousand times larger than the human sperm. The consequences of this gametic dimorphism ramify throughout the biology and psychology of human sex. The most important immediate result is that the female places a greater investment in each of her sex cells. A woman can expect to produce only about four hundred eggs in her lifetime. Of these a maximum of about twenty can be converted into healthy infants. The costs of bringing an infant to term and caring for it afterward are relatively enormous. In contrast, a man releases 100 million sperm with each ejaculation. Once he has achieved fertilization his purely physical commitment has ended. His genes will benefit equally with those of the female, but his investment will be far less than hers unless she can induce him to contribute to the care of the offspring. If a man were given total freedom to act, he could theoretically inseminate thousands of women in his lifetime.

The resulting conflict of interest between the sexes is a property of not only human beings but also the majority of animal species. Males are characteristically aggressive, especially toward one another and most intensely during the breeding season. In most species, assertiveness is the most profitable male strategy. During the full period of time it takes to bring a fetus to term, from the fertilization of the egg to the birth of the infant, one male can fertilize many females but a female can be fertilized by only one male. Thus if males are able to court one female after another, some will be big winners and others will be absolute losers, while virtually all healthy females will succeed in being fertilized. It pays males to be aggressive, hasty, fickle, and undiscriminating. In theory it is more profitable for females to be coy, to hold back until they can identify males with the best genes. In species that rear young, it is also important for the females to select males who are more likely to stay with them after insemination.

Human beings obey this biological principle faithfully. It is true that the thousands of existing societies are enormously variable in the details of their sexual mores and the division of labor between the sexes. This variation is based on culture. Societies mold their customs to the requirements of the environment and in so doing duplicate in totality a large fraction of the arrangements encountered throughout the remainder of the animal kingdom: from strict monogamy to extreme forms of polygamy, and from a close approach to unisex to extreme differences between men and women in behavior and dress. People change their attitudes consciously and at will; the reigning fashion of a society can shift within a generation. Nevertheless, this flexibility is not endless, and beneath it all lie general features that conform closely to the expectations from evolutionary theory. So let us concentrate initially on the biologically significant generalities and defer, for the moment, consideration of the undeniably important plasticity controlled by culture.

We are, first of all, moderately polygynous, with males initiating most of the changes in sexual partnership. About three-fourths of all human societies permit the taking of multiple wives, and most of them encourage the practice by law and custom. In contrast, marriage to multiple husbands is sanctioned in less than one percent of societies. The remaining monogamous societies usually fit that category in a legal sense only, with concubinage and other extramarital stratagems being added to allow de facto polygyny.

Because women are commonly treated by men as a limiting resource and hence as valued property, they are the beneficiaries of hypergamy, the practice of marrying upward in social position. Polygyny and hypergamy are essentially complementary strategies. In diverse cultures men pursue and acquire, while women are protected and battered. Sons sow wild oats and daughters risk being ruined. When sex is sold, men are usually the buyers. It is to be expected that prostitutes are the despised members of society; they have abandoned their valuable reproductive investment to strangers. . . .

Anatomy bears the imprint of the sexual division of labor. Men are on the average 20 to 30 percent heavier than women. Pound for pound, they are stronger and quicker in most categories of sport. The proportion of their limbs, their skeletal torsion, and the density of their muscles are particularly suited for running and throwing, the archaic specialties of the ancestral hunter-gatherer males. The world track records reflect the disparity. . . .

It is of equal importance that women match or surpass men in a few other sports, and these are among the ones further removed from the primitive techniques of hunting and aggression: long-distance swimming, the more acrobatic events of gymnastics, precision (but not distance) archery, and small-bore rifle shooting. As sports and sport-like activities evolve into more sophisticated channels dependent on skill and agility, the overall achievements of men and women can be expected to converge more closely.

The average temperamental differences between the human sexes are also consistent with the generalities of mammalian biology. Women as a group are less assertive and physically aggressive. The magnitude of the distinction depends on the culture. It ranges from a tenuous, merely statistical difference in egalitarian settings to the virtual enslavement of women in some extreme polygynous societies. But the variation in degree is not nearly so important as the fact that women differ consistently in this qualitative manner regardless of the degree. The fundamental average difference in personality traits is seldom if ever transposed.

The physical and temperamental differences between men and women have been amplified by culture into universal male dominance. History records not a single society in which women have controlled the political and economic lives of men. Even when queens and empresses ruled, their intermediaries remained primarily male. At the present writing not a single country has a woman as head of state, although Golda Meir of Israel and Indira Gandhi of India were, until recently, assertive, characteristic leaders of their countries. In about 75 percent of societies studied by anthropologists, the bride is expected to move from the location of her own family to that of her husband, while only 10 percent require the reverse exchange. Lineage is reckoned exclusively through the male line at least five times more frequently than it is through the female line. Men have traditionally assumed the positions of chieftains, shamans, judges, and warriors. Their modern technocratic counterparts rule the industrial states and head the corporations and churches.

These differences are a simple matter of record—but what is their significance for the future? How easily can they be altered?

It is obviously of vital social importance to try to make a value-free assessment of the relative contributions of heredity and environment to the differentiation of behavioral roles between the sexes. Here is what I believe the evidence shows: modest genetic differences exist between the sexes; the behavioral genes interact with virtually all existing environments to create a noticeable divergence in early psychological development; and the divergence is almost always widened in later psychological development by cultural sanctions and training. Societies can probably cancel the modest genetic differences entirely by careful planning and training, but the convergence will require a conscious decision based on fuller and more exact knowledge than is now available.

The evidence for a genetic difference in behavior is varied and substantial. In general, girls are predisposed to be more intimately sociable and less physically venturesome. From the time of birth, for example, they smile more than boys. This trait may be especially revealing, since as I showed earlier the infant smile, of all human behaviors, is most fully innate in that its form and function are virtually invariant. Several independent studies have shown that newborn females respond more frequently than males with eyes-closed, reflexive smiling. The habit is soon replaced by deliberate, communicative smiling that persists into the second year of life. Frequent smiling then becomes one of the more persistent of female traits and endures through adolescence and maturity. By the age of six months, girls also pay closer attention to sights and sounds used in communication than they do to nonsocial stimuli. Boys of the same age make no such distinction. The ontogeny then proceeds as follows: one-year-old girls react with greater fright and inhibition to clay faces, and they are more reluctant to leave their mothers' sides in novel situations. Older girls remain more affiliative and less physically venturesome than boys of the same age. . . .

In Western cultures boys are also more venturesome than girls and more physically aggressive on the average. Eleanor Maccoby and Carol Jacklin, in their review *The Psychology of Sex Differences,* concluded that this male trait is deeply rooted and could have a genetic origin. From the earliest moments of social play, at age 2 to 2¹/₂ years, boys are more aggressive in both words and actions. They have a larger number of hostile fantasies and engage more often in mock fighting, overt threats, and physical attacks, which are directed preferentially at other boys during efforts to acquire dominance status. Other studies, summarized by Ronald P. Rohner, indicate that the differences exist in many cultures. . . .

So at birth the twig is already bent a little bit—what are we to make of that? It suggests that the universal existence of sexual division of labor is not entirely an accident of cultural evolution. But it also supports the conventional view that the enormous variation among societies in the degree of that division is due to cultural evolution. Demonstrating a slight biological component delineates the options that future societies may consciously select. Here the second dilemma of human nature presents itself. In full recognition of the struggle for women's rights that is now spreading throughout the world, each society must make one or the other of the three following choices:

Condition its members so as to exaggerate sexual differences in behavior. This is the pattern in almost all cultures. It results more often than not in domination of women by men and exclusion of women from many professions and activities. But this need not be the case. In theory at least, a carefully designed society with strong sexual divisions could be richer in spirit, more diversified, and even more productive than a unisex society. Such a society might safeguard human rights even while channeling men and women into different occupations. Still, some amount of social injustice would be inevitable, and it could easily expand to disastrous proportions.

Train its members so as to eliminate all sexual differences in behavior. By the use of quotas and sex-biased education it should be possible to create a society in which men and women *as groups* share equally in all professions, cultural activities, and even, to take the absurd extreme, athletic competition. Although the early predispositions that characterize sex would have to be blunted, the biological differences are not so large as to make the undertaking impossible. Such control would offer the great advantage of eliminating even the hint of group prejudice (in addition to individual prejudice) based on sex. It could result in a much more harmonious and productive society. Yet the amount of regulation required would certainly place some personal freedoms in jeopardy, and at least a few individuals would not be allowed to reach their full potential.

Provide equal opportunities and access but take no further action. To make no choice at all is of course open to all cultures. Laissez-faire on first thought might seem to be the course most congenial to personal liberty and development, but this is not necessarily true. Even with identical education for men and women and equal access to all professions, men are likely to maintain disproportionate representation in political life, business, and science. Many would fail to participate fully in the equally important, formative aspects of child rearing. The result might be legitimately viewed as restrictive of the complex emotional development of individuals. Just such a divergence and restriction has occurred in the Israeli kibbutzim, which represents one of the most powerful experiments in egalitarianism conducted in modern times.

From the time of the greatest upsurge of the kibbutz movement, in the 1940s and 1950s, its leaders promoted a policy of complete sexual equality, of encouraging women to enter roles previously reserved for men. In the early years it almost worked. The first generation of women were ideologically committed, and they shifted in large numbers to politics, management, and labor. But they and their daughters have regressed somewhat toward traditional roles, despite being trained from birth in the new culture. Furthermore, the daughters have gone further than the mothers. They now demand and receive a longer period of time each day with their children, time significantly entitled "the hour of love." Some of the most gifted have resisted recruitment into the higher levels of commercial and political leadership, so that the representation in these roles is far below that enjoyed by the same generation of men. It has been argued that this reversion merely represents the influence of the strong patriarchal tradition that persists in the remainder of Israeli society, even though the role division is now greater inside the kibbutzim than outside. The Israeli experience shows how difficult it is to predict the consequences and assess the meaning of changes in behavior based on either heredity or ideology.

From this troubling ambiguity concerning sex roles one firm conclusion can be drawn: the evidences of biological constraint alone cannot prescribe an ideal course of action. However, they can help us to define the options and to assess the price of each. The price is to be measured in the added energy required for education and reinforcement and in the attrition of individual freedom and potential. And let us face the real issue squarely: since every option has a cost, and concrete ethical principles will rarely find universal acceptance, the choice cannot be made easily. In such cases we could do well to consider the wise counsel of Hans Morgenthau: "In the combination of political wisdom, moral courage and moral judgment, man reconciles his political nature and his moral destiny. That this conciliation is nothing more than a *modus vivendi,* uneasy, precarious, and even paradoxical, can disappoint only those who prefer to gloss over and to distort the tragic contradictions of human existence with the soothing logic of a specious concord." I am suggesting that the contradictions are rooted in the surviving relics of our prior genetic history, and that one of the most inconvenient and senseless, but nevertheless unavoidable of these residues is the modest predisposition toward sex role differences. . . .

The Political Nature of "Human Nature"

Ruth Hubbard[*]

Biologists, social scientists, and philosophers have speculated about human nature. Is there such a thing, and if so, how does one describe it? Fortunately I do not need to review the history of such speculations, since Alison Jaggar has provided a lucid discussion of the main issues and has located the debates in their historical and political contexts.[1] What I can do is evaluate the biological suppositions that underlie the concept of a human nature.

The ambiguity of the term *biology* is at the heart of questions about what scientists do when they try to examine nature. We use the word to denote what scientists tell us about the nature of organisms and also the living experience. When I speak of "my biology," I am usually referring to how I experience my biological functions, not to what scientists tell me about them. I can also use the word as the name of the scientific discipline, as in "I am studying biology." These multiple meanings for *biology* reflect confusions and ambiguities about the connections between scientific descriptions and the phenomena in the real world that scientists try to describe. It is important that we be aware of this ambiguity when we think about "human nature." Are we describing the natures of real people—you and me—or an abstraction or reification that biologists construct? "Human nature" does not describe people. It is a normative concept that incarnates historically based beliefs about what human beings are and how they should behave.

Biologists' claims about human nature are embedded in the ways they learn about and describe living organisms. Most biologists, like other scientists, accept the notion that nature can best be described in terms of different levels of organization. These levels extend from ultimate particles, through atoms and molecules, to cells, tissues, and organs, to organisms considered individually, and then to groups of organisms—societies. Biology nowadays is concerned with the range of levels from atoms and molecules through organisms, and also with groups of organisms and their relations with each other over time (evolution) and space (animal behavior and ecology). Some biologists learn about organisms by taking them apart; others observe whole organisms in the laboratory or in the field. Yet these levels are not credited with equal authority. Most biologists (as well as chemists and physicists) believe that the "lower" atomic and molecular levels are more basic and have intrinsically greater explanatory potential. Thus we find scientists and science writers describing genes (which are molecules) as keys to "the secret of life" or as "blueprints" of the organism. Numerous biologists believe that we would understand a great deal more about ourselves and other animals if we knew the composition and sequence of all the genes on our chromosomes. This belief in the superior explanatory content of "lower" levels is usually referred to as *reductionism,* and at this time reductionism is the dominant mode of thinking among biologists.

Reductionists assert that the study of organs, tissues, and molecules can yield

[*]I want to thank Robin M. Gillespie for critical comments and discussion.

important information about how organisms, and hence societies, operate. For example, they attribute the existence of crime to the "criminal personality," and criminals are said to behave as they do because they have diseased brains, too much or too little of certain hormones or other critical substances, or defective genes. Reductionism is a hierarchical theory that proceeds from the bottom up.

The converse is sometimes called *holism*. It can be based on a similar analysis that accepts hierarchies of levels, but it assigns superior authority to the "higher" levels, the organism as a whole or the organism in its surroundings. It is a less popular system of explanation among scientists, but one that carries considerable weight among practitioners of "alternative" methods of healing such as acupuncture and massage, and among feminists and environmentalists. They see reductionist ways of conceptualizing nature as a threat to people and our environment because these focus on specific areas of interest as though they could be isolated from their context.

Biodeterminism is a form of reductionism that explains individual behavior and characteristics of societies in terms of biological functions. Feminists know it best in the form of Freud's notorious statement, "Biology is destiny." During the nineteenth and twentieth centuries, biologists have produced numerous biodeterminist explanations for the obvious differences in women's and men's access to social, economic, and political power. Among them are Darwin's descriptions of the greater "vigour" and more highly developed weapons of males, acquired over eons of evolution through competition among males for access to females. At the same time, Darwin claimed, females sharpened their skills at discerning the most fit among their suitors and acquired coyness and the other wiles needed to captivate the best males. Biodeterminism has also prompted comparisons between the sizes of men's and women's brains and between brains of men of different races—which scientists used to "prove" the superiority of Caucasian men over men of other races and over all women.

A good deal of present-day research into presumed causes of social and behavioral differences between women and men relies upon reductionist explanations. These draw on hypothesized differences in hormone levels of female and male fetuses or on hypothetical genes for spatial skills, mathematical ability, and competitiveness and aggression in men and for domesticity and nurturance in women. The most pervasive and comprehensive of contemporary biodeterminist theories is sociobiology, which has as its project "the systematic study of the *biological basis* of all social behavior" (my italics).[2] Sociobiologists claim that the fundamental elements of human nature can be identified in traits that characterize all people (and selected animals as well) irrespective of their cultural or historical differences. Once these supposedly universal traits have been identified, for example, male aggression and female nurturance, sociobiologists argue that their universality is evidence that they are adaptive. The term *adaptive* in this context means that individuals who exhibit these traits leave more descendants than do other individuals and that they pass the traits on to their descendants. In this way the genes for more adaptive traits come to outnumber the genes for less adaptive ones until the more adaptive traits become universal.

Sociobiologists argue that animals, including humans, do things that help spread their genes about. Behaviors that let them do that most effectively become universal traits. Among males, these are behaviors that lead them to inseminate as many females as possible, hence male promiscuity; for females they are behaviors that optimize the ability to spot and attach themselves to genetically well endowed males and to take good care of the few precious offspring they can produce in their lifetime, hence female fidelity and nurturance.

This basic difference between male and female reproductive strategies is said to arise from the fact that males can produce large numbers of small sperm, whereas females can produce fewer but larger eggs.[3] From this seemingly trivial asymmetry, sociobiologists draw two conclusions that they assume are crucial for the evolution of important differences between females and males: (1) females are the scarce resource (few eggs) and (2) females invest more energy in each egg than males do in each sperm.

But there is no reason to believe that females expend more energy (whatever that means) in the biological components of reproduction than males do. Among mammals, females indeed produce fewer eggs than males do sperm, and females gestate the embryos, but it is not obvious how to translate these facts into energy expenditures. Is it reasonable to count only the energy males require to produce the few sperm that actually end up fertilizing eggs, or should one not count the total energy they expend in producing and ejaculating semen (that is, sperm plus spermatic fluid) throughout their lives (however one would do that)? What is more, a woman's eggs are laid down ("produced") while she is still in her mother's womb. So should they be credited to her mother's energy expenditures or to her own (however one might calculate them)?

There are other puzzles. Sociobiologists describe the growth of a fetus as an investment of energy on the part of the pregnant woman. But the metabolism of a mammalian embryo is part of a pregnant woman's metabolic functions. As she eats, breathes, and metabolizes, some of the food she takes in is used to build the embryo. Why does that represent an investment of *her* energies? I can see that an embryo that grows inside an undernourished woman may be a drain on her because it uses her body for its growth. But healthy, well nourished women have been known to live normal active lives, create art, compete in Olympic events, and feel "energized" rather than drained by their pregnancies.

In the nineteenth century, physicians argued that girls would not be able to grow up to bear children if they diverted the energy required by their developing reproductive organs to their brains by going to school and becoming educated, like boys.[4] And they spoke of menstruation and pregnancy as requiring energy as part of the self-serving ideology by which they portrayed all female reproductive functions as diseases that required medical (hence, of course, male) supervision. Sociobiological arguments that posit differences in the energy women and men invest in procreation to explain why men take less responsibility for the care of their children than women do may ring with scientific plausibility. But there is no way even to specify the variables, much less to do the necessary calculations to turn such hand-waving into scientific statements.

Sociobiologist Richard Dawkins takes sociobiological reductionism to its extreme by asserting that organisms are merely the gene's way of making more genes. He claims that everything organisms do is done out of self-interest, since organisms are only living manifestations of "selfish genes" engaged in the process of replicating themselves.[5] One of the obvious problems with this kind of formulation is that genes do not replicate *themselves.* Nor do eggs or sperm. Even many organisms do not reproduce themselves—at least not organisms that procreate sexually, like humans and most other animals discussed by sociobiologists. Sexual procreation involves a coming together of individuals with different genetic makeups, who produce individuals who are genetically different from their parents and from each other. This has made it difficult for biologists to know how to analyze the ways in which even simple Mendelian traits that involve differences in only one gene become established in a population, not to speak of the ill-defined behaviors that sociobiologists label selfishness, aggression, or nurturance.

Sociobiology can be criticized on many levels. Even within the reductionist, biodeterminist paradigm, human sociobiology allows far too much leeway for identifying and naming traits that are observed in different cultures and under different historical circumstances as the same and hence "universal," especially when these "same" traits are generalized to animals as well. In such an exercise everything—from sharp business practices and warfare to toddlers and young animals roughhousing to interactions scientists have observed among animals in the field, in zoos, or in crowded laboratory cages—becomes "aggression." The term *rape,* which refers ordinarily to the violent, sexualized assertion of power men impose on unconsenting women and occasionally on other men, has been used by sociobiologists as though it denoted nothing more sinister than males' efforts to spread their genes around. Hence sociobiologists have described what they choose to call rape among birds, fishes, insects, and even plants.[6] Contexts and cultural meanings are erased, and all that is left is reified traits, which are universalized when the same name is given to a multiplicity of behaviors. In this way sociobiological reductionism leads to absurd extremes of lumping diverse behaviors together and naming them to suit the scientist's purpose.

Obviously similarities exist between the ways animals and people behave. But the variety of animal behaviors on which to draw for models of human behavior is so great that one can prove any human behavior is "natural" if the criterion is merely that one can point to an animal that behaves that way. This brings me to a crucial problem with efforts to construct lines of evolutionary descent for behaviors among animals, as well as between animals and people. In attempting to establish continuities between different species that may be of historical—evolutionary—significance, biologists have learned to distinguish between two types of similarities: analogies and homologies. Analogies are similarities in appearance or function that have diverse biological origins. Examples are the wings of birds, bats, and insects, and the eyes of frogs, lobsters, and octopuses. Homologous structures may look less similar, but they exhibit important similarities of structure and function that point to a common ancestry. An example is the scales of reptiles and the feathers of birds. To establish lines of historical continuity, analogies are irrelevant. One must look for homologies, which usually requires culling the fossil record.

Behavior leaves no fossils. There are only observations of how contemporary animals (including people) act and interpretations of what their actions signify. This offers too much leeway for postulating connections and imagining possible lines of descent for similar behaviors in particular groups of people and kinds of animals. If we want to use biological observations to try to trace and describe our natural history (which is what sociobiologists want to do), we have to follow more rigorous rules. Resemblances in the ways different animals and people act should not alone lead us to conclude that a behavior has evolutionary significance and is genetically determined.

INTERACTIVE, DIALECTICAL, AND COMPLEMENTARY MODELS OF NATURE

To get away from reductionism *and* holism and from futile arguments about whether nature or nurture is more significant in shaping behavior, a number of scientists have stressed that both genetics and environment are important, and that their effects cannot be separated. The simplest model suggests that the effects are additive. On the basis of that kind of model Arthur Jensen and Richard Herrnstein have argued that 80 percent of intelligence is inherited, 20 percent due to environment.

Other scientists have pointed out that this interpretation is too simplistic and that nature and nurture interact in ways that cannot be numerically quantified because they are not additive but simultaneous, and always act together. For example, Lewontin has argued that we can assess the separate contributions of genetic and environmental factors that act jointly only under strictly controlled conditions that permit the experimenter to change just one variable at a time.[7] On the basis of such experiments one can construct graphs called norms of reaction that describe how specific changes in each variable affect the phenomenon under observation (such as the growth of a plant in various types of soil and under various conditions of moisture, temperature, and cultivation). But these graphs do not permit one to predict the reactions of different varieties of the same organism under the same experimental conditions, or the reactions of a single variety under conditions that one has not yet measured. Such experiments illustrate the complexity of the situation but do not yield information about the real world, in which changes do not occur one variable at a time or in controlled or controllable ways.

More recently, Lewontin, Rose, and Kamin, as well as Birke, have argued that this kind of interactive model, though less limited than simple additive ones, is still too static.[8] Lewontin, Rose, and Kamin propose a dialectical model that acknowledges levels of organization, such as the ones I have enumerated. They argue that no one level is more fundamental than any other. None "causes" or "determines" another, but all are related dialectically, mutually drawing upon and modifying the changes that may be produced at any particular level. Properties observed at a particular level cannot be inferred from properties at other levels because the levels are related dialectically. For example, one cannot predict the physics and chemistry of water from the properties of hydrogen and oxygen atoms. Nor can one predict the structures and functions of proteins from the properties of the amino acids of which they are composed, and even less from the properties of the atoms that make up the amino acids. This is not because we do not know enough about atoms or amino acids, but because new properties emerge when atoms or amino acids come together in different combinations. These properties must be discovered empirically. The same goes for the relationships between organisms and their genes or between societies and the individuals who live in them.

I like to call the dialectical model *transformationism,* an awkward term, but one that tries to signify that biological and environmental factors can utterly change an organism so that it responds differently to other concurrent or subsequent, biological or environmental changes than it might have done. At the same time, the organism transforms its environment, which includes other organisms.

We can visualize this kind of interaction or transformation by thinking about the interplay between biological and cultural factors that affects the ways boys and girls grow up in our society. If a society puts half its children into short skirts and warns them not to move in ways that reveal their panties, while putting the other half into jeans and overalls and encouraging them to climb trees, play ball, and participate in other vigorous outdoor games; if later, during adolescence, the children who have been wearing trousers are urged to "eat like growing boys," while the children in skirts are warned to watch their weight and not get fat; if the half in jeans runs around in sneakers or boots, while the half in skirts totters about on spike heels, then these two groups of people will be biologically as well as socially different. Their muscles will be different, as will their reflexes, posture, arms, legs and feet, hand-eye coordination, and so on. Similarly, people who spend eight hours a day in an office working at a typewriter or a visual display terminal will be biologically different from those who work on construction jobs. There is no way to sort the biological and social components that produce these differences. We cannot sort nature from nurture when we confront group differences in societies in which people from different races, classes, and sexes do not have equal access to resources and power, and therefore live in different environments. Sex-typed generalizations, such as that men are heavier, taller, or stronger than women, obscure the diversity among women and among men and the extensive overlaps between them for all traits except those directly involved with procreation. Most women and men fall within the same range of heights, weights, and strengths, three variables that depend a great deal on how we have grown up and live. We all know that first-generation Americans, on average, are taller than their immigrant parents and that men who do physical labor, on average, are stronger than male college professors. But we forget to look for the obvious reasons for differences when confronted with assertions like "Men are stronger than women." We should be asking: "Which men?" and "What do they do?" There may be biologically based average differences between women and men, but these are interwoven with a host of social differences from which we cannot disentangle them.

Recently some of us have begun to use yet another model to look at the different levels of organization, a model that draws on Niels Bohr's principle of complementarity. Bohr proposed complementarity as a way to think about the fact that light and other electromagnetic radiation can be described equally well as bursts of particles (quanta) or as waves spreading out from a point source. Classical physicists argued over which they really are; Bohr and other quantum theorists asserted that they are both. By complementarity Bohr meant that they are both at all times, not sometimes one, sometimes the other. Which description is appropriate depends on the instruments an observer uses to examine the radiation. When observed with a phototube or a photoelectric cell, light looks like a random succession of packets of energy; with a diffraction grating or a prism, it looks like waves.

Complementarity provides a fruitful model to integrate the different levels of organization and describe living organisms. The phenomena we observe at the subatomic, atomic, molecular, cellular, organismic, and societal levels are all taking place simultaneously and constitute a single reality. The distinctions between them are not part of nature. It is an outcome of Western cultural history and of the history of professionalization that we have developed separate academic specialties that describe these levels as though they were different phenomena. The only reason we think in terms of such levels is that we have developed specialties that draw distinctions between them. But physicists do not have access to more fundamental truths than molecular biologists have, and molecular biologists do not provide more basic descriptions than do the biologists who study cells or organisms. Biologists do not probe deeper realities than anthropologists or historians, only different ones. The fact that academic professionals value the explanatory power of these disciplines differently tells us something about the history and sociology of professionalization and about the alliances different disciplines have been able to forge with economic and political power, not about nature.

HUMAN NATURE

It is questionable whether the concept of human nature means anything. People's "nature" can be described only by looking at the things we do. To try to abstract or reify a human essence from the ways in which different groups of people have grappled with issues of survival in the range of geographical, ecological, and demographic settings that our species has populated is a dubious enterprise, because what one labels as "natural" depends on one's experience and viewpoint. People with different backgrounds are not likely to agree. Margaret Mead pointed out years ago that in societies with different, even opposite, sexual divisions of labor, people tend to believe that what women and men do follows from inherent differences in our natures.[9]

Sociobiologists presume that certain traits are inherent in our biological nature. Primary among them is selfishness, since it supposedly gets us to perpetuate our genes. A variant on selfishness is altruism of the kind that benefits the altruist (something like, "I'll scratch your back if you'll scratch my children's"). Then there are territoriality and a tendency toward establishing dominance hierarchies, which entered descriptions of animal behavior around the beginning of World War I, when a so-called pecking order was described among barnyard chickens,[10] a not very "natural" population. There are also the sex-differentiated characteristics of male aggressiveness and competitiveness and female coyness and nurturance, which supposedly follow from the asymmetry in our reproductive interests that I questioned earlier. Wilson includes in "human nature" various behaviors that make sexual relationships between women and men emotionally satisfying, such as fondling and kissing, religious and spiritual aspirations that generate the need to believe in something beyond oneself, and the incest taboo.[11] He acknowledges cultural influences but insists that biology contributes a "stubborn kernel" that "cannot be forced without cost."[12] Because sociobiologists posit that "kernel" of biological traits, honed over eons of evolutionary history, their human nature theories tend to be conservative and portray competitive, hierarchical, capitalist societies in which men dominate women and a small, privileged group of men dominates everyone else as the natural outcome of inborn biological propensities.[13] But competition and dominance hierarchies do not characterize all human societies,[14] and there is no reason to believe that our biology determines the ways we construct them.

Stimulated in part by insights gained in the women's liberation movement, a number of sociobiologists have recently published accounts that round out the traditional descriptions of female animals as reproducers.[15] They present females as active participants in the social life of the group, as aggressive, competitive, involved in dominance hierarchies of their own, and as initiators of sexual contact and promiscuous. It seems that the sexual revolution has overtaken the dominant, competitive male and the coy, submissive female.

Carl Degler points out that sociobiologists as individuals have a range of political views and commitments. This is true, but the sociobiological definition of human nature lends itself to conservative politics. It is not inconsistent for a sociobiologist to assert that Marxism is "based on an inaccurate description of human nature,"[16] or that women's liberation is doomed because "human societies have evolved toward sexual domination as though sliding down a ratchet,"[17] and that "even with identical education and equal access to all professions, men are likely to play a disproportionate role in political life, business, and science."[18]

Biology imposes limits on what people can do, but when we feel the need we usually try to overcome them—at times all too recklessly. Bareskinned, we live in the arctic; wingless we fly; we live under water without benefit of gills. In view of the ingenuity with which we have overcome our limitations, it might seem odd that scientists call on sometimes quite subtle hypothetical differences between women and men to explain gender inequalities and that research into sex differences arouses so much scientific and public interest. We must recognize that differences among people are of interest only if they are correlated with differences in power. Little, if any, research is done on biological or psychosocial correlates of differences in height, although folk wisdom suggests there may be some. But when it comes to dark-skinned and light-skinned people or women and men, every possibility of difference is explored—and always some scientists predict that it will be hard to overcome.

Yet people have undergone substantial physical as well as psychological changes during times of major political and economic transformation. For example, as a result of rationing and the social policies the British government enacted during World War II, a generation of children grew up in Britain that was healthier and looked significantly different from any that had gone before. People who participate in major political or personal changes that drastically alter the ways they live often experience simultaneous changes in the ways their bodies function—changes in their ability to work and concentrate, in sleep and eating patterns, muscle mass, shape and strength, body weight, skin color and texture, and many others. It is not that changes in our way of life *cause* our biology to change. All the changes are interconnected: *we* change. Women who have participated in the women's liberation movement are well aware of such changes—changes in our bodies as well as in our lives.

Another example: We tend to think of menstruation as purely biological, yet menstrual patterns and experiences are profoundly affected by the ways women live, and the menstrual and reproductive patterns of women whose ways of life differ can be very different. Research conducted with female college athletes has demonstrated menstrual changes induced by exercise and diet.[19] !Kung women who forage for food in the Kalahari desert in southern Africa have entirely different menstrual and reproductive histories from the ones we are accustomed to think of as normal or natural. These women walk a great deal as part of their foraging and eat food that, although nutritionally adequate, supplies very different proportions and kinds of carbohydrates, fats and proteins than do our Western diets. Also, they nurse their babies for longer times and much more frequently than we do.[20] As a result, the !Kung establish patterns of ovulation and menstruation that produce only four or five pregnancies and very few menstruations in a lifetime.[21] It seems quite possible that the regular monthly cycle that some Western ideologies have put at the core of female personality is an accompaniment of ways of life that have developed in the last few thousand years. During this time increasing numbers of people have ceased to live as nomadic foragers and have begun to cultivate land, form settlements, and build the kinds of cultural and political structures that have yielded historical records.[22] But even now, women (and no doubt men) in different parts of the world live diverse biological, as well as social and economic, lives. As I have tried to say, these aspects of our lives cannot be separated.

Biological differences between the sexes prevent us from achieving gender equality only in procreation, narrowly defined. To date, only men can produce sperm and only women can produce eggs and gestate. Women *and* men can now feed infants reasonably healthful imitations of mother's milk, at least in affluent societies. People's capacities to work at socially useful tasks and to nurture children and form nonexploitative and mutually satisfying relationships are not limited by biology, but by discriminatory economic and social practices.

NOTES

1 Alison Jaggar, *Feminist Politics and Human Nature* (Totowa, N.J.: Rowman and Allanheld, 1983).

2 Edward O. Wilson, *Sociobiology: The New Synthesis* (Cambridge: Harvard University Press, 1975), 4.

3 George C. Williams, *Sex and Evolution* (Princeton: Princeton University Press, 1975).

4 Edward H. Clarke, *Sex in Education* (Boston: James R. Osgood, 1874).

5 Richard Dawkins, *The Selfish Gene* (Oxford: Oxford University Press, 1976).

6 David Barash, *The Whispering Within* (New York: Harper & Row, 1979).

7 R. C. Lewontin, "The Analysis of Variance and the Analysis of Causes," *American Journal of Human Genetics* 26 (1974): 400–11.

8 R. C. Lewontin, Steven Rose, and Leon J. Kamin, *Not in Our Genes* (New York: Pantheon, 1984); Lynda Birke, *Women, Feminism and Biology* (New York: Methuen, 1986).

9 Margaret Mead, *Male and Female* (New York: Dell, 1949).

10 Donna Haraway, "Signs of Dominance," *Studies in History of Biology* 6 (1983): 129–219.

11 Edward O. Wilson, *On Human Nature* (Cambridge: Harvard University Press, 1978).

12 Wilson, *On Human Nature,* 147.

13 Idem, *Sociobiology,* chap. 27; "Human Decency Is Animal," *New York Times Magazine* (October 12, 1975).

14 Eleanor Burke Leacock, *Myths of Male Dominance* (New York: Monthly Review Press, 1981).

15 Samuel K. Wasser, ed., *Social Behavior of Female Vertebrates* (New York: Academic, 1983); Sarah Blaffer Hrdy, "Empathy, Polyandry, and the Myth of the Coy Female," in Ruth Bleier, ed., *Feminist Approaches to Science* (New York: Pergamon, 1986), 119–46.

16 Wilson, *On Human Nature,* 190.

17 Ibid., 134.

18 Wilson, "Human Decency Is Animal."

19 Rose Frisch et al., "Delayed Menarche and Amenorrhea of College Athletes in Relation to Age of Onset of Training," *Journal of the American Medical Association* 246 (1981): 1559–63.

20 Melvin Konner and Carol Worthman, "Nursing Frequency, Gonadal Function, and Birth Spacing among !Kung Hunter-Gatherers," *Science* 207 (1980): 788–90.

21 Nancy Howell, *Demography of the Dobe !Kung* (New York: Academic, 1979).

22 Barbara B. Harrell, "Lactation and Menstruation in Cultural Perspective," *American Anthropologist* 83 (1982): 796–823.

Women's Subordination Through the Lens of Gender: Liberalism

The Subjection of Women

John Stuart Mill

The object of this Essay is to explain as clearly as I am able, the grounds of an opinion which I have held from the very earliest period when I had formed any opinions at all on social or political matters, and which, instead of being weakened or modified, has been constantly growing stronger by the progress of reflection and the experience of life: That the principle which regulates the existing social relations between the two sexes—the legal subordination of one sex to the other—is wrong in itself, and now one of the chief hindrances to human improvement; and that it ought to be replaced by a principle of perfect equality, admitting no power or privilege on the one side, nor disability on the other.

The very words necessary to express the task I have undertaken, show how arduous it is. But it would be a mistake to suppose that the difficulty of the case must lie in the insufficiency or obscurity of the grounds of reason on which my conviction rests. The difficulty is that which exists in all cases in which there is a mass of feeling to be contended against. So long as an opinion is strongly rooted in the feelings, it gains rather than loses in stability by having a preponderating weight of argument against it. For if it were accepted as a result of argument, the refutation of the argument might shake the solidity of the conviction; but when it rests solely on feeling, the worse it flares in argumentative contest, the more persuaded its adherents are that their feeling must have some deeper ground, which the arguments do not reach; and while the feeling remains, it is always throwing up fresh intrenchments of argument to repair any breach made in the old. And there are so many causes tending to make the feelings connected with this subject the most intense and most deeply-rooted of all those which gather round and protect old institutions and customs, that we need not wonder to find them as yet less undermined and loosened than any of the rest by the progress of the great modern spiritual and social transition; nor suppose that the barbarisms to which men cling longest must be less barbarisms than those which they earlier shake off. . . .

In the first place, the opinion in favour of the present system, which entirely subordinates the weaker sex to the stronger, rests upon theory only; for there never has been trial made of any other; so that experience, in the sense in which it is vulgarly opposed to theory, cannot be pretended to have pronounced any verdict. And in the second place, the adoption of this system of inequality never was the result of deliberation, or forethought, or any social ideas, or any notion whatever of what conducted to the benefit of humanity or the good order of society. It arose simply from the fact that from the very earliest twilight of human society, every woman (owing to the value attached to her by men, combined with her inferiority in muscular strength) was found in a state of bondage to some man. Laws and systems of polity always begin by recognising the relations they find already existing between individuals. They convert what was a mere physical fact into a legal right, give it the sanction of society, and principally aim at the substitution of public and organized means of asserting and protecting these rights, instead of the irregular and lawless conflict of physical strength. Those who had already been compelled to obedience became in this manner legally bound to it. Slavery, from being a mere affair of force between the master and the slave, became regularized and a matter of compact among the masters, who, binding themselves to one another for common protection, guaranteed by their collective strength the private possessions of each, including his slaves. In early times, the great majority of the male sex were slaves, as well as the whole of the female. And many ages elapsed, some of them ages of high cultivation, before any thinker was bold enough to question the rightfulness and the absolute social necessity, either of the one slavery or of the other. . . .

If people are mostly so little aware how completely, during the greater part of the duration of our species, the law of force was the avowed rule of general conduct, any other being only a special and exceptional consequence of peculiar ties—and from how very recent a date it is that the affairs of society in general have been even pretended to be regulated according to any moral law; as little do people remember or consider, how institutions and customs which never had any ground but the law of force, last on into ages and states of general opinion which never would have permitted their first establishment. Less than forty years ago, Englishmen might still by law hold human beings in bondage as saleable property; within the present century they might kidnap them and carry them off, and work them literally to death. This absolutely extreme case of the law of force, condemned by those who can tolerate almost every other form of arbitrary power, and which, of all others, presents features the most revolting to the feelings of all who look at it from an impartial position, was the law of civilized and Christian England within the memory of persons now living: and in one half of Anglo-Saxon America three or four years ago, not only did slavery exist, but the slave trade, and the breeding of slaves expressly for it, was a general practice between slave states. Yet not only was there a greater strength of sentiment against it, but, in England at least, a less amount either of feeling or of interest in favour of it, than of any other of the customary abuses of force: for its motive was the love of gain, unmixed and undisguised; and those who profited by it were a very small numerical fraction of the country, while the natural feeling of all who were not personally interested in it, was unmitigated abhorrence. So extreme an instance makes it almost superfluous to refer to any other; but consider the long duration of absolute monarchy. In England at present it is the almost universal conviction that military despotism is a case of the law of force, having no other origin or justification. Yet in all the great nations of Europe except England it either still exists, or has only just ceased to exist, and has even now a strong party favourable to it in all ranks of the people, especially among persons of station and consequence. Such is the power of an established system, even when far from universal, when not only in almost every period of history there have been great and well-known examples of the contrary system, but these have almost invariably been afforded by the most illustrious and most prosperous communities. In this case, too, the possessor of the undue power, the person directly interested in it, is only one person, while those who are subject to it and suffer from it are literally all the rest. The yoke is naturally and necessarily humiliating to all persons, except the one who is on the throne, together with, at most, the one who expects to succeed to it. How different are these cases from that of the power of men over women! I am not now prejudging the question of its justifiableness. I am showing how vastly more permanent it could not but be, even if not justifiable, than these other dominations which have nevertheless lasted down to our own time. Whatever gratification of pride there is in the possession of power, and whatever personal interest in its exercise, is in this case not confined to a limited class, but common to the whole male sex. Instead of being, to most of its supporters, a thing desirable chiefly in the abstract, or, like the political ends usually contended for by factions, of little private importance to any but the leaders; it comes home to the person and hearth of every male head of a family, and of every one who looks forward to being so. The clodhopper exercises, or is to exercise, his share of the power equally with the highest nobleman. And the case is that in which the desire of power is the strongest: for every one who desires power, desires it most over those who are nearest to him, with whom his life is passed, with whom he has most concerns in common, and in whom any independence of his authority is oftenest likely to interfere with his individual preferences. If, in the other cases specified, powers manifestly grounded only on force, and having so much less to support them, are so slowly and with so much difficulty got rid of, much more must it be so with this, even if it rests on no better foundation than those. We must consider, too, that the possessors of the power have facilities in this case, greater than in any other, to prevent any uprising against it. Every one of the subjects lives under the very eye, and almost, it may be said, in the hands, of one of the masters—in closer intimacy with him than with any of her fellow-subjects; with no means of combining against him, no power of even locally overmastering him, and, on the other hand, with the strongest motives for seeking his favour and avoiding to give him offence. In struggles for political emancipation, everybody knows how often its champions are bought off by bribes, or daunted by terrors. In the case of women, each individual of the subject-class is in a chronic state of bribery and intimidation combined. In setting up the standard of resistance, a large number of the leaders, and still more of the followers, must make an almost complete sacrifice of the pleasures or the alleviations of their own individual lot. If ever any system of privilege and enforced subjection had its yoke tightly riveted on the necks of those who are kept down by it, this has. . . .

All causes, social and natural, combine to make it unlikely that women should be collectively rebellious to the power of men. They are so far in a position different from all other subject classes, that their masters require something more from them than actual service. Men do not want solely the obedience of women, they want their senti-ments. All men, except the most brutish, desire to have, in the woman most nearly connected with them, not a forced slave but a willing one, not a slave merely, but a favourite. They have therefore put everything in practice to enslave their minds. The masters of all other slaves rely, for maintaining obedience, on fear; either fear of them-selves, or religious fears. The masters of women wanted more than simple obedience, and they turned the whole force of education to effect their purpose. All women are brought up from the very earliest years in the belief that their ideal of character is the very opposite to that of men; not self-will, and government by self-control, but sub-mission, and yielding to the control of others. All the moralities tell them that it is the duty of women, and all the current sentimentalities that it is their nature, to live for others; to make complete abnegation of themselves, and to have no life but in their affections. And by their affections are meant the only ones they are allowed to have— those to the men with whom they are connected, or to the children who constitute an additional and indefeasible tie between them and a man. When we put together three things—first, the natural attraction between opposite sexes; secondly, the wife's entire dependence on the husband, every privilege or pleasure she has being either his gift, or depending entirely on his will; and lastly, that the principal object of human pursuit, consideration, and all objects of social ambition, can in general be sought or obtained by her only through him, it would be a miracle if the object of being attractive to men had not become the polar star of feminine education and formation of character. And, this great means of influence over the minds of women having been acquired, an instinct of selfishness made men avail themselves of it to the utmost as a means of holding women in subjection, by representing to them meekness, submissiveness, and resignation of all individual will into the hands of a man, as an essential part of sexual attractiveness. Can it be doubted that any of the other yokes which mankind have suc-ceeded in breaking, would have subsisted till now if the same means had existed, and had been as sedulously used, to bow down their minds to it? If it had been made the object of the life of every young plebeian to find personal favour in the eyes of some patrician, of every young serf with some seigneur; if domestication with him, and a share of his personal affections, had been held out as the prize which they all should look out for, the most gifted and aspiring being able to reckon on the most desirable prizes; and if, when this prize had been obtained, they had been shut out by a wall of brass from all interests not centering in him, all feelings and desires but those which he shared or inculcated; would not serfs and seigneurs, plebeians and patricians, have been as broadly distinguished at this day as men and women are? and would not all but a thinker here and there, have believed the distinction to be a fundamental and unalterable fact in human nature?

The preceding considerations are amply sufficient to show that custom, however universal it may be, affords in this case no presumption, and ought not to create any prejudice, in favour of the arrangements which place women in social and political subjection to men. But I may go farther, and maintain that the course of history, and the tendencies of progressive human society, afford not only no presumption in favour of this system of inequality of rights, but a strong one against it; and that, so far as the whole course of human improvement up to this time, the whole stream of modern tendencies, warrants any inference on the subject, it is, that this relic of the past is discordant with the future, and must necessarily disappear.

For, what is the peculiar character of the modern world—the difference which chiefly distinguishes modern institutions, modern social ideas, modern life itself, from those of times long past? It is, that human beings are no longer born to their place in life, and chained down by an inexorable bond to the place they are born to, but are free to employ their faculties, and such favourable chances as offer, to achieve the lot which may appear to them most desirable. Human society of old was constituted on a very different principle. All were born to a fixed social position, and were mostly kept in it by law, or interdicted from any means by which they could emerge from it. As some men are born white and others black, so some were born slaves and others freemen and citizens; some were born patricians, others plebeians; some were born feudal nobles, others commoners and *roturiers*. A slave or serf could never make himself free, nor, except by the will of his master, become so. In most European countries it was not till towards the close of the middle ages, and as a consequence of the growth of regal power, that commoners could be ennobled. Even among nobles, the eldest son was born the exclusive heir to the paternal possessions, and a long time elapsed before it was fully established that the father could disinherit him. Among the industrious classes, only those who were born members of a guild, or were admitted into it by its members, could lawfully practise their calling within its local limits; and nobody could practise any calling deemed important, in any but the legal manner—by processes authoritatively prescribed. Manufacturers have stood in the pilory for presuming to carry on their business by new and improved methods. In modern Europe, and most in those parts of it which have participated most largely in all other modern improvements, diametrically opposite doctrines now prevail. Law and government do not undertake to prescribe by whom any social or industrial operation shall or shall not be conducted, or what modes of conducting them shall be lawful. These things are left to the unfettered choice of individuals. Even the laws which required that workmen should serve an apprenticeship, have in this country been repealed: there being ample assurance that in all cases in which an apprenticeship is necessary, its necessity will suffice to enforce it. The old theory was, that the least possible should be left to the choice of the individual agent; that all he had to do should, as far as practicable, be laid down for him by superior wisdom. Left to himself he was sure to go wrong. The modern conviction, the fruit of a thousand years of experience is, that things in which the individual is the person directly interested, never go right but as they are left to his own discretion; and that any regulation of them by authority, except to protect the rights of others, is sure to be mischievous. This conclusion, slowly arrived at, and not adopted until almost every possible application of the contrary theory had been made with disastrous result, now (in the industrial department) prevails universally in the most advanced countries, almost universally in all that have pretensions to any sort of advancement. It is not that all processes are supposed to be equally good, or all persons to be equally qualified for everything; but that freedom of individual choice is now known to be the only thing which procures the adoption of the best processes, and throws each operation into the hands of those who are best qualified for it. Nobody thinks it necessary to make a law that only a strong-armed man shall be a blacksmith. Freedom and competition suffice to make blacksmiths strong-armed men, because the weak-armed can earn more by engaging in occupations for which they are more fit. In consonance with this doctrine, it is felt to be an overstepping of the proper bounds of authority to fix beforehand, on some general presumption, that certain persons are not fit to do certain things. It is now thoroughly known and admitted that if some such presumptions exist, no such presumption is infallible. Even if it be well grounded in a majority of cases, which it is very likely not to be, there will be a minority of exceptional cases in which it does not hold; and in those it is both an injustice to the individuals, and a detriment to society, to place barriers in the way of their using their faculties for their own benefit and for that of others. In the cases, on the other hand, in which the unfitness is real, the ordinary motives of human conduct will on the whole suffice to prevent the incompetent person from making, or from persisting in, the attempt.

If this general principle of social and economical science is not true; if individuals, with such help as they can derive from the opinion of those who know them, are not better judges than the law and the government, of their own capacities and vocation; the world cannot too soon abandon this principle, and return to the old system of regulations and disabilities. But if the principle is true, we ought to act as if we believed it, and not to ordain that to be born a girl instead of a boy, any more than to be born black instead of white, or a commoner instead of a nobleman, shall decide the person's position through all life—shall interdict people from all the more elevated social positions, and from all, except a few, respectable occupations. Even were we to admit the utmost that is ever pretended as to the superior fitness of men for all the functions now reserved to them, the same argument applies which forbids a legal qualification for members of Parliament. If only once in a dozen years the conditions of eligibility exclude a fit person, there is a real loss, while the exclusion of thousands of unfit persons is no gain; for if the constitution of the electoral body disposes them to choose unfit persons, there are always plenty of such persons to choose from. In all things of any difficulty and importance, those who can do them well are fewer than the need, even with the most unrestricted latitude of choice; and any limitation of the field of selection deprives society of some chances of being served by the competent, without ever saving it from the incompetent.

At present, in the more improved countries, the disabilities of women are the only case, save one, in which laws and institutions take persons at their birth, and ordain that they shall never in all their lives be allowed to compete for certain things. . . .

The social subordination of women thus stands out an isolated fact in modern social institutions; a solitary breach of what has become their fundamental law; a single relic of an old world of thought and practice exploded in everything else, but retained in the one thing of most universal interest. . . .

The least that can be demanded is, that the question should not be considered as prejudged by existing fact and existing opinion, but open to discussion on its merits, as a question of justice and expediency; the decision on this, as on any of the other social arrangements of mankind, depending on what an enlightened estimate of tendencies and consequences may show to be most advantageous to humanity in general, without distinction of sex. And the discussion must be a real discussion, descending to foundations, and not resting satisfied with vague and general assertions. It will not do, for instance, to assert in general terms, that the experience of mankind has pronounced in favour of the existing system. Experience cannot possibly have decided between two courses, so long as there has only been experience of one. If it be said that the doctrine of the equality of the sexes rests only on theory, it must be remembered that the contrary doctrine also has only theory to rest upon. All that is proved in its favour by direct experience, is that mankind have been able to exist under it, and to attain the degree of improvement and prosperity which we now see; but whether that prosperity has been attained sooner, or is now greater, than it would have been under the other system, experience does not say. On the other hand, experience does say, that every step in improvement has been so invariably accompanied by a step made in raising the social position of women, that historians and philosophers have been led to adopt their elevation or debasement as on the whole the surest test and most correct measure of the civilization of a people or an age. Through all the progressive period of human history, the condition of women has been approaching nearer to equality with men. This does not of itself prove that the assimilation must go on to complete equality; but it assuredly affords some presumption that such is the case.

Neither does it avail anything to say that the *nature* of the two sexes adapts them to their present functions and position, and renders these appropriate to them. Standing on the ground of common sense and the constitution of the human mind, I deny that any one knows, or can know, the nature of the two sexes, as long as they have only been seen in their present relation to one another. If men had ever been found in society without women, or women without men, or if there had been a society of men and women in which the women were not under the control of the men, something might have been positively known about the mental and moral differences which may be inherent in the nature of each. What is now called the nature of women is an eminently artificial thing—the result of forced repression in some directions, unnatural stimulation in others. It may be asserted without scruple, that no other class of dependents have had their character so entirely distorted from its natural proportions by their relation with their masters; for, if conquered and slave races have been, in some respects, more forcibly repressed, whatever in them has not been crushed down by an iron heel has generally been let alone, and if left with any liberty of development, it has developed itself according to its own laws; but in the case of women, a hot-house and stove cultivation has always been carried on of some of the capabilities of their nature, for the benefit and pleasure of their masters. . . .

Hence, in regard to that most difficult question, what are the natural differences between the two sexes—a subject on which it is impossible in the present state of society to obtain complete and correct knowledge—while almost everybody dogmatizes upon it, almost all neglect and make light of the only means by which any partial insight can be obtained into it. This is, an analytic study of the most important department of psychology, the laws of the influence of circumstances on character. For, however great and apparently ineradicable the moral and intellectual differences between men and women might be, the evidence of their being natural differences could only be negative. Those only could be inferred to be natural which could not possibly be artificial—the residuum, after deducting every characteristic of either sex which can admit of being explained from education or external circumstances. The profoundest knowledge of the laws of the formation of character is indispensable to entitle any one to affirm even that there is any difference, much more what the difference is, between the two sexes considered as moral and rational beings; and since no one, as yet, has that knowledge, (for there is hardly any subject which, in proportion to its importance, has been so little studied), no one is thus far entitled to any positive opinion on the subject. Conjectures are all that can at present be made; conjectures more or less probable, according as more or less authorized by such knowledge as we yet have of the laws of psychology, as applied to the formation of character.

Even the preliminary knowledge, what the differences between the sexes now are, apart from all questions as to how they are made what they are, is still in the crudest and most incomplete state. . . .

One thing we may be certain of—that what is contrary to women's nature to do, they never will be made to do by simply giving their nature free play. The anxiety of mankind to interfere in behalf of nature, for fear lest nature should not succeed in effecting its purpose, is an altogether unnecessary solicitude. What women by nature cannot do, it is quite superfluous to forbid them from doing. What they can do, but not so well as the men who are their competitors, competition suffices to exclude them from; since nobody asks for protective duties and bounties in favour of women; it is only asked that the present bounties and protective duties in favour of men should be recalled. If women have a greater natural inclination for some things than for others, there is no need of laws or social inculcation to make the majority of them do the former in preference to the latter. Whatever women's services are most wanted for, the free play of competition will hold out the strongest inducements to them to undertake. And, as the words imply, they are most wanted for the things for which they are most fit; by the apportionment of which to them, the collective faculties of the two sexes can be applied on the whole with the greatest sum of valuable result.

The general opinion of men is supposed to be, that the natural vocation of a woman is that of a wife and mother. I say, is supposed to be, because, judging from acts—from the whole of the present constitution of society—one might infer that their opinion was the direct contrary. They might be supposed to think that the alleged natural vocation of women was of all things the most repugnant to their nature; insomuch that if they are free to do anything else—if any other means of living, or occupation of their time and faculties, is open, which has any chance of appearing desirable to them—there will not be enough of them who will be willing to accept the condition said to be natural to them. If this is the real opinion of men in general, it would be well that it should be spoken out. I should like to hear somebody openly enunciating the doctrine (it is already implied in much that is written on the subject)—"It is necessary to society that women should marry and produce children. They will not do so unless they are compelled. Therefore it is necessary to compel them." The merits of the case would then be clearly defined. It would be exactly that of the slaveholders of South Carolina and Louisiana. "It is necessary that cotton and sugar should be grown. White men cannot produce them. Negroes will not, for any wages which we choose to give. *Ergo* they must be compelled." An illustration still closer to the point is that of impressment. Sailors must absolutely be had to defend the country. It often happens that they will not voluntarily enlist. Therefore there must be the power of forcing them. How often has this logic been used! and, but for one flaw in it, without doubt it would have been successful up to this day. But it is open to the retort—First pay the sailors the honest value of their labour. When you have made it as well worth their while to serve you, as to work for other employers, you will have no more difficulty than others have in obtaining their services. To this there is no logical answer except "I will not": and as people are now not only ashamed, but are not desirous, to rob the labourer of his hire, impressment is no longer advocated. Those who attempt to force women into marriage by closing all other doors against them, lay themselves open to a similar retort. If they mean what they say, their opinion must evidently be, that men do not render the married condition so desirable to women, as to induce them to accept it for its own recommendations. It is not a sign of one's thinking the boon one offers very attractive, when one allows only Hobson's choice, "that or none." And here, I believe, is the clue to the feelings of those men, who have a real antipathy to the equal freedom of women. I believe they are afraid, not lest women should be unwilling to marry, for I do not think that any one in reality has that apprehension; but lest they should insist that marriage should be on equal conditions; lest all women of spirit and capacity should prefer doing almost anything else, not in their own eyes degrading, rather than marry, when marrying is giving themselves a master, and a master too of all their earthly possessions. And truly, if this consequence were necessarily incident to marriage, I think that the apprehension would be very well founded. I agree in thinking it probable that few women, capable of anything else, would, unless under an irresistible *entrainement,* rendering them for the time insensible to anything but itself, choose such a lot, when any other means were open to them of filling a conventionally honourable place in life: and if men are determined that the law of marriage shall be a law of despotism, they are quite right, in point of mere policy, in leaving to women only Hobson's choice. But, in that case, all that has been done in the modern world to relax the chain on the minds of women, has been a mistake. They never should have been allowed to receive a literary education. Women who read, much more women who write, are, in the existing constitution of things, a contradiction and a disturbing element: and it was wrong to bring women up with any acquirements but those of an odalisque, or of a domestic servant.

Bill of Rights

National Organization for Women (NOW)

I   Equal Rights Constitutional Amendment
II   Enforce Law Banning Sex Discrimination in Employment
III   Maternity Leave Rights in Employment and in Social Security Benefits
IV   Tax Deduction for Home and Child Care Expenses for Working Parents
V   Child Care Centers
VI   Equal and Unsegregated Education
VII   Equal Job Training Opportunities and Allowances for Women in Poverty
VIII   The Right of Women to Control Their Reproductive Lives

WE DEMAND:

I   That the United States Congress immediately pass the Equal Rights Amendment to the Constitution to provide that "Equality of rights under the law shall not be denied or abridged by the United States or by any State on account of sex," and that such then be immediately ratified by the several States.

II   That equal employment opportunity be guaranteed to all women, as well as men, by insisting that the Equal Employment Opportunity Commission enforces the prohibitions against sex discrimination in employment under Title VII of the Civil Rights Act of 1964 with the same vigor as it enforces the prohibitions against racial discrimination.

III   That women be protected by law to ensure their rights to return to their jobs within a reasonable time after childbirth without loss of seniority or other accrued benefits, and be paid maternity leave as a form of social security and/or employee benefit.

IV   Immediate revision of tax laws to permit the deduction of home and child care expenses for working parents.

V   That child care facilities be established by law on the same basis as parks, libraries, and public schools, adequate to the needs of children from the pre-school years through adolescence, as a community resource to be used by all citizens from all income levels.

VI   That the right of women to be educated to their full potential equally with men be secured by Federal and State Legislation, eliminating all discrimination and segregation by sex, written and unwritten, at all levels of education, including colleges, graduate and professional schools, loans and fellowships, and Federal and State training programs such as the Job Corps.

VII   The right of women in poverty to secure job training, housing, and family allowances on equal terms with men, but without prejudice to a parent's right to remain at home to care for his or her children; revision of welfare legislation and poverty programs which deny women dignity, privacy and self-respect.

VIII   The right of women to control their own reproductive lives by removing from penal codes laws limiting access to contraceptive information and devices and laws governing abortion.

Women's Subordination Through the Lens of Class: Classical Marxism

Origin of the Family, Private Property, and the State

Friedrich Engels

. . . According to the materialistic conception, the determining factor in history is, in the final instance, the production and reproduction of immediate life. This, again, is of a twofold character: on the one side, the production of the means of existence, of food, clothing and shelter and the tools necessary for that production; on the other side, the production of human beings themselves, the propagation of the species. The social organization under which the people of a particular historical epoch and a particular country live is determined by both kinds of production: by the stage of development of labor on the one hand and of the family on the other. The lower the development of labor and the more limited the amount of its products, and consequently, the more limited also the wealth of the society, the more the social order is found to be dominated by kinship groups. However, within this structure of society based on kinship groups the productivity of labor increasingly develops, and with it private property and exchange, differences of wealth, the possibility of utilizing the labor power of others, and hence the basis of class antagonisms: new social elements, which in the course of generations strive to adapt the old social order to the new conditions, until at last their incompatibility brings about a complete upheaval. In the collision of the newly developed social classes, the old society founded on kinship groups is broken up. In its place appears a new society, with its control centered in the state, the subordinate units of which are no longer kinship associations, but local associations; a society in which the system of the family is completely dominated by the system of property, and in which there now freely develop those class antagonisms and class struggles that have hitherto formed the content of all *written* history. . . .

Morgan was the first person with expert knowledge to attempt to introduce a definite order into the history of primitive man; so long as no important additional material makes changes necessary, his classification will undoubtedly remain in force.

Of the three main epochs—savagery, barbarism, and civilization—he is concerned, of course, only with the first and the transition to the third. . . .

Reconstructing thus the past history of the family, Morgan, in agreement with most of his colleagues, arrives at a primitive stage when unrestricted sexual freedom prevailed within the tribe, every woman belonging equally to every man and every man to every woman. . . .

According to Morgan, from this primitive state of promiscuous intercourse there developed, probably very early:

1 THE CONSANGUINE FAMILY, THE FIRST STAGE OF THE FAMILY

Here the marriage groups are separated according to generations: all the grandfathers and grandmothers within the limits of the family are all husbands and wives of one another; so are also their children, the fathers and mothers; the latter's children will form a third circle of common husbands and wives; and their children, the great-grandchildren of the first group, will form a fourth. In this form of marriage, therefore, only ancestors and progeny, and parents and children, are excluded from the rights and duties (as we would say) of marriage with one another. Brothers and sisters, male and female cousins of the first, second, and more remote degrees, are all brothers and sisters of one another, and *precisely for that reason* they are all husbands and wives of one another. At this stage the relationship of brother and sister also includes as a matter of course the practice of sexual intercourse with one another. In its typical form, such a family would consist of the descendants of a single pair, the descendants of these descendants in each generation being again brothers and sisters, and therefore husbands and wives, of one another. . . .

2 THE PUNALUAN FAMILY

If the first advance in organization consisted in the exclusion of parents and children from sexual intercourse with one another, the second was the exclusion of sister and brother. On account of the greater nearness of age, this second advance was infinitely more important, but also more difficult, than the first. It was effected gradually, beginning probably with the exclusion from sexual intercourse of one's own brothers and sisters (children of the same mother) first in isolated cases and then by degrees as a general rule (even in this century exceptions were found in Hawaii), and ending with the prohibition of marriage even between collateral brothers and sisters, or, as we should say, between first, second, and third cousins. It affords, says Morgan, "a good illustration of the operation of the principle of natural selection." There can be no question that the tribes among whom inbreeding was restricted by this advance were bound to develop more quickly and more fully than those among whom marriage between brothers and sisters remained the rule and the law. How powerfully the influence of this advance made itself felt is seen in the institution which arose directly out of it and went far beyond it—the gens, which forms the basis of the social order of most, if not all, barbarian peoples of the earth and from which in Greece and Rome we step directly into civilization.

After a few generations at most, every original family was bound to split up. The practice of living together in a primitive communistic household which prevailed without exception till late in the middle stage of barbarism set a limit, varying with the conditions but fairly definite in each locality, to the maximum size of the family community. As soon as the conception arose that sexual intercourse between children of the same mother was wrong, it was bound to exert its influence when the old households split up and new ones were founded (though these did not necessarily coincide with the family group). One or more lines of sisters would form the nucleus of the one household and their own brothers the nucleus of the other. It must have been in some such manner as this that the form which Morgan calls the punaluan family originated out of the consanguine family. According to the Hawaiian custom, a number of sisters, natural or collateral (first, second or more remote cousins) were the common wives of their common husbands, from among whom, however, their own brothers were excluded. These husbands now no longer called themselves brothers, for they were no longer necessarily brothers, but punalua—that is, intimate companion, or partner. Similarly, a line of natural or collateral brothers had a number of women, *not* their sisters, as common wives, and these wives called one another *punalua*. This was the classic form of family structure [*Familienformation*] in which later a number of variations was possible, but whose essential feature was the mutually common possession of husbands and wives within a definite family circle, from which, however, the brothers of the wives—first one's own and later also collateral—and conversely also the sisters of the husbands, were excluded. . . .

In all forms of group family, it is uncertain who is the father of a child; but it is certain who its mother is. Though she calls *all* the children of the whole family her children and has a mother's duties toward them, she nevertheless knows her own children from the others. It is therefore clear that in so far as group marriage prevails, descent can only be proved on the *mother's* side and that therefore only the *female* line is recognized. And this is in fact the case among all peoples in the period of savagery or in the lower stage of barbarism. . . .

3 THE PAIRING FAMILY

A certain amount of pairing, for a longer or shorter period, already occurred in group marriage or even earlier; the man had a chief wife among his many wives (one can hardly yet speak of a favorite wife), and for her he was the most important among her husbands. This fact has contributed considerably to the confusion of the missionaries, who have regarded group marriage sometimes as promiscuous community of wives, sometimes as unbridled adultery. But these customary pairings were bound to grow more stable as the gens developed and the classes of "brothers" and "sisters" between whom marriage was impossible became more numerous. The impulse given by the gens to the prevention of marriage between blood relatives extended still further. Thus among the Iroquois and most of the other Indians at the lower stage of barbarism, we find that marriage is prohibited between *all* relatives enumerated in their system—which includes several hundred degrees of kinship. The increasing complication of these prohibitions made group marriages more and more impossible; they were displaced by the *pairing family*. In this stage, one man lives with one woman, but the relationship is such that polygamy and occasional infidelity remain the right of the men, even though for economic reasons polygamy is rare, while from the woman the strictest fidelity is generally demanded throughout the time she lives with the man and adultery on her part is cruelly punished. The marriage tie can, however, be easily dissolved by either partner; after separation, the children still belong as before to the mother alone. . . .

Thus the history of the family in primitive times consists in the progressive narrowing of the circle, originally embracing the whole tribe, within which the two sexes have a common conjugal relation. The continuous exclusion, first of nearer, then of more and more remote relatives, and at last even of relatives by marriage, ends by making any kind of group marriage practically impossible. Finally, there remains only the single, still loosely linked pair, the molecule with whose dissolution marriage itself ceases. This in itself shows what a small part individual sex love, in the modern sense of the word, played in the rise of monogamy. Yet stronger proof is afforded by the practice of all peoples at this stage of development. Whereas in the earlier forms of the family, men never lacked women but, on the contrary, had too many rather than too few, women had now become scarce and highly sought after. Hence it is with the pairing marriage that there begins the capture and purchase of women—widespread *symptoms*, but no more than symptoms, of the much deeper change that had occurred. . . .

The pairing family, itself too weak and unstable to make an independent household necessary or even desirable, in no wise destroys the communistic household inherited from earlier times. Communistic housekeeping, however, means the supremacy of women in the house; just as the exclusive recognition of the female parent, owing to the impossibility of recognizing the male parent with certainty, means that the women—the mothers—are held in high respect. One of the most absurd notions taken over from 18th century enlightenment is that in the beginning of society woman was the slave of man. Among all savages and all barbarians of the lower and middle stages, and to a certain extent of the upper stage also, the position of women is not only free, but honorable. As to what it still is in the pairing marriage, let us hear the evidence of Ashur Wright, for many years missionary among the Iroquois Senecas:

> As to their family system, when occupying the old long houses [communistic households comprising several families], it is probable that some one clan [gens] predominated, the women taking in husbands, however, from the other clans [gentes]. . . . Usually, the female portion ruled the house. . . . The stores were in common; but woe to the luckless husband or lover who was too shiftless to do his share of the providing. No matter how many children, or whatever goods he might have in the house, he might at any time be ordered to pick

up his blanket and budge; and after such orders it would not be healthful for him to attempt to disobey. The house would be too hot for him; and . . . he must retreat to his own clan [gens]; or, as was often done, go and start a new matrimonial alliance in some other. The women were the great power among the clans [gentes], as everywhere else. They did not hesitate, when occasion required, "to knock off the horns," as it was technically called, from the head of a chief, and send him back to the ranks of the warriors [Morgan, 1963: 464 *fn*].

The communistic household, in which most or all of the women belong to one and the same gens, while the men come from various gentes, is the material foundation of that supremacy of the women which was general in primitive times, and which it is Bachofen's third great merit to have discovered. The reports of travelers and missionaries, I may add, to the effect that women among savages and barbarians are overburdened with work in no way contradict what has been said. The division of labor between the two sexes is determined by quite other causes than by the position of women in society. Among peoples where the women have to work far harder than we think suitable, there is often much more real respect for women than among our Europeans. The lady of civilization, surrounded by false homage and estranged from all real work, has an infinitely lower social position than the hard-working woman of barbarism, who was regarded among her people as a real lady (lady, *frowa, Frau*—mistress) and who was also a lady in character. . . .

The first beginnings of the pairing family appear on the dividing line between savagery and barbarism; they are generally to be found already at the upper stage of savagery, but occasionally not until the lower stage of barbarism. The pairing family is the form characteristic of barbarism, as group marriage is characteristic of savagery and monogamy of civilization. To develop it further, to strict monogamy, other causes were required than those we have found active hitherto. In the single pair the group was already reduced to its final unit, its two-atom molecule: one man and one woman. Natural selection, with its progressive exclusions from the marriage community, had accomplished its task; there was nothing more for it to do in this direction. Unless new, *social* forces came into play, there was no reason why a new form of family should arise from the single pair. But these new forces did come into play.

We now leave America, the classic soil of the pairing family. No sign allows us to conclude that a higher form of family developed here or that there was ever permanent monogamy anywhere in America prior to its discovery and conquest. But not so in the Old World.

Here the domestication of animals and the breeding of herds had developed a hitherto unsuspected source of wealth and created entirely new social relations. Up to the lower stage of barbarism, permanent wealth had consisted almost solely of house, clothing, crude ornaments and the tools for obtaining and preparing food—boat, weapons, and domestic utensils of the simplest kind. Food had to be won afresh day by day. Now, with their herds of horses, camels, asses, cattle, sheep, goats, and pigs, the advancing pastoral peoples—the Semites on the Euphrates and the Tigris, and the Aryans in the Indian country of the Five Streams (Punjab), in the Ganges region, and in the steppes then much more abundantly watered by the Oxus and the Jaxartes—had acquired property which only needed supervision and the rudest care to reproduce itself in steadily increasing quantities and to supply the most abundant food in the form of milk and meat. All former means of procuring food now receded into the background; hunting, formerly a necessity, now became a luxury.

But to whom did this new wealth belong? Originally to the gens, without a doubt. Private property in herds must have already started at an early period, however. It is difficult to say whether the author of the so-called first book of Moses regarded the patriarch Abraham as the owner of his herds in his own right as head of a family community or by right of his position as actual hereditary head of a gens. What is certain is that we must not think of him as a property owner in the modern sense of the word. And it is also certain that at the threshold of authentic history we already find the herds everywhere separately owned by heads of families, as are the artistic products of barbarism (metal implements, luxury articles and, finally, the human cattle—the slaves).

For now slavery had also been invented. To the barbarian of the lower stage, a slave was valueless. Hence the treatment of defected enemies by the American Indians was quite different from that at a higher stage. The men were killed or adopted as brothers into the tribe of the victors; the women were taken as wives or otherwise adopted with their surviving children. At this stage human labor power still does not produce any considerable surplus over and above its maintenance costs. That was no longer the case after the introduction of cattle breeding, metalworking, weaving, and lastly, agriculture. Just as the wives whom it had formerly been so easy to obtain had now acquired an exchange value and were bought, so also with labor power, particularly since the herds had definitely become family possessions. The family did not multiply so rapidly as the cattle. More people were needed to look after them; for this purpose use could be made of the enemies captured in war, who could also be bred just as easily as the cattle themselves.

Once it had passed into the private possession of families and there rapidly begun to augment, this wealth dealt a severe blow to the society founded on pairing marriage and the matriarchal gens. Pairing marriage had brought a new element into the family. By the side of the natural mother of the child it placed its natural and attested father with a better warrant of paternity, probably, than that of many a "father" today. According to the division of labor within the family at that time, it was the man's part to obtain food and the instruments of labor necessary for the purpose. He therefore also owned the instruments of labor, and in the event of husband and wife separating, he took them with him, just as she retained her household goods. Therefore, according to the social custom of the time, the man was also the owner of the new source of subsistence, the cattle, and later of the new instruments of labor, the slaves. But according to the custom of the same society, his children could not inherit from him. For as regards inheritance, the position was as follows:

At first, according to mother right—so long, therefore, as descent was reckoned only in the female line—and according to the original custom of inheritance within the gens, the gentile relatives inherited from a deceased fellow member of their gens. His property had to remain within the gens. His effects being insignificant, they probably always passed in practice to his nearest gentile relations—that is, to his blood relations on the mother's side. The children of the dead man, however, did not belong to his gens, but to that of their mother; it was from her that they inherited, at first conjointly with her other blood-relations, later perhaps with rights of priority; they could not inherit from their father because they did not belong to his gens within which his property had to remain. When the owner of the herds died, therefore, his herds would go first to his brothers and sisters and to his sister's children, or to the issue of his mother's sisters. But his own children were disinherited.

Thus on the one hand, in proportion as wealth increased it made the man's position in the family more important than the woman's, and on the other hand created an impulse to exploit this strengthened position in order to overthrow, in favor of his children, the traditional order of inheritance. This, however, was impossible so long as descent was reckoned according to mother right. Mother right, therefore, had to be overthrown, and overthrown it was. This was by no means so difficult as it looks to us today. For this revolution—one of the most decisive ever experienced by humanity—could take place without disturbing a single one of the living members of a gens. All could remain as they were. A simple decree sufficed that in the future the offspring of the male members should remain within the gens, but that of the female should be excluded by being transferred to the gens of their father. The reckoning of descent in the female line and the matriarchal law of inheritance were thereby overthrown, and the male line of descent and the paternal law of inheritance were substituted for them. As to how and when this revolution took place among civilized peoples, we have no knowledge. It falls entirely within prehistoric times. But that it *did* take place is more than sufficiently proved by the abundant traces of mother right which have been collected. . . .

The overthrow of mother right was the *world historical defeat of the female sex.* The man took command in the home also; the woman was degraded and reduced to servitude; she became the slave of his lust and a mere instrument for the production of children. This degraded position of the woman, especially conspicuous among the Greeks of the heroic and still more of the classical age, has gradually been palliated and glossed over, and sometimes clothed in a milder form; in no sense has it been abolished.

The establishment of the exclusive supremacy of the man shows its effects first in the patriarchal family, which now emerges as an intermediate form. Its essential characteristic is not polygyny, of which more later, but "the organization of a number of persons, bond and free, into a family under paternal power for the purpose of holding lands and for the care of flocks and herds. . . . (In the Semitic form) the chiefs, at least, lived in polygamy. . . . Those held to servitude and those employed as servants lived in the marriage relation" [Morgan, 1963: 474].

Its essential features are the incorporation of unfree persons and paternal power; hence the perfect type of this form of family is the Roman. The original meaning of the word "family" (*familia*) is not that compound of sentimentality and domestic strife which forms the ideal of the present-day philistine; among the Romans it did not at first even refer to the married pair and their children but only to the slaves. *Famulus* means domestic slave, and *familia* is the total number of slaves belonging to one man. As late as the time of Gaius, the *familia, id est patrimonium* (family, that is, the patrimony, the inheritance) was bequeathed by will. The term was invented by the Romans to denote a new social organism whose head ruled over wife and children and a number of slaves, and was invested under Roman paternal power with rights of life and death over them all.

This term, therefore, is no older than the ironclad family system of the Latin tribes, which came in after field agriculture and after legalized servitude, as well as after the separation of the Greeks and Latins [Morgan, 1963: 478].

Marx adds:

The modern family contains in germ not only slavery (*servitus*) but also serfdom, since from the beginning it is related to agricultural services. It contains *in miniature* all the contradictions which later extend throughout society and its state.

Such a form of family shows the transition of the pairing family to monogamy. In order to make certain of the wife's fidelity and therefore of the paternity of the children, she is delivered over unconditionally into the power of the husband; if he kills her, he is only exercising his rights. . . .

4   THE MONOGAMOUS FAMILY

It develops out of the pairing family, as previously shown, in the transitional period between the upper and middle stages of barbarism; its decisive victory is one of the signs that civilization is beginning. It is based on the supremacy of the man, the express purpose being to produce children of undisputed paternity; such paternity is demanded because these children are later to come into their father's property as his natural heirs. It is distinguished from pairing marriage by the much greater strength of the marriage tie, which can no longer be dissolved at either partner's wish. As a rule, it is now only the man who can dissolve it and put away his wife. The right of conjugal infidelity also remains secured in him, at any rate by custom (the *Code Napoleon* explicitly accords it to the husband as long as he does not bring his concubine into the house), and as social life develops he exercises his right more and more; should the wife recall the old form of sexual life and attempt to revive it, she is punished more severely than ever.

. . . It is the existence of slavery side by side with monogamy, the presence of young, beautiful slaves belonging unreservedly to the *man,* that stamps monogamy from the very beginning with its specific character of monogamy *for the woman only,* but not for the man. And that is the character it still has today. . . .

This is the origin of monogamy as far as we can trace it back among the most civilized and highly developed people of antiquity. It was not in any way the fruit of individual sex love, with which it had nothing whatever to do; marriages remained as before marriages of convenience. It was the first form of the family to be based not on natural but on economic conditions—on the victory of private property over primitive, natural communal property. The Greeks themselves put the matter quite frankly; the sole exclusive aims of monogamous marriage were to make the man supreme in the family and to propagate, as the future heirs to his wealth, children indisputably his own. Otherwise, marriage was a burden, a duty which had to be performed whether one liked it or not to gods, state, and one's ancestors. In Athens the law exacted from the man not only marriage but also the performance of a minimum of so-called conjugal duties.

Thus when monogamous marriage first makes its appearance in history, it is not as the reconciliation of man and woman, still less as the highest form of such a reconciliation. Quite the contrary monogamous marriage comes on the scene as the subjugation of the one sex by the other; it announces a struggle between the sexes unknown throughout the whole previous prehistoric period. In an old unpublished manuscript written by Marx and myself in 1846, I find the words: "The first division of labor is that between man and woman for the propagation of children." And today I can add: The first class opposition that appears in history coincides with the development of the antagonism between man and woman in monogamous marriage, and the first class oppression coincides with that of the female sex by the male. Monogamous marriage was a great historical step forward; nevertheless, together with slavery and private wealth, it opens the period that has lasted until today in which every step forward is also relatively a step backward, in which prosperity and development for some is won through the misery and frustration of others. It is the cellular form of civilized society in which the nature of the oppositions and contradictions fully active in that society can be already studied. . . .

. . . With the rise of the inequality of property—already at the upper stage of barbarism, therefore—wage labor appears sporadically side by side with slave labor, and at the same time, as its necessary correlate, the professional prostitution of free women side by side with the forced surrender of the slave. Thus the heritage which group marriage has bequeathed to civilization is double-edged, just as everything civilization brings forth is double-edged, double-tongued, divided against itself, contradictory: here monogamy, there hetaerism with its most extreme form, prostitution. For hetaerism is as much a social institution as any other; it continues the old sexual freedom—to the advantage of the men. Actually, not merely tolerated but gaily practiced by the ruling classes particularly, it is condemned in words. But in reality this condemnation never falls on the men concerned, but only on the women; they are despised and outcast in order that the unconditional supremacy of men over the female sex may be once more proclaimed as a fundamental law of society. . . .

Thus, wherever the monogamous family remains true to its historical origin and clearly reveals the antagonism between the man and the woman expressed in the man's exclusive supremacy, it exhibits in miniature the same oppositions and contradictions as those in which society has been moving, without power to resolve or overcome them, ever since it split into classes at the beginning of civilization. . . .

Our jurists, of course, find that progress in legislation is leaving women with no further ground of complaint. Modern civilized systems of law increasingly acknowledge first, that for a marriage to be legal it must be a contract freely entered into by both partners and secondly, that also in the married state both partners must stand on a common footing of equal rights and duties. If both these demands are consistently carried out, say the jurists, women have all they can ask.

This typically legalist method of argument is exactly the same as that which the radical republican bourgeois uses to put the proletarian in his place. The labor contract is to be freely entered into by both partners. But it is considered to have been freely entered into as soon as the law makes both parties equal on *paper*. The power conferred on the one party by the difference of class position, the pressure thereby brought to bear on the other party—the real economic position of both—that is not the law's business. Again, for the duration of the labor contract, both parties are to have equal rights in so far as one or the other does not expressly surrender them. That economic relations compel the worker to surrender even the last semblance of equal rights—here again, that is no concern of the law.

In regard to marriage, the law, even the most advanced, is fully satisfied as soon as the partners have formally recorded that they are entering into the marriage of their own free consent. What goes on in real life behind the juridical scenes, how this free consent comes about—that is not the business of the law and the jurist. And yet the most elementary comparative jurisprudence should show the jurist what this free consent really amounts to. In the countries where an obligatory share of the paternal inheritance is secured to the children by law and they cannot therefore be disinherited—in Germany, in the countries with French law and elsewhere—the children are obliged to obtain their parents' consent to their marriage. In the countries with English law, where parental consent to a marriage is not legally required, the parents on their side have full freedom in the testamentary disposal of their property and can disinherit their children at their pleasure. It is obvious that in spite and precisely because of this fact freedom of marriage among the classes with something to inherit is in reality not a whit greater in England and America than it is in France and Germany.

As regards the legal equality of husband and wife in marriage, the position is no better. The legal inequality of the two partners bequeathed to us from earlier social conditions is not the cause but the effect of the economic oppression of the woman. In the old communistic household, which comprised many couples and their children, the task entrusted to the women of managing the household was as much a public, a socially necessary industry as the procuring of food by the men. With the patriarchal family and still more with the single monogamous family, a change came. Household management lost its public character. It no longer concerned society. It became a *private service;* the wife became the head servant, excluded from all participation in social production. Not until the coming of modern large-scale industry was the road to social production opened to her again—and then only to the proletarian wife. But it was opened in such a manner that, if she carries out her duties in the private service of her family, she remains excluded from public production and unable to earn; and if she wants to take part in public production and earn independently, she cannot carry out family duties. And the wife's position in the factory is the position of women in all branches of business, right up to medicine and the law. The modern individual family is founded on the open or concealed domestic slavery of the wife, and modern society is a mass composed of these individual families as its molecules.

In the great majority of cases today, at least in the possessing classes, the husband is obliged to earn a living and support his family, and that in itself gives him a position of supremacy without any need for special legal titles and privileges. Within the family he is the bourgeois, and the wife represents the proletariat. In the industrial world, the specific character of the economic oppression burdening the proletariat is visible in all its sharpness only when all special legal privileges of the capitalist class have been abolished and complete legal equality of both classes established. The democratic republic does not do away with the oppression of the two classes; on the contrary, it provides the clear field on which the fight can be fought out. And in the same way, the peculiar character of the supremacy of the husband over the wife in the modern family, the necessity of creating real social equality between them and the way to do it, will only be seen in the clear light of day when both possess legally complete equality of rights. Then it will be plain that the first condition for the liberation of the wife is to bring the whole female sex back into public industry, and that this in turn demands that the characteristic of the monogamous family as the economic unit of society be abolished.

Women: Caste, Class, or Oppressed Sex?

Evelyn Reed

The new stage in the struggle for women's liberation already stands on a higher ideological level than did the feminist movement of the last century. Many of the participants today respect the Marxist analysis of capitalism and subscribe to Engels's classic explanation of the origins of women's oppression. It came about through the development of class society, founded upon the family, private property, and the state.

But there still remain considerable misunderstandings and misinterpretations of Marxist positions, which have led some women who consider themselves radicals or socialists to go off course and become theoretically disoriented. Influenced by the myth that women have always been handicapped by their childbearing functions, they tend to attribute the roots of women's oppression, at least in part, to biological sexual differences. In actuality its causes are exclusively historical and social in character.

Some of these theorists maintain that women constitute a special class or caste. Such definitions are not only alien to the views of Marxism but lead to the false conclusion that it is not the capitalist system but men who are the prime enemy of women. I propose to challenge this contention. The findings of the Marxist method, which have laid the groundwork for explaining the genesis of women's degradation, can be summed up in the following propositions:

First, women were not always the oppressed or "second" sex. Anthropology, or the study of prehistory, tells us the contrary. Throughout primitive society, which was the epoch of tribal collectivism, women were the equals of men and recognized by man as such.

Second, the downfall of women coincided with the breakup of the matriarchal clan commune and its replacement by class-divided society with its institutions of the patriarchal family, private property and state power.

The key factors which brought about this reversal in woman's social status came out of the transition from a hunting and food-gathering economy to a far higher mode of production based upon agriculture, stock raising and urban crafts. The primitive division of labor between the sexes was replaced by a more complex social division of labor. The greater efficiency of labor gave rise to a sizable surplus product, which led first to differentiations and then to deepgoing divisions among the various segments of society.

By virtue of the directing roles played by men in large-scale agriculture, irrigation and construction projects, as well as in stock raising, this surplus wealth was gradually appropriated by a hierarchy of men as their private property. This, in turn, required the institution of marriage and the family to fix the legal ownership and inheritance of a man's property. Through monogamous marriage the wife was brought under the complete control of her husband who was thereby assured of legitimate sons to inherit his wealth.

As men took over most of the activities of social production, and with the rise of the family institution, women became relegated to the home to serve their husbands and families. The state apparatus came into existence to fortify and legalize the institutions of private property, male dominion and the father-family, which later were sanctified by religion.

This, briefly, is the Marxist approach to the origins of woman's oppression. Her subordination did not come about through any biological deficiency as a sex. It was the result of the revolutionary social changes which destroyed the equalitarian society of the matriarchal gens or clan and replaced it with a patriarchal class society which, from its birth, was stamped with discriminations and inequalities of many kinds, including the inequality of the sexes. The growth of this inherently oppressive type of socioeconomic organization was responsible for the historic downfall of women.

But the downfall of women cannot be fully understood, nor can a correct social and political solution be worked out for their liberation, without seeing what happened at the same time to men. It is too often overlooked that the patriarchal class system which crushed the matriarchy and its communal social relations also shattered its male counterpart, the fratriarchy—or tribal brotherhood of men. Woman's overthrow went hand in hand with the subjugation of the mass of toiling men to the master class of men.

Speaking in a loose and popular way, it is possible to refer to women as an inferior "caste"—as is sometimes done when they are also called "slaves" or "serfs"—when the intent is merely to indicate that they occupy the subordinate position in male-dominated society. The use of the term "caste" would then only expose the impoverishment of our language, which has no special word to indicate womankind as the oppressed sex. But more than this seems to be involved, if we judge from the paper by Roxanne Dunbar dated February 1970 which supersedes her previous positions on this question.

In that document she says that her characterization of women as an exploited caste is nothing new; that Marx and Engels likewise "analyzed the position of the female sex in just such a way." This is simply not the case. Neither Marx in *Capital,* nor Engels in *The Origin of the Family, Private Property, and the State,* nor in any writings by noted Marxists from Lenin to Luxemburg on this matter, has woman been defined by virtue of her sex as a "caste." Therefore this is not a mere verbal squabble over the misuse of a term. It is a distinct departure from Marxism, although presented in the name of Marxism.

I would like clarification from Roxanne Dunbar on the conclusions she draws from her theory. For, if all women belong to an inferior caste, and all men belong to the superior caste, it would consistently follow that the central axis of a struggle for liberation would be a "caste war" of all women against all men to bring about the liberation of women. This conclusion would seem to be confirmed by her statement that "we live under an international caste system. . . ."

This assertion is equally non-Marxist. What Marxists say is that we live under an international *class* system. And they further state that it will require not a caste war, but a *class struggle*—of all the oppressed, male and female alike—to consummate women's liberation along with the liberation of all the oppressed masses. Does Roxanne Dunbar agree or disagree with this viewpoint on the paramount role of the class struggle?

Her confusion points up the necessity for using precise language in a scientific exposition. However downtrodden women are under capitalism, they are not chattel slaves any more than they are feudal serfs or members of an inferior caste. The social categories of slave, serf and caste refer to stages and features of past history and do not correctly define the position of women in our society.

If we are to be precise and scientific, women should be defined as an "oppressed *sex*."

Turning to the other position, it is even more incorrect to characterize women as a special "class." In Marxist sociology a class is defined in two interrelated ways: by the role it plays in the processes of production and by the stake it has in the ownership of property. Thus the capitalists are the major power in our society because they own the means of production and thereby control the state and direct the economy. The wage workers who create the wealth own nothing but their labor power, which they have to sell to the bosses to stay alive.

Where do women stand in relation to these polar class forces? They belong to all strata of the social pyramid. The few at the top are part of the plutocratic class; more among us belong to the middle class; most of us belong to the proletarian layers of the population. There is an enormous spread from the few wealthy women of the Rockefeller, Morgan and Ford families to the millions of poor women who subsist on welfare dole. *In short, women, like men, are a multiclass sex.*

This is not an attempt to divide women from one another but simply to recognize the actual divisions that exist. The notion that all women as a sex have more in common than do members of the same class with one another is false. Upper-class women are not simply bedmates of their wealthy husbands. As a rule they have more compelling ties which bind them together. They are economic, social and political bedmates, united in defense of private property, profiteering, militarism, racism—and the exploitation of other women.

To be sure, there can be individual exceptions to this rule, especially among young women today. We remember that Mrs. Frank Leslie, for example, left a $2 million bequest to further the cause of women's suffrage, and other upper-class women have devoted their means to secure civil rights for our sex. But it is quite another matter to expect any large number of wealthy women to endorse or support a revolutionary struggle which threatens their capitalist interests and privileges. Most of them scorn the liberation movement, saying openly or implicitly, "What do we need to be liberated from?"

Is it really necessary to stress this point? Tens of thousands of women went to the Washington antiwar demonstrations in November 1969 and again in May 1970. Did they have more in common with the militant men marching beside them on that life-and-death issue—or with Mrs. Nixon, her daughters, and the wife of the attorney general, Mrs. Mitchell, who peered uneasily out of her window and saw the specter of another Russian Revolution in those protesting masses? Will the wives of bankers, generals, corporation lawyers, and big industrialists be firmer allies of women fighting for liberation than working-class men, black and white, who are fighting for theirs? Won't there be both men and women on both sides of the class struggle? If not, is the struggle to be directed against men as a sex rather than against the capitalist system?

It is true that all forms of class society have been male-dominated and that men are trained from the cradle on to be chauvinistic. But it is not true that men as such represent the main enemy of women. This crosses out the multitudes of downtrodden, exploited men who are themselves oppressed by the main enemy of women, which is the capitalist system. These men likewise have a stake in the liberation struggle of the women; they can and will become our allies.

Although the struggle against male chauvinism is an essential part of the tasks that women must carry out through their liberation movement, it is incorrect to make that the central issue. This tends to conceal or overlook the role of the ruling powers who not only breed and benefit from all forms of discrimination and oppression but are also responsible for breeding and sustaining male chauvinism. Let us remember that male supremacy did not exist in the primitive commune, founded upon sisterhood and brotherhood. Sexism, like racism, has its roots in the private property system.

A false theoretical position easily leads to a false strategy in the struggle for women's liberation. Such is the case with a segment of the Redstockings who state in their *Manifesto* that "women are an oppressed *class*." If all women compose a class then all men must form a counterclass—the oppressor class. What conclusion flows from this premise? That there are no men in the oppressed class? Where does this leave the millions of oppressed white working men who, like the oppressed blacks, Chicanos and other minorities, are exploited by the monopolists? Don't they have a central place in the struggle for social revolution? At what point and under what banner do these oppressed peoples of all races and both sexes join together for common action against their common enemy? To oppose women as a class against men as a class can only result in a diversion of the real class struggle.

Isn't there a suggestion of this same line in Roxanne Dunbar's assertion that female liberation is the basis for social revolution? This is far from Marxist strategy since it turns the real situation on its head. Marxists say that social revolution is the basis for full female liberation—just as it is the basis for the liberation of the whole working class. In the last analysis the real allies of women's liberation are all those forces which are impelled for their own reasons to struggle against and throw off the shackles of the imperialist masters.

The underlying source of women's oppression, which is capitalism, cannot be abolished by women alone, nor by a coalition of women drawn from all classes. It will require a worldwide struggle for socialism by the working masses, female and male alike, together with every other section of the oppressed, to overthrow the power of capitalism, which is centered today in the United States. . . .

Women's Subordination Through the Lens of Sex/Gender and Sexuality: Radical Feminism

Lesbians in Revolt

Charlotte Bunch

The development of Lesbian-Feminist politics as the basis for the liberation of women is our top priority: this article outlines our present ideas. In our society which defines all people and institutions for the benefit of the rich, white male, the Lesbian is in revolt. In revolt because she defines herself in terms of women and rejects the male definitions of how she should feel, act, look, and live. To be a Lesbian is to love oneself, woman, in a culture that denigrates and despises women. The Lesbian rejects male sexual/political domination; she defies his world, his social organization, his ideology, and his definition of her as inferior. Lesbianism puts women first while the society declares the male supreme. Lesbianism threatens male supremacy at its core. When politically conscious and organized, it is central to destroying our sexist, racist, capitalist, imperialist system.

Male society defines Lesbianism as a sexual act, which reflects men's limited view of women: they think of us only in terms of sex. They also say Lesbians are not real women, so a real woman is one who gets fucked by men. We say that a Lesbian is a woman whose sense of self and energies, including sexual energies, center around women—she is woman identified. The woman-identified-woman commits herself to other women for political, emotional, physical, and economic support. Women are important to her. She is important to herself. Our society demands that commitment from women be reserved for men.

The Lesbian, woman-identified-woman, commits herself to women not only as an alternative to oppressive male/female relationships but primarily because she *loves* women. Whether consciously or not, by her actions, the Lesbian has recognized that giving support and love to men over women perpetuates the system that oppresses her. If women do not make a commitment to each other, which includes sexual love, we deny ourselves the love and value traditionally given to men. We accept our second class status. When women do give primary energies to other women, then it is possible to concentrate fully on building a movement for our liberation.

Woman-identified Lesbianism is, then, more than a sexual preference, it is a political choice. It is political because relationships between men and women are essentially political, they involve power and dominance. Since the Lesbian actively rejects that relationship and chooses women, she defies the established political system.

Of course, not all Lesbians are consciously woman-identified, nor are all committed to finding common solutions to the oppression they suffer as women and Lesbians. Being a Lesbian is part of challenging male supremacy, but not the end. For the Lesbian or heterosexual woman, there is no individual solution to oppression.

The Lesbian may think that she is free since she escapes the personal oppression of the individual male/female relationship. But to the society she is still a woman, or worse, a visible Lesbian. On the street, at the job, in the schools, she is treated as an inferior and is at the mercy of men's power and whims. (I've never heard of a rapist who stopped because his victim was a Lesbian.) This society hates women who love women, and so, the Lesbian, who escapes male dominance in her private home, receives it doubly at the hands of male society; she is harassed, outcast, and shuttled to the bottom. Lesbians must become feminists and fight against woman oppression, just as feminists must become Lesbians if they hope to end male supremacy.

U.S. society encourages individual solutions, apolitical attitudes, and reformism to keep us from political revolt and out of power. Men who rule, and male leftists who seek to rule, try to depoliticize sex and the relations between men and women in order to prevent us from acting to end our oppression and challenging their power. As the question of homosexuality has become public, reformists define it as a private question of who you sleep with in order to sidetrack our understanding of the politics of sex. For the Lesbian-Feminist, it is not private; it is a political matter of oppression, domination, and power. Reformists offer solutions which make no basic changes in the system that oppresses us, solutions which keep power in the hands of the oppressor. The only way oppressed people end their oppression is by seizing power: People whose rule depends on the subordination of others do not voluntarily stop oppressing others. Our subordination is the basis of male power.

SEXISM IS THE ROOT OF ALL OPPRESSION

The first division of labor, in pre-history, was based on sex: men hunted, women built the villages, took care of children, and farmed. Women collectively controlled the land, language, culture, and the communities. Men were able to conquer women with the weapons that they developed for hunting when it became clear that women were leading a more stable, peaceful, and desirable existence. We do not know exactly how this conquest took place, but it is clear that the original imperialism was male over female: the male claiming the female body and her service as his territory (or property).

Having secured the domination of women, men continued this pattern of suppressing people, now on the basis of tribe, race, and class. Although there have been numerous battles over class, race, and nation during the past 3000 years, none has brought the liberation of women. While these other forms of oppression must be ended, there is no reason to believe that our liberation will come with the smashing of capitalism, racism, or imperialism today. Women will be free only when we concentrate on fighting male supremacy.

Our war against male supremacy does, however, involve attacking the latter day dominations based on class, race, and nation. As Lesbians who are outcasts from every group, it would be suicidal to perpetuate these man-made divisions among ourselves. We have no heterosexual privileges, and when we publicly assert our Lesbianism, those of us who had them lose many of our class and race privileges. Most of our privileges as women are granted to us by our relationships to men (fathers, husbands, boyfriends) whom we now reject. This does not mean that there is no racism or class chauvinism within us, but we must destroy these divisive remnants of privileged behavior among ourselves as the first step toward their destruction in the society. Race, class, and national oppressions come from men, serve ruling class white men's interests, and have no place in a woman-identified revolution.

LESBIANISM IS THE BASIC THREAT TO MALE SUPREMACY

Lesbianism is a threat to the ideological, political, and economic basis of male supremacy. The Lesbian threatens the ideology of male supremacy by destroying the lie about female inferiority, weakness, passivity, and by denying women's "innate" need for men. Lesbians literally do not need men (even for procreation if the science of cloning is developed).

The Lesbian's independence and refusal to support one man undermines the personal power that men exercise over women. Our rejection of heterosexual sex challenges male domination in its most individual and common form. We offer all women something better than submission to personal oppression. We offer the beginning of the end of collective and individual male supremacy. Since men of all races and classes depend on female support and submission for practical tasks and feeling superior, our refusal to submit will force some to examine their sexist behavior, to break down their own destructive privileges over other humans, and to fight against those privileges in other men. They will have to build new selves that do not depend on oppressing women and learn to live in social structures that do not give them power over anyone.

Heterosexuality separates women from each other; it makes women define themselves through men; it forces women to compete against each other for men and the privilege which comes through men and their social standing. Heterosexual society offers women a few privileges as compensation if they give up their freedom: for example, mothers are respected and "honored," wives or lovers are socially accepted and given some economic and emotional security, a woman gets physical protection on the street when she stays with her man, etc. The privileges give heterosexual women a personal and political stake in maintaining the status quo.

The Lesbian receives none of these heterosexual privileges or compensations since she does not accept the male demands on her. She has little vested interest in maintaining the present political system since all of its institutions—church, state, media, health, schools—work to keep her down. If she understands her oppression, she has nothing to gain by supporting white rich male America and much to gain from fighting to change it. She is less prone to accept reformist solutions to women's oppression.

Economics is a crucial part of woman oppression, but our analysis of the relationship between capitalism and sexism is not complete. We know that Marxist economic theory does not sufficiently consider the role of women or Lesbians, and we are presently working on this area.

However, as a beginning, some of the ways that Lesbians threaten the economic system are clear: In this country, women work for men in order to survive, on the job and in the home. The Lesbian rejects this division of labor at its roots; she refuses to be a man's property, to submit to the unpaid labor system of housework and childcare. She rejects the nuclear family as the basic unit of production and consumption in capitalist society.

The Lesbian is also a threat on the job because she is not the passive/part-time woman worker that capitalism counts on to do boring work and be part of a surplus labor pool. Her identity and economic support do not come through men, so her job is crucial and she cares about job conditions, wages, promotion, and status. Capitalism cannot absorb large numbers of women demanding stable employment, decent salaries, and refusing to accept their traditional job exploitation. We do not understand yet the total effect that this increased job dissatisfaction will have. It is, however, clear that as women become more intent upon taking control of their lives, they will seek more control over their jobs, thus increasing the strains on capitalism and enhancing the power of women to change the economic system.

LESBIANS MUST FORM OUR OWN MOVEMENT TO FIGHT MALE SUPREMACY

Feminist-Lesbianism, as the most basic threat to male supremacy, picks up part of the Women's Liberation analysis of sexism and gives it force and direction. Women's Liberation lacks direction now because it has failed to understand the importance of heterosexuality in maintaining male supremacy and because it has failed to face class and race as real differences in women's behavior and political needs. As long as straight women see Lesbianism as a bedroom issue, they hold back the development of politics and strategies which would put an end to male supremacy and they give men an excuse for not dealing with their sexism.

Being a Lesbian means ending identification with, allegiance to, dependence on, and support of heterosexuality. It means ending your personal stake in the male world so that you join women, individually and collectively, in the struggle to end your oppression. Lesbianism is the key to liberation and only women who cut their ties to male privilege can be trusted to remain serious in the struggle against male dominance. Those who remain tied to men, individually or in political theory, cannot always put women first. It is not that heterosexual women are evil or do not care about women. It is because the very essence, definition, and nature of heterosexuality is men first. Every woman has experienced that desolation when her sister puts her man first in the final crunch: heterosexuality demands that she do so. As long as women still benefit from heterosexuality, receive its privileges and security, they will at some point have to betray their sisters, especially Lesbian sisters who do not receive those benefits.

Women in women's liberation have understood the importance of having meetings and other events for women only. It has been clear that dealing with men divides us and saps our energies and that it is not the job of the oppressed to explain our oppression to the oppressor. Women also have seen that collectively, men will not deal with their sexism until they are forced to do so. Yet, many of these same women continue to have primary relationships with men individually and do not understand why Lesbians find this oppressive. Lesbians cannot grow politically or personally in a situation which denies the basis of our politics: that Lesbianism is political, that heterosexuality is crucial to maintaining male supremacy.

Lesbians must form our own political movement in order to grow. Changes which will have more than token effects on our lives will be led by woman-identified Lesbians who understand the nature of our oppression and are therefore in a position to end it.

One Is Not Born a Woman

Monique Wittig

A materialist feminist approach to women's oppression destroys the idea that women are a "natural group": "a social group of a special kind, a group perceived *as natural,* a group of men considered as materially specific in their bodies." A lesbian society destroys the artificial (social) fact constituting women as a "natural group." A lesbian society pragmatically reveals that the division from men of which women have been the object is a political one and shows how we have been ideologically re-built into a "natural group." In our case, ideology goes far since our bodies as well as our minds are the product of this manipulation. We have been compelled in our bodies and in our minds to correspond, feature by feature, with the *idea* of nature that has been established for us. Distorted to such an extent that our deformed body is what they call "natural," is what is supposed to exist as such before oppression. Distorted to such an extent that at the end oppression seems to be a consequence of this "nature" in ourselves (a nature which is only an *idea*). What a materialist analysis does by reasoning, a lesbian society accomplishes in fact: not only is there no natural group "women" (we lesbians are a living proof of it) but as individuals as well we question "woman," which for us, as for Simone de Beauvoir thirty years ago, is only a myth. She said: "One is not born, but becomes a woman. No biological, psychological, or economic fate determines the figure that the human female presents in society; it is civilization as a whole that produces this creature, intermediate between male and eunuch, which is described as feminine."

However, most of the feminists and lesbian-feminists in America and elsewhere still believe that the basis of women's oppression *is biological as well as* historical. Some of them even claim to find their sources in Simone de Beauvoir. The belief in mother-right and in a "prehistory" when women would have created civilization (because of a biological predisposition), while the coarse and brutal men would have hunted (because of a biological predisposition), does not make the biological approach any better. It is still the same method of finding in women and men a biological explanation of their division, outside of social facts. For me this could never constitute a lesbian approach since it assumes that the basis of society or the beginning of society lies in heterosexuality. Matriarchies are no less heterosexual than patriarchies: it's only the sex of the oppressor that changes. Furthermore, not only is this conception still a prisoner of the categories of sex (woman and man), but it keeps to the idea that the capacity to give birth (biology) is what defines a woman. Although practical facts and ways of living contradict this theory in lesbian society, there are lesbians who affirm that "women and men are different species or races (the words are used interchangeably); men are biologically inferior to women; male violence is a biological inevitability . . ." By doing this, by admitting that there is a "natural" division between women and men, we naturalize history, we assume that men and women have always existed and will always exist. Not only do we naturalize history, but also consequently we naturalize the social phenomena which express our oppression, making change impossible. For example, instead of seeing giving birth as a forced production, we see it as a "natural," "biological" process, forgetting that in our societies births are planned (demography), forgetting that we ourselves are programmed to produce children, while this is the only social activity "short of war" that presents such a great danger of death. Thus, as long as we will be "unable to abandon by will or impulse a lifelong and centuries old commitment to childbearing as *the* female creative act," having control of the production of children will mean much more than the mere control of the material means of this production. Women will have to abstract themselves from the definition "woman" which is imposed upon them.

A materialist feminist approach shows that what we take for the cause or origin of oppression is in fact only the *mark* imposed by the oppressor: the "myth of woman," plus its material effects and manifestations in the appropriated consciousnesses and bodies of women. Thus, the mark does not preexist oppression. Colette Guillaumin, a French sociologist, has shown that before the socio-economical reality of black slavery, the concept of race did not exist (at least not in its modern meaning: it was applied to the lineage of families). However, now, race, exactly like sex, is taken as an "immediate given," a "sensible given," "physical features." They appear as though they existed prior to reasoning, belonging to a natural order. But what we believe to be a physical and direct perception is only a sophisticated and mythic construction, an "imaginary formation" which reinterprets physical features through the network of relationships in which they are perceived. (They are seen *black,* therefore they *are* black; they are seen *women,* therefore they *are* women. But before being *seen* that way, they first had to be *made* that way.) A lesbian consciousness should always remember how "unnatural," compelling, totally oppressive, and destructive being "woman" was for us in the old days before the women's liberation movement. It was a political obligation and those who resisted it were accused of not being "real" women. But then we were proud of it, since in the accusation there was already something like a shadow of victory: the avowal by the oppressor that "woman" is not something that goes without saying, since to be one, one has to be a "real" one (what about the others?). We were also confronted by the accusation of wanting to be men. We still are by certain lesbians and feminists who believe that one has to become more and more of a woman as a political obligation. But to refuse to be a woman does not mean that one has to become a man. And for her who does want to become a man: in what way is her alienation different from wanting to become a woman? At least for a woman, wanting to become a man proves that she escaped her initial programming. But even if she wants to, she cannot become a man. For becoming a man would demand from a woman having not only the outside appearance of a man but his consciousness as well, that is, the consciousness of one who disposes by right of at least two natural "slaves" during his life span. This is impossible since precisely one feature of lesbian oppression consists of making women out of reach for us, since women belong to men. Thus a lesbian *has to* be something else, not-woman, not-man, a product of society not a product of "nature," for there is no "nature" in society.

The refusal to become heterosexual always meant to refuse to become a man or a woman, consciously or not. For a lesbian this goes further than the refusal of the role "woman." It is the refusal of the economic, ideological and political power of a man. This, we lesbians, and non-lesbians as well, have experienced before the beginning of the lesbian and feminist movement. However, as Andrea Dworkin emphasizes, many lesbians recently "have increasingly tried to transform the very ideology that has enslaved us into a dynamic, religious, psychologically compelling celebration of female biological potential." Thus, some avenues of the feminist and lesbian movement lead us back to the myth of woman which was created by men especially for us, and with it we sink back into a natural group. Thirty years ago Simone de Beauvoir destroyed the myth of woman. Ten years ago we stood up to fight for a sexless society. Now we find ourselves entrapped in the familiar deadlock of "woman is wonderful." Thirty years ago Simone de Beauvoir underlined particularly the false consciousness which consists of selecting among the features of the myth (that women are different from men) those which look good and using them as a definition for women. What the concept of "woman is wonderful" accomplishes is that it retains for defining women the best features which oppression has granted us and it does not radically question the categories "man" and "woman." It puts us in a position of fighting within the class "women" not as the other classes do, for the disappearance of our class, but for the defense of "woman" and its reinforcement. It leads us to develop with complacency "new" theories about our specificity: thus, we call our passivity "non-violence." The ambiguity of the term "feminist" sums up the whole situation. What does "feminist" mean? Feminist is formed with the word "femme," "woman," and means "someone who fights for women." For many of us it means "someone who fights for women as a class and for the disappearance of this class." For many others it means "someone who fights for woman and her defense"—for the myth then and its reinforcement. But why was the word "feminist" chosen? We chose to call ourselves "feminists" ten years ago, not in order to identify ourselves with the oppressor's definition of us, but rather to affirm that our movement had a history and to emphasize the political link with the old feminist movement.

It is, then, this movement that we can question for its meaning of "feminism." It so happens that feminism in the last century could never resolve its contradictions on the subject of nature/culture, woman/society. Women started to fight for themselves as a group and rightly considered that they shared common features. But for them these features were natural and biological rather than social. They went so far as to adopt pseudo-Darwinist theories of evolution. They did not believe like Darwin, however, "that women were less evolved than men, but they did believe that male and female natures had diverged in the course of evolutionary development and that society at large reflected this polarization . . . The failure of early feminism was that it only attacked the Darwinist charge of female inferiority, while accepting the foundations of this charge—namely, the view of woman as 'unique.'" And finally it was women scholars—and not feminists—who scientifically destroyed this theory. But the early feminists had failed to regard history as a dynamic process which develops from conflicts of interests. Furthermore, they still believed that the cause (origin) of their oppression lay within themselves (among black people only the Uncle Toms believed this). And therefore feminists, after some astonishing victories, found themselves at an impasse for lack of reasons for fighting. They upheld the illogical principle of "equality in difference," an idea now being born again. They fell back into the trap which threatens us once again: the myth of woman.

Thus it remains historically for us to define our oppression in materialist terms, to say that women are a class, which is to say that the category "woman," as well as "man," is a political and economic category, not an eternal one. Our fight aims to suppress men as a class, not through a genocidal, but a political struggle. Once the class "men" disappears, women as a class will disappear as well, for there are no slaves without masters. Our first task, it seems, is to always thoroughly disassociate "women" (the class within which we fight) and "woman," the myth. For "woman" does not exist for us: it is only an imaginary formation, while "women" is the product of a social relationship. Furthermore we have to destroy the myth within and outside ourselves. "Woman" is not each one of us, but the political and ideological formation which negates "women" (the product of a relation of exploitation). "Woman" is there to confuse us, to hide the reality of "women." In order to become a class and to be aware of it, we have first to kill the myth "woman" even in its most seductive aspects. . . .

To destroy "woman" does not mean to destroy lesbianism, for a lesbian is not a woman and does not love a woman, given that we agree with Christine Delphy that what "makes" woman is a personal dependency on a man (as opposed to an impersonal dependency on a boss). Lesbian is the only concept that I know of which is beyond the categories of sex (woman and man), because lesbian societies are not based upon women's oppression and because the designated subject (lesbian) is *not* a woman either economically or politically or ideologically. Furthermore, what we aim at is not the disappearance of lesbianism, which provides the only social form that we can live in, but the destruction of heterosexuality—the political system based on women's oppression, which produces the body of thought of the difference between the sexes to explain women's oppression.

Beyond or within this class consciousness, this science/experience, while in the separateness of one's ego, do we still have to fight to exist as an autonomous entity? There is no doubt that we have to fight for this entity, since we are left with nothing, once we reject the basic determination "woman" and "man," once we have no more attributes by which to identify ourselves (I am this or that). We are for the first time in history confronted with the necessity of existing as a person.

Sex Equality: Difference and Dominance
Catharine MacKinnon

There is one thing of which one can say neither that it is one meter long nor that it is not one meter long, and that is the standard meter in Paris.

Ludwig Wittgenstein

The measure of man is man.

Pythagoras

[Men] think themselves superior to women, but they mingle that with the notion of equality between men and women. It's very odd.

Jean-Paul Sartre

Inequality because of sex defines and situates women as women. If the sexes were equal, women would not be sexually subjected. Sexual force would be exceptional, consent to sex could be commonly real, and sexually violated women would be believed. If the sexes were equal, women would not be economically subjected, their desperation and marginality cultivated, their enforced dependency exploited sexually or economically. Women would have speech, privacy, authority, respect, and more resources than they have now. Rape and pornography would be recognized as violations, and abortion would be both rare and actually guaranteed.

In the United States, it is acknowledged that the state is capitalist; it is not acknowledged that it is male. The law of sex equality, constitutional by interpretation and statutory by joke, erupts through this fissure, exposing the sex equality that the state purports to guarantee.[1] If gender hierarchy and sexuality are reciprocally constituting—gender hierarchy providing the eroticism of sexuality and sexuality providing an enforcement mechanism for male dominance over women—a male state would predictably not make acts of sexual dominance actionable as gender inequality. Equality would be kept as far away from sexuality as possible. In fact, sexual force is not conventionally recognized to raise issues of sex inequality, either against those who commit the acts or against the state that condones them. Sexuality is regulated largely by criminal law, occasionally by tort law, neither on grounds of equality.[2] Reproductive control, similarly, has been adjudicated primarily as an issue of privacy. It is as if a vacuum boundary demarcates sexual issues on the one hand from the law of equality on the other. Law, structurally, adopts the male point of view: sexuality concerns nature not social arbitrariness, interpersonal relations not social distributions of power, the sex difference not sex discrimination.

Sex discrimination law, with mainstream moral theory, sees equality and gender as issues of sameness and difference. According to this approach, which has dominated politics, law, and social perception, equality is an equivalence not a distinction, and gender is a distinction not an equivalence. The legal mandate of equal treatment—both a systemic norm and a specific legal doctrine—becomes a matter of treating likes alike and unlikes unlike, while the sexes are socially defined as such by their mutual unlikeness. That is, gender is socially constructed as difference epistemologically, and sex discrimination law bounds gender equality by difference doctrinally. Socially, one tells a woman from a man by their difference from each other, but a woman is legally recognized to be discriminated against on the basis of sex only when she can first be said to be the same as a man. A built-in tension thus exists between this concept of equality, which presupposes sameness, and this concept of sex, which presupposes difference. Difference defines the state's approach to sex equality epistemologically and doctrinally. Sex equality becomes a contradiction in terms, something of an oxymoron. The deepest issues of sex inequality, in which the sexes are most constructed as socially different, are either excluded at the threshold or precluded from coverage once in. In this way, difference is inscribed on society as the meaning of gender and written into law as the limit on sex discrimination. . . .

In [the] mainstream epistemologically liberal approach,[3] the sexes are by nature biologically different, therefore socially properly differentiated for some purposes. Upon this natural, immutable, inherent, essential, just, and wonderful differentiation, society and law are thought to have erected some arbitrary, irrational, confining, and distorting distinctions. These are the inequalities the law against sex discrimination targets. As one scholar has put it, "any prohibition against sexual classifications must be flexible enough to accommodate two legitimate sources of distinctions on the basis of sex: biological differences between the sexes and the prevailing heterosexual ethic of American society."[4] The proposed federal ERA's otherwise uncompromising prohibition on sex-based distinctions provides parallel exceptions for "unique physical characteristics" and "personal privacy."[5] Laws or practices that express or reflect sex "stereotypes," understood as inaccurate overgeneralized attitudes often termed "archaic" or "outmoded," are at the core of this definition of discrimination.[6] Mistaken illusions about real differences are actionable, but any distinction that can be accurately traced to biology or heterosexuality is not a discrimination but a difference.

From women's point of view, gender is more an inequality of power than a differentiation that is accurate or inaccurate. To women, sex is a social status based on who is permitted to do what to whom; only derivatively is it a difference. For example, one woman reflected on her gender: "I wish I had been born a doormat, or a man."[7] Being a doormat is definitely different from being a man. Differences between the sexes do descriptively exist. But the fact that these are a woman's realistic options, and that they are so limiting, calls into question the perspective that considers this distinction a "difference." Men are not called different because they are neither doormats nor women, but a woman is not socially permitted to be a woman and neither doormat nor man.

From this perspective, considering gender a matter of sameness and difference covers up the reality of gender as a system of social hierarchy, as an inequality. The differences attributed to sex become lines that inequality draws, not any kind of basis for it. Social and political inequality begins indifferent to sameness and difference. Differences are inequality's post hoc excuse, its conclusory artifact, its outcome presented as its origin, its sentimentalization, its damage that is pointed to as the justification for doing the damage after the damage has been done, the distinctions that perception is socially organized to notice because inequality gives them consequences for social power. Gender might not even code as difference, might not mean distinction epistemologically, were it not for its consequences for social power. Distinctions of body or mind or behavior are pointed to as cause rather than effect, with no realization that they are so deeply effect rather than cause that pointing to them at all is an effect. Inequality comes first; difference comes after. Inequality is material and substantive and identifies a disparity; difference is ideational and abstract and falsely symmetrical. If this is so, a discourse and a law of gender that center on difference serve as ideology to neutralize, rationalize, and cover disparities of power, even as they appear to criticize or problematize them. Difference is the velvet glove on the iron fist of domination. The problem then is not that differences are not valued; the problem is that they are defined by power. This is as true when difference is affirmed as when it is denied, when its substance is applauded or disparaged, when women are punished or protected in its name.

Doctrinally speaking, two alternative paths to sex equality for women exist within the mainstream approach to sex discrimination, paths that follow the lines of the sameness/difference tension. The leading one is: be the same as men. This path is termed "gender neutrality" doctrinally and the single standard philosophically. It is testimony to how substance becomes form in law that this rule is considered formal equality. Because it mirrors the values of the social world, it is considered abstract, meaning transparent to the world and lacking in substance. Also for this reason it is considered to be not only *the* standard, but *a* standard at all. Legally articulated as conforming normative standards to existing reality, as law reflecting life, the strongest doctrinal expression of sameness would prohibit taking gender into account in any way, with exceptions for "real differences." This is so far the leading rule that the words "equal to" are code for, or/and equivalent to, the words "the same as"—with the referent for both unspecified.

To women who want equality yet find themselves "different," the doctrine provides an alternative route: be different from men. This equal recognition of difference is termed the special benefit rule or special protection rule legally, the double standard philosophically. It is in rather bad odor, reminiscent of women's exclusion from the public sphere and of protective labor laws.[8] Like pregnancy, which always brings it up, it is something of a doctrinal embarrassment. Considered an exception to true equality and not really a rule of law at all, it is the one place where the law of sex discrimination admits it is recognizing something substantive. Together with the Bona Fide Occupational Qualification (BFOQ) and the exception for unique physical characteristics under ERA policy, compensatory legislation, and sex-conscious relief in particular litigation, affirmative action is thought to live here.[9] Situated differences can produce different treatment—indulgences *or* deprivations. This equality law is agnostic as to which.

The philosophy underlying the sameness/difference approach applies liberalism to women. Sex is a natural difference, a division, a distinction, beneath which lies a stratum of human commonality, sameness.[10] The moral thrust of the sameness branch of the doctrine conforms normative rules to empirical reality by granting women access to what men have: to the extent women are no different from men, women deserve what men have. The differences branch, which is generally regarded as patronizing and unprincipled but necessary to avoid absurdity, exists to value or compensate women for what they are or have become distinctively as women—by which is meant, unlike men, or to leave women as "different" as equality law finds them.

Most scholarship on sex discrimination law concerns which of these paths to sex equality is preferable in the long run or more appropriate to any particular issue, as if they were all there is.[11] As a prior matter, however, treating issues of sex equality as issues of sameness and difference is to take a particular approach. This approach is here termed the sameness/difference approach because it is obsessed with the sex difference. Its main theme is: "we're the same, we're the same, we're the same." Its counterpoint theme (in a higher register) goes: "but we're different, but we're different, but we're different." Its story is: on the first day, difference was; on the second day, a division was created upon it; on the third day, occasional dominance arose. Division may be rational or irrational. Dominance either seems or is justified or unjustified. Difference *is*.

Concealed is the substantive way in which man has become the measure of all things. Under the sameness rubric, women are measured according to correspondence with man, their equality judged by proximity to his measure. Under the difference rubric, women are measured according to their lack of correspondence from man, their womanhood judged by their distance from his measure. Gender neutrality is the male standard. The special protection rule is the female standard. Masculinity or maleness is the referent for both. Approaching sex discrimination in this way, as if sex questions were difference questions and equality questions were sameness questions, merely provides two ways for the law to hold women to a male standard and to call that sex equality. . . .

NOTES

1 Sex inequality was first found unconstitutional by interpretation of the equal protection clause of the Fourteenth Amendment in 1971. Reed v. Reed, 404 U.S. 71 (1971). When Title VII of the Civil Rights Act of 1964 was debated, racist southern congressmen attempted to defeat the provisions on racial discrimination by adding "sex" to the prohibited bases. Their *reductio ad absurdum* failed when it passed; *Congressional Record*, February 8, 1964, p. 2577. See also Willingham v. Macon Telegraph Publishing Co., 507 F.2d 1084, 1090 (5th Cir. 1975).

2 The law of sexual harassment, recognized only recently under sex equality law, is an exception, achieved by putting into practice the analysis argued in this book. See Catharine A.

MacKinnon, *Sexual Harassment of Working Women: A Case of Sex Discrimination* (New Haven: Yale University Press, 1979). Sex equality cases that address sexual issues such as rape (Michael M. v. Superior Court of Sonoma County, 450 U.S. 464 [1981]; Dothard v. Rawlinson, 433 U.S. 321 [1977]) do so in a context of the drawing of gender lines.

3 There is another approach, gaining ascendancy, discussed in Chapter 13.

4 G. Rutherglen, "Sexual Equality in Fringe-Benefit Plans," 65 *Virginia Law Review* 199, 206 (1979).

5 Brown, Emerson, Falk, and Freedman, "The Equal Rights Amendment."

6 Nadine Taub, "Keeping Women in Their Place: Stereotyping Per Se as a Form of Employment Discrimination," 21 *Boston College Law Review* 345 (1980); See also Barbara Kirk Cavanaugh, "'A Little Dearer than His Horse': Legal Stereotypes and the Feminine Personality," 6 *Harvard Civil Rights-Civil Liberties Law Review* 260 (1971).

7 Jean Harris, quoted by Shana Alexander in *Very Much a Lady,* in a review by Anne Bernays, *New York Times Book Review,* March 27, 1983, p. 13.

8 See B. Babcock, A. Freedman, E. Norton, and S. Ross, *Sex Discrimination and the Law* (Boston: Little, Brown, 1975), pp. 23–53.

9 The Bona Fide Occupational Qualification exception to Title VII of the Civil Rights Act of 1964, 42 U.S.C. Section 2000e-2(e), permits sex to be a job qualification when it is a valid one. For ERA, theory, see Brown, Emerson, Falk, and Freedman, "The Equal Rights Amendment," 80 *Yale Law Journal* 871 (1971).

10 This observation applies even to enlightened liberals like John Rawls, who rejects the naturalism of social orderings as prescriptive but accepts them as descriptive of unjust societies. Inequality exists in nature; society can accept or reject it. It is not in itself a social construct, nor are differences a function of it; John Rawls, *A Theory of Justice* (Cambridge, Mass.: The Belknap Press of Harvard University Press, 1971), p. 102.

11 For examples, see Wendy Williams, "The Equality Crisis: Some Reflections on Culture, Courts, and Feminism," 7 *Women's Rights Law Reporter* 175 (1982); Herma Kay, "Models of Equality," 1985 *University of Illinois Law Review* 39; Fran Olsen, "Statutory Rape: A Feminist Critique of Rights Analysis," 63 *Texas Law Review* 387 (1984); Wendy Williams, "Equality's Riddle: Pregnancy and the Equal Treatment/Special Treatment Debate," 13 *New York University Review of Law and Social Change* 325 (1985); Sylvia Law, "Rethinking Sex and the Constitution," 132 *University of Pennsylvania Law Review* 955 (1984); Stephanie Wildman, "The Legitimation of Sex Discrimination: A Critical Response to Supreme Court Jurisprudence," 63 *Oregon Law Review* 265 (1984); Herma Kay, "Equality and Difference: The Case of Pregnancy," 1 *Berkeley Women's Law Journal* 1 (1985); Dowd, "Maternity Leave: Taking Sex Differences into Account," 54 *Fordham Law Review* 699 (1986). Frances Olsen, "From False Paternalism to False Equality: Judicial Assaults on Feminist Community, Illinois 1869–1895," 84 *Michigan Law Review* 1518 (1986), sees the definition of the issues as limiting.

Women's Subordination Through the Lens of Sex/Gender, Sexuality, and Class: Socialist Feminism

A View of Socialist Feminism

Charlotte Perkins Gilman Chapter of the New American Movement

We believe that socialist feminism is essential to the struggle for the liberation of all women and the destruction of capitalism. We derive roots, strength, and direction from the feminist movement and from the socialist movement. Yet we believe that neither approach alone can achieve our goals for economic justice and a society where all women and men are equal. Socialist feminism provides a synthesis of both movements, while providing its unique perspective, vision, strategies, and contributions to theory.

AS FEMINISTS

As feminists, we see sexism as a primary focus; we fight against all forms and facets of sexism. We attack the inferior economic and legal status of women. We oppose the sexual division of labor, in which men and women have different responsibilities for home and family and unequal work divisions in the outside work place. We struggle for control of reproduction: for the freedom to choose contraception, abortion, or sterilization when we want them, but never to have any imposed, as they are on many poor and minority women. We challenge societal definitions of "femininity" and "masculinity" and seek freedom to define ourselves as we wish. We see "personal" issues as aspects of ourselves and society that are basic to change—sexuality, life-style, and family.

AS SOCIALISTS

As socialists, we see ourselves involved in the historic struggle of working people against a system which creates poverty in the midst of wealth; alienating work in a technological society; divisions between black and white, male and female, workers in this country and abroad; capitalism. All people who struggle against capitalism and for a socialist society must work together to challenge that system and its institutions.

THE TENSION

There remains a tension between socialism and feminism. Each regards its own particular focus as primary, and the other as secondary. Socialists insist on their unifying analysis, yet feminists can point to past failures of the left to address either the oppression women face, or the sexism within the left itself.

We must insist on a socialist-feminist movement because:

1 Sexism has a life of its own. It has existed throughout human history, under every economic system.

2 Capitalism determines the particular forms of sexism in a capitalist society. The subjugation of women contributes to capitalists' domination of society.

Any movement which fails to deal with *both* of these fundamental realities cannot succeed. Thus, we believe socialist-feminism is the necessary approach for both feminists and socialists.

WHY SOCIALIST FEMINISM?

The demands of feminism cannot be met by capitalist society. In order to achieve such goals as the elimination of sex roles, free 24-hour day care, and women's control over their own bodies, women must not only struggle to build a strong women's movement, but must work along with other oppressed groups. Socialist feminism moves beyond an attempt to create equality of women within the system to a struggle for equality within a new system that is not dependent on male domination or any exploitation of one group by another. This results in seeing feminism within a larger revolutionary context. For example, when we organize for day care, we challenge the power structure and economic system that are responsible for the present inadequacies. We expose the priorities and interests of those people who are determining and carrying out the current policies. We explore the implications of socialized child care, and its effect on working women and men.

WHY FEMINIST SOCIALISM?

Even though women are divided by class society, we are all united by our oppression as women. Just as women cannot achieve their full liberation except under socialism, so socialism cannot truly succeed unless all people are free from exploitation, manipulation, and prejudice.

Feminism provides the key to the cultural dimension of any successful revolutionary movement. Traditional socialist politics has focused on the public realms of "politics," goods production outside the home, and material needs. But feminism has taught us that the personal *is* political; that production in the "private" world of the home, while invisible under capitalism, is economically and socially critical; and that our culture, as well as our economic system, gives some people power over other people's lives. Any movement which ignores these learnings will surely fail, for it warps its vision and cuts itself off from the strength and knowledge of the female half of the working class. The fight against sexism reinforces the essential recognition that what is important is not just redistribution of goods, but a change in authority, control, and ideas.

Sexism's roots are deep; we must struggle not only against the institutions that maintain it, but against our own roles and attitudes. Feminism brings to the movement an attention to relationships *within* the movement, to the nature and functions of leadership, and to the importance of working collectively.

Women's pain and anger are real. When the broad interests of women and the interests of the working class seem to conflict, it is our task to clarify the interrelationships of those movements and seek programs that speak to all women's needs from a class perspective. Socialists committed to working for a society that is against all forms of oppression and exploitation must join in the struggle against sexism and together with other oppressed people fight for a new social and economic order.

Woman's Estate

Juliet Mitchell

Radical feminism attempts to solve the problem of analyzing the oppression of women by making it *the* problem. The largest, first and foremost. While such a theory remains descriptive of the experience, it *does* nevertheless stress the magnitude of the problem. What we need is a theory that is at once large enough and yet is capable of being specific. We have to see *why* women have always been oppressed, and *how* they are oppressed now, and how differently elsewhere. As radical feminists demand, we must dedicate ourselves to a theory of the oppression of all women and yet, at the same time, not lose sight of the historical specificity in the general statement. We should ask the feminist questions, but try to come up with some Marxist answers.

The situation of women is different from that of any other oppressed social group: they are half of the human species. In some ways they are exploited and oppressed like, and along with, other exploited classes or oppressed groups—the working-class, Blacks, etc. . . . Until there is a revolution in production, the labour situation will prescribe women's situation within the world of men. But women are offered a universe of their own: the family. Women are exploited at work, and relegated to the home: the two positions compound their oppression. Their subservience in production is obscured by their assumed dominance in their own world—the family. What is the family? And what are the actual functions that a woman fulfills within it? Like woman herself, the family appears as a natural object, but is actually a cultural creation. There is nothing inevitable about the form or role of the family, any more than there is about the character or role of women. It is the function of ideology to present these given social types as aspects of Nature itself. Both can be exalted, paradoxically, as ideals. The "true" woman and the "true" family are images of peace and plenty: in actuality they may both be sites of violence and despair. The apparently natural condition can be made to appear more attractive than the arduous advance of human beings towards culture. But what Marx wrote about the bourgeois myths of the Golden Ancient World describes precisely women's realm.

> . . . in one way the child-like world of the ancients appears to be superior; and this is so, insofar as we seek for closed shape, form and established limitation. The ancients provide a narrow satisfaction, whereas the modern world leaves us unsatisfied, or, where it appears to be satisfied with itself, is *vulgar* and *mean*.[1]

The ideology of "woman" presents her as an undifferentiated whole—"a woman," alike the world over, eternally the same. Likewise the "concept" of the family is of a unit that endures across time and space, there have always been families. . . . Within its supposed permanent structure, eternal woman finds her place. So the notion goes. . . . Any analysis of woman, and of the family, must uncoil this ideological concept of their permanence and of their unification into a monolithic whole, mother and child, a woman's place . . . her natural destiny. Theoretical analysis and revolutionary action must destructure and destroy the inevitability of this combination.

Past socialist theory has failed to differentiate woman's condition into its separate structures, which together form a complex—not a simple—unity. To do this will mean rejecting the idea that woman's condition can be deduced derivatively from the economy (Engels), or equated symbolically with society (early Marx). Rather, it must be seen as a *specific* structure, which is a unity of different elements. The variations of woman's condition throughout history will be the result of different combinations of these elements—we will thus have not a linear narrative of economic development (De Beauvoir) for the elements will be combined in different ways at different times. In a complex totality each independent sector has its own autonomous reality though each is ultimately, but only ultimately, determined by the economic factor. This complex totality means that no contradiction in society is ever simple. As each sector can move at a different pace, the synthesis of the different time-scales in the total structure means that sometimes contradictions cancel each other out, and sometimes they reinforce one another. Because the unity of woman's condition at any time is in this way the product of several structures, moving at different paces, it is always "overdetermined."[2]

The key structures of woman's situation can be listed as follows: Production, Reproduction, Sexuality and the Socialization of Children. The concrete combination of these produce the "complex unity" of her position; but each separate structure may have reached a different "moment" at any given historical time. Each then must be examined separately in order to see what the present unity is, and how it might be changed. . . .

NOTES

1 Karl Marx: *Pre-Capitalist Economic Formations,* ed. Hobsbawm, Lawrence & Wishart, 1964, p. 85.
2 See Louis Althusser: "Contradiction and Overdetermination," in *For Marx,* Allen Lane, London, 1970. To describe the movement of this complexity, as I have mentioned above, Althusser uses the Freudian term "overdetermination." The phrase *"unité de rupture"* (mentioned below) refers to the moment when the contradictions so reinforce one another as to coalesce into the conditions for a revolutionary change.

The Unhappy Marriage of Marxism and Feminism: Towards a More Progressive Union[1]

Heidi I. Hartmann

The "marriage" of marxism and feminism has been like the marriage of husband and wife depicted in English common law: marxism and feminism are one, and that one is marxism.[2] Recent attempts to integrate marxism and feminism are unsatisfactory to us as feminists because they subsume the feminist struggle into the "larger" struggle against capital. To continue our simile further, either we need a healthier marriage or we need a divorce.

The inequalities in this marriage, like most social phenomena, are no accident. Many marxists typically argue that feminism is at best less important than class conflict and at worst divisive of the working class. This political stance produces an analysis that absorbs feminism into the class struggle. Moreover, the analytic power of marxism with respect to capital has obscured its limitations with respect to sexism. We will argue here that while marxist analysis provides essential insight into the laws of historical development, and those of capital in particular, the categories of marxism are sex-blind. Only a specifically feminist analysis reveals the systemic character of relations between men and women. Yet feminist analysis by itself is inadequate because it has been blind to history and insufficiently materialist. Both marxist analysis, particularly its historical and materialistic method, and feminist analysis, especially the identification of patriarchy as a social and historical structure, must be drawn upon if we are to understand the development of western capitalist societies and the predicament of women within them. In this essay we suggest a new direction for marxist feminist analysis. . . .

I MARXISM AND THE WOMAN QUESTION

The woman question has never been the "feminist question." The feminist question is directed at the causes of sexual inequality between women and men, of male dominance over women. Most marxist analyses of women's position take as their question the relationship of women to the economic system, rather than that of women to men, apparently assuming the latter will be explained in their discussion of the former. Marxist analysis of the woman question has taken [several] forms. All see women's oppression in our connection (or lack of it) to production. Defining women as part of the working class, these analyses consistently subsume women's relation to men under workers' relation to capital. . . . All attempt to include women in the category working class and to understand women's oppression as another aspect of class oppression. In doing so all give short shrift to the object of feminist analysis, the relations between women and men. While our "problems" have been elegantly analyzed, they have been misunderstood. The focus of marxist analysis has been class relations; the object of marxist analysis has been understanding the laws of motion of capitalist society. While we believe marxist methodology *can* be used to formulate feminist strategy, these marxist feminist approaches discussed above clearly do not do so; their marxism clearly dominates their feminism. . . .

Marxism enables us to understand many aspects of capitalist societies: the structure of production, the generation of a particular occupational structure, and the nature of the dominant ideology. Marx's theory of the development of capitalism is a theory of the development of "empty places." Marx predicted, for example, the growth of the proletariat and the demise of the petit bourgeoisie. More precisely and in more detail, Braverman among others has explained the creation of the "places" clerical worker and service worker in advanced capitalist societies.[3] Just as capital creates these places indifferent to the individuals who fill them, the categories of marxist analysis, class, reserve army of labor, wage-laborer, do not explain why particular people fill particular places. They give no clues about why *women* are subordinate to *men* inside and outside the family and why it is not the other way around. *Marxist categories, like capital itself, are sex-blind.* The categories of marxism cannot tell us who will fill the empty places. Marxist analysis of the woman question has suffered from this basic problem. . . .

II RADICAL FEMINISM AND PATRIARCHY

The great thrust of radical feminist writing has been directed to the documentation of the slogan "the personal is political." Women's discontent, radical feminists argued, is not the neurotic lament of the maladjusted, but a response to a social structure in which women are systematically dominated, exploited, and oppressed. Women's inferior position in the labor market, the male-centered emotional structure of middle class marriage, the use of women in advertising, the so-called understanding of women's psyche as neurotic—popularized by academic and clinical psychology—aspect after aspect of women's lives in advanced capitalist society was researched and analyzed. The radical feminist literature is enormous and defies easy summary. At the same time, its focus on psychology is consistent. The New York Radical Feminists' organizing document was "The Politics of the Ego." "The personal is political" means for radical feminists, that the original and basic class division is between the sexes, and that the motive force of history is the striving of men for power and domination over women, the dialectic of sex.[4] . . .

Radical feminists use patriarchy to refer to a social system characterized by male domination over women. Kate Millett's definition is classic:

> our society . . . is a patriarchy. The fact is evident at once if one recalls that the military, industry, technology, universities, science, political offices, finances—in short, every avenue of power within the society, including the coercive force of the police, is entirely in male hands.[5]

This radical feminist definition of patriarchy applies to most societies we know of and cannot distinguish among them. The use of history by radical feminists is typically limited to providing examples of the existence of patriarchy in all times and places.[6] For both marxist and mainstream social scientists before the women's movement, patriarchy referred to a system of relations between men, which formed the political and economic outlines of feudal and some pre-feudal societies, in which hierarchy followed ascribed characteristics. Capitalist societies are understood as meritocratic, bureaucratic, and impersonal by bourgeois social scientists; marxists see capitalist societies as systems of class domination.[7] For both kinds of social scientists neither the historical patriarchal societies nor today's western capitalist societies are understood as systems of relations between men that enable them to dominate women.

Towards a Definition of Patriarchy

We can usefully define patriarchy as a set of social relations between men, which have a material base, and which, though hierarchical, establish or create interdependence and solidarity among men that enable them to dominate women. Though patriarchy is hierarchical and men of different classes, races, or ethnic groups have different places in the patriarchy, they also are united in their shared relationship of dominance over their women; they are dependent on each other to maintain that domination. Hierarchies "work" at least in part because they create vested interests in the status quo. Those at the higher levels can "buy off" those at the lower levels by offering them power over those still lower. In the hierarchy of patriarchy, all men, whatever their rank in the patriarchy, are bought off by being able to control at least some women. There is some evidence to suggest that when patriarchy was first institutionalized in state societies, the ascending rulers literally made men the heads of their families (enforcing their control over their wives and children) in exchange for the men's ceding some of their tribal resources to the new rulers.[8] Men are dependent on one another (despite their hierarchical ordering) to maintain their control over women.

The material base upon which patriarchy rests lies most fundamentally in men's control over women's labor power. Men maintain this control by excluding women from access to some essential productive resources (in capitalist societies, for example, jobs that pay living wages) and by restricting women's sexuality.[9] Monogamous heterosexual marriage is one relatively recent and efficient form that seems to allow men to control both these areas. Controlling women's access to resources and their sexuality, in turn, allows men to control women's labor power, both for the purpose of serving men in many personal and sexual ways and for the purpose of rearing children. The services women render men, and which exonerate men from having to perform many unpleasant tasks (like cleaning toilets) occur outside as well as inside the family setting. Examples outside the family include the harassment of women workers and students by male bosses and professors as well as the common use of secretaries to run personal errands, make coffee, and provide "sexy" surroundings. Rearing children, whether or not the children's labor power is of immediate benefit to their fathers, is nevertheless a crucial task in perpetuating patriarchy as a system. Just as class society must be reproduced by schools, work places, consumption norms, etc., so must patriarchal social relations. In our society children are generally reared by women at home, women socially defined and recognized as inferior to men, while men appear in the domestic picture only rarely. Children raised in this way generally learn their places in the gender hierarchy well. Central to this process, however, are the areas outside the home where patriarchal behaviors are taught and the inferior position of women enforced and reinforced: churches, schools, sports, clubs, unions, armies, factories, offices, health centers, the media, etc.

The material base of patriarchy, then, does not rest solely on childbearing in the family, but on all the social structures that enable men to control women's labor. The aspects of social structures that perpetuate patriarchy are theoretically identifiable, hence separable from their other aspects. Gayle Rubin has increased our ability to identify the patriarchal element of these social structures enormously by identifying "sex/gender systems":

> a "sex/gender system" is the set of arrangements by which a society transforms biological sexuality into products of human activity, and in which these transformed sexual needs are satisfied.[10]

We are born female and male, biological sexes, but we are created woman and man, socially recognized genders. *How* we are so created is that second aspect of the *mode* of production of which Engels spoke, "the production of human beings themselves, the propagation of the species."

How people propagate the species is socially determined. If, biologically, people are sexually polymorphous, and society were organized in such a way that all forms of sexual expression were equally permissible, reproduction would result only from some sexual encounters, the heterosexual ones. The strict division of labor by sex, a social invention common to all known societies, creates two very separate genders and a need for men and women to get together for economic reasons. It thus helps to direct their sexual needs toward heterosexual fulfillment, and helps to ensure biological reproduction. In more imaginative societies, biological reproduction might be ensured by other techniques, but the division of labor by sex appears to be the universal solution to date. Although it is theoretically possible that a sexual division of labor not imply inequality between the sexes, in most known societies, the socially acceptable division of labor by sex is one which accords lower status to women's work. The sexual division of labor is also the underpinning of sexual subcultures in which men and women experience life differently; it is the material base of male power which is exercised (in our society) not just in not doing housework and in securing superior employment, but psychologically as well.

How people meet their sexual needs, how they reproduce, how they inculcate social norms in new generations, how they learn gender, how it feels to be a man or a woman—all occur in the realm Rubin labels the sex/gender system. Rubin emphasizes the influence of kinship (which tells you with whom you can satisfy sexual needs) and the development of gender specific personalities via childbearing and the "oedipal machine." In addition, however, we can use the concept of the sex/gender system to examine all other social institutions for the roles they play in defining and reinforcing gender hierarchies. Rubin notes that theoretically a sex/gender system could be female dominant, male dominant, or egalitarian, but declines to label various known sex/gender systems or to periodize history accordingly. We choose to label our present sex/gender system patriarchy, because it appropriately captures the notion of hierarchy and male dominance which we see as central to the present system.

Economic production (what marxists are used to referring to as *the* mode of production) and the production of people in the sex/gender sphere both determine "the social organization under which the people of a particular historical epoch and a particular country live," according to Engels. The whole of society, then, can be understood by looking at both these types of production and reproduction, people and things.[11] There is no such thing as "pure capitalism," nor does "pure patriarchy" exist, for they must of necessity coexist. What exists is patriarchal capitalism, or patriarchal feudalism, or egalitarian hunting/gathering societies, or matriarchal horticultural societies, or patriarchal horticultural societies, and so on. There appears to be no necessary connection between *changes* in the one aspect of production and changes in the other. A society could undergo transition from capitalism to socialism, for example, and remain patriarchal.[12] Common sense, history, and our experience tell us, however, that these two aspects of production are so closely intertwined, that change in one ordinarily creates movement, tension, or contradiction in the other.

Racial hierarchies can also be understood in this context. Further elaboration may be possible along the lines of defining color/race systems, arenas of social life that take biological color and turn it into a social category, race. Racial hierarchies, like gender hierarchies, are aspects of our social organization, of how people are produced and reproduced. They are not fundamentally ideological; they constitute that second aspect of our mode of production, the production and reproduction of people. It might be most accurate then to refer to our societies not as, for example, simply capitalist, but as patriarchal capitalist white supremacist. In Part III below, we illustrate one case of capitalism adapting to and making use of racial orders and several examples of the interrelations between capitalism and patriarchy.

Capitalist development creates the places for a hierarchy of workers, but traditional marxist categories cannot tell us who will fill which places. Gender and racial hierarchies determine who fills the empty places. *Patriarchy is not simply hierarchical organization,* but hierarchy in which *particular* people fill *particular* places. It is in studying patriarchy that we learn why it is women who are dominated and how. While we believe that most known societies have been patriarchal, we do not view patriarchy as a universal, unchanging phenomenon. Rather patriarchy, the set of interrelations among men that allow men to dominate women, has changed in form and intensity over time. It is crucial that the hierarchy among men, and their differential access to patriarchal benefits, be examined. Surely, class, race, nationality, and even marital status and sexual orientation, as well as the obvious age, come into play here. And women of different class, race, national, marital status, or sexual orientation groups are subjected to different degrees of patriarchal power. Women may themselves exercise class, race, or national power, or even patriarchal power (through their family connections) over men lower in the patriarchal hierarchy than their own male kin.

To recapitulate, we define patriarchy as a set of social relations which has a material base and in which there are hierarchical relations between men and solidarity among them which enable them in turn to dominate women. The material base of patriarchy is men's control over women's labor power. That control is maintained by excluding women from access to necessary economically productive resources and by restricting women's sexuality. Men exercise their control in receiving personal service work from women, in not having to do housework or rear children, in having access to women's bodies for sex, and in feeling powerful and being powerful. The crucial elements of patriarchy as we *currently* experience them are: heterosexual marriage (and consequent homophobia), female childbearing and housework, women's economic dependence on men (enforced by arrangements in the labor market), the state and numerous institutions based on social relations among men—clubs, sports, unions, professions, universities, churches, corporations, and armies. All of these elements need to be examined if we are to understand patriarchal capitalism. . . .

III THE PARTNERSHIP OF PATRIARCHY AND CAPITAL

How are we to recognize patriarchal social relations in capitalist societies? It appears as if each woman is oppressed by her own man alone; her oppression seems a private affair. Relationships among men and among families seem equally fragmented. It is hard to recognize relationships among men, and between men and women, as *systematically* patriarchal. We argue, however, that patriarchy as a system of relations between men and women exists in capitalism, and that in capitalist societies a healthy and strong partnership exists between patriarchy and capital. Yet if one begins with the concept of patriarchy and an understanding of the capitalist mode of production, one recognizes immediately that the partnership of patriarchy and capital was not inevitable; men and capitalists often have conflicting interests, particularly over the use of women's labor power. Here is one way in which this conflict might manifest itself: the vast majority of men might want their women at home to personally service them. A smaller number of men, who are capitalists, might want most women (not their own) to work in the wage labor market. In examining the tensions of this conflict over women's labor power . . . we will be able to identify the material base of patriarchal relations in capitalist societies, as well as the basis for the partnership between capital and patriarchy.

Industrialization and the Development of Family Wages

. . . Family wages may be understood as a resolution of the conflict over women's labor power which [occurred] between patriarchal and capitalist interests [in the nineteenth century].

Family wages for most adult men imply men's acceptance, and collusion in, lower wages for others, young people, women and socially defined inferior men as well (Irish, blacks, etc., the lowest groups in the patriarchal hierarchy who are denied many of the patriarchal benefits). Lower wages for women and children and inferior men are enforced by job segregation in the labor market, in turn maintained by unions and management as well as by auxiliary institutions like schools, training programs, and even families. Job segregation by sex, by insuring that women have the lower paid jobs, both assures women's economic dependence on men and reinforces notions of appropriate spheres for women and men. For most men, then, the development of family wages secured the material base of male domination in two ways. First, men have the better jobs in the labor market and earn higher wages than women. The lower pay women receive in the labor market both perpetuates men's material advantage over women and encourages women to choose wifery as a career. Second, then, women do housework, childcare, and perform other services at home which benefit men directly.[13] Women's home responsibilities in turn reinforce their inferior labor market position.[14]

The resolution that developed in the early twentieth century can be seen to benefit capitalist interests as well as patriarchal interests. Capitalists, it is often argued, recognized that in the extreme conditions which prevailed in the early nineteenth century industrialization, working class families could not adequately reproduce themselves. They realized that housewives produced and maintained healthier workers than wage-working wives and that educated children became better workers than noneducated ones. The bargain, paying family wages to men and keeping women home, suited the capitalists at the time as well as the male workers. Although the terms of the bargain have altered over time, it is still true that the family and women's work in the family serve capital by providing a labor force and serve men as the space in which they exercise their privilege. Women, working to serve men and their families, also serve capital as consumers.[15] The family is also the place where dominance and submission are learned, as Firestone, the Frankfurt School, and many others have explained.[16] Obedient children become obedient workers, girls and boys each learn their proper roles.

While the family wage shows that capitalism adjusts to patriarchy, the changing status of children shows that patriarchy adjusts to capital. Children, like women, came to be excluded from wage labor. As children's ability to earn money declined, their legal relationship to their parents changed. At the beginning of the industrial era in the United States, fulfilling children's need for their fathers was thought to be crucial, even primary, to their happy development; fathers had legal priority in cases of contested custody. As children's ability to contribute to the economic well-being of the family declined, mothers came increasingly to be viewed as crucial to the happy development of their children, and gained legal priority in cases of contested custody.[17] Here patriarchy adapted to the changing economic role of children: when children were productive, men claimed them; as children became unproductive, they were given to women. . . .

With respect to capitalism and patriarchy, the adaptation, or mutual accommodation, took the form of the development of the family wage in the early twentieth century. The family wage cemented the partnership between patriarchy and capital. Despite women's increased labor force participation, particularly rapid since World War II, the family wage is still, we argue, the cornerstone of the present sexual division of labor—in which women are primarily responsible for housework and men primarily for wage work. Women's lower wages in the labor market (combined with the need for children to be reared by someone) assure the continued existence of the family as a necessary income pooling unit. The family, supported by the family wage, thus allows the control of women's labor by men both within and without the family.

Though women's increased wage work may cause stress for the family (similar to the stress Kautsky and Engels noted in the nineteenth century), it would be wrong to think that as a consequence, the concepts and the realities of the family and of the sexual division of labor will soon disappear. The sexual division of labor reappears in the labor market, where women work at women's jobs, often the very jobs they used to do only at home—food preparation and service, cleaning of all kinds, caring for people, and so on. As these jobs are low-status and low-paying patriarchal relations remain intact, though their material base shifts somewhat from the family to the wage differential, from family-based to industrially-based patriarchy[18]. . . .

Many people have argued that though the partnership between capital and patriarchy exists now, it may *in the long run* prove intolerable to capitalism; capital may eventually destroy both familial relations and patriarchy. The argument proceeds logically that capitalist social relations (of which the family is not an example) tend to become universalized, that women will become increasingly able to earn money and will increasingly refuse to submit to subordination in the family, and that since the family is oppressive particularly to women and children, it will collapse as soon as people can support themselves outside it.

We do not think that the patriarchal relations embodied in the family can be destroyed so easily by capital, and we see little evidence that the family system is presently disintegrating. Although the increasing labor force participation of women has made divorce more feasible, the incentives to divorce are not overwhelming for women. Women's wages allow very few women to support themselves and their children independently and adequately. The evidence for the decay of the traditional family is weak at best. The divorce rate has not so much increased, as it has evened out among classes; moreover, the remarriage rate is also very high. Up until the 1970 census, the first-marriage age was continuing its historic decline. Since 1970 people seem to have been delaying marriage and childbearing, but most recently, the birth rate has begun to increase again. It is true that larger proportions of the population are now living outside traditional families. Young people, especially, are leaving their parents' homes and establishing their own households before they marry and start traditional families. Older people, especially women, are finding themselves alone in their own households, after their children are grown and they experience separation or death of a spouse. Nevertheless, trends indicate that the new generations of young people will form nuclear families at some time in their adult lives in higher proportions than ever before. The cohorts, or groups of people, born since 1930 have much higher rates of eventual marriage and childbearing than previous cohorts. The duration of marriage and childbearing may be shortening, but its incidence is still spreading.[19]

The argument that capital destroys the family also overlooks the social forces which make family life appealing. Despite critiques of nuclear families as psychologically destructive, in a competitive society the family still meets real needs for many people. This is true not only of long-term monogamy, but even more so for raising children. Single parents bear both financial and psychic burdens. For working class women, in particular, these burdens make the "independence" of labor force participation illusory. Single parent families have recently been seen by policy analysts as transitional family formations which become two-parent families upon remarriage.[20]

It could be that the effects of women's increasing labor force participation are found in a declining sexual division of labor within the family, rather than in more frequent divorce, but evidence for this is also lacking. Statistics on who does housework, even in families with wage-earning wives, show little change in recent years; women still do most of it.[21] The double day is a reality for wage-working women. This is hardly surprising since the sexual division of labor outside the family, in the labor market, keeps women financially dependent on men—even when they earn a wage themselves. The future of patriarchy does not, however, rest solely on the future of familial relations. For patriarchy, like capital, can be surprisingly flexible and adaptable.

Whether or not the patriarchal division of labor, outside the family and elsewhere, is "ultimately" intolerable to capital, it is shaping capitalism now. . . .

IV   TOWARDS A MORE PROGRESSIVE UNION

Many problems remain for us to explore. Patriarchy as we have used it here remains more a descriptive term than an analytic one. If we think marxism alone inadequate, and radical feminism itself insufficient, then we need to develop new categories. What makes our task a difficult one is that the same features, such as the division of labor, often reinforce both patriarchy and capitalism, and in a thoroughly patriarchal capitalist society, it is hard to isolate the mechanisms of patriarchy. Nevertheless, this is what we must do. We have pointed to some starting places: looking at who benefits from women's labor power, uncovering the material base of patriarchy, investigating the mechanisms of hierarchy and solidarity among men. The questions we must ask are endless.

Can we speak of the laws of motion of a patriarchal system? How does patriarchy generate feminist struggle? What kinds of sexual politics and struggle between the sexes can we see in societies other than advanced capitalist ones? What are the contradictions of the patriarchal system and what is their relation to the contradictions of capitalism?. . .

Feminism and the Class Struggle

. . . The struggle against capital and patriarchy cannot be successful if the study and practice of the issues of feminism is abandoned. A struggle aimed only at capitalist relations of oppression will fail, since their underlying supports in patriarchal relations of oppression will be overlooked. And the analysis of patriarchy is essential to a definition of the kind of socialism useful to women. While men and women share a need to overthrow capitalism they retain interests particular to their gender group. It is not clear—from our sketch, from history, or from male socialists—that the socialism being struggled for is the same for both men and women. For a humane socialism would require not only consensus on what the new society should look like and what a healthy person should look like, but more concretely, it would require that men relinquish their privilege.

As women we must not allow ourselves to be talked out of the urgency and importance of our tasks, as we have so many times in the past. We must fight the attempted coercion, both subtle and not so subtle, to abandon feminist objectives.

This suggests two strategic considerations. First, a struggle to establish socialism must be a struggle in which groups with different interests form an alliance. Women should not trust men to liberate them after the revolution, in part, because there is no reason to think they would know how; in part, because there is no necessity for them to do so. In fact their immediate self-interest lies in our continued oppression. Instead we must have our own organizations and our own power base. Second, we think the sexual division of labor within capitalism has given women a practice in which we have learned to understand what human interdependence and needs are. While men have long struggled *against* capital, women know what to struggle *for*.[22] As a general rule, men's position in patriarchy and capitalism prevents them from recognizing both human needs for nurturance, sharing, and growth, and the potential for meeting those needs in a nonhierarchical, nonpatriarchal society. But even if we raise their consciousness, men might assess the potential gains against the potential losses and choose the status quo. Men have more to lose than their chains.

As feminist socialists, we must organize a practice which addresses both the struggle against patriarchy and the struggle against capitalism. We must insist that the society we want to create is a society in which recognition of interdependence is liberation rather than shame, nurturance is a universal, not an oppressive practice, and in which women do not continue to support the false as well as the concrete freedoms of men.

NOTES

1 Earlier drafts of this essay appeared in 1975 and 1977 coauthored with Amy B. Bridges. Unfortunately, because of the press of current commitments, Amy was unable to continue with this project, joint from its inception and throughout most of its long and controversial history. Over the years many individuals and groups offered us comments, debate, and support. . . . This is a substantially abridged version of the essay as it appeared in *Women and Revolution,* edited by Lydia Sargent (Boston: South End Press, 1981). A more complete version was also published in *Capital and Class* in the summer of 1979. . . .

2 Often paraphrased as "the husband and wife are one and that one is the husband," English law held that "by marriage, the husband and wife are one person in law: that is, the very being or legal existence of the women is suspended during the marriage, or at least is incor-

porated and consolidated into that of the Husband," I. Blackstone, *Commentaries,* 1965, pp. 442–445, cited in Kenneth M. Davidson, Ruth B. Ginsburg, and Herma H. Kay, *Sex Based Discrimination* (St. Paul, Minn.: West Publishing Co., 1974), p. 117.

3 Harry Braverman, *Labor and Monopoly Capital* (New York: Monthly Review Press, 1975).

4 "Politics of Ego: A Manifesto for New York Radical Feminists," can be found in *Rebirth of Feminism,* ed. Judith Hole and Ellen Levine (New York: Quadrangle Books, 1971), pp. 440–443. "Radical feminists" are those feminists who argue that the most fundamental dynamic of history is men's striving to dominate women. 'Radical' in this context does *not* mean anti-capitalist, socialist, counter-cultural, etc., but has the specific meaning of this particular set of feminist beliefs or group of feminists. Additional writings of radical feminists, of whom the New York Radical Feminists are probably the most influential, can be found in *Radical Feminism,* ed. Ann Koedt (New York: Quadrangle Press, 1972).

5 Kate Millett, *Sexual Politics* (New York: Avon Books, 1971), p. 25.

6 One example of this type of radical feminist history is Susan Brownmiller's *Against Our Will, Men, Women, and Rape* (New York: Simon & Schuster, 1975).

7 For the bourgeois social science view of patriarchy, see, for example, Weber's distinction between traditional and legal authority, *Max Weber: The Theories of Social and Economic Organization,* ed. Talcott Parsons (New York: The Free Press, 1964), pp. 328–357. These views are also discussed in Elizabeth Fee, "The Sexual Politics of Victorian Social Anthropology," *Feminist Studies,* Vol. 1, nos. 3–4 (Winter–Spring 1973), pp. 23–29, and in Robert A. Nisbet, *The Sociological Tradition* (New York: Basic Books, 1966), especially Chapter 3, "Community."

8 See Viana Muller, "The Formation of the State and Oppression of Women: Some Theoretical Considerations and a Case Study in England and Wales," *Review of Radical Political Economics,* Vol. 9, no. 3 (Fall 1977), pp. 7–21.

9 The particular ways in which men control women's access to important economic resources and restrict their sexuality vary enormously, both from society to society, from subgroup to subgroup, and across time. The examples we use to illustrate patriarchy in this section, however, are drawn primarily from the experience of whites in western capitalist countries. The diversity is shown in *Toward an Anthropology of Women,* ed. Rayna Rapp Reiter (New York: Monthly Review Press, 1975), *Woman, Culture and Society,* ed. Michelle Rosaldo and Louise Lamphere (Stanford, California: Stanford University Press, 1974), and *Females, Males, Families: A Biosocial Approach,* by Liba Leibowitz (North Scituate, Massachusetts: Duxbury Press, 1978). The control of women's sexuality is tightly linked to the place of children. An understanding of the demand (by men and capitalists) for children is crucial to understanding changes in women's subordination.

Where children are needed for their present or future labor power, women's sexuality will tend to be directed toward reproduction and childbearing. When children are seen as superfluous, women's sexuality for other than reproductive purposes is encouraged, but men will attempt to direct it towards satisfying male needs. The Cosmo girl is a good example of a woman "liberated" from childbearing only to find herself turning all her energies toward attracting and satisfying men. Capitalists can also use female sexuality to their own ends, as the success of Cosmo in advertising consumer products shows.

10 Gayle Rubin, "The Traffic in Women," in *Anthropology of Women,* ed. Reiter, p. 159.

11 Himmelweit and Mohun point out that both aspects of production (people and things) are logically necessary to describe a mode of production because by definition a mode of production must be capable of reproducing itself. Either aspect alone is not self-sufficient. To put it simply the production of things requires people, and the production of people requires things. Marx, though recognizing a capitalism's need for people did not concern himself with how they were produced or what the connections between the two aspects of produc-

tion were. See Himmelweit and Mohun, "Domestic Labour and Capital," *Cambridge Journal of Economics,* Vol. 1, no. 1 (March 1977), pp. 15–31.

12 For an excellent discussion of one such transition to socialism, see Batya Weinbaum, "Women in Transition to Socialism: Perspectives on the Chinese Case," *Review of Radical Political Economics,* Vol. 8, no. 1 (Spring 1976), pp. 34–58.

13 The importance of the fact that women perform labor services for men in the home cannot be overemphasized. As Pat Mainardi said in "The Politics of Housework," "[t]he measure of your oppression is his resistance" (in *Sisterhood is Powerful,* ed. Robin Morgan [New York: Vintage Books, 1970], p. 451). Her article, perhaps as important for us as Firestone on love, is an analysis of power relations between women and men as exemplified by housework.

14 Libby Zimmerman has explored the relation of membership in the primary and secondary labor markets to family patterns in New England. See her *Women in the Economy: A Case Study of Lynn, Massachusetts, 1760–1974* (Unpublished Ph.D. dissertation, Heller School, Brandeis, 1977). Batya Weinbaum is currently exploring the relationship between family roles and places in the labor market. See her "Redefining the Question of Revolution," *Review of Radical Political Economics,* Vol. 9, no. 3 (Fall 1977), pp. 54, 78, and *The Curious Courtship of Women's Liberation and Socialism* (Boston: South End Press, 1978). Additional studies of the interaction of capitalism and patriarchy can be found in Zillah Eisenstein, ed., *Capitalist Patriarchy and the Case for Socialist Feminism* (New York: Monthly Review Press, 1978).

15 See Batya Weinbaum and Amy Bridges, "The Other Side of the Paycheck: Monopoly Capital and the Structure of Consumption," *Monthly Review,* Vol. 28, no. 3 (July–August 1976), pp. 88–103, for a discussion of women's consumption work.

16 For the view of the Frankfurt School, see Max Horkheimer, "Authority and the Family," in *Critical Theory* (New York: Herder & Herder, 1972) and Frankfurt Institute of Social Research, "The Family," in *Aspects of Sociology* (Boston: Beacon, 1972).

17 Carol Brown, "Patriarchal Capitalism and the Female-Headed Family," *Social Scientist* (India); no. 40–41 (November–December 1975), pp. 28–39.

18 Carol Brown, in "Patriarchal Capitalism," argues, for example, that we are moving from "family based" to "industrially-based patriarchy within capitalism."

19 For the proportion of people in nuclear families, see Peter Uhlenberg, "Cohort Variations in Family Life Cycle Experiences of U.S. Females," *Journal of Marriage and the Family,* Vol. 36, no. 5 (May 1974), pp. 284–92. For remarriage rates see Paul C. Glick and Arthur J. Norton, "Perspectives on the Recent Upturn in Divorce and Remarriage," *Demography,* Vol. 10 (1974), pp. 301–14. For divorce and income levels see Arthur J. Norton and Paul C. Glick, "Marital Instability: Past, Present, and Future," *Journal of Social Issues,* Vol. 32, no. 1 (1976), pp. 5–20. Also see Mary Jo Bane, *Here to Stay: American Families in the Twentieth Century* (New York: Basic Books, 1976).

20 Heather L. Ross and Isabel B. Sawhill, *Time of Transition: The Growth of Families Headed by Women* (Washington, D.C.: The Urban Institute, 1975).

21 See Kathryn E. Walker and Margaret E. Woods, *Time Use: A Measure of Household Production of Family Goods and Services* (Washington, D.C.: American Home Economics Association, 1976); and Heidi I. Hartmann, "The Family as the Locus of Gender, Class, and Political Struggle: The Example of Housework," *Signs: Journal of Women in Culture and Society,* Vol. 6, no. 3 (Spring 1981).

22 Lise Vogel, "The Earthly Family," *Radical America,* Vol. 7, no. 4–5 (July–October 1973), pp. 9–50.

Women's Subordination Through the Lens of Sex/Gender, Sexuality, Class, and Race: Multicultural Feminism

From a Long Line of Vendidas: Chicanas and Feminism[*]

Cherríe Moraga

If somebody would have asked me when I was a teenager what it means to be Chicana, I would probably have listed the grievances done me. When my sister and I were fifteen and fourteen, respectively, and my brother a few years older, we were still waiting on him. I write "were" as if now, nearly two decades later, it were over. But that would be a lie. To this day in my mother's home, my brother and father are waited on, including by me. I do this out of respect for my mother and her wishes. In those early years, however, it was mainly in relation to my brother that I resented providing such service. For unlike my father, who sometimes worked as much as seventy hours a week to feed my face every day, the only thing that earned my brother my servitude was his maleness.

[*]*Editor's Note:* This contribution is excerpted from Moraga's essay "A Long Line of Vendidas," originally published in her book *Loving in the War Years: Lo que nunca pasó por sus labios* (Boston: South End Press, 1983), pp. 90–144. The essay, combining critical analysis with poems, journal entries, and other autobiographical material, was dedicated to Gloria Anzaldúa. The excerpts are reprinted here with the author's permission. Gracias, Cherríe.

203

What looks like betrayal between women on the basis of race originates, I believe, in sexism/heterosexism. Chicanas begin to turn our backs on each other either to gain male approval or to avoid being sexually stigmatized by them under the name of puta, vendida, jota. This phenomenon is as old as the day is long, and first learned in the school yard, long before it is played out with a vengeance within political communities.

In the seventh grade, I fell in love with Manuel Poblano. A small-boned boy. Hair always perfectly combed and oiled. Uniform shirt pressed neatly over shoulder blades jutting out. At twelve, Manuel was growing in his identity—sexually, racially—and Patsy Juárez, my one-time fifth-grade friend, wanted him too. Manuel was pals with Leticia and Connie. I remember how they flaunted a school picture of his in front of my face, proving how *they* could get one from him, although I had asked first. The two girls were conspiring to get him to "go" with Patsy, which in the end, he finally did. I, knowing all along I didn't have a chance. Not brown enough. And the wrong last name.

At puberty, it seemed identity alliances were beginning to be made along rigid and immovable lines of race, as it combined with sex. And everyone—boy, girl, anglo, and Chicano—fell into place. Where did *I* stand?

I did not move away from other Chicanos because I did not love my people. I gradually became anglocized because I thought it was the only option available to me toward gaining autonomy as a person without being sexually stigmatized. I can't say that I was conscious of all this at the time, only that at each juncture in my development, I instinctively made choices which I thought would allow me greater freedom of movement in the future. This primarily meant resisting sex roles as much as I could safely manage and this was far easier in an anglo context than in a Chicano one. That is not to say that anglo culture does not stigmatize its women for "gender-transgressions"—only that its stigmatizing did not hold the personal power over me which Chicano culture did.

Chicanas' negative perceptions of ourselves as sexual persons and our consequential betrayal of each other find their roots in a four-hundred-year-long Mexican history and mythology. They are further entrenched by a system of anglo imperialism which long ago put Mexicanos and Chicanos in a defensive posture against the dominant culture.

The sexual legacy passed down to the Mexicana/Chicana is the legacy of betrayal, pivoting around the historical/mythical female figure of Malintzin Tenepal. As translator and strategic advisor and mistress to the Spanish conqueror of México, Hernan Cortez, Malintzin is considered the mother of the mestizo people. But unlike La Virgen de Guadalupe, she is not revered as the Virgin Mother, but rather slandered as La Chingada, meaning the "fucked one," or La Vendida, sell-out to the white race.[1]

Upon her shoulders rests the full blame for the "bastardization" of the indigenous people of México. To put it in its most base terms: Malintzin, also called Malinche, fucked the white man who conquered the Indian peoples of México and destroyed their culture. Ever since, brown men have been accusing her of betraying her race, and over the centuries continue to blame her entire sex for this "transgression."

As a Chicana and a feminist, I must, like other Chicanas before me, examine the effects this myth has on my/our racial/sexual identity and my relationship with other

Chicanas. There is hardly a Chicana growing up today who does not suffer under her name even if she never hears directly of the one-time Aztec princess.

The Aztecs had recorded that Quetzalcoatl, the feathered serpent god, would return from the east to redeem his people in the year One Reed according to the Aztec calendar. Destiny would have it that on this very day, April 21, 1519 (as translated to the Western calendar), Cortez and his men, fitting the description of Quetzalcoatl, light-haired and bearded, landed in Vera Cruz.[2]

At the time of Cortez's arrival in México, the Aztecs had subjugated much of the rest of the Indian population, including the Mayans and Tabascans, who were much less powerful militarily. War was a necessity for the Aztecs in order to take prisoners to be used for sacrificial offerings to the warrior-god, Huitzilopochtli. As slaves and potential sacrificial victims to the Aztecs, then, these other Indian nations, after their own negotiations and sometimes bloody exchanges with the Spanish, were eager to join forces with the Spanish to overthrow the Aztec empire. The Aztecs, through their systematic subjugation of much of the Mexican Indian population, decreed their own self-destruction.[3]

Aleida Del Castillo, Chicana feminist theorist, contends that as a woman of deep spiritual commitment, Malinche aided Cortez because she understood him to be Quetzalcoatl returned in a different form to save the peoples of México from total extinction. She writes, "The destruction of the Aztec empire, the conquest of México, and as such, the termination of her indigenous world," were, in Malinche's eyes, "inevitable" in order to make way for the new spiritual age that was imminent.[4]

Del Castillo and other Chicana feminists who are researching and re-interpreting Malinche's role in the conquest of México are not trying to justify the imperialism of the Spanish. Rather, they are attempting to create a more realistic context for, and therefore a more sympathetic view of, Malinche's actions.

The root of the fear of betrayal by a woman is not at all specific to the Mexican or Chicano. The resemblance between Malinche and the Eve image is all too obvious. In chronicling the conquest of México and founding the Catholic Church there, the Spanish passed on to the mestizo people as legacy their own European-Catholic interpretation of Mexican events. Much of this early interpretation originated from Bernal del Castillo's eye-witness account of the conquest. As the primary source of much contemporary analysis as well, the picture we have of Mexican Indian civilization during that period often contains a strong Catholic and Spanish bias.

In his writings, Bernal Diaz del Castillo notes that upon the death of Malinche's father, the young Aztec princess was in line to inherit his estate. Malinche's mother wanted her son from her second marriage to inherit the wealth instead. She therefore sold her own daughter into slavery.

According to Gloria Anzaldúa, there are writings in México to refute this account.[5] But it was nevertheless recorded—or commonly believed—that Malinche was betrayed by her own mother. It is this myth of the inherent unreliability of women, our natural propensity for treachery, which has been carved into the very bone of Mexican/Chicano collective psychology.

Traitor begets traitor.

Little is made of this early betrayal, whether or not it actually occurred, probably because no man was immediately affected. In a way, Malinche's mother would only have been doing her Mexican wifely duty: *putting the male first.*

There is none so beautiful as the Latino male. I have never met any kind of Latino who, although he may have claimed his family was very woman-dominated ("mi mamá made all the real decisions"), did not subscribe to the basic belief that men are better. It is so ordinary a statement as to sound simplistic and I am nearly embarrassed to write it, but that's the truth in its kernel.

Ask, for example, any Chicana mother about her children and she is quick to tell you she loves them all the same, but she doesn't. *The boys are different.* Sometimes I sense that she feels this way because she wants to believe that through her mothering, she can develop the kind of man she would have liked to have married, or even have been. That through her son she can get a small taste of male privilege, since without race or class privilege that's all there is to be had. The daughter can never offer the mother such hope, straddled by the same forces that confine the mother. As a result, the daughter must constantly earn the mother's love, prove her fidelity to her. The son—he gets her love for free.

After ten years of feminist consciousness and activism, why does this seem so significant to me—to write of the Mexican mother favoring the son? I think because I had never quite gone back to the source. Never said in my own tongue, *the boys, they are men, they can do what they want . . . after all, he's a man.*

Journal Entry: April 1980
Three days ago, my mother called me long distance full of tears, loving me, wanting me back in her life after such a long period of separation. My mother's tears succeed in getting me to break down the edge in my voice, the protective distance. My mother's pleading "mi'jita, I love you, I hate to feel so far away from you," succeeds in opening my heart again to her.

I don't remember exactly why my heart had been shut, only that it had been very necessary to keep my distance, that in a way we had agreed to that. But, it only took her crying to pry my heart open again.

I feel myself unriveting. The feelings begin to flood my chest. Yes, this is why I love women. This woman is my mother. There is no love as strong as this, refusing my separation, never settling for a secret that would split us off, always at the last minute, like now, pushing me to the brink of revelation, speaking the truth.

I am as big as a mountain! I want to say, "Watch out, Mamá! I love you and I am as big as a mountain!" And it is on the brink of this precipice where I feel my body descending into the places where we have not spoken, the times I did not fight back. I am descending, ready to speak the truth, finally.

And then suddenly, over the phone, I hear another ring. My mother tells me to wait. There is a call on my father's work phone. Moments later, "It is your brother," she says. My knees lock under me, bracing myself for the fall . . . Her voice lightens up. "Okay, mi'jita. I love you. I'll talk to you later," cutting off the line in the middle of the connection.

I am relieved when I hang up that I did not have the chance to say more. The graceful reminder. This man doesn't have to earn her love. My brother has always come first.

Seduction and betrayal. Since I've grown up, no woman cares for me for free. There is always a price. My love.

What I wanted from my mother was impossible. It would have meant her going against Mexican/Chicano tradition in a very fundamental way. You are a traitor to your race if you do not put the man first. The potential accusation of "traitor" or "vendida" is what hangs above the heads and beats in the hearts of most Chicanas seeking to develop our own autonomous sense of ourselves, particularly through sexuality.

Because heterosexism—the Chicana's sexual commitment to the Chicano male—is proof of her fidelity to her people, the Chicana feminist attempting to critique the sexism in the Chicano community is certainly between a personal rock and a political hard place.

Although not called "the sexism debate," as it has been in the literary sectors of the Black movement, the Chicana discussion of sexism within our community has like that movement been largely limited by heterosexual assumption: "How can we get our men right." The feminist-oriented material which appeared in the late 70s and early 80s for the most part strains in its attempt to stay safely within the boundaries of Chicano—male-defined and often anti-feminist—values.

Over and over again, Chicanas trivialize the women's movement as being merely a white middle-class thing, having little to offer women of color. They cite only the most superficial aspects of the movement. For example, in "From Woman to Woman," Silvia S. Lizarraga writes:

> class distinction is a major determinant of attitudes toward other subordinated groups. In the U.S. we see this phenomenon operating in the goals expressed in the Women's Liberation Movement. . . . The needs represent a large span of interests—from those of *capitalist women,* women in business and professional careers, to *witches* and *lesbians.* However, the needs of the unemployed and working class women of different ethnic minorities are generally overlooked by this movement.[6] (my emphasis)

This statement typifies the kind of one-sided perspective many Chicanas have given of the women's movement in the name of Chicana liberation. My question is *who* are they trying to serve? Certainly not the Chicana who is deprived of some very critical information about a ten-year grassroots feminist movement where women of color, including lesbians of color (certainly in the minority and most assuredly encountering "feminist" racism) have been actively involved in reproductive rights, especially sterilization abuse, battered women's shelters, rape crisis centers, welfare advocacy, Third World women's conferences, cultural events, health and self-help clinics and more.

Interestingly, it is perfectly acceptable among Chicano males to use white theoreticians, e.g. Marx and Engels, to develop a theory of Chicano oppression. It is unacceptable, however, for the Chicana to use white sources by women to develop a theory of Chicana oppression. Even if one subscribes to a solely economic theory of oppression, how can she ignore that over half of the world's workers are females who suffer discrimination not only in the workplace, but also at home and in all the areas of sex-related abuse I just cited? How can she afford not to recognize that the wars against imperialism occurring both domestically and internationally are always accompanied by the rape of women of color by both white and Third World men? Without a feminist analysis what name do we put to these facts? Are these not deterrents to the Chicana developing a sense of "species being"? Are these "women's issues" not also "people's issues"? It is far easier for the Chicana to criticize white women who on the face of things could never be familia, than to take issue with or complain, as it were, to a brother, uncle, father. . . .

In recent years, however, truly feminist Chicanas are beginning to make the pages of Chicano, feminist, and literary publications. This, of course, is only a reflection of a fast-growing Chicana/Third World feminist movement. I am in debt to the research and writings of Norma Alarcón, Martha Cotera, Gloria Anzaldúa, and Aleida Del Castillo, to name a few. Their work reflects a relentless commitment to putting the female first, even when it means criticizing el hombre.[7] . . .

I remain amazed at how often so-called "Tercermundistas" in the U.S. work to annihilate the concept and existence of white supremacy, but turn their faces away from male supremacy. Perhaps this is because when you start to talk about sexism, the world becomes increasingly complex. The power no longer breaks down into neat little hierarchical categories, but becomes a series of starts and detours. Since the categories are not easy to arrive at, the enemy is not easy to name. It is all so difficult to unravel. It *is* true that some men hate women even in their desire for them. And some men oppress the very women they love. But unlike the racist, they allow the object of their contempt to share the table with them. The hatred they feel for women does not translate into separatism. It is more insidiously intra-cultural, like class antagonism. But different, because it lives and breathes in the flesh and blood of our families, even in the name of love.

In Toni Cade Bambara's novel, *The Salt Eaters,* the curandera asks the question, "Can you afford to be whole?"[8] This line represents the question that has burned within me for years and years through my growing politicization. *What would a movement bent on the freedom of women of color look like?* In other words, what are the implications of not only looking outside of our culture, but into our culture and ourselves and from that place beginning to develop a strategy for a movement that could challenge the bedrock of oppressive systems of belief globally?

The one aspect of our identity which has been uniformly ignored by every existing political movement in this country is sexuality, both as a source of oppression and a means of liberation. Although other movements have dealt with this issue, sexual oppression and desire have never been considered specifically in relation to the lives of women of color. Sexuality, race, and sex have usually been presented in contradiction to each other, rather than as part and parcel of a complex web of personal and political identity and oppression.

Unlike most white people, with the exception of the Jews, Third World people have suffered the threat of genocide to our races since the coming of the first European expansionists. The family, then, becomes all the more ardently protected by oppressed peoples, and the sanctity of this institution is infused like blood into the veins of the

Chicano. At all costs, la familia must be preserved: for when they kill our boys in their own imperialist wars to gain greater profits for American corporations; when they keep us in ghettos, reservations, and barrios which ensure that our own people will be the recipients of our frustrated acts of violence; when they sterilize our women without our consent because we are unable to read the document we sign; when they prevent our families from getting decent housing, adequate child care, sufficient fuel, regular medical care; then we have reason to believe—although they may no longer technically be lynching us in Texas or our sisters and brothers in Georgia, Alabama, Mississippi—they intend to see us dead.

So we fight back, we think, with our families—with our women pregnant, and our men, the indisputable heads. We believe the more severely we protect the sex roles within the family, the stronger we will be as a unit in opposition to the anglo threat. And yet, our refusal to examine *all* the roots of the lovelessness in our families is our weakest link and softest spot.

Our resistance as a people to looking at the relationships within our families—between husband and wife, lovers, sister and brother, father, son, and daughter, etc.—leads me to believe that the Chicano male does not hold fast to the family unit merely to safeguard it from the death-dealings of the anglo. Living under Capitalist Patriarchy, what is true for "the man" in terms of misogyny is, to a great extent, true for the Chicano. He, too, like any other man, wants to be able to determine how, when, and with whom his women—mother, wife, and daughter—are sexual. For without male imposed social and legal control of our reproductive function, reinforced by the Catholic Church, and the social institutionalization of our roles as sexual and domestic servants to men, Chicanas might very freely "choose" to do otherwise, including being sexually independent *from* and/or *with* men. In fact, the forced "choice" of the gender of our sexual/love partner seems to precede the forced "choice" of the form (marriage and family) that partnership might take. The control of women begins through the institution of heterosexuality.

Homosexuality does not, in and of itself, pose a great threat to society. Male homosexuality has always been a "tolerated" aspect of Mexican/Chicano society, as long as it remains "fringe." A case can even be made that male homosexuality stems from our indigenous Aztec roots.[9] But lesbianism, in any form, and male homosexuality which openly avows both the sexual and emotional elements of the bond, challenges the very foundation of la familia. The "faggot" is the object of the Chicano/Mexicano's contempt because he is consciously choosing a role his culture tells him to despise. That of a woman.

The question remains. Is the foundation as it stands now sturdy enough to meet the face of the oppressor? I think not. There is a deeper love between and amongst our people that lies buried between the lines of the roles we play with each other. It is the earth beneath the floor boards of our homes. We must split wood, dig barefisted into the packed ground to find out what we really have to hold in our hands as muscle.

Family is *not* by definition the man in a dominant position over women and children. Familia is cross-generational bonding, deep emotional ties between opposite sexes, and within our sex. It is sexuality, which involves, but is not limited to, intercourse or orgasm. It springs forth from touch, constant and daily. The ritual of kissing and the sign of the cross with every coming and going from the home. It is finding familia among friends where blood ties are formed through suffering and celebration shared.

The strength of our families never came from domination. It has only endured in spite of it—like our women. . . .

The woman who defies her role as subservient to her husband, father, brother, or son by taking control of her own sexual destiny is purported to be a "traitor to her race" by contributing to the "genocide" of her people—whether or not she has children. In short, even if the defiant woman is *not* a lesbian, she is purported to be one; for like the lesbian in the Chicano imagination, she is una *Malinchista*. Like the Malinche of Mexican history, she is corrupted by foreign influences which threaten to destroy her people. Norma Alarcón elaborates on this theme of sex as a determinant of loyalty when she states:

> The myth of Malinche contains the following sexual possibilities: woman is sexually passive, and hence at all times open to potential use by men whether it be seduction or rape. The possible use is double-edged: that is, the use of her as pawn may be intracultural—"amongst us guys"—or intercultural, which means if we are not using her then "they" must be using her. Since woman is highly pawnable, nothing she does is perceived, as choice.[10]

Lesbianism can be construed by the race then as the Chicana being used by the white man, even if the man never lays a hand on her. The choice is never seen as her own. Homosexuality is *his* disease with which he sinisterly infects Third World people, men and women alike. (Because Malinche is female, Chicano gay men rebelling against their prescribed sex roles, although still considered diseased, do not suffer the same stigma of traitor.) Further, the Chicana lesbian who has relationships with white women may feel especially susceptible to such accusations, since the white lesbian is seen as the white man's agent. The fact that the white woman may be challenging the authority of her white father, and thereby could be looked upon as a potential ally, has no bearing on a case closed before it was ever opened.

The line of reasoning goes:

Malinche sold out her indio people by acting as courtesan and translator for Cortez, whose offspring symbolically represent the birth of the bastardized mestizo/Mexicano people. My mother then is the modern-day Chicana, Malinche marrying a white man, my father, to produce the bastards my sister, my brother, and I are. Finally, I—a half-breed Chicana—further betray my race by *choosing* my sexuality which excludes all men, and therefore most dangerously, Chicano men.

I come from a long line of Vendidas.

I am a Chicana lesbian. My own particular relationship to being a sexual person; and a radical stand in direct contradiction to, and in violation of, the woman I was raised to be. . . .

In failing to approach feminism from any kind of materialist base, failing to take race, ethnicity, class into account in determining where women are at sexually, many feminists have created an analysis of sexual oppression (often confused with sexuality itself) which is a political dead-end. "Radical Feminism," the ideology which sees men's oppression of women as the root of and paradigm for all other oppressions, allows women to view ourselves as a class and to claim our sexual identity as the *source* of our oppression and men's sexual identity as the *source* of the world's evil. But this ideology can never then fully integrate the concept of the "simultaneity of oppression" as Third World feminism is attempting to do. For, if race and class suffer the woman of color as much as her sexual identity, then the Radical Feminist must extend her own "identity" politics to include her "identity" as oppressor as well. (To say nothing of having to acknowledge the fact that there are men who may suffer more than she.) This is something that, for the most part, Radical Feminism as a movement has refused to do.

Radical Feminist theorists have failed to acknowledge how their position in the dominant culture—white, middle-class, often Christian—has influenced every approach they have taken to implement feminist political change—to "give women back their bodies." It follows then that the anti-pornography movement is the largest organized branch of Radical Feminism. For unlike battered women's, anti-rape, and reproductive rights workers, the anti-porn "activist" never has to deal with any live woman outside of her own race and class. The tactics of the anti-pornography movement are largely symbolic and theoretical in nature. And, on paper, the needs of the woman of color are a lot easier to represent than in the flesh. Therefore, her single-issued approach to feminism remains intact.

It is not that pornography is not a concern to many women of color. But the anti-materialist approach of this movement makes little sense in the lives of poor and Third World women. Plainly put, it is our sisters working in the sex industry. . . .

Among Chicanas, it is our tradition to conceive of the bond between mother and daughter as paramount and essential in our lives. It is the daughters that can be relied upon. Las hijas who remain faithful a la madre, a la madre de la madre.

When we name this bond between the women of our race, from this Chicana feminism emerges. For too many years, we have acted as if we held a secret pact with one another never to acknowledge directly our commitment to one another. Never to admit the fact that we count on one another *first*. We were never to recognize this in the face of el hombre. But this is what being a Chicana feminist means—making bold and political the love of the women of our race.

A political commitment to women does not equate with lesbianism. As a Chicana lesbian, I write of the connection my own feminism has had with my sexual desire for women. This is my story. I can tell no other one than the one I understand. I eagerly await the writings by heterosexual Chicana feminists that can speak of their sexual desire for men and the ways in which their feminism informs that desire. What is true, however, is that a political commitment to women must involve, by definition, a political commitment to lesbians as well. To refuse to allow the Chicana lesbian the right to the free expression of her own sexuality, and her politicization of it, is in the deepest sense to deny one's self the right to the same. I guarantee you, there will be no change among heterosexual men, there will be no change in heterosexual relations, as long as the Chicano community keeps us lesbians and gay men political prisoners among our own people. Any movement built on the fear and loathing of anyone is a failed movement. The Chicano movement is no different.

NOTES

1 Norma Alarcón examines this theme in her article "Chicana's Feminist Literature: A Re-Vision Through Malintzin/or Malintzin: Putting Flesh Back on the Object," in *This Bridge Called My Back: Writings by Radical Women of Color,* ed. Cherríe Moraga and Gloria Anzaldúa (Watertown, Mass.: Persephone Press, 1981).

2 Aleida R. Del Castillo, "Malintzin Tenepal: A Preliminary Look into a New Perspective," in *Essays on La Mujer,* ed. Rosaura Sánchez and Rosa Martínez Cruz (University of California at Los Angeles: Chicano Studies Center Publications, 1977), p. 133.

3 Ibid., p. 131.

4 Ibid., p. 141.

5 Gloria Anzaldúa, unpublished work in progress. Write: The Third World Women's Archives, Box 159, Bush Terminal Station, Brooklyn, NY 11232.

6 Silvia S. Lizarraga, "From a Woman to a Woman," in *Essays on La Mujer,* p. 91.

7 Some future writings by Latina feminists include: Gloria Anzaldúa's *La Serpiente Que Se Come Su Cola: The Autobiography of a Chicana Lesbian* (Write: The Third World Women's Archives, see address above); *Cuentos: Stories by Latinas,* ed. Alma Gómez, Cherríe Moraga, and Mariana Romo-Carmona (Kitchen Table: Women of Color Press, Box 2753 Rockefeller Center Station, New York, NY 10185, 1983); and *Compañeras: Antología Lesbiana Latina,* ed. Juanita Ramos and Mirtha Quintanales (Write: The Third World Women's Archives, see address above).

8 Toni Cade Bambara, *The Salt Eaters* (New York: Random House, 1980), pp. 3 and 10.

9 Bernal Díaz del Castillo, *The Bernal Diaz Chronicles,* trans. and ed. Albert Idell (New York: Doubleday, 1956), pp. 86–87.

10 Norma Alarcón, in *This Bridge Called My Back,* p. 184.

The Feminist Movement: Where Are All the Asian American Women?

Esther Ngan-Ling Chow

From its inception the feminist movement in the United States has been predominantly white and middle class. Like blacks, Hispanics, and other women of color, Asian American women have not joined white women and, thus far, have not made a great impact on the movement. Since the late 1960s, Asian Americans have begun to organize themselves and build bonds with other women's groups to advocate for their civil rights as a racial minority and as women. Their relative lack of political activism stems from cultural, psychological, and social oppressions which historically discouraged them from organizing. This resulted in their apparent political invisibility and powerlessness.

BARRIERS TO POLITICAL ACTIVISM

In order to become and remain politically active, Asian American women must over-come many barriers at various levels: in individuals, in racial relations, in the cultural system, in the class structure, in gender-role stratification, and in the legal-political system. These constitute the main sources of multiple oppression faced by this group of minority women and can be classified into two major types: internal and external barriers.

The former refers to those factors that are specifically inherent to Asian American women as a group, including psychological constraints, cultural restrictions, and patri-archy and structural impediments. The latter refers to those elements existing primari-ly in American society at large that have kept them from full involvement in the women's liberation movement, including legal-political barriers, racial insensitivity and unreceptivity, and class cleavage. External barriers are more invidious and harder for Asian American women to overcome than internal ones. These two types of barrier may be dialectical in nature, providing stability as well as contradiction in the life ex-perience of many Asian American women.[1]

Internal Barriers

Psychological Constraints.   Because of their dual status, Asian American women derive their identification and self-esteem from both ethnicity and gender.[2] Although Asian American women may benefit from and contribute significantly to the feminist movement, joining such a movement seems to be a double bind for them because it pits ethnic identity against gender identity. It could also lead to absorption or coopta-tion into the larger society, resulting in an eventual loss of ethnic identity. In any case, Asian American women must deal with this identity crisis. The key issue here is how to balance one's ethnic and sexual or gender identification in order to develop a healthy self-concept.

Research has indicated that gender-role stereotypes are psychologically and social-ly detrimental to the personality and achievement of women.[3] And Asian American women suffer from racial stereotypes as well. All stereotypes, whether positive or neg-ative, serve as self-fulfilling prophecies when contending with them gradually leads to internalizing them as part of an illusionary reality. Being perceived generally as sub-servient, obedient, passive, hard working, and exotic, Asian American women them-selves become convinced that they should behave in accordance with these stereo-typed expectations. But if they act accordingly, they are then criticized for doing so, becoming victims of the stereotypes imposed by others.[4] For Asian American women to develop their political potential, they must develop a positive self-concept and maintain psychological well-being.

Cultural Restrictions.   Although certain Asian values emphasizing education, achievement, and diligence account for the high level of aspiration and success of some Asian American women, other values hinder active political participation. Such cultural limitation is further compounded by the adjustment to American culture, which is often in conflict and contradiction with their ethnic one.

Four cultural dilemmas frequently face Asian American women: (1) obedience vs. independence; (2) collective (or familial) vs. individual interest; (3) fatalism vs. change; and (4) self-control vs. self-expression or spontaneity.[5] On the one hand, adherence to Asian values, that is, obedience, familial interest, fatalism, and self-control, tends to foster submissiveness, passivity, pessimism, timidness, inhibition, and adaptiveness, which are not necessarily conducive to political activism. On the other hand, acceptance of the American values of independence, individualism, mastery of one's environment through change, and self-expression generates self-interest, aggressiveness, initiative, and expressive spontaneity. All these traits tend to encourage political activism, but at the same time are incompatible with the family upbringing of most Asian American women. The key problem here is how to maintain a bicultural existence by selecting appropriate elements of both cultural worlds to make the best adaptation according to the demands of social circumstances. . . .

Unfamiliarity with the language is another factor that hinders the acculturation and political participation of Asian immigrant women. This barrier limits the extent to which Asian American women can express themselves, reduces their ability to make demands, restricts their access to many types of information, curtails the flow and scope of communication with others, and eventually limits the development of political efficacy in America. Although the English proficiency level of many Asian American women of foreign birth is generally adequate for functioning well in the workplace and in social circles, language remains a handicap for some. These women tend to prefer speaking in their native tongue, feel inhibited from engaging in open dialogue with others in English, and subsequently increase their political powerlessness and decrease their ability to influence others. The American-born are better able to overcome this communication difficulty and thereby can participate readily in the larger society. However, their physical features still remind others of their foreign backgrounds, thus presumably limiting full acceptance by others in the larger society. The integration of Asian American women of diverse backgrounds and generations into both the Asian American communities and the larger feminist movement remains key for their future political activism.

Patriarchy and Structural Impediments. As long as patriarchy persists, the social institutions that encompass Asian American women will continue to perpetuate the devaluation and subjugation of women. School, family, workplace, and other social institutions within and outside the Asian communities all reinforce this gender-role conditioning. The education system has frequently failed to provide women with knowledge of their legal rights. The doctrine of three obediences for a Chinese woman to her father, husband, and son well illustrates her subservient roles. The male is still perceived as major breadwinner and the woman as homemaker. For many employed Asian American women, managing multiple roles is a significant problem. Those with young children are more likely than their white counterparts to stay at home.[6] Overburdened with family and work, and without much support and cooperation from their spouses and sometimes from other family members, Asian American women find political participation beyond their own ethnic group difficult, if not impossible.[7]

Although many Asian American women do engage in political organizing within ethnic communities, their activity in white feminist organizations is often perceived by their male partners and even their female peers as a move toward separatism. They are warned that the consequences of separation will threaten the male ego, damage working relationships between Asian men and women, and dilute efforts and resources for the Asian American cause. All these forces have impeded Asian American women from more active participation in the larger feminist movement.

External Barriers

Legal-Political Barriers.   Historically, structural receptivity to Asian Americans, men and women alike, has been low in the United States. Legal and political barriers deeply rooted in the social system can be documented from the first immigration of Asians to this country. For example, fourteen pieces of legislation were written by state and federal governments to discriminate against the Chinese in America and to strip them of their rights as lawful members of society.[8] The economic exploitation and deprivation that frequently go hand in hand with legal exclusion under political dominance are strongly evident in the century-old history of Asian Americans.[9]

To prevent Asian Americans from forming a strong coalition and political force, U.S. immigration policies emphasized the importance of cheap labor and discouraged the formation of family unity by setting up restrictive quotas for women and children of Asian laborers. The virtual absence of Asian women until the 1950s and the enforcement of antimiscegenation laws made it difficult for these laborers to find mates in this country. As a result, bachelor communities consisting mainly of single males became characteristic of many Asian ethnic groups.

Although many of these discriminatory laws have been revoked, the community still bears the long-term effects of cultural, socioeconomic, and political exploitation and oppression. Institutional discrimination and deprivation continue, but in new forms, such as the Immigration Reform and Control Act of 1986, which disproportionately affects people of color, including Asians, and exclusion elsewhere of Asian Americans as minorities entitled to special services and opportunities. As long as Asian Americans are not treated as full citizens of this country, their political participation and contribution will remain limited.

Racial Insensitivity and Unreceptivity.   Along with other women of color, some Asian American women criticize the role that white women, in partnership with white men, play in defending and perpetuating racism.[10] The capitalist patriarchy has differential effects on white women and Asian American women. While white women experience sexism, Asian American women suffer from both racism and sexism. For example, sexual stereotypes compounded with racial stereotypes continue to degrade the self-image of Asian American women. White supremacy and male dominance, both individually and in combination, have detrimental effects on the political functioning of Asian American women. For this reason, white women are seen as partly responsible for perpetuating racial prejudice and discriminatory practices.

More specifically, Asian American women who are committed to fighting both sexism and racism feel that white feminists are not aware of or sympathetic to the differences in concerns and priorities of Asian American women. Although Asian American women share many common issues and concerns with white feminists, many tend to place a higher priority on eradicating racism than sexism. They prefer to join groups that advocate improved conditions for people of their own ethnic background rather than groups oriented toward women's issues only. They advocate for multiculturally sensitive programs, not ones just aimed at reforming gender inequality. For instance, they prefer multilingual childcare programs and counseling services that bridge communication gaps and promote cultural understanding.

Some white feminists may accept Asian American women and other women of color as an integral part of the movement in the abstract. But entrance into the predominantly white feminist organizations has not been extended to include them in actuality. The open-door policy allows Asian American women as members, but closed attitudes limit their efforts to work on issues and problems concerning Asian American women, to build coalitions, and to influence decision making. Without understanding the history and culture of Asian American women, some white feminists are impatient with the relatively low level of consciousness and apparent slow progress made by Asian American women in organizing. Their token presence indicates the superficial nature of the invitation to join. The same frustrations of voicelessness, namelessness, and powerlessness run parallel to the experience of white women trying to break into a male-dominated system, the "old-boy" network.[11] While white feminists belong to the center of the movement, Asian American women and women of color remain on its margin.[12]

Class Cleavage.   In addition to racial insensitivity, the typical middle- and upper-class composition of the feminist movement repels many Asian American women who feel more concern about working-class women.[13] The economic class structure has unfortunately created social barriers between working-class women and middle- or upper-class women. While affluent white women, because of their class entitlement, have more resources, extra time, and the personal energy for political organizing, working-class Asian American women struggle to survive and have little time to question the economic structure. They may not therefore fully understand how the class structure of America limits their aspirations and achievements. Furthermore, greater acceptance of traditional sex-typed ideology by Asian American women and their perception of the feminist movement as alien, radical, and irrelevant to their needs also account for their lack of participation. As a result, it is difficult for them to relate their own economic issues to other women's concerns and place them in a larger sociopolitical context.

Class cleavage exists not only in the larger feminist movement, but also among Asian American women as well. While Asian American working-class women tend to see economic survival as a primary concern, those with high levels of education, social status, and income tend to be more concerned with job advancement, professional licensing requirements, and career development. Regardless of occupational levels, the immigrant status of Asian American women and their families does not enable them to adapt easily to current demands and requirements of the American labor market. Many experience tremendous status and financial losses as the result of immigration.

Ethnicity, however, cuts across all the class sectors, and provides a form of identification and social bonding among Asian American women from different classes. Limited efforts, such as providing tutoring, social, legal, and health services, women's shelters, counseling, job-training programs, and outreach, are helping bridge the gap between class groups. Class barriers are thus much easier to overcome among Asian American women than between the white feminists and Asian American women from working-class backgrounds.

IMPLICATIONS AND CONCLUSION

Asian American women confront problems on multiple fronts. Thus no social movement that addresses only one of the problem areas can adequately resolve their multiple oppressions sexually, racially, legally, economically, and culturally. The feminist movement is not an exception to this, for the specific concerns of Asian American women are often not those of white feminists. Without recognizing these multiple oppressions, political participation in the larger movement will be incompatible with the definition, goals, and interests of the Asian American cause. In this case, the concept of feminism needs to be broadly defined to address the interconnectedness of sex, gender, race, class, and culture so that its defining character and meaning are grounded in the experience of various kinds of women, including Asian American women. Broadening feminism implies that sisterhood is inclusive regardless of one's race, class background, national origin, sexual preference, physical condition, and life-style. Then strategies of collective action are needed to address the specific needs of Asian American women, to overcome the barriers that block their political participation, and to strengthen their relationship with others in the feminist movement as well as human liberation as a whole. . . .

To effect their political course of action Asian American women must develop strategies and programs to overcome internal and external barriers. When developing appropriate courses of action, the differences in their historical pasts, the uniqueness of their subculture, and structural arrangements within the Asian American communities and in the larger society must be taken into account. What has successfully advanced the cause of other women's groups cannot be simply imposed on Asian American women.

Five major suggestions are outlined here. First, strategies targeted to overcome psychological barriers may include consciousness-raising techniques to deal directly with identity crises and conflicting loyalties resulting from the double status as women and as members of a racial minority group. Asian American women might develop a transcendent type of gender consciousness that encompasses concern for all forms of multiple oppression.[14] Education is one of the necessary ingredients for increasing political awareness and the power of Asian American women. The women need to develop leadership and organizational skills in order to become active in the political arena. They may identify outstanding women leaders as role models to emulate. Networking and coalition building would provide them mutual support and contact with other women's groups. Programs designed to overcome language difficulties and to improve communication skills and image management are also needed. The goal is to develop a healthy self-concept, positive in outlook, assertive in behavior, and androgynous in style.

Second, self-awareness and cultural programs aimed toward cultural pluralism may be designed to educate Asian American women. They can learn what past conditions and ineffectual activities have led to their current plight. These programs will assist them in seeking cultural resolutions by combining the parts of the Asian and American cultures that are compatible with one another and most appropriate given the demands of current social circumstances. By exposing Asian American women to a wide range of life options, they will learn to demand self-determination, to explore ways of self-expression, and to seek strategies for self-empowerment. They will realize that they can change the course of their life by their own actions.

Third, the role of males in the life struggle of Asian American women is a critical but unanswered question to be explored. As long as patriarchy persists, male dominance will exist inside and outside Asian American communities. While some Asian American women are willing to work with men in partnership for happiness and success, others may opt for independence from males politically and/or sexually. The issue here is that freedom of choice must be available to women if they are to be totally liberated.[15] Whatever choices Asian American women make, others, whoever they are, have to accept these women's definition of gender relationship and respect their choice of self-determination.

Fourth, white feminists and Asian American women should work to build a foundation for feminist solidarity and deal together with racism and classism. White feminists must first critically examine their attitudes and behavior toward women of color and different classes. They need to demonstrate consistency in attitudes and behavior when relating to Asian American women. They need to show sensitivity toward Asians and place the eradication of racism and classism as the top priority in the larger feminist movement. They should take responsibility for educating the general public about cultural and ethnic differences and join Asian American women in protesting and stopping actions that reinforce racism and classism.

Finally, Asian American women must unite with other women of color who, for the most part, share similar life circumstances, experience multiple oppression, and struggle for common goals. Unless the whole social structure is uprooted, many institutional barriers in law, housing, education, employment, economics, and politics that are deeply embedded in the system will remain unchanged. Only when different groups work effectively and strategically together as a political force will all women achieve a new political consciousness and gain collective strength, to supersede the race, gender, sexual, class, and cultural differences that now divide them.

NOTES

1 Patricia Madoo Lengermann and Jill Niebrugge-Brantley, "Contemporary Feminist Theory," in *Contemporary Sociological Theories,* ed. George Ritzer (New York: Alfred A. Knopf, 1988), 430–432.

2 Esther Ngan-Ling Chow, *Acculturation of Asian American Professional Women,* research monograph (Washington, D.C.: National Institute of Mental Health, Department of Health and Human Services, 1982); Chow, "Acculturation Experience of the Asian American Woman," in *Beyond Sex Roles,* ed. Alice Sargent (St. Paul: West, 1985), 238–251.

3 Inge K. Broverman, Susan Raymond Vogel, Donald M. Broverman et al., "Sex-Role Stereotypes: A Current Appraisal," *Journal of Social Issues* 28 (1972), 59–78, and Susan A. Basow, *Gender Stereotypes: Traditions and Alternatives,* 2d ed. (Monterey, Calif.: Brooks/Cole, 1986).

4 Esther Ngan-Ling Chow, "The Politics of Racial and Sexual Stereotypes at Work," paper presented at the annual meeting of the society for the Study of Social Problems, San Francisco, 1982.

5 Few significant variations were found among different subgroups in their adherence to Asian values and acceptance of American values in two survey samples of Asian American women on both the East and West Coasts. See Chow, *Acculturation of Professional Women.*

6 Pauline Fong and Amado Y. Cabezas, "Employment of Asian-Pacific-American Women," in *Conference on the Educational and Occupational Needs,* 255–321.

7 Esther Ngan-Ling Chow, "Job Decision, Household Work and Gender Relations in Asian American Families," paper presented at the annual meeting of the American Sociological Association, Chicago, 1987.

8 Major legislation passed to ban and discriminate against Asians in America includes the 1850 Anti-Prostitution Law, the Naturalization Act of 1870, the Chinese Exclusion Act of 1882, the 1906 California Anti-Miscegenation Law, the California Alien Land Acts of 1913 and 1920, the Cabel Act of 1922, the Exclusion Act of 1924, and Executive Order 9066 in 1942–45, which put 112,000 Japanese Americans in concentration camps.

9 American history is filled with examples of such injustice, including anti-Chinese riots and massacres that forced the relocation of Chinese communities in many cities, mass internment and relocation of Japanese Americans during World War II, and land invasions and colonization in the Pacific Islands. See Judy Yung, *Chinese Women in America: A Pictorial History* (Seattle: University of Washington Press, 1986).

10 Chalso Loo and Paul Ong, "Slaying Demons with a Sewing Needle: Feminist Issues for Chinatown Women," *Berkeley Journal of Sociology* 27 (1982), 77–88; and Esther Ngan-Ling Chow, "Development of Feminist Consciousness."

11 Rosabeth Moss Kanter, *Men and Women of the Corporation* (New York: Basic Books, 1977).

12 Bell Hooks, *Feminist Theory: From Margin to Center* (Boston: South End Press, 1984) and *Ain't I a Woman: Black Women and Feminism* (Boston: South End Press, 1981).

13 Mitsuye Yamada, "Asian Pacific American Women and Feminism," in *This Bridge Called My Back: Writings by Radical Women of Color,* ed. C. Moraga and G. Anzaldúa (Watertown, Mass.: Persephone, 1981), 71–75; Loo and Ong, "Slaying Demons"; Chow, "Development of Feminist Consciousness"; and Cheng, "Social Mobility of Asian Women."

14 Chow, "Development of Feminist Consciousness."

15 See Alice Jardine and Paul Smith, eds., *Men in Feminism* (New York: Methuen, 1987).

Multiple Jeopardy: The Context of a Black Feminist Ideology

Deborah King[*]

Black women have long recognized the special circumstances of our lives in the United States: the commonalities that we share with all women, as well as the bonds that connect us to the men of our race. We have also realized that the interactive oppressions that circumscribe our lives provide a distinctive context for black womanhood. For us, the notion of double jeopardy is not a new one. Near the end of the nineteenth century, Anna Julia Cooper, who was born a slave and later became an educator and earned a Ph.D., often spoke and wrote of the double enslavement of black women and of our being "confronted by both a woman question and a race problem."[1] In 1904, Mary Church Terrell, the first president of the National Association of Colored Women, wrote, "Not only are colored women . . . handicapped on account of their sex, but they are almost everywhere baffled and mocked because of their race. Not only because they are women, but because they are colored women."[2]

The dual and systematic discriminations of racism and sexism remain pervasive, and, for many, class inequality compounds those oppressions. Yet, for as long as black women have known our numerous discriminations, we have also resisted those oppressions. Our day-to-day survival as well as our organized political actions have demonstrated the tenacity of our struggle against subordination. In the mid-nineteenth century, Sojourner Truth, an antislavery activist and women's rights advocate, repeatedly pronounced the strength and perseverance of black women.[3] More than one hundred years later, another black woman elaborated on Truth's theme. In addressing the National Association for the Advancement of Colored People (NAACP) Legal Defense Fund in 1971, Fannie Lou Hamer, the daughter of sharecroppers and a civil rights activist in Mississippi, commented on the special plight and role of black women over 350 years: "You know I work for the liberation of all people because when I liberate myself, I'm liberating other people . . . her [the white woman's] freedom is shackled in chains to mine, and she realizes for the first time that she is not free until I am free."[4] The necessity of addressing all oppressions is one of the hallmarks of black feminist thought.

THE THEORETICAL INVISIBILITY OF BLACK WOMEN

Among the first and perhaps most widely used approaches for understanding women's status in the United States has been the race-sex analogy. In essence, the model draws parallels between the systems and experiences of domination for blacks and those for women, and, as a result, it assumes that political mobilizations against racism and sexism are comparable. In 1860, Elizabeth Cady Stanton observed, "Prejudice against

*I am greatly indebted to Elsa B. Brown, Elaine Upton, Patricia Palmieri, Patricia Hill Collins, Dianne Pinderhughes, Rose Brewer, and *Signs'* referees for their thoughtful and critical comments on this paper.

color, of which we hear so much, is no stronger than that against sex."[5] Scholars in various disciplines have drawn similar analogies between racism and sexism. Sociologist Helen Hacker and historian William Chafe have both noted that unlike many ethnic groups, women and blacks possess ineradicable physical attributes that function "systematically and clearly to define from birth the possibilities to which members of a group might aspire."[6] In the first formal typology of the race-sex analogy, Helen Hacker identifies four additional dimensions on which the castelike status of blacks and women are similar: (1) ascribed attributes of emotionality, immaturity, and slyness; (2) rationalizations of status as conveyed in the notions of appropriate "place" and the contented subordinate; (3) accommodating and guileful behaviors; and (4) economic, legal, educational, and social discriminations.[7] Feminist theorists, including Simone de Beauvoir, Kate Millett, Mary Daly, and Shulamith Firestone, have all drawn extensively on this analogy in their critiques of the patriarchy.[8]

This analogy has served as a powerful means of conveying an image of women's subordinate status, and of mobilizing women and men for political action. The social movements for racial equality in the United States, whether the abolitionist movement in the nineteenth century or the civil rights movement in the mid-twentieth century, were predecessors, catalysts, and prototypes for women's collective action. A significant segment of feminist activists came to recognize and understand their own oppression, as well as to develop important organizing skills through their participation in efforts for racial justice.[9] In sum, the race-sex correspondence has been used successfully because the race model was a well-established and effective pedagogical tool for both the theoretical conceptualization of and the political resistance to sexual inequality.

We learn very little about black women from this analogy.[10] The experience of black women is apparently assumed, though never explicitly stated, to be synonymous with that of either black males or white females; and since the experiences of both are equivalent, a discussion of black women in particular is superfluous. It is mistakenly granted that either there is no difference in being black and female from being generically black (i.e., male) or generically female (i.e., white). The analogy obfuscates or denies what Chafe refers to as "the profound substantive differences" between blacks and women. The scope, both institutionally and culturally, and the intensity of the physical and psychological impact of racism is qualitatively different from that of sexism. The group experience of slavery and lynching for blacks, genocide for Native Americans, and military conquest for Mexican-Americans and Puerto Ricans is not substantively comparable to the physical abuse, social discrimination, and cultural denigration suffered by women. This is not to argue that those forms of racial oppressions are greater or more unjust but that the substantive differences need to be identified and to inform conceptualizations. Althea Smith and Abigail Stewart point out that "the assumption of parallelism led to research that masked the differences in these processes [i.e., racism, sexism, and their effects on self-image] for different groups."[11] A similar point has been forcefully made by bell hooks: "No other group in America has so had their identity socialized out of existence as have black women. We are rarely recognized as a group separate and distinct from black men, or a present part of the larger group 'women' in this culture. . . . When black people are talked about the focus tends to be on black men; and when women are talked about the focus tends to be on white women."[12] It is precisely those differences between blacks and women, between black men and black women, between black women and white women that are crucial to understanding the nature of black womanhood.

THE PROMISE AND LIMITATIONS OF DOUBLE JEOPARDY

In 1972, Frances Beale, a founding member of the Women's Liberation Committee of the Student Nonviolent Coordinating Committee (SNCC) and, later, a member of the Third World Women's Alliance, introduced the term "double jeopardy" to describe the dual discriminations of racism and sexism that subjugate black women. Concerning black women, she wrote, "As blacks they suffer all the burdens of prejudice and mistreatment that fall on anyone with dark skin. As women they bear the additional burden of having to cope with white and black men."[13] Beale also astutely observed that the reality of dual discriminations often entailed economic disadvantage; unfortunately she did not incorporate that understanding into the conceptualization. Perhaps she viewed class status as a particular consequence of racism, rather than as an autonomous source of persecution; but such a preponderant majority of black women have endured the very lowest of wages and very poorest conditions of rural and urban poverty that some scholars have argued that economic class oppression must necessarily constitute a third jeopardy.[14] Still others have suggested that heterosexism or homophobia represents another significant oppression and should be included as a third or perhaps fourth jeopardy.[15] The triple jeopardy of racism, sexism, and classism is now widely accepted and used as the conceptualization of black women's status. However, while advancing our understanding beyond the erasure of black women within the confines of the race-sex analogy, it does not yet fully convey the dynamics of multiple forms of discrimination.

Unfortunately, most applications of the concepts of double and triple jeopardy have been overly simplistic in assuming that the relationships among the various discriminations are merely additive. These relationships are interpreted as equivalent to the mathematical equation, racism plus sexism plus classism equals triple jeopardy. In this instance, each discrimination has a single, direct, and independent effect on status, wherein the relative contribution of each is readily apparent. This simple incremental process does not represent the nature of black women's oppression but, rather, I would contend, leads to nonproductive assertions that one factor can and should supplant the other. For example, class oppression is the largest component of black women's subordinate status, therefore the exclusive focus should be on economics. Such assertions ignore the fact that racism, sexism, and classism constitute three, interdependent control systems. An interactive model, which I have termed multiple jeopardy, better captures those processes.[16]

The modifier "multiple" refers not only to several, simultaneous oppressions but to the multiplicative relationships among them as well. In other words, the equivalent formulation is racism multiplied by sexism multiplied by classism. The sexual exploitation of black women in slavery is a historical example. While black women workers suffered the same demanding physical labor and brutal punishments as black men, as females, we were also subject to forms of subjugation only applicable to women. Angela Davis, in *Women, Race and Class,* notes, "If the most violent punishments of men consisted in floggings and mutilations, women were flogged and mutilated, as well as raped."[17] At the same time, our reproductive and child-rearing activities served to enhance the quantity and quality of the "capital" of a slave economy. Our institutionalized exploitation as the concubines, mistresses, and sexual slaves of white males distinguished our experience from that of white females' sexual oppression because it could only have existed in relation to racist and classist forms of domination.

The importance of any one factor in explaining black women's circumstances thus varies depending on the particular aspect of our lives under consideration and the reference groups to whom we are compared. In some cases, race may be the more significant predictor of black women's status; in others, gender or class may be more influential. Table 1 presents the varied and conditional influence of race and gender and, presumably, of racism and sexism on socioeconomic and educational status. White males earn the highest median incomes, followed in decreasing order by black males, white females, and black females. The educational rankings are different. White males are again on top; but whites, males and females, have more years of schooling than black males and females. While gender is more critical in understanding black women's income ranking, race is more important in explaining their level of educational attainment. But in both examples, black females have the lowest status.

Table 2 shows a more complex relationship between race, gender, and class (here represented by educational attainment), and the influence of these variables on income. Overall, education is an important determinant of income, and despite race or gender, those with more education earn more money than those with less. Men earn more than women at the same level of education, and whites earn more than blacks at the same level of education. But among women, the relationship of education to income is confounded by race. Given our subordinate statuses as female and black, we might expect black women to receive the lowest incomes regardless of their educational attainment. However, the returns of postsecondary education, a college degree or higher, are greater for black females than for white females, while among those with less than a college degree, black females earn less than white females. A similar pattern is not

TABLE 1
RACE AND GENDER INTERACTIVE EFFECTS ON SOCIOECONOMIC STATUS

	Economic status ($)	Educational status (yrs.)
White males	16,467	12.7
Black males	9,448	12.2
White females	6,949	12.6
Black females	6,164	12.2

Note: Income figures are 1984 median incomes for those fifteen years or older. Educational attainment is for 1984, median years of school completed.
Source: U.S. Department of Commerce. Bureau of the Census. *Statistical Abstract of the United States, 1987* (Washington, D.C.: Government Printing Office, 1987).

TABLE 2
MULTIPLICATIVE EFFECTS OF RACE, GENDER, AND CLASS ON INCOME

	Income ($)			
	White males	Black males	White females	Black females
Less than a high school diploma	9,525	6,823	3,961	3,618
4 years of high school	13,733	9,260	6,103	5,954
1–3 years of college	14,258	10,532	6,451	6,929
Bachelor's degree	19,783	14,131	9,134	10,692
5 or more years of post-baccalaureate education	23,143	18,970	12,980	14,537

Note: Income is 1979 median income. Educational attainment is used as a measure of economic class.
Source: Detailed Population Characteristics, U.S. Summary, Sec. A, 1980 (Washington, D.C.: Government Printing Office, 1980).

found among males. In this three-way analysis, black women are not consistently in the lowest status, evidence that the importance of the multiple discriminations of race, gender, and class is varied and complex.

In the interactive model, the relative significance of race, sex, or class in determining the conditions of black women's lives is neither fixed nor absolute but, rather, is dependent on the socio-historical context and the social phenomenon under consideration. These interactions also produce what to some appears a seemingly confounding set of social roles and political attitudes among black women. Sociologist Bonnie Thornton Dill has discussed the importance of scholars' recognizing, incorporating, and interpreting the complex variety of social roles that black women have performed in reaction to multiple jeopardies. She argues that the constellation of "attitudes, behaviors, and interpersonal relationships . . . were adaptations to a variety of factors, including the harsh realities of their environment, Afro-American cultural images of black womanhood, and the sometimes conflicting values and norms of the wider society."[18]

A black woman's survival depends on her ability to use all the economic, social, and cultural resources available to her from both the larger society and within her community. For example, black women historically have had to assume economically productive roles as well as retain domestic ones, and until recently our labor force participation rate well exceeded that of white women.[19] Labor, whether unpaid and coerced (as under slavery) or paid and necessary employment, has been a distinctive characteristic of black women's social roles. It has earned us a small but significant degree of self-reliance and independence that has promoted egalitarian relations with black men and active influence within the black family and community.[20] But it also has had costs. For instance, black women have most often had to work in low status and low paying jobs since race and sex discrimination have historically limited our employment options. The legacy of the political economy of slavery under capitalism is the fact that employers, and not black women, still profit the most from black women's labor. And when black women become the primary or sole earners for households, researchers and public analysts interpret this self-sufficiency as pathology, as deviance, as a threat to black family life.[21] Yet, it is black women's well-documented facility to encompass seemingly contradictory role expectations of worker, homemaker, and mother that has contributed to the confusion in understanding black womanhood.[22] These competing demands (each requiring its own set of resistances to multiple forms of oppression) are a primary influence on the black woman's definition of her womanhood, and her relationships to the people around her. To reduce this complex of negotiations to an addition problem (racism + sexism = black women's experience) is to define the issues, and indeed black womanhood itself, within the structural terms developed by Europeans and especially white males to privilege their race and their sex unilaterally. Sojourner's declaration, "ain't I a woman?" directly refutes this sort of conceptualization of womanhood as one dimensional rather than dialectical.

MULTIPLE JEOPARDY WITHIN THE POLITICS OF LIBERATION

In order to understand the concept of multiple jeopardy, it is necessary to look beyond the social structure and process of the dominant society that insidiously pervade even the movements for race, gender, and class liberation. Thus, the confrontations among blacks about sexism and classism, among women about racism and classism, and among the various economic classes about racism and sexism compose a second feature of the context of black feminist ideology. A formidable impediment in these battles is the "monist" approach of most liberation ideologies. In *Liberating Theory,* monism is described as a political claim "that one particular domination precipitates all really important oppressions. Whether Marxist, anarchist, nationalist, or feminist, these 'ideal types' argue that important social relations can all be reduced to the economy, state, culture, or gender."[23] For example, during the suffrage debates, it was routinely asserted that only one group might gain voting privileges—either blacks or women, that is black men or white women. For black women, the granting of suffrage to either group would still mean our disenfranchisement because of either our sex or our race. Faced with this dilemma, many black women and most black men believed that the extension of suffrage to black males was imperative in order to protect race interests in the historical period of postbellum America. But because political empowerment for black women would require that both blacks and women gained the right to vote, some of these same black women also lobbied strenuously for women's suffrage.[24]

The contemporary efforts of black women to achieve greater equal opportunity and status present similar dilemmas, whether in the areas of reproductive rights, electoral politics, or poverty. Our history of resistance to multiple jeopardies is replete with the fierce tensions, untenable ultimatums, and bitter compromises between nationalism, feminism, and class politics. In a curious twist of fate, we find ourselves marginal to both the movements for women's liberation and black liberation irrespective of our victimization under the dual discriminations of racism and sexism. A similar exclusion or secondary status typifies our role within class movements. Ironically, black women are often in conflict with the very same subordinate groups with which we share some interests. The groups in which we find logical allies on certain issues are the groups in which we may find opponents on others. To the extent that we have found ourselves confronting the exclusivity of monistic politics, we have had to manage ideologies and activities that did not address the dialectics of our lives. We are asked to decide with whom to ally, which interests to advance. Should black women's primary ideological and activist commitment be to race, sex, or class-based social movements? Can we afford to be monist? Can we afford not to be?

In the following consideration of the dialectics within each of three liberation movements, I hope to describe the tensions and priorities that influence the construction of a black feminist ideology. To the extent that any politic is monistic, the actual victims of racism, sexism, or classism may be absent from, invisible within, or seen as antagonistic to that politic. Thus, prejudicial attitudes and discriminatory actions may be overt, subtle, or covert; and they may have various manifestations through ideological statements, policies and strategies, and interpersonal relations. That is, black and/or poor women may be marginal to monistic feminism, women's concerns may be excluded from nationalistic activism, and indifference to race and gender may pervade class politics. This invisibility may be due to actual exclusion or benign neglect, while marginality is represented in tokenism, minimization, and devalued participation. Antagonism involves two subordinate groups whose actions and beliefs are placed in opposition as mutually detrimental. From this conceptual framework, the following discussion highlights the major aspects of multiple jeopardy within liberation politics.

Intraracial Politics

Racial solidarity and race liberation have been and remain a fundamental concern for black Americans. Historically and currently, slavery, segregation, and institutional as well as individual discrimination have been formative experiences in most blacks' socialization and political outlook. The inerasable physical characteristics of race have long determined the status and opportunities of black women in the United States. Since race serves as a significant filter of what blacks perceive and how blacks are perceived, many black women have claimed that their racial identity is more salient than either their gender or class identity.[25]

Since the 1800s, however, the writings of such prominent black women as Sojourner Truth, Maria Stewart, Anna Julia Cooper, Josephine St. Pierre Ruffin, Frances Watkins Harper, Pauli Murray, Frances Beale, Audre Lorde, and Angela Davis have described a broader view of black consciousness.[26] Even among those black women who expressed grave reservations about participating in the women's movement, most recognized sexism as a factor of their subordination in the larger society and acknowledged sexual politics among blacks. They could identify the sexual inequities that resulted in the images of black women as emasculating matriarchs; in the rates of sexual abuse and physical violence; and in black men assuming the visible leadership positions in many black social institutions, such as the church, the intelligentsia, and political organizations.[27] During the civil rights and black nationalist movements of the

1960s and 1970s, men quite effectively used the matriarchy issue to manipulate and coerce black women into maintaining exclusive commitments to racial interests and redefining and narrowing black women's roles and images in ways to fit a more traditional Western view of women. Black feminists Pauli Murray and Pauline Terrelonge Stone both agree that the debates over this issue became an ideological ploy to heighten guilt in black women over their supposed collusion with whites in the oppression of black men.[28] Consequently, these intraracial tensions worked against the public articulations of a feminist consciousness by most black women. Nevertheless, a point of concern and contention within the black community was how sexual inequalities might best be addressed, not whether they existed. A few black women responded by choosing monistic feminism, others sought a distinct black feminist activism. While many organized feminist efforts within race-oriented movements, some also adopted a strict nationalist view. Over time, there were also transformations of perspectives. For example, the black women of SNCC created within it a women's liberation group which later became an independent feminists-of-color organization, the Third World Women's Alliance, which is today the only surviving entity of SNCC.

The politics of race liberation have rarely been exclusively race-based. Because so many blacks historically have been economically oppressed, race liberation has out of necessity become more pluralistic through its incorporation of economic interests. Whether civil rights or a nationalist activism, the approach to class injustice generally promotes greater economic opportunities and rewards within the existing capitalist order. At the turn of the century, for instance, the collective action known as racial uplift involved the efforts of educated, middle-class blacks to elevate the moral, physical, social, and economic conditions of lower income blacks. The National Association of Wage Earners was established in the 1920s by women like Nannie Burroughs, Maggie Wallace, and Mary McCleod Bethune to assist black female domestic and factory workers.[29]

The civil rights movement initially seemed to avoid the value-laden implications of this pattern of middle-class beneficence toward those with fewer economic resources. Both Aldon Morris, a sociologist, and Clayborne Carson, a historian, have written of the genuine grass roots orientation of the black southern strategy in the 1950s and early 1960s.[30] The majority of the participants were rural, poorly educated, and economically disadvantaged, but more important, these same individuals set the priorities and the strategies of the movement. The legacy was an affirmation of the strength of seemingly powerless people, and particularly of the black women who were among the principal organizers and supporters.[31]

Despite these auspicious beginnings, Cornell West, a black theologian, described the 1960s as a time when the interests of poor blacks were often betrayed.[32] Middle-class blacks were better able to take advantage of the relatively greater opportunities made possible through the race-oriented, legal liberalism of equal opportunity and affirmative action policies and electoral politics. Only such groups as the Nation of Islam and the League of Revolutionary Black Workers, like Marcus Garvey's United Negro Improvement Association earlier in this century, continued to represent the interests of working class and impoverished blacks. The contemporary controversy over class polarization in the black community is a consequence of the movement not effectively addressing the economic status of all blacks. Given the particularly precarious economic status of black women, this neglect and marginalization of class is especially problematic for them. The National Welfare Rights Organization, founded in 1967, was one of the few successful, though short-lived, efforts to address the class divisions. Only recently have race-focal groups, including the Urban League and the National Association for the Advancement of Colored People, addressed the plight of impoverished black women.

Racial solidarity has been a fundamental element of black women's resistance to domination. However, the intraracial politics of gender and class have made a strictly nationalistic approach overly restrictive and incalculably detrimental to our prospects for full liberation. Given a social condition that is also compounded by other oppressions, black women have necessarily been concerned with affecting, at the very least, an amelioration of economic and gender discriminations. Consequently, some black women have sought an association with feminism as one alternative to the limitations of monistic race politics.

Politics Among Women

At one level, black women, other women of color, and white women, share many common contemporary concerns about their legal status and rights, encounters with discrimination, and sexual victimization. It is on these shared concerns that feminists have sought to forge a sense of sisterhood and to foster solidarity. This effort is manifest in a variety of ways, but the slogan, "sisterhood is powerful," best exemplifies the importance and the hoped for efficacy of such solidarity in the achievement of women's equality and liberation. For example, all-female restrictions for consciousness-raising sessions, intellectual and artistic programs and publications, organizations, businesses, and communities reflect this singular orientation; and lesbian feminist separatism represents the absolute ideological expression of the monistic tendencies in feminism.

Presumably, black women are included in this sisterhood, but, nonetheless, invisibility and marginality characterize much of our relationship to the women's movement. The assertion of commonality, indeed of the universality and primacy of female oppression, denies the other structured inequalities of race, class, religion, and nationality, as well as denying the diverse cultural heritages that affect the lives of many women. While contending that feminist consciousness and theory emerged from the personal, everyday reality of being female, the reality of millions of women was ignored. The phrase, "the personal is the political" not only reflects a phenomenological approach to women's liberation—that is, of women defining and constructing their own reality—but it has also come to describe the politics of imposing and privileging a few women's personal lives over all women's lives by assuming that these few could be prototypical. For black women, the personal is bound up in the problems peculiar to multiple jeopardies of race and class, not the singular one of sexual inequality. This has not necessarily meant that black women rejected feminism, but merely that they were not singlemindedly committed to the organizations and some of the agenda that have come to be called the women's movement, that is, the movement of white, often protestant, middle-class women.

Feminism has excluded and devalued black women, our experiences, and our interpretations of our own realities at the conceptual and ideological level. Black feminists and black women scholars have identified and critically examined other serious flaws in feminist theorizing. The assumption that the family is by definition patriarchal, the privileging of an individualistic worldview, and the advocacy of female separatism are often antithetical positions to many of the values and goals of black women and thus are hindrances to our association with feminism.[33] These theoretical blinders obscured the ability of certain feminists first to recognize the multifaceted nature of women's oppressions and then to envision theories that encompass those realities. As a consequence, monistic feminism's ability to foresee remedies that would neither abandon women to the other discriminations, including race and class, nor exacerbate those burdens is extremely limited. Without theories and concepts that represent the experiences of black women, the women's movement has and will be ineffectual in making ideological appeals that might mobilize such women. Often, in fact, this conceptual invisibility has led to the actual strategic neglect and physical exclusion or nonparticipation of black women.

Many white feminist activists have often assumed that their antisexism stance abolished all racial prejudice or discriminatory behaviors. At best, this presumption is naive and reflects a serious ignorance of the pervasiveness of racism in this society. Many blacks, women and men alike, see such postures as arrogant, racist, and dangerous to their own interests. Diane Lewis concluded that the status of black women and our interests within the women's movement and its organizations essentially replicates our structurally subordinate position to white women in the larger society.[34] Different opportunity structures and life options make interracial alliances and feminist solidarity problematic. Conceptually invisible, interpersonally misunderstood and insulted, and strategically marginal, black women have found that much in the movement has denied important aspects of our history and experience. Yet, despite the critical obstacles and limitations, the imperatives of multiple jeopardy necessitate recognizing and resisting sexism.

Beyond the race politics in feminism, many black women share concerns of impoverished and working-class women about class politics. What has become mainstream feminism rests on traditional, liberal economic aspirations of equal employment opportunities for women. In practice, however, the emphasis is often on the professional careers of those women who are already economically privileged and college educated. It could be argued, for instance, that equal access to all types of vocational training and jobs may not be desirable as a necessary or primary goal. While it is true that men on average earn more than women, all men do not have equally attractive jobs in terms of working conditions, compensation and benefits, prestige, and mobility. Those male jobs may represent, at best, only a minimal improvement over the jobs of many working women. White feminist economic concerns have concentrated on primary sector employment, but these are not the positions that are most critical and accessible to lower- or no-income women. Referring to the equal opportunity approach, Karen Kollias points out that "the majority of nonwhite, lower- and working-class women don't have the power to utilize these benefits because their primary, objective economic conditions haven't changed."[35]

Class stratification becomes an insignificant issue if economic disadvantage is seen as only relevant for feminism to the extent that women are unequal vis-à-vis men. The difference between male and female incomes is dramatically less among blacks than among whites (see table 1), suggesting that sex alone is not the sole determinant of economic status. From a monist feminist perspective, class exploitation is not understood as an independent system of oppression. Consequently, broad class dynamics are not addressed in liberal and some radical feminisms. Marxist and socialist feminists have sought to correct this biased view of class.[36] While the Marxists attempted to incorporate a concern for gender within traditional Marxist analysis, socialist feminists tried to develop a nonmonist perspective of feminism that saw sexism and classism as co-equal oppressions. Ellen Willis concludes that within various feminisms there was limited politics beyond an assertion that class hierarchy was oppressive. A radical feminist, she observes that the consciousness-raising, personal politics approach did not effectively challenge the structural, political economy of class oppression. She concludes that as a consequence, "women were implicated in the class system and had real class interests, that women could oppress men on the basis of class, and that class differences among women could not be resolved within a feminist context alone."[37]

First, the memberships of these class-oriented groups remained mostly middle class. Economically disadvantaged women have not directly contributed to a feminist theoretical understanding of class dynamics or the development of programs and strategies. Black feminist and literary critic, bell hooks notes that "had poor women set the agenda for feminist movement, they might have decided that class struggle would be a central feminist issue."[38] She further contends that class oppression has not become central among women liberationists because their "values, behaviors, and lifestyles continue to be shaped by privilege."[39] In a similar fashion, feminist and race politics have not informed or established ties between poor and working-class black and white women. Phyllis M. Palmer reasons that from the perspective of a poor black woman, white women individually may suffer wage discrimination because of their sex, but their relations to white males, the top income earners, as daughters and wives grants them a relatively better quality of material well-being. "Most white women do not *in reality* live on what they earn; they have access to the resources of white male income earners."[40] Rejecting what she views as the hollow efforts of "slumming" or nonhierarchical organizing, she observes that no serious strategies have been developed for convincing bourgeois women that class liberation is critical for women's liberation or for organizing with poor and working-class women.

This lack of attention to economic issues has significant implications for the participation of black women. Many of the differences of priorities between black and white women are related to class. Issues of welfare, hunger, poor housing, limited health care, and transportation are seldom seen as feminist interests and are rarely the subject of feminist social policies. As Brenda Eichelberger maintains, "the black woman's energy output is more often directed toward such basic survival issues, while the white woman's is more often aimed at fulfillment."[41]

In summary, feminism's neglect, misunderstanding, or deemphasis of the politics of race and class have direct implications for the actions of black women in relationship to the movement. Often, our response has been to avoid participation in white female, middle-class dominated organizations and to withhold our support from policies that are not in our race and class interests. Nevertheless, just as the importance of race led many black women to commitments to racially based politics, and gender interests compelled our feminist efforts, economic injustices have brought many to consider class politics as a major avenue of liberation. . . .

MULTIPLE CONSCIOUSNESS IN BLACK FEMINIST IDEOLOGY

Black women have been feminists since the early 1800s, but our exclusion from the white women's movement and its organizations has led many incorrectly to assume that we were not present in the (white) women's movement because we were not interested in resisting sexism both within and without the black community. What appears recently to be a change in black women's position, from studied indifference to disdain and curiosity to cautious affirmation of the women's movement, may be due to structural changes in relationships between blacks and whites that have made black women "more sensitive to the obstacles of sexism and to the relevance of the women's movement."[42] Black women's apparent greater sensitivity to sexism may be merely the bolder, public articulation of black feminist concerns that have existed for well over a century. In other words, black women did not just become feminists in the 1970s. We did, however, grant more salience to those concerns and become more willing to organize primarily on that basis, creating the Combahee River Collective, the National Black Feminist Organization, and Sapphire Sapphos. Some black women chose to participate in predominantly white, women's movement activities and organizations, while others elected to develop the scholarship and curriculum that became the foundation of black women's studies, while still others founded black feminist journals, presses, and political organizations.[43]

Several studies have considered the relevance of black women's diverse characteristics in understanding our political attitudes; these reports seem fairly inconsistent, if not contradictory.[44] The various findings do suggest that the conditions that bring black women to feminist consciousness are specific to our social and historical experiences. For black women, the circumstances of lower socioeconomic life may encourage political, and particularly feminist, consciousness.[45] This is in contrast to feminist as well as traditional political socialization literature that suggests that more liberal, that is, feminist, attitudes are associated with higher education attainment and class standing. Many of the conditions that middle-class, white feminists have found oppressive are perceived as privileges by black women, especially those with low incomes. For instance, the option not to work outside of the home is a luxury that historically has been denied most black women. The desire to struggle for this option can, in such a context, represent a feminist position, precisely because it constitutes an instance of greater liberty for certain women. It is also important to note, however, that the class differences among black women regarding our feminist consciousness are minimal. Black women's particular history thus is an essential ingredient in shaping our feminist concerns.

Certainly the multifaceted nature of black womanhood would meld diverse ideologies, from race liberation, class liberation, and women's liberation. The basis of our feminist ideology is rooted in our reality. To the extent that the adherents of any one ideology insist on separatist organizational forms, assert the fundamental nature of any one oppression, and demand total cognitive, affective, and behavioral commitment, that ideology and its practitioners exclude black women and the realities of our lives.

A black feminist ideology, first and foremost, thus declares the visibility of black women. It acknowledges the fact that two innate and inerasable traits, being both black and female, constitute our special status in American society. Second, black feminism asserts self-determination as essential. Black women are empowered with the right to interpret our reality and define our objectives. While drawing on a rich tradition of struggle as blacks and as women, we continually establish and reestablish our own priorities. As black women, we decide for ourselves the relative salience of any and all identities and oppressions, and how and the extent to which those features inform our politics. Third, a black feminist ideology fundamentally challenges the interstructure of the oppressions of racism, sexism, and classism both in the dominant society and within movements for liberation. It is in confrontation with multiple jeopardy that black women define and sustain a multiple consciousness essential for our liberation, of which feminist consciousness is an integral part.

Finally, a black feminist ideology presumes an image of black women as powerful, independent subjects. By concentrating on our multiple oppressions, scholarly descriptions have confounded our ability to discover and appreciate the ways in which black women are not victims. Ideological and political choices cannot be assumed to be determined solely by the historical dynamics of racism, sexism, and classism in this society. Although the complexities and ambiguities that merge a consciousness of race, class, and gender oppressions make the emergence and praxis of a multivalent ideology problematical, they also make such a task more necessary if we are to work toward our liberation as blacks, as the economically exploited, and as women.

NOTES

1 Gerda Lerner, ed., *Black Women in White America: A Documentary History* (New York: Vintage, 1973), 573.

2 Mary Church Terrell, "The Progress of Colored Women," *Voice of the Negro* 1, no. 7 (July 1904): 292.

3 See Lerner, ed., esp. 566–72; and Bert James Loewenberg and Ruth Bogin, eds., *Black Women in Nineteenth-Century American Life* (University Park: Pennsylvania State University Press, 1976), 234–42.

4 See Lerner, ed., 609, 610, 611.

5 Elizabeth Cady Stanton as quoted by William Chafe, *Women and Equality: Changing Patterns in American Culture* (New York: Oxford University Press, 1977), 44. Some eighty years after Stanton's observation, Swedish social psychologist Gunnar Myrdal, in an ap-

pendix to his *An American Dilemma: The Negro Problem and Modern Democracy* (New York: Harper & Row, 1962), also saw the woman problem as parallel to the Negro problem.

6 Chafe, 77.

7 Helen Hacker, "Women as a Minority Group," *Social Forces* 30 (1951): 60–69.

8 For examples of feminist writings using the race-sex analogy or the master-slave model, see Simone de Beauvoir, *The Second Sex,* trans. and ed. H. M. Parshley (New York: Random House, 1974); Kate Millett, *Sexual Politics* (New York: Avon, 1969); Shulamith Firestone, *The Dialectics of Sex* (New York: Morrow, 1970); and Mary Daly, *Beyond God the Father: Toward a Philosophy of Women's Liberation* (Boston: Beacon, 1973).

9 See Sara Evans, *Personal Politics: The Roots of Women's Liberation in the Civil Rights Movement and the New Left* (New York: Vintage, 1980); Catharine Stimpson, "Thy Neighbor's Wife, Thy Neighbor's Servants: Women's Liberation and Black Civil Rights," in *Woman in Sexist Society: Studies in Power and Powerlessness,* ed. Vivian Gornick and Barbara Moran (New York: Basic, 1971), 452–79; and Angela Davis, *Women, Race and Class* (New York: Random House, 1981). Recently, there has been some debate concerning precisely what lessons, if any, women learned from their participation in the abolitionist and civil rights movements. For an argument against the importance of race-oriented movements for feminist politics, see E. C. DuBois, *Feminism and Suffrage* (Ithaca, N.Y.: Cornell University Press, 1978).

10 Other limitations have been noted by Linda LaRue, who contends that the analogy is an abstraction that falsely asserts a common oppression of blacks and women for rhetorical and propagandistic purposes ("The Black Movement and Women's Liberation," in *Female Psychology: The Emerging Self,* ed. Sue Cox [Chicago: Science Research Assoc., 1976]). In *Ain't I a Woman* (Boston: South End Press, 1981), bell hooks questions whether certain women, particularly those self-identified feminists who are white and middle class, are truly oppressed as opposed to being discriminated against. Stimpson bluntly declares that the race-sex analogy is exploitative and racist. See also Margaret A. Simons, "Racism and Feminism: A Schism in the Sisterhood," *Feminist Studies* 5 (1979): 384–401, for a critical review of this conceptual approach in feminist theorizing.

11 Chafe, 76; Althea Smith and Abigail J. Stewart, "Approaches to Studying Racism and Sexism in Black Women's Lives," *Journal of Social Issues* 39 (1983): 1–15.

12 hooks, *Ain't I a Woman,* 7.

13 Frances Beale, "Double Jeopardy: To Be Black and Female," in *The Black Woman: An Anthology,* ed. Toni Cade (New York: New American Library, 1979), 90–100.

14 See, e.g., Beverly Lindsay, "Minority Women in America: Black American, Native American, Chicana, and Asian American Women," in *The Study of Woman: Enlarging Perspectives of Social Reality,* ed. Eloise C. Synder (New York: Harper & Row, 1979), 318–63. She presents a paradigm wherein whiteness, maleness, and money are advantageous: a poor, black woman is triply disadvantaged. Lindsay argues that triple jeopardy, the interaction of sexism, racism, and economic oppression, is "the most realistic perspective for analyzing the position of black American women; and this perspective will serve as common linkage among the discussions of other minority women" (328).

15 See Barbara Smith, ed., *Home Girls: A Black Feminist Anthology* (New York: Kitchen Table Press, 1983), esp. sec. 3; and Audre Lorde, "Scratching the Surface: Some Notes on Barriers to Women and Loving," *Black Scholar* 13 (Summer 1982): 20–24, and *Sister Outsider: Essays and Speeches* (Trumansberg, N.Y.: Crossing Press, 1984).

16 For other attempts at nonadditive models, see Smith and Stewart; Elizabeth M. Almquist, "Untangling the Effects of Race and Sex: The Disadvantaged Status of Black Women," *Social Science Quarterly* 56 (1975): 129–42; Margaret L. Andersen, *Thinking about Women:*

Sociological and Feminist Perspectives (New York: Macmillan, 1983). The term "ethnogender" is introduced in Vincent Jeffries and H. Edward Ransford, *Social Stratification: A Multiple Hierarchy Approach* (Boston: Allyn & Bacon, 1980); and Edward Ransford and Jon Miller, "Race, Sex, and Feminist Outlook," *American Sociological Review* 48 (1983): 46–59.

17 Davis, *Women, Race and Class,* 7.

18 Bonnie Thornton Dill, "The Dialectics of Black Womanhood," *Signs: Journal of Women in Culture and Society* 4 (1979): 543–55, esp. 547. Smith and Stewart, 1, make a similar point.

19 In slavery, there was 100 percent labor force participation by black women. In 1910, 34 percent were in the official labor force. In 1960, the figure was 40 percent, and by 1980, it was over 50 percent. Comparable figures for white women are 18 percent in 1890, 22 percent in 1910, 37 percent in 1960, and 51 percent in 1980. For a more detailed discussion, see Phyllis A. Wallace, *Black Women in the Labor Force* (Cambridge, Mass.: MIT Press, 1980).

20 Angela Davis, "Reflections of the Black Woman's Role in the Community of Slaves," *Black Scholar* 3 (December 1971): 2–16, offers an enlightening discussion of the irony of independence out of subordination. See also Deborah Gray White, *Ar'n't I a Woman? Female Slaves in the Plantation South* (New York: Norton, 1985), for a more detailed analysis of the contradictions of the black female role in slavery. For a discussion of the role of black women in the family, see Robert Staples, *The Black Woman in America* (Chicago: Nelson Hall, 1973); Robert Hill, *The Strengths of Black Families* (New York: Emerson Hall, 1972); Herbert Guttman, *The Black Family in Slavery and Freedom, 1750 to 1925* (New York: Random House, 1976); Carol Stack, *All Our Kin: Strategies for Survival in a Black Community* (New York: Harper & Row, 1974); and Charles Willie, *A New Look at Black Families* (New York: General Hall, 1976). For a discussion of black women's community roles, see Bettina Aptheker, *Woman's Legacy: Essays on Race, Sex, and Class in American History* (Amherst: University of Massachusetts Press, 1982); Paula Giddings, *When and Where I Enter: The Impact of Black Women on Race and Sex in America* (New York: William Morrow, 1983); Lerner, ed. (n. 1 above); Sharon Harley and Rosalyn Terborg-Penn, eds., *The Afro-American Woman: Struggles and Images* (Port Washington, N.Y.: Kennikat Press, 1978); Linda Perkins, "The Impact of the 'Cult of True Womanhood' on the Education of Black Women," *Journal of Social Issues* 39 (1983): 17–28; and the special issue, "The Impact of Black Women in Education," *Journal of Negro Education* 51, no. 3 (Summer 1982).

21 See Robert Staples, "The Myth of the Black Matriarchy," in his *The Black Family: Essays and Studies* (Belmont, Calif.: Wadsworth, 1971), and *The Black Woman in America*. Also see hooks, *Ain't I a Woman* (n. 10 above); and Cheryl T. Gilkes, "Black Women's Work as Deviance: Social Sources of Racial Antagonism within Contemporary Feminism," Working Paper no. 66 (Wellesley, Mass.: Wellesley College, Center for Research on Women, 1979). However, more recently Robert Staples has argued that black women who are too independent will be unable to find black mates and that black men are justified in their preference for a more traditionally feminine partner ("The Myth of Black Macho: A Response to Angry Black Feminists," *Black Scholar* 10 [March–April 1979]: 24–32).

22 See White; and Jacqueline Jones, *Labor of Love, Labor of Sorrow: Black Women, Work and the Family, From Slavery to the Present* (New York: Basic, 1985).

23 Michael Albert et al., *Liberating Theory* (Boston: South End Press, 1986), 6.

24 For further discussion of suffrage and racism, see Davis, *Women, Race and Class* (n. 9 above); Giddings; Harley and Terborg-Penn; and Barbara H. Andolsen, *"Daughters of Jefferson, Daughters of Bootblacks": Racism and American Feminism* (Macon, Ga.: Mercer University Press, 1986).

25 See Gloria Joseph and Jill Lewis, *Common Differences: Conflicts in Black and White Feminist Perspectives* (New York: Avon, 1981); Diane K. Lewis, "A Response to Inequality:

Black Women, Racism, and Sexism," *Signs* 3 (1977): 339–61; and bell hooks, *Feminist Theory: From Margin to Center* (Boston: South End Press, 1984), for extended discussions of the dynamics of structural subordination to and social conflict with varying dominant racial and sexual groups.

26 For statements by Truth, Stewart, Cooper, Ruffin, and Harper, see Loewenberg and Bogin, eds. (n. 3 above); and Lerner, ed. (n. 1 above); for Lorde, see Lorde (n. 15 above); for Davis, see Davis, *Women, Race and Class;* for Beale, see Frances Beale, "Double Jeopardy" (n. 13 above), and "Slave of a Slave No More: Black Women in the Struggle," *Black Scholar* 12, no. 6 (November/December 1981): 16–24; and for Murray, see Pauli Murray, "'The Liberation of Black Women," in *Women: A Feminist Perspective,* ed. Jo Freeman (Palo Alto, Calif.: Mayfield, 1975), 351–63.

27 Regarding the church, see Pauline Terrelonge Stone, "Feminist Consciousness and Black Women," in Freeman, ed., 575–88; Joseph and Lewis; Jacqueline Grant, "Black Women and the Church," in *But Some of Us Are Brave: Black Women's Studies,* ed. Gloria T. Hull et al. (Old Westbury, N.Y.: Feminist Press, 1982), 141–52; and Cheryl Townsend Gilkes, "'Together and in Harness'; Women's Traditions in the Sanctified Church," *Signs* 10, no. 4 (Summer 1985): 678–99. Concerning politics, see LaRue (n. 10 above); Mae C. King, "The Politics of Sexual Stereotypes," *Black Scholar* 4 (March/April 1973): 12–22; and Manning Marable, *How Capitalism Underdeveloped Black America* (Boston: South End Press, 1983), esp. chap. 3. For a discussion of sexual victimization, see Barbara Smith, "Notes for Yet Another Paper on Black Feminism, or Will the Real Enemy Please Stand Up," *Conditions* 5 (1979): 123–27, as well as Joseph and Lewis. For a critique of the notion of the matriarch, see Stone; and Staples, "The Myth of the Black Matriarchy" (n. 21 above).

28 See Murray; and Stone.

29 Evelyn Brooks Bennett, "Nannie Burroughs and the Education of Black Woman," in Harley and Terborg-Penn (n. 20 above), 97–108.

30 Aldon Morris, *The Origins of the Civil Rights Movement: Black Communities Organizing for Change* (New York: Free Press, 1984); and Carson.

31 See the recent publication by Jo Ann Gibson Robinson, *The Montgomery Bus Boycott and the Women Who Started It* (Knoxville: University of Tennessee Press, 1987).

32 Cornell West, "The Paradox of the Afro-American Rebellion," in *The Sixties without Apology,* ed. Sohnya Sayres, Anders Stephanson, Stanley Aronowitz, Fredric Jameson (Minneapolis: University of Minnesota Press, 1984).

33 Lorde, *Sister Outsider,* esp. 66–71; hooks, *Feminist Theory* (n. 25 above); Linda Burnham, "Has Poverty Been Feminized in Black America?" *Black Scholar* 16, no. 2 (March/April 1985): 14–24; Maria C. Lugones and Elizabeth V. Spelman, "Have We Got A Theory for You! Feminist Theory, Cultural Imperialism and the Demand for 'The Woman's Voice,'" *Women's Studies International Forum* 6, no. 6 (1983): 573–81.

34 Lewis (n. 25 above).

35 Karen Kollias, "Class Realities: Create a New Power Base," in *Building Feminist Theory: Essays from Quest,* ed. *Quest* staff (New York: Longman, 1981), 125–38, esp. 134.

36 See Josephine Donovan, *Feminist Theory: The Intellectual Traditions of American Feminism* (New York: Ungar, 1985); and Lydia Sargent, ed., *Woman and Revolution: A Discussion of the Unhappy Marriage of Marxism and Feminism* (Boston: South End Press, 1981); and Zillah R. Eisenstein, ed., *Capitalist Patriarchy and the Case for Socialist Feminism* (New York: Monthly Review Press, 1979), for fuller discussions.

37 Ellen Willis, "Radical Feminism and Feminist Radicalism," in Sayres et al., eds. (n. 32 above), 91–118, esp. 110–11.

38 hooks, *Feminist Theory* (n. 25 above), 60–61.

39 Ibid., 61.

40 Phyllis Marynick Palmer, "White Women/Black Women: The Dualism of Female Identity and Experiences in the United States," *Feminist Studies* 91 (Spring 1983): 162.

41 Brenda Eichelberger, "Voices on Black Feminism," *Quest: A Feminist Quarterly* 4 (1977): 16–28, esp. 16.

42 Lewis (n. 25 above), 341.

43 For information on the development of black feminist scholarship and academic programs, see Patricia Bell Scott, "Selective Bibliography on Black Feminism," in Hull et al., eds. (n. 27 above); Black Studies/Women's Studies Faculty Development Project, "Black Studies/Women's Studies: An Overdue Partnership" (Women's Studies, University of Massachusetts—Amherst, mimeograph, 1983); Nancy Conklin et al., "The Culture of Southern Black Women: Approaches and Materials" (University: University of Alabama Archives of American Minority Cultures and Women's Studies Program, Project on the Culture of Southern Black Women, 1983); the premier issue of *Sage: A Scholarly Journal on Black Women* 1, no. 1 (Spring 1984); and the establishment of Kitchen Table: A Women of Color Press, New York. The Center for Research on Women at Memphis State University, the Women's Research and Resource Center at Spelman College, and the Minority Women's Program at Wellesley College are among the academic centers.

44 See Andrew Cherlin and Pamela Waters, "Trends in United States Men's and Women's Sex-Role Attitudes: 1972–1978," *American Sociological Review* 46 (1981): 453–60. See also, Janice Gump, "Comparative Analysis of Black Women's and White Women's Sex-role Attitudes," *Journal of Consulting and Clinical Psychology* 43 (1975): 858–63; and Marjorie Hershey, "Racial Difference in Sex-Role Identities and Sex Stereotyping: Evidence against a Common Assumption," *Social Science Quarterly* 58 (1978): 583–96. For various opinion polls, see "The 1972 Virginia Slims American Women's Opinion Poll" and "The 1974 Virginia Slims American Women's Opinion Poll," conducted by the Roper Organization (Williamstown, Mass.: Roper Public Opinion Research Center, 1974). See Barbara Everitt Bryant, "American Women: Today and Tomorrow," National Commission on the Observance of International Women's Year (Washington, D.C.: Government Printing Office, March 1977). Gloria Steinem, "Exclusive Louis Harris Survey: How Women Live, Vote and Think," *Ms. Magazine* 13 (July 1984): 51–54.

45 For analyses of the influence of socioeconomic class and race on feminist attitudes, see Willa Mae Hemmons, "The Women's Liberation Movement: Understanding Black Women's Attitudes," in *The Black Woman,* ed. LaFrances Rodgers-Rose (Beverly Hills, Calif.: Sage Publications, 1960), 285–99; and Ransford and Miller (n. 16 above).

Reconceptualizing Differences Among Women

Gerda Lerner[*]

The development of women's history in the past twenty years has not only helped to bring new subject matter to history, but has forced us to deal with the concepts and values underlying the organization of historical studies and of all intellectual fields. It has forced us to question not only why certain content was previously omitted, ignored, and trivialized, but also to consider who decides what is to be included. In short, we have begun first to question and then to challenge the conceptual framework for the organization of traditional knowledge. We challenge it because of its omissions: it leaves out the experiences, activities, and ideas of half or more of humankind. We challenge it because it is elitist: it leaves out not only all women, but most men, those of non-white races, those of various ethnicities, and, until quite recently, those of lower classes. In so doing, it defines all the groups omitted as less significant than the groups included. Patently, this is untrue and therefore it is unacceptable. We challenge it because what traditional history teaches us denies our own experience of reality. We live in a world in which nothing happens without the active participation of men and women and yet we are constantly being told of a past world in which men are presumed to act and women presumed to be acted upon. Women's history, even in its short development, has proven this judgement to be false, for the past as well as the present. Women are and always have been active participants in the shaping of events. One of the basic errors of patriarchal thought has been to make claims of universality for descriptions of the activities of a small elite group of upper-class white males. Traditional historians have described the activities of this group and called it the history of all of humankind. They have subsumed all women under the term "men" and have ignored the actual differences that exist among people by asserting that the small group whose activities they describe can stand for the rest of us. It obviously cannot. In rejecting this androcentric distortion of the past, we have opened the way to other insights and challenges.

Historians of women have long ago come to see that "women" cannot be treated as

[*]This article was first prepared for delivery as a keynote address for the Lowell Conference on Women's History, sponsored by the Lowell National Historical Park, the Harvard Graduate School of Education, the Massachusetts Department of Education, the New Hampshire Department of Education, and the New England Center for Equity Assistance, held at Lowell, MA on March 2, 1988. I benefited from the discussion and comments by over two hundred high school and college teachers attending this conference.

I am grateful also for the comments and suggestions made by Professor Nellie Y. McKay, Afro-American Studies Department, University of Wisconsin-Madison, and by Professor Nell Painter, Princeton University. Over the years, I have learned much from discussions of my ideas on "differences" with my colleagues Florencia Mallon, Steve Stern, and Steven Feierman, who helped me to sharpen my thinking in the light of their expertise in Latin-American and African history. Finally, the concepts on which this article is based were tested and applied in an undergraduate lecture course, "Sex, Gender, Class and Race in Comparative Historical Perspective," which I have twice given at the University of Wisconsin-Madison. The interest and enthusiasm of my students for this conceptual framework encouraged me to write this article.

I am indebted to the participants of the Conference on Graduate Training in U.S. Women's History, held at Wingspread, Racine, WI, October 21–23, 1988, who shared their course syllabi and experiences in attempts to reconstruct Women's History and US History survey courses along non-racist, non-sexist lines.

a unified category any more than "men-as-a-group" can.[1] Women differ by class, race, ethnic and regional affiliation, religion, and any number of other categories. Thus, historians of women have stressed the need for using such categories as tools for analysis.[2] What we mean by that is that whenever we study a group of women, past or present and make generalizations about them, we must take not only the similarities but the differences among them into consideration. We must ask, does this hold true for women of different races? for women of different classes? It simply will no longer do to design a research project or to teach without taking the differences among women into account. Anyone can, of course, study any particular group of women, but then one is not entitled to making claims of universality based solely on the study of that particular group.

The problem one encounters when using race, class, ethnicity, and gender as tools of analysis is that one seems to add endless variation to any problem without gaining greater analytical clarity. One drowns in illustrative detail regarding the various groups. The traditionalists describe this as losing sight of the unity of events in the past, the so-called "common core."[3] Different groups of the population may have experienced the Civil War in different ways, but the common core was provided by the political and military events, which is, they say, what we should be teaching. I would argue that we should be teaching both the common core and the particular in all its variations, and that we distort reality and the truth if we do not.

The problem is that we have an inadequate conceptual framework for dealing with "differences." The model we have is the model of liberal pluralism, according to which America represents not a melting pot but a salad bowl. Presumably this is an advance over the "melting pot" which assumed a national identity into which all alien elements—alien by race, ethnicity, religion, and sex—would need to "melt." The liberal pluralism of the salad bowl assumes not a "melting" but a sharing of space by multiple parts which add up to a whole. This is indeed a conceptual advance, but it is insufficient as a model of reality because it ignores power, dominance, hegemony. It assumes that the process of doing justice to "differences" is additive—leave the whole concept intact and add the infinite variety in which humankind appears in society and history.

If one ignores "differences" one distorts reality. If one ignores the power relations built on differences one reinforces them in the interest of those holding power. I would like to propose a different conceptual model for dealing with "differences."[5]

When men discovered how to turn "difference" into dominance they laid the ideological foundation for all systems of hierarchy, inequality, and exploitation. They found a way of justifying such systems and of keeping them functioning with the cooperation of the dominated. This "invention of hierarchy" can be traced and defined historically: it occurs everywhere in the world under similar circumstances, although not at the same time. It occurs when the development of militarism due to the technological innovations of the Bronze Age coincides with the economic shifts occasioned by the agricultural revolution. Small groups of men, usually military leaders, usurp power in their domain, usually following some conquest of foreigners, and consolidate such power by ideological and institutional means. These means always rest upon the discovery that "difference" can justify dominance. For Western civilization, these events occur in the Ancient Near East in the third and second millennium B.C. and take the form of state formation.[6]

States formed through the consolidation of early military conquests by tribal chiefs or kings become legitimized by the creation of myths of origin, which confer divine or semi-divine power upon their rulers, and by the formation of laws, which set up rules increasing hierarchy and regulating dominance. Everywhere, the first step toward turning "difference into dominance" is the institution of patriarchal privileges of men over women.

A small group of men dominate resources and allocate them to the women they have acquired as sexual property and to their children, to other less powerful men, and to a newly-created underclass of slaves. The texture of power relationships thus created balances privileges and obligations for each group in such a way as to make the whole arrangement acceptable and to continue it in the interest of the dominant male group. Women and their children, in an age of rampant militarism and constant warfare and in an age of high infant and maternal mortality, needed protection in order for the tribe as a whole to survive. Such reasoning led women in the first place to accept and cooperate with the "patriarchal bargain"—in exchange for their sexual and reproductive services to one man, they will be guaranteed protection and resources for themselves and their children. Slavery, which develops at a time when men first acquire sufficient resources to keep captives alive instead of killing them, initially starts with a similar bargain. Slave women and later men accept that bargain the moment they accept the gift of their life after military conquest in exchange for their enslavement.[7]

It is no accident that everywhere the first slaves known are women of foreign tribes. Often such tribes are racially and visibly different from their conquerors, which makes it easier for the conquerors to designate them permanently as an underclass. But where such racial differences do not exist, it is possible to create them by "marking" the slaves—with a brand, a peculiar way of cutting the hair, a special way of dressing or other means. Always, what is accentuated is "difference." The slave is different from the master and because he is different he can be designated as inferior. Because he or more likely she is designated as inferior she can be exploited, commodified, and designated as in some way sub-human. The institutionalization of militarism as a way of life presupposes hierarchical thinking—some people who dominate have the right to dominate because they are superior; the dominated must accept being dominated because they are inferior.

How can one tell who is to be dominant and who is to be dominated? By force, first of all—the victors dominate; the conquered are dominated. But rule by force alone is untenable in the long run. Even the fiercest warriors could not long enslave other warriors unless they had several conquerors watching each conquered warrior day and night. Dominance is only possible if it can be justified and accepted both by the dominant and the dominated and by the large majority of people who are neither. And, historically, what makes dominance acceptable is putting a negative mark on difference. This group or that group is different from us; they are our "Other." And because they are our "Other" we can rule them. It is upon such ideological foundations that class dominance was made acceptable even to people who did not directly benefit from it.

At the time of the formation of the archaic states non-slaveholding men accepted the bargain of being dominated and exploited in regard to resources by more powerful men of their own group because they were simultaneously offered the chance to dominate and control the resources of others, the "different" others, namely the women and children of their own class. Even to men who did not themselves hold slaves, the existence of an underclass raises their own sense of status and made them accept their own relative inequality as a fair arrangement.

Once the system of dominance and hierarchy is institutionalized in custom, law, and practice, it is seen as natural and just and people no longer question it, unless historical circumstances change very dramatically. For the dominated, the benefits the original bargain conferred upon them are lost, once slavery becomes hereditary—it is then simply exploitation based on arbitrary power.

What I have briefly outlined here is a pattern of development which took many hundreds of years to consolidate. What is important is that this analysis shows, in its simplest and rudimentary form, the connectedness of various forms of difference-turned-into-dominance. It shows that sex, class, and race dominance are interrelated and inseparable, from the start. The difference between men and women was the first, most easily notable difference and therefore dominance by men could first be acted out on that terrain. But class and race dominance (in the form of the enslavement of conquered foreign people) developed almost immediately upon this first human "discovery" of how to use power so as to benefit people unequally. The function of all designations of "otherness" or deviance is to keep hierarchy in place for the benefit of the dominant. I am not here trying to set up priorities of oppression. Which system of oppression came first and which second is insignificant, if we understand that we are dealing with one, inseparable system with different manifestations.

But we do need richer, more complex, and more relational definitions of terms with which we usually work, such as "class" and "race." In Marxist terms "Class" is defined as a group "who play the same part in the mechanism of production" or, alternatively, "men's relationship to the means of production." The Weberian definition is "people who have life chances in common, as determined by their power to dispose of goods and skills for the sake of income."[8] No matter what the definition, class has been so defined that women are subsumed under the category "men." Males and females are considered as belonging to the same class, without definite distinctions between them. But "class" never describes a single set of locations, relations, and experiences. "Class" is genderic, that is it is expressed and institutionalized in terms that are *always different* for men and women. For men, "class" describes their relationship to the means of production and their power over resources and women and children. For women, "class" describes their relationship to the means of production *as mediated* through the man to whom they render sexual and reproductive services and/or the man on whom they are dependent in their family of origin. In the case of women who enjoy economic independence, "class" still describes not only their relationship to the means of production, but their control (or lack thereof) over their reproductive capacity and their sexuality.

The concept "race" will similarly have to be expanded and re-defined. The definition of "race" as a mark of difference and, thereby, inferiority antedates the formation of Western civilization, as I have shown. From its inception, "race" as a defining term was created generically, that is it was applied in a different way to men and women. Men of oppressed races were primarily exploited as workers; women were *always* exploited as workers, as providers of sexual services, and as reproducers. Dominant elites, once they had institutionalized slavery, acquired the unpaid labor of enslaved men and women, but they also acquired the sexual and reproductive services of slave women as a commodity. That is, the children of slave women became an actual commodity to be worked, sold, and traded; the unrewarded sexual services of slave women to their master enhanced the master's status among his peers, as in the form of harems; slave women's sexual services were and could be commodified in the form of prostitution.[9]

The binary gendered opposition (male/female) which is so firmly rooted in our culture and cultural product as well as in our language and thought, makes it difficult for us to see the complexity of other structural relationships in society. We have thought of classifications such as "class" and "race" as being vertical boxes into which to sort people in history, but it has been difficult for us to conceptualize the overlapping boundaries of the two concepts.[10] When we think not in terms which compare two separate oppressive systems which may show some overlap, but in terms of one system with several, fully integrated aspects which depend for their existence one upon the other, a truer relationship can be visualized.[11] We can then discuss not "priorities" of oppression or primacies (is a black woman more oppressed because of her sex or of her race?) but we can show the inter-relatedness of both aspects of oppression and their interdependency. Once we do that, a richer description, more closely related to actual relationships, can be drawn.[12]

The system of male dominance over resources and women, called patriarchy, depends for its existence on creating categories of "deviants" or "others." Such groups, variously constituted in different times and places, are always defined as being "different" from the hegemonic group and assumed to be inferior. It is upon this assumption of the inferiority of presumed "deviant" groups that hierarchy is instituted and maintained. Hierarchy is institutionalized in the state and its laws, in military, economic, educational, and religious institutions, in ideology and the hegemonic cultural product created by the dominant elite. The system which has historically appeared in different forms, such as ancient slavery, feudalism, capitalism, industrialism, depends, for its continuance, on its ability to split the dominated majority into various groups and to mystify the process by which this is done. The function of various forms of oppression, which are usually treated as separate and distinct, but which in fact are aspects of the same system, is to accomplish this division by offering different groups of the oppressed various advantages over other groups and thus pit them one against the other. Racism, anti-Semitism, various forms of ethnic prejudice, sexism, classism, and homophobia are all means to this end. If we see these various forms of creating "deviance" and "otherness" as aspects of one and the same system of dominance, we can demystify the process by which the system constructs a reality which constantly sustains and reinforces it.

Let me illustrate this by a concrete example. In the antebellum South lower-class white males, whose long-range economic interests were actually opposed to the economic interests of the planter class, derived psychological and status benefits from racism. They had control over the sexuality and reproduction of women of their own class and enjoyed sexual privileges over Black women. This combination of sexual and status privileges made them cooperative with the planter's hegemonic system, despite the fact that they were deprived of educational opportunities, had limited access to political power and had to subordinate their economic interest to that of the planters.[13]

White and Black women of all classes in the antebellum South were also denied political and legal rights and access to education. Although neither group controlled their sexuality nor their reproduction, the differences between them were substantial. White women, regardless of class, owed sexual and reproductive services to the men to whom they were married. Black women, in addition to the labor extracted from them, owed sexual and reproductive services to their white masters and to the Black men their white masters had selected for them. Since the white master of Black women could as well be a white woman, it is clear that racism was for Black women and men the decisive factor which structured them into society and controlled their lives. Conversely, white women could offset whatever economic and social disadvantages they suffered by sexism by the racist advantages they had over both Black men and women. Practically speaking, this meant that white women benefited from racism economically, insofar as they owned slaves; that they could relieve themselves of child-rearing (and at times even childbearing) responsibilities by using the enforced services of their female slaves; that they were relieved of doing unpaid domestic labor by using slave labor. In addition white men and women of all classes derived a sense of higher status from the racist system which decisively affected their consciousness.

Another way of saying this is that dominant elite, white, upper-class men benefit from all aspects of their dominance—economic and educational privilege, sexual and reproductive control, and higher status. Women of their own class benefit sufficiently from racist and economic privilege so as to mask for them the disadvantages and discrimination they experience because of sexism. Whites of the lower classes benefit sufficiently from racism and (in the case of males) from sexism so that they support the system, even in face of obvious economic and political disadvantages. For those dominated and oppressed by racism, classism, and sexism, all aspects of the oppressive system work to make their emancipation more difficult.

The fact that in the case of antebellum slavery the dominant elite understood the importance of all aspects of the oppressive system to the continuance of their privileges is shown in the increasing severity with which laws against educating slaves were enforced in that period and in the continuous existence of unequal laws in regard to sexual crimes. From the middle of the eighteenth century on, sexual crimes of Black men against white women were punished by death, while sexual crimes of white men against Black women were not only not considered crimes but were considered white male rights. The denial to African-American men not only of sexual privilege over women of their own race, but of their ability to protect women of their families from the attacks of white men was a further means of dehumanizing them, defining them as "other" and forcing them to accept lower-status self-definitions.[14] Racism never succeeded in actually making Black men internalize such self-definitions; yet dominant whites never gave up the attempt to impose them on slaves and later on freedmen.

That Black men were well aware of the intended effect of this strategy can be seen in the Reconstruction period when they first claimed male privilege over their women as a symbol of their "manhood." Black women were to render domestic and nurturant services to their own families only (a goal many Black women understandably supported); Black men were to be breadwinners; Black men were to be able to protect their women from sexual assault by whites.[15] One of the marks of the failure of Reconstruction and of the continuing existence of the racist system was precisely that these goals were not realizable in the nineteenth-century South.

The importance of sexism as a means of enforcing racism can also be seen in the way racist double standards were used in the post-Civil War period to keep freedmen and later all southern Blacks in subordinate status despite the end of slavery. The rise of violence against Black males and the sharp increase in lynchings, always excused as being "in defense of white womanhood," served to intimidate the free Black community in the post-Reconstruction period and again at the turn of the century, when Blacks in the South were virtually disfranchised. It was African-American women in their clubs, and especially Ida B. Wells, who first uncovered the workings of this sexist-racist double standard and who exposed the falsity of the charge that white women needed protection from Black men.[16] Similarly, the history of the U.S. trade union movement abounds with evidence of the ways employers were able to exploit ethnic and racial differences among their work force in order to retard or prevent unionization, sometimes for decades. Racially or ethnically defined status privileges often induced white workers to act against their best economic self-interest, as did lower-class whites in the antebellum South.[17]

The inter-relatedness of distinctions based on race, class, ethnicity, and sex is not so clearly demonstrable in contemporary industrial society as it is in the society of the antebellum South. Gender-relations have undergone considerable change, and some of the more obvious male sexual privileges have altered under the impact of women's political struggle and economic changes. Men no longer have property rights in women and children; women have, at least on a formal level, equal access to education and are entitled to equality of political representation, even if they do not actually enjoy it in practice. Large numbers of women, except for the poor, now have access to economic resources directly, that is, not mediated through a man, although this does not hold for married women who are full-time homemakers. The control of women's reproductive resources is no longer exerted by individual men but instead by male-dominated institutions such as the courts, the state, the churches, and the medical professional establishment.

Still, in contemporary USA, white males of elite groups continue to control the major corporations, the legal and political establishment, the news media, the academic establishment (despite some inroads made by women), the trade union movement, the churches. The economic dependency of women (and, with it, the basic inequality in access to and control of resources) continues. It is secured through the definition of heterosexuality as the norm; through gender-indoctrination; the continued existence of women's unpaid domestic labor and child-rearing services; the gender-based wage discrimination against women and their concentration in low-paid, temporary, or dead-end service jobs. Male dominance and privilege is further expressed through the definition of professionalism to fit the male model and through the denial to women of professional career patterns suited to their life cycles. It also is manifested in sexual harassment on the job as a means of keeping women out of better jobs. Male control of women's sexuality and reproduction is now exerted through the politicization of issues of reproductive choice, the continuing growth of the pornography establishment and the sex industry, and of prostitution, which, as it has been for millennia, is predominantly an occupation of lower-class women. The ever growing phenomenon of violence against women and children is another distorted and perverted form of male dominance.

All whites derive tangible benefits from racism, but such benefits vary by class and sex so that upper-class males benefit more from racism than do lower-class people of both sexes and upper-class women. Racism, by splitting people from one another, helps to prevent alliances of lower-class people which might effectively challenge the system. Racism gives the illusion of superiority to lower-class whites, which convinces them to support the dominant elites, often against their true economic interests.

The benefits to upper- and middle-class women of the race/class system are so tangible that it is easy for them to overlook and disregard its oppressive aspects, even to themselves. The gains made by women over a century of struggle have benefited upper-class women disproportionally. This group has control over its own property; it reaps the economic benefits of racism and classism and shares them with upper-class men. Women of this group share, even if on a lower level, the benefits of education and of opportunities for professional careers. Class and race privileges allow such women to fulfill their domestic and child-rearing services by substituting another woman for themselves. Their economic independence allows them to define sexual relations in their own interest and to secure divorces without great economic loss. In short, it is their class privilege which helps them offset any disadvantages arising from their subordinate status as women.

The women less privileged economically are more vulnerable since they are in a worse bargaining position. For many middle- and lower-class women, gaining some economic independence by working means assuming the burden of a double working day. Such women are usually not in a position to support themselves and their children in case of divorce, which means they are unable to bargain for better conditions within their marriages or to make other choices. This is the large group of women of whom it can be said that they are "one man away from poverty." This is also the group of white women most committed against feminism since their security and economic opportunities seem to them entirely to rest on the maintenance of their marriages and the good will of the men with whom they are affiliated. Such women have a direct economic investment in maintaining their "respectability" against people of other races or ethnicities or against the most dangerous "other"—non-respectable women. Black women of this economic group do not necessarily expect Black men to support them and their children; thus, their attitude toward a feminism of their own definition is more positive than that of white women of the same economic class.[18]

In modern industrial society, the majority of the poor are women and children. The "feminization of poverty" is the modern expression of the multifaceted system of patriarchal dominance. Women become poor because they are abandoned by men; because they are oppressed by being in a lower class or a nonwhite race; because they are members of a "deviant" group (lesbians, drug users, handicapped, "immoral," single mothers) or because they are old. Modern society has created new adaptations for the old definitions of "Otherness," but the function of defining "Otherness" as deviance has not changed. It helps to raise the status of dominant males to define themselves against despised outgroups; such raised status perceptions secure the collaboration of middle- and lower-class people in the system that robs them of equity and justice.

Historians who understand the inter-relatedness of the various aspects of the system of patriarchal dominance are in a better position to interpret the history of women than are those who continue to regard class, race, and gender dominance as separate though intersecting and overlapping systems. The intellectual construct of separate systems inevitably marginalizes the subordination of women.

Race, class, and gender oppression are inseparable; they construct, reinforce, and support one another. The form which class first took historically was genderic and racist. The form racism first took was genderic and classist. The form the state first took was patriarchal. These are the starting points for re-conceptualization. . . .

All re-conceptualization must start with a new conceptual framework. We must have our goal firmly in mind and approach our task by finding new analytic questions. If we do this, the integration of new materials will not have to come at the expense of omitting something else of importance. Rather, the question will arise: why is this important and not that? It is not an easy task, and it will challenge the best of our collective minds and energies. But it is a worthwhile enterprise from every point of view. What we are trying to do is to create a holistic history in which men and women, in the various aspects of their lives, interact in various ways, reflecting the differences among them. The textured richness of such a reconstruction of the past depends on our ability to embrace difference, hear many languages, and see interdependencies rather than separation. Learning from female language and modes of perception, we will need to be relational, existential, and aware of our own involvement even as we use the male mode to categorize, order, and analyze. The point is that the two modes always have been coexisting and complementary. We must adapt our own craft to that reality by ourselves becoming conscious and accepting of it.

NOTES

1 I first called attention to the need of including class differences among women in any generalization made about women in my 1969 article, "The Lady and the Mill Girl: Changes in the Status of Women in the Age of Jackson," *American Studies* 10, no. 1 (Spring 1969), reprinted in Gerda Lerner, *The Majority Finds its Past: Placing Women in History* (New York: Oxford University Press, 1979), chap. 2.

For discussion of the problem of "differences" among women, see *ibid.,* chaps. 4–7.

For a review of the historiography of Women's History in the first decade of its twentieth-century revival, see Barbara Sicherman, "Review Essay; American History," *SIGNS: Journal of Women in Culture and Society* 1, no. 2 (Winter 1975) 461–85; Mary Beth Norton, "Review Essay; American History," *SIGNS: Journal of Women in Culture and Society* 5, no. 2 (Winter 1979): 324–37. For a review of this topic covering the years 1975–80 see Hilda Smith, "Recent Trends in Women's History," in Paula A. Treichler, et al., ed. *For Alma Mater: Theory and Practice in Feminist Scholarship* (Urbana: University of Illinois Press, 1985).

2 The need for considering race and ethnicity as factors in Women's History was raised in

Gerda Lerner, ed. *Black Women in White America: A Documentary History* (New York: Pantheon, 1972). The theoretical implications were discussed in Lerner, *Majority,* chaps. 5–7.

See also: William Chafe, *Women and Equality: Changing Patterns in American Culture* (New York: Oxford University Press, 1977); Sharon Harley and Rosalyn Terborg-Penn, eds. *The Afro-American Woman: Struggles and Images* (Port Washington, New York: National University Publications, 1978); Gloria T. Hull, Patricia Bell Scott and Barbara Smith, eds. *All the Women are White, All the Blacks are Men, But Some of Us are Brave* (Old Westbury, NY: The Feminist Press, 1981); Bell Hooks, *Ain't I a Woman: Black Women and Feminism* (Boston: South End Press, 1981); Bettina Aptheker, *Woman's Legacy: Essays on Race, Sex, and Class in American History* (Amherst: University of Massachusetts Press, 1982).

For background on issues of ethnicity see: *Frontiers,* Special issue "Native American Women" 6, no. 3 (Fall 1981); *SIGNS,* Special issue on Hispanic-American Women 3, no. 1 (Autumn 1977); Maria Linda Apodaca, "The Chicana Woman: A Historical Materialist Perspective," *Latin American Perspectives* 4 nos. 1/2 (1977): 74–89; Louisa Ano Nuevo Kerr, *Chicanos* (Bloomington: Indiana University Press, 1978); Alfredo Mirande and Evangelina Enriquez, *La Chicana: The Mexican-American Woman* (Chicago: University of Chicago Press, 1979); Magdelena Mora and Adelaida R. Del Castillo, eds. *Mexican Women in the United States: Struggles Past and Present* (Los Angeles: University of California Chicano Studies Research Center, 1980); Verna Abe et al., *Asian American Women* (Stanford: Stanford University Press, 1976).

3 This argument has recently appeared in several influential works in the form of an attack on the "new history." See cf: Gertrude Himmelfarb, *The New History and the Old: Critical Essays and Reappraisals* (Cambridge: Belknap Press of Harvard University Press, 1987); Theodore S. Hamerow, *Reflections on History and Historians* (Madison: The University of Wisconsin Press, 1987). See also the contributions of Theodore S. Hamerow, Gertrude Himmelfarb, Lawrence W. Levine, Joan Wallach Scott, and John E. Toews in "AHR *Forum,* Perspectives on The Old History and the New," *The American Historical Review* 94, no. 3 (June 1989): 654–98.

4 The concept of America as the "melting pot" became popularized in 1903 through a play by that name by Israel Zangwill, which also had wide distribution in book form. The "salad bowl" metaphor was popularized in the widely used one-volume textbook on American History by Carl Degler, *Out of Our Past: The Forces that Shaped Modern America* (New York: Harper & Row, 1959), 296. Degler states: "A more accurate analogy would be a salad bowl, for, though the salad is an entity, the lettuce can still be distinguished from the chicory, the tomatoes from the cabbage." For a general background on questions of ethnicity and prejudice, see Gordon W. Allport, *The Nature of Prejudice* (Garden City, NY: Doubleday, 1954); George Eaton Simpson & J. Milton Yinger, *Racial and Cultural Minorities: An Analysis of Prejudice and Discrimination* (New York: Harper & Bros., 1953); Peter Rose, *They and We: Racial and Ethnic Relations in the United States* (New York: Random House, 1964); Albert Memmi, *Dominated Men* (Boston: Beacon Press, 1968).

5 For a forceful argument on the need to make "gender" a primary tool of historical analysis, see Joan W. Scott, "Gender: A Useful Category of Historical Analysis," *The American Historical Review* 91, no. 5 (December 1986) 1053–75. Particularly important is her definition of gender as always connected to power: "[G]ender is a constitutive element of social relationships based on perceived differences between the sexes, and gender is a primary way of signifying relationships of power" (*Ibid.,* 1067). I share her conviction that the connection between these two propositions is "integral," and I am here trying to show that this integral connection embraces relationships of power expressed not only in terms of gender, but of race, ethnicity, and class.

6 The following analysis is based on the research and findings detailed in my book, Gerda Lerner, *The Creation of Patriarchy* (New York: Oxford University Press, 1986). Since it would be cumbersome to repeat here the extensive documentation of the argument, interested readers are referred to the book, esp. to chaps. 3–6 and 11.

7 This point is elaborated in Orlando Patterson, *Slavery and Social Death: A Comparative Study* (Cambridge: Harvard University Press, 1982).

8 David Sills, ed. *Encyclopedia of the Social Sciences* (New York: The Macmillan Co. and the Free Press, 1968), Vol. 15, 298 and 300–01. Essay by Seymour Martin Lipset.

9 These generalizations are based on my detailed study of the development of slavery in the Ancient Near East in the second and first millennium B.C. I tested them out in comparative studies of Chinese and South American slavery and of the slave systems of Antiquity and of medieval Europe. Although most of the generalizations hold for the specific case of antebellum U.S. slavery, this relatively late slave system showed some peculiarities that cannot be detailed here due to lack of space. The development of African slavery, in its early and native form, was quite different.

10 There is a vast literature of modern Marxist-Feminism that tries to reconceptualize the social constructs "class" and "gender," while attempting to retain the basic structure of marxist thought. The discussion is well summarized in Zillah R. Eisenstein, *Capitalist Patriarchy and the Case for Socialist Feminism* (New York: Monthly Review Press, 1979) and Zillah R. Eisenstein, *The Radical Future of Liberal Feminism* (New York: Longman, 1981).

For a reconceptualization based on two separate, but interrelated, systems, see Gayle Rubin, "The Traffic in Women: Notes on the Political Economy of Sex," in Rayna Rapp Rieter, *Toward an Anthropology of Women* (New York: Monthly Review Press, 1975), 157–210, and Mary O'Brien, *The Politics of Reproduction* (Boston: Routledge & Kegan Paul, 1981). Joan Kelly came closest to breaking out of the constraints of this approach in her "The Doubled Vision of Feminist Theory," reprinted in Joan Kelly, *Women, History and Theory* (Chicago: University of Chicago Press, 1984), 51–64.

For a flexible analysis that still remains within the Marxist framework, see Heidi Hartmann, "Capitalism, Patriarchy, and Job Segregation by Sex," *SIGNS* 1, no. 3, Part 2 (Spring 1976): 137–70, and her "The Family as the Locus of Gender, Class, and Political Struggle: The Example of Housework," *SIGNS* 6, no. 3 (Spring 1981): 366–94.

11 African-American women have in the past decade expressed their acute unease and dissatisfaction with the racism they experienced in the modern feminist movement and with the inadequacy of feminist theoretical work in regard to race. They have proposed a variety of alternative theoretical approaches and have insisted that the complexity of their own life experience as Black women be recognized and expressed in dialogue with white feminists.

Important work in this redefinition was done by Frances Beale, "Double Jeopardy: To Be Black and Female" in Tony Cade, ed. *The Black Woman* (New York: New American Library, 1970), 90–100; Pauli Murray, "Jim Crow and Jane Crow," and Fannie Lou Hamer, "It's in your Hands," both reprinted in Gerda Lerner, ed. *Black Women in White America: A Documentary History* (New York: Pantheon, 1972) 592–98, 609–14; Angela Davis, *Women, Race and Class* (New York: Random House, 1981); Paula Giddings, *When and Where I Enter: The Impact of Black Women on Race and Sex in America* (New York: William Morrow & Co., 1984); Audre Lorde, *Sister Outsider: Essays and Speeches* (Trumansburg, NY: Crossing Press, 1984); Alice Walker, *In Search of our Mothers' Garden: Womanist Prose* (New York: Harcourt, Brace Jovanovich, 1983); June Jordan, *Political Essays* (Boston: Southend Press, n.d.), and by Bell Hooks, Gloria Hull et al., Sharon Harley and Rosalind Terborg-Penn in the works cited in fn. 2.

Michelle Wallace, *Black Macho and the Myth of the Super Woman* (New York: Dial Press, 1978) confronted the issue of Black sexism.

Linda M. Perkins, "The Impact of the 'Cult of True Womanhood' on the Education of Black Women," *Journal of Social Issues* 39, no. 3 (1983): 17–38 compares differing educational goals and self-concepts of white and Black women in the nineteenth century.

12 A model somewhat similar to my own, although restricted to "race" and "gender," is proposed by Althea Smith and Abigail J. Stewart in their "Approaches to Studying Racism and Sexism in Black Women's Lives" in *ibid.*, 1–16. The authors call for a "contextual interactive model" in which all generalizations would be tested on "gender-race groups" (i.e., white women and men, Black women and men) to assure a more varied, accurate, and sophisticated analysis. I have added class as a factor in the concrete historical example I am offering.

13 C. Vann Woodward, *The Strange Career of Jim Crow* (New York: Oxford University Press, 1957), chap. 2; W. J. Cash, *The Mind of the South* (New York: Vintage, 1941) discusses the ideology and politics of planter and non-slaveholding whites; Frank L. Owsley *Plain Folk of the Old South* (Chicago: Quadrangle PB, 1965), chap. 4.

My generalizations on the antebellum South are based on extensive readings in slave narratives and primary sources. For specific discussion of the position of women in antebellum society see: Anne Firor Scott, *The Southern Lady: From Pedestal to Politics: 1830–1930* (Chicago: University of Chicago Press, 1970); Catherine Clinton, *The Plantation Mistress: Women's World in the Old South* (New York: Pantheon Books, 1983); Suzanne Lebsock, *The Free Women of Petersburg: Status and Culture in a Southern Town, 1784–1860* (New York: Norton, 1984); Jacqueline Jones, *Labor of Love, Labor of Sorrow: Black Women, Work and Family from Slavery to the Present* (New York: Basic Books, 1985); Deborah Gray White, *Ar'n't I a Woman? Female Slaves in the Plantation South* (New York: W.W. Norton & Co., 1985); Elizabeth Fox-Genovese, *Within the Plantation Household: Black and White Women of the Old South* (Chapel Hill: The University of North Carolina Press, 1988).

14 The subject is fully explored in Winthrop Jordan, *White over Black: American Attitudes toward the Negro: 1550–1812* (New York: Norton, 1968), and George M. Frederickson, *The Black Image in the White Mind: The Debate on Afro-American Character and Destiny: 1817–1914* (New York: Harper & Row, 1971), esp. chap. 2.

15 Leon S. Litwack, *Been in the Storm So Long: The Aftermath of Slavery* (New York: Alfred A. Knopf, 1979), 244–45.

16 Ida B. Wells, *A Red Record* (Chicago: Donohue & Henneberry, 1895); Alfreda M. Duster, ed. *Crusade for Justice: The Autobiography of Ida B. Wells* (Chicago and London: University of Chicago Press, 1970).

See also: Mary Church Terrell, "Lynching from a Negro's Point of View," *North American Review* 178, no. 571 (June 1904): 853–68.

17 David Brody, *Steelworkers in America: The Nonunion Era* (Cambridge: Harvard University Press, 1960).

18 According to a *New York Times* poll conducted June 20–25, 1989, eighty-five percent of African-American women questioned supported the women's movement, compared to only sixty-seven percent of white women.

Three more recent texts succeed in more fully integrating women, race, and ethnicities, and the new scholarship on these topics in their texts: David Burner, with Eugene D. Genovese and Forrest McDonald, *The American People* (St. James, N.Y.: Revisionary Press, 1980); Mary Beth Norton et al., *A People and A Nation: A History of the United States,* 2nd ed., 2 vols. (Boston: Houghton Mifflin, 1986); James A. Henretta et al., *America's History* (Chicago: The Dorsey Press, 1987). The Henretta and Norton texts handle the invasion better than any of the others, and pay more attention to women and ethnic groups. Yet, I find the treatment of the latter two subjects disappointing, because the authors are still grafting these groups on to a traditional framework.

Women's Subordination Worldwide: Global Feminism

Prospects for Global Feminism

Charlotte Bunch

I have chosen to talk of global feminism, not international feminism, because I see feminism as a movement of people working for change across and despite national boundaries, not of representatives of nation-states or national governments. As a people seeking change, we must move beyond the concept of nation-state, which is another expression of patriarchy whereby groups battle for domination over each other on the basis of geographical territory. Instead, we must be global, recognizing that the oppression of women in one part of the world is often affected by what happens in another, and that no woman is free until the conditions of oppression of women are eliminated everywhere.

When talking of feminism, we also need to be clear what we mean by the term, which, as the Forum in Copenhagen demonstrated, is often misunderstood. While I do not want to see a narrow "correct line" on feminism emerge, it is important for women to develop some general understandings of the concept so that it is not defined by the media and other sectors of the Establishment. To date, Western mass media have dominated in controlling the images of feminism and have tended to portray feminism either as the prerogative of a few token women rising to the top of corporate structures or as the province of a group of crazies who simply can't live a "normal" life. These distorted stereotypes are meant to keep women both in industrialized countries and in the developing world from identifying with a movement that in fact asks very basic, root or radical, questions about existing structures of society, and particularly about the injustice of all forms of domination, whether based on sex, sexual preference, race, class, age, religion, or nationality.

This problem was discussed extensively at an international workshop held in Bangkok on "Feminist Ideology and Structures in the First Half of the Decade for Women," sponsored by the UN Asian and Pacific Centre for Women and Development in June 1979. In that workshop, we chose to affirm the term "feminist" and to define it for ourselves, rather than to allow the media to frighten us away from it or to divide us through stereotypes and name-calling. The workshop then defined feminism in terms of two long-term goals:

1 The freedom from oppression for women involves not only equity, but also the right of women to freedom of choice, and the power to control our own lives within and outside of the home. Having control over our lives and our bodies is essential to ensure a sense of dignity and autonomy for every woman.

2 The second goal of feminism is the removal of all forms of inequity and oppression through the creation of a more just social and economic order, nationally and internationally. This means the involvement of women in national liberation struggles, in plans for national development, and in local and global struggles for change.

On the basis of our definition, it is clear that feminism *is* and *must be* a *transformational politics* that addresses every aspect of life. It is not simply a laundry list of so-called women's issues such as child care and equal pay. While these issues are important, feminism is not a new ghetto where women are confined to concerning ourselves about only a select list of topics separated from the overall social and economic context of our lives. Similarly, feminism is not just "add women and stir" into existing institutions, ideologies, or political parties. Yes, feminists want more power for women, but we desire more than simply "equality" within a system of injustice: we seek a change in existing institutions and a new approach to power in our lives. Thus, for instance, the problem with the UN official conference in Copenhagen was not that it was "politicized," but that it failed to consider issues from a feminist political perspective or even in terms of how they were specifically viewed by or affected women.

Developing feminist political perspectives on issues such as the New International Economic Order, the nuclear arms race, or the international slave traffic in women is still work in progress. We have much to do in order to demonstrate the potential of feminism for providing new ways of viewing the world that can help build a just future. In approaching this task, feminists can draw on the insights of our movements, but we are primarily building from the base of experience and analysis begun by women in motion politically in many countries. This experience is diverse and rich. In building a global politics we must link and affirm the struggles and insights gained from feminist demands on a variety of fronts: from woman's fight to control her body through reproductive freedom to her demands for control through adequate standards of nutrition and sanitation to her right to define and embrace her own sexuality to her demand for an end to violence against her body and her mind. We must show that violence to and degradation of the body are connected to alienation and exploitation at work; we must demonstrate that a world committed to domination at its intimate core in the home more readily accepts ever-escalating levels of domination and imperialism not only between peoples but throughout all its structures. Thus, through examining and struggling to end the oppression of women, feminism is providing new insights into various forms of domination, new visions for how societies might exist without injustice at their core and new energy for working to bring these visions into reality.

In the formation of a transformational feminist politics that is global in perspective, the particular issues and forms of struggle for women in different situations will vary. Nevertheless, we must strive to understand and expand the commonality and solidarity of that struggle. Doing this requires that we recognize the social forces that divide women from each other—forces such as race, class, sexual orientation, colonialism, poverty, religion, nationality—and work to end the forms of oppression that are based on these factors. Yet fighting on these fronts should go hand in hand with challenging oppression on the basis of sex—not before or after, but as a single struggle with many faces.

One problem that feminists confront is how to value cultural diversity without allowing it to be used to justify traditions that are oppressive to women. Cultural imperialism from the dominant world powers often worsens women's status and certainly offers little of benefit to women in developing countries; moreover, the experience of women in the Western world illustrates the inadequacy of the Western mode of "development" as a humane model for others. At the same time, efforts by some males to justify the continuation or adoption of practices oppressive to women by labeling them "resistance to Western influence" is also onerous to feminists. Most cultures as we know them today are patriarchal. Hope for the future therefore requires that women create new models, allowing for diversity and drawing from the best of the past, but refusing to accept any form of domination in the name of either tradition or modernization.

To make global feminist consciousness a powerful force in the world demands that we make the local, global and the global, local. Such a movement is not based on international travel and conferences, although these may be useful, but must be centered on a sense of connectedness among women active at the grass roots in various regions. For women in industrialized countries, this connectedness must be based in the authenticity of our struggles at home, in our need to learn from others, and in our efforts to understand the global implications of our actions, not in liberal guilt, condescending charity, or the false imposition of our models on others. Thus, for example, when we fight to have a birth control device banned in the United States because it is unsafe, we must simultaneously demand that it be destroyed rather than dumped on women in the Third World.

Too often international contact takes place only between the experts of government or of the university and not among the activists involved in creating and maintaining a political struggle. For instance, I have found that most women in developing countries only get to meet U.S. women who are considered experts on their regions, and rarely have contact with local feminists with whom they might exchange ideas and experiences on organizing projects or protests. This lack of contact is unfortunate since feminism in the U.S. is primarily a decentralized, indigenous people's struggle and has much to learn from women elsewhere as well as to offer from its own endeavors. It is this diverse local base of feminism that needs to develop a greater global awareness and be connected to women in struggle around the world if the feminist perspective is to advance.

If any lesson was clear in Copenhagen, it was that a global feminist movement will only come through people connecting to people, not from governments. The Forum gave us a hint of how powerful such a movement could be as well as a taste of the conflicts and creativity inherent in such a possibility. The challenge is great, but so are the stakes. The crisis of survival on our planet demands that we take the risk of trying to develop a global feminism that can add to the forces for sanity and justice at work in the world.

Surviving Beyond Fear: Women and Torture in Latin America

Ximena Bunster-Bunalto

Military regimes in Latin America have developed patterns of punishments specifically designed for women who are perceived as actively fighting against or in any way resisting the oppression and exploitation visited upon their peoples by dictatorial governments. The attempts to dominate and coerce women through terrorism and torture have become organized and systematic—administered by the military state. The more generalized and diffused female sexual enslavement through the patriarchal state has been crystallized and physically literalized through the military state as torturer.

Punitive sexual enslavement of female political prisoners is found throughout Latin America. However, the armed, organized terrorizing of women may best be understood in the context of political, economic, and social forces present in a given historical-national situation. We, therefore, see a somewhat different profile in the victimization of women taking place in Nicaragua, Salvador, Guatemala, and Honduras than that which has become characteristic of the countries of the Southern Cone—Argentina, Chile, Uruguay, Paraguay, and Bolivia.

In the first cluster of countries—those forming part of Central America—political torture reaches women as daily terror. Women are most often injured or killed in contexts of generalized violence: in massacres, attacks on churches during mass, and the burning of villages. This generalized violence affects different segments of the population who happen to be present during the attacks—men, older people, children, and even domestic animals. By contrast, in the countries of the Southern Cone, where a military government or succession of military governments have been entrenched for decades, women are *systematically identified*—with names, address, and family composition—as "enemies" of the government. They are methodically tracked down and incarcerated. There are institutions within the military government dedicated specifically and exclusively to this task. . . .

In the state torturers' efforts to force confessions, elicit information, or to punish, a pattern in structure and in content is clearly discernible. These common elements experienced by female political prisoners in violent sexual attacks upon her body and psyche are consciously designed to violate her sense of herself, her female human dignity. The combination of culturally defined moral debasement and physical battering is the demented scenario whereby the prisoner is to undergo a rapid metamorphosis from madonna—"respectable woman and/or mother"—to whore. To women through processes of socialization, this violent sexual treatment administered by the state becomes most cruelly doubly disorienting; it exacerbates and magnifies the woman's already subservient, prescribed, passive, secondary position in Latin American society and culture. . . .

In order to better understand—while maintaining an awareness of the pitfalls that cultural generalization entails—how societal archetypes and stereotypes are manipulated by the torturers, it is important to look briefly at the delicate balance and complementarity of the male and female roles and the culturally assigned gender differences in Latin American society.

Many authors have discussed the bipolar conception of *machismo/Marianismo* underlying the socialization of men and women in Latin America. *Machismo,* or the cult of virility, has been described as embracing an "exaggerated aggressiveness and intransigence in male-to-male interpersonal relationships and arrogance and sexual aggression in male-to-female relationships"; *Marianismo,* as "the cult of feminine spiritual superiority which teaches that women are semi-divine, morally superior to and spiritually stronger than men" (Stevens 1973:91). Machismo and marianismo are New World variations on Old World themes.

Machismo is obviously a Latin American manifestation of global patriarchy, whereby males enjoy special privileges within the society and within the family and are considered superior to women. "Marianismo, Mariology," or the cult of the Virgin Mother—she who embodies simultaneously the ideal of nurturance/motherhood and chastity—permeates the world view of Latin America and all aspects of its culture and institutions. Latin American women are supposed to pattern their role as women after this perfect model inspired through pervasive Catholicism. . . .

Two important characteristics, then, of Latin American culture are crucial to an understanding of the specific nature of female sexual torture in these countries. First, women are basically recognized and valued only as mothers, after the Blessed Virgin Mother. Second, women have adopted and internalized these patterns under the historical weight of Hispanic-Arab and Christian heritage and are now faced and overburdened by contemporary underdevelopment—a situation that must be felt and understood in its dailiness. Latin America has undergone conquest and colonization, and with these has seen Western values imposed over those autochthonic belief systems represented through high Indian civilizations at the time of the conquest. It is in this context that we hear the resonance of the Latin American/Caribbean Women's Collective in exile in Europe today: "domination in Latin America has been a prolongation of the history of man's exploitation of man and of men's domination of women." (Latin American and Caribbean Women's Collective 1980:8). . . .

There is a distinctive pattern of torture when female political prisoners are involved. We must recognize and have recognized the fact that when the issue of torture of political prisoners is raised as a human rights issue it never deals with women. We must recognize that the physical and psychic torture of *women as women*—female sexual slavery in patriarchal societies reaching its "logical" extension and quintessential crystallization in the military state—is made invisible. As the military state so often tortures women as a mode of punishing their "man," so even to many human rights advocates the "desecration" of the female is processed as torture of the male. . . .

The aim of the first phase in the psychological and physical maltreatment of female political prisoners staged by military, navy, air force or police torturers is to intimidate and create a sense of anxiety in their victims. Two categories of women are targeted for attention.

Captors representing the state as torturer direct their established institutions of violence at the many Latin American women whose political consciousness has spurred them into political activism on behalf of the establishment of a more just social order within their own countries. This has been the case of Chilean women who worked within the Allende government toward the construction of a more egalitarian socioeconomic order. This has also been the case of Argentinian, Uruguayan, and—following the coup—Chilean women who became active in the struggle to liberate their countries and peoples from repressive dictatorships and the complicity of those regimes with foreign interests exploiting the human and natural resources of their nations. This group of women, many with public roles—as union leaders, lawyers, doctors, professors—are targeted because of their commitment to a people's struggle.

Institutionalized violence, torture, is also aimed at a second category of women—women who do not have a publicly recognized identity of their own, but, from the perspective of the state, derive their identity from their relationship to a male. These women are targeted because of the activism of a husband, lover, son, father, or brother. The "super-macho" military system brutalizes these women as an extension of the ego and as a possession of the male whom they consider the "enemy" in an "internal war." The women undergo imprisonment as hostages in this "internal war" and are then savagely tortured to get even with their men—the enemies of the military regime in power. The sexual enslavement of women belonging to this category is used to intimidate, emasculate, bring forth confessions from, and, in many cases, destroy the men to whom they are legally or emotionally attached. . . .

TORTURE DESIGNED FOR FEMALE POLITICAL PRISONERS

Female and male prisoners, then, are subjected to many of the same torturing practices, whose aim is to inflict physical pain, mental distress, and general suffering. However, the torture of men, while horrible, has as its object something less than the extinction of their sexual, gender identity. The primary form of sexual torture of men is directed toward their sexual confidence; their humanity is debased by placing them in powerless situations, where they cannot defend a female political prisoner—usually a wife, daughter, mother, lover, or friend—from brutal sexual torture performed in their presence.

Women's torment is comparatively much worse than men's because it is painfully magnified a thousand times by the most inhuman, cruel, and degrading methods of torture consciously and systematically directed at her female sexual identity and female anatomy. The process of imprisonment and torture of women political prisoners is female sexual slavery in its most hideous and blatantly obvious forms. It represents "macho" patriarchal contempt and misogyny crystallized and implemented through military-police structures of organized violence. These are not simply males "out of control with permission," with a demonic irony, the sexual torture of women is named "control" and is authorized state "security." This fact should not surprise us; the military is, by definition, the most sexist and patriarchal institution of the many institutions that reinforce ideological subordination of women in the family and in society at large (Chapkis 1981).

The sexual violence unleashed against women political prisoners is seen as the key in controlling them, through punishment and interrogations. Gang rape, massive rape becomes the standard torture mechanism for the social control of the imprisoned women. Politically committed, active women who have dared to take control of their own lives by struggling against an oppressive regime demand sexual torture—as do the women who have stood by their men in an organized political effort to liberate their country and themselves from a coercive military regime. One of the essential ideas behind the sexual slavery of a woman in torture is to teach her that she must retreat into the home and fulfill the traditional role of wife and mother. It is this role only that provides her with respect in a society where she is ideologically defined as inferior to the men from whom she derives her secondary identity—she is some male's mother, sister, wife, and *companera*. With a too usual contradiction and reversal, the method of the "lesson" forcing a return to the *marianissimo* ideal simultaneously violates that possibility. There seems to be not only a willingness to violate cultural notions of what the "natural" social order is, but in fact to direct torment with excruciating precision just to those areas of societal definition. We can only describe these patterns of state torture, we cannot make them rational.

Behind the sequence of brutal sexual acts committed on a woman's body and mind while she is in captivity lurks the criminal attempt to humiliate, degrade, and morally and physically destroy her through and within the social, cultural, and political environment that is familiar to her. It is, in an important sense, too distancing to speak of culturally accepted and defined gender distinctions. The ideological conceptions, the myths, and the realities of the paradigmatic vision of Woman, are much of the ground from which springs a woman's sense of herself and from which she derives the emotional needs and the gratifications that give meaning to her life—the love and respect of her family and the esteem and caring of her coworkers.

A woman's self-respect, sense of dignity, and physical integrity are shattered when at the hands of her captors she unwillingly becomes the participant-observer of the planned and enforced destruction of her culturally defined womanhood. In every sense of the word, in every level of her being, the torturers' invasion involves radical disorientation.

The sequence of types and examples of torture that follows is from cases of women in Argentina, Chile, and Uruguay. There is always a danger, when cases of the torture of people are summarized and then classified. As painful as it is we must not allow ourselves to forget, even for a moment, that we are speaking of pain and torment inflicted upon individuals. Even in the notions of selection of "evidence" of what is held to be a viable methodology we neutralize the FACT of the agony for these women, woman by woman.

The woman prisoner is brought blindfolded and hooded to one of the many *casas de tortura* (torture houses) administered by the security forces of these countries. They are most often established in regiments, police quarters, naval and air force bases, and academies, and in houses rented and equipped for purposes of torturing. The woman has already undergone the trauma of arrest and the geographical disorientation of being taken blindfolded to the torture house. She has been cut off from her family; or, if her arrest went unobserved by relatives, neighbors or passers-by, she has "disappeared"—she knows that no one knows where to look for her. Some victims captured on the streets start shouting their own names aloud so that the family will know they were dragged away.

While she is presumably at the information desk or in the "reception room" of the detention center—"presumably" because survivors report that it takes a while to look from under the blindfold without being discovered and beaten—her name and address are taken and entered into files with a number. While she is giving the information demanded, her body—especially her breasts, buttocks and entire genital area—is fingered and pawed by countless male hands. Her body is squeezed and explored producing in her a sense of outrage, sometimes physical pain, shame, and despair.

She is then taken to another room, where a group of men undress her, literally tear her clothing and start slapping and beating her up continuously. No sooner has she been able to get on her feet when she is again thrown to the floor or against a wall. Her nose starts bleeding and she aches all over. During the course of this brutal battering, she is given orders to sit down—there is never a chair—so she falls to the floor. She is then given contradictory orders to march in a given direction, obeying, hits herself against a wall, then she is told to kneel and squat because she has to go under a table. In the meantime she is the target of crude verbal abuse and vile ridicule of her naked body. She becomes the pathetic jester who amuses the torturers by her aimless movements directed to make her fall, roll on the floor, crawl on all fours, and jump over obstacles that are nonexistent. Fun is made of the shape of the woman's breasts, her birthmarks, or the scars left on her abdomen after a cesarean birth. This stage of torture is marked by the captors sadistic objectification of the women at their mercy.

Questions are interjected during the process of physical and verbal abuse. Depending on her presumed "profile," the woman is interrogated concerning the whereabouts of her husband, or a key male political figure who is in hiding, or about whether or not she is active in a specific political party. If the woman political prisoner claims ignorance or refuses to cooperate, the sexual violence of the torture escalates. She is thrown to the floor, splashed with cold water all over her body, and the electric prod is applied to her eyelids, gums, nipples and genital area.

As interrogations continue, sexual torture is increased. Cigarettes are extinguished on the woman's breasts and nipples; her breasts are slashed with sharpened instruments; blades, hot irons and electrical surgical "pens" are used to brand different parts of her body. . . .

Many women have had the words "Marxist" or "Mirista"—(Mir is a political party that the military junta in Chile calls the revolutionary leftist movement: its members have been systematically murdered), "extremist," and/or "dangerous" tattooed across their breasts. These words are often also imprinted on their foreheads. It must be understood that this organized political torture is not applied only to women thought to be Marxists. It is applied to women from a variety of political parties, to women who are active in center political parties, and to women who are not involved in politics at all. Women are branded if their captors believe them to be against the military government.

There is a male-bonding in the violence of massive criminal rape—performed in succession, by three to twenty-seven men in some cases—against women political prisoners. Rape is part of almost every torture sequence endured by a woman, especially women from twelve to forty-nine years of age. Power and domination are exerted on the victims of sexual slavery in a torture situation where women cannot leave nor fight back. Testimonies of older women political prisoners who have survived correspond in their hair-raising accounts of massive rapes perpetrated on the younger women upon arrival at the "houses of torture." Following these vile sessions of rape and other forms of sexual abuse, many women suffered severe hemorrhaging for days with no medical attention.

The use of animals to physically and psychically torture women is yet another phase in this unutterable process. Women's mental stability and physical health have been seriously threatened, sometimes destroyed, by the introduction of mice into their vaginas. Foreign objects, such as sticks and dull instruments, have also been introduced into the vagina and anus; but it is difficult to compare even such abuse with the psychological and physical suffering brought about by a scratching, biting, disoriented mouse forced into a female's genital region. Women, now in exile, who survived this torture, explain that they have not, nor do they believe they ever can, really recover from the trauma of this experience. Many of them developed ulcers within their vaginal walls as a result of the rodent's action inside them.

Many female political prisoners in Chile have been raped by trained dogs—usually boxers (Denuncia y Testimonio 1975:99). This is evidently one of the most brutalizing and traumatic experiences suffered by women in prison. The survivors of this torment find it very difficult to report their exposure to this extreme sexual debasement. With sickening canniness, the torturers traumatize their victims into feeling shame for their own bodies. The women who are able to do so are willing to recall these events in an effort to make known these atrocities although they suffer anew by speaking of them.

The military state—the patriarchal state in distillation—with its dependence on coercion to mold human beings to the ideology that will sustain its authority, uses the paradigm of female sexual enslavement, rape, in as many forms as it can imagine. Patriarchy under stress tends to reveal itself with contradictory zeal. The notion of Madonna/Whore in the context of male linearity of thinking (Barry 1979:262) as it melds with rape systematically applied to exert absolute control is illustrated through the case of A.N.M.R. This courageous young widow, whose husband had been assassinated during a "military" operation, was seized by the police and mercilessly tortured for long periods. As she refused to talk, she was given electric shocks, sent to her cell for a short while, and then dragged out again by the officer in charge of the supervision of her sexual torture. Officers would shout to groups of soldiers inviting them to rape her with the following order: "Come and have a good time with this whore, because she needs it!" They did rape her. She sums it up in her own words, "Thus I was debased and raped countless times." As if continual rape were not enough "control," her uterus was later ruptured by a high-voltage shock with an electric prod.

Rape is used during sessions of "family torture," usually to extract information from a noncooperative male prisoner. It is for this reason, for leverage in interrogations, that women in the family are kidnapped along with the male "subversive." Numerous wives and daughters of male prisoners have been sexually debased and massively raped in front of their husbands, lovers, or fathers. If a man is wanted and in hiding, his wife and female children are incarcerated in a manipulative attempt to extract information concerning his activities and hiding place. If the wife does not cooperate with her captors, she is raped. If this does not produce the desired information, she is threatened with the rape of her daughters. In addition to the physical suffering, the psychic strain of having to deal with such a confrontation of loyalties and the consequences of any so-called "decision" are devastating. Unfortunately, many threats are made good by the torturers, and mothers are forced to witness in shock and powerless pain violent sexual acts committed upon their innocent female youngsters. (See further discussion of this below.)

The case of L. de las N.A.M., single, is, unfortunately, a typical example of a most vile form of "family torture." At the time of the arrest she was twenty-three years old. She was imprisoned together with her father and fifteen-year-old brother. To extract information from the father and the daughter, the torturers first applied electricity to the father in front of her, she in turn was administered electricity in front of her father so that he would talk. Her fifteen-year-old brother was savagely tortured in her presence. Watching this suffering was the only time in her prolonged torture when her blindfold was removed. In order to psychologically and physically weaken her further, L. de las N.A.M. was battered and bruised all over her body; her breasts and other parts of her body were slashed with a blade and her nipples brutally squeezed and pulled while at the same time the torturers introduced their dirty hands into her vagina and stuck a variety of metal objects inside her. Later on she was submitted to electric shocks, then hung by the knees from a horizontal plank, with hands and ankles tied together (the dreaded pau de arara). She fainted, and when she recovered, her five tormentors started threatening her with rape. Her father and her brother were brought in and the captors started forcing the father and daughter into having intercourse. L. de las N.A.M., screaming in terror, fainted again. She was revived with slaps, thrown onto a mattress on the floor, and raped by many men—she cannot recall exactly how many they were. She describes herself (after the massive rape) as "waking up soiled ["impure," her chastity taken away from her by force] and bleeding." What she describes as "waking up" is the realization that the culturally defined dignity of her womanhood had been shattered; she had fought back so bravely, like a caged animal at the mercy of her executioners. Further suffering was inflicted on this brave woman by introducing mice into her vagina. She describes mice as "going berserk inside me and painfully inserting their paw nails in my flesh."

An extension of the notion of degradation of a woman in the "community" of her family is the forced abuse and humiliation of a woman through her peers. As with "family torture" this method produces pain and humiliation in all those forced to participate in this particular type of sexual torment. A naked woman political prisoner is placed in the middle of a human circle formed by her naked male coprisoners, many of whom know her. In cases where she is not known personally, she stands as the representative of "one of their own" ideologically. The men are forced at gunpoint to masturbate while looking at the naked body of the woman and having her as a target when they ejaculate. Once again the woman who finds herself in this type of situation, from which she cannot escape, is further degraded in a painfully debasing incident in which male domination not only increases her inferiority as a woman but robs her of her dignity and individuality as a person.

It should be noted that there appears to be a class element and racial component in the most extreme cases of sexual violence. Proletarian women and women with markedly *meztizo* features—the fusion of European and Indian admixtures—have been even more brutalized than their lighter sisters coming from bourgeois families. It is, however, also important to stress that the fact that in the highly class-conscious society of Latin America, the sexual torture of female political prisoners has cut across class lines. The common denominator has been the definition as enemy by the fascist military governments whether the "security threat" comes directly through the woman's— real or supposed—political activism or through the identity she is seen to derive from a male who is politically active.

TORTURE OF THE FEMALE PSYCHE

Although, as is quite evident by now, it is impossible to separate physical abuse from psychological abuse, the state torturers have designed methods specifically aimed at the mental torment of their prisoners—methods that underscore their domination and control. This harrowing of the psyche of these women is used by their tormentors as complement to the sexual violence that their bodies are undergoing. Psychological torture leaves scars that are almost impossible to heal. A woman's sympathy and empathy for others is played upon; her deep sense of herself as nurturer is manipulated and torn. . . .

The young offspring of women and men who are sought by a dictatorial regime for their clandestine activities against the government and the children of women and men considered a threat to the "internal security" of the government have been kidnapped by force from their homes. These children are placed in so-called Homes for Children run by the armed forces; they are hostages used to exert pressure on their parents. Most often, a message will reach the mother of the child with an ultimatum—if she does not turn herself in to the security forces, the little girl or boy will remain in captivity and undergo torture or be placed "under the vigilance of sexual perverts who prefer children."

Tho bureaucratic torture machines of Argentina and Chile use both threats of the torture of children and the actual torture of children to further heighten a woman's suffering while still physically brutalizing her. Examples already on the record include:

Tamara, a child of three, was tortured in Chile. Her mother, now in exile, described the treatment her daughter received in detention:

> They undressed my little daughter and whipped her with a leather whip. They put her in a barrel with ice water and held her head under the water until she almost drowned. They threatened to rape her and whipped her again. This was repeated four times a day for four days. (Children 1979:15).

N.B.L., a young mother, was kidnapped by Argentinian Task Force No. 3, Military Personnel, November 1977. The task force made her son "Facundo cry in the operating theatre"—torture chamber—next to the one in which she was being tortured.

Christina was abducted along with her mother, M. del C. J., by a special task force in October 1978. M., during her own interrogation, was forced to listen to her young daughter's screams. (Testimony 1980: 18-19)

Evidence has been on the record and continued to mount showing that babies and children are not safeguarded from torture; their torment is sadistically aimed at their mothers.

Under the threat of having a child tortured or "disappear" altogether, mothers have sometimes confessed the hiding place of their husband or *companero*. Here again is a most diabolical form of psychological torture: The Latin American mother placed in a situation of conflict between her role as wife/lover and her role as mother will almost always opt for her "sacred" maternal duty of protecting the vulnerable child. In addition to living with the brutal assault her body has taken while under interrogation, she must live now, as well, with the "guilt" of having revealed the whereabouts or activities of her husband. There is shattering moral pain brought about by the disintegration of her family. This is the cruelest attack upon a woman's psyche; it shows us so clearly how the torture of these dictatorial military regimes pierces to the essentials of female sexual slavery. The woman must not only suffer in every part of her being; she must also be faced with a shame that is called a "choice" and feel herself a "collaborator" with her torturer, no matter what she does or does not do. . . .

If the segment of the population that dares criticize the totalitarian military state is female, the punishment is administered through female sexual slavery in torture. The subservient, dependent, passive, and unequal position in society that women experience as opposed to men in a "machista"-patriarchal society is exacerbated in torture. The courageous women who have managed to survive this brutal appropriation, colonization, and objectification of their bodies, as well as the psychological suffering derived from the cruelly premeditated deprivation of their human womanly dignity have set an example of bravery for us all. They have also handed us the banner of struggle by surviving, by not succumbing at the feet of their tormentors, by transcending their sense of shame and humiliation and offering their personal testimonies to make known the criminal acts of the military state. Their cry is for justice, for the elimination of sexual slavery in torture, for the diffusion of the awareness of its existence and its monstrosity so that it may be stopped, so that it will never happen again.

Thousands of women in countries of the Southern Cone—Peru, Argentina, Chile, Uruguay, Bolivia, and Paraguay—have dared struggle for a more just socioeconomic order. Many of them have died. Thousands have disappeared and thousands are still fighting dictatorships. By so doing they have acquired an identity of their own; they have become full persons in their own right and thus challenged the passive, submissive, dependent role assigned to women based on the conservative religious archetype of the Virgin Mother that the patriarchal institutions have imprinted through the socialization of all women. These are the women who, by their direct actions, are transforming the cultural content of *marianismo, Mariology*. They have contributed, and are contributing to rapid and radical changes in the societies to which they belong, they are also creating new female models for the younger generations to follow. *This is the legacy of the women political prisoners who have survived sexual slavery in torture. . . .*

Bananas, Bases, and Patriarchy

Cynthia Enloe[*]

. . . WHERE ARE THE WOMEN?

It seems like such a simple question, why is it so rarely asked? What in fact would we see if we looked at women's lives in Central America and the Carribbean, for example?

One possibility is that we would understand how the policies of the American government and its local allies intensify the hardships of women's lives. If we take women's lives seriously, we cannot assume that local or international politics affect women and men in identical ways. For example, some of the issues named and contested by feminism become visible as integral parts of U.S. intervention policy. The denigration of women intensifies with the U.S. militarization of Central America. There is increased rape and battering. The male role as protector and sexual exploiter is affirmed and extended; prostitution is a mainstay of preserving military organization. More difficult, but equally important, we need to understand the full costs of Nicaraguan militarization to the future of the revolution. While U.S. policy has forced such a mobilization, the way in which the Nicaraguan government views its defense and appeals to its people to join the effort may deepen the power of men over women, as well as endangering democratic goals.

There is also a second possibility. If we keep asking "Where are the women?" we may find that we will have to modify our understanding of the requirements for U.S. policies to succeed in the Third World. In other words, it might be that women's lives are worth considering not only for the sake of detailing the *impact* of militarism and imperialism, but also for the sake of clarifying their basic underpinnings: how U.S. power locks into existing power relations within the countries it seeks to control.

This, in turn, has an impact on how we would rethink our organizing strategy around Central America. For instance, what sorts of campaigns would we launch if we discovered that American corporate executives weighed their overseas investments, not just in terms of profits, but in terms of gender relations; or if we knew that U.S.-Honduran joint military maneuvers depended as much on shared notions of masculinity as they did on shared state paranoia? At this stage we don't have a fully articulated

[*]Through the months of writing and revising this article I have benefitted especially from suggestions made by Ann Withorn, Lois Wasserspring, Joni Seager, Saralee Hamilton, Kirsten Johnson, Marla Erlien, and Margaret Cerullo.

feminist theory to explain how imperialism and militarism have structured our relations with Central America and the Caribbean. But we do have the makings of such a theory. We do know enough about how power operates *inside* societies to urge that men-as-men and women-as-women be made visible in any investigation of how power operates *between* societies.

COLONIALISM AND THE REPRODUCTION OF GENDER

Sugar. Coffee. Cotton. Limes. Cocoa. Bauxite. Rice. Bananas. These are the raw products for which the countries of Central America and the Caribbean are famous. Each has its own peculiar politics. Each has its own history. Most have been nurtured not just by the region's warm climate and rich soil, but by foreign capital and hierarchies of class and skin color. When militaries have been sent into these countries it has usually been to protect those hierarchies and the rewards they have garnered from their control of sugar, coffee, bananas and other products for export.

In the last decades other, less traditional industries have been added: tourism, cattle, garment-making, electronics assembly, oil refining and, most recently, office work.

Both the more traditional and the recently introduced products have been enmeshed in global power struggles from the outset. The colonizing governments (Spain, Britain, the Netherlands, the United States, France) and the internationally competitive companies (Gulf and Western, Tate and Lisle, Bookers, United Fruit, Alcan, Kaiser, Del Monte and Dole) have waxed and waned in their fortunes, have bargained and fought each other, and have withdrawn from some places in order to intervene in others. But remaining constant has been the extreme vulnerability of the local peoples to decisions made outside their own societies.

Most historical accounts we have of these decisions and how Caribbean and Central American people have tried to cope with, or at times resist, these decisions are written as though no one ever had gender on their mind. But is this true? For instance, did British and Spanish colonizers never consider whether female Africans made less valuable slave laborers than male Africans? New work being done in this country by black women historians suggests that it is misleading to imagine that sexist strategies didn't shape the ways in which racism was developed to rationalize and organize slave labor. They suggest that these early uses of sexist strategies have had lasting effects, helping to sustain patriarchal notions within the black communities, notions which present obstacles to effective political action even a century or more after slavery's abolition. What then of the present day politics of Jamaica, Trinidad, Dominica, Guyana? Until shown otherwise, it seems unwise to theorize about post slavery "plantation societies" of the Caribbean as if women and men experienced slavery in identical ways or as if the politics of post slavery communities were free of the legacies of the colonists' patriarchal strategizing.

Essentially we would be asking how divisions of labor have been constructed, divisions that have made the cultivation of sugar and bananas, for instance, profitable enough that they reaped profits for the overseas companies and their local allies. Furthermore, questions about how racist bases of such profitable divisions are dependent on sexism aren't relevant solely to those countries in the region with histories of slavery. In Central American societies, where colonists' use of African slaves was less prevalent, racism nonetheless was wielded in order to create domestic stratifications of color that served to coopt the Hispanicized and exploit the Indian. Were the formulation and, even more interesting for us today, the persistence of these divisions of Central American labor accomplished without any dependence on sexism?

We have heard a lot about the potency of *machismo* ideology, about how women in the insurgent movements of El Salvador, Guatemala and Nicaragua have had to struggle against the presumption of male privilege inside their own organizations, but we rarely ask how *machismo* has supported the racist stratifications on which most of the coffee, sugar and banana companies depend for their own operations. We often proceed as if ideologies of male dominance have their place in Central American history, ideologies of Indian inferiority in turn have their place, and never the twain shall meet. Moreover, in most of our political organizing it is the latter that gets treated with more seriousness, as if Hispanicization and its complementary exploitation of Indians is what "really" explains how profits are squeezed out of sugar cane, banana trees or coffee beans. *Machismo*'s role in the process is hardly considered, or, if it is, it is not discussed in ways that could tell us how sexual divisions of labor have been used to support racial and class divisions of labor.

BANANAS AND PATRIARCHY

Take the banana. The banana's history is embedded in the history of European colonial expansion and, later, North American neocolonial control. It is also integrally tied to the ways that women's relations to men have been shaped by local governments and foreign companies, bolstered from time to time by U.S. military intervention. So the banana perhaps is a good place to start in our fashioning of a feminist analysis of American militarization of the region.

The banana is not native to Central America. Its original home was Southeast Asia. By the 1400s the banana had spread westward to become a basic food on the Guinean coast of Africa. When Spanish slavers began raiding the coast and shipping captured Africans to the West Indies and South America, they shipped bananas as well. The banana, then, entered this hemisphere as the slavers' choice of a cheap and popular African staple to feed enslaved women and men.

The yellow bananas familiar to North American consumers were not developed as a distinct variety until the 19th century. They were first served at the homes of wealthy Bostonians in 1875. United Fruit's corporate empire, which over the next century came to behave like a surrogate state in much of Central America, grew out of the American popularization of this humble globe-trotting fruit. That marketing success wove an invisible but crucial political link of interdependence between the women of North America and the women of Central America.

In the 1950s United Fruit took the lead in launching a brand name for its own bananas—"Chiquita." Standard Fruit, its chief competitor, followed quickly on its heels with its own brand name—"Cabana." Thus began a marketing way to win the allegiance of the American and European housewife and her local grocer. The goal remains today, to persuade predominantly female consumers that bananas from one company are of higher quality, and possess longer shelf life and greater overall reliability.

The conventional way of thinking about how and why it's "banana republics" that American officials want to preserve—by force, if necessary—in Central America is one that focuses on class alliances made by United Fruit and Del Monte executives with local political and economic elites on the one hand, and with Washington policy makers on the other. They all have a common stake in keeping banana workers' wages low and their political consciousness undeveloped. But who are these workers? Pictures that I have seen of Honduran banana worker union members always appear full of men. Do only men work on the major banana plantations, or is it only the male workers who are employed in the banana industry in ways that allow for unionization? Where are the women? One reality is that women do work that makes bananas profitable for this triple alliance of elites, but the work they do (weeding) is so marginalized that they develop a different sort of political consciousness and are excluded from the unions by their fathers and brothers who imagine their conflicts with management more "political," more "serious." Another reality is that women do not do any waged work on the plantations of United Fruit or Del Monte, that they are at home doing unpaid subsistence farming, child care and cooking. Feminists in scores of industrialized and Third World countries have revealed how even mining and agricultural operations that recruit only male workers still depend on women's work. For without women being relegated to doing the hard but unpaid work of subsistence farming and household maintenance the companies would not be able to pay their male workers such low wages. The unpaid work that women do—and the patriarchal assumptions on which that work depends—allows for the survival and reproduction of those paid workers.

Given these realities, the "banana republics" that U.S. militarization is intended to sustain are patriarchal in at least two ways. First, the colonially seeded culture of *machismo* serves to legitimize local class and racial stratifications in ways that make the subjugation of all women perpetuate the inequalities among the country's men. Second, the gender, class, and ethnic strategies of labor and profit that foreign companies use serve to perpetuate low wages and attenuate union organizing. If we thought these propositions were worth investigating, we would also find how they operate *together* so as to sustain the kind of internationally dependent, militarized society we have come to call a "banana republic."

The economies of Central America and the Caribbean have been undergoing important changes during the 1970s and 80s. Most of those changes have been initiated by foreign corporations and governments in order to resecure their hold on the region. In part because of the growing militarization and its resultant social unrest and in part out of their own in-house global strategies, some of the largest banana companies are threatening to cut back their Central American operations. Both Honduras and Nicaragua have been told that countries such as Ecuador and the Philippines now look greener for banana operations. The corporate decisions have been reported in terms of their effects on unemployment in already fragile Central American economies. Scarcely anything has been said about what it has meant for relations between women and men.

If we knew that women and men in Nicaragua and Honduras had identical roles in the international banana industry, then it would be superfluous to ask those questions. But we know this is not the case. Women and men have been affected by these recent corporate decisions in very different ways. For instance, Honduran peasant women reportedly are trying to develop cash generating projects such as the making of straw hats and the processing of cashew nuts. This is a political development, a step women are taking to reduce their earlier dependence on exploitative middlemen, *coyotes,* and to gain some social autonomy as women. But the pressure to start these new cooperative projects is also coming from the gendered ripple effects of the banana companies' cutbacks. For the unemployed banana workers are overwhelmingly the men in these women's families. Women as mothers and wives are joining women's straw hat and cashew nut cooperatives at least in part to offset the decline in household income. But what are the long range implications of male banana workers' unemployment and women's cash-producing projects? Will the political prominence of the Honduran banana workers' union fade? Will Honduran women demand a larger say in leftist political organizations? It is not unreasonable to predict that whatever change or resistance to change does occur will get played out not in the plaza but in thousands of peasant homes.

Sugar. Coffee. Cotton. Limes. Cocoa. Bauxite. Rice. Bananas. Each deserves consideration on its own in order to spell out how they are woven together into an imperialist web over the last three hundred years. And if we look at how sexual divisions of labor have been created as the pillars of these industries we should not expect to find precisely the same patterns.

Women in the region have been making their own critiques to address the presumptions of gender's political irrelevance or women's uninvolvement. For instance, the Jamaican populist women's theater collective, *Sistren,* has created a play about women sugar workers. They are reminding Jamaican poor women (and us, as well) that though Jamaican post-independence politics has been dominated by men in part because it was men who led and filled the ranks of the pre-independence militant sugar workers' unions, the sugar industry was not an all-male affair. Women too worked to make profits for the giant British company. Yet they and their labor have been made politically invisible in ways that continue to obstruct Jamaican women's entry into the nation's political life.

Similarly, before the U.S. military invasion, Grenadian women were organizing to make their work in the cocoa industry (a principle export sector) more visible. Grenadian women in the revolutionary movement began to insist that the men take their work seriously. Beyond that, they began developing government policies which would dismantle the sexual divisions of labor on which the island's cocoa business has relied. These important sexual politics were cut short by the landing of the U.S. Marines. It is likely that the post-invasion Grenadian society is being "developed" on an even more stark sexual division of labor by the expansion of the tourist industry and by the (not terribly successful) attempts by Washington officials to "secure" Grenada by inviting American light industries to establish cost-cutting assembly plants there. Both tourism and light assembly are notoriously feminized industries. The chief political difference between them and the cocoa industry is that women's cheap labor contribution is a lot harder to make invisible in the former.

A NATION OF CHAMBERMAIDS

As landlessness increases in Central America, women and men may be making quite different choices about how to survive. There is no reason to believe *a priori* that landlessness is any less gendered than plantation labor. One indication that this is happening is the rising numbers of women migrating from the countryside to the towns to seek jobs as low paid seamstresses and, if they are less lucky, domestic workers. According to one estimate, 64 per cent of all women working for wages in Guatemala City today are employed as domestic workers. Many of these women are Indian women working for Latino families. Many of these women are the sole caretakers of children.

The fact that more Latin American women work in domestic servant jobs than in any other type of waged employment is an important clue to what kind of class transformations are occurring in the 1980s as a consequence of changes in the international economy. Having household servants is one of the most visible signs of having joined the middle class. The push of more and more peasant women out of the countryside, where they no longer can support themselves and their children, and into the towns, where they must accept low paid jobs with minimal workers' rights, allows more and more Central Americans with relatively secure incomes to imagine that they have arrived in the middle or even upper middle class. For many a man of this class it is an arrival that is accompanied by peculiarly masculine privileges, sexual access to a young rural woman under his own roof who has only minimal resources with which to resist his demands. For the woman of this growing middle class the role of employer—of another woman—may serve to reconfirm her sense of upward mobility and blunt her sense of shared destiny with other, poorer women in her own country.

Simultaneously, prostitution is being integrated into this gendered and globalized political economy. A woman working as a domestic servant may be fired by her employers if she becomes pregnant—by the man of the house who wants to cover up his own actions, or by the woman of the house who prefers to deal with her husband's "indiscretions" by turning her anger on the victim. Those women, as well as women from the countryside who never were lucky enough to find jobs (or who found jobs in a factory assembling bras or transistor radios only to be laid off soon afterwards), still have children or parents to support. Thus they often turn to the last resort, prostitution.

Our understanding of what changes are occurring in Central America needs to go beyond simply talk of "landless peasants" or "peasant mobilization." What kind of politics does a woman learn from being the sole caretaker of one's own child as well as surrogate mother to someone else's child? What are the understandings about power that come from working as an Indian maid in a Latino home? At what point does sexual harassment by the father or son of that household begin to inspire resistance—resistance supported by whom?[1]

In the Caribbean as well, the resort to domestic work has been a growing trend among poor women. Some of those women have sought domestic servant jobs in their own countries. Thousands of women have migrated to Canada, the U.S. and Europe in search of income with which to support themselves and their children. Some of them have started to overcome the isolating effects of such work to speak out and to politically organize. In the United States one such organization includes both Caribbean and Central American women, as well as U.S.-born Latina and black women.[2] What would our political analysis look like if we took these domestic workers' political messages and organizing efforts as seriously as we did those of male activists and social theorists?

Even more striking and noticeable than the increase of domestic work has been the emergency of the tourist industry. Tourism seems to be the Caribbean replacement for the world's declining sugar demand. Sometimes the shift happens very explicitly, such as in the Dominican Republic last year when Gulf and Western, the hydra-headed American conglomerate, sold off more than 200,000 acres of sugar cane fields to American entrepreneurs who plan to turn the land into tourist havens. Already, by 1984, tourism had leaped ahead of sugar to become the Dominican Republic's top foreign exchange earner.

Typically, this rapid rise of foreign-capitalized tourism is condemned by critics because it is turning the countries of the Caribbean into "nations of busboys." That is, it is in the very character of these sprawling Holiday Inn chains to deskill their workers, institutionalize racism and keep crucial decision-making prerogatives in the overseas headquarters. Furthermore, the lengths to which Holiday Inn, Club Med, et al. will go to make their American, Canadian, French, and British patrons comfortable with familiar foods and decor ends up siphoning off whatever foreign exchange the friendly regimes may hope to keep for themselves.

But is it a "nation of busboys" that is replacing the region's plantation society? Is this the most accurate way for us to make sense of the kind of transformation that is taking place in Grenada, Jamaica, Barbados, the Dominican Republic and other countries that Washington is trying to pull more tightly into its security orbit? Fear of becoming a "nation of busboys" may raise insecurities around manhood to nationalist political mobilizations but it may not reflect the real gender dynamics of tourism.

Observers who bother to put on their gender-glasses note that tourism is a blatantly feminized industry in its lowest ranks. Approximately 75 per cent of all the 250,000 Caribbean tourism workers are women.[3] Many of these women are seeking hotel jobs in the wake of jobs lost in agriculture. Many women are also in desperate search for income because it has been women who, even more than men, have had to find daily ways of coping with their government's decisions to give in to International Monetary Fund pressure to cut public services and raise food prices.[4] In other words, one way we might understand how the Reagan administration is transforming American influence in the Caribbean is to trace the lines between the decline in foreign-funded agribusiness, the growth of tourism, imposition of the IMF austerity programs, and the spread of U.S. control. It appears that each of these trends, as well as their underlying connections, are illuminated by taking the experiences of Caribbean women—as workers, as copers, and as challengers.

WOMEN AND "LIGHT INDUSTRY"

Light industry is the newest economic sector to be opened up in the Caribbean and Central America. Much of this development is based on the lessons derived from Puerto Rico's earlier "Operation Bootstrap," a thoroughly feminized formula that depended on forced sterilization and making women's wages cheap. "Light industry" usually encompasses such labor-intensive forms of manufacture as used in garment and toy manufacture, food processing, and electronics assembly. Taking a page out of the textile industry's history book, light industry's executives have defined their operations' assembly jobs as "unskilled," requiring a high tolerance for repetition, without loss of precision, and thus low-waged and ideal for women.

Reagan's advisors are urging friendly regimes of what they now misleadingly call the "Caribbean Basin" (which includes Central America and Colombia) to accept more light industry foreign investment. The aim is not so much the promotion of Caribbean economic development or even American profits. Rather, the aim is to cement a security alliance between those weaker regimes and the United States with the glue of economic dependency. But this security scheme ultimately won't work unless the local regimes and American investors can attract women workers. This in turn will depend on their success in sustaining those myths of masculinity, femininity, motherhood, skill, and family which together make and keep women's labor cheap. Women who write plays about wife battering, women who risk overseas migration, women who unionize, women who demand more training, women who see single motherhood as a political category—these will not be the sorts of women that will guarantee the success of Reagan's Caribbean Basin Initiative and the security objectives the CBI is designed to serve.

But along with older light industries, corporate newcomers are taking up Washington's invitation, seemingly sure that the patriarchal myths can be kept alive.

Office work is becoming globalized. American Airlines has been in the forefront, shifting its reservations operations to Barbados. Thanks to the wonders—and cost-effectiveness—of satellite communications, companies in the insurance, banking, credit and reservations businesses have begun to look outside the United States for office workers. International lending agencies like the World Bank and the IMF have been enthusiastic. A Washington-based organization called the "Free Zone Authority" is currently urging Jamaica's Seaga regime to open up a "teleport." It has the added attraction of being only a stone's throw from Jamaica's tourist mecca, Montego Bay.

It is clear that it is the feminization of cheap labor, plus the legacy of English language in post-colonial countries, that is making this new stage in the global reach feasible. As one of the off-shore office work boosters told a journalist, "These workers are really good . . . Typing skills are impressive, and accuracy is about 99 per cent."[5] They also can be hired at wage rates far below those paid their American counterparts.

Diana Roos, researcher for the national office of 9 to 5, says that American executives are still weighing alternatives. They are busy comparing the costs, productivity and controllability of three groups of women office workers: American women employed at the companies' own offices; American women contracted to do office work as home work in the suburbs (without the costs of overhead and in a setting that is harder to unionize); finally Caribbean and Asian (especially Indian) women working offshore.

For American feminists this corporate strategizing presents at least two interlocking challenges. First, politically active office workers and their supporters must find ways to understand these global maneuvers that don't play into the hands of divide and rule union busters. Second, office workers and their supporters here and in countries like Barbados, the Bahamas and Jamaica will have to try to get the attention of women and men active in the anti-intervention movement. In the future, anti-intervention campaigns will have to be shaped out of an awareness of how women in the United States and other countries of the region are being linked to one another in ways that could serve to smooth the way for Caribbean militarization or, alternatively, *could* permit them to subvert Washington's grand security scheme.

BASES AND PATRIARCHY

Feminists in the Philippines, South Korea and Thailand have described in alarming detail just how U.S. military bases have distorted the sexual politics of the countries. A military base isn't simply an installation for servicing bombers, fighters and aircraft carriers or a launch-pad for aggressive forays into surrounding territories. A military base is also a package of presumptions about male soldier's sexual needs and about the local society's resources for satisfying those needs. Massage parlors are as integral to Subic Bay, the mammoth U.S. naval base in the Philippines, as its dry docks.

If Honduran and Salvadoran women met with Thai and Filipina women, what common stories would they have to tell? What light would those common stories shed on what it takes for militarization to proceed?

Lucy Komisar, a freelance reporter, has written an account of how sexual politics in Honduras are being fashioned so as to meet the alleged needs of the American military there.[6] Komisar went to visit the shanty town of brothels that has grown up near the Palmerole military base, one of the bases used by the U.S. military in its series of "Big Pine" joint maneuvers. She found Honduran women serving as prostitutes to both Honduran and American soldiers. Her report revealed in microcosm what Honduran public health officials have noted more generally: that there has been a notable rise in the cases of venereal disease in Honduras in the three years since the start of U.S. military build-up. Hondurans refer to the particularly virulent strain of vd as "Vietnam Rose." While the nickname once again wrongly blames the victim, it suggests that Hondurans see the Vietnamization of their country in terms of sexuality as well as money and hardware.

Lucy Komisar lets us hear from some of the people behind the statistics. First there are the young Honduran women, as young as 16 years old, who have been virtually kidnapped and brought to the brothels as captives. One woman who tried to escape was caught and returned by Honduran policemen. There are other women who on the surface seem to have come to the brothels "freely," driven by the need for money. They split their fees with the owners of the shabby cantinas where they conduct their business. But many of the women living on the fringes of the base fall somewhere in between. They have been drawn so deeply into debt to the men who supply their food and minimal housing that they never seem able to pay off their debts and gain their freedom.

The men involved are both American and Honduran. Komisar found that local policemen acted as the enforcers of the prostitution system. They in turn are controlled by Honduran army officers, a reflection of the growing capacity of the military to intimidate other Honduran institutions. American men involved are from both the enlisted and officer ranks. It may be the construction of militarized masculinity that is most responsible for American enlisted men's belief that one of the prerogatives due an American male GI overseas is the sexual services of local women. It's not clear yet how this presumption is being affected by the fact that, unlike Vietnam where most American military women were nurses, in Honduras American field units include several dozen women soldiers. So far the most common complaint that these women have had is that they have not been issued proper sanitary supplies. But where do American women soldiers go for *their* "R and R" when their male comrades head for the cantinas?

It would be wrong to imagine that this sort of sexual exploitation is sustained solely by Honduran military intimidation and diffuse American patriarchal culture. As is true in other base towns around the world, the system requires explicit American policy making. Komisar reports, for example, that it is American army doctors from the Palmerole base who routinely conduct medical exams on Honduran women working in the nearby brothels. Their job is to insure that American male soldiers will get access to the sex they want without jeopardizing the army's operational readiness. . . .

NOTES

1 For moving descriptions of the daily lives of domestic workers in Lima, Peru, see the new book by Ximena Bunster and Elsa Chaney, *Sellers and Servant* (New York: Praeger, 1985). Other excellent descriptions of working women's lives in Central America are: Laurel H. Bossen, *The Redivision of Labor: Women and Economic Choice in Four Guatemalan Communities* (Albany: SUNY Press, 1984) and Audrey Bronstein, *The Triple Struggle* (Boston: South End Press, 1982). The U.S.A.I.D. Women and Development section has also published a statistical overview of selected Latin American and Caribbean countries, *Women of the World,* Washington, D.C. May 1984.

2 Interviews with West Indian women working as domestic workers in Canada are included in Makeda Silvera, *Silenced* (Toronto: Wallace Williams Publishers) distributed in the U.S. by Kitchen Table Women of Color Press in New York. Latina, black, Asian, and white women have organized Household Workers' Rights, 330 Ellis St. Rm. 501, San Francisco, CA 94102.

3 This figure comes from one of the few general books critiquing neo-imperialism in the Caribbean to include information on women: Tom Barry, Beth Wood, and Deb Preusch, *The Other Side of Paradise* (New York: Grove Press, 1984).

4 Lynne Bolles, "Kitchens Hit by Priorities: Employed Working Class Jamaican Women Confront the IMP," in June Nash and Maria Patricia Fernandez-Kelley, *Women, Men and the International Division of Labor* (Albany: SUNY Press, 1983). Another excellent discussion of the domestic politics of underdevelopment in the Caribbean and women's responses is in *Daughters of the Nightmare: Caribbean Women,* 1984. This useful short booklet and others

like it about and by women from Chile, Peru, Ethiopia, Thailand, and the Philippines can be obtained by writing Georgian Ashworth, Change: International Reports on Women, 29 Great James St., London WC1N, England.

5 *Boston Globe,* Sept. 15, 1985.

6 The full version of Lucy Komisar's article appeared in *Honduras Update,* Vol. 3, No. 11, 1985, available from them at *Update,* 1 Summer St., Somerville, MA 02143.

Black Women, Identity, and the Quest for Humanhood and Wholeness: Wild Women in the Whirlwind

Andrée Nicola McLaughlin

One of the last poems I wrote was based on an old song called "Every time me 'memba Liza. . . ." I changed that into "Every time me 'memba Elaine (Elaine Clair)," "Every time me 'memba Colin (Colin Roach) . . ." and I talk about the youths in Soweto and Atlanta, Georgia, all the young Black people who are being killed. And what I'm saying in that poem is that they're killing Black children because they are trying to wipe out the part of the race which is militant. And although it's not stated openly, I'm also saying that the youths are coming up militant, thanks to the Black women who raised them.

Nefertiti, poet, quoted in *Heart of the Race: Black Women's Lives in Britain* by
Beverley Bryan, Stella Dadzie, and Suzanne Scafe

Nnu Ego had allowed herself to wonder where she had gone wrong. She had been brought up to believe that children made a woman. She had had children, nine in all and luckily seven were alive, much more than many women of that period could boast. . . . Still, how was she to know that by the time her children grew up the values of her country, her people and her tribe would have changed so drastically, to the extent where a woman with many children could face a lonely old age, and maybe a miserable death all alone, just like a barren woman? She was not even certain that worries over children would not send her to her grave before her chi was ready for her. Nnu Ego told herself that she would have been better off had she had time to cultivate those women who had offered her hands of friendship; but she had never had the time.

The Joys of Motherhood by Nigeria's Buchi Emecheta

How can a magistrate judge determine whether an Aboriginal tribal mother is looking after her child properly. It is not for him to decide. Aboriginal people tie the removal of their children closely with the taking of the land. The children are the only resource we've got. We're fighting to get our land back but, we say, what's the use of it if they're taking our children.

Marjorie Thorpe, national co-ordinator of the Secretariat of Aboriginal and Islander Child Care
in Gwondana Land (Australia)

By 1927 the French had reduced the Kanak population 200,000 to 26,000. Our grandmothers used to hide their children from the massacring colonial army, and thanks to them we are 56,000 strong today. We are organised, and we are ready to fight.

Sousanna Ounei, revolutionary independence activist, Kanaky (New Caledonia)

The basic unit for change is the mother and her child, and the turning around of Te Kohanga Reo ["Language Nests"—preschool Maori language programs], from a palliative into a tidal wave of self-determination, rests basically on the efforts and struggle of thousands of young Maori mothers. It will be up to them to heal the breach formed by the wedge white culture has forced through our young and old. Leadership can be simply defined as leading. And it is women in every sphere and in all current phases who are doing it.

Maori Sovereignty by Donna Awatere, Maori activist of Aotearoa (New Zealand)

It is imperative that young people be told that we have come a long way, otherwise they are likely to become cynical. A cynical young person is almost the saddest sight to see, because it means that he or she has gone from knowing nothing to believing in nothing. Young people must not get to the point of saying, "You mean to tell me we had Malcolm X, Martin Luther King, Medgar Evers? You mean to tell me we had the Kennedys, Fannie Lou Hamer and Mary McLeod Bethune? You mean to tell me we had all these men and women and we have made no progress? Then what the hell—there is no progress to be made. It can't be made." So it must be simultaneous—how far we have come and how far we have to go.

Maya Angelou, artist, quoted in *I Dream a World: Portraits of Black Women Who Changed America* by Brian Lanker

You could smell gunfire everywhere. Children were dying in the street, and as they were dying, the others marched forward, facing guns. No one has ever underestimated the power of the enemy. We know that he is armed to the teeth. But the determination, the thirst for freedom in children's hearts, was such that they were prepared to face those machine guns with stones. This is what happens when you hunger for freedom, when you want to break those chains of oppression. Nothing else seems to matter. We couldn't stop our children. We couldn't keep them off the streets.

Part of My Soul Went with Him by Winnie Mandela, on the June 1976 Uprising of Soweto, Azania (South Africa)

I came down from the Sierra / to put an end to capital and usurer / to generals and to bourgeois / Now I exist: only today do we own, do we create / Nothing is foreign to us / The Land is ours / Ours the sea and the sky / the magic and the vision.

"The Black Woman" in *Where the Island Sleeps Like a Wing* by Nancy Morejón, *Cuban poet*

Black women's realities, concerns, and analyses are being brought to world attention today by their political activism globally and by their artistic and written expression.[1] In spite of pervasive illiteracy and still limited opportunities for publication, distribution, or translation of their writings, many more Black women are making their stories known in print. The significance of this work is evident in the fact that the theories expressed in Black women's writings have become a part of the general discourse regarding the major questions of our times—social justice and human freedom.

The power of the theory being put forth by these writers largely rests in the interpretative penning of the Black female experience through the prism of their activism. An enhanced role in the political struggles of the modern world has given Black women an embryonic prominence as social and political theoreticians, and their writings are motivating further efforts to creatively render, explicate, or redress Black women's existence. A cross-cultural discussion of Black feminism by two Black women writers in Britain, for example, notes that theoretical works by Amerafrican women in the United States "have acted as a catalyst for discussion, and reaffirmed that similar kinds of consciousness were being explored."[2] As a result of increased literary endeavors, the correlative and comparative dimensions of Black women's lives and issues are perceptible in ways that previously they have not been.

This intercontinental surge of consciousness reflects a variety of complementary factors: a desire by Black women to foster understanding of their lives and legacies in a durable form; a will to build links with Black women and other people; and a passion to stir human consciousness through accounts of political struggles, expositions of history, present events and trends, and visions of new social orders. Black women's literature, by purposeful intent, emerges as a force in the dialogue about the quality and future of all human existence. Of equal primacy with their literary voices, however, are the societies Black women create and the identities they simultaneously forge to attain their aims of humanhood and wholeness.

The philosophic world-views guiding Black women's new self-definitions bring into focus a consciousness movement. Signaled by the resurgence in Black female activism and expression, this intercontinental Black women's consciousness movement is a motion to have power of the *word, the idea,* and *the ideal.* Black women, thus engaged, are not only redefining themselves and society but also the realm of resistance and, ultimately, the future. These Wild Women in the Whirlwind strive to create a new global culture by a pro-active connection to the universe, working across real boundaries of human existence while challenging those which are artificial.

The following discussion presents a cross-cultural treatment of the consciousness and theory undergirding socio-political identities Black women have adopted in endeavoring to govern their destinies. It contextualizes the Black female experience before offering another theoretical paradigm for exploring variations in self-definition relating to the term "Black" and to different identities Black women have chosen. A survey of how Black women—primarily in English-speaking, economically developed nations—have named themselves and defined their experiences is instructive about their distinct socio-political realities and the diversity and complexity of the Black female experience. The examination concludes by analyzing the social applicability of Black women's activism and self-definition to the quality of global order that is required for a truly liberated humanity.

MULTIPLE JEOPARDY AND THE HUMAN EXPERIENCE

The human experience in the twentieth century has been significantly shaped by two interrelated but divergent factors: economic class oppression and the quest for self-determination. In this regard, the United Nations' *Universal Declaration of Human Rights* and *Declaration on the Granting of Independence to Colonial Countries and Peoples* have comprised a primary basis of legitimization, if not an actual impetus, for continuing political movements for social justice. The breadth of efforts by the world's women to transform unjust systems is rivaled only by the scope of their experiences of oppression.

While the condition of most women's lives has been attributed to economic class oppression based upon race (racialism) or nationality (colonialism and imperialism) and gender (sexism and patriarchy), such a view is too simplified. Women's lives—as they experience them—are far more complex. For instance, the oppression of Burakumin women in Japan suggests a unique configuration of "triple jeopardy" in an industrialized society—gender, economic class, and caste. More pervasively, women experience national *and* racial oppression, not one to the exclusion of the other. Some examples are: indigenous women who belong to internal colonized groups and, in this way, suffer both racial and national oppression, such as Namibian, South African, (Japan's) Ainu, Palestinian, Northern Irish, Amerindian, and many Pacific women; Latin American women of African descent who experience imperialist domination along with their fellow nationals and, because of their countries' racial hierarchies, also experience racial oppression; and a large number of migrant women who were among the economically "locked-out" (or politically repressed) in their native countries and who, because of race, remain locked out in the developed societies to which they have immigrated. Reinforced and maintained by the world economic order, diverse configurations of structural inequities exist in both industrialized and developing nations. To look at the concept of women's class oppression as one solely based on race or nationality and gender is a Western notion that does not speak to the intricacy of class contradictions in other societies.

Symptomatic of the array of tensions in the world community are the possibilities for women experiencing *multiple jeopardy.* On a large scale, the oppression of women is compounded by various structural inequities which have their origins in colonialism or feudalism: differences of religion (e.g., Muslim vis-à-vis Catholic Philippine society) and ethnicity (e.g., Tamil minority vis-à-vis Sinhalese majority of Sri Lanka); and the contradictions of region (e.g., rural vis-à-vis urban Ugandans), caste (e.g., "untouchables" vis-à-vis post Gandhian India), social class (e.g., descendants of Americo-Liberian immigrants vis-à-vis indigenous peoples of Liberia), and color (e.g., status determined by complexion vis-à-vis Jamaica). Even as the bases for these structural inequities and divisions are being undermined by political revolutions, new ones are being produced by the globalization of capital (moving into those regions of "the periphery" traditionally outside "the center" of concentrated capital) and of labor (whereby new populations are relocating in foreign contexts as cheap labor). Furthermore, patriarchal oppression ensures that women experience any other oppression twice over—as a member of the dominated group and as a woman. To the extent that multiple structural inequities dictate human existence, they also define the experience of Black women.

If these forces are not complex enough already, Black women's multiple jeopardy is further complicated by a great range of geopolitical realities such as, for example, famine in the Sudan, discriminatory immigration laws in France, foreign military intervention in Nicaragua, an upsurge in racist violence in the United States, political repression in Haiti, counterrevolution in Mozambique, military occupation of East Timor, narco-terrorism in Colombia, civil war in Ethiopia, radioactive uranium mining on Aboriginal lands in Australia, nuclear testing in the Marshall Islands, apartheid in South Africa. The temptation to oversimplify and generalize about Black women's experiences and issues originates from several sources: 1) the pathos and insignificance ascribed to the cultures and lives of people of colony and promoted by Western cultural chauvinism and racism;[3] 2) the patriarchal devaluation of all women and the trivialization of their lives; 3) the great emphasis oppressed groups put upon both the commonalities in the roots of their respective circumstances and the unity of representations of their subordinate station—a means of garnering moral, political, and material support for social change; and 4) a wide-scale proclivity by many people and institutions to resort exclusively to pre-twentieth-century social thought for evaluating contemporary social phenomena.

Within the frameworks of historically evolved variations in their societies and concerns, Black women initiate new, socio-political identities, commonly spurred by the imperative of social transformation. They define themselves according to their experiences of oppression and their unique priorities for achieving a higher quality of life. These experiences and priorities in their own societies also constitute the bases for Black women's determining the relative importance of nationality, ethnicity, race, social class, culture, gender, sexuality, and so forth to their struggles for social justice.

BLACK AS POLITICAL-CLASS IDENTIFICATION

Many scholars have documented that, in antiquity, "black" was a physical characteristic, a color. "Black" first developed as a social category of low station when the Arab trade in African slaves increased; a hierarchy that valued cultural, religious, and social homogeneity assigned a negative status to slaves.[4] With Europeans' subordination of world peoples as laboring classes in subsequent centuries, the designation of social groups by color and nationality was entrenched in the Western psyche. "Black," in this context, shifted in the seventeenth century from mere association with color. As a term and a social category, "black" came to form part of a system of oppositional and hierarchical cultural constructs that patterned and justified power constellations of the colonizer and the colonized, the slave owner and the slave. That which was "white" (or Anglo, male, Christian, wealthy) was extolled and infused with connotations of benevolence and superiority, while that which was not white (or not Anglo, female, non-Christian, poor) was debased and associated with malevolence and inferiority. As such, the concept of "race" as ideological taxonomy, with "white" occupying the apical position, has represented a social construction inherent in Anglo-Saxon racism. Imposing racial identity had, in many instances, the impact of dual processes, deculturation as well as racialization of economic class arrangements. The varying sets of assumptions which Black people today assign to "black" identity mirror the range of their historical experiences and point to "Black" as a political-class identification.

Poignant evidence of the diversity of the Black experience is the difficulty in applying just one term or one definition to label or define the collective realities of Black women. For example, Black women in English-speaking North America employ a definition of Black identity which assumes that all women of African descent are Black and, conversely, that all Black women are of African descent. Yet, the majority of women in the African nations of Algeria, Tunisia, Mauritania, and elsewhere represent a cultural heritage distinct from Africans south of the Sahara and claim "Arab," not Black, identity based on linguistic and cultural unity (although there are obviously black-skinned Arabs). Furthermore, phenotypically black (physiologically classified as "Negroid") people of islands in the Pacific—many of whom embrace Black identity— are indigenous to this region, not the African continent (speculatively, a result of a glacial epoch). In areas of Europe, Black self-definition is increasingly inclusive of women of Asian, Middle Eastern, and Pacific as well as African ancestries. The Black Dutch of Holland, for instance, include immigrants and descendants of peoples from "Indonesia, South Africa, Nigeria, Turkey, the Moluccans, the Caribbean, China and other parts of the world where Black people are aboriginals."[5]

While assigning Black identity to Asian, Middle Eastern, and Pacific women in North America would invariably be interpreted as a misnomer, these women and those of African ancestry in both Canada and the United States are, to a large extent, linked by the shared designation of "women of color." But, in parts of southern Africa, stark political realities have included schematic stratifications of privileges based upon racial classification; referring to a Black woman as a "woman of color" in South Africa, for example, may lead her to believe that the referent assumes she is of the so-called "colored" category of inhabitants or that she accepts the apartheid regime's practice of legalized racialism. In Latin America, the literal translation of "woman of color" similarly has negative associations. Even so, some Latin American and Caribbean countries possess intricate racial hierarchies based on phenotype (and, sometimes, social status) in which black is a low-status social classification. Exemplary of Black self-identification in this situation is Afro-Brazilians' descriptive definition that includes those who "possess Black racial characteristics in skin color, facial characteristics and hair texture" among Brazil's more than three dozen racial categories.[6] Black identity can also break down along lines of ethnicity: those of English-speaking Caribbean background in Central America's Panama consider themselves to be Black in contrast to Spanish-speaking descendants of African slaves. In various regions of the world where self-definition is exclusively linked to nationality, tribal affiliation, and/or kinship systems (family and/or clan), the relevance of Black identity can span associations of no meaning at all, color, material condition, and/or cultural unity. Thus, there are limitations to the applicability of Black women's terms for and definitions of themselves when they move outside given social contexts.

In the absence of a universally applied taxonomy, however, Black still exists as culture, social class, and political class. As a cultural group, Black people, in their distinct geographical and interactive historical contexts, are bound by what Frantz Fanon defined as "the whole body of efforts made by a people in the sphere of thought to describe, justify and praise the action through which that people has created itself and keeps itself in existence," including its belief systems, social structures, idioms, aesthetics, art, customs, traditions, and technology.[7] As a social class, Black people are among the world's disfranchised whose plight is characterized by a condition of poverty, violence, misery, and inequality. A Black political class exists when the oppressed—self-defined as "Black"—act in behalf of their social class to oppose the prevailing socio-economic interests of the dominant group. There is a dialectical relationship among all three—culture, social class, and political class—with each influencing the way the others are expressed.

According to sociologist Oliver C. Cox, a political class seeks "control of the state" in order to fulfill the aspirations of a social class. "Different political factions may represent the same political class" when they share the same motivating premise; in this case, the factions are only separate organs for meeting the demands of the same social class.[8] Cox further argued that *"as a function of the economic order, the political class has potential existence, but as the result of agitation it becomes organized for conflict"* (emphasis mine).[9] While economic determinants are common to both classes, the political class—unlike the social class—exhibits "social solidarity" and is an actual "power group," not merely a concept. Basically, social class defines status whereas political class organizes and performs political action to empower a social class. The absence of political power to reorder unsatisfactory economic arrangements is the catalyst for political-class movement.[10] Within this theoretical framework, then, from the mid-1960's to the present, "Black" has constituted a political-class identity internationally adopted in disparate ways by oppressed women (and men) as a vehicle for liberating themselves from man-made systems of human suffering.

WILD WOMEN IN THE WHIRLWIND

The overall philosophy of Black liberation for which Malcolm X searched in his final days takes shape in the ongoing movement of Black women intercontinentally. They have sought to extend the body politic of Black nationalism to other oppressions not specific to race, and to develop an even broader frame for political-class movement. This motion, which aims to address biological life, the standard of living, and their ways of life, motivates Black women's continual redefinition of self as Azanians, indigenous peoples, feminists, and people and women of color.

Culture being the only real expression of human existence, the derogation and impairment of group character and, consequently, the threatened survival of the group propel Black women to move from being a class *in* itself—a social class, to a class *for* itself—a political class. Both social class and political class are aspects of culture, and oppressed women in either case are responding to what they are in the culture differently. However, Black women are conscious of the need for political power to ensure a future, embodied in the children, which spurs Black women's political-class identification and movement. In global perspective, Black political-class exhibits no particular geographic, racial, ethnic, religious, sexual, phenotypical, or ideological reference point outside of a uniform political opposition to imperialism, namely monopoly capitalism, colonialism, and racism, which relegates Black people to a life-threatening condition.

The political-class consciousness of Black women cross culturally evinces a quintessential unity. As a popular means through which they empower themselves, political-class, most profoundly, expresses a sentiment for autonomy. This moral sensibility demands freedom from social homogenization by means of new economic arrangements and a new definition of the human community. It insists on the reunification of the universe based on the inseparability of body, mind, and spirit, and the interdependence of all living things and life sources, and asserts a will to be self-determining in every situational locus—the home, workplace, community, and broader society. This quest for autonomy ultimately translates as a desire to free culture at the levels of the group and the individual.

The universal import of Black women's political-class action lies in both its political premise and its intrinsic sentiment for autonomy. The battle against multiple jeopardy—that is, the international and national divisions of labor with all their attendant configurations, including racialism, sexism, ethnocentrism, colorism, sectarianism, regionalism, and caste—embodies the struggle of and for humanity. The modern epoch also brings to light the contest for freedom of culture—that is, real existence: from the Tibetans in China to the Eritreans in Ethiopia, the Basque in Spain to the Kurds in Iraq, the French Canadians to the Sikhs in India, and many other peoples. The struggle for autonomy embraces to another degree the world's women who, living under patriarchal domination, seek to liberate their respective women's cultures.

Black women's activism manifests multiple consciousness, indicating a recognition that political class is a demand for the end of oppression *whatever* the basis and, further, that the vision for autonomy is shared by *all* people. Moreover, their contemporaneous political-class identities suggest qualitative change is brought about by the community who opposes domination and not by a "nationality," a "race," a "gender," or an ethnic group per se. Multiply-identified, Black women in various regions of the world are offering a holistic conception of the struggle for social justice and human freedom. This poses another challenge to transcend the vocabulary and limitations of Western language and secularism.

Political-class identity, even as it is necessary to achieve humanhood, obscures the basis of humanhood—culture. For if culture is the commonly real expression of human existence, then, in the final analysis, true human identity will not be based upon social class or political class. This premise makes Fanon's contention ring with import: What does it mean to be Black when the person who created the nigger is losing control of the world?[11] Overcoming domination requires that Black women leave aside the imperialist-derived secularism of Western culture that fragments the universe, including human existence, the struggle for human freedom, and human identity.

To establish a new relationship to the planet and cosmos, Black women are not redefining women-qua-women but redefining themselves in their entirety and, hence, the men, children, Earth, and the universe. By symbolmaking, ideamaking, and world-making, they are creators in the preeminent sense. Through this activity, Black women—from Holland to Brazil, South Africa to New Zealand, Britain to the United States, and elsewhere—expose the truths of their existence. Demythified by the intensity of their own actions, they turn Western imagery of Black women and their experiences on its head. Their primary instruments are the traditional world-views and fearlessness of their maligned foremothers. Assuming the mantle of the foremothers to regain their lost autonomy, these Wild Women in the Whirlwind make real change in the real world through real means.

With this reassertion of their world-views in tandem with efforts to reorder the world economy, Wild Women in the Whirlwind are attempting to establish a meaning-ful and nondestructive basis for human interaction and all life's coexistence. In so doing, they reclaim their land, labor, fellow human being, history, language, and cul-ture—elements of humanhood and wholeness. They are receptive to multiple perspec-tives and concepts of being, cognizant that there is not one truth but many, and, there-by, they represent a humanistic social force. These Black women's proactive connection to the living global community is grounded in the acceptance of the diver-sity and integrity of life as a means and ends for existence. The political-class move-ment of Black women conveys that autonomy must be true for all people and that human fulfillment rests in the harmonious integration of all life systems. Their visions instruct that there is only one humanity, one Earth, one cosmos, one reality.

Creating a new identity in the course of creating a new world, Wild Women in the Whirlwind invoke the birth of a new global culture based on an ethos of human libera-tion and harmony with the universe. In the lyric of Gwendolyn Brooks's prophecy, they urgently impart that

. . .we are the last of the loud.
Nevertheless, live.
conduct your blooming in the noise and whip of the whirlwind.[12]

NOTES

1 Sections of this paper are based on a presentation, "Redefining Parameters for Comparative Research on Black Women," for the Centre for Multicultural Education and the Centre for Research and Education on Gender, the University of London Institute of Education, June 4, 1986.

2 Dorothea Smartt and Val Mason-John, "Black Feminists Organizing on Both Sides of the Atlantic," *Spare Rib: A Women's Liberation Magazine* [London], no. 171 (October 1986), 22.

3 "People of colony" in this context designates peoples who currently are or have formerly been subjugated by European colonialism.

4 For discussion of concerns for homogeneity in the Muslim order as they apply to "the men of low estate," namely African slaves, see Fatna A. Sabbah, "The Omnisexual Woman in Action: Subversion of the Social Order," in *Women in the Muslim Unconscious* (New York: Pergamon Press, 1984).

5 Black Women's Centre, Amsterdam, Holland, letter to attendees of the 1985 Non-Govern-mental World Meeting of Women in Nairobi, Kenya (n.d.).

6 Niani [Dee Brown], "Black Consciousness vs. Racism in Brazil," *The Black Scholar*, 11, no. 3 (January/February 1980), 68.

7 Frantz Fanon, "On National Culture," in *The Wretched of the Earth* (New York: Internation-al Publishers, 1968), p. 233.

8 Oliver C. Cox, "The Political Class," in *Caste, Class & Race: A Study in Social Dynamics* (New York: Modern Readers Paperbacks, 1948), pp. 156, 155. In this Chapter 10 of his work, Cox distinguished "political class" and "social class" as two different phenomena. He contended that social class was a type of "social-status system": "Social classes form a sys-tem of co-operating conceptual status entities; political classes, on the other hand, do not constitute a system at all, for they are antagonistic." Regarding political class, he said "the

designation 'economic class' might have been used, but economic determinants are evidently at the base of social classes also."

9 Ibid., p. 157.
10 Ibid., pp. 154, 155, 159.
11 Fanon, "On National Culture," p. 234.
12 Gwendolyn Brooks, "Second Sermon on the Warplan," in *Blacks* (Chicago: The David Company, 1987), p. 456.

Suggestions for Further Reading: Part 3

The literature on various aspects of feminism is now so extensive that we have made no attempt to provide exhaustive bibliographies. Instead, we have suggested just a few books that provide accessible introductions to various topics or have become classics in the field.

Allen, Jeffner: *Lesbian Philosophies and Cultures,* State University of New York Press, Albany, 1990.

Anzaldúa, Gloria: *Making Face, Making Soul: Haciendo Caras: Creative and Critical Perspectives by Women of Color,* Aunt Lute Foundation Books, San Francisco, 1990.

de Beauvoir, Simone: *The Second Sex,* Knopf, New York, 1953.

Bernard, Jessie: *The Female World from a Global Perspective,* Indiana University Press, Bloomington and Indianapolis, 1987.

Building Feminist Theory: Essays from Quest, Longman, New York, 1981.

Bunch, Charlotte: *Passionate Politics: Feminist Theory in Action,* St. Martin's Press, New York, 1986.

Butler, Judith: *Gender Trouble: Feminism and the Subversion of Identity,* Routledge, New York, 1990.

Collins, Patricia Hill: *Black Feminist Thought: Knowledge, Consciousness, and the Politics of Empowerment,* Unwin Hyman, Boston, 1990.

Daly, Mary: *Gyn/Ecology: The Metaethics of Radical Feminism,* Beacon, Boston, 1978.

Davis, Angela Y.: *Women, Race and Class,* Vintage, New York, 1983.

Davis, Angela Y.: *Women, Culture and Politics,* Random House, New York, 1990.

Eisenstein, Zillah R.: *Capitalist Patriarchy and the Case for Socialist Feminism,* Monthly Review Press, New York, 1979.

Engels, Frederick: *The Origin of the Family, Private Property and the State,* International Publishers, New York, 1972.

Ferguson, Ann: *Blood at the Root: Motherhood, Sexuality and Male Dominance,* Unwin Hyman, Boston, 1989.

Frye, Marilyn: *The Politics of Reality: Essays in Feminist Theory,* The Crossing Press, Trumansburg, N.Y., 1983.

Hartsock, Nancy C. M.: *Money, Sex and Power: Toward a Feminist Historical Materialism,* Longman, New York, 1983.

hooks, bell: *Feminist Theory: From Margin to Center,* South End, Boston, 1983.

Jaggar, Alison M., *Feminist Politics and Human Nature,* Rowman and Allanheld, Totowa, N.J., 1983.

Koedt, Anne, Ellen Levine, and Anita Rapone: *Radical Feminism,* Quadrangle, New York, 1973.

Lowe, Marian, and Ruth Hubbard: *Woman's Nature: Rationalizations of Inequality,* Pergamon, New York, 1983.

MacKinnon, Catharine A., *Feminism Unmodified: Discourses on Life and Law,* Harvard University Press, Cambridge, Mass., 1987.

MacKinnon, Catharine A.: *Toward a Feminist Theory of the State,* Harvard University Press, Cambridge, Mass., 1989.

Mill, John Stuart, and Harriet Taylor Mill: *Essays on Sex Equality,* edited and with an introductory essay by Alice S. Rossi, University of Chicago Press, Chicago and London, 1970.

Mitchell, Juliet: *Women's Estate,* Pantheon, New York, 1971.

Mitchell, Juliet: *Psychoanalysis and Feminism: Freud, Reich, Laing and Women,* Vintage, New York, 1974.

Mohanty, Chandra Talpade, Ann Russon, and Lourdes Torres (eds.): *Third World Women and the Politics of Feminism,* University of Indiana Press, Bloomington and Indianapolis, 1991.

Moraga, Cherrie, and Gloria Anzaldua: *This Bridge Called My Back: Writings by Radical Women of Color,* Persephone Press, Watertown, Mass., 1981.

Rothenberg, Paula S., *Race, Class and Gender in the United States: An Integrated Study,* St. Martin's, New York, 1992.

Sargent, Lydia (ed.): *Women and Revolution: A Discussion of the Unhappy Marriage of Marxism and Feminism,* South End, Boston, 1981.

Spelman, Elizabeth V.: *Inessential Woman: Problems of Exclusion in Feminist Thought,* Beacon, Boston, 1988.

Wollstonecraft, Mary: *A Vindication of the Rights of Woman,* 1792.

A few of the many journals of feminist theory

Differences: A Journal of Feminist Cultural Studies
Feminist Studies
Frontiers: A Journal of Women Studies
Genders
Sage: A Scholarly Journal on Black Women
Signs: Journal of Women in Culture and Society

Practice: Contemporary Issues Through the Lenses

Although the particular issues that capture our attention and provoke our passion change over time and place, many arise out of our ongoing efforts to survive economically and emotionally by obtaining enough material resources to sustain us, by creating some form of family, and by dealing with our sexuality and the ways in which society seeks to direct or control it. In this final section of the book, we again turn our attention to some of the practical issues that women and men confront in their daily lives. Unlike the articles in Part 1, however, which remain more on the level of experience and description, the articles and essays in Part 4 attempt to go beyond description to explanation and analysis. As they do so, they adopt, often implicitly, one or more of the various lenses we have identified in Part 3, using the priorities that the lenses reflect as the basis for defining and analyzing the problems on which they focus.

In previous editions of *Feminist Frameworks* we grouped the selections in the last part of the book according to the frameworks identified earlier, treating each article as if it were an example of the kind of practice generated by one and only one theoretical framework. The sophistication and complexity of much feminist theorizing about contemporary issues makes this organization no longer possible or desirable. A careful reading of many of the articles in this section reveals their subtle or sometimes not so subtle adoption of more than one lens in identifying problems and framing solutions. The challenge to the reader, then, is to read each selection critically with an eye to ferreting out the theoretical commitments that determine various authors' points of departure, as well as the categories and values implicit in their formulation of the issues and recommendations for a just resolution.

The ability to identify the theoretical or ideological underpinnings of various approaches to political, social, and economic problems becomes increasingly important at a time when many analyses of social problems are presented as if they were value-free or "neutral," even though in fact they assume a particular way of defining who and what counts and consequently privilege the interests of some while devaluing or dismissing those of others. In place of the impossible goal of value neutrality, we suggest the desirability of learning to identify competing or opposing interests and values hidden within theoretical analyses. This will allow us to make conscious and deliberate choices about which interests to address instead of pretending that our choices are ever entirely "objective" in the sense of being "value-free."

A good example of how easy it is for assumptions and value judgments to be concealed in particular ways of theorizing about women emerges from a question as seemingly straightforward as how to title the readings that appear under our subhead "Staying Alive." In previous editions, we grouped similar readings first under the heading "Work" and later under "Paid Labor." Although dismissed by some as mere semantics, the ability to name and categorize carries with it the power to structure people's perceptions and even their experience. One of the early observations of feminist theory was that capitalism's insistence upon reserving the term "work" exclusively for paid labor had the effect of emphasizing men's productive activity while rendering invisible those productive activities generally assigned to women such as child rearing and homemaking. As a result of this peculiar use of language, many women when asked "What kind of work do you do?" found themselves forced to reply "I don't work" if their primary productive activities were centered in the home and did not result in a wage. Even today, when a majority of women are in the paid labor force, questions about work continue to ignore the economic and social contributions of women's (and some men's) household labor.

This devaluation of women's work is not without consequences. By denying women's contribution to the world's economy, it becomes easier to rationalize the extraordinarily unequal distribution of income and wealth that exists throughout the world. According to the first article in this section, women do two-thirds of the world's work, receive only about 5 percent of the income, and own less than 1 percent of the assets. In the United States, where the statistics are not quite as dramatic, popular conceptions of what counts as work, as well as the social values reflected in how various occupations are remunerated, effectively rationalize the gap between male and female earnings as well as the ongoing sex and race segregation of the labor force. After all, if women's work is less important than men's, women should not be surprised to be paid less. If women's primary role in life is to serve as wife and mother, then the income she derives from part- or even full-time work can be regarded as "pin money," "extra" earnings that provide a few extras for the family, and her lower rate of pay, lack of health and pension benefits, and other discriminatory aspects of women's employment can be ignored or dismissed. And if women's caregiving activities in the home aren't real work, no wonder that social service and teaching and other traditionally female occupations, which can be represented as extensions of those activities, are paid at abysmally low rates. These ways of defining and denying work render discriminatory treatment invisible by making it appear natural or reasonable. For this reason, we chose to talk about "paid labor" rather than "work" in our second edition where our focus was clearly on work outside the home, and for this reason we now choose to use the more inclusive heading "Staying Alive" in order to more adequately capture the interrelatedness among economic survival and homophobia, racism, sexism, and sexual harassment.

Not only the categories implicit in the language we choose but also the relative importance we place upon these categories plays a role both in how we formulate problems and how we propose solving them. A clear example of how prioritizing different lenses that emphasize different aspects of reality can lead to different though not necessarily incompatible analyses of data can be found by comparing Diana Pearce's article "The Feminization of Poverty" with the one by Margaret B. Wilkerson and Jewell Handy Gresham entitled "The Racialization of Poverty." Pearce and other white feminists who have sought to call attention to the economic plight of women in the United States during the past decade have coined the phrase "the feminization of poverty." By this they mean to highlight the unique aspects of women's employment that have resulted in female-headed families having a significantly higher poverty rate than two-parent families or single-parent families headed by men. A striking aspect of such poverty-level female-headed families is that in some cases the women heading them are actually employed as full-time workers.

While talk about the feminization of poverty is dramatic and has succeeded on occasion in directing media attention to the plight of poor women, some argue that the phrase itself is problematic insofar as it obscures the distinctive problems of certain other groups, rendering those groups and their problems invisible. In contrast to Pearce, Wilkerson and Gresham argue that "the feminization of poverty is real, but the *racialization* of poverty is at its heart." They object to the former term because they maintain that "it negates the role played by racial barriers to black employment, particularly among males."

When we scrutinize the implications of each analysis, we can see how much is at stake in the way we frame issues, i.e., in our choice of lenses and the emphasis we place on them. Each of these ways of defining the problem leads to very different public policy proposals. If we define the problem in terms of the feminization of poverty, it is likely that we will seek to generate a public policy that improves both the availability and the quality of child care, provides public income support for children with absent or long-term unemployed parents, and dismantles occupational segregation, pay inequities, and other forms of labor force discrimination that impact directly on women. If we choose to employ a conceptual and theoretical apparatus which explains the poverty of women and children in the African-American community in terms of the plight of African-American men in this country, we will press for increased educational and employment opportunities for black men as well as related social policies. The latter problem statement and solution implicitly privilege the patriarchal family insofar as it ties the fate of black women and children directly to that of African-American men rather than treating black women as autonomous. Other ways of framing the issues at stake might adopt additional lenses in order to capture the complex interrelations among race, class, and gender that shape and limit our lives.

The power inherent in naming and categorizing is further illustrated by the continuing and highly politicized debate in the United States over what constitutes a family. As Phillip Gutis reports in "Family Redefines Itself," the debate revolves around whether the family is to be defined primarily by structure or by function. Where conservatives would reserve the term "family" for legally married heterosexual couples, their children, and immediate blood relatives, others argue that people can be said to have formed a family if they assume long-term responsibility for contributing to the physical and emotional well-being of each other. While conservatives might have no difficulty treating the married couple described by John Krich in his account of mail-order brides as a family, they usually wish to deny that title and status to lesbian or gay couples living together in long-term committed relationships, perhaps including children which they coparent, and even might wish to withhold the title from a woman of color living alone with her child at or below the poverty line or to an unmarried heterosexual couple with earnings in the highest income bracket. Other readings in this section explore the ways in which wealth and patriarchal privilege determine what constitutes a family. The various definitions of family have direct consequences for women's lives. They influence whether women are allowed or forced to bear children or prevented from giving birth, whether they are valued and respected or despised as mothers, and even whether women who are "employed" to bear children for others have the right to be called the mothers of the children they bear.

Equally problematic is the way in which we as women and men have been taught to define our sexuality. For some, the carefully coiffed, well-manicured, painfully slender young woman wearing the latest fashion is a symbol of femininity and material success, worthy of being idealized and emulated; to others she is the victim of a culture that urges women to become doll-like objects, dependent on men and a carefully constructed and enforced compulsory heterosexuality for their sense of personal self-worth and their attainment of satisfaction. For many conservatives, heterosexual sex within marriage represents the ultimate realization of our physical and emotional needs which they believe are grounded in our biology. According to liberals, by contrast, consenting adults should be free to express and explore their sexuality in whatever way they choose within the context of a mature and private relationship. Some feminists share the liberal view, but others argue that liberals are blind to the unequal economic and social realities that form the context in which this so-called free sexual expression occurs. In addition, feminists disagree strongly over whether certain sexual practices are so inherently degrading to women that they should not be tolerated under any conditions. For example, Alice Walker is repelled by sadomasochistic fantasies and practices based on master/slave paradigms of dominance and subordination which she sees as perversely replicating the physical and emotional brutality inflicted upon African-American women by their slave masters. Other feminists place what they take to be issues of free speech at the center of their focus and are willing to tolerate pornographic portrayals of women and sexuality, no matter how offensive, because they believe that protecting First Amendment freedoms must take precedence. Still other feminists argue in favor of tolerating conventionally abhorrent practices because they believe that women must be free to define the difference between pornography and eroticism for themselves outside or beyond the context established by a male-dominated, homophobic, racist, capitalist society.

In each of these cases the way particular thinkers or essays define the problem and identify or prioritize the issues reflects which lens or combination of lenses they are employing. For example, those who employ only the lenses of gender and class are likely to focus on the coercive nature of sexual interaction between individuals with unequal access to economic resources. Feminists like Angela Davis, who also employ the lens of race, may be as concerned about the way in which charges of raping white women have been used against African-American men to perpetuate race and class domination in the United States as they are about rape as violence against women, an issue that was ignored in the past by many white feminists who looked at the issue exclusively through the lens of gender. Feminists like Charlotte Bunch, who place issues of race, class, and gender in a global context, may be more likely to identify a worldwide systemic mobilization of patriarchy and international capital in the interest of exploiting women's sexuality for male enjoyment and profit than feminists whose understandings are more limited because they use fewer lenses.

We cannot overstate the importance of making explicit the moral and political commitments inherent in various theoretical frameworks employed for analyzing social problems and formulating proposals for resolving them. Nor can we overstate the need to replace monodimensional analyses and recommendations with multiple perspectives or lenses. Nothing less will reveal the biases endemic to so many existing social policy analyses. In a world where the few have spoken for the many for so long, only such a commitment to utilizing a multiplicity of perspectives and an insistence upon learning to see the world in its enormous richness and complexity can give us any confidence in the adequacy of the positions we adopt. Only a serious commitment to hearing every voice and the understanding that new voices are always in the process of emerging can embolden any of us to speak, however tentatively. In the final analysis, the differences that separate us are certainly no greater than the problems that we face, problems that will have to be defined and solved with an understanding of their global implications and consequences if we are to move beyond the realities of exploitation, oppression, and deprivation to a more just and humane existence for us all.

Staying Alive

Women Count—Count Women's Work

A Petition for All Women to All Governments

WHEREAS women do 2/3 of the world's work, receive only 5 percent of the income and own less than 1 percent of the assets;

WHEREAS women are the poorer sex, Black and Third World women are the poorest of all, and the poorer we are the harder we are forced to work;

WHEREAS women produce all the workers of the world, but this is not considered work and we are not considered workers;

WHEREAS women, with the help of children, grow at least half the world's food, yet we are often denied ownership of or even access to land, credit and loans, and the technology of our choice;

WHEREAS women do most or all of the work of caring for children, but are often threatened with loss of child custody;

WHEREAS we are often forced to cross national boundaries for economic and political survival, and do the invisible work of resettling whole communities in new and hostile environments;

WHEREAS most of the work women do is invisible and unwaged, and any welfare benefits, pensions or services we receive are considered not a right, not a wage, but charity;

WHEREAS despite our enormous contribution and despite lip service to women's equality, women are often denied food, healthcare, housing, the right to have or not to have children in conditions we choose, safety from rape and other violence in the home and outside, sexual choices, education, childcare, job opportunities and pay equity — in other words, our basic human rights;

WHEREAS there is no peace as long as people anywhere, beginning with women and children, most struggle to survive the holocaust of poverty, overwork, famine and ecological devastation;

288

WHEREAS according to State definitions, raising a child is not counted as "work," but being in the military and killing is;

WHEREAS because of women's pressure internationally, in 1980 the United Nations called on all governments to count "the contribution of the unpaid work that women do in the farms, at home and in other fields" (UN Decade for Women Draft Program of Action);

WHEREAS at the final World Conference of the UN Decade for Women in Nairobi in 1985, governments agreed that: "The remunerated and, in particular, the unremunerated contributions of women to all aspects and sectors of development should be recognized, and appropriate efforts should be made to measure and reflect these contributions in national accounts and economic statistics and in the gross national product. Concrete steps should be taken to quantify the unremunerated contribution of women to agriculture, food production, reproduction and household activities" (Paragraph 120 of *Forward Looking Strategies for the Advancement of Women*) and this was ratified by the UN General Assembly on 6 November 1985;

THEREFORE we petition every government to implement the 1985 UN decision and to count the contribution to the economy of all women's work, so that it is recognized and reflected in every Gross National Product.

The Gross National Product (GNP) — sometimes referred to as the Gross Domestic Product (GDP) — is defined as the total value of goods and services produced, but includes only goods and services exchanged for money. Women's unwaged work, estimated to produce as much as 50 percent of the GNP, has been left out.

Issued by International Wages for Housework Campaign and International Black Women for Wages for Housework. Address in US: P.O. Box 86681, Los Angeles, CA 90086-0681. Tel: (213) 221-1698; Fax (213) 227-9353.

The Women Count — Count Women's Work petition was issued jointly in 1984 by International Black Women for Wages for Housework and the International Wages for Housework Campaign. A wide range of individuals and community groups have endorsed counting women's work, including women's, civil and human rights, labor, religious, civic, peace, and ecology organizations. The National Women's Studies Association has passed a recommendation in support.

Legislative and international progress includes a Bill in the U.S. Congress in 1991 by Rep. Barbara-Rose Collins with the backing of the Congressional Black Caucus, entitled "The Unremunerated Work Act" (HR 3625), which has subsequently been endorsed by the Congressional Caucus for Women's Issues; the report "The Assessment of Women's Unwaged Work" in committee of the European Parliament; and, in 1989, a Bill in the British Parliament, "Counting Women's Unremunerated Work," introduced by Labour MP Mildred Gordon. In March 1990, the UN Commission on the Status of Women reaffirmed the 1985 UN decision to count women's unwaged work and set 1995 as a deadline for governments to act on the decision. The Committee for the Elimination of Discrimination Against Women (CEDAW) has prioritized counting women's unwaged work as crucial to equality for women. Trinidad and Tobago's national policy says women's work should be counted.

The Women Count — Count Women's Work petition is available in 24 languages and in Braille and on tape in English.

For more information, write P.O. Box 86681, Los Angeles, CA 90086-0681 or call (213) 221-1698.

Further Reading (*orders available from the above address*):
The Power of Women and the Subversion of the Community, by Selma James with Mariarosa Dalla Costa, 3rd ed., 1975.
Black Women and the Peace Movement, by Wilmette Brown, 2nd ed., 1984.
The Disinherited Family, by Eleanor Rathbone with an Introductory Essay by Suzie Fleming, 1986.
Strangers and Sisters: Women, Race & Immigration, edited and with an Introduction by Selma James, 1985.
Black Women: Bringing It All Back Home, by Margaret Prescod, 2nd ed., 1984.

The Feminization of Poverty: Update

Diana M. Pearce

This paper is a second look at the "feminization of poverty," a decade after the phenomenon was first documented. It begins by carefully defining the "feminization of poverty," and then evaluates whether the trends, especially recent ones, indicate a continuing pattern of the "feminization of poverty." Three ways in which official poverty measures underestimate the extent and depth of women's poverty are discussed briefly. The next section looks closely at the dynamics of women's poverty as they relate to macro-economic changes in the economy, the labor market and child rearing. Finally, new public policy priorities are outlined.

I. IS THERE STILL A FEMINIZATION OF POVERTY?

A. Defining the Feminization of Poverty

What is the "feminization of poverty"? As the term was first used in 1978, it described the trend toward more and more of the burden of poverty being borne by women. This can be measured by two different methods. One, which will be called the **individual-base method,** is simply to count all persons, or adults,[1] who are poor by gender, and examine the changes over time in the proportion female. Thus wives and daughters in poor families with male householders are counted as well as women maintaining households alone. The other way, which will be called the **household-base method,** is to examine the number of people who are poor by the gender of the person(s) maintaining the household, i.e., the proportion of the poor in households which are maintained by women alone,[2] and how that proportion changes over time. The **household-base** measure will be used here, for it has two distinct advantages: (1) it is consistent with the way poverty is actually measured, which is at the level of the household, not the individual, and (2) it more closely reflects the concept of the feminization of poverty, i.e., the idea that women have increasingly borne the burden of poverty alone.

B. The Trends

Over the last quarter of a century, the number of poor women-maintained families, particularly those with children, has more than doubled, increasing at a remarkably steady rate of roughly 100,000 families each year. There are now 3.6 million poor, women-maintained families. The proportion of poor families maintained by women alone has risen from 23 to over 51% of all families. There has been a parallel growth of women-maintained families in each racial group: between 1959 and 1986, the proportion of poor white families maintained by women alone increased from 20 to 42%, and the proportion of poor black families from 30 to 75%. Likewise, the proportion of poor hispanic families maintained by women alone increased from 45% in 1973 (the first year for which data was available) to 49% in 1986.

C. The Depth of Women's Poverty

The poverty of women-maintained families is greater, and more persistent, than the poverty experienced by married couples and their families. In 1984, about half of poor women-maintained families, but less than a third of all other poor families, had incomes below **half** the poverty line. The median deficit, i.e., the amount of money per family needed for them to reach the poverty level, was 25% greater for poor women-maintained families than for all other poor families. The only survey which has followed the same people year after year, the Panel Survey on Income Dynamics at the University of Michigan, found that about 60% of the persistently poor, i.e., people poor at least 8 out of 10 years, lived in woman-maintained families (Duncan, et al, 1984).[3] With the same data set, Hill and Corcoran estimate that once poor, the likelihood of staying poor is ten times greater if one is in a woman-maintained family compared to a family with an adult male in it.[4]

Altogether, women-maintained households have experienced a steady decline in their economic status relative to that of married couples. The median income of women-maintained households, as a percentage of that of married couples, has steadily fallen from 70% in 1947 to 42% in 1987.[5] Even when the comparison is to married couples in which the wife is not working, there is a decline in the relative status of women-maintained families.

D. Is Poverty Underestimated?

Clear as these trends are, there are three ways in which these numbers *underestimate* the number of poor, and particularly underestimate number of poor women-maintained families.

First, poor families who are doubled-up with other families, but are not the owners or renters of the unit which they are sharing, (since 1980) have not been in the count of poor families. Statistically speaking, these families, whom the Census Bureau calls sub-families, have thus been made invisible. Since these families are disproportionately women-maintained, these changes also underestimate the nature and extent of women's poverty.

Second, the method used since 1980 to calculate poverty thresholds creates systematically lower thresholds for single parent—compared to two-parent—families;[6] since most single parent families are women-maintained, this leads to an underestimate of the number of poor families that seriously undercounts women's poverty.

Third, because the official annual poverty counts are based on a survey of households, they do not include the homeless. Women-maintained families are the most rapidly increasing group among the homeless. Thus excluding the homeless from the count of the poor underestimates poverty generally, and women's poverty especially.

II. THE DYNAMICS OF POVERTY: ARE THEY DIFFERENT FOR WOMEN?

To further examine the phenomenon of the "feminization of poverty," this paper will examine the nature of the feminization of poverty, why the number of poor women has increased, and the specific characteristics of women's poverty, including how women's poverty is related to the labor market and to child rearing.

A. What Is the Nature of the Feminization of Poverty?

How much of this trend towards the feminization of poverty is a function of "changing demographics"—the increase in the number of women-maintained households—how much is due to the pauperization (increase in poverty rates) of women, and how much to the depauperization (decrease in poverty rates) of other groups?

Basically, what has been happening are two opposite trends. First, "demographic changes" have increased the number of and proportion of the population who are in woman-maintained households, with a corresponding decrease in married-couple households. Second, there has been a "depauperization" of several groups that have historically experienced disproportionate rates of poverty. Many workers, who used to be labeled "the working poor," have been lifted out of poverty by postwar economic growth and are now economically secure enough to be seen as the working class or the middle class. Older Americans, whose poverty frequently occurred because of a health crisis or the lack of housing, and inadequate social security, have benefited from programs targeted to their needs: Medicare, elderly housing, and broadened and indexed social security benefits. As a result, the overall poverty rate for the elderly is actually less than that of the population as a whole.

It is important to understand the dynamics of women's poverty, including what it is not. The feminization of poverty is not the result of increased numbers of women suddenly becoming impoverished. Instead it is due to a consistent, year after year, systematic increase in the number of poor women-maintained households, coupled with a systematic decrease in the number of other poor households, the elderly and male-present families.

B. Why Have Women Not Shared in the Poverty Reduction Experienced by Other Groups?

Why have women-maintained households not experienced the depauperization that has allowed other demographic groups to exit poverty? The answer to this question lies in the dynamics of poverty over the past quarter century. The most dramatic decrease in poverty occurred during the decade of the 1960's with most of the progress occurring among males (unrelated individuals) and male-present families. During the seventies and early eighties, a cyclical pattern appeared for married-couple and male-headed households: each recession resulted in the poverty population expanding rapidly with the influx of unemployed (disproportionately male) workers and their families, and during the recoveries that followed, these families left poverty relatively quickly. Even during and after the 1982 recession, which resulted in the highest unemployment levels in the last half-century, the increase and decrease in the numbers of families in poverty was much sharper among married-couple and male-headed families than among women-maintained families.

Women-maintained families do not experience, to the same extent, the sharp increase in poverty during a recession that is experienced by men and married couples, and their families, nor do they benefit when the economy is in recovery. This is reflected in the feminization of poverty index: for example, at the depths of the most recent recession, the "index" for families fell to 46%, meaning that 46% of the poor were in women-maintained families, but in the following two years it rose again, reaching 51.5% in 1987, its highest point ever. Similar patterns can be observed for the earlier, smaller, recessions in 1975 and 1980. Because the proportion of poor families which are women-maintained is higher at the end of each recession than it was before it began, the entire period of 1959 to 1987, the proportion of poor families who are women-maintained has risen.

C. The Specific Characteristics of Women's Poverty

1. Women in the Labor Market   While trends in women's poverty do not follow closely macroeconomic changes or cycles in the economy, that does not mean that the economy is not relevant to women's poverty. On the contrary, increasingly women's poverty is a direct result of the disadvantaged position women hold in the labor market, their structural position. Women experience discrimination not only in getting a job, but also once they have gotten one. Many poor women are employed women, i.e., they are poor in spite of their paid employment.

a. Wages, Hours, and Benefits   The nature of women's disadvantage in the labor market is to be found not just in higher unemployment rates, but in employment itself. Due to child-rearing responsibilities and the lack of affordable day care, women who maintain households alone find it extremely difficult to become full-time year-round workers, and even when they do, the new jobs created by the economy's expansion are often part-time and part-year. Job growth is clearly most rapid in such sectors as service and retail trade, sectors that are dominated by part-time, part-year jobs. In 1985, for example, one-third of the new jobs were part-time. Women workers, especially those who are newly entering or reentering the labor market, are likely to take a disproportionate share of these new jobs. Thus less than half of all women workers, and 40% of women who head households alone, work full-time year-round.

The disparity between part-time/seasonal jobs and "good" jobs in terms of non-wage fringe benefits is even greater than the differences in wages alone. In addition, their marginal labor force status is reinforced for many women by their lack of coverage under unemployment insurance programs. Altogether, the wages of full-time, year-round women workers are not improving significantly or consistently, while the proportion of women with poor paying, deadend, part-time and/or part-year jobs seems likely to increase.

2. Women and Children   An equally important dynamic of the feminization of poverty is the economic burden of children. Over the past two-plus decades, the proportion of poor women-maintained households that have children in them has risen from 80 to 90%. At the same time, divorce today occurs at younger ages of both mother and children, and an increased proportion of single mothers have never been married. As a consequence, single parents have greater needs, for example, younger children require more costly child care, and fewer resources with which to meet them: in general, shorter marriages, or no marriages at all, result in fewer resources, including subsequent child support, than do longer marriages.

In spite of these increasing economic burdens, neither private transfers nor public transfers adequately meet the costs of caring for children. Indeed, both types of income support, private and public, have *decreased* in recent years, exacerbating this dynamic of women's poverty. As for *private transfers,* only half of absent fathers are even *supposed* to pay child support, and less than half of those paid the full amount owed. Moreover, while the proportion of non-custodial parents, mostly fathers, who pay child support has remained virtually unchanged in recent years, the amount of support has actually decreased in constant dollars—about 12% between 1983 and 1985, and it averages only about $2200 annually (per family, not per child). Even if enforcement was thorough, however, and every penny owed were paid, it would do little to reduce poverty for the simple reason that the amounts of child support ordered are too low to raise most family incomes above the poverty line.

Since 1970, the real value of *public transfers,* in the form of welfare benefits, has decreased by about one-third. The 1981 Omnibus Budget Reconciliation Act also decreased both the number of persons eligible, and benefit levels, through changes in eligibility rules and benefit calculation formulas. And the 1988 Family Support Act further restricts the availability of income support by pushing welfare recipients into employment with only minimal support and training of the kind needed for women-maintained families to become not only self-sufficient, but no longer poor. Related programs providing subsidies to low-income families have also been cut significantly, particularly, low-income housing, but also child care, medical care, etc. Even non-welfare income support programs, such as unemployment insurance, are reaching fewer single parent families, and are lifting fewer of those out of poverty than was true before 1980.

3. Older Women and Poverty   The nature of women's disadvantages, in the labor market, and as a result of childrearing, is such that it even contributes to the feminization of poverty among older women. While women over 65 have experienced decreased poverty *rates* in recent years, this is not likely to continue; moreover, all of the progress in poverty reduction among the elderly has happened among married couples and men.[7] Most married women choose to receive Social Security benefits as wives, rather than in their own right as workers, because of their husbands' substantially higher earnings and thus higher Social Security benefits. As the proportion of women turning 65 who have not been married long enough to qualify for their ex-husbands' Social Security benefits increases, they are likely to have far less Social Security income.

Likewise, many divorced women, even those divorced near or during their husbands' retirement, receive little or no money from their ex-husbands' private pensions. Women's increased labor force participation still leaves them, because of their low wages, with very low Social Security benefits. Finally, women tend to outlive not only their husbands, but also their joint resources, as much or all of their savings are spent, and his pension often stops with his death. Until we develop policies to better protect women against these losses of income, increasing numbers of older women will spend their last years as impoverished widows.

III. THE IMPLICATION OF THE FEMINIZATION OF POVERTY PERSPECTIVE FOR UNDERSTANDING POVERTY: TOWARDS A NEW PUBLIC POLICY

Current public policy debate has begun to recognize the importance of some of the roots of women's poverty, but quite unevenly. In the area of childrearing, the importance of child care, both the need to cover the costs, and issues of availability of safe and decent child care, are being at least debated. And for poor women, the creation of essentially an entitlement to child care in the Family Support Act of 1988 for those entering employment or education and training programs is significant for its implicit recognition of this need among poor women. At the same time, current debates, much less enacted legislation, do not address the inadequacy of income support for dependent children with absent or long-term unemployed parents. Without income support in the form of adequate AFDC benefits, or a public back-up child support for those children who have inadequate or no private child support, women will continue to be impoverished by the economic burdens of raising children alone.

In the area of employment disadvantage, it is clear that decreasing the incidence of working poverty among women requires addressing the inequalities women face in the labor market. Compared to the nascent recognition of needs created by childrearing, in the area of employment policy, there is virtually no recognition of the connections between women's labor force position and women's poverty. Thus the recent federal welfare reform mandates a range of education, training, and employment programs without a single reference to the occupational segregation, pay inequities, and other disadvantages women experience that were described above. Just as the War on Poverty saw anti-discrimination civil rights laws as integral to efforts to reduce black poverty, current employment policy must incorporate comparable anti-discrimination efforts if programs are going to effectively raise women's wages and reduce women's poverty. Moreover, efforts to portray the growth of part-time and seasonal employment as positive for women, on the theory that their "flexibility" facilitates balancing work and family obligations, obscures the ways in which these new jobs impoverish women and lock them into jobs that are deadend.

NOTES

1 Since it is reasonable to assume that poor and non-poor households have roughly equal numbers of boys and girls, there would be little difference between counting adults only or persons of all ages. Most individual-base analyses by gender count only adults.

2 Throughout this paper, the term "women-maintained" will be used instead of the Census Bureau designation "female householder, no husband present," for two reasons: first, it describes the household's economic structure straightforwardly by who is there and maintaining the household, rather than by who is not there, and second, it has the advantage of being concise.

3 This is probably under-estimated, because residence in a woman-maintained family was measured once, at the end of the decade. Thus if one was poor as a member of a mother-only family for the first eight years, but not in a mother-only family for the last two years, one would be counted as "persistently poor, non-female headed household."

4 Duncan, et al, *Years of Poverty, Years of Plenty,* Ann Arbor, Michigan: Institute for Social Research, 1984.

5 *Money Income and Poverty Statistics in the United States: 1987,* US Commerce, Bureau of the Census, March 1988. Figures for intervening years are: 56% in 1950, to 50% in 1960, to 48% in 1970, to 45% in 1980, to 44% in 1984.

6 In 1980, the Census Bureau did away with the distinction in poverty thresholds between "male-headed" households and "female-headed" households. However, this was misleading, because rather than using the previous poverty threshold for "male-headed households," and agreeing that all families need an equal amount of money to survive, the Census Bureau took a *weighted average* of the "male-headed" and "female-headed" thresholds. Since the majority of single parents are female, the figures they arrived at for single adult householders was very close to the previous *female-headed* thresholds, and therefore, about 3% on the average lower than the *male-headed* threshold on the average. Since the threshold is lower, fewer single parent households, which are mostly women-maintained households, are below that threshold. Thus although the categorical distinction between male-headed and female-headed no longer exists, the distinction remains imbedded in the thresholds which are used each year to arrive at the number of poor.

7 Since 1959, the *total* number of poor persons over 65 has dropped from 5.4 million to 3.4 million. In contrast, there has been virtually no change in the number of the poor elderly who are women alone, or in women-maintained households; in 1959, they numbered 2.0 million, and by 1986, the number actually increased slightly to 2.1 million poor elderly who were women or in women-maintained households.

The Racialization of Poverty

Margaret B. Wilkerson and Jewell Handy Gresham

American policymakers have an uncanny ability to obfuscate and compartmentalize social problems—to recognize on the one hand that the United States has an unacceptably high level of unemployment, particularly among specific groups, and to recognize that we also have an incredibly high number of female-headed families, particularly within the same groups, but to avoid the cause-and-effect relationship between the two phenomena.

Ruth Sidel
Women and Children Last

The term "feminization of poverty," which was devised to describe the significant numbers of women and children living in poverty, is a distortion that negates the role played by racial barriers to black employment, particularly among males. The feminization of poverty is real, but the *racialization* of poverty is at its heart. To discuss one without the other is to play a mirror game with reality.

In *Women and Children Last: The Plight of Poor Women in Affluent America,* sociologist Ruth Sidel observes that in contemporary America, "welfare" has become a euphemism for Aid to Families with Dependent Children (A.F.D.C.). More, the term is now used to mask, barely, negative images of teeming black female fecundity—particularly among teen-agers—and of feckless black males who abandon their children. The fact that it is specifically black unwed mothers who evoke this atavistic response shows that race, not gender, is the source of revulsion.

Currently, the most critical problem relating to the plight of black unwed mothers is the massive unemployment of the males who would otherwise be potential mates for them. Sidel ties her discussion of black male unemployment to a survey of black versus white incomes. In 1981, for example, 47 percent of black college graduates earned $20,000 to $40,000 a year, the income spread for the majority of white *high school* graduates. This is only one of many facts evidencing the degree of discrimination against blacks in the workplace.

Although the number of black men holding professional, technical, managerial and sales jobs has increased significantly, the number who are unemployed is "astronomical," Sidel observed. "It is estimated that approximately 45 percent of black men do not have jobs, including not only those officially classified by the Census Bureau but also those who are counted as 'discouraged and no longer looking for work.' " In addition, she wrote,

> according to a statistician with the Children's Defense Fund, approximately 15–29 percent of black men aged twenty to forty *could not be found by the Bureau in 1980.* They are presumed to have neither permanent residences nor jobs. If they are added to the number of unemployed, the number of black men without jobs can be estimated to be well over 50 percent. (Emphasis added.)

This level of unemployment is more than double the figure for all workers at the height of the Great Depression. William Julius Wilson, author of *The Truly Disadvantaged,* states that in one of the Chicago ghetto neighborhoods he studied, the ratio of employed black males to their impoverished female counterparts was 18 to 100.

Such a "shockingly high rate of male unemployment," Sidel points out, "has had a direct bearing on the dramatic rise in black female-headed families." Yet we still look for "the 'causes' of the rise in black-female families, debate whether the welfare system encourages their proliferation, blame the mothers for having babies outside of marriage—but largely ignore the impact of male unemployment on family life."

One of the most pernicious aspects of the white patriarchal definition of an acceptable household (one headed by a male who is able to provide for his family) is that the masses of black youth and men who are excluded from the opportunities and rewards of the economic system cannot possibly meet this requirement. Then both males and females of the subjugated class are castigated as being morally unfit because they have not held their reproductive functions in abeyance.

At the same time, there is the insidious notion that households headed by black women are *destined* for poverty, not because of the absence of economic means but because of the absence of the male. (Unwed mothers who happen to be affluent are sometimes dubbed "bachelor mothers" to distinguish them from this group.) Feminists who omit race and racism as a possible decisive variable in any analysis of American poverty—and most particularly the poverty of black women—unwittingly contribute to this notion. When sociologist Diana Pearce coined the term "feminization of poverty" in 1978, she had in mind "two characteristics of women's poverty that distinguish it from the poverty experienced by men: children and labor market discrimination."

But in view of the astronomical levels of black males who are excluded from the labor market, the plight of black children must be examined in light of the circumstances of both their mothers and fathers, even though the mothers are usually left with the responsibility of caring for the children after the fathers depart under economic duress.

"ALL THEY'LL DO IS HAVE MORE CHILDREN"

In her recent book *Regulating the Lives of Women: Social Welfare Policy from Colonial Times to the Present,* Mimi Abramovitz provides a comprehensive account of the welfare policies of this society from their beginnings in 1935, when the Social Security Act legitimized the idea of social insurance. The immediate predecessor of the act was a pension to widows with young children, limited almost entirely to white women. In the 1930s, Aid to Dependent Children (A.D.C.) was born in the provisions for a "means-tested" public assistance program for the impoverished elderly, blind adults and poor children with absent fathers.

With the passage of this program, Abramovitz notes, the state took direct responsibility for reproduction in female-headed households under certain conditions, foremost among them that the mothers stay at home to rear their children. While that patriarchal model was set up for some women, however, an opening was left to insure that an ample supply of low-paid female domestic and casual labor reached the market through provisions denying aid to "undeserving" women.

By race, black women fell collectively into the category of "the undeserving." By class, so did large numbers of white women. Some states drew up, Abramovitz noted, "employable mother" rules that disqualified able-bodied women with school-age children, especially black women, on the ground that they should work. In the late 1930s, one Southern public assistance field supervisor reported the following:

> The number of Negro cases is few due to the unanimous feeling on the part of the staff and board that there are more work opportunities for Negro women and to their intense desire not to interfere with local labor conditions. The attitude that they have always gotten along, and that "all they'll do is have more children" is definite. . . . There is hesitancy on the part of lay boards to advance too rapidly over the thinking of their own communities, which see no reason why the employable Negro mother should not continue her usual sketchy seasonal labor or indefinite domestic service rather than receive a public assistance grant.

This commonplace form of discrimination is only one example of the vicissitudes of the marketplace to which black women and children, like black men, have historically been subjected.

The A.D.C. program, which grew from 372,000 families in 1940 to 803,000 in 1960, declined temporarily during World War II and the Korean War. In 1962, it became Aid to Families with Dependent Children. In the face of its rapid expansion and a shift in the composition of the caseload from white widows to unwed mothers and women of color, A.D.C. was attacked for faltering in the task of regulating the lives of poor women by excluding the undeserving. With the entry of significant numbers of black women into the program, the attacks upon it became widespread and systematically racist.

The black women who are caught in oppressive circumstances can articulate better than anyone else the flavor of their predicament. Abramovitz quotes Johnnie Tillmon, welfare mother and a leader of the National Welfare Rights Organization in the 1960s and 1970s, who calls the relationship between A.F.D.C. mothers and the system a "super-sexist marriage." Tillmon explains:

> You trade in "a" man for "The" man. But you can't divorce him if he treats you bad. He can divorce you of course, cut you off anytime he wants. But in that case "he" keeps the kids, not you. "The" man runs everything. In ordinary marriage, sex is supposed to be for your husband. On AFDC you're not supposed to have any sex at all. You give up control over your body. It's a condition of aid. . . . "The" man, the welfare system, controls your money. He tells you what to buy and what not to buy, where to buy it, and how much things cost. If things—rent, for instance—really cost more than he says they do, it's too bad for you.

Clearly, the impact of race, class and gender cannot be adequately examined by focusing on the status of women alone; it must also be viewed in the context of prescribed black and white women's roles in the labor marketplace vis-à-vis those of privileged males. It is interesting, for instance, to reflect on the significance of the polar extremes to which women, by race and class, are currently assigned. Felice Schwartz's article on "Management Women and the New Facts of Life," which caused such a furor when it appeared in the January-February issue of the *Harvard Business Review,* has little relevance to black women, whose presence in corporate management positions is negligible.

Schwartz recommended that a double-track system be set up to permit part-time work by women who wanted to spend time with their children (the so-called Mommy track) and full-time employment for "career primary" women who can be "worked like men." The corporate world's enthusiastic response to this proposal raises a question: Did it do so because the proposal offered desirable adjustments relating to the reproductive roles of women, or because it would lessen the economic competition coming from women of the corporate class and provide highly skilled female labor at a lower cost? Whatever the case, the issues affect only upper-class women, who can choose whether they work full- or part-time.

THE MOYNIHAN-ARMSTRONG "REFORM"

It is instructive to contrast Schwartz's plan with the welfare reform legislation enacted last fall for which New York Democratic Senator Daniel Patrick Moynihan and Republican Senator William Armstrong of Colorado took major public credit. Under this program, A.F.D.C. mothers, in keeping with Tillmon's description, will *not* be the ones making the decision as to whether they should remain at home with their children. Those who have children older than 3 *must* go forth as cheaply paid laborers unless they are under 19, in which case they are required to seek educational advancement, assuming the states chip in to fund such programs.

When one considers that a single Chicago housing project may hold as many as 20,000 largely jobless people packed into high-rise buildings of thirty or more stories, just how this program's proponents intend to insure adequate child care services for the poor mothers forced to leave their children is not clear, especially when day care facilities and personnel are unavailable even to large numbers of middle-class and upper-class mothers. And what means of transportation will these poor (and frequently inexperienced) mothers use when they pack themselves and their children off to babysitters? One wonders how many of the men who sit in the halls of Congress have ever played a parenting role in which they had the opportunity to engage in such tasks for even, let us say, one week.

For tens of thousands of the urban poor in housing projects, the length of time it takes for the elevators in their buildings merely to rise to their floors and descend again—assuming they work at all—can present a crisis. How far a mother and her child or children must travel after that—and by what means—before the youngsters can be deposited and mothers continue on their way may represent another; what arrangements can be made with the employer when the children are ill, yet another. What surcease will be available for the women themselves if they are ill, or harried, or weary beyond bearing? How can they summon up sufficient energy to help their school-age children with homework, assuming they have sufficient education to do so? And so on, endlessly.

Ponder just a fraction of the problems in populations in which babies, children, youth and adults die off at unconscionably high ratios from preventable or manageable diseases and conditions (and whose mothers, and fathers when they are present, must be particularly vigilant to guard their children against becoming casualties of the pervasive scourge of drugs, in psychologically and physically violent neighborhoods) and it becomes apparent why some "experts" and officials take refuge in abstract solutions, or none at all.

When one further reflects on where any jobs will come from, and—in the case of teen-age mothers ordered to finish high school—what miraculous educational services are contemplated, the picture for those deprived by race *and* class appears not brighter but potentially even more retrogressive.

In a chapter of her book entitled "Welfare," Sidel provides a picture of the intolerable treatment systematically accorded the nation's poor when applying for or receiving A.F.D.C. aid. In spite of the attempts of many caseworkers to preserve a sense of personal compassion, the weight of the system overwhelms them.

More than any other single factor, women on welfare report that the most damaging traumas they suffer are the humiliations daily meted out in welfare offices all over the country, which are designed to demean and punish them for being in need. Besides a barrage of examples drawn from A.F.D.C. mothers, Sidel quotes from an analysis of the working class, *The Hidden Injuries of Class,* by Richard Sennett and Jonathan Cobb.

"Dignity is as compelling a human need as food or sex," these men wrote, "and yet here is a society which casts the mass of its people into limbo, never satisfying their hunger for dignity." In describing the "plight of blue-collar workers who feel shamed and demeaned by their position in American society," the authors point out that these workers survive by keeping

> a certain distance from the problems of class and class consciousness, by separating themselves from their feelings when they are interacting with the world the same way as the poor attempt to protect themselves from the not-so-hidden injuries of poverty. They try to deal with the welfare bureaucracies with resignation and deadened emotions. They leave "the real me" somewhere else when they must cope with the intrusive questions, the unspoken (and all-too-often spoken) criticisms, the disregard for their humanness.

White blue-collar workers humiliated in such fashion may be able, in general, to hide behind a blanket of public anonymity, but black welfare recipients are seldom permitted even this refuge. Sidel quotes a black social worker in Atlanta, who describes the county offices that administer A.F.D.C. as "little nations" and the client population as "very fearful":

> They will use all of their resources rather than go to welfare. They're not going to take that ugliness, that humiliation. . . . Georgia will not give welfare to a two-parent family. These people are treated so badly that they would rather sell dope and steal instead.

The director of Family and Children Services in DeKalb County, Georgia, reports a dramatic increase over the past years in requests for emergency aid arising out of the state's "trimming the rolls." County workers may give emergency aid only once to a family. "When asked what a family did if it had received emergency aid once and was in dire need again, one worker replied dryly, 'Pray a lot.'"

Sidel recounts numerous tales of fortitude among welfare recipients, such as that of the mother of two children who took two buses to get her children to her grandmother's every day so that she could attend a community college. When she completed her work and, with the help of scholarships, went on to a four-year school, she could not tell her caseworker—because A.F.D.C. did not support students in four-year programs, only two-year or vocational schools. In such blatant fashion is revealed A.F.D.C.'s policy of keeping the poor poor.

The role of racism in the system is the traditional one of making racial and class exploitation easier. Dangerous precedents that will be harmful to the welfare of major segments of the society can be established by first applying them only to blacks. One can gain some idea of how this works by examining the way the national political leadership treats the masses. An example is the targeting of black adolescents by top "centrist" echelons of the Democratic Party. On the one hand, teen-age mothers are projected as carriers of a particular strain of pathology against which drastic measures must be taken. (Only recently, Moynihan ascribed malignancy to the black "matriarchy"!) Concomitantly, black male teen-agers are propelled to the forefront of black criminality, which must be destroyed. This may be the first time in history that a nation has singled out a specific race of youths against whom to direct its frustration and fury.

SAM NUNN'S "NATIONAL SERVICE" SOLUTION

Writing in *The New York Times* on May 30, 1987, Frances Fox Piven and Barbara Ehrenreich argued that the welfare reform act will accomplish little more than creating a new form of "mass peonage." Some idea of what is in store for youthful black males and females bound into a single package for manipulation may be glimpsed in the legislation currently sponsored in the Senate by Sam Nunn. The ill-conceived proposal would eliminate all forms of Federal educational grants for higher education to poor students and replace them with a "Citizenship and National Service Act," which is, in effect, a "workfare" program. For two years of labor, young people would receive a stipend of $10,000 annually at the conclusion of their "service." If they volunteered for the military, their reward would be $12,000 per year. Virtually the only way that most of the poor could get into college would be through this "national service."

In combination, the two programs—welfare and national service—would create bureaucratic machinery for manipulating black young people. It would channel a pool of cheap black female labor, composed of welfare mothers, into the work force and harness the energies of their male counterparts through the national service plan. Disproportionate numbers of young black males would be drawn to the military by the added stipend, and thereby rendered disproportionately vulnerable to wartime death. (America has always found it easier to propel its black youths toward death than to educate them.)

One might also ask whether the stipends will help many deprived young people to enter college. Not very much in the way of higher education can be purchased for $10,000 or $12,000, and the temptation would be great for black and white families of limited means to spend the money on a dozen needs having higher priority.

In the case of A.F.D.C. mothers, former Secretary of Labor Ray Marshall points out that 86 percent of all social welfare spending since the 1960s has gone to America's elderly, and only a small proportion to A.F.D.C. mothers or their offspring. The result has been that poverty among the elderly has declined almost by half, from more than 25 percent at the beginning of the War on Poverty to 14 percent in 1983. Just the opposite is true with regard to America's children, primarily blacks and others of color whose parents are poor. In a 1986 article in *Southern Changes* titled "The War Against the Poor," Robert Greenstein, director of the Washington-based Center on Budget and Policy Priorities, wrote:

> If you look at the statistics of American poverty today, one set—the figures for children's poverty—hits you over the head. Fifteen years ago the child poverty rate was between thirteen and fourteen percent. Last year it was over twenty-one percent. . . . And, while there has been a very slight recent reduction in the overall poverty rate during the past year, and in the overall child poverty rate, all the reduction in child poverty has occurred among white children. None of it has occurred among black or Hispanic children.
>
> The poverty rate for black children under the age of six now has reached just over fifty-one percent.

If one out of every two black children in this country is born poor, and the national leadership regards black adolescents as exemplars of pathology instead of promise, what must black Americans do? What must society do?

For one thing, we might begin by reviewing the attitudes of officials of the national government—of the Bush Administration and members of Congress of both political parties—toward the well-being of *all* members of the society. In particular, we should make certain that the political conditions are created and sustained that will encourage those who serve in positions of leadership to do so not by ignoring race, gender and class as determining variables affecting the lives of the people, but by developing infinitely more sophisticated means to address and redress what is wrong. And we, who are most directly affected by race, class and gender, should advance our own knowledge accordingly.

Even, for example, if we were concerned simply with the reproductive roles, functions and rights of women, it would still be necessary to develop a keener awareness of the interrelated roles of race, gender and class oppression—including the institutionalized white-male-over-black-male oppression, which in this patriarchal (not matriarchal) society underpins everything else.

Black women must address the enormous problems within the black community, including black male sexism and rage, particularly the violence and, yes, the pathology of anger and frustration that is taken out against them and other members of the community. But we cannot turn our attention to any condition besetting black people without consideration of the terrible toll of the white racism and sexism which undergird and perpetuate an oppressive system.

Barbara Ommolade, a single-mother college counselor, activist and writer who has been on welfare, neatly and eloquently summed up the picture in "It's a Family Affair: The Real Lives of Black Single Mothers" (*Village Voice,* July 15, 1986):

Today, the context of the struggle to have a black family is legal desegregation and superficial political gains for black people, along with high unemployment among black men, depressed wages for black women, and public denigration of poor people. The concept of a pathological underclass has become the rationale for continued racism and economic injustice; in attempting to separate racial from economic inequality and [in] blaming family pathology for black people's condition, current ideology obscures the system's inability to provide jobs, decent wages, and adequate public services for the black poor. And in a racist-patriarchal society, the effects of the system's weaknesses fall most heavily on black women and children. Just as black family life has always been a barometer of racial and economic injustice and at the same time a means of transcending and surviving those injustices, black families headed by women reflect the strength and the difficulty of black life in the 80's.

Black women know the critical problems of our communities, but we also know their strengths. We have to call on those strengths collectively from blacks now, but we also call on more. It is the obligation of all concerned Americans to join forces in seeking to remove the stigma from government assistance to citizens in need. And to make certain that channels exist for people who are temporarily down to recover their footing, thankful that a nurturing society exists for them and conscious of their responsibility to be nurturing too.

"There's No Place Like Home"

Cynthia R. Daniels

THE HISTORY OF HOMEWORK

Once tucked away in urban industrial kitchens, homework has a long and buried history. At the turn of the century, over 250,000 tenement women and children in New York City did piecework at home: hand-finishing pants, assembling artificial flowers and feathers, sewing buttons on cards, stitching doll's clothing, cracking nuts, or sorting coffee beans.

Most of these women were poor immigrants who had to care for underemployed husbands and young children. In New York, they were primarily Italian, Polish, and Russian. In Boston, most were Irish or French Canadian. They earned an average of 6 cents per hour, a little more than half of what a woman doing the same work in a factory could earn. The hours they kept were long. In an interview a homeworker in the garment industry remarked, "You can't count homework by the day, for a day is really two days sometimes because people often work half the night."

In 1911, one New York City investigator described a typical homeworking family. Mrs. Rapallo was a 30-year-old immigrant from southern Italy. She had seven children. The Rapallos cut and pasted the petals of artificial flowers. Together, the family could make 18,000 violets per week, for which they were paid 75 cents per day.

In the early part of this century, homework was banned in some industries as part of the crusade against child labor. The National Child Labor Committee, an association of middle-class social reformers, called for the abolition of homework (while blaming immigrant parents for the "exploitation of their children"). Garment and textile unions finally succeeded in prohibiting homework in seven industries through the Federal Fair Labor Standards Act of 1938. This act banned homework in garments and textiles, and extended protective hour and wage legislation to cover homework for the first time.

HOMEWORK IN THE EIGHTIES

Four decades later, business and government are rolling back the gains of labor. Corporate management once again has found that home-based work (like part-time and temporary work) is good for business because it increases productivity, decreases office costs and staff turnover, and provides flexibility in hiring. Business can transfer the costs of rent, heating, and lighting a workplace to those who take work home. What used to be the company's responsibility for health and safety concerns—proper work stations for VDT workers, proper lighting for detailed work, adequate ventilation around paints or chemicals—are now the homeworker's burden.

To attract workers into the world of homework, the mass media portrays the homeworker as a young entrepreneur, often male, who is free from the routines and supervision of office work. But a closer look reveals that most homeworkers are women—pieceworkers whose hours and wages are controlled by the whims of their bosses and the swings of a seasonal market. A worker who refuses to do overtime often won't get any work at all.

From garment workers in Los Angeles to clericals in New Jersey, the story remains the same: Homework encourages the exploitation of workers, especially mothers with young children who lack access to day care. With few options for work and a pressing need for family income, these women are pushed into becoming "supermoms," caring for children and earning a wage for piecework all at the same time.

Homework is no longer confined to urban industrial centers. A study done by Jamie Faricellia Dangler at SUNY Binghamton revealed that hundreds of rural, working- and middle-class women located in central New York were engaged in the assembly of electronic transformers, resistors, capacitors, and circuit boards at home for both national and international firms. And in California's high-tech Silicon Valley, although management claims they employ few people outside the plant, an underground economy has homeworkers doing assembly in the microchip business.

Precise estimates of homeworkers are notoriously difficult to calculate because neither the Census records nor the tax codes contain categories appropriate for home-based workers. Most people who work at home are listed simply as "self-employed" and are included in the same category as free-lance professionals and home-based businessmen. But in contrast to most homeworking women, these professionals exercise much more control over their hours, their income, and the quality of their worklife in general.

In an examination of information collected in the 1980 Census on "white collar" homeworkers (those employed primarily at clerical and administrative support work), Robert Kraut and Patricia Grambsch at the Bell Communications Lab in New Jersey found that 1.3 million people listed their home as their "primary place of employment" (excluding farm-based work). Of those, over 180,000 were clericals. Homeworkers received only 70% of what non-homeworkers earned. In addition, homeworkers were *twice* as likely to live in households below the poverty line.

High-tech futurists such as Alvin Toffler argue that homework offers a brave new alternative to alienation in the workplace and the jam-ups of rush-hour traffic. But like Toffler, many fail to distinguish between professional and non-professional homework. The director of the Chicago-based International Association of Home Businesses, Coralee Smith Kern, was quoted in *American Way* (12/24/85) characterizing homework as "one of America's best-kept secrets. Working at home is a real movement that is as significant as the civil rights, women's, and disabled movements. . . . The president works at home and most governors work at home and the rest of us are going to be doing it, too."

If the use of homework is to expand, it is not likely to be professional, skilled work that people do at home. In test programs studied by Margrethe Olson of the New York University Graduate School of Business, business managers expressed reservations about letting professional staff work at home. In addition, homeworking professionals complain of the isolation of working at home and the career disadvantages of being separated from others at work.

As one homeworking insurance saleswoman said, "I didn't want to become a high-rise hermit." In fact, in a 1984 survey conducted by Management Recruiters International, Inc., only 28% of those interviewed liked the idea of working at home, while 54% said they would not like to work at home. Jeffrey Heath, general manager of MRI, told *American Way,* "We thought nearly everyone would say they'd love to crawl out of bed in the morning and work in their bathrobe. We thought support for the idea would run into the 80th percentile. What came through instead is that people need their fellow workers for their camaraderie and the assistance and support they give."

Despite reluctance to promote professional homework, more industrial forms of homework continue to grow. In the high-tech industry, more and more companies subcontract out labor-intensive work to rural areas in the United States and to third world countries as well. Such international homework is found not only in electronics, but also in the garment industries of the Philippines, Japan, Mexico, and Puerto Rico.

According to Eileen Boris of Howard University, some rural and poor immigrant women in the United States earn as little as 37 cents per hour for sewing women's sportswear. The exploitation of homeworkers is compounded by the fact that they are often immigrants (sometimes without legal status) who face the threat of deportation and the limits imposed by extreme poverty and language barriers. In an interview with Patricia Fernandez Kelley and Anna M. Garcia of the University of California, San Diego, one immigrant Mexican woman who works in the garment industry in Los Angeles stated, "The problem was language; how to make yourself understood when you are looking for a job. So I ended up sewing. . . . Then I got pregnant. I didn't want to live with relatives then, so I had to work at home."

HOME AND WORK CONFLICT

In spite of the drawbacks of homework, many women are still attracted to the promises of the homework system. The allure of flexibility and control over work, combined with freedom from the scrutiny or harassment of bosses are, for some homeworkers, worth the sacrifice in wages.

In a study done for the Office Homework Program at the Wisconsin Physician's Service Insurance Company by Cynthia Costello, women explained their preference for homework. For a woman at an insurance company in Wisconsin, homework provided the satisfaction of "being able to do it at my own time, setting my own hours. No one was watching over my shoulder all the time." For others, homework offered the only way to earn an income, thereby promising a renewed sense of self-worth: "I didn't want people to think [all I had been doing was] sitting around eating potato chips and dip." Though still done at home, the option of paid work gives many women a new sense of self.

Nevertheless, whether in clerical work, electronics or garment work, such freedoms are limited. Control over the pace or quantity of work remains in the hands of the contractor. For homeworkers, the rules and restrictions set by the foreman are replaced by the threat of losing work if quotas are not met. Finally, common in all forms of homework are seasonal rushes broken only by spells when no work at all can be found.

Contrary to the myth that women want to work at home so that they can also mind their children, a 1985 *Family Circle* survey of over 7,000 homeworkers revealed that the vast majority do not even try to work when their children are awake and active (cited in a study by Kathy Christensen, CUNY Graduate Center). Most women squeeze frantic periods of work in between family responsibilities. One insurance processor brings to mind stories from the turn of the century as she describes her schedule: "When I get the claims at night, I try to put in an hour while the kids are watching TV. Then I get up at 4:30 am to work before the kids get up . . . I work between 5:50 and 7:30 am . . . During the day, I turn on the TV and tell my preschooler to watch. When she takes a nap, I can work."

The stress of working and caring for children at the same time is obscured by the fact that women's domestic responsibilities are not only underpaid but are also undervalued by society as a whole. Husbands compound the burden by expecting homeworking wives to continue to keep house as if they weren't working at all. One homeworker who earns a living by typing hospital records said, "Just try to imagine bringing your three-year-old to work with you and you'll get some idea of the frustrations I face every day. How many men would try that?"

Homework is no solution to the conflict women face between wage-earning and caring for children. Lifting the bans on homework, especially in the garment industry, would instead give birth to a new genre of U.S. sweatshops patterned after the kind that exist now in parts of Asia and Latin America. The real solution lies in empowering homeworkers, ensuring their right to organize and to have the same benefits, such as unemployment and social security, that other workers still have. Critical to the organization of homeworkers everywhere is a recognition of the need to address the double day these working mothers face: homeworkers need both quality childcare as well as higher wages and more stable work opportunities.

In the short run, the conditions of homework could be improved by helping home-workers organize themselves in industries where homework is legal (the ban prohibits homework only in those industries cited by law). For instance "homeworking centers" could be established. At these community sites, homeworkers could meet to compare wages and working conditions or to find better work. Centers that have been estab-lished in several European countries and in India have encouraged the close regulation of homework by both unions and government agencies.

In India, for instance, the Self-Employed Women's Association (SEWA) was es-tablished to organize homeworkers. SEWA has set up a bank which offers women credit, and has sponsored programs to upgrade skills and to improve working condi-tions. As a grassroots organization that has helped to build cooperatives of homework-ers, SEWA provides a model for alternative organizing strategies. Similarly, the three-year-old Leicester Outwork Campaign in England provides "Fact Packs" of information about homeworkers' rights and distributes a newsletter to women working at home.

In the long run, until homeworkers have the ability to defend their rights to decent wages and working conditions, lifting federal bans on homework will only encourage the exploitation of working mothers.

Homophobia: A Weapon of Sexism

Suzanne Pharr

Patriarchy—an enforced belief in male dominance and control—is the ideology and sexism the system that holds it in place. The catechism goes like this: Who do gender roles serve? Men and the women who seek power from them. Who suffers from gen-der roles? Women most completely and men in part. How are gender roles main-tained? By the weapons of sexism: economics, violence, homophobia.

Why then don't we ardently pursue ways to eliminate gender roles and therefore sexism? It is my profound belief that all people have a spark in them that yearns for freedom, and the history of the world's atrocities—from the Nazi concentration camps to white dominance in South Africa to the battering of women—is the story of at-tempts to snuff out that spark. When that spark doesn't move forward to full flame, it is because the weapons designed to control and destroy have wrought such intense damage over time that the spark has been all but extinguished.

Sexism, that system by which women are kept subordinate to men, is kept in place by three powerful weapons designed to cause or threaten women with pain and loss. As stated before, the three are economics, violence, and homophobia. . . .

Economics must be looked at first because many feminists consider it to be the root cause of sexism. Certainly the United Nations study released at the final conference of the International Decade on Women, held in Nairobi, Kenya, in 1985, supports that belief: of the world's population, women do 75% of the work, receive 10% of the pay and own 1% of the property. In the United States it is also supported by the opposition of the government to the idea of comparable worth and pay equity, as expressed by Ronald Reagan who referred to pay equity as "a joke." Obviously, it is considered a dangerous idea. Men profit not only from women's unpaid work in the home but from our underpaid work within horizontal female segregation such as clerical workers or upwardly mobile tokenism in the workplace where a few affirmative action promotions are expected to take care of all women's economic equality needs. Moreover, they profit from women's bodies through pornography, prostitution, and international female sexual slavery. And white men profit from both the labor of women and of men of color. Forced economic dependency puts women under male control and severely limits women's options for self-determination and self-sufficiency.

This truth is borne out by the fact that according to the National Commission on Working Women, on average, women of all races working year round earn only 64 cents to every one dollar a man makes. Also, the U.S. Census Bureau reports that only 9 percent of working women make over $25,000 a year. There is fierce opposition to women gaining employment in the nontraditional job market, that is, those jobs that traditionally employ less than 25 percent women. After a woman has gained one of these higher paying jobs, she is often faced with sexual harassment, lesbian baiting, and violence. It is clear that in the workplace there is an all-out effort to keep women in traditional roles so that the only jobs we are "qualified" for are the low-paid ones.

Actually, we have to look at economics not only as the root cause of sexism but also as the underlying, driving force that keeps all the oppressions in place. In the United States, our economic system is shaped like a pyramid, with a few people at the top, primarily white males, being supported by large numbers of unpaid or low-paid workers at the bottom. When we look at this pyramid, we begin to understand the major connection between sexism and racism because those groups at the bottom of the pyramid are women and people of color. We then begin to understand why there is such a fervent effort to keep those oppressive systems (racism and sexism and all the ways they are manifested) in place to maintain the unpaid and low-paid labor.

Susan DeMarco and Jim Hightower, writing for *Mother Jones,* report that *Forbes* magazine indicated that "the 400 richest families in America last year had an average net worth of $550 million each. These and less than a million other families—roughly one percent of our population—are at the prosperous tip of our society. . . . In 1976, the wealthiest 1 percent of America's families owned 19.2 percent of the nation's total wealth. (This sum of wealth counts all of America's cash, real estate, stocks, bonds, factories, art, personal property, and anything else of financial value.) By 1983, those at this 1 percent tip of our economy owned 34.3 percent of our wealth. . . . *Today, the top 1 percent of Americans possesses more net wealth than the bottom 90 percent.* " (My italics.) *(May, 1988, pp. 32–33)*

In order for this top-heavy system of economic inequity to maintain itself, the 90 percent on the bottom must keep supplying cheap labor. A very complex, intricate system of institutionalized oppressions is necessary to maintain the status quo so that the vast majority will not demand its fair share of wealth and resources and bring the system down. Every institution—schools, banks, churches, government, courts, media, etc.—as well as individuals must be enlisted in the campaign to maintain such a system of gross inequity.

What would happen if women gained the earning opportunities and power that men have? What would happen if these opportunities were distributed equitably, no matter what sex one was, no matter what race one was born into, and no matter where one lived? What if educational and training opportunities were equal? Would women spend most of our youth preparing for marriage? Would marriage be based on economic survival for women? What would happen to issues of power and control? Would women stay with our batterers? If a woman had economic independence in a society where women had equal opportunities, would she still be thought of as owned by her father or husband?

Economics is the great controller in both sexism and racism. If a person can't acquire food, shelter, and clothing and provide them for children, then that person can be forced to do many things in order to survive. The major tactic, worldwide, is to provide unrecompensed or inadequately recompensed labor for the benefit of those who control wealth. Hence, we see women performing unpaid labor in the home or filling low-paid jobs, and we see people of color in the lowest-paid jobs available.

The method is complex: limit educational and training opportunities for women and for people of color and then withhold adequate paying jobs with the excuse that people of color and women are incapable of filling them. Blame the economic victim and keep the victim's self-esteem low through invisibility and distortion within the media and education. Allow a few people of color and women to succeed among the profit-makers so that blaming those who don't "make it" can be intensified. Encourage those few who succeed in gaining power now to turn against those who remain behind rather than to use their resources to make change for all. Maintain the myth of scarcity—that there are not enough jobs, resources, etc., to go around—among the middleclass so that they will not unite with laborers, immigrants, and the unemployed. The method keeps in place a system of control and profit by a few and a constant source of cheap labor to maintain it.

If anyone steps out of line, take her/his job away. Let homelessness and hunger do their work. The economic weapon works. And we end up saying, "I would do this or that—be openly who I am, speak out against injustice, work for civil rights, join a labor union, go to a political march, etc.—if I didn't have this job. I can't afford to lose it." We stay in an abusive situation because we see no other way to survive. . . .

Violence is the second means of keeping women in line, in a narrowly defined place and role. First, there is the physical violence of battering, rape, and incest. Often when battered women come to shelters and talk about their lives, they tell stories of being not only physically beaten but also raped and their children subjected to incest. Work in the women's anti-violence movement during almost two decades has provided significant evidence that each of these acts, including rape and incest, is an attempt to seek power over and control of another person. In each case, the victim is viewed as an object and is used to meet the abuser's needs. The violence is used to wreak punishment and to demand compliance or obedience.

Violence against women is directly related to the condition of women in a society that refuses us equal pay, equal access to resources, and equal status with males. From this condition comes men's confirmation of their sense of ownership of women, power over women, and assumed right to control women for their own means. Men physically and emotionally abuse women because they *can,* because they live in a world that gives them permission. Male violence is fed by their sense of their *right* to dominate and control, and their sense of superiority over a group of people who, because of gender, they consider inferior to them.

It is not just the violence but the threat of violence that controls our lives. Because the burden of responsibility has been placed so often on the potential victim, as women we have curtailed our freedom in order to protect ourselves from violence. Because of the threat of rapists, we stay on alert, being careful not to walk in isolated places, being careful where we park our cars, adding incredible security measures to our homes—massive locks, lights, alarms, if we can afford them—and we avoid places where we will appear vulnerable or unprotected while the abuser walks with freedom. Fear, often now so commonplace that it is unacknowledged, shapes our lives, reducing our freedom. . . .

The threat of violence against women who step out of line or who are disloyal is made all the more powerful by the fact that women do not have to do anything—they may be paragons of virtue and subservience—to receive violence against our lives: the violence still comes. It comes because of the woman-hating that exists throughout society. Chance plays a larger part than virtue in keeping women safe. Hence, with violence always a threat to us, women can never feel completely secure and confident. Our sense of safety is always fragile and tenuous.

Many women say that verbal violence causes more harm than physical violence because it damages self-esteem so deeply. Women have not wanted to hear battered women say that the verbal abuse was as hurtful as the physical abuse: to acknowledge that truth would be tantamount to acknowledging that *virtually every woman is a battered woman.* It is difficult to keep strong against accusations of being a bitch, stupid, inferior, etc., etc. It is especially difficult when these individual assaults are backed up by a society that shows women in textbooks, advertising, TV programs, movies, etc., as debased, silly, inferior, and sexually objectified, and a society that gives tacit approval to pornography. When we internalize these messages, we call the result "low self-esteem," a therapeutic individualized term. It seems to me we should use the more political expression: when we internalize these messages, we experience *internalized sexism,* and we experience it in common with all women living in a sexist world. The violence against us is supported by a society in which woman-hating is deeply imbedded. . . .

Homophobia works effectively as a weapon of sexism because it is joined with a powerful arm, heterosexism. Heterosexism creates the climate for homophobia with its assumption that the world is and must be heterosexual and its display of power and privilege as the norm. Heterosexism is the systemic display of homophobia in the institutions of society. Heterosexism and homophobia work together to enforce compulsory heterosexuality and that bastion of patriarchal power, the nuclear family. The central focus of the rightwing attack against women's liberation is that women's equality, women's self-determination, women's control of our own bodies and lives will damage what they see as the crucial societal institution, the nuclear family. The attack has been led by fundamentalist ministers across the country. The two areas they have focused on most consistently are abortion and homosexuality, and their passion has led them to bomb women's clinics and to recommend deprogramming for homosexuals and establishing camps to quarantine people with AIDS. To resist marriage and/or heterosexuality is to risk severe punishment and loss. . . .

There was a time when the two most condemning accusations against a woman meant to ostracize and disempower her were "whore" and "lesbian." The sexual revolution and changing attitudes about heterosexual behavior may have led to some lessening of the power of the word *whore,* though it still has strength as a threat to sexual property and prostitutes are stigmatized and abused. However, the word *lesbian* is still fully charged and carries with it the full threat of loss of power and privilege, the threat of being cut asunder, abandoned, and left outside society's protection.

To be a lesbian is to be *perceived* as someone who has stepped out of line, who has moved out of sexual/economic dependence on a male, who is woman-identified. A lesbian is perceived as someone who can live without a man, and who is therefore (however illogically) against men. A lesbian is perceived as being outside the acceptable, routinized order of things. She is seen as someone who has no societal institutions to protect her and who is not privileged to the protection of individual males. Many heterosexual women see her as someone who stands in contradiction to the sacrifices they have made to conform to compulsory heterosexuality. A lesbian is perceived as a threat to the nuclear family, to male dominance and control, to the very heart of sexism.

Gay men are perceived also as a threat to male dominance and control, and the homophobia expressed against them has the same roots in sexism as does homophobia against lesbians. Visible gay men are the objects of extreme hatred and fear by heterosexual men because their breaking ranks with male heterosexual solidarity is seen as a damaging rent in the very fabric of sexism. They are seen as betrayers, as traitors who must be punished and eliminated. In the beating and killing of gay men we see clear evidence of this hatred. When we see the fierce homophobia expressed toward gay men, we can begin to understand the ways sexism also affects males through imposing rigid, dehumanizing gender roles on them. The two circumstances in which it is legitimate for men to be openly physically affectionate with one another are in competitive sports and in the crisis of war. For many men, these two experiences are the highlights of their lives, and they think of them again and again with nostalgia. War and sports offer a cover of all-male safety and dominance to keep away the notion of affectionate openness being identified with homosexuality. When gay men break ranks with male roles through bonding and affection outside the arenas of war and sports, they are perceived as not being "real men," that is, as being identified with women, the weaker sex that must be dominated and that over the centuries has been the object of male hatred and abuse. Misogyny gets transferred to gay men with a vengeance and is increased by the fear that their sexual identity and behavior will bring down the entire system of male dominance and compulsory heterosexuality.

If lesbians are established as threats to the status quo, as outcasts who must be punished, homophobia can wield its power over all women through lesbian baiting. Lesbian baiting is an attempt to control women by labeling us as lesbians because our behavior is not acceptable, that is, when we are being independent, going our own way, living whole lives, fighting for our rights, demanding equal pay, saying no to violence, being self-assertive, bonding with and loving the company of women, assuming the right to our bodies, insisting upon our own authority, making changes that include us in society's decision-making; lesbian baiting occurs when women are called lesbians because we resist male dominance and control. And it has little or nothing to do with one's sexual identity.

To be named as lesbian threatens all women, not just lesbians, with great loss. And any woman who steps out of role risks being called a lesbian. To understand how this is a threat to all women, one must understand that any woman can be called a lesbian and there is no real way she can defend herself: there is no way to credential one's sexuality. ("The Children's Hour," a Lillian Hellman play, makes this point when a student asserts two teachers are lesbians and they have no way to disprove it.) She may be married or divorced, have children, dress in the most feminine manner, have sex with men, be celibate—but there are lesbians who do all those things. *Lesbians look like all women and all women look like lesbians.* There is no guaranteed method of identification, and as we all know, sexual identity can be kept hidden. (The same is true for men. There is no way to prove their sexual identity, though many go to extremes to prove heterosexuality.) Also, women are not necessarily born lesbian. Some seem to be, but others become lesbians later in life after having lived heterosexual lives. Lesbian baiting of heterosexual women would not work if there were a definitive way to identify lesbians (or heterosexuals). . . .

If, then, any woman can be named a lesbian and be threatened with terrible losses, what is it she fears? Are these fears real? Being vulnerable to a homophobic world can lead to these losses:

• *Employment.* The loss of job leads us right back to the economic connection to sexism. This fear of job loss exists for almost every lesbian except perhaps those who are self-employed or in a business that does not require societal approval. Consider how many businesses or organizations you know that will hire and protect people who are openly gay or lesbian.

• *Family.* Their approval, acceptance, love.

• *Children.* Many lesbians and gay men have children, but very, very few gain custody in court challenges, even if the other parent is a known abuser. Other children may be kept away from us as though gays and lesbians are abusers. There are written and unwritten laws prohibiting lesbians and gays from being foster parents or from adopting children. There is an irrational fear that children in contact with lesbians and gays will become homosexual through influence or that they will be sexually abused. Despite our knowing that 95 percent of those who sexually abuse children are heterosexual men, there are no policies keeping heterosexual men from teaching or working with children, yet in almost every school system in America, visible gay men and lesbians are not hired through either written or unwritten law.

• *Heterosexual privilege and protection.* No institutions, other than those created by lesbians and gays—such as the Metropolitan Community Church, some counseling centers, political organizations such as the National Gay and Lesbian Task Force, the National Coalition of Black Lesbians and Gays, the Lambda Legal Defense and Education Fund, etc.—affirm homosexuality and offer protection. Affirmation and protection cannot be gained from the criminal justice system, mainline churches, educational institutions, the government.

• *Safety.* There is nowhere to turn for safety from physical and verbal attacks because the norm presently in this country is that it is acceptable to be overtly homophobic. Gay men are beaten on the streets; lesbians are kidnapped and "deprogrammed." The National Gay and Lesbian Task Force, in an extended study, has documented violence against lesbians and gay men and noted the inadequate response of the criminal justice system. One of the major differences between homophobia/heterosexism and racism and sexism is that because of the Civil Rights Movement and the women's movement racism and sexism are expressed more covertly (though with great harm); because there has not been a major, visible lesbian and gay movement, it is permissible to be overtly homophobic in any institution or public forum. Churches spew forth homophobia in the same way they did racism prior to the Civil Rights Movement. Few laws are in place to protect lesbians and gay men, and the criminal justice system is wracked with homophobia.

• *Mental health.* An overtly homophobic world in which there is full permission to treat lesbians and gay men with cruelty makes it difficult for lesbians and gay men to maintain a strong sense of well-being and self-esteem. Many lesbians and gay men are beaten, raped, killed, subjected to aversion therapy, or put in mental institutions. The impact of such hatred and negativity can lead one to depression and, in some cases, to suicide. The toll on the gay and lesbian community is devastating.

• *Community.* There is rejection by those who live in homophobic fear, those who are afraid of association with lesbians and gay men. For many in the gay and lesbian community, there is a loss of public acceptance, a loss of allies, a loss of place and belonging.

• *Credibility.* This fear is large for many people: the fear that they will no longer be respected, listened to, honored, believed. They fear they will be social outcasts.

The list goes on and on. But any one of these essential components of a full life is large enough to make one deeply fear its loss. A black woman once said to me in a workshop, "When I fought for Civil Rights, I always had my family and community to fall back on even when they didn't fully understand or accept what I was doing. I don't know if I could have borne losing them. And you people don't have either with you. It takes my breath away."

What does a woman have to do to get called a lesbian? Almost anything, sometimes nothing at all, but certainly anything that threatens the status quo, anything that steps out of role, anything that asserts the rights of women, anything that doesn't indicate submission and subordination. Assertiveness, standing up for oneself, asking for more pay, better working conditions, training for and accepting a non-traditional (you mean a man's?) job, enjoying the company of women, being financially independent, being in control of one's life, depending first and foremost upon oneself, thinking that one can do whatever needs to be done, but above all, working for the rights and equality of women.

In the backlash to the gains of the women's liberation movement, there has been an increased effort to keep definitions man-centered. Therefore, to work on behalf of women must mean to work against men. To love women must mean that one hates men. A very effective attack has been made against the word *feminist* to make it a derogatory word. In current backlash usage, *feminist* equals *man-hater* which equals *lesbian.* This formula is created in the hope that women will be frightened away from their work on behalf of women. Consequently, we now have women who believe in the rights of women and work for those rights while from fear deny that they are feminists, or refuse to use the word because it is so "abrasive.". . .

Women in many of these organizations, out of fear of all the losses we are threatened with, begin to modify our work to make it more acceptable and less threatening to the male-dominated society which we originally set out to change. The work can no longer be radical (going to the root cause of the problem) but instead must be reforming, working only on the symptoms and not the cause. Real change for women becomes thwarted and stopped. The word *lesbian* is instilled with the power to halt our work and control our lives. And we give it its power with our fear.

In my view, homophobia has been one of the major causes of the failure of the women's liberation movement to make deep and lasting change. (The other major block has been racism.) We were fierce when we set out but when threatened with the loss of heterosexual privilege, we began putting on brakes. Our best-known nationally distributed women's magazine was reluctant to print articles about lesbians, began putting a man on the cover several times a year, and writing articles about women who succeeded in a man's world. We worried about our image, our being all right, our being "real women" despite our work. Instead of talking about the elimination of sexual gender roles, we stepped back and talked about "sex role stereotyping" as the issue. Change around the edges for middleclass white women began to be talked about as successes. We accepted tokenism and integration, forgetting that equality for all women, for all people—and not just equality of white middleclass women with white men—was the goal that we could never put behind us.

But despite backlash and retreats, change is growing from within. The women's liberation movement is beginning to gain strength again because there are women who are talking about liberation for all women. We are examining sexism, racism, homophobia, classism, anti-Semitism, ageism, ableism, and imperialism, and we see everything as connected. This change in point of view represents the third wave of the women's liberation movement, a new direction that does not get mass media coverage and recognition. It has been initiated by women of color and lesbians who were marginalized or rendered invisible by the white heterosexual leaders of earlier efforts. The first wave was the 19th and early 20th century campaign for the vote; the second, beginning in the 1960s, focused on the Equal Rights Amendment and abortion rights. Consisting of predominantly white middleclass women, both failed in recognizing issues of equality and empowerment for all women. The third wave of the movement, multi-racial and multi-issued, seeks the transformation of the world for us all. We know that we won't get there until everyone gets there; that we must move forward in a great strong line, hand in hand, not just a few at a time.

We know that the arguments about homophobia originating from mental health and Biblical/religious attitudes can be settled when we look at the sexism that permeates religious and psychiatric history. The women of the third wave of the women's liberation movement know that *without the existence of sexism, there would be no homophobia.*

Finally, we know that as long as the word lesbian can strike fear in any woman's heart, then work on behalf of women can be stopped; the only successful work against sexism must include work against homophobia.

The Feminist Majority Report: Corporate Women and the Mommy Track

Katherine Spiller

Many women have been blocked from the "top" of corporate America by a set of myths that suggest they are not suited for senior management and that employing women is "more costly" to the corporation. The "mommy track" is just the latest in this series of myths—myths that work to justify the lack of progress for women. Worse yet, the myths often place blame on the women themselves rather than sex discrimination.

This mythology needs to be exposed for what it is once and for all.

Myth: It is just a matter of time before women reach equality in the board rooms and the executive suites of the corporate world.

Fact: Women, for the most part, are stuck in middle management—and it has nothing to do with how long they have been in business or whether they have the right professional degrees for advancement. Despite persistence and hard work, women have made only incremental gains at the top levels of business over the past 15 to 20 years.

A 1986 study of the top Fortune 500 companies by Mary Ann Von Glinow and Anna Krzyczkowsky Mercer of the University of Southern California showed that *women were only 1.65% of the Corporate Officers* at the vice presidential level and up. Women officers registered only slightly higher in the service industries. At the current rates of increase, it will be 478 years—or until the year 2466—before women reach equality in the executive suites.

The story is not much better on the Corporate Boards. *Only 3.55% of the Fortune 500 Directorships are held by women.* The rate of increase is so slow that parity with men on Corporate Boards will not be achieved until the year 2116—or for 128 years.

Only one woman in 1986 held the rank of CEO and Chair of the board of a Fortune 500 company. She came into the top management post by inheriting the company from her father and husband. Today there are three more women at the top. One of these women executives founded the company she oversees. Another shares the job with her husband. The third took over as acting CEO in the summer of 1988 when her predecessor was struck and killed by lightning while on vacation.

Not even the right credentials are enough to guarantee a woman a fair shot at the top: Two sepafate studies show that women MBAs "have always had less opportunity for management careers than their male counterparts." Very simply, women in business are slamming into a "glass ceiling" that prevents them from moving up.

Myth: Conflicts with family and home responsibilities keep executive women from getting "to the top."

Fact: Of women executives who do have families, "only a tiny minority (3%) feel that family responsibilities have hindered their careers," according to a 1984 *Wall Street Journal*/Gallup Survey. In fact, many believe their jobs have benefited their family lives. Few of the women executives surveyed reported that family conflicts had ever "prevented them from accepting a job change that would have required relocation" (only 9% of the one-third who say they ever turned down a transfer).

Besides, women executives with children are more likely to get help from their husbands with household chores and family responsibilities according to the *Wall Street Journal* survey. What's more, it is easier for executive level women to combine their careers with motherhood because they can better afford to pay for child care and other services.

The "mommy track" is never talked about for women who work in traditional, female-dominated, low wage jobs. It is the woman vice president of the bank—not the cleaning woman who works nights at the bank and who probably holds one or two other jobs—who is asked "can women really have it all."

The cleaning woman is never offered a "mommy track" option.

Myth: Women are not as serious about their careers and often "drop out" or "interrupt" their careers to have children. As a result, they cost corporations more than male executives, and they are poor investments for companies that must spend considerable amounts on executive recruitment, training and development.

Fact: According to studies of mobility patterns and turnover rates, *women executives are no more likely to leave their jobs than men.* If anything, women in executive positions have traditionally exhibited *lower turnover rates* than men, because their chances of finding another high level post were more limited. The *Wall Street Journal* summed it up best in a 1978 headline: "Debunking a Myth: Women Managers Don't Leave Jobs More Often than Men."

There is also no evidence that executive women leave the corporation to have children. In fact, a 1980 study by Catalyst found that 37% of women in two-career families return to work within two months of childbirth and 87% are back in eight months. A follow-up study in 1986 found that women at the top took even shorter leaves of 6 to 8 weeks. These executive women returned quickly, worried about "jeopardizing the positions they had achieved."

Myth: The "mommy track" is a practical way for women to "have it all" and get to the top while still fulfilling their "child rearing responsibilities."

Fact: The "mommy track" is an excuse to pay women less, to swell the ranks of middle-management and to keep women from competing for the top jobs. In effect, the "mommy track" penalizes women who have children by placing them in dead-end jobs while asking them to do essentially the same work as their male counterparts on the "fast track to the top"—but with less pay.

The problem is *not* that corporations need to provide more flexibility for their women executives to enable them to balance their career and family responsibilities. The real issue is to provide women executives the same flexibility that male executives have *always* enjoyed. For example, corporations think nothing of providing paid extended leaves of absence for men executives who have suffered a heart attack.

Myth: Frustrated with trying to balance family and work, women executives are leaving the corporation in droves to start their own businesses.

Fact: There is no evidence that women are dropping off the corporate fast track to start their own businesses *because* of the desire to balance family and work. While it's true more women than ever are starting their own businesses, most do so after age 40 when child-rearing responsibilities for many are ending, according to a 1984 study by Hisrich and Brush. For men executives who start their own companies their move is seen as a bold and positive career maneuver. For women, entrepreneurial ventures are seen as retreats from the corporate world and a chance to devote more time to the family.

Besides, business ventures require never-ending attention from the owners—not leaving much time for taking on even *more* family duties. Any "exodus" by women from the corporate ranks is more likely the result of carefully calculated decisions by women who have slammed into the glass ceiling and see little advantage in staying with the corporation.

Myth: Any woman can make it to the top if she's competent and works hard. That's how men make it and after all, the corporation is looking for the "best person to fill a job."

Fact: Don't we wish. Who makes it to the top" appears to be determined as much by "who you are" as by "what you know." The most blatant example is found in looking at who's currently at the top of corporate America: 276 of the current board chairmen of the Fortune 500 companies are the sons of former chairmen. (Didn't these men ever have daughters?)

Corporate women are increasingly bumping into the "glass ceiling." From their vantage point on the corporate ladder, women can see the top, but are blocked from reaching the high-level corporate positions.

Women executives are frequently locked out of assignments in the "business mainstream," concentrated into jobs that offer little opportunity for getting to the top. Women executives are often treated differently from men in comparable executive positions. One of the biggest concerns is that the best assignments go to men, particularly the ones that would allow women to distinguish themselves as high performers.

Women executives are often excluded from the informal corporate networks where decisions are made and business relationships forged. Even on a more formal level, women report there are "certain kinds of meetings" they are not invited to because they're not seen as policymakers.

Given the overwhelming evidence, no one should be surprised that when women executives are asked what they consider the most serious obstacle in their business careers, they most frequently cite sex discrimination, *not* conflicts between career and family.

The "mommy track" is so dangerous because it provides a rationale for keeping women out of the top, while it helps to keep women at the middle and the bottom low paid. Obviously if women can't keep up they deserve less pay—these jobs must be easier or how could they do them?

If companies were really concerned about the conflicts employed women and men face, surely we would have seen more changes in corporate policies and practices by now. Instead it seems "the mommy track" and the constant drumbeat that "women can't have it all" are a way of keeping women in power controversial. This in turn provides an excuse for segregating women into dead-end jobs and low wages.

Middle-Class Women in Trouble

Katherine S. Newman

Women are in double jeopardy in terms of downward mobility. Some, like their male counterparts, lose well-paid jobs and plunge from the middle class for that reason.[1] But for most middle-class women, one must look closer to home to find the main cause for downward mobility. It is in the aftermath of divorce that once-secure women find themselves sliding right out of the middle class. When men, who enjoy far greater earning power and job mobility than their wives, no longer contribute to household support, the "female-headed" families left behind are pushed into downward mobility.[2] Losses are particularly steep for middle-class women who typically have to make do with 29 to 39 percent of the family income they had before divorce.[3]

The economic impact of divorce disadvantages women far more than it does men:

> While most divorced men find that their standard of living *improves* after divorce, most divorced women and the minor children in their households find that their standard of living plummets. . . . When income is compared to needs, divorced men experience an average 42% rise in their standard of living in the first year after divorce, while divorced women (and their children) experience a 73% decline.
>
> These apparently simple statistics have far-reaching social and economic consequences. For most women and children, divorce means precipitous downward mobility—both economically and socially. The reduction in income brings residential moves and inferior housing, drastically diminished or nonexistent funds for recreation and leisure, and intense pressures due to inadequate time and money.[4]

A series of obstacles stand in the way of divorced mothers struggling to maintain a decent standard of living for their children. High on the list of hurdles they face is the difficulty of securing child support payments. Over four million women in the United States were entitled to receive some form of child support in 1985. Fewer than half were able to collect the payments awarded by the courts, and average child support awards have been declining.[5]

Labor market segregation adds to the woes of the divorced woman trying to support her family, particularly if she has interrupted her career to raise small children.[6] For, as she returns to the job market, she often finds her prospects limited to jobs that are sex segregated and poorly paid. If her children are young, she must find child care for them while she is working, which increases the cost of supporting a family. Clerical workers, waitresses, sales clerks—these are the jobs open to women who lack professional credentials—and they do not, by themselves, pay enough to sustain a middle-class standard of living. And despite recent improvement in America's attitude toward working women, their wages are still comparatively low: Women still earn only seventy cents for every dollar earned by men.[7]

Legal reforms implemented in the 1970s—the end of alimony and the rise of no-fault divorce—once hailed as the equitable solution to property settlements, have only exacerbated the situation.[8] Among the most valuable property built up during marriage is the occupational training, the track record on the job, and the professional licenses that accrue to men while their wives are at home raising the family.[9] With these credentials, men can hold on to a middle-class lifestyle after divorce, while their wives are left behind with half the financial assets but without the occupational wherewithal to a comparable standard of living.[10]

These economic facts have contributed to "the feminization of poverty."[11] Welfare rolls are increasingly filled by women and children who have been abandoned economically by husbands and fathers. Many of these families were low income to start with, but a growing number of single-headed households are outcasts from the middle class who have suffered a wrenching dislocation. They have seen the end of affluence not in the guise of a pink slip—which is hard enough to bear—but in the form of marital dissolution. They must find their bearings as members of the new poor, while simultaneously coming to grips with the painful emotional loss of husbands and fathers. For these women and their children, downward mobility is cloaked in the disappointment of failed marriages, the financial irresponsibility of ex-husbands, and the difficulty of reconstructing the family in a new form which, for all its ubiquitousness in the 1980s, is still perceived as a cultural anomaly.[12]

Jacqueline Johansen found all this out the hard way. She was married for twenty-five years to John Johansen, a dentist in northern California. She worked for a time to put him through school, but her main career was raising three children, something to which she devoted her full attention during the years John was compiling a professional track record in dentistry. His income continued to increase over the years, and it supported an affluent, country-club lifestyle. When he left Jacqueline for a younger woman, John was earning a big salary; Jacqueline was "earning" nothing, though she maintains she was working pretty hard. The divorce was a bitter affair, with lawyers battling on both sides. Once the dust settled, Jacqueline had the huge house (and a huge mortgage to go with it) and monthly support payments that will terminate when her children, who are in their mid- to late teens, turn twenty-one. Since Jacqueline lacks a college degree, she has only been able to find a part-time clerical job that pays a small salary that cannot begin to cover the expenses of three children and a big house. She is having trouble making ends meet and the child support payments are becoming increasingly erratic. She is adamant that her children go to college, but she has no idea how she will manage to pay for it. The pressures are enough to keep her awake at night, but her skills are not enough to do very much to change her long-term prospects for recovery. Slowly, but surely, Jacqueline is seeing the end of her tenure in the middle class. And, since she is forty-seven, it seems unlikely that things are going to improve with time.

Jacqueline's story has been repeated over and over again across the country. It has been the subject of countless academic studies and government reports. Politicians and advocates from women's groups have termed the situation a "public disgrace" and have warned that the nation's children are at risk.[13]

When downward mobility is generated by occupational disaster, the finger of blame must be pointed at forces that are in some sense abstract. But where divorce is the culprit, the causal connections are quite direct and personal. In these families, downward mobility is cast not in terms of the job market, the crisis atmosphere of a strike, or the changing nature of the American economy. Instead, dislocation is seen through the intimate lens of family life. Husbands who vowed to love, protect, and support their wives, now maneuver to protect their incomes from the demands of alimony or child support. Wives accustomed to the comforts of middle-class life — nice homes, good schools, freedom from worry and want — now see these mainstays pulled out from under them by the very men who were their most intimate and trusted partners. . . .

NOTES

1 But despite impressive gains in the last decade, most working women are not in managerial and professional jobs. Instead, they continue to populate "pink collar ghettos" where pay and promotion prospects are comparatively low. Reskin and Hartmann (1986:9), Blau (1984). Hence the stories of occupational displacement among well-paid, middle-class employees discussed earlier are disproportionately about men.

2 Bane and Weiss (1980); Bradbury et al. (1979); Espenshade (1979); Kriesberg (1970); Mott (1977); Ross and Sawhill (1975); Wattenberg and Reinhardt (1979).

3 Weitzman (1985:325). Divorced women from low-income families retain a greater percentage of the family income (71 percent), but this is still less than what their husbands enjoy. (Weitzman [1985:325]). Her figures represent household income one year after divorce. My research is based on the experiences of women who have been divorced for two years or more. While still hard pressed, they show a degree of recovery (50 to 75 percent of predivorce income). Nevertheless it is clear that economic decline follows divorce for all classes of women (Weiss [1984]), but middle-class women slide farthest.

4 Weitzman (1985:323).

5 The U.S. Bureau of the Census reports that between 1983–1985, the average payment for child support dropped 12.4 percent—from $2,528 per year to $2,215. The decline was confined to white families, who are more likely to receive child-support awards in the first place. While white women receive court awarded support decrees in 71 percent of divorces, Hispanic women do so only 42 percent of the time, and black women only 35 percent. The amount of the awards to minority women is also lower, on average, than white women, reflecting the poorer economic standing of men in these minority groups (U.S. Bureau of the Census [1987b]).

6 Corcoran et al. (1984) argue that although "women who drop out of the labor force have lower real wages when they return to work than they had when they left work," the net effects are small. Nevertheless, when these losses are tacked on to the fact that women are generally poorly paid anyway, the result is still significant.

7 The U.S. Bureau of the Census (1987a) reports that the wage gap between men and women who work full time is narrowing, mainly because young women (those in their twenties) are entering relatively high-paying occupations (those once dominated by men) in ever-increasing numbers. While this may eventually mean that divorced women reach a par with their husbands in earning power, it is no comfort to the women of the generations examined here. For women forty-five to sixty-four, earnings are still only 60 percent of men's wages. Moreover, it remains to be seen what will happen to the women in the youngest age group as they begin to have children and face the need to interrupt their labor force participation. It will also be interesting to see whether wage rates remain high in the formerly male-dominated occupations as women enter them in increasing number.

It is entirely possible that the closing of the wage gap within the youngest cohort is an artifact of time spent in the labor market. Brandwein (1987) points out that "at the start of their careers, there is a small gap between the salaries of women and men. . . . However, the longer they are employed, the larger the gap." Hence "unless women's advancement chances substantially improve, we will see, in 10 or 20 years, the earnings gap for this [younger] cohort increasing."

8 Nationwide only 14% of women receive alimony awards and only 7 percent receive it on a regular basis. In New Jersey, where extensive research has been done on court awards, Bruch and Wickler (1985) discovered that judges generally give wives no more than 30 percent of the husband's salary to maintain themselves and their children, leaving husbands with the remaining 70 percent. New Jersey women rarely receive more than 35 to 40 percent of marital assets. Even so, New Jersey judges are under the impression that alimony is awarded half the time, and have completely unrealistic ideas about the cost of raising children.

9 Weitzman (1985:110) calls these "career assets" and includes among them pension benefits and education. She points out that these are among the most important valuables in the modern economy, but they are not subject to the community property laws (which include only tangible property) and are therefore not taken into account in divorce settlements.

10 Weitzman (1985:15–52).

11 Thirty-four percent of all female-headed families are below the poverty level, and nearly half of them are divorced. If the proportion of the poor who are in female-headed households continues to increase at the same rate that it did in the 1960s and 1970s, "the poverty population would be composed solely of women and their children before the year 2000" (National Advisory Council on Economic Opportunity [1981]).

12 Up until the mid-1980s, one in every two American marriages ended in divorce, many of them without children. Yet our cultural conceptions of the family lag behind this reality. The single-parent household has yet to achieve the status of a "normal" family that its numbers might bear out.

13 *New York Times* (1987).

REFERENCES

Bane, M.J., and R. Weiss. 1980. "Alone Together: The World of Single-Parent Families." *American Demographics* 2(5):323–330

Blau, Francine. 1984. "Occupational Segregation and Labor Market Discrimination." In *Sex Segregation in the Workplace: Trends, Explanations, Remedies*, edited by B. Reskin, pp. 117–143. Washington, D.C.: National Academy of Sciences Press.

Bradbury, K.,S. Danziger, E. Smolensky, and P. Smolensky. 1979. "Public Assistance, Female Headship, and Economic Well-Being." *Journal of Marriage and the Family* 41(3):519–535.

Brandwein, R. 1987. "Time Widens Male-Female Earnings Disparity." Letter to the Editor, *New York Times*, 27 September, E22.

Bruch, C., and N. Wickler. 1985. "The Economic Consequences of Divorce." *Juvenile and Family Court Journal* 36(3):5–26

Corcoran, Mary, Greg Duncan, and Michael Ponza. 1984. "Work Experience, Job Segregation and Wages." In *Sex Segregation in the Workplace: Trends, Expectations, Remedies*, edited by B. F. Reskin, pp. 171–191. Washington, D.C.: National Academy of Sciences Press.

Espenshade, T. 1979. "The Economic Consequences of Divorce." *Journal of Marriage and the Family* 41(3):615–625.

Kriesberg, L. 1970. *Mothers in Poverty*. Chicago: Aldine Publishing Co.

Mott, F. 1977. "The Socioeconomic Status of Households Headed by Women. Results from the National Longitudinal Surveys" (R & D. Monograph 72). Washington, D.C.: U.S. Department of Labor.

National Advisory Council on Economic Opportunity. 1981. *The American Promise: Equal Justice and Economic Opportunity* (Final Report). Washington, D.C.: U.S. Government Printing Office.

New York Times. 1987. "Average Child Support Payment Drops by 12%." 23 August, 26.

Reskin, Barbara, and Heidi Hartman, eds. 1986. *Women's Work, Men's Work: Sex Segregation on the Job.* Washington, D.C.: National Academy of Sciences Press.

Ross, H., and I. Sawhill. 1975. *Time of Transition: The Growth of Families Headed by Women.* Washington, D.C.: The Urban Institute.

U.S. Bureau of the Census. 1986. "Characteristics of the Population Below the Poverty Level: 1984." *Current Population Reports* (Series P- 60, No. 152). Washington, D.C.: U.S. Government Printing Office.

Wattenburg, E., and H. Reinhardt. 1979. "Female-Headed Families: Trends and Implications. " *Social Work* 24:460–467.

Weiss, R. 1984. "The Impact of Marital Dissolution on Income and Consumption in Single-Parent Households." *Journal of Marriage and the Family* 46(1):115–128.

Weitzman, Lenore. 1985. *The Divorce Revolution: The Unexpected Social and Economic Consequences for Women and Children in America.* New York: Free Press.

The Lecherous Professor

Billie Wright Dziech and Linda Weiner

"When I use a word," Humpty Dumpty said, in a rather scornful tone, "it means just what I choose it to mean—neither more nor less." "The question is," said Alice, "whether you can make words mean so many different things." "The question is," said Humpty Dumpty, "which is to be the master—that's all."

Lewis Carroll, *Alice in Wonderland*

In a recent *Cosmopolitan* article on sexual harassment, Adrian L., a student at a large Midwestern state university, described Tom, one of her professors:

[He's] like a rabid wolf hovering at the edge of a sheep pack—the incoming class of freshmen.

When he's selected a girl who's unusually attractive, intelligent, and naive, he moves right in. Believe me, he's *predatory*—I've seen him in action. First, he'll "rap and relate" with the freshman over drinks at the college bar. In a couple of weeks, he has her dizzy with the "existential nihilism of Sartre" or "archetypal patterns of Jung." All this may sound exciting, but the results are tragicomic. Two years ago, he "shared" a girl with a friend of his, another faculty member. The three of them made it while watching a particularly beautiful sunrise—very aesthetic, you know. His current ploy is backgammon. You see him shaking those dice at a table in the rathskeller with this hazy-eyed kid. Several dormitory assistants have seen him leaving her room at six in the morning, and the campus security guard once caught him with a student in the stacks of the library. You can guess what he found.

Is Tom exploiting his pupils? You bet he is. Does he know what he's doing? Of course. Is the administration aware of what he's up to? Sure they are, but these days, to get fired for what they used to call "moral turpitude," you'd have to rape an entire cheerleading squad at half time. Tom's like a pothead turned loose in a Twinkies factory.

Although there is limited evidence of the number of harassers who may be "loose" on the nation's campuses, one point is clear. They are tolerated because society doubts that men are capable of sexual restraint. Sexual harassers are often defended with the shrugged observation, "After all, they're only human." A middle-aged professor, notorious for pursuing sexual relations with female students, offered a variation on this view. "If you put me at a table with food (with coeds), I eat."

The appeal to "human nature" is a reminder that even in an era of ostensible sexual liberalism and freedom, both men and women suffer and stereotypes die hard. Even in the 1980s, society has not freed itself of the Victorian notion that men are creatures barely capable of controlling their bestial appetites and aggressions. All the contemporary rhetoric about liberating the sexes from stereotypes has done little to change the popular view of the male as a kind of eternal tumescence, forever searching and forever unsatisfied.

Such an attitude demeans the notion of "human." To be human does not mean that a man is at the mercy of his genitalia. Whatever it is that constitutes "humanness" is located in the mind and heart, not the libido. "Human" implies reason, compassion, control—all the qualities that distinguish college professors from their cats and dogs. Without these, they are "only animal," a defense few find appealing. Sexual harassment unquestionably harms females, but men are equally debased when it is allowed to flourish. On the college campus, a very small number of men damage the reputations of colleagues who perform difficult tasks for relatively low wages without "succumbing" to the "irresistible" temptations of women students. . . .

A crucial concern for both students and academicians is learning to recognize the characteristics that differentiate the lecherous professor from his colleagues. There are no infallible predictors for recognizing sexual harassment. The most pernicious behavior can occur exclusive of "giveaways," or isolated actions can be misinterpreted as sinister when they are simply examples of clumsy professional or social style. However, a tentative list of warning signs might include the following:

• *Staring, leering, ogling.* These behaviors may be surreptitious or very obvious. In any case, college faculty should possess knowledge of social decorum, and must avoid such activities.

• *Frequently commenting on personal appearance of the student.* In the academic setting, most professors refrain from discussing the apparel and physical traits of their students.

• *Touching out of context.* Every physical gesture should be appropriate to the occasion, setting, and need and character of the individual student. Professional educators may legitimately be expected to possess the ability to make such determinations.

• *Excessive flattery and praise of the student.* This behavior, exhibited with others present, is especially seductive to students with low self-esteem *or* high aspirations.

By convincing a student that she is intellectually and/or physically exceptional, the lecherous professor gains psychological access to her.

• *Deliberately avoiding or seeking encounters with the student in front of colleagues.* Depending on the type of harasser, he may either attempt to hide from or to perform for colleagues in interactions with the student. The key is that in either case his behavior with the student changes when he is being observed.

• *Injecting a "male versus female" tone into discussions with the students or colleagues.* A frequent behavior of verbal harassers, this conduct signals a generally disparaging attitude toward women. Its initial effect is to make them feel outsiders in the academic environment, but it may also be an indicator of other potential forms of abuse.

• *Persistently emphasizing sexuality in all contexts.* Pervasive, inordinate emphasis on sex can occur in class or outside. For the lecherous professor, sexuality becomes, in effect, the prism through which all topics are focused. Students, male and female, can usually detect this behavior readily, and such professors often acquire a reputation for "being fixated on sex" in papers, tests, and discussions.

Such behaviors can serve as signals to the student. Another key to understanding the lecherous professor is assessing the setting or context in which he works. There are both public and private harassers, and they act in very different fashions. The public harasser engages in observable, flagrant posturing toward women. He is the most likely to intimidate or seek control through sexist remarks and advances that may be offensive but are essentially free from sanctions. Students sometimes refer to him as "hands," "touchy-feelly," or "mouth." Colleagues describe him as "patronizing," "always performing," "convinced of his own cuteness." He frequently costumes himself by extreme dressing up or down and seldom employs standard academic vocabulary—except to punctuate a witticism. He is articulate, glib, sarcastic and/or funny. His general image is that of a casual "good guy" or an imposing man of the world. . . .

The style and intent of the private harasser are directly opposite. He may be the more genuinely "lecherous" of the two, for he uses his authority to gain private access to the student. Unlike his counterpart, he deliberately avoids notoriety. He not only seeks but depends upon privacy because he requires a domain in which there are no witnesses to his behavior. He is the harasser of greatest interest to the public and the media, the one who demands sexual favors of students, the one most readily cast in the image of despoiler of innocence and molester of youth.

His personal and professional styles lend credence to the epithets. The private harasser often adheres to academic stereotypes. He usually dresses conservatively. His language and demeanor are generally formal, perhaps even intimidating, to the student. Because he appears so circumspect, he is the last to be suspected by colleagues. The Levi-clad professor who sits casually before the class seems more culpable than the imposing man with the resonant voice who stands behind the lectern.

The lectern symbolizes the private harasser's teaching style. Characteristically removed and aloof, he lectures while the class listens. Just as the public harasser uses his openness to move the student to compliance, the private offender employs authority to lure her into acquiescence. The ability to control the setting gives him special access to the women under his power. He can seduce them into his private domain with a simple oral or written directive. "Please see me" or "I would like a conference with you" are familiar demands.

But, few are prepared for the deception that occurs when the professor closes the office door and sheds the professorial for the male role. Whether he begins with overt sexual advances or the more subtle verbal approach ("My wife doesn't love me anymore," "Young women like you are so lovely"), his sudden role change causes the student surprise and confusion. Her role submissiveness, female self-doubt, and shock combine with the privacy of the interaction to provide a cover for the harasser. When there are no witnesses and the student experiences extreme disorientation, there are seldom sexual harassment grievances.

Another way of understanding sexual harassers is to describe the roles they most commonly assume:

• *The Counselor-Helper.* This type of professor uses the guise of nurturer and caretaker to gain access to the student. If she feels lonely and anonymous on campus, she may be flattered or consoled by his interest. He invites her confidence and uses information about her private life to discover her vulnerabilities, commitments, and attitudes about men and sex. Then he can tailor his "line" to her specific need. One professor, after encouraging a student's anguished account of rejection by a boyfriend, replied earnestly, "I'd never treat you like that." To her, it was a terribly moving assertion. To the witness to the incident, it was far less compelling because she had observed the professor making the statement to at least three other female students from whom he later sought sexual favors.

The counselor-helper may act as a go-between in male-female relationships of students. This behavior, described by one ombudsman as "pimping," encourages the student to see the professor as a broker or gatekeeper in her relationship with a significant male. The professor's intent can be to derive vicarious sexual pleasure from thus involving himself or to use the male as a foil to increase his own stature in the eyes of the female. One administrator describes this as "seduction with an agent." An accomplished harasser in one university was fond of acting as go-between and then reporting to the female that he had advised her boyfriend, "She's a real woman. Are you prepared to satisfy her?" The motive was to win the seduction when the student became attracted to the professor's image of her as experienced and voluptuous.

• *The Confidant.* This individual approaches the student not as a superior who can help her but as an equal and friend. Sharing is an essential element in their interaction. He may invite her confidences, but he also offers his own. In an attempt to impress or win sympathy from the student, he may relate or invent stories about his private and professional life. Placed in this role, the student often feels that he values and trusts her, so she becomes an involuntary confidante. Without genuine mutual agreement, the relationship is moved to an intimate domain from which she may find it difficult to extricate herself.

Another method a harasser may employ is creating indebtedness through gestures of friendship. Offers from a professor to lend the student books, money, notes, a place to study or providing her with free tickets or rides may signal an attempt to make her feel obligated.

• *The Intellectual Seducer.* Called "mind fucking" or "intellectual intercourse" by some, this kind of seduction results from the professor's ability to impress students with his skill and knowledge. He may use class content to gain access to personal information about the student. Self-disclosure on the part of the student is often invited in disciplines like psychology, sociology, philosophy, and literature where personal values, beliefs, and experiences are easily related to course content. At one college, students told of being required to write about their sex fantasies. Such information may be used to identify areas of vulnerability and/or accessibility in the student. A psychology professor bragged to a colleague about requiring students to take personality inventories. He told them the demonstrated uses of the test, but his real motivation was to gain personal information about respondents in whom he was interested.

A professor's avocations may also be engaging or dangerous. A common example is the faculty member who uses his knowledge of books or movies to move the student into discussions of erotic topics. Another is that of the professor who hypnotizes students outside the classroom. While some use hypnosis appropriately, it can be dangerous when done by a sexual harasser. Finally, there is the case of the art professor who employs female students as nude models for private studio work.

• *The Opportunist.* This person takes advantage of the physical setting and unusual or occasional circumstances to obscure his inappropriate behavior and to gain intimacy with students. He may rely on equipment or subject matter to gain physical access to the student. A serious problem in clinical, laboratory, counseling, performance, and vocational-technical settings, this behavior is often described by students as stealing "cheap feels." The lecherous professor discovers ways to touch the student by using proximity to equipment as an excuse or by employing parts of her body in class demonstrations. One student complained that her woodwind professor persisted in touching her breasts while telling her he was illustrating the movements of her diaphragm; another that her nursing instructor "felt [her] up" while using her body to demonstrate physical disabilities in patients.

The opportunist may also use field trips, meetings, and conventions as occasions to escape institutional restraints. The problem for the student is that these are often described as scholastic or professional honors and/or necessities, and she feels compelled to attend.

• *The Power Broker.* The most familiar type of harasser, the power broker, trades on his ability to control grades, credentials, recommendations, or jobs. The assumption that he works only through crude and raw assertions of power is inaccurate. Direct promises of rewards or threats of punishment can exert enormous influence on students, but they feel equally victimized by promises and threats that are implied rather than stated openly. Because so much may be at stake, the student is unlikely to risk a complaint unless the harasser has been very overt about his intentions.

Regardless of the role he assumes or the type of harassment in which he engages, the lecherous professor always controls the circumstances surrounding the student victim. Sexual harassment is a power issue, and the power of the professoriate is enormous. . . .

The Managed Heart

Arlie Russell Hochschild

On a 15-hour flight from Hong Kong to New York, a young businessman puts his drink down, leans back and takes in a flight attendant, who is pushing a 300-pound meal cart on its third voyage up the aisle. "Hey, Honey," he calls out, "give me a smile." The flight attendant stops the cart, wipes her brow and looks him in the eye. "I'll tell you what," she says. "You smile first, then I'll smile. O.K.?" The business-man smiles at her. "Good," she replies. "Now freeze and hold that for 15 hours." And she turns to push the cart up the aisle. The smiling passenger got more than he asked for—he got the flight attendant's real feeling. Which was this: "The company may sell my smile to you in an ad. And reading that ad, you may think you have bought the right to my smile. But it's for me to decide when I smile, because it's my face." De-tails come and go when a story is as worn with the telling and as relished as this one. In some versions of this smile war the flight attendant works for United; in others, TWA or World Airways. In some versions the businessman says, "What's the matter, not smiling today?" or "Baby, where's my smile?" In some versions the man is old, in others young. But in all the times I've heard this story, one detail goes unchanged. It is always a man who claims the smile and always a woman's smile that he claims. For the businessman, that smile holds a promise—not so much of her interest in him as a man, perhaps, as of her interest in him as a child with a need for care. Behind the "Hey, honey" is perhaps his unnamed dread that the whole supply of female nurtu-rance is drying up around him.

Long before the current labor struggles in the airline industry, sensitive observers could have seen the trouble coming: they could have read it in the flight attendants' faces. Ever since deregulation sent the airlines into a competitive frenzy, the compa-nies have asked flight attendants to shoulder an increasingly heavy share of winning in the marketplace. Like workers on an assembly line that has been speeded up, flight at-tendants have been asked to hand out commercial love at an ever faster rate, to more people in the same amount of time.

Unable to keep up, attendants have countered with a slowdown. They could not slow down their actual physical labor—they had to serve meals in the flight time allot-ted—but they could slow down their emotional labor. And, in a way not quite articu-lated, that is what they have been doing. Passengers no longer get the steady, good-hearted cheer promised ever more boldly by smiling young women in ads.

"Flight attendants never even look at me as they go by," one woman complained. "I figure it's because I'm a woman and they figure I'm not a big business customer." In fact, something else is going on. As one flight attendant explained, "We keep our eyes down. We avoid eye contact and focus on the aisle, on the plates. I know the guy in 7-B is patiently waiting to catch my eye and ask for another Coke. But we can't do a cocktail and meal service for 200 passengers in two and a quarter hours and take spe-cial requests, too. I'd like to, but I'm like a dispensing machine as it is. How can I give personal service the way it is now?"

For decades, flight attendants have been mothering frightened passengers. With the breakdown of this familiar service system over the past ten years, we can see the form of exploitation on which it has depended: the exploitation of emotional labor—the managing of hearts for the company good.

One crisp autumn week, I went to the Flight Attendant Training Center of Delta Air Lines in Atlanta, Georgia, to see how they prepared people to do emotional labor. The center was near the Atlanta airport, not far from the airplane hangars that new recruits toured. Each day of the four-week training course began at eight a.m. in a large assembly hall with talks by an array of supervisors, pilots, company officials. The trainees— 123 of them, nearly all white females in their early 20s—sat nervously with notepads in their laps.

Where were the blacks? I thought. Where were the men? Why is this a white woman's job? It is white, one of the few black flight attendants suggested to me, because Delta caters to what it takes to be a prejudiced white traveling public. It is female, she explained, because women and "friendly service" go together, especially in a nonunion company in the South. The young woman sitting to my left, like many others, felt lucky to be chosen: "This sure beats workin' a desk job in Memphis. That's where I come from. All my girlfriends are working as secretaries or having babies. They think I'm real liberated to be here."

The program proved to be harder than they had thought. Quizzes came daily—on what to do if you see a passenger slumped over; on the location of the oxygen masks on the L-1011, on the 767; on whether to board a handcuffed convict; on how to inflate the life rafts. They had been told that if they didn't measure up in any way, many eager applicants were waiting to replace them. In the hall that morning there were nervous, sidelong glances and hushed talk. Finally a pilot, crew-cut, in his mid-50s, walked with a slow authoritative stride to the microphone, paused and looked around. After a few good morning remarks, he came to the point: "The pilot commands the plane, wing to wing and nose to tail. Now," he said in a thick Southern drawl, "if you girls have any trouble in the cabin that you can't handle, you take it to your A-line [the flight attendant in charge], and if she can't handle it, she should come to me. Now if you're the A-line you take time to collect yourself. You go powder your nose in the ladies' room. Then come in the cockpit and politely say, 'Captain? I hate to disturb you but I think we have a problem.'"

Having first established the emotional labor due *him*, he went on to describe what was due the passengers. "Now, girls, I want to tell you something else," he said moving slowly, with authority. "I want you to think of the cabin as the living room in your very own home. At home, wouldn't you go out of your way to make friends feel at ease and have a good time? Well, it's the same thing in the L-1011." Then he said what other pilots were to repeat after him: "Girls, I want you to smile. Your smile is your best asset. So I want you to go out there and use it. Smile. Really lay it on. Smile." The young woman from Memphis wrote in her notebook, "Must smile— impt."

If a passenger is "demanding" or "drinking too much," the flight attendants were told in a later session, "think of him as a child. Maybe he's afraid of flying." From the trainer's point of view, all this is just a sensible way to generate commercial affection—evoking the warm feelings flight attendants have for children, for friends, for people they would invite into their own homes and give smiles to easily, naturally. The trainers are not unpleasant people with malicious intentions. On the contrary, the trainers I saw conducting the classes from eight to five each day were helpful, friendly women who had been and probably would again be flight attendants themselves.

I have many times thought, since meeting her, of the center's director, a distinguished woman in her early 50s. She had a tough exterior that kept trainees in awe and allowed her to be at ease with the nearly solidly male management above her. (Her job, she had been told, was to *quarterback* the training division. Now that's language to make a woman feel right at home.) But her gentleness and thoughtfulness shone through; a small table by her desk was crammed with photos of former trainees, some with new husbands and babies—her "family." She was there at 7:30 every morning, keeping an eye out, ripples of laughter surrounding her from time to time as she cracked jokes, shoring up morale, year after year after year. Like the flight attendants themselves, she and the other trainers seemed to me deeply decent people.

At the same time, something struck me as terribly wrong with the whole commercial logic they had been drawn into—a logic that uses Southern white womanhood as a marketing gimmick, that trades in female niceness. When young recruits, armed with mental images of passengers as children and friends, actually begin work, the experience is often a shock. Yes, a drunk may fear flying, poor fellow, but what if he has his hand between your legs? What if he's cursing at you? What if he's putting out his cigarette on your arm? These things happen. And in recessionary times, when people are coping with more failures in their personal lives, these things happen more often.

The technique of seeing a passenger through images that bring him closer and help you empathize gets in the way of quickly depersonalizing him when he does not act like a child or a friend in your home. The trainers helped workers learn how to extend their empathy to strangers. But they didn't want to discourage their young trainees by telling it like it is, or make them too uppity by spelling out what abuse they were paid to withstand and what they were not. The trainers taught flight attendants how to send out their feelings but not how to take them back.

Flight attendants who worked during the 1960s speak nostalgically of times when there was one worker to 25 passengers, when planes were smaller and slower, when layovers were longer and flights less crowded, and some personal attention was actually possible. Once a cruise ship, the airplane has become a Greyhound bus. During the recession of the early 1970s, many airlines began "cost-efficient" flying. They began using planes that could hold more people and fly longer without fuel stops. That meant longer workdays and more workdays bunched together. Flight attendants had less time to adjust to time-zone changes on layovers and less time to enjoy a major attraction of their work: personal travel.

One measure of cost-efficiency has always been how long the plane is kept in the air. Now, like the airplane, the flight attendant is kept in use as long and as intensively as possible. One American Airlines union official describes the speedup: "They rush us through the emergency briefing. They're even briefing us on the buses getting out there. When you get on the plane, you just start counting all the food and everything and start loading the passengers. They'll shut the door and pull away and we'll find we're 20 meals short."

It is as if a giant conveyor belt carrying human beings has begun to move faster. There is no longer one flight attendant to 25 passengers; there is now about one to 50.

With deregulation in the early 1970s and a subsequent but short-lived drop in fares, the "discount people" boarded: more mothers with small children who left behind nests of toys, gum wrappers and food scraps; more elderly, "white-knuckle" flyers; and more people who did not know where the restrooms were or who wandered around wanting to go "downstairs." The flight attendant was called on to do far more, with far less time to do it.

The current recession has made matters worse. Some airlines have laid off baggage handlers, gate personnel, ticket clerks and managers. Lines are longer. More bags are lost. Connecting flights are missed. Mishaps multiply. Most passengers can take a moderate number of mishaps with moderate good grace. But one passenger in, say, every 100 is a grumbler who needs to fix blame on someone—usually the flight attendant. Taking blame from such grumblers makes up a large part of the attendant's workday. A passenger's frustration at a missed connection, mixed with the usual anxiety about air travel, can erupt as an angry complaint about the food. Eyes ablaze, a man may suddenly glare at a flight attendant and shout, "This meat is not *cooked!*"

Flight attendants have a name for the blaze-eyed man. He is an "irate," a term attendants use as a noun, as in, "Irene, I had three irates this morning." In flush times, a flight attendant can soothe her irates with a free drink or deck of cards, but on some airlines those frills are gone. Only extra friendly service is left to appease the ever longer stream of irates, frustrated by baggage handlers, ticket agents, late flights, missed flights and the fact that the passenger in the next seat got a ticket for $100 less by buying at the right hour of the right day.

With so much riding on service, airlines—now a highly competitive and volatile industry—keep a keen eye on their relative ratings. They wait for Egon Ronay's yearly *Lucas Guide* with the eagerness of networks waiting for Neilsen ratings. This white-and-green paperback, available in many airport drugstores and geared to traveling businessmen (ads for sherry and cigars often adorn the pages), lets the airlines and their passengers know who's ahead in the intercompany smile wars.

A *Lucas Guide* ranking of Delta Airlines says, "[Drinks were served] not only with a smile but with concerned inquiries such as, 'Anything else I can get you, Madam?' The atmosphere was that of a civilized party—with the passengers, in response, behaving like civilized guests. . . . Once or twice our inspectors tested stewardesses by being deliberately exacting, but they were never roused, and at the end of the flight they lined up to say farewell with undiminished brightness. . . . [Passengers are] quick to detect strained or forced smiles, and they come aboard wanting to *enjoy* the flight. One of us looked forward to his next trip on Delta 'because it was fun.' Surely that is how passengers ought to feel."

Being friendly or enjoying your work is one thing, but having your enjoyment advertised, promised—in essence, sold—is quite another. A recent Delta ad featuring a close-up of a pretty smiling woman advertised "people [who] love their work." The ad coyly explained the glow of her smile: "And if you're wondering where all this comes from, well, it comes from inside." And one PSA slogan bragged, "On PSA, our smiles are not just painted on . . . So smile your way from L.A. to San Francisco."

By creating expectations, advertisements in effect rewrite the job description, since part of the job is to cope with what people expect and enjoy it. Ads promise on-time service though planes are late up to 50 percent of the time. Ads picture half-empty planes and leisurely service. Ads imply prompt, quiet, smoke-free flights in comfortable seats with reading lights that work. In promising all this, ads create an extra job—dealing with the inevitable disgruntlement of passengers who sit out a half-hour delay in crowded seating, contemplating the connection they are going to miss. The smile in the ad makes the passengers view ordinary nonsmiling as facial loafing. Across the pages of one magazine after another, the happy worker of one company competes with the still happier worker of another. And the ads of both diverge ever more wildly from the hard work this smiling really is.

The connection between profits, service and self—the commercial logic of the managed heart—is not slipped quietly over the workers' heads. The company tries to bring the workers in on it. One male worker, who had seven years' experience resisting this logic at United Airlines, observed: "We get told how we're doing. Periodically we get sent passenger evaluations. They show how United, American, Continental and TWA are competing. The passengers are asked to rank the flight attendants: 'Genuinely concerned, made me feel welcome. Spoke to me more than required. Was wide awake, energetic and eager to help. Seemed sincere when talking to passengers. Helped establish a relaxed cabin atmosphere. Enjoyed their jobs. Treated passengers as individuals.' We see how United is doing in the competition. We're supposed to really get into that."

Why did this flight attendant resist the performance questionnaire? Not because he believed capitalism had no right to program and sell a person's feelings. He had not thought things out that far; anyway, it's nothing to think about when a recession is on and he's lucky to have work. No, he resisted having his friendliness rated because he couldn't be sincerely friendly to 700 people a day. And while he took the job far less seriously and gave it much less than many women workers I talked with, even he wanted to be sincerely friendly. He withdrew only when sheer numbers made that impossible.

In response to any industry speedup, workers experience stress. A company base manager at Delta used that term as she explained frankly, "The job is getting harder. There's no question about it. We see more sick forms. We see more cases of situational depression. We see more alcoholism and drugs, more trouble sleeping and relaxing."

Flight attendants I talked to said stress comes when they are faced with a rapid flow of demands but have little power over the conditions that would help them meet those demands. They can't make passenger requests disappear. They can't leave. They feel torn—and they feel helpless to stop the flow of demands that make them feel torn.

I was having dinner one evening with a flight attendant, seven years with Delta, who tried to get across what it feels like:

"I had this woman complain to me—bitterly—that the seat was small, that her bag didn't fit under it as it did on other airlines. And she was mad at *me* for that. I was trying to deal with her when a guy came up to complain his earphones didn't work. I offered to give him new ones but he was still mad. Then at the end of the trip, this man sitting opposite my jump seat began staring at me and finally propositioned me. 'How much do you charge?' he asked. He made me feel like a prostitute. Maybe I could have handled any one of these episodes without getting upset. But they happened one after another, one after another. I had different feelings about each one. But I didn't get a chance to work out my feelings before —*bang*—the next thing happened."

Another worker told me how she reached her breaking point: "I thought I'd heard them all. I had a lady tell me her doctor gave her a prescription for playing cards. I had a man ask me to tell the pilot to use the cockpit radio to reserve his Hertz car. I had a lady ask me if we gave enemas on board. But the time I finally cracked was when a lady just took her tea and threw it on my arm. That was it."

Another flight attendant, who took pride in her resiliency and love of people and who felt she had grown in both areas during her ten years at Pan Am, also reached the point at which she could not continue: "I guess it was on a flight when a lady spat at me that I decided I'd had enough. I tried. God knows, I tried my damnedest."

We know what the old kind of exploitation looks like: an assembly-line worker, bent over his machine, works long hours in terrible conditions for desperately low wages. But there is another kind—the exploitation of service workers, many of them women, and it looks markedly different. The labor it demands is less physical than emotional, less in the hands than in the managed heart. And the occupational hazards of this work are not back injuries or cataracts but emotional stress and burnout.

A surprising number of modern workers are, in a sense, flight attendants: as part of their jobs, they manage their clients' feelings and, in doing so, they manage their own. Some have brief encounters with many people—radio and television announcers, waitresses and waiters, hotel receptionists. Some have more prolonged contact—hairdressers, social workers, dental hygienists. And some have extended, close contact—therapists, nurses, doctors, teachers.

Just as the airlines invite customers to rate service, so too, other companies come up with ways of making sure their employees do their emotional work. An article headlined "A Grumpy Winn-Dixie Clerk Could Make You a Dollar Richer" ran in the *St. Petersburg Times* on April 17, 1982: "The cashiers at six St. Petersburg and Pinellas Park Winn-Dixie stores are wearing dollar bills pinned to their uniforms these days. It's all part of a company courtesy campaign. If the cashier doesn't come up with a friendly greeting and a sincere thank you, the customer is supposed to get a dollar. And a cashier who gives away too many dollars may wind up with a lecture from the boss."

As the shift from an industrial to a service economy continues, less and less will people make things for a living and more and more will they deliver services that require face-to-face or voice-to-voice contact. A capacity to deal with things will matter relatively less on the job, while the capacity to deal with people, relationships and feelings will matter relatively more. In a capitalist, postindustrial culture, what this means, I think, is that a commercial logic will penetrate deeper and deeper into what we used to think of as a private, psychological, sacred part of a person's self and soul.

Emotional labor is the silent work of evoking and suppressing feeling—in ourselves and in others. When you drive a truck or swing a hammer for a living, you give the company your time and sweat. But you don't relinquish your way of seeing things. You don't give the company your face or your feelings. Those aren't used. Those aren't exploited. But when you do emotional labor to express the company's disposition toward the public, and to make a profit for the company, you put your feelings to work.

What an employer actually sees and buys, of course, is what you can *see*—how we seem. To maintain that outward appearance, people use one of two techniques of professional acting. The first is surface acting—the putting on of an outward appearance. A social worker, say, might lean over slightly, head tilted, with a closed smile to express the official feeling—concern. But surface acting carries us only so far. In the long run, it is hard to feel one thing while seeming to feel another. What lasts longer is the acting that Konstantin Stanislavsky proposed: what I call deep acting. To do deep acting, we actually evoke in ourselves the feelings we need in order to seem to feel the right feeling for the job. The social worker, then, might think of a surly client as the mother of a boy she knows down the street and in this way evoke the empathy she needs for the job.

If a service worker learns how to do deep acting, to evoke and retract the appropriate images and metaphors at the appropriate time, if she can extend herself when a client is friendly but contract herself when the client isn't, if she is good at detecting who is likely to be which, then she can minimize the stress. But she may come to recognize that she is acting, and that the actor is both the "real" her and not the "real" her. And she can become confused and troubled over which is which. The issue of falseness came up again and again as I interviewed flight attendants. They often said to me, "Oh, I'm not a phony, but . . ." or "X is a real phony, but, now, I feel like myself in the cabin." Some seemed to blame themselves for what was really a necessity of the job: putting on an act.

While flight attendants are the actors, the airlines write the script. In an example of near-Orwellian Newspeak, the companies seem to have officially eliminated the very idea of getting angry at a passenger, the source of revenue. Supervisors never speak officially of an "obnoxious" or "outrageous" passenger, only of an "uncontrolled" passenger. The term suggests that a fact has somehow attached itself to this passenger—not that the passenger has lost control or even had any control to lose. Again, the common phrase "mishandled passenger" suggests a bungle somewhere up the line, by someone destined to remain lost in the string of workers that stretches from curbside to airplane cabin. By linguistically avoiding any attribution of blame, the companies smuggle out of discourse the very idea of a right to be angry at a passenger.

In one passenger-handling class, a trainer described how she passed a dinner tray to a man in a window seat. To do this, she had to pass it across a woman sitting on the aisle. As the tray went by, the woman snitched the man's dessert. The flight attendant politely responded, "I notice this man's dessert is on your tray." The dirty deed was done, but, the implication was, not by anyone in particular. With the help of industry language, emotional labor was done, but its tracks were hidden with words.

Seeing in company ways, the worker learns to feel in company ways that make a smile easier to sustain. But then it becomes more difficult for the worker to listen to her or his own feelings. Our own feelings may not be good feelings but they are our feelings. They tell us who we are. Yet for more workers nowadays, it's hard to tell where, in a face or a feeling, the company stops and the person begins. . . .

Deference and Maternalism

Judith Rollins

The baseness of the domestic must not seem to be the result of the airs, contortions or ruses suffered under the yoke. On the contrary, the more the domestic is crushed, the more the master is justified. This is not surprising once one has understood the general phenomenon of the reversal of the accusation in all oppressive relationships.[1]

The relationship between domestics and their employers is extraordinarily multi-dimensional and complex but, at its essence, I will argue, it is one of exploitation. It may appear too obvious to even state that domestic servants have always been an exploited group of workers. But I submit that this labor arrangement goes far beyond the exploitation in the economic sense in which the term is usually used. What makes domestic service as an occupation more profoundly exploitive than other comparable occupations grows out of the precise element that makes it unique: the personal relationship between employer and employee. What might appear to be the basis of a more humane, less alienating work arrangement allows for a level of psychological exploitation unknown in other occupations. The typical employer extracts more than labor. This fact was suggested by the employers' preference for an individual woman over a cleaning service and the numerous statements in which employers made clear that work performance was not their highest priority in evaluating their domestics. The personality of the workers and the kinds of relationships employers were able to establish with them were as or more important considerations. As historian David Katzman has stated, "In domestic employment a personal relationship is part of the job, and the worker is hired not for her labor alone but also for her personality traits."[2]

Why are these aspects so important? And what, exactly, are employers seeking from these relationships? The psychological exploitation of domestics is highly significant for, I submit, it has the two essential functions of affording the employers the self-enhancing satisfactions that emanate from having the presence of an inferior and validating the employers' lifestyle, ideology, and social world, from their familial interrelations to the economically and racially stratified system in which they live.

These aspects of domestic service—these ego and system-supporting psychological functions—as well as the low-cost labor it provides may constitute part of the explanation for its immemorial and ubiquitous world history and its tenacious presence in contemporary American life. And it is in the examination of these dynamics that we can begin to identify the impact this occupation has on the social structure—an impact, I hope to show, fundamentally conservative and reproductive of hierarchical social forms.

Psychological exploitation need not be overtly harsh. It is indeed easily identifiable in deference demands, in the treatment of others as invisible or non-humans, and in the use of them as "windows to exotica." But the exploitation may be just as powerful when it is disguised in maternalism, in gift-giving, and in tolerance for irresponsibility. It is the motivation for and the belief system behind such apparently benevolent gestures that make them, in fact, highly beneficial to the employer at the psychological expense of the domestic.

The psychological exploitation of female domestics by female employers is based in the two dynamics that I contend form the foundation of the relationship between the women: rituals of deference and maternalism. . . .

DEFERENCE

Erving Goffman has defined deference as a type of ceremonial activity "which functions as a symbolic means by which appreciation is regularly conveyed to a recipient."[3] Although deference may exist between status equals (called "symmetrical deference"), it is more commonly thought of, and its use in this discussion will be, "as something a subordinate owes to his superordinate."[4] What is important about deferential behavior between non-equals is that it confirms the inequality and each party's position in the relationship to the other. If the superordinate believes the relationship to be unequal, one might ask, why are such behaviors necessary? Because one's consciousness is confirmed only by that of another; one's superior position exists only in relation to another. The inferior other must recognize the superior as such and must exhibit confirming behaviors. To do otherwise is to "disconfirm the selves of the participants" and risk eliciting a negative response from the more powerful superordinate.[5] When the superordinate is an employer who expects elaborate forms of deference, the risk is job loss. The domestics I interviewed fully understood that the deferential performance was an integral part of the job expectations of their work.[6]

Goffman has stated that deference behaviors, as all ceremonial acts, are quite varied in character: they may be linguistic, gestural, spatial, task-embedded (related to the attitude and manner with which the individual performs tasks), or part of the communication structure (who initiates speech, speaks more frequently, receives more attention, et cetera). And deference may take the form of avoidance rituals or presentation rituals.[7]

It was not surprising that I encountered instances of all of the above forms of deference within this highly deferential occupation. Three types of linguistic deference are extremely common: most domestics are called by their first names and are expected to call their employers by their last names; both employers and domestics refer to domestics as "girls," regardless of age; and employers appreciate respectful and deferential terms like "Ma'am.". . .

How do domestics feel about being called by their first names and being referred to as "girls"? A few seemed indifferent ("No, it doesn't bother me none. That's just what people say") but most, like Odette Harris, disliked such language (a dislike, however, never expressed to employers):

> I didn't like it. Why am I your "girl"? I didn't like it because it sounded like ownership. Like masters and slaves, talking about "my." . . . But you had to accept being called a "girl" and being called by your first name. You would prefer to be addressed as "Miss" but there wasn't anything you could do so you accepted it. . . . They never referred to us as "ladies." They figured it's too nice for us. We're not "ladies."

That employers used "girl" was not unexpected; that domestics used it also was intriguing. My attempts at probing this with domestics yielded little: "Everybody says that": "I don't know. I always say 'girl.' " The explanations that were offered by domestics for their using "girl" for themselves and "lady" and "woman" for employers indicated only that they did it out of habit, conforming to the language use they heard around them. I consider their using these terms an unexamined remnant of what Fanon called the "colonized mind." Language, like other socially constructed systems, usually serves the interests of the powerful. Even when one is conscious of oppressive elements in a language, it is difficult to eliminate them from one's vocabulary. (For example, try avoiding the myriad negative uses of "black" and "dark" that form the foundation of racism in English: blacklist, blackball, the black market, a black heart, a dark day in history, the forces of darkness, a dark mood, et cetera.) The powerless may accept some of the vocabulary and definitions of the dominant society even when degrading and inaccurate; more often than not, however, they retrieve their dignity by altering definitions and operating on the basis of different values.[8]

Domestics concurred that employers enjoyed being called deferential terms like "ma'am." Recall that Margo Townsend, the director of a social service and training program for domestics, had said this was part of the reason Northern employers preferred Southern black women over Northern: "They would stipulate, 'I want a Southern girl.' They liked the 'Yes, Ma'am' and the 'Yes, Sir.' They *loved* that." May Lund's remarks exemplify those of all the domestics: "Before, I used to 'Yes, Ma'am' and 'Yes, Sir' them to death. No matter how much work they piled on: 'OK, all right.' They just want you to agree." . . .

My own way of discovering the power of such deferential language was revealing. Although Ms. Caton and I had agreed at our interview that I would start working for her the following week, she called me the night before I was to begin and expressed hesitancy about hiring me because "you seem so well educated." Because I had completed my first set of domestic jobs, I had, in fact, gone to this interview somewhat carelessly relaxed: I carried myself and spoke in a natural way, without the deliberately subservient manner I had feigned during my first set of job interviews (when I questioned if I could successfully pass myself off as a domestic). Because her call caused me concern about retaining the job, I arrived the following day looking especially shabby (baggy slacks, old work shirt, cotton headscarf tied Southern-style) and with an exaggeratedly subservient demeanor (standing less erect, eyes usually averted from hers, a tentativeness of movement). Most important, I said almost nothing, asked the few necessary questions in a soft unassertive voice, and responded to her directions with "Yes, Ma'am." I was rather shocked at her obvious pleasure over and total lack of suspicion about this performance, especially since she had encountered me without it the previous week. To me I felt like an absurd and transparent caricature of Stepin Fetchit; her mind, however, was clearly eased of the apprehensions she had had about my suitability for the job. She did not question the change; my behavior now expressed my belief in my inferiority in relation to her and thus my acceptance of her superiority in relation to me. Her desire for that confirmation from me was apparently strong enough to erase from her memory the contradiction of my previous behavior. . . .

This privilege of familiarity affords the employer another kind of opportunity beyond reinforcing inequality. For many, their contact with their domestic is the closest relationship they have with a lower-class or Third World person. Talking with the domestic is a chance to explore what they assume is a very different lifestyle. The domestics I interviewed reported having been asked "very personal questions"—about their finances, children, marital situations—that clearly had made them uncomfortable. Some dismissed it casually ("They're the biggest gossips in the world!") or felt it came from the women's leading lonely and boring lives. But others felt it was more significant. Nancy Clay said:

> They want to know all your business so they know just where you're coming from. They tell you some of their problems so that you'll tell them your business. It's knowledge for control they want. They're uneasy if they don't know enough about you, if they don't know what you're thinking.

And May Lund attributes it to racial curiosity:

> They've read or heard a lot about black people. They know we've been an oppressed people and they want to know what keeps us going. And they want to know how you handle stress, how you manage to do all you have to do. They want to know your secrets.

However, giving an answer that in some way satisfied the employer was a necessary survival strategy. No domestic reported having told an employer that what she had asked was none of her business or was something about which the domestic did not choose to talk. A few suggested they sometimes fabricated stories ("Oh, I tell her anything") but most said they answered in a way that would both satisfy the employer and protect some of their privacy. It is reasonable to assume, however, that the more powerless the domestic felt, the more she might acquiesce to the mistress' inquisitiveness and actually reveal more about her personal life than she wanted or would later choose to admit to me. Live-in workers, particularly recent migrants and the foreign-born, would be more vulnerable to this type of exploitation because of their precarious positions.

In his 1953 study of blacks in Amherst, David Chaplin, too, discovered that domestic servants "found themselves drawn into a peculiar relationship involving self-abasing exposés of the most intimate details of their private lives as part of a quite unconscious bargain with paternalistic employers. Female domestics were subject to a sort of verbal voyeurism on the part of their mistresses.[9] And he, too, found lies to be sometimes employed to satisfy the mistresses' needs:

> This situation suggested to the servants, consciously or otherwise, the possibility of playing on the sympathy or lurid imagination of their employers by elaborating and often inventing debasing anecdotes about their private lives. They were, in effect, catering to the least complimentary elements of the Negro stereotype.[10]

Chaplin's comments lead us to another aspect of this type of "verbal voyeurism." Beyond the fact that by asking such questions the mistresses are asserting that their superior position gives them the right to such intrusive familiarity, beyond displaying a natural curiosity about another person and culture, they may also be looking for titillation and for confirmation of their negative stereotypes about the personal lives of black people. A part of traditional American racist stereotyping is the belief in the less inhibited social and sexual life of black people. This belief reinforces the overall image of black inferiority, since mental activity and self discipline are valued in the Western ethos while sensuality and lack of discipline are disdained.[11] Employers' encouragement of lively stories about domestics' personal lives both satisfies their desire for gossip and, more significantly, confirms their belief in the inferiority of black/domestic workers/the lower classes—a belief that is part of the justification of a system that maintains such people in a disadvantaged position. The use of domestics as "windows to exotica," then, is hardly the innocuous interchange it appears to be.

A related, though less prevalent, type of familiarity between the women is employers' using domestics as confidantes. Some domestics heard details of their employers' extramarital affairs; many heard about strains in employers' marriages. In the South, Elizabeth Roy's employer, after sharing the details of the causes and incidents leading to her divorce, told Ms. Roy: "I've told you things that I wouldn't even tell my mother.' We were friends! When she was in trouble, I was too. When she cried, I cried." Domestics as confidantes are not rare. Former domestic Jane Louis explains it this way:

> Most employers like to talk to the people who work for them because you're not in their circle, you're not going to tell anybody who's important to them. I've been like a confidante. . . . They talk to you anyplace. A white person will go up to a black stranger and tell them very private things—because they know it's not going to go.

Using a domestic as a confidante may, in fact, be evidence of the distance in even the closest of these relationships. Employers can feel free to tell domestics secrets they would not share with their friends or family precisely because the domestic is so far from being socially and psychologically significant to the employer. As physically close as the domestic may be, she is so existentially distant in the mind of the employer that the employer does not even entertain the possibility of the domestic's divulging secrets to those within the employer's social universe. And the employer does not care what the domestic thinks of her for, as Fanon suggested, a person cannot be hurt or insulted by the judgments of those she genuinely believes to be her inferior. . . .

Ingratiating behavior has been displayed by many categories of subordinate people because of dominant groups' desire for it. Domestic servants, Afro-Americans, and women are three such groups that have been encouraged to incorporate ingratiation into their encounters with employers, whites, and men, respectively. It was not surprising that a few of the domestics were ingratiating even during our interviews (all older Southern-born women) and many more described having so performed when on their jobs. I watched the personalities of two of the domestics with whom I worked change dramatically when they interacted with their employers and their employers' teenage children. I watched this performance and knew how much it hid. In interacting with employers, these women put on a mask that covered their real selves most effectively. For some domestics, Jacklyn Cock's observation is unquestionably true: "The domestic worker's main mode of adaption is the adoption of a mask of deference as a protective disguise.[12]

Throughout the literature on "Uncle Tomming" runs the debate about the degree to which the person consciously performs without accepting its premises of inferiority or actually comes to believe its premises and thus becomes the role. This debate is a microcosmic version of the discussion among British sociologists about whether there are genuine "deferential workers"—that is, categories of workers who both behave deferentially and accept their subordinate position" as a necessary, acceptable, and even desirable part in a natural system of inequality.[13] Both of these debates entertain the possibility that there may be some groups of people who believe that their own group is innately inferior and is justifiably on the bottom of a legitimately inegalitarian social system. Both discussions are sophisticated versions of the search for the "happy slave." Empirical efforts to find such "deferential workers" have failed.[14] As they must. . . .

. . . The words "paternalism" and "maternalism" are not equivalent in their conceptual or social meanings. If paternalism is indeed part of the tradition of patriarchal authority, an authority that stretched from the household head to the kings and church leaders to God himself, there is no comparable "matriarchal authority" in the West of which maternalism is a part. Paternalism is one aspect of a political-economic-ideological power base, the aspect that relates to the exchange of patriarchal protections for service and loyalty; maternalism, on the other hand, is a concept related to women's supportive intrafamilial roles of nurturing, loving, and attending to affective needs. The very different connotations of these apparently parallel words reflect the distinct gender roles in the social structures of the West.

The importance of the employer's being female in affecting the position, tone, and dynamics of the relationship cannot be overestimated. Though the role of employer is a masculine one, a woman in the position alters the way it is both viewed and executed. . . .

All females share a secondary gender position in the society. The female employer of a domestic has lower social and familial status than her male counterpart. Her knowledge of that, her awareness of the limitations on her options because of that status, and her internalization, to whatever degree, of the legitimacy of her inferiority place her in a different position from the male employer in relation to the domestic.

Both the female employer and the female domestic have been socialized to consider themselves and other women inferior. Additionally, both women know that the female employer is not the ultimate authority in the household. Though the husband of the employer usually plays an indirect role, it may be pivotal. Recall that in every case in which an employer wanted to withhold Social Security tax, it was her husband's decision to do so. And a number of my interviewees described situations in which misunderstandings between the mistress and the domestic were reported to him for resolution. . . .

Both women's having internalized some belief about their inherent inferiority as women, both knowing there is an external power holding more social status than either of them can ever attain and holding final say over various aspects and even the existence of their arrangements, make their interrelations different from those in which one or both parties is male. The employer might herself be a material and psychological dependent. She has the luxury of identifying with power but she is not the ultimate power. Both she and the domestic know this. The domestic must show deference to an agent of a real power; she must show deference to a second-class power figure for survival. Might the fact that the employer is "inferior" in gender and a pseudo-authority contribute to both women's and the society's low regard for the occupation of domestic servant?

And might the fact that the work is what has traditionally been "women's work" have a similar result? The low regard for this sphere of labor—whether paid or unpaid—has been well documented.[15] The female employer, regardless of the degree to which she may have chosen to buy her way out of it, knows that she is seen as responsible for all household maintenance and that this is devalued work. She perceives the person she hires to do such work as doing *her* work in a way the male employer does not. The domestic is something more than an employee; she is an extension of, a surrogate for, the woman of the house. And she operates in what is increasingly the least prestigious realm of women's activities. This view of the domestic on the part of the employer—as an extension of the more menial part of herself rather than as an autonomous employee—may help to explain why the women tend to see domestic service as a more informal arrangement than other occupations.

And, more important, the employer's low regard for this "women's work" can combine with her own sexism, racism, and class prejudice to further degrade the work and the groups already subordinate in the "three structures of power" in the United States (women, people of color, and the lower classes). For some employers, like Alberta Putnam, it is incongruous to hire a man to do such work: "I would feel uncomfortable with a man in that position. I wouldn't feel right giving him orders like that. I even feel funny asking my husband to clean the dishes." For some, like Holly Woodward's husband, it is incongruous to hire a middle-class person: "Then there was Patricia, a fascinating British girl. Her father was an actor and she wasn't sure what she wanted to do. My husband was against hiring her. He told me, 'You don't want help like that around.' " And it may be assumed that for some employers—particularly in the South, Southwest, and Far West, where the servant population has been almost exclusively black, Mexican-American, Native American, and Asian-American—it is incongruous to hire a white. One can begin to see why the lower-class woman of color, just *because* of this society's sexism, racism, and class prejudice, might be psychologically the most desirable "type" for a position of servitude and why being associated with this archetypical "women's work" further degrades her—even, or perhaps especially, in the eyes of her female employer. The employer benefits from the degradation because it underscores the power and advantage (easily interpreted as the rightness) of being white and middle-class.

And the employer simultaneously contributes to the continuation of gender subordination in the society: by hiring another woman to do her work, she solves the problems of the tediousness of housework and (if she is employed) of women having "double duty" in a way that does not challenge patriarchal ideas of appropriate "women's work." None of my interviewees—not the young Ph.D.'s any more than the older employers who had never worked—was pressuring her husband to take more household responsibility. For these women, the masculist idea that housework is "women's work" remained unchallenged. They were willing to take full advantage of the class and racial inequities generated by this social system to mitigate against their gender disadvantage.

It is clearly significant that the domestic represents the employer in the most devalued area of the employer's activities. If, indeed, she sees the domestic as an extension of herself, it is of her least capable and least "feminine" self. Any identification the employer has with the domestic is a negative identification. The menial, unintelligent, physically strong, irresponsible, weak-charactered servant provides a convenient contrast figure upon whom might be projected those aspects of herself most despised and feared. As stated, for this kind of role, the lower-class black domestic, removed from the employer by class, culture, and color, might be particularly useful.[16]

Another important consequence of both parties' being women is the fact that the success of the arrangement is measured by both more in terms of the quality of the relationship than the practical work aspects. Comments like those of domestic Elizabeth Roy and employer Karen Edwards were common:

> The worst thing that can happen in domestic work is a poor understanding with your employer. A bad relationship makes the work that much harder. That's it; a bad relationship. Then you've really got a hard job. You dread it. (Ms. Roy)

> I want reliability, honesty, niceness. The quality of the work is probably the least important thing. (Ms. Edwards)

That women's value system and morality are different from men's has been demonstrated by a number of writers.[17] Though explanations of this vary, the conclusions are consistent: women are more empathetic, caring, service-oriented, relationship oriented, and concerned with others' feelings. Women "judge themselves in terms of their ability to care" and the "feminine personality comes to define itself in relation and connection to other people."[18] This tendency to emphasize relationships helps explain why many employers and domestics placed a higher value on working with an amiable and pleasant person than on more practical aspects of the work situation. (As would be expected, this attitude was more pervasive with domestics than with employers, and more true of employers who wanted childcare, were not working, or were widowed than those not needing childcare or companionship from the domestic.) But this "caring" and "empathy" that are unquestionably a part of the maternalism from employer to domestic must be scrutinized carefully.

The maternalism dynamic is based on the assumption of a superordinate-subordinate relationship. While maternalism may protect and nurture, it also degrades and insults. The "caring" that is expressed in maternalism might range from an adult-to-child to a human-to-pet kind of caring but, by definition (and by the evidence presented by my data), it is not human-to-equal-human caring. The female employer, with her motherliness and protectiveness and generosity, is expressing in a distinctly feminine way her lack of respect for the domestic as an autonomous, adult employee. While the female employer typically creates a more intimate relationship with a domestic than her male counterpart does, this should not be interpreted as meaning she values the human worth of the domestic any more highly than does the more impersonal male employer. Her ideas about the domestic are not different; her style and her needs are. . . .

My interviewees' statements make it clear that this remains an important part of employers' conceptualizations of domestics. For example, when describing a time when her housecleaner criticized her for working outside the home, Jocelyn Minor said:

I remember there was a kind of veiled reproach. I said to her, "What will you do after you get married?" She said, "Oh, I'm going to stay home. I believe a wife should stay home after she marries." And I'm quite certain that was meant as a reproach. But I didn't take it seriously. I regarded her as an ignorant child.

How old was she?

About twenty-two going on ten. . . .

Viewing the domestic as childlike justifies treating her maternalistically. Her acceptance of such treatment "proves" she deserves the treatment, which further justifies the attitude. But it should be kept in mind that the employer has the power in this relationship (enhanced by her greater power by virtue of race and class in the society); the domestic behaves as she must in order to survive. She must accept maternalistic treatment as surely as she must accept being relegated to the kitchen and verbal familiarities that are offensive. These conventions are all very much a "part of the job."

Expressions of maternalism that were related to me included giving gifts, the loaning of money, explaining bills, demanding to meet and approve friends, making business calls for the employee, making travel arrangements for her, and (in the South) interceding on her behalf with the legal system. Because the giving of gifts—especially old clothes—has been an integral part of the domestic service experience all over the world and because it persists today as one of the unique "benefits" of household work, a closer examination of this phenomenon, this ubiquitous expression of maternalism, is considered appropriate.

Ava Pearson's way of operating was typical of employers: "I am an easy person to work for. I'm not hard to get along with and I think that's part of their compensation. But I always gave Alice gifts—old children's clothes, pieces of furniture. And, of course, there was the Christmas bonus." And May Lund's response to such generosity was typical of domestics:

This woman was always giving me her old size five-and-a-half shoes. I wear an eight! But my mother always said, and she did domestic work for years, she said, "No matter what they give you, you take it because one day they're going to give you something worth having." And I dragged those damned five-and-a-half *double A* shoes home! I'd give them to somebody else or throw them away. . . .

Domestics do, indeed, "take . . . whatever they give"—and not only because it might be useful. Domestics know that gifts, like other expressions of maternalism, *must* be accepted. And, further, as Ellen Samuel points out, they know they must appear grateful . . .

I didn't want most of that junk. But you have to take it. It's part of the job, makes them feel like they're being so kind to you. And you have to *appear* grateful. That makes them feel good too. . . .

On some level, the women involved in this one-way gift-giving are aware that it reinforces the inequality of the relationship. It strengthens and provides evidence for the view of the relationship the employer, the initiator of the gifts, prefers—that it is a relationship between a superior and her inferior. For this purpose, it is far more useful than giving a comparable amount in wages. (In fact, raising the wages, another medium of exchange, could threaten to weaken the employer's belief in the inferiority of the domestic; for does not the fact that she will work for low wages help prove her inferiority? "To pay more in cash would be to admit the greater worth of the servant, to give more in kind retains the servant as a dependant whilst reducing his moral worth."[19]) Thus the pervasiveness of gift-giving in domestic service: it, like the many forms of deference demanded and the other manifestations of maternalism, serves to reify the differences between the women—be they in terms of class, race, or human worth. . . .

The purpose of this maternalism is *not* to nurture and enhance growth (as is that, for instance, toward the employer's real children). The main function of the maternalism from employer to domestic is the confirmation of the inferiority of the domestic (and, by extension, her class and racial group). . . .

Because the stealing and drinking supported the negative stereotypes about the lower classes and black people, the presence of such weak-charactered employees benefitted the employers by making them feel superior. Such an employee does more psychologically for her employers than any efficient but dignified domestic ever could.

Just as "it is the anti-Semite who *makes* the Jew" and "it is the racist who creates his inferior," indeed, it is the mistress with her class and racial preconceptions who creates the obsequious, incompetent servant. And for the same reason. The anti-Semite, the racist, and the mistress (obviously not mutually exclusive categories) want the despised others to exist as they have defined them in order to define their own identity as superiors. To maintain the presence of an inferior is to create a setting for the constant enhancement of one's ego by means of the inevitable comparison.

David Katzman, who has done one of the finest historical books on American servitude, recognizes this attraction to the inferior worker, but offers what I consider an inadequate explanation of the phenomenon:

> Some women (like some men) find fulfillment in exercising power over another woman's life. Rather than seeking an intelligent, resourceful, and independent worker, they may want a servant to whom they can feel superior and dominating. Employing a domestic offers them a position of power not otherwise available to housewives.[20]

Employing a domestic to whom one can feel superior offers far more, in my opinion, than "a position of power." And it is largely because of these non-material benefits to employers, I submit, that the occupation has existed in such diverse stratified social systems throughout the world. The presence of the "inferior" domestic, an inferiority evidenced by the performance she is encouraged to execute and her acceptance of demeaning treatment, offers the employer justification for materially exploiting the domestic, ego enhancement as an individual, and a strengthening of the employer's class and racial identities. Even more important, such a presence supports the idea of unequal human worth: it suggests that there might be categories of people (the lower classes, people of color) who are inherently inferior to others (middle and upper classes, whites). And this idea provides ideological justification for a social system that institutionalizes inequality.

This ideological function of domestic servitude is part of what has made this occupation a profoundly conservative element in the varied hierarchical societies in which it has existed. This ideological function—based in rituals of deference and maternalism that are as integral to this occupation as are low pay and low prestige—cannot be overestimated in its importance to the perpetuation of the occupation and the perpetuation of a social system of class, racial, and gender stratification.

NOTES

1 Albert Memmi, *Dominated Man* (New York: Orion Press, 1968), p. 169.
2 David Katzman, "Domestic Service: Woman's Work," in *Women Working,* ed. Ann Stromberg and Shirley Harkness (Palo Alto, Calif.: Mayfield, 1978), p. 382.
3 Erving Goffman, "The Nature of Deference and Demeanor," *American Anthropologist* 58 (1956): 473–502.
4 Ibid., p. 479.
5 Ibid., p. 475.
6 Some of the younger domestics were clearly struggling with this aspect of their work. May Lund, for example, has recently begun to introduce herself to prospective employers as "Mrs. Lund" and has deliberately stopped using "Ma'am."
7 Goffman, "Nature of Deference and Demeanor," pp. 477 and 481.
8 The narratives in John L. Gwaltney's *Drylongso* (New York: Vintage, 1981) illustrate aspects of the alternative value system of some Afro-Americans.
9 David Chaplin, "Domestic Service and the Negro," *Blue Collar World,* ed. Arthur Shostak and William Gomberg (Englewood Cliffs, N.J.: Prentice-Hall, 1964), p. 540.
10 Ibid.
11 See Joel Kovel, *White Racism: A Psychohistory* (New York: Vintage, 1971), ch. 6.
12 Jacklyn Cock, *Maids and Madams* (Johannesburg: Ravan, 1980), p. 103.
13 David Lockwood, "Sources of Variation in Working Class Images of Society," *Sociological Review* 14, no. 3 (1966): 249–67.
14 In addition to Lockwood, see Cock, *Maids and Madams,* and Howard Newby, *The Deferential Worker* (Madison: University of Wisconsin Press, 1979).
15 See Ann Oakley, *The Sociology of Housework* (New York: Pantheon, 1974).
16 This psychodynamic is similar to that described by Winthrop Jordan and Joel Kovel. Both convincingly argue that blacks have been used as "contrast conceptions" to strengthen and unify white America. See Jordan, *White Over Black* (Baltimore: Penguin, 1968), and Kovel, *White Racism.*
17 See especially Nancy Chodorow, *The Reproduction of Mothering* (Berkeley: University of California Press, 1978), and Carol Gilligan, *In A Different Voice* (Cambridge: Harvard University Press, 1982).
18 Nancy Chodorow, "Family Structure and Feminine Personality," *Women, Culture and Society,* ed. Michelle Rosaldo and Louise Lamphere (Stanford, Calif.: Stanford University Press, 1974), p. 44.
19 Michael G. Whisson and William Weil, *Domestic Servants: A Microcosm of "The Race Problem"* (Johannesburg: South African Institute of Race Relations, 1971), p. 43.
20 Katzman, "Domestic Service," p. 384.

"Their Logic Against Them": Contradictions in Sex, Race, and Class in Silicon Valley

Karen J. Hossfeld

The bosses here have this type of reasoning like a seesaw. One day it's "you're paid less because women are different than men," or "immigrants need less to get by." The next day it's "you're all just workers here—no special treatment just because you're female or foreigners."

Well, they think they're pretty clever with their doubletalk, and that we're just a bunch of dumb aliens. But it takes two to use a seesaw. What we're gradually figuring out here is how *to use their own logic against them.*

Filipina circuit board assembler in Silicon Valley (emphasis added)

This chapter examines how contradictory ideologies about sex, race, class, and nationality are used as forms of both labor control and labor resistance in the capitalist workplace today. Specifically, I look at the workplace relationships between Third World immigrant women production workers and their predominantly white male managers in high-tech manufacturing industry in Silicon Valley, California. My findings indicate that in workplaces where managers and workers are divided by sex and race, class struggle can and does take gender- and race-specific forms. Managers encourage women immigrant workers to identify with their gender, racial, and national identities when the managers want to "distract" the workers from their *class* concerns about working conditions. Similarly, when workers have workplace needs that actually *are* defined by gender, nationality, or race, managers tend to deny these identities and to stress the workers' generic class position. Immigrant women workers have learned to redeploy their managers' gender and racial tactics to their own advantage, however, in order to gain more control over their jobs. As the Filipina worker quoted at the beginning of the chapter so aptly said, they have learned to use managers' "own logic against them."

One of the objectives of this chapter is to expand traditional definitions of workplace resistance and control. All too frequently, these definitions have failed to consider the dynamics of gender and racial diversity. Another goal is to add to current theoretical debates about the changing conditions of capitalist, patriarchal, and national labor arrangements. My empirical data verify what Diane Elson and Ruth Pearson (1981a), Maria Patricia Fernandez-Kelly (1983), June Nash and Fernandez-Kelly (1983), Helen Safa (1981), and many others have documented: namely, that the "new" international division of labor is increasingly based on gender, as well as class and nation. In addition, my findings confirm what Rachel Grossman (1979), Lenny Siegel (1980), and Linda Lim (1978) have each suggested: that high-tech industry is at the forefront of these trends toward a globalized, "gendered" labor division. Finally, I hope to inform strategic questions posed by organizers and workers who are faced with the struggle against this increasingly hierarchical and fragmented division of labor. . . .

SILICON VALLEY

The Prototype

"Silicon Valley" refers to the microelectronics-based high-tech industrial region located just south of San Francisco in Santa Clara County, California. The area has been heralded as an economic panacea and as a regional prototype for localities around the globe that seek rapid economic growth and incorporation into the international market. Representatives from more than two thousand local and national governments, from People's Republic of China delegations to the queen of England, have visited the valley in search of a model for their own industrial revitalization. They have been awed by the sparkling, clean-looking facilities and the exuberant young executives who claim to have made riches overnight.[1] But the much-fetishized Silicon Valley "model" that so many seek to emulate implies more than just the potential promise of jobs, revenue, growth, and participation in the technological "revolution.". . .

Since the 1960s, the large U.S. microelectronics manufacturers have been shifting production facilities to "offshore" locations, primarily in Southeast Asia, but also in Mexico, Puerto Rico, and other locations in both the Third World and Europe. Assembly work has been particularly easy to shift abroad since the materials involved are light in weight, small in size, and of relatively low per-unit value. Materials and assembled products are thus easy to transport. Assembly requires little special equipment or skilled labor when performed manually: the work involves relatively low capital investment but is labor-intensive. Frequently, semiconductors are manufactured in the United States, shipped abroad, where they are assembled and sometimes tested, and then shipped back to the United States for final inspection, packaging, and distribution. Increasingly, any one circuit board on the U.S. market represents labor performed in several countries.

The major motivating force in shifting production has been to cut labor costs. Assembly workers in most Third World high-tech outposts are paid only a few dollars a day. According to my informants at the American Electronics Association, assembly workers in the Philippines, for example, earn one-tenth of what they do in Silicon Valley. But which countries the companies choose to go to has depended on other labor and investment considerations as well. The Singapore government, for example, has actively courted multinational high-tech firms and has offered them economic and tax incentives. The governments of Singapore, Korea, and the Philippines have strongly discouraged and in some cases outlawed labor organizing and strikes (although the "investment climate" in the Philippines may change under Corazon Aquino's government). In a global economy that is short on both capital and jobs, microelectronics firms have been able to shop around the world for the most advantageous labor market conditions. . . .

Although most low-paying, high-tech jobs are sent to the periphery and semiperiphery of the world economy, firms continue to employ production workers in Silicon Valley to meet the ongoing need for quickly available prototypic and short-term projects. Thus, during the 1980s, the *percentage* of production work done in the valley declined drastically, as the industry expanded, but the number of production jobs did not decrease significantly. Although most manufacturing done on-site in Silicon Valley involves "higher-tech" stages of the production process, the assembly work that immigrant women engage in closely resembles the same "low-tech" labor done by their "sisters" overseas.

What Silicon Valley offers the numerous other "Silicon dales" and "deserts" that are springing up around the world is not only a model of technological know-how and development, but also—and equally important—a model of labor control based on highly stratified divisions of race, sex, and class. This study suggests that this division of labor stratifies not only Singapore and San Francisco—core and periphery—but workers within the core metropole itself.

Class Structure and the Division of Labor

Close to 200,000 people—one out of every four employees in the San Jose Metropolitan Statistical Area labor force—work in Silicon Valley's microelectronics industry. There are more than 800 manufacturing firms that hire ten or more people each, including 120 "large" firms that each count over 250 employees. An even larger number of small firms hire fewer than ten employees apiece. Approximately half of this high-tech labor force—100,000 employees—works in production-related work: at least half of these workers—an estimated 50,000 to 70,000—are in low-paying, semiskilled operative jobs (Siegel and Borock 1982; *Annual Planning Information* 1983).[2]

The division of labor within the industry is dramatically skewed according to gender and race. Although women account for close to half of the total paid labor force in Santa Clara County both inside and outside the industry, only 18 percent of the managers, 17 percent of the professional employees, and 25 percent of the technicians are female. Conversely, women hold at least 68 percent and by some reports as many as 85 to 90 percent of the valley's high-tech operative jobs. In the companies examined in my study, women made up an average of 90 percent of the assembly and operative workers. Only rarely do they work as production managers or supervisors, the management area that works most closely with the operatives.

Similar disparities exist vis-à-vis minority employment. According to the 1980 census, 26.51 percent of the civilian work force of Santa Clara County was composed of racial minorities. Fifteen percent were Hispanic (all races); 7.5 percent were Asian–Pacific Islanders; 3 percent were Black; 0.5 percent were Native-American; and 0.2 percent were listed as "other races—not Hispanic" (*Annual Planning Information* 1983:96–97). Over 75 percent of the Hispanics were of Mexican descent. Of the 102,000 Asian–Pacific Islanders counted in the 1980 census as living in the area, roughly 28 percent were Filipino or of Filipino descent; 22 percent each were Japanese and Chinese; 11 percent were Vietnamese; 6 percent were Korean; 5 percent were Asian Indian; and less than 2 percent each were of other national origins (*Annual Planning Information* 1983:64). . . .[3]

Both employers and workers interviewed in this study agreed that the lower the skill and pay level of the job, the higher the percentage of Third World immigrant women who were employed. Thus assembly work, which is the least skilled and lowest-paying production job, tends to be done predominantly by Third World women. Entry-level production workers, who work in job categories such as semiconductor processing and assembly, earn an average of $4.50 to $5.50 an hour; experienced workers in these jobs earn from $5.50 to $8.50. At the subcontracting assembly plants I observed, immigrant women accounted for 75 to 100 percent of the production labor force. At only one of these plants did white males account for more than 2 percent of the production workers. More than 90 percent of the managers and owners at these businesses were white males, however.

This occupational structure is typical of the industry's division of labor nationwide. The percentage of women of color in operative jobs is fairly standardized throughout various high-tech centers; what varies is *which* minority groups are employed, not the job categories in which they are employed.[4] . . .

LABOR CONTROL ON THE SHOP FLOOR

Gender and Racial Logic

In Silicon Valley production shops, the ideological battleground is an important arena of class struggle for labor control. Management frequently calls upon ideologies and arrangements concerning sex and race, as well as class, to manipulate worker consciousness and to legitimate the hierarchical division of labor. Management taps both traditional popular stereotypes about the presumed lack of status and limited abilities of women, minorities, and immigrants and the workers' own fears, concerns, and sense of priorities as immigrant women.

But despite management's success in disempowering and devaluing labor, immigrant women workers have co-opted some of these ideologies and have developed others of their own, playing on management's prejudices to the workers' own advantage. In so doing, the workers turn the "logic" of capital against managers, as they do the intertwining logics of patriarchy and racism. The following section examines this sex- and race-based logic and how it affects class structure and struggle. I then focus on women's resistance to this manipulation and their use of gender and racial logics for their own advantage.

From interviews with Silicon Valley managers and employers, it is evident that high-tech firms find immigrant women particularly appealing workers not only because they are "cheap" and considered easily "expendable" but also because management can draw on and further exploit preexisting patriarchal and racist ideologies and arrangements that have affected these women's consciousness and realities. In their dealings with the women, managers fragment the women's multifaceted identities into falsely separated categories of "worker," "ethnic," and "woman." The effect is to increase and play off the workers' vulnerabilities and splinter their consciousness. But I also found limited examples of the women drawing strength from their multifaceted experiences and developing a unified consciousness with which to confront their oppressions. These instances of how the workers have manipulated management's ideology are important not only in their own right but as models. To date, though, management holds the balance of power in this ideological struggle. . . .

I focus primarily on managers' "gender-specific" tactics because management uses race-specific (il)logic much less directly in dealing with workers. Management clearly draws on racist assumptions in hiring and dealing with its work force, but usually it makes an effort to conceal its racism from workers. Management recognizes, to varying degrees, that the appearance of blatant racism against workers is not acceptable, mainly because immigrants have not sufficiently internalized racism to respond to it positively. Off the shop floor, however, the managers' brutal and open racism toward workers was apparent during "private" interviews. Managers' comments demonstrate that racism is a leading factor in capital logic but that management typically disguises racist logic by using the more socially acceptable "immigrant logic." Both American and immigrant workers tend to accept capital's relegation of immigrants to secondary status in the labor market.

Conversely, "gender logic" is much less disguised: management uses it freely and directly to control workers. Patriarchal and sexist ideology is *not* considered inappropriate. Because women workers themselves have already internalized patriarchal ideology, they are more likely to "agree" with or at least accept it than they are racist assumptions. This chapter documents a wide range of sexist assumptions that management employs in order to control and divide workers.

Gender Ideology

A growing number of historical and contemporary studies illustrate the interconnections between patriarchy and capitalism in defining both the daily lives of working women and the nature of work arrangements in general. Sallie Westwood, for example, suggests that on-the-job exploitation of women workers is rooted in part in patriarchal ideology. Westwood states that ideologies "play a vital part in calling forth a sense of self linked to class and gender as well as race. Thus, a patriarchal ideology intervenes on the shopfloor culture to make anew the conditions of work under capitalism" (1985:6).

One way in which patriarchal ideology affects workplace culture is through the "gendering" of workers—what Westwood refers to as "the social construction of masculinity and femininity on the shop floor" (page 6). The forms of work culture that managers encourage, and that women workers choose to develop, are those that reaffirm traditional forms of femininity. This occurs in spite of the fact that, or more likely because, the women are engaged in roles that are traditionally defined as nonfeminine: factory work and wage earning. My data suggest that although factory work and wage earning are indeed traditions long held by working-class women, the dominant *ideology* that such tasks are "unfeminine" is equally traditional. For example, I asked one Silicon Valley assembler who worked a double shift to support a large family how she found time and finances to obtain elaborate manicures, makeup, and hair stylings. She said that they were priorities because they "restored [her] sense of femininity." Another production worker said that factory work "makes me feel like I'm not a lady, so I have to try to compensate.". . .

Specific examples of informal ways in which individual managers encourage gender identification, such as flirting, dating, sexual harassment, and promoting "feminine" behavior, are given below. The most widespread company practice that encourages engenderment, of course, is hiring discrimination and job segregation based on sex.

An example of a company policy that divides workers by gender is found in a regulation one large firm has regarding color-coding of smocks that all employees in the manufacturing division are required to wear. While the men's smocks are color-coded according to occupation, the women's are color-coded by sex, regardless of occupation. This is a classic demonstration of management's encouragement of male workers to identify according to job and class and its discouragement of women from doing the same. Regardless of what women do as workers, the underlying message reads, they are nevertheless primarily women. The same company has other practices and programs that convey the same message. Their company newsletter, for example, includes a column entitled "Ladies' Corner," which runs features on cooking and fashion tips for "the working gal." A manager at this plant says that such "gender tactics," as I call them, are designed to "boost morale by reminding the gals that even though they do unfeminine work, they really are still feminine." But although some women workers may value femininity, in the work world, management identifies feminine traits as legitimation for devaluation.

In some places, management offers "refeminization" perks to help women feel "compensated" for their perceived "defeminization" on the job. A prime example is the now well-documented makeup sessions and beauty pageants for young women workers sponsored by multinational electronics corporations at their Southeast Asian plants (Grossman 1979; Ong 1985). While such events are unusual in Silicon Valley, male managers frequently use flirting and dating as "refeminization" strategies. Flirting and dating in and of themselves certainly cannot be construed as capitalist plots to control workers; however, when they are used as false compensation for and to divert women from poor working conditions and workplace alienation, they in effect serve as a form of labor control. In a society where women are taught that their femininity is more important than other aspects of their lives—such as how they relate to their work—flirting can be divisive. And when undesired, flirting can also develop into a form of sexual harassment, which causes further workplace alienation.

One young Chinese production worker told me that she and a co-worker avoided filing complaints about illegal and unsafe working conditions because they did not want to annoy their white male supervisor, whom they enjoyed having flirt with them. These two women would never join a union, they told me, because the same supervisor told them that all women who join unions "are a bunch of tough, big-mouthed dykes." Certainly these women have the option of ignoring this man's opinions. But that is not easy, given the one-sided power he has over them not only because he is their supervisor, but because of his age, race, and class.

When women workers stress their "feminine" and female characteristics as being counter to their waged work, a contradictory set of results can occur. On one hand, the women may legitimate their own devaluation as workers, and, in seeking identity and solace in their "femininity," discard any interest in improving their working conditions. On the other hand, if turning to their identities as female, mother, mate, and such allows them to feel self-esteem in one arena of their lives, that self-esteem may transfer to other arenas. The outcome is contingent on the ways in which the women define and experience themselves as female or "feminine." Femininity in white American capitalist culture is traditionally defined as passive and ineffectual, as Susan Brownmiller explores (1984). But there is also a female tradition of resistance.

The women I interviewed rarely pose their womanhood or their self-perceived femininity as attributes meriting higher pay or better treatment. They expect *differential* treatment because they are women, but "differential" inevitably means lower paid in the work world. The women present their self-defined female attributes as creating additional needs that detract from their financial value. Femininity, although its definition varies among individuals and ethnic groups, is generally viewed as something that subtracts from a woman's market value, even though a majority of women consider it personally desirable.

In general, both the women and men I interviewed believe that women have many needs and skills discernible from those of male workers, but they accept the ideology that such specialness renders them less deserving than men of special treatment, wages, promotions, and status. . . .

Definitions of femininity and masculinity not only affect the workplace but are in turn affected by it. Gender is produced and reproduced in and through the workplace, as well as outside it. Gender identities and relationships are formed on the work floor both by the labor process organized under capitalism and by workers' resistance to that labor process. "Femininity" in its various permutations is not something all-bad and all-disempowering: women find strength, pride, and creativity in some of its forms. But the ideological counterpositioning of "feminine" as weak, powerless, and submissive and of "masculine" as strong, powerful, and dominant raises yet another problem in the workplace: sexual harassment. For reasons of space, I will not discuss this here. I turn now to one of the other tenets of women workers' multitiered consciousness that employers find advantageous: gender logic that poses women's work as "secondary."

THE LOGIC OF "SECONDARY" WORK

Central to gender-specific capital logic is the assumption that women's paid work is both secondary and temporary. More than 70 percent of the employers and 80 percent of the women workers I interviewed stated that a woman's primary jobs are those of wife, mother, and homemaker, even when she works full time in the paid labor force. Because employers view women's primary job as in the home, and they assume that, prototypically, every woman is connected to a man who is bringing in a larger paycheck, they claim that women do not need to earn a full living wage. Employers repeatedly asserted that they believed the low-level jobs were filled only by women because men could not afford to or would not work for such low wages.

Indeed, many of the women would not survive on what they earned unless they pooled resources. For some, especially the nonimmigrants, low wages did mean dependency on men—or at least on family networks and household units. None of the women I interviewed—immigrant or nonimmigrant—lived alone. Yet most of them would be financially better off without their menfolk. For most of the immigrant women, their low wages were the most substantial and steady source of their family's income. *Eighty percent of the immigrant women workers in my study were the largest per annum earners in their households.*

Even when their wages were primary—the main or only family income—the women still considered men to be the major breadwinners. The women considered their waged work as secondary, both in economic value and as a source of identity. . . .

The majority of women who are earning more than their male family members view their situation negatively and hope it will change soon. They do not want to earn less than they currently do; rather, they want their menfolk to earn more. This was true of women in all the ethnic groups. The exceptions—a vocal minority—were mainly Mexicanas. Lupe, a high-tech worker in her twenties, explained:

> Some of the girls I work with are ridiculous—they think if they earn more than their husbands it will hurt the men's pride. They play up to the machismo. . . . I guess it's not entirely ridiculous, because some of them regularly come in with black eyes and bruises, so the men are something they have to reckon with. But, my God, if I had a man like that I would leave. . . .
>
> My boyfriend's smart enough to realize that we need my paycheck to feed us and my kids. He usually brings home less than I do, and we're both damn grateful for every cent that either of us makes. When I got a raise he was very happy—I think he feels more relieved, not more resentful. But then, he's not a very typical man, no? Anyway, he'd probably change if we got married and had kids of his own—that's when they start wanting to be the king of their castle.

A Korean immigrant woman in her thirties told how her husband was so adamant that she not earn more than he and that the men in the household be the family's main supporters that each time she cashed her paycheck she gave some of her earnings to her teenaged son to turn over to the father as part of his earnings from his part-time job. She was upset about putting her son in a position of being deceitful to his father, but both mother and son agreed it was the only alternative to the father's otherwise dangerous, violent outbursts. . . .

Almost without exception, the women production workers I interviewed—both immigrant and nonimmigrant—saw their present jobs as temporary.

Employers are thus at an advantage in hiring these women at low wages and with little job security. They can play on the women's *own* consciousness as wives and mothers whose primary identities are defined by home and familial roles. While the division of labor prompts the workers to believe that women's waged work is less valuable than men's, the women workers themselves arrive in Silicon Valley with this ideology already internalized. . . .

Any attempts to organize the women workers of Silicon Valley—by unions, communities, political or social groups and by the women themselves—must deal with the articulation of gender, race, and class inequalities in their lives.

RESISTANCE ON THE SHOP FLOOR

There is little incidence in Silicon Valley production shops of *formal* labor militancy among the immigrant women, as evidenced by either union participation or collectively planned mass actions such as strikes. . . .

There is, however, an important, although often subtle, arena in which the women do engage in struggle with management: the ideological battleground. Just as employers and managers harness racist, sexist, and class-based logic to manipulate and control workers, so too workers use this logic against management. In the ideological arena, the women do not merely accept or react to the biased assumptions of managers: they also develop gender-, class-, and race-based logic of their own when it is to their advantage. The goal of these struggles is not simply ideological victory but concrete changes in working conditions. Further, in Silicon Valley, immigrant women workers have found that managers respond more to workers' needs when they are couched in ethnic or gender terms, rather than in class and labor terms. Thus, class struggle on the shop floor is often disguised as arguments about the proper place and appropriate behavior of women, racial minorities, and immigrants.

When asked directly, immigrant women workers typically deny that they engage in any form of workplace resistance or efforts to control their working conditions. This denial reflects not only workers' needs to protect clandestine activities, but also their consciousness about what constitutes resistance and control. In their conversations with friends and co-workers, the women joke about how they outfoxed their managers with female or ethnic "wisdom." Yet most of the women do not view their often elaborate efforts to manipulate their managers' behavior as forms of struggle. Rather, they think of their tactics "just as ways to get by," as several workers phrased it. It is from casual references to these tactics that a portrait of worker logic and resistance emerges.

The workers overwhelmingly agreed that the challenges to management in which they could and did engage were on a small-scale, individual, or small-group level. Several women said they engaged in forms of resistance that they considered "quiet" and unobtrusive: acts that would make a difference to the woman and possibly her co-workers but that management would probably not recognize as resistance. Only rarely was resistance collectively articulated.

The vast majority of these women clearly wish to avoid antagonizing management. Thus, rather than engaging in confrontational resistance strategies, they develop less obvious forms than, say, work stoppages, filing grievances, and straightforwardly refusing to perform certain tasks, all of which have frequently been observed in other industrial manufacturing sectors. Because the more "quiet" forms of resistance and struggle for workplace control engaged in by the women in Silicon Valley are often so discrete and the workers are uncomfortable discussing them, it is probable that there are more such acts and they are broader in scope than my examples imply. As a Chinese woman in her forties who has worked as an operative in the valley for six years explained:

> Everybody who does this job does things to get through the day, to make it bearable. There are some women who will tell you they never do anything unproper or sneaky, but you are not to believe them. The ones that look the most demure are always up to something. . . . There's not anybody here who has never purposefully broken something, slowed down work, told fibs to the supervisor, or some such thing. And there's probably no one but me with my big mouth who would admit it!

As discussed above, it is clear that managers have found effective ways to play off workers' gender, racial, and immigrant consciousness. At the same time, white male managers in particular often have striking misconceptions about the gender and cultural experiences of their workers, and workers can thus frequently confuse them with bogus claims about the women's special needs. Workers can also use real claims that supervisors have tried to co-opt.

A Salvadorean woman, fed up with her supervisor for referring to his Hispanic workers as "mamacitas" and "little mothers" and with admonishing them to "work faster if you want your children to eat," had her husband bring both her own children and several nieces and nephews to pick her up one day. She lined all the children up in front of the supervisor and asked him how fast she would have to work to feed all those mouths. One of the children had been coached, and he told the supervisor that his mother was so tired from working that she did not have time to play with them anymore. The guilt-ridden supervisor, astonished by the large number of children and the responsibility they entailed, eased up on his admonishments and speed-up efforts and started treating the woman with more consideration.

The most frequently mentioned acts of resistance against management and work arrangements were ones that played on the white male managers' consciousness—both false and real—about gender and ethnic culture. Frequently mentioned examples involved workers who turned management's ideologies against them by exploiting their male supervisors' misconceptions about "female problems." A white chip tester testified:

> It's pretty ironic because management seems to have this idea that male supervisors handle female workers better than female supervisors. You know, we're supposed to turn to mush whenever he's around and respect his authority or something. But this one guy we got now lets us walk all over him. He thinks females are flighty and irresponsible because of our hormones—so we make sure to have as many hormone problems as we can. I'd say we each take hormone breaks several times a day. My next plan is to convince him that menstrual blood will turn the solvents bad, so on those days we have to stay in the lunchroom!

A Mexican wafer fabricator, whose unit supervisor was notorious for the "refeminization" perks discussed above, told of how she manipulated the male supervisor's gender logic to disguise what was really an issue of class struggle:

> I was getting really sick from all the chemicals we have to work with, and I was getting a rash from them on my arms. [The manager] kept saying I was exaggerating and gave the usual line about you can't prove what caused the rash. One day we had to use an especially harsh solvent, and I made up this story about being in my sister's wedding. I told him that the solvents would ruin my manicure, and I'd be a mess for the wedding. Can you believe it? He let me off the work! This guy wouldn't pay attention to my rash, but when my manicure was at stake, he let me go!

Of course, letting this worker avoid chemicals for one day because of a special circumstance is more advantageous to management than allowing her and others to avoid the work permanently because of health risks. Nonetheless, the worker was able to carve out a small piece of bargaining power by playing off her manager's gender logic. The contradiction of these tactics that play up feminine frailty is that they achieve short-term, individual goals at the risk of reinforcing damaging stereotypes about women, including the stereotype that women workers are not as productive as men. From the workers' point of view, however, the women are simply using the prejudices of the powerful to the advantages of the weak. . . .

Although the above are isolated examples, they represent tactics that workers can use either to challenge or play off sexist ideology that employers use to legitimate women's low position in the segregated division of labor. Certainly there are not enough instances of such behavior to challenge the inequality between worker and boss, but they do demonstrate to managers that gender logic cannot always be counted on to legitimate inequality between male and female workers. And dissolving divisions between workers *is* a threat to management hegemony.

RACIAL AND ETHNIC LOGIC

Typically, high-tech firms in Silicon Valley hire production workers from a wide spectrum of national groups. If their lack of a common language (both linguistically and culturally) serves to fragment the labor force, capital benefits. Conversely, management may find it more difficult to control workers with whom it cannot communicate precisely. Several workers said they have feigned a language barrier in order to avoid taking instructions; they have also called forth cultural taboos—both real and feigned—to avoid undesirable situations. One Haitian woman, who took a lot of kidding from her employer about voodoo and black magic, insisted that she could not work the night shift because evil spirits were out then. Because she was a good worker, the employer let her switch to days. When I tried to establish whether she believed the evil spirits were real or imagined, she laughed and said, "Does it matter? The result is the same: I can be home at night with my kids."

Management in several plants believed that racial and national diversity minimized solidarity. According to one supervisor, workers were forbidden from sitting next to people of their own nationality (i.e., language group) in order to "cut down on the chatting." Workers quickly found two ways to reverse this decision, using management's own class, racial, and gender logic. Chinese women workers told the supervisor that if they were not "chaperoned" by other Chinese women, their families would not let them continue to work there. Vietnamese women told him that the younger Vietnamese women would not work hard unless they were under the eyes of the older workers and that a group of newly hired Vietnamese workers would not learn to do the job right unless they had someone who spoke their language to explain it to them. Both of these arguments could also be interpreted as examples of older workers wanting to control younger ones in a generational hierarchy, but this was not the case. Afterwards both the Chinese and the Vietnamese women laughed among themselves at their cleverness. Nor did they forget the support needs of workers from other ethnic groups: they argued with the supervisor that the same customs and needs held true for many of the language groups represented, and the restriction was rescinded.

Another example of a large-scale demonstration of interethnic solidarity on the shop floor involved workers playing off supervisors' stereotypes regarding the superior work of Asians over Mexicans. The incident was precipitated when a young Mexicana, newly assigned to an assembly unit in which a new circuit board was being assembled, fell behind in her quota. The supervisor berated her with racial slurs about Mexicans' "laziness" and "stupidity" and told her to sit next to and "watch the Orientals." As a group, the Asian women she was stationed next to slowed down their production, thereby setting the average quota on the new boards at a slower than usual pace. The women were in fits of laughter after work because the supervisor had assumed that the speed set by the Asians was the fastest possible, since they were the "best" workers.

Hispanic workers also turn management's anti-Mexican prejudices against them, as a Salvadorean woman explained:

> First of all, the bosses think everyone from Latin America is Mexican, and they think all Mexicans are dumb. So, whenever they try to speed up production, or give us something we don't want to do, we just act dumb. It's not as if you act smart and you get a promotion or a bonus anyway.

A Mexicana operative confided, "They [management] assume we don't understand much English, but we understand when we want to."

A Chinese woman, who was under five feet tall and who identified her age by saying she was a "grandmother," laughingly told how she had her white male supervisor "wrapped around [her] finger." She consciously played into his stereotype that Asian women are small, timid, and obedient by frequently smiling at and bowing to him and doing her job carefully. But when she had a special need, to take a day or a few hours off, for example, she would put on her best guileless, ingratiating look and, full of apologies, usually obtained it. She also served as a voice for co-workers whom the supervisor considered more abrasive. On one occasion, when three white women in her unit complained about poor lighting and headaches, the supervisor became irritated and did not respond to their complaint. Later that week the Chinese "grandmother" approached him, saying that she was concerned that poor lighting was limiting the workers' productivity. The lighting was quickly improved. This incident illustrates that managers can and do respond to workers' demands when they result in increased productivity.

Some workers see strategies to improve and control their work processes and environments as contradictory and as "Uncle Tomming." Two friends, both Filipinas, debated this issue. One argued that "acting like a China doll" only reinforced white employers' stereotypes, while the other said that countering the stereotype would not change their situation, so they might as well use the stereotype to their advantage. The same analysis applies to women workers who consciously encourage male managers to view women as different from men in their abilities and characteristics. For women and minority workers, the need for short-term gains and benefits and for long-term equal treatment is a constant contradiction. And for the majority of workers, short-term tactics are unlikely to result in long-term equality.

POTENTIAL FOR ORGANIZING

Obviously, the lesson here for organizing is contradictory. Testimonies such as the ones given in these pages clearly document that immigrant women are not docile, servile people who always follow orders, as many employers interviewed for this study claimed. Orchestrating major actions such as family migration so that they could take control of and better their lives has helped these women develop leadership and survival skills. Because of these qualities, many of the women I interviewed struck me as potentially effective labor and community organizers and rank-and-file leaders. Yet almost none of them were interested in collective organizing, because of time limitations and family constraints and because of their lack of confidence in labor unions, the feminist movement, and community organizations. Many were simply too worn out from trying to make ends meet and caring for their families. And for some, the level of inequality and exploitation on the shop floor did not seem that bad, compared to their past experiences. A Salvadorean woman I interviewed exemplified this predicament. Her job as a solderer required her to work with a microscope all day, causing her to develop severe eye and back strain. Although she was losing her eyesight and went home exhausted after working overtime, she told me she was still very happy to be in the United States and very grateful to her employer. "I have nothing to complain about," she told me. "It is such a luxury to know that when I go home all of my children will still be alive." After losing two sons to government-backed terrorist death squads in El Salvador, her work life in Silicon Valley was indeed an improvement. . . .

My findings indicate that Silicon Valley's immigrant women workers have a great deal to gain from organizing, but also a great deal to contribute. They have their numeric strength, but also a wealth of creativity, insight, and experience that could be a shot in the arm to the stagnating national labor movement. They also have a great deal to teach—and learn from—feminist and ethnic community movements. But until these or new alternative movements learn to speak and listen to these women, the women will continue to struggle on their own, individually and in small groups. In their struggle for better jobs and better lives, one of the most effective tactics they have is their own resourcefulness in manipulating management's "own logic against them."

NOTES

1 For a comprehensive analytical description of the development of Silicon Valley as a region and an industry, see Saxenian 1981.

2 These production jobs include the following U.S. Department of Labor occupational titles: semiconductor processor; semiconductor assembler; electronics assembler; and electronics tester. Entry-level wages for these jobs in Silicon Valley in 1984 were $4.00 to $5.50; wages for workers with one to two years or more experience were $5.50 to $8.00 an hour, with testers sometimes earning up to $9.50.

3 "Minority" is the term used by the California Employment Development Department and the U.S. Department of Labor publications in reference to people of color. The statistics do not distinguish between immigrants and nonimmigrants within racial and ethnic groupings.

4 In North Carolina's Research Triangle, for example, Blacks account for most minority employment, whereas in Albuquerque and Texas, Hispanics provide the bulk of the production labor force. Silicon Valley has perhaps the most racially diverse production force, although Hispanics—both immigrant and nonimmigrant—still account for the majority.

Life on the Global Assembly Line

Barbara Ehrenreich and Annette Fuentes

In Ciudad Juarez, Mexico, Anna M. rises at 5 A.M. to feed her son before starting on the two-hour bus trip to the maquiladora (factory). He will spend the day along with four other children in a neighbor's one-room home. Anna's husband, frustrated by being unable to find work for himself, left for the United States six months ago. She wonders, as she carefully applies her new lip gloss, whether she ought to consider herself still married. It might be good to take a night course, become a secretary. But she seldom gets home before eight at night, and the factory, where she stitches brassieres that will be sold in the United States through J. C. Penney, pays only $48 a week.

In Penang, Malaysia, Julie K. is up before the three other young women with whom she shares a room, and starts heating the leftover rice from last night's supper. She looks good in the company's green-trimmed uniform, and she's proud to work in a modern, American-owned factory. Only not quite so proud as when she started working three years ago—she thinks as she squints out the door at a passing group of women. Her job involves peering all day through a microscope, bonding hair-thin gold wires to a silicon chip destined to end up inside a pocket calculator, and at 21, she is afraid she can no longer see very clearly.

Every morning between four and seven, thousands of women like Anna and Julie head out for the day shift. In Ciudad Juárez, they crowd into *ruteras* (run-down vans) for the trip from the slum neighborhoods to the industrial parks on the outskirts of the city. In Penang they squeeze, 60 or more at a time, into buses for the trip from the village to the low, modern factory buildings of the Bayan Lepas free trade zone. In Taiwan, they walk from the dormitories—where the night shift is already asleep in the still-warm beds—through the checkpoints in the high fence surrounding the factory zone.

This is the world's new industrial proletariat: young, female. Third World. Viewed from the "first world," they are still faceless, genderless "cheap labor," signaling their existence only through a label or tiny imprint—"made in Hong Kong," or Taiwan, Korea, the Dominican Republic, Mexico, the Philippines. But they may be one of the most strategic blocks of womenpower in the world of the 1980s. Conservatively, there are 2 million Third World female industrial workers employed now, millions more looking for work, and their numbers are rising every year. Anyone whose image of Third World women features picturesque peasants with babies slung on their backs should be prepared to update it. Just in the last decade, Third World women have become a critical element in the global economy and a key "resource" for expanding multinational corporations.

It doesn't take more than second-grade arithmetic to understand what's happening. In the United States, an assembly-line worker is likely to earn, depending on her length of employment, between $3.10 and $5 an hour. In many Third World countries, a woman doing the same work will earn $3 to $5 a *day*. According to the magazine "Business Asia," in 1976 the average hourly wage for unskilled work (male or female) was 55 cents in Hong Kong, 52 cents in South Korea, 32 cents in the Philippines, and 17 cents in Indonesia. The logic of the situation is compelling: why pay someone in Massachusetts $5 an hour to do what someone in Manila will do for $2.50 a day? Or, as a corollary, why pay a male worker anywhere to do what a female worker will do for 40 to 60 percent less?

And so, almost everything that can be packed up is being moved out to the Third World; not heavy industry, but just about anything light enough to travel—garment manufacture, textiles, toys, footwear, pharmaceuticals, wigs, appliance parts, tape decks, computer components, plastic goods. In some industries, like garment and textile, American jobs are lost in the process, and the biggest losers are women, often black and Hispanic. But what's going on is much more than a matter of runaway shops. Economists are talking about a "new international division of labor," in which the process of production is broken down and the fragments are dispersed to different parts of the world. In general, the low-skilled jobs are farmed out to the Third World, where labor costs are minuscule, while control over the overall process and technology remains safely at company headquarters in "first world" countries like the United States and Japan.

The American electronics industry provides a classic example: circuits are printed on silicon wafers and tested in California; then the wafers are shipped to Asia for the labor-intensive process by which they are cut into tiny chips and bonded to circuit boards; final assembly into products such as calculators or military equipment usually takes place in the United States. Garment manufacture too is often broken into geographically separated steps, with the most repetitive, labor-intensive jobs going to the poor countries of the southern hemisphere. Most Third World countries welcome whatever jobs come their way in the new division of labor, and the major international development agencies—like the World Bank and the United States Agency for International Development (AID)—encourage them to take what they can get.

So much any economist could tell you. What is less often noted is the *gender* breakdown of the emerging international division of labor. Eighty to 90 percent of the low-skilled assembly jobs that go to the Third World are performed by women—in a remarkable switch from earlier patterns of foreign-dominated industrialization. Until now, "development" under the aegis of foreign corporations has usually meant more jobs for men and—compared to traditional agricultural society—a diminished economic status for women. But multinational corporations and Third World governments alike consider assembly-line work—whether the product is Barbie dolls or missile parts—to be "women's work."

One reason is that women can, in many countries, still be legally paid less than men. But the sheer tedium of the jobs adds to the multinationals' preference for women workers—a preference made clear, for example, by this ad from a Mexican newspaper: *We need female workers; older than 17, younger than 30; single and without children; minimum education primary school, maximum education one year of preparatory school* [high school]; *available for all shifts.*

It's an article of faith with management that only women can do, or will do, the monotonous, painstaking work that American business is exporting to the Third World. Bill Mitchell, whose job is to attract United States businesses to the Bermudez

Industrial Park in Ciudad Juárez told us with a certain macho pride: "A man just won't stay in this tedious kind of work. He'd walk out in a couple of hours." The personnel manager of a light assembly plant in Taiwan told anthropologist Linda Gail Arrigo: "Young male workers are too restless and impatient to do monotonous work with no career value. If displeased, they sabotage the machines and even threaten the foreman. But girls? At most, they cry a little."

In fact, the American businessmen we talked to claimed that Third World women genuinely enjoy doing the very things that would drive a man to assault and sabotage. "You should watch these kids going into work," Bill Mitchell told us. "You don't have any sullenness here. They smile." A top-level management consultant who specializes in advising American companies on where to relocate their factories gave us this global generalization: "The [factory] girls genuinely enjoy themselves. They're away from their families. They have spending money. They can buy motorbikes, whatever. Of course it's a regulated experience too—with dormitories to live in—so it's a healthful experience."

What is the real experience of the women in the emerging Third World industrial work force? The conventional Western stereotypes leap to mind: You can't really compare, the standards are so different. . . . Everything's easier in warm countries. . . . They really don't have any alternatives. . . . Commenting on the low wages his company pays its women workers in Singapore, a Hewlett-Packard vice-president said, "They live much differently here than we do. . . ." But the differences are ultimately very simple. To start with, they have less money.

The great majority of the women in the new Third World work force live at or near the subsistence level for one person, whether they work for a multinational corporation or a locally owned factory. In the Philippines, for example, starting wages in U.S.-owned electronics plants are between $34 to $46 a month, compared to a cost of living of $37 a month; in Indonesia the starting wages are actually about $7 a month less than the cost of living. "Living," in these cases, should be interpreted minimally: a diet of rice, dried fish, and water—a Coke might cost a half-day's wages—lodging in a room occupied by four or more other people. Rachael Grossman, a researcher with the Southeast Asia Resource Center, found women employees of U.S. multinational firms in Malaysia and the Philippines living four to eight in a room in boardinghouses, or squeezing into tiny extensions built onto squatter huts near the factory. Where companies do provide dormitories for their employees, they are not of the "healthful," collegiate variety implied by our corporate informant. Staff from the American Friends Service Committee report that dormitory space is "likely to be crowded with bed rotation paralleling shift rotation—while one shift works, another sleeps, as many as twenty to a room." In one case in Thailand, they found the dormitory "filthy," with workers forced to find their own place to sleep among "splintered floorboards, rusting sheets of metal, and scraps of dirty cloth."

Wages do increase with seniority, but the money does not go to pay for studio apartments or, very likely, motorbikes. A 1970 study of young women factory workers in Hong Kong found that 88 percent of them were turning more than half their earnings over to their parents. In areas that are still largely agricultural (such as parts of the Philippines and Malaysia), or places where male unemployment runs high (such as northern Mexico), a woman factory worker may be the sole source of cash income for an entire extended family.

But wages on a par with what an 11-year-old American could earn on a paper route and living conditions resembling what Engels found in 19th-century Manchester are only part of the story. The rest begins at the factory gate. The work that multinational corporations export to the Third World is not only the most tedious, but often the most hazardous part of the production process. The countries they go to are, for the most part, those that will guarantee no interference from health and safety inspectors, trade unions, or even free-lance reformers. As a result, most Third World factory women work under conditions that already have broken or will break their health—or their nerves—within a few years, and often before they've worked long enough to earn any more than a subsistence wage.

Consider first the electronics industry, which is generally thought to be the safest and cleanest of the exported industries. . . .

One study in South Korea found that most electronics assembly workers developed severe eye problems after only one year of employment: 88 percent had chronic conjunctivitis; 44 percent became near-sighted; and 19 percent developed astigmatism. A manager for Hewlett-Packard's Malaysia plant, in an interview with Rachael Grossman, denied that there were any eye problems. "These girls are used to working with 'scopes.' We've found no eye problems. But it sure makes me dizzy to look through those things."

Electronics, recall, is the "cleanest" of the exported industries. Conditions in the garment and textile industry rival those of any 19th-century (or 20th—see below) sweatshop. The firms, generally local subcontractors to large American chains such as J. C. Penney and Sears, as well as smaller manufacturers, are usually even more indifferent to the health of their employees than the multinationals. Some of the worst conditions have been documented in South Korea, where the garment and textile industries have helped spark that country's "economic miracle." Workers are packed into poorly lit rooms, where summer temperatures rise above 100 degrees. Textile dust, which can cause permanent lung damage, fills the air. When there are rush orders, management may require forced overtime of as much as 48 hours at a stretch, and if that seems to go beyond the limits of human endurance, pep pills and amphetamine injections are thoughtfully provided. In her diary (originally published in a magazine now banned by the South Korean government) Min Chong Suk, 30, a sewing-machine operator, wrote of working from 7 A.M. to 11:30 P.M. in a garment factory: "When [the apprentices] shake the waste threads from the clothes, the whole room fills with dust, and it is hard to breathe. Since we've been working in such dusty air, there have been increasing numbers of people getting tuberculosis, bronchitis, and eye diseases. Since we are women, it makes us so sad when we have pale, unhealthy, wrinkled faces like dried-up spinach. . . . It seems to me that no one knows our blood dissolves into the threads and seams, with sighs and sorrow."

In all the exported industries, the most invidious, inescapable health hazard is stress. On their home ground United States corporations are not likely to sacrifice productivity for human comfort. On someone else's home ground, however, anything goes. Lunch breaks may be barely long enough for a woman to stand in line at the canteen or hawkers' stalls. Visits to the bathroom are treated as privilege; in some cases, workers must raise their hands for permission to use the toilet, and waits up to a half hour are common. Rotating shifts—the day shift one week, the night shift the next—wreak havoc with sleep patterns. Because inaccuracies or failure to meet production quotas can mean substantial pay losses, the pressures are quickly internalized; stomach ailments and nervous problems are not unusual in the multinationals' Third World female work force. In some situations, good work is as likely to be punished as slow or shoddy work. . . .

As if poor health and the stress of factory life weren't enough to drive women into early retirement, management actually encourages a high turnover in many industries. "As you know, when seniority rises, wages rise," the management consultant to U.S. multinationals told us. He explained that it's cheaper to train a fresh supply of teenagers than to pay experienced women higher wages. "Older" women, aged 23 or 24, are likely to be laid off and not rehired.

We estimate, based on fragmentary data from several sources, that the multinational corporations may already have used up (cast off) as many as 6 million Third World workers—women who are too ill, too old (30 is over the hill in most industries), or too exhausted to be useful any more. Few "retire" with any transferable skills or savings. The lucky ones find husbands. . . .

One of the most serious occupational hazards that Julie and millions of women like her may face is the lifelong stigma of having been a "factory girl." Most of the cultures favored by multinational corporations in their search for cheap labor are patriarchal in the grand old style: any young woman who is not under the wing of a father, husband, or older brother must be "loose." High levels of unemployment among men, as in Mexico, contribute to male resentment of working women. . . .

Anthropologist Patricia Fernandez, who has worked in a *maquiladora* herself, believes that the stigmatization of working women serves, indirectly, to keep them in line. "You have to think of the kind of socialization that girls experience in a very Catholic—or, for that matter, Muslim—society. The fear of having a 'reputation' is enough to make a lot of women bend over backward to be 'respectable' and ladylike, which is just what management wants." She points out that in northern Mexico, the tabloids delight in playing up stories of alleged vice in the *maquiladoras*—indiscriminate sex on the job, epidemics of venereal disease, fetuses found in factory rest rooms. "I worry about this because there are those who treat you differently as soon as they know you have a job at a *maquiladora*," one woman told Fernandez. "Maybe they think that if you have to work, there is a chance you're a whore."

And there is always a chance you'll wind up as one. Probably only a small minority of Third World factory workers turn to prostitution when their working days come to an end. But it is, as for women everywhere, the employment of last resort, the only thing to do when the factories don't need you and traditional society won't—or, for economic reasons, can't—take you back. In the Philippines, the brothel business is expanding as fast as the factory system. If they can't use you one way, they can use you another.

There has been no international protest about the exploitation of Third World women by multinational corporations—no thundering denunciations from the floor of the United Nations' general assembly, no angry resolutions from the Conference of the

Non-Aligned Countries. Sociologist Robert Snow, who has been tracing the multinationals on their way south and eastward for years, explained why: "The Third World governments *want* the multinationals to move in. There's cutthroat competition to attract the corporations.". . .

In the competition for multinational investment, local governments advertise their women shamelessly, and an investment brochure issued by the Malaysian government informs multinational executives that: "The manual dexterity of the Oriental female is famous the world over. Her hands are small, and she works fast with extreme care. . . . Who, therefore, could be better qualified by nature and inheritance, to contribute to the efficiency of a bench-assembly production line than the Oriental girl?". . .

Many "host" governments are willing to back up their advertising with whatever amount of brutality it takes to keep "their girls" just as docile as they look in the brochures. Even the most polite and orderly attempts to organize are likely to bring down overkill doses of police repression:

In Inchon, South Korea, women at the Dong-II Textile Company (which produces fabrics and yarn for export to the United States) had succeeded in gaining leadership in their union in 1972. But in 1978 the government-controlled, male-dominated Federation of Korean Trade Unions sent special "action squads" to destroy the women's union. Armed with steel bars and buckets of human excrement, the goons broke into the union office, smashed the office equipment, and smeared the excrement over the women's bodies and in their hair, eyes, and mouths.

Crudely put (and incidents like this do not inspire verbal delicacy), the relationship between many Third World governments and the multinational corporations is not very different from the relationship between a pimp and his customers. The governments advertise their women, sell them and keep them in line for the multinational "johns." But there are other parties to the growing international traffic in women— such as the United Nations' Industrial Development Organization (UNIDO), the World Bank, and the United States government itself.

UNIDO, for example, has been a major promotor of "free trade zones." These are enclaves within nations that offer multinational corporations a range of creature comforts, including: freedom from paying taxes and export duties; low-cost water power, and buildings; exemption from whatever labor laws may apply in the country as a whole; and, in some cases, such security features as barbed-wire, guarded checkpoints, and government-paid police.

Then there is the World Bank, which over the past decade has lent several billion dollars to finance the roads, airports, power plants, and even the first-class hotels that multinational corporations need in order to set up business in Third World countries. The Sri Lankan garment industry, which like other Third World garment industries survives by subcontracting to major Western firms, was set up on the advice of the World Bank and with a $20 million World Bank loan. This particular experiment in "development" offers young women jobs at a global low of $5 for a six-day week. Gloria Scott, the head of the World Bank's Women and Development Program, sounded distinctly uncomfortable when we asked her about the bank's role in promoting the exploitation of Third World women. "Our job is to help eliminate poverty. It is not our responsibility if the multinationals come in and offer such low wages. It's the responsibility of the governments." However, the Bank's 1979 World Development Report speaks strongly of the need for "wage restraint" in poor countries.

But the most powerful promoter of exploitative conditions for Third World women workers is the United States government itself. For example, the notoriously repressive Korean textile industry was developed with the help of $400 million in aid from the U.S. State Department. Malaysia became a low-wage haven for the electronics industry, thanks to technical assistance financed by AID and to U.S. money (funneled through the Asian Development Bank) to set up free trade zones. Taiwan's status as a "showcase for the free world" and a comfortable berth for multinationals is the result of three decades of financial transfusions from the United States. On a less savory note, the U.S. funds an outfit called the Asian-American Free Labor Institute, whose ostensible purpose is to encourage "free" (*i.e.,* non-Communist) trade unions in Asia, but whose actual mission is to discourage any truly militant union activity. AAFLI works closely with the Federation of Korean Trade Unions, which was responsible for the excrement-smearing incident described above.

But the most obvious form of United States involvement, according to Lenny Siegel, the director of the Pacific Studies Center, is through "our consistent record of military aid to Third World governments that are capitalist, politically repressive, and are not striving for economic independence." Ironically, says Siegel, there are "cases where the United States made a big investment—through groups like AAFLI or other kinds of political pressure—to make sure that any unions that formed would be pretty tame. Then we put in even more money to support some dictator who doesn't allow unions at all." And if that doesn't seem like a sufficient case of duplicate spending, the U.S. government also insures (through the Overseas Private Investment Corporation) outward-bound multinationals against any lingering possibility of insurrection or expropriation.

What does our government have to say for itself? It's hard to get a straight answer—the few parts of the bureaucracy that deal with women and development seem to have little connection with those that are concerned with larger foreign policy issues. A spokesman for the Department of State told us that if multinationals offer poor working conditions (which he questioned), this was not their fault: "There are just different standards in different countries." Offering further evidence of a sheltered life, he told us that "corporations today are generally more socially responsible than even ten years ago. . . . We can expect them to treat their employees in the best way they can." But he conceded in response to a barrage of unpleasant examples, "Of course, you're going to have problems wherever you have human beings doing things." Our next stop was the Women's Division within AID. Staffer Emmy Simmons was aware of the criticisms of the quality of employment multinationals offer, but cautioned that "we can get hung up in the idea that it's exploitation without really looking at the alternatives for women." AID's concern, she said, was with the fact that population is outgrowing the agricultural capacity of many Third World countries, dislocating millions of people. From her point of view, multinationals at least provide some sort of alternative: "These people have to go somewhere." . . .

Yet thousands of women in the Third World's industrial work force have chosen to fight for better wages and working conditions. Few of these struggles reach the North

American media. We know of them from reports, often fragmentary, from church and support groups.

• Nuevo Laredo, Mexico, 1973: 2,000 workers at Transitron Electronics walked out in solidarity with a small number of workers who had been unjustly fired. Two days later, 8,000 striking workers met and elected a more militant union leadership.

• Mexicali, Mexico, 1974: 3,000 workers, locked out by Mextel (a Mattel subsidiary), set up a 24-hour guard to prevent the company from moving in search of cheaper labor. After two months of confrontations, the company moved away.

• Bangkok, Thailand, 1976: 70 young women locked their Japanese bosses out and took control of the factory. They continued to make and sell jeans and floppy hats for export, paying themselves 150 percent more than their bosses had.

• South Korea, 1977: 3,000 women at the American-owned Signetics plant went on a hunger strike for a 46.8 percent wage hike above the 39 cents an hour they were receiving. Since an actual walkout would have been illegal, they remained in the plant and held a sit-in in the cafeteria. They won a 23 percent increase.

• South Korea, 1978: 1,000 workers at the Mattel toy company in Seoul, which makes Barbie dolls and Marie Osmond dolls, staged a work slowdown to protest their 25 cents-an-hour wages and 12-hour shifts.

• South Korea, 1979: 200 young women employees of the YH textile-and-wig factory staged a peaceful vigil and fast to protest the company's threatened closing of the plant. On August 11, the fifth day of the vigil, more than 1,000 riot police, armed with clubs and steel shields, broke into the building where the women were staying and forcibly dragged the women out. Twenty-one-year-old Kim Kyong-suk was killed during the melee. It was her death that touched off widespread rioting throughout Korea that many thought led to the overthrow of President Park Chung Hee.

• Ciudad Juá rez, Mexico; September, 1980: 1,000 women workers occupied an American Hospital Supply Corporation factory. They demanded better working conditions, paid vacations, and recognition of the union of their choice. The women, who are mostly in their teens and early twenties, began the occupation when 180 thugs, which the company claims were paid by a rival union, entered the factory and beat up the women's leaders. The occupation is over, but the struggle goes on.

Saralee Hamilton, an AFSC staff organizer of a 1978 conference on "Women and Global Corporations" (held in Des Moines, Iowa) says: "The multinational corporations have deliberately targeted women for exploitation. If feminism is going to mean anything to women all over the world, it's going to have to find new ways to resist corporate power internationally." She envisions a global network of grass-roots women capable of sharing experiences, transmitting information, and—eventually—providing direct support for each other's struggles. It's a long way off; few women anywhere have the money for intercontinental plane flights or even long-distance calls, but at least we are beginning to see the way. "We all have the same hard life," wrote Korean garment worker Min Chong Suk. "We are bound together with one string."

Family

A Marriage Agreement
Alix Kates Shulman

When my husband and I were first married a decade ago, "keeping house" was less of a burden than a game. We both worked full-time jobs and we each pretty much took care of ourselves. We had a small apartment which stayed empty most of each day so that taking care of it was very little trouble. Every couple of weeks we'd spend a Saturday morning cleaning and taking our laundry to the laundromat. Though I usually did the cooking, our meals were casual and simple. We shopped for food together after work; sometimes we ate out; we had our breakfast at a diner near work; sometimes my husband cooked; there were few dishes. In the evenings we went for long walks and weekends we spent in Central Park. Our domestic life was beautifully uncomplicated.

Then our first child was born. I quit my job to stay home with him. Our domestic life was suddenly very complicated. When our second child was born, domestic life, the only life I had any longer, became a tremendous burden.

Once we had children, we totally accepted the sex-roles society assigns. My husband worked all day in an office and I was at home, so the domestic burden fell almost entirely on me. We had to move to a larger apartment to accommodate the children. Keeping it minimally livable was no longer a matter of an hour or two a week but took hours of every day: children make unbelievable messes. Our one meal a day for two people turned into a half a dozen meals a day for anywhere from one to four people at a time, and everyone ate different food. To shop for this brood—or even just to run out for a quart of milk—became a major project. It meant putting on snowsuits, boots, and mittens, getting strollers or carriages up and down stairs, and scheduling the trip so it did not interfere with someone's feeding or nap or illness or some other domestic job. Laundry turned from a weekly to a daily chore. And all this tumult started for me at six in the morning and didn't let up until nine at night, and *still* there wasn't time enough to do everything.

But even more burdensome than the physical work of child-rearing was the relentless responsibility I had for the children. There was literally nothing I could do or even contemplate without having to consider first how the children would be affected. Answering their questions alone ruled out for me such a minimum of privacy as a private *mental* life. They were always *there*. I couldn't read or think. If there ever was a moment to read, I read to them.

My husband's job began keeping him at work later and later, and sometimes took him out of town. If I suffered from too much domesticity, he suffered from too little. The children were usually asleep when he got home and I was too exhausted to talk. He became a stranger. Though he had sometimes, when we were first married, cooked for the two of us, that was no longer possible. A meal had become a major complicated production, in which timing counted heavily and someone might be crying in the background. No longer could we decide at the last moment what we felt like having for supper. And there were always dishes in the sink.

As the children grew up, our domestic arrangement seemed increasingly odious to me. I took free-lance work to do at home in order to keep some contact with the world, but I had to squeeze it into my "free" time. My husband, I felt, could always change his job if the pressure was too great, but I could never change mine. When I finally began to see my situation from a woman's liberation point of view, I realized that the only way we could possibly survive as a family (which we wanted to do) was to throw out the old sex roles we had been living by and start again. Wishing to be once more equal and independent as we had been when we had met, we decided to make an agreement in which we could define our roles our own way. We wanted to share completely the responsibility for caring for our household and for raising our children, by then five and seven. We recognized that after a decade of following the traditional sex roles we would have to be extremely vigilant and wary of backsliding into our old domestic habits. If it was my husband's night to take care of the children, I would have to be careful not to check up on how he was managing; if the baby sitter didn't show up for him, it would have to be *his* problem.

When our agreement was merely verbal, it didn't work; our old habits were too firmly established. So we made a formal agreement instead, based on a detailed schedule of family duties and assignments. Eventually, as the old roles and habits are replaced, we may be able to abandon the formality of our arrangement, but now the formality is imperative. Good intentions are simply not enough.

Our agreement is designed for our particular situation only in which my husband works all day at a job of his choice, and I work at home on a free-lance basis during the hours the children are in school (from 8:30 till 3:00). If my husband or I should change jobs, income, or working hours, we would probably have to adjust our agreement to the altered circumstances. Now, as my husband makes much more money than I do, he pays for most of our expenses.

MARRIAGE AGREEMENT

I Principles

We reject the notion that the work which brings in more money is the more valuable. The ability to earn more money is already a privilege which must not be compounded by enabling the larger earner to buy out of his/her duties and put the burden on the one who earns less, or on someone hired from outside.

We believe that each member of the family has an equal right to his/her own time, work, value, choices. As long as all duties are performed, each person may use his/her extra time any way he/she chooses. If he/she wants to use it making money, fine. If he/she wants to spend it with spouse, fine. If not, fine.

As parents we believe we must share all responsibility for taking care of our children and home—not only the work, but the responsibility. At least during the first year of this agreement, *sharing responsibility* shall mean:

1 Dividing the *jobs* (see "Job Breakdown" below); and
2 Dividing the *time* (see "Schedule" below) for which each parent is responsible

In principle, jobs should be shared equally, 50–50, but deals may be made by mutual agreement. If jobs and schedule are divided on any other than a 50–50 basis, then either party may call for a re-examination and redistribution of jobs or a revision of the schedule at any time. Any deviation from 50–50 must be for the convenience of both parties. If one party works overtime in any domestic job, she/he must be compensated by equal extra work by the other. For convenience, the schedule may be flexible, but changes must be formally agreed upon. The terms of this agreement are rights and duties, not privileges and favors.

II JOB BREAKDOWN

A Children

1 Mornings: Waking children; getting their clothes out, making their lunches; seeing that they have notes, homework, money, passes, books, etc.; brushing their hair; giving them breakfast; making coffee for us.

2 Transportation: Getting children to and from lessons, doctors, dentists, friends' houses, park, parties, movies, library, etc. Making appointments.

3 Help: Helping with homework, personal problems, projects like cooking, making gifts, experiments, planting, etc.; answering questions, explaining things.

4 Nighttime: Getting children to take baths, brush their teeth, go to bed, put away their toys and clothes; reading with them; tucking them in and having night-talks, handling if they wake and call in the night.

5 Babysitters: Getting babysitters, which sometimes takes an hour of phoning.

6 Sickcare: Calling doctors, checking out symptoms, getting prescriptions filled, remembering to give medicine, taking days off to stay home with sick child; providing special activities.

7 Weekends: All above, plus special activities (beach, park, zoo, etc.).

B Housework

8 Cooking: Breakfasts; dinners; (children, parents, guests).
9 Shopping: Food for all meals; housewares; clothing and supplies for children.
10 Cleaning: Dishes daily; apartment weekly, bi-weekly, or monthly.
11 Laundry: Home laundry; making beds; drycleaning (take and pick up).

III SCHEDULE

(The numbers on the following schedule refer to Job Breakdown list.)

1 Mornings: Every other week each parent does all.

2 and **3** Transportation and Help: Parts occurring between 3:00 and 6:30 pm, fall to wife. She must be compensated (see 10 below). Husband does all weekend transportation and pickups after 6:00. The rest is split.

4 Nighttime (and all Help after 6:30): Husband does Tuesday, Thursday, and Sunday. Wife does Monday, Wednesday, and Saturday. Friday is split according to who has done extra work during the week.

5 Babysitters must be called by whoever the sitter is to replace. If no sitter turns up, the parent whose night it is to take responsibility must stay home.

6 Sickcare: This must still be worked out equally, since now wife seems to do it all. (The same goes for the now frequently declared school closings for so-called political protest, whereby the mayor gets credit at the expense of the mothers of young children. The mayor only closes the schools, not the places of business or the government offices.)

7 Weekends: Split equally. Husband is free all of Saturday, wife is free all of Sunday, except that the husband does all weekend transportation, breakfasts, and special shopping.

8 Cooking: Wife does all dinners except Sunday nights; husband does all weekend breakfasts (including shopping for them and dishes). Sunday dinner, and any other dinners on his nights of responsibility if wife isn't home. Breakfasts are divided week by week. Whoever invites the guests does shopping, cooking, and dishes; if both invite them, split work.

9 Shopping: Divide by convenience. Generally, wife does local daily food shopping, husband does special shopping for supplies and children's things.

10 Cleaning: Husband does all the house-cleaning, in exchange for wife's extra childcare (3:00 to 6:30 daily) and sick care. Dishes: same as 4.

11 Laundry: Wife does most home laundry. Husband does all dry cleaning delivery and pick up. Wife strips beds, husband remakes them.

After only four months of strictly following our agreement, our daughter said one day to my husband, "You know, Daddy, I used to love Mommy more than you, but now I love you both the same."

Black Women in Poverty: Some Comments on Female-Headed Families

Rose M. Brewer

A substantial amount of data, both statistical and anecdotal, have been collected that indicate that much of black poverty in the United States is experienced by black women living in households with their dependent children.[1] Most analyses of the underlying causes have been filled with normative assumptions about what is proper and improper familial behavior, and, consequently, social scientists often have labeled the family formation practices of the black population "inappropriate."[2] Such empirical findings and analyses lack critical perspectives on the political and economic structures that provide the milieu for family formation strategies and emphasize the human capital disabilities of the black population generally, and of black women specifically.[3]

The purpose of this essay is to place current debate on poor black women heading households within a structural and political economic context. Cultural arguments alone have never satisfactorily explained the reason for the persistence of black poverty, and it is unlikely such arguments will do so today as poverty embraces ever larger numbers of women and children.[4] Nonetheless, even scholars sensitive to the limitations of "the culture of poverty" can fail to incorporate a full appreciation of the powerful and complex interplay between capitalism, racial oppression, and black family life.[5] For instance, Eleanor Holmes Norton may acknowledge the destructive force of economic marginalization on black families, but she separates this from the cultural forces she also damns: acceptance of premarital pregnancy, unwed parenthood, street life, and a destructive "ghetto ethos."[6]

There is an intense American cultural bias that assumes that the male-headed household, with woman as homemaker, is the norm—despite the fact that only about 14 percent of American households now have such an arrangement.[7] The nuclear family imperative is rooted in upper-class, white, patriarchal prerogatives that are unevenly shared across race and class lines. Married and single women in increasing numbers are entering the labor force in this society, and the rigid sexual division of labor embodied in the old nuclear family form appears to be giving way to more shared arrangements among whites. Black nuclear families have always been egalitarian in role division,[8] but the traditional sex-role divisions prevail here too: women of all races do most of the private domestic work in addition to working outside the home.[9] Nevertheless, the popular ideology of what constitutes an appropriate family—black or white—remains strong, and this has special ramifications for households headed by black women.

My argument is that theories centered in the human capital deficit notion (lack of training, skills, or education) are insufficient and inadequate for explaining the poverty of female-headed families. Human capital variables explain only a small amount of the difference in status attainment between poor people and other groups in the society.[10] The emphasis instead should be on analyzing family structure changes that occur within the context of an advanced industrial capitalist order and its welfare-state practices. At the center of such an approach would be an explication of the changing family dynamics of a people who have been systematically excluded from the economy of the wider society. Currently, blacks have one of the highest rates of unemployment in the country and are heavily marginalized into the secondary and casual sectors of the labor market.[11] These private economic delimiters should be examined as they occur in interaction with public welfare-state transfer payments and with group cultural dynamics and practices. It is this relationship between the microlevel cultural/familial sphere and the macrolevel political economic sphere that is central to understanding the persisting poverty in the majority of black female-headed households.

A bias against black family diversity has persisted in social science literature despite the fact that blacks historically have generally lived in nuclear family arrangements.[12] More specifically, two principal forms of black family life have been maintained in the history of Afro-Americans despite the difficulties imposed by slavery and racial discrimination. The first form, according to research based on censuses of 1800 and 1900, derived from a pattern of premarital intercourse (indicated by the birth of a child less than eight months after marriage) and the birth of a child prior to marriage. The rates of such births for blacks during that period were higher than for white immigrants and native whites. This did not, however, mean that black households were headed mainly by women. In fact, the two-parent household predominated.[13] Other research confirms that another important form of black households in the nineteenth century was the household formed around marriage.[14]

The pronounced trend toward black female-headed households, then, is a recent historical phenomenon, though their poverty is not. Whatever the debate about the reasons behind it, there is today no doubt that the black American community still lives within profound economic impoverishment.[15] And though in particular it is black women and children who are poor, it is not simply because they are more likely to live in female-headed households. Mary Jo Bane found that two out of three blacks living in female-headed households were already poor before a change put them in female-headed households.[16] Recent research by the Center for the Study of Social Policy suggests that the declining economic status of black men is the "flipside" of the increase in female-headed families: "The increase in single parent Black families has been a deterioration in the economic status of Black men. Recent figures show that only 55 percent of Black men are currently in the labor force; the remainder are unemployed, discouraged and not seeking work, in correctional facilities, or unaccounted for."[17]

Given black female and male economic realities, relying on normative assumptions about family structure is not only misleading; it also reinforces an uncritical acceptance of upper-class, white, patriarchal prerogatives as normative in American society. More specifically, an emphasis on female-headed households misses an essential truth about black women's poverty: black women are also poor in households with male heads. With or without a male present, there is a strong likelihood that black women and children will be living in poverty in America today.

It is not, then, the household arrangement that should be at issue but, rather, the prevalence of poverty in female-headed households and in all black households, even with a male head, that should be the center of concern. Essentially, black women's poverty is reflective of and complicated by interrelated forces involving culture, politics, and economics, as well as race, gender, and class inequality. Understanding black women's poverty requires a hard look at political and economic changes in urban inner cities, in rural southern towns, and in the marginalization of black men and women from the labor market.[18] Indeed, the racial/sexual division of labor intensifies the effects of underemployment and low wages. That is, women generally are segregated in low paying, secondary jobs, but black women are highly concentrated in the lowest paying and lowest status women's work, from nurse's aid to private household worker.[19] And whether they work or not, the other economic networks on which they depend—support from friends, family, and spouses, the irregular, informal, or illegal economy—need to be understood, including the American welfare state, which must be viewed in terms of the other political and economic disabilities structuring racial and gender hierarchies.

Unlike other institutional structures, the black family is often treated as an aside when dealing with issues of racial inequality.[20] When it does become the center of discussion, as it did following the Moynihan report of 1965, rhetoric and polemics distort the analyses.[21] I make the assumption here that manifestations of exclusionary practices that lead to black inequality occur in all American institutions. The family is one such institutional structure; but if it is examined as if it were an autonomous, self-sufficient cultural unit, the family holds little analytical power. However, if the family is understood to be an institution influenced by the confluence of economic, state, racial, gender, and external cultural forces, on the one hand, and as a cultural meaning system and social structure, on the other hand, the black family becomes a strategic unit for understanding the convergence of macro and micro social forces.

The revisionist literature on black families has not addressed these complex interactions.[22] Although these works document the resiliency of black families, no one has systematically investigated the transformation and reconstitution of black families under twentieth-century historical conditions of economic change and crisis.[23] Revisionists either have focused on specific time and place (such as slavery or post-Reconstruction) or on cross-sectional, or qualitative, approaches that do not incorporate historical perspectives. There is a vacuum of knowledge about changes in urban black family life from 1900 to the present. For instance, we have very sketchy information on what happened to black families after they migrated to northern and southern cities during the early twentieth century, their confrontations with urban labor markets and work patterns, and the impact of these converging forces on family dynamics—the relationship between family and work and the modification in meaning systems about kinship and family. It would be useful to know how preexistent forms of kinship and family formation, as well as cultural meaning systems, helped shape responses to the urban setting and economy. We do know that in addition to continued racial discrimination the most immediate and perhaps most profound changes with consequences for black families have been the growth and development of the welfare state and the economic marginalization of the urban black population.[24]

Again, the economic dynamics shaping black family forms are complex. We do not know the precise relationship between unemployment, economic marginalization, and welfare dependency, but we do know that the pronounced contemporary trend toward black female-headed households is a recent phenomenon. The number of these households has risen dramatically in the 1960 to 1980 period. Now, nearly one-half of all black children are living in a family headed by a single parent.[25]

A historically grounded argument that considers change and transformation over time can avoid accounting for contemporary black family change in terms of disabilities while at the same time it can presume that the most crucial separation of blacks from the rest of the social order occurred within the context of slavery. The unique labor role played by the black population and the peculiar cultural position the group came to occupy are fundamental to the differences between the ways black families emerged in the United States and the ways families of other populations emerged. The fact that the black family as a cultural institution outlived slavery does not mean that it remained unaltered by historical change. Continued antebellum racism—including legal, social, and economic practices of exclusion—caused the black family to assume distinctive characteristics.[26] In this context, the unique cultural practices that some have traced to Africa in the actual lifeways of black Americans played a yet to be determined role in the interplay between culture, economy, and black family life.[27]

The most distinct differences between blacks and other groups are related to household forms. The black family historically has respected extended relations, including family forms involving higher rates of out-of-marriage births and female-headed households.[28] Such an inclusive family system was necessary in a context in which the private sphere of black life could be disrupted by external forces that were much more powerful than the cultural practices internal to the group. Moreover, black family change is continually filtered through the cultural practices, resistances, and innovations of the group. Given the fact that state policy has not worked to ensure black family wholeness, two-parent households can only be extremely difficult to maintain under such conditions.[29] Although in certain historical periods the two-parent household has existed as the primary black family form, this has not occurred consistently across time or place.[30]

What appears to be distinctive about the economics of black family life is that the difficulties of tying work and family together in a way that consistently cushions the private sphere are accentuated by welfare-state capitalism.[31] Though sharecroppers in the nineteenth century were poor families working together as a unit, economic resources and the private sphere came together in a way that strengthened a household structure by requiring the contributions of everyone.[32] This remained the situation to some extent in the urban North and South until the mid-twentieth century as black Americans migrated to the cities.[33] But since the post–World War II period there has been an abrupt change as black unemployment rates began to double that of whites and as black households became more firmly linked to Aid for Families with Dependent Children (AFDC) and the general public assistance aspects of the welfare state.[34] Apparently, the welfare state has generated a tension between work and family life that appears to undermine family stability for some sectors of the black population.

In recent years, changes in household forms also have been influenced by two other major trends: the increasing economic marginalization of blacks in the urban economy and a general normative devaluation of the nuclear family by the wider society as expressed in higher divorce rates, more single-parent households, and a rising number of out-of-wedlock births for all groups in the society.[35] Again, although job skills, education, and training explain small amounts of the variation in status attainment differences between poor people and other groups in the society, they cannot explain the vast inequalities of income that mark the differences between races in the American economic system.[36]

Today, there are virtually no differences in the educational attainment of workers, yet great disparities continue in median income between the sexes and races. Black women who have attended high school have less income than white men or black men who have attended only elementary school. This also holds true for high school–educated white women.[37] Diana Pearce, who strongly emphasizes the feminization of poverty, concedes that poor women share many characteristics in common with poor men. These include high drop-out rates in the schools and lack of market-relevant job skills and job training opportunities. However, Pearce moves beyond these traditional human capital variables and stresses the costs of being a woman heading a family: "First of all, women who head their families often bear most or all the economic burden of raising the children. Secondly, because of sex discrimination, occupational segregation in a segmented labor market, and sexual harassment, women who seek to support themselves and their families through paid work are disadvantaged in the labor force."[38]

Furthermore, labor market segmentation is not only gender but also race specific. Though there have been some changes in the job categories in which black women primarily work, they are still disproportionately represented among the underemployed, unemployed, and wards of the welfare state.[39] Thus the major assumption of the human capital approach to women's poverty—that lack of education, training, and experience prevents people from getting the jobs that will solve their problems—is challenged by the realities of gender-based operations of the labor force.

The evidence is still coming in on the precise relationship between the nuclear family, urbanization, and industrialization,[40] but one thing is certain: whatever the causal ordering, a private sphere was made economically possible for white families under industrial capitalism. White nuclear family life has been sustained and protected historically and explicitly by state labor legislation.[41] The same relationship between work and family has not been consistently possible for blacks. The American economy, in other words, has not been shaped by concerns about preserving the private sphere of black life. Consequently, the move beyond slavery and early industrial capitalism to a more advanced industrial society and the welfare state has not improved the integration of work with family life for some sectors of the black population. Given the high rates of unemployment and underemployment for black women and men in urban labor markets, and given the combination of work and welfare that often sustains this portion of the black population, black female-headed households become the logical end product of a whole series of social, political, and economic forces.

NOTES

1 Phyllis Wallace, *Black Women in the Labor Force* (Cambridge, Mass.: MIT Press, 1980), indicates that "in 1976, black families headed by women accounted for two-thirds of all black families below the poverty level (1,122,000 black female-headed families versus

1,617,000 black families). Thus, the overwhelming component of black poverty occurs where families are headed by women" (82)

2 See Maxine Baca Zinn and D. Stanley Eitzen, *Diversity in American Families* (New York: Harper & Row, 1987), 163–64, for a discussion of the so-called deficit model of racial minority family formation that is prevalent in social science literature.

3 Jacqueline Jones, *Labor of Love, Labor of Sorrow* (New York: Basic Books, 1985), 325–26, gives a cogent summary of the peculiar position of black women in today's economy.

4 Even though the culture of poverty debate is an old one, it is being resurrected. Oscar Lewis's arguments about how poverty is transmitted intergenerationally go back to 1966 (*La Vida: A Puerto Rican Family in the Culture of Poverty—San Juan and New York* [New York: Random House, 1966]). It was rebutted rather resoundingly by Charles Valentine, *Culture and Poverty* (Chicago: University of Chicago Press, 1968). It has emerged again in updated form in the work of Charles Murray, *Losing Ground: American Social Policy* (New York: Basic Books, 1984); and Nicholas Lemann, "The Origins of the Underclass," *The Atlantic* 257, no. 6 (June 1986): 54–66.

5 Eleanor Holmes Norton, "Restoring the Traditional Black Family," *New York Times Magazine* (June 2, 1985).

6 For an extended discussion of this point, see Angela Davis and Fania Davis, "The Black Family and the Crisis of Capitalism," *Black Scholar* 17, no. 5 (September/October 1986): 33–40.

7 Jerome Skolnick and Elliot Curry, *America's Problems* (Boston: Little, Brown & Co., 1984).

8 Robert Staples, ed., *The Black Family: Essays and Studies,* 3d ed. (Belmont, Calif.: Wadsworth Publishing Co., 1986).

9 Skolnick and Curry.

10 For an excellent review and critique of this literature, see William A. Darity, Jr., "Current Empirical Research on Black-White Income Inequality: A Survey and Critique," Center for Economic Research, Discussion Papers (Austin: University of Texas, Department of Economics, 1982).

11 Center for the Study of Social Policy, "The 'Flip-Side' of Black Families Headed by Women: The Economic Status of Black Men," in Staples, ed., 232–38.

12 For an example of work that assumes the worst of black female-headed households, see Daniel P. Moynihan, *The Negro Family: The Case for National Action,* Office of Policy Planning and Research, United States Department of Labor (Washington, D.C.: Government Printing Office, March 1965). Deborah White, *Ain't I a Woman?* (New York: W. W. Norton & Co., 1985), argues historically for the diversity and nuclear nature of black families. Yet this diversity is defined as pathological in mainstream social science. Such tunnel vision, which narrowly defines black families, is reflected in the work of Moynihan.

13 Carl Degler, *At Odds* (New York: Oxford University Press, 1980).

14 See Theodore Herschberg, "Free Blacks in Antebellum Philadelphia: A Study of Ex-Slaves, Free Born and Socioeconomic Decline," *Journal of Social History* 5 (1972): 183–209; Paul Lammermeier, "The Urban Black Family of the Nineteenth Century: A Study of Black Family Struggle in the Ohio Valley, 1850–1880," *Journal of Marriage and the Family* 35, no. 3 (1973): 404–56; and William J. Wilson and Kathryn Neckerman, "Poverty and Family Structure: The Widening Gap between Evidence and Public Policy Issues" (Chicago: University of Chicago, Department of Sociology, February 1985), 2–5.

15 See Arthur I. Blaustein, *The American Promise: Equal Justice and Economic Opportunity* (New Brunswick, N.J.: Transaction Books, 1982); Beverly L. Johnson and Elizabeth Waldman, "Most Women Who Head Families Received Poor Market Returns," *Monthly Labor*

Review (December 1983), 30–34; and Harriet McAdoo, "Factors Related to Stability in Up-wardly Mobile Black Families," *Journal of Marriage and the Family* 40, no. 4 (1978): 761–66.

16 Mary Jo Bane, "Household Composition and Poverty: Which Comes First?" (Albany: New York State Department of Social Services, January 1985).

17 Center for the Study of Social Policy (n. 11 above), 232.

18 The decreasing labor-force participation of black men and women is one indicator of eco-nomic marginalization. The point is that fewer black men and women have any work at all relative to white men and women. That is, their labor-force participation is down severely, especially that of black men (see Center for the Study of Social Policy).

19 Alexis M. Herman, "Still . . . Small Change for Black Women," in *Feminist Frameworks,* ed. Alison M. Jaggar and Paul S. Rothenberg (New York: McGraw-Hill Book Co., 1984).

20 In discussions of racism and racial inequality, the focus is often on education, the state, and racial attitudes. Recently, the black family has taken center stage in a debate rooted in old is-sues: Is the culprit culture or poverty, values or class? Which one accounts for the high num-ber of female-headed households? (See William Darity, Jr., and Samuel L. Myers, Jr., "Changes in Black Family Structure: Implications for Welfare Dependency," *American Eco-nomic Review* 73, no. 2 [May 1983]: 59–64, for a critique of economic and value argu-ments.)

21 Today, the debate is likely to be among a community of black scholars. Wilson and Necker-man argue for economic and structural causes, whereas Norton (n. 5 above) equivocates be-tween structural and cultural arguments. Glen Loury, in "Beyond Civil Rights," in *The State of Black America 1986* (Washington, D.C.: National Urban League, 1986), 163–74, argues strongly for cultural factors. None of these scholars attempts an integrated analysis of cultur-al and social forces.

22 Some examples of this revisionist literature include Joyce Ladner, *Tomorrow's Tomorrow* (New York: Doubleday & Co., 1971); Eugene Genovese, *Roll, Jordan, Roll* (New York: Pantheon Books, 1974); Herbert Gutman, *The Black Family in Slavery and Freedom* (New York: Pantheon Books, 1976); and Staples, ed. (n. 8 above).

23 Wilson and Neckerman (n. 14 above) and Staples, ed., have made some moves in this direc-tion, but they do not take on the task of a historical and contemporary discussion of political, economic, gender-based cultural and social forces.

24 Bogart R. Leashore, "Social Policies, Black Males and Black Families," in Staples, ed., 280–86.

25 U.S. Bureau of the Census, "Money Income and Poverty Status of Families and Persons in the United States: 1984," *Current Population Reports,* series P-60, no. 149; and Suzanne M. Bianchi, *Household Composition and Racial Inequality* (New Brunswick, N.J.: Rutgers Uni-versity Press, 1981).

26 See Jones (n. 3 above), 112–27, for a discussion of changing family formation as rural blacks first met southern urban labor markets then northern urban labor markets.

27 Wades Nobles, "African-American Family Life: An Instrument of Culture," in *Black Fami-lies,* ed. Harriette Pipes McAdoo (Beverly Hills, Calif.: Sage Publications, 1981), argues for an African influence on black family forms and practices, although the specifics of this influ-ence are still being worked out.

28 Degler (n. 13 above).

29 Eli Zaretsky, *Capitalism, the Family and Personal Life* (New York: Harper & Row, 1986), points out how forces of capitalism created, albeit at a cost, a personal sphere for white fami-lies. I argue that the dynamics worked differently for black families because racism and eco-nomic discrimination were continually disruptive of black personal life.

30 Gutman (n. 22 above).

31 Harrell R. Rodgers, Jr., *The Cost of Human Neglect: America's Welfare Failure* (New York: M. E. Sharpe, Inc., 1982).

32 Jones (n. 3 above).

33 Although, as noted earlier, the stresses of urban occupational segregation and social discrimination began taking a toll on black families at the beginning of the twentieth century as blacks migrated first to urban southern cities, then northern (see Jones).

34 The data are quite mixed on this. Apparently disruption occurs in certain circumstances and not in others. Wilson and Neckerman (n. 14 above) discuss this welfare/family disruption conundrum.

35 "Since 1950 such births have more than quadrupled, rising from 142,000 in 1950 to 666,000 in 1980," according to Harrell R. Rodgers, Jr., *Poor Women, Poor Families* (New York: M. E. Sharpe, Inc., 1986), 40.

36 Darity (n. 10 above).

37 Herman (n. 19 above), 39.

38 Diana Pearce, "The Feminization of Ghetto Poverty," *Transaction: Social Science and Modern Society* 21, no. 1 (November, December 1983): 70.

39 U. S. Commission on Civil Rights, *Unemployment and Underemployment among Blacks, Hispanics, and Women,* Clearinghouse Publication no. 74 (Washington, D.C.: Clearinghouse Publication, November 1982); Diana Pearce, "The Feminization of Poverty: Women, Work and Welfare," *Urban and Social Change Review,* no. 11 (1978), 28–36.

40 Michael Gordon, ed., *The American Family in Social-Historical Perspective,* 3d ed. (New York: St. Martin's Press, 1983).

41 Eli Zaretsky, "The Place of the Family in the Origins of the Welfare State," in *Rethinking the Family,* ed. Barrie Thorne with Marilyn Yalom (New York: Longman, Inc., 1982), 188–224.

Family Redefines Itself, and Now the Law Follows

Philip S. Gutis

As a growing number of unmarried couples claim legal rights, governments, courts and private employers are struggling to decide how to define a family.

Last week, the San Francisco Board of Supervisors approved a law that would allow unmarried partners, both heterosexual and homosexual, to register their relationships with the city, in much the same way that a couple applies for a marriage license.

Mayor Art Agnos has said he will sign the bill, making San Francisco the first city to grant legal recognition to unmarried partners. Less certain is whether the city will follow the board's recommendation that unmarried city employees be allowed to extend their health benefits to their partners, an issue that has taken on great importance because of the AIDS epidemic. Such a policy is already in effect in Berkeley, Calif.

In March the Los Angeles City Council passed a law that gives unmarried city employees sick leave to care for a partner and bereavement leave benefits if they have filed a "domestic partnership" affidavit. But the recognition of unmarried couples does not extend to people who do not work for the city.

In New York, the state's highest court is now deciding whether the surviving partner of a 10-year gay relationship can be considered a family member and keep the lease to an apartment under rent-control guidelines.

In 1988, 27 percent, or 24.6 million, of the country's 91.1 million households fit the traditional definition of a family—two parents living with children. In 1970, the proportion was 40 percent. "The structure of the family has changed quite a bit since the stereotype of 'Leave It to Beaver' days," said Michael Woo, a Los Angeles council member who introduced the measure. The issue not only affects unmarried couples but also handicapped, elderly and other single people living in group homes.

Some groups oppose tinkering with the definition of family, arguing that the effort is not a reaction to a changed environment but an attempt to promote a new social agenda.

"When government begins to legally recognize other kinds of relationships, it educates the citizenry," said Gary L. Bauer, the former Reagan Administration domestic affairs adviser who is now president of the Family Research Council, a conservative research group in Washington. "It says—particularly to the young—that this is a way of living that their society feels to be just as acceptable as married couples."

Redefining the family is not only a gay rights issue. The New York Court of Appeals recently ruled in a case involving four former mental patients who were living with a family in Brookhaven on Long Island. The town fined the family for having too many unrelated people living in a house zoned for single family use, but the court ruled that for zoning purposes the group was the "functional equivalent" of a family.

In another New York case, now awaiting a decision from the Appellate Division of the State Supreme Court, a mother and son are fighting eviction from a rent-controlled apartment in Harlem that they shared with an unrelated man for about 20 years before his death in 1985. In December 1987, a Manhattan Civil Court judge found that although unrelated by blood, marriage or adoption, the mother and son had formed a family with the man and ruled that they could not be evicted.

Still, in most places, gay rights organizations are leading the push for changes in government regulations defining a family. "That is almost a matter of necessity since there is no identified constituency of unmarried heterosexual couples," said Shelly F. Cohen of the Mayor's Lesbian-Gay Task Force in Seattle, where a law similar to the one in Los Angeles was recently proposed.

Although cities are free to extend family benefits to their unmarried employees, they are prohibited by Federal law from requiring that private companies do the same. But some experts believe that broader changes are likely.

"There is a trend toward defining family by functions rather than by structure," said Thomas F. Coleman, a member of the California State Task Force on the Changing Family, which was established in 1987 by the state legislature to make recommendations on social, economic and demographic trends. The panel said those functions include maintaining physical health and safety of members, providing conditions for emotional growth, helping to shape a "belief system," and encouraging shared responsibility.

The private sector has not been immune from pressures to extend the definition of family. The San Francisco Chamber of Commerce has put together a task force to survey its members on policies about unrelated people living together.

"No employer that we know of has extended fringe benefits, such as health care, to people outside the traditional definition of family," said Richard Morten, a vice president of the Chamber of Commerce. "But on a case-by-case basis, certain of our companies are taking a little bit broader interpretation of a family since they know that many of their employees are in nontraditional relationships."

Motherhood: The Annihilation of Women

Jeffner Allen

I would like to affirm the rejection of motherhood on the grounds that motherhood is dangerous to women. If woman, in patriarchy, is she who exists as the womb and wife of man, every woman is by definition a mother: she who produces for the sake of men. *A mother is she whose body is used as a resource to reproduce men and the world of men, understood as the biological children of patriarchy and as the ideas and material goods of patriarchal culture.* Motherhood is dangerous to women because it continues the structure within which females must be women and mothers and, conversely, because it denies to females the creation of a subjectivity and world that is open and free.

An active rejection of motherhood entails the development and enactment of a *philosophy of evacuation.*[1] Identification and analysis of the multiple aspects of motherhood not only show what is wrong with motherhood, but also point to a way out. A philosophy of evacuation proposes women's collective removal of ourselves from all forms of motherhood. Freedom is never achieved by the mere inversion of an oppressive construct, that is, by seeing motherhood in a "new" light. Freedom is achieved when an oppressive construct, motherhood, is vacated by its members and thereby rendered null and void. . . .

Speaking of motherhood as the annihilation of women does not disclaim either women's past or present as mothers. Women as mothers make the best of motherhood. Women are mothers because within patriarchy women have no choice except motherhood. Without the institution of motherhood women could and would live otherwise. Just as no single woman, or particular mother, is free in patriarchy, no group of token women, mothers in general, are free in patriarchy. Until patriarchy no longer exists, all females, as historical beings, must resist, rebel against, and avoid producing for the sake of men. Motherhood is not a matter of women's psychological or moral character. As an ideology by which men mark females as women, motherhood has nothing to do with a woman's selfishness or sacrifice, nurturance or nonviolence. Motherhood has everything to do with a history in which women remain powerless by reproducing the world of men and with a present in which women are expected to do the same. . . .

The mark imposed by patriarchy on the bodies of all women compels all women to exist as mothers. The mark of motherhood inscribes the domination of men into woman's body, making motherhood appear as a natural phenomenon. Yet, motherhood is not a natural phenomenon and mothers do not exist as a natural group. On the contrary, female biological possibilities are first "naturalized" by men as women's specific difference and then claimed as the reason for the existence of motherhood.[2] Through such "naturalization," the female's biological possibility to give birth is made to appear as the intrinsic cause of woman's place in motherhood and as the origin of woman's social, economic, and political place in the world. The female's biological capacity to bear a child becomes the defining characteristic of all women.

Marking focuses on isolated fragments of the female body.[3] Such fragments, vagina, breasts, etc., are marked with a significance that is presumed to be intrinsic, eternal, and to characterize the whole of the female body. Forms of activity and character traits termed "natural" to women are then deduced from the marking imposed on the body fragments.

The closer a mark is to the body, the more indelibly it is associated with the body and the more the individual as a whole is pursued, hunted, trapped.[4] In the case of woman, the mark has absolute permanence, for woman's entire body, and the body of her world, is marked: MOTHER. The permanence of the mark is the sign of the permanence of the male domination that marks all women as mothers.

The object marked, woman as mother, experiences the mark as pain. The inscription of the mark of motherhood on women's bodies is never without pain—the pain of not "owning" our bodies, the pain of physical injury, the pain of being compelled to never produce a life or world of our own. Pain [from Greek *poinē,* punishment, penalty, payment] is the punishment, the penalty we must pay, for being marked by men as woman and mother. Pain has nothing to do with what we do, that is, our success or failure at being good, well-informed, or willing mothers. Pain is a sign that we, as women, are endangered by men who mark us. *If and when* the pain of the mark is not successfully "naturalized" by men, that is, is not or does not remain imprinted on females as belonging to our nature either physiologically or psychologically, we attempt to evade pain. Our pain breaks through the force of the mark. We do not endure the pain. We do not put up with the mark. We avoid, resist, the mark. We neither need nor desire the mark. We will get out of the mark. The immense amount of pain that marking entails is both an experience that accompanies the mark of motherhood and an experience that can lead to the end of the mark of motherhood.

Among those institutions created by marking, the institution of motherhood is unique: there is no other institution in which so many persons can be destroyed by the mark, and yet, a sufficient supply of persons to be marked remains. In all other forms of war, attrition eventually threatens the supply of persons who can be marked and thereby limits the activity of marking, at least for a time. The mark of motherhood is distinctive in that one of its by-products is the regeneration of more females to be marked as women and mothers.

Outside the social power relationship within which marking occurs, the mark does not exist.[5] Outside patriarchy, the mark of motherhood cannot even be imagined.

Women's daily life within patriarchy is shaped by the mark of motherhood. The genitalia and stomach are among the primary fragments of the female body which are so marked, as is woman's body as a whole.

Cut, carved, and literally burned into women's bodies are both the conditions under which our bodies will be open to the world, i.e., when, where, and to which individual men, and the world to which our bodies will be open, i.e., the world of men. From the mark of virginity to that of genital mutilation, our genitalia are marked: MOTHER.

In all modern culture, the marking of women's genitalia is indelible, permanently closing us to alternative decisions within patriarchy, as well as to the decision to create other possible and non-patriarchal worlds. On 42nd Street in New York City, movies on excision are featured attractions.[6] Our genitalia are marked to give us "worth": the smaller the artificial passage made by genital mutilation, the greater our "value," the higher our brideprice. Without the operation we cannot get a husband. We are "worthless."[7] Our genitalia are marked to improve heterosexual intercourse: Dr. James Burt, a Dayton, Ohio, gynecologist, "reconstructs" women for "better" intercourse. For a fee of $1,500, he surgically tightens the vaginal opening of female patients to bring the vagina and the clitoris closer together.[8] To make us desire marriage our genitalia are marked: "Only when they [young girls] are ready to procreate is it [the clitoris] removed—and once it is they feel deprived. Their desire then is concentrated in one place only and they promptly get married."[9] To regulate "madness" our genitalia are marked: "Circumcision, which . . . is confined to the clitoris, sets a barrier to the mad life of the girls," to the "lasciviousness" of eight year old females.[10] Marking is used as "social protection" against teenage heterosexual intercourse and pregnancy: "Why should not the United States and Europe be investigating the possibilities of hygienic experimentation with female circumcision as a social safeguard" from "teen sex" and "teen parenthood."[11] Marking as a "social safeguard" against rape: "infibulation is necessary to protect women from being raped."[12] Or, to "protect" the family.[13] One hundred percent of the female population of Somalia, Sudan, and Djibouti,[14] sixty-five million women in those areas of Africa from which such estimates are available,[15] and increasing numbers of females in France, Norway, and Australia experience genital mutilation as the mark of motherhood.[16] Pain, illness, and death accompany the mark that initiates us into motherhood.[17]

The mark of motherhood imprints on us patriarchal (male) sexuality. It cuts, carves, and literally burns into our bodies men's "needs," men's "desires":

> A virgin body . . . what he alone is to take and to penetrate seems to be in truth created by man. And more, one of the ends sought by all desire is the using up of the desired object, which implies its destruction.[18]

From the idea of virginity to the act of genital mutilation, the mark of motherhood controls where we may walk in the world of men, and that we must walk only in the world of men. . . .

PRIORITIES AND ALTERNATIVES

To show how motherhood, in its many forms, is dangerous to women is also to suggest how women may get out of motherhood. *Central to a philosophy of evacuation from motherhood is the primacy of women's daily lives and the power of our possible, and sometimes actual, collective actions.* In breaking free from motherhood, I no longer focus on birth and death as the two most important moments of my life. I give priority, rather, to that which is always already given: my life and my world. I—my activities, body, sexuality—am articulated by my actions and choices which, apart from patriarchy, may be made in the openness of freedom. I no longer give a primacy to that which I have reproduced. New modes of thinking and existing emerge. I, as an individual female, and we, as the community of all females, lay claim to our own freely chosen subjectivities, to the priorities and alternatives we create as our own.

The evacuation from motherhood does not simply seek to alter motherhood as it exists currently. Its focus is not specifically the development of alternative means of intercourse, pregnancy, or child care.[19] Women who use artificial insemination and whose children have no known father and women who live as lesbian mothers clearly challenge, but need not break with, the ideology and institution of motherhood. Each of these alternatives is significant for women's survival within patriarchy, but none is sufficient for women's effective survival, that is, for the creation of a female's self-chosen, non-patriarchal, existence.

A precondition for women's effective survival may be established, instead, by a female's power to not have children. A decision not to have children may be made, not because a female's biological capacity causes the ideology of motherhood, but because:

1 To not have children opens a time-space for the priority of claiming my life and world as my own and for the creative development of radically new alternatives.

2 The biology from which a child is born does not determine or control the course of that child's life. Females and males, younger and older, create the shapes of our lives through our actions.

3 Women who wish to be with younger females or males can do so collectively, with others of similar interests, or individually, through adoption.

At present, and for several thousands of years past, women have conceived, borne, and raised multitudes of children without any change in the conditions of our lives as women. In the case that all females were to decide not to have children for the next twenty years, the possibilities for developing new modes of thought and existence would be almost unimaginable.

The necessary condition for women's evacuation from motherhood is the claiming of our bodies as a source. Our bodies are not resources to be used by men to reproduce men and the world of men while, at the same time, giving death to ourselves. If necessary, women must bear arms, but not children, to protect our bodies from invasion by men.[20] For our effective survival, women's repetitive reproduction of patriarchy must be replaced by the creative production of ourselves. In particular, the areas of food, literacy, and energy sources and supplies for women must be examined anew.

Women's hunger is one of the specific conditions affecting the possibility for men's continuing success in representing and marking women as mothers. In the current patriarchal economy, women are the majority of the world's farmers, but women, on a global basis, do not have access to sufficient food to feed ourselves.[21] Nor do women have access to the money necessary to purchase food: women living in poverty constitute twelve percent of the total, world-wide, female population and seventy-five percent of all people living in poverty.[22]

Women's literacy is the second specific condition that enhances the possibility for men's continuing success in maintaining the ideology and institution of women as mothers. Women have insufficient access to the basics of literacy, that is, reading, writing, and simple arithmetic. From a global perspective, women are two-thirds of the illiterate people of the world.[23] In almost all countries, "girls already begin school in fewer numbers than boys; on the average, the difference even at the start of school is ten to twenty percent. By the time higher education is reached, the ratio between boys and girls is at least two to one, but in many cases more."[24] The education gap between men and women is growing throughout the developing world.[25] Even in industrialized societies, women have no access to determining which areas of research are the most urgent, or what constitutes an education.

Energy sources and supplies for women are a third area that undermines women's endeavors to break free of motherhood. In many villages in Africa and Asia, women work about three hours per day more than men because women are expected to gather the food, water, and fuel necessary for survival.[26] Technological information on alternative means of energy is usually not made available to these women, any more than it is to most women in industrialized countries. In all societies, women's non-control of energy sources and supplies necessary to our survival keeps us in subordination to men.

Female-defined access to food, education, and energy forms a necessary condition for women's collective evacuation from motherhood, for such access claims as a source the whole of our bodies and world. To get out of the reproduction of motherhood, females of all ages must work together to establish alternatives that express and fulfill our current needs and desires. As females who engage in evacuation from motherhood, we shape the whole of ourselves and our world in the present of our own lifetimes.

NOTES

1 I would like to thank Julie Murphy for suggesting the phrase, "a philosophy of evacuation."
2 Colette Guillaumin, "Race et Nature: Système des marques. Idée de groupe naturel et rapports sociaux," *Pluriel,* no. 11 (1977), pp. 48, 54, 55. Guillaumin develops the concept of the mark to analyze racial oppression.
3 Ibid., p. 49.
4 Ibid., p. 45.
5 Ibid., p. 55.
6 Fran Hosken, "The Case Histories: The Western World," *The Hosken Report,* 2d rev. ed. (Lexington Massachusetts, 1979), p. 11.
7 Ibid., "Medical Facts and Summary," p. 2.
8 Ibid., "Case Histories," p. 9.
9 Ibid., "The Reasons Given," p. 5.
10 Ibid., p. 6.
11 *WIN News,* vol. 7, no. 2 (1981), p. 39. Citation from *The New National Black Monitor,* (October, 1980).
12 Hosken, "Forward," *The Hosken Report,* p. 3.
13 Ibid.

14 *WIN News,* vol. 6, no. 2 (1980), p. 30. From Edna Adan Ismail, *Genital Operations: Their Physical and Mental Effects and Complications.*

15 Hosken, "Medical Facts and Summary," *The Hosken Report,* p. 6.

16 *WIN News,* vol. 6, no. 4 (1980), p. 45. From the New South Wales Humanist Society, "Report on Genital Mutilation from Australia."

17 Hosken, "The Reasons Given," *The Hosken Report,* p. 4.

18 *WIN News,* vol. 7, no. 4 (1981), p. 34. Report by Dr. Abu Hassan Abu in "Workshop on Eradicating Female Circumcision in the Sudan."

19 *WIN News,* vol. 7, no. 4 (1981), p. 19. *The American Journal of Obstetrics and Gynecology* (July, 1981), shows that the mortality rate in the United States for infants aided by midwife-assisted deliveries is nine per thousand births, in comparison with nearly seventeen per thousand births among physician-aided deliveries. Such alternative means have positive implications for women as mothers.

20 Julie Murphy, personal communication, December, 1981.

21 *WIN News,* vol. 7, no. 4 (1981), pp. 23, 24. From The Population Institute, *International Dateline.* See Jeffner Allen, "Women and Food: Feeding Ourselves," *The Journal of Social Philosophy,* 1984, pp. 34–41.

22 *WIN News,* vol. 7, no. 4 (1981), p. 73. From the National Commission on Working Mothers, "Women at Work: News about the 80%."

23 Hosken, "Editorial," *WIN News,* vol. 7, no. 2 (1981), p. 1.

24 *WIN News,* vol. 7, no. 1 (1981), p. 21. From World Bank Headquarters, "Education: A World Bank Sector Policy Paper."

25 Hosken, "Editorial," *WIN News,* vol. 6, no. 3 (1980), p. 1.

26 *WIN News,* vol. 7, no. 4 (1981), p. 6. From U.N. Conference on New and Renewable Sources of Energy, "Conference Report."

The Strange Case of Baby M

Katha Pollit

I think I understand Judge Harvey Sorkow's ruling in the Baby M case. It seems that a woman can rent her womb in the state of New Jersey, although not her vagina, and get a check upon turning over the product to its father. This transaction is not baby selling (a crime), because a man has a "drive to procreate" that deserves the utmost respect and, in any case, the child is genetically half his. The woman he pays for help in fulfilling that drive, however, is only "performing a service" and thus has no comparable right to a child genetically half hers. Therefore, despite the law's requirements in what the layperson might think are similar cases (women who change their minds about giving up a child for adoption, for example), a judge may terminate a repentant mother-for-money's parental rights forever without finding that she abused or neglected her child—especially if he finds her "manipulative, exploitive and deceitful." In other words, so-called surrogacy agreements are so unprecedented that the resulting human arrangements bear no resemblance to adoption, illegitimacy, custody after divorce, or any other relationship involving parents and children, yet, at the same time, bear an uncanny resemblance to the all-sales-final style of a used-car lot.

The State Supreme Court will hear Mary Beth Whitehead's appeal in September and has meanwhile granted her two hours of visiting time a week—a small sign, perhaps, that in jettisoning the entire corpus of family law, Judge Sorkow may have gone a bit too far. (*The New York Times* had trouble finding a single legal scholar who supported the judge's reasoning in full.) Maybe not, though. Despite the qualms of pundits, the outrage of many feminists and the condemnation of many religious leaders, every poll to date has shown overwhelming approval of Judge Sorkow's ruling. Twenty-seven states are considering bills that would legalize and regulate bucks-for-baby deals. What on earth is going on here?

Some of this support surely comes from the bad impression Mrs. Whitehead made every time she opened her mouth—most damningly, in her tape-recorded threat to kill Baby M and herself. And some comes from the ineptitude of her lawyer. (Where was the National Organization for Women? Where was the American Civil Liberties Union?) The Sterns said they would drag the Whiteheads through the mud, and they did. We learned as much about the Whiteheads' marital troubles, financial woes and quarrelsome relatives as if they were characters on *All My Children*. Distinguished experts testified that Mrs. Whitehead, who has raised two healthy, normal kids, is a bad mother and emotionally unbalanced: she was "overenmeshed" with her kids, disputed the judgment of school officials, gave Baby M teddy bears to play with instead of pots and pans (*pots and pans?*) and said "hooray" instead of "patty-cake" when the tot clapped her hands. I know that, along with two-thirds of the adult female population of the United States, I will never feel quite the same about dyeing my hair now that Dr. Marshall Schechter, professor of child psychiatry at the University of Pennsylvania, has cited this little beauty secret as proof of Mrs. Whitehead's "narcissism" and "mixed personality disorder." Will I find myself in custody court someday, faced with the damning evidence of Exhibit A: a half-empty bottle of Clairol's Nice 'N' Easy?

Inexplicably, Mrs. Whitehead's lawyer never challenged the Sterns's self-representation as a stable, sane, loving pair, united in their devotion to Baby M. And neither did the media. Thus, we never found out why Dr. Elizabeth Stern claimed to be infertile on her application to the Infertility Center of New York when, in fact, she had diagnosed herself as having multiple sclerosis, which she feared pregnancy would aggravate; or why she didn't confirm that diagnosis until shortly before the case went to trial, much less consult a specialist in the management of M.S. pregnancies. Could it be that Elizabeth Stern did not share her husband's zeal for procreation? We'll never know, any more than we'll know why a disease serious enough to bar pregnancy was not also serious enough to consider as a possible bar to active mothering a few years down the road. If the Sterns's superior income could count as a factor in determining "the best interests of the child," why couldn't Mary Beth Whitehead's superior health?

The trial was so riddled with psychobabble, class prejudice and sheer callousness that one would have expected public opinion to rally round Mrs. Whitehead. Imagine openly arguing that a child should go to the richer parent! (Mr. Whitehead drives a garbage truck; Dr. Stern is a professor of pediatrics, and Mr. Stern is a biochemist.) And castigating a mother faced with the loss of her baby as hyperemotional because she wept! But Mrs. Whitehead (who, it must be said, did not help her case by perjuring herself repeatedly) made a fatal mistake: she fell afoul of the double standard of sexual morality. Thus, in the popular mind, Mrs. Whitehead was "an adult" who "knew what she was doing," while Mr. Stern, presumably, was not an adult and did not know what he was doing. Mrs. Whitehead was mercenary for agreeing to sell, but not Mr. Stern for proposing to buy. That victim-as-seducer mentality hasn't got such a workout since a neighborhood matron decided to stop for a drink at Big Dan's bar in New Bedford, Massachusetts.

The personalities of the Whiteheads and the Sterns, so crucial during the custody phase of the trial, will soon fade from public memory. The extraordinary welter of half-truths, bad analogies, logical muddles and glib catch phrases that have been mustered in defense of their bargain are apparently here to stay. If we are really about to embark on an era of reproductive Reaganomics—and most Americans seem to be saying, Why not?—we at least ought to clear away some of the more blatantly foolish things being said in support of it. For example:

Mary Beth Whitehead is a surrogate mother.

"Mother" describes the relationship of a woman to a child, not to the father of that child and his wife. Everything a woman does to produce her own child Mary Beth Whitehead did, including giving it half the genetic inheritance regarded by the judge as so decisive an argument on behalf of William Stern. If anyone was a surrogate mother, it was Elizabeth Stern, for she was the one who substituted, or wished to substitute, for the child's actual mother.*

What's in a name? Plenty. By invariably referring to Mrs. Whitehead as a surrogate, the media, the courts and, unwittingly, Mrs. Whitehead herself tacitly validated the point of view of the Sterns, who naturally wanted to render Mrs. Whitehead's role in producing Baby M as notional as possible, the trivial physical means by which their desire—which is what really mattered—was fulfilled. And if Mrs. Whitehead was the substitute, then Dr. Stern must be the real thing.

Oddly enough, Mr. Stern, whose paternity consisted of ejaculating into a jar, was always referred to as the father or natural father or, rarely, biological father of Baby M, except by Mrs. Whitehead, who called him "the sperm donor." Although that is a far more accurate term for him than "surrogate mother" is for her (let alone "surrogate uterus," which is how the distinguished child psychologist Lee Salk referred to her), her use of it was widely taken as yet another proof of her irrational and cruel nature. Why was this harpy persecuting this nice man?

Surrogacy is a startling new technological development.

This claim is a favorite of columnists and other instant experts, who, having solemnly warned that reproductive science is outstripping society's ability to deal with it, helplessly throw up their hands because—what can you do?—progress marches on. But a maternity contract is not a scientific development; it is a piece of paper. Physically, as

---

*In this article I will use the terms "contract mother," "maternity contract" and their variants, except where I am indirectly quoting others.

Mary Beth Whitehead pointed out, it involves merely artificial insemination, a centuries-old technique which requires a device no more complicated than a turkey baster. And artificial insemination itself is a social contrivance, the purpose of which is to avert not infertility but infidelity.

What is new about contract motherhood lies in the realm of law and social custom. It is a means by which women sign away rights that, until the twentieth century, they rarely had: the right to legal custody of their children, and the right not to be bought, sold, lent, rented or given away. Throughout most of Western history and in many countries even today, there has been no need for such contracts because the father already owned the child, even if the child was illegitimate (unless the child's mother was married, in which case her husband owned the child). If a father chose to exercise his right to custody, the mother had no legal standing. In most societies, furthermore, a man in William Stern's position could have legally or semilegally acquired another female whose child, as per above, would be legally his: a second (or third or tenth) wife, a concubine, a slave, a kept woman. This is the happy state of affairs to which the maternity contract seeks to return its signers.

Those who comb history, literature and the Bible for reassuring precedents ignore the social context of oppression in which those odd little tales unfold. Yes, Sarah suggested that Abraham impregnate Hagar in order "that I may obtain children by her," but Hagar was a slave. What's modern about the story is that once pregnant, Hagar, like Mary Beth Whitehead, seemed to think that her child was hers no matter what anyone said. The outcome of that ancient domestic experiment was, in any case, disastrous, especially for Baby Ishmael. So perhaps the Bible was trying to tell us something about what happens when people treat people like things.

Surrogacy is the answer to female infertility.

It has widely and properly been noted that only the well-to-do can afford to contract for a baby. (The Sterns, with a combined income of more than $90,000, paid $25,000 all told for Baby M, with $10,000 going to Mrs. Whitehead.) Less often has it been remarked that contract maternity is not a way for infertile women to get children, although the mothers often speak as though it were. It is a way for men to get children. Elizabeth Stern's name does not even appear on the contract. Had Mr. Stern filed for divorce before Baby M was born, had he died or become non compos, Dr. Stern would have been out of luck. Even after she became Baby M's primary caretaker, until the adoption went through, she had no more claim on the child than a baby sitter. Rather than empower infertile women through an act of sisterly generosity, maternity contracts make one woman a baby machine and the other irrelevant.

And there is no reason to assume that contracts will be limited to men married to infertile women—indeed, the Sterns have already broken that barrier—or even to men married at all. I can hear the precedent-setting argument already: Why, your honor, should a man's drive to procreate, his constitutional right to the joys of paternity, be dependent on the permission of a woman? No doubt, this further innovation will be presented as a gesture of female altruism too ("I just wanted to give him the One Thing a man can't give himself"). But take away the mothers' delusion that they are making babies for other women, and what you have left is what, in cold, hard fact, we already have: the limited-use purchase of women's bodies by men—reproductive prostitution.

So what? A woman has the right to control her body.

The issue in contract motherhood is not whether a woman can bear a child for whatever reason she likes, but whether she can legally promise to sell that child—a whole other person, not an aspect of her body—to its father. Judge Sorkow is surely the only person on earth who thinks William Stern paid Mary Beth Whitehead $10,000 merely to conceive and carry a baby and not also to transfer that baby to him.

Actually, maternity contracts have the potential to do great harm to the cause of women's physical autonomy. Right now a man cannot legally control the conduct of a woman pregnant by him. He cannot force her to have an abortion or not have one, to manage her pregnancy and delivery as he thinks best, or to submit to fetal surgery or a Caesarean. Nor can he sue her if, through what he considers to be negligence, she miscarries or produces a defective baby. A maternity contract could give a man all those powers, except, possibly, the power to compel abortion, the only clause in the Stern-Whitehead contract that Judge Sorkow found invalid. Mr. Stern, for instance, seemed to think he had the right to tell Mrs. Whitehead's doctors what drugs to give her during labor. We've already had the spectacle of policemen forcibly removing 5-month-old Baby M from the arms of Mrs. Whitehead, the only mother she knew (so much for the best interests of the child!). What's next? State troopers guarding contract mothers to make sure they drink their milk?

Even if no money changed hands, the right-to-control-your-body argument would be unpersuasive. After all, the law already limits your right to do what you please with your body: you can't throw it off the Brooklyn Bridge, or feed it Laetrile, or even drive it around without a seat belt in some places. But money does change hands, and everybody, male and female, needs to be protected by law from the power of money to coerce or entice people to do things that seriously compromise their basic and most intimate rights, such as the right to health or life. You can sell your blood, but you can't sell your kidney. In fact, you can't even donate your kidney except under the most limited circumstances, no matter how fiercely you believe that this is the way you were meant to serve your fellow man and no matter how healthy you are. The risk of coercion is simply too great, and your kidney just too irreplaceable.

Supporters of contract motherhood talk about having a baby for pay as if it were like selling blood, or sperm, or breast milk. It is much more like selling a vital organ. Unlike a man, who produces billions of sperm and can theoretically father thousands of children at zero physical risk to himself, a woman can bear only a small number of children, and the physical cost to her can be as high as death. She cannot know in advance what a given pregnancy will mean for her health or for her ability to bear more children. (Interestingly, both the Sterns, who delayed parenthood until they found pregnancy too risky, and the Whiteheads, who foreclosed having more children with Mr. Whitehead's vasectomy, show just how unpredictable extrapolations from one's reproductive present are as guides to the future.) How can it be acceptable to pay a woman to risk her life, health and fertility so that a man can have his own biological child, yet morally heinous to pay healthy people to sacrifice "extra" organs to achieve the incomparably greater aim of saving a life? We're scandalized when we read of Asian sterilization campaigns in which men are paid to be vasectomized—and not just because of the abuses to which those campaigns are notoriously subject but because they seem, by their very nature, to take advantage of people's shortsightedness in order to deprive them forever of something precious. Why is hiring women to have babies and give them away any better?

The question of payment is crucial because although contract mothers prefer to tell the television cameras about their longing to help humanity, studies have shown that almost nine out of ten wouldn't help humanity for free. (Well, it's a job. Would you do your job for free?) But women to whom $10,000 is a significant amount of money are the ones who live closest to the economic edge and have the fewest alternative ways of boosting their income in a crisis. Right now contract motherhood is still considered a rather *outré* thing to do, and women often have to talk their families into it. But if it becomes a socially acceptable way for a wife to help out the family budget, how can the law protect women from being coerced into contracts by their husbands? Or their relatives? Or their creditors? It can't. In fact, it can't even insure uncoerced consent when no money changes hands. *The New York Times* has already discovered a case in which a family matriarch successfully pressured one relative to produce a child for another.

If contract motherhood takes hold, a woman's "right to control her body" by selling her pregnancies will become the modern equivalent of "she's sitting on a fortune." Her husband's debts, her children's unfixed teeth, the kitchen drawer full of unpaid bills, will all be her fault, the outcome of her selfish refusal to sell what nature gave her.

A deal's a deal.

This is what it's really all about, isn't it? To hear the chorus of hosannas currently being raised to this sacred tenet of market economics, you'd think the entire structure of law and morality would collapse about our ears if one high-school-dropout housewife in New Jersey was allowed to keep her baby. "One expects a prostitute to fulfill a contract," intoned Lawrence Stone, the celebrated Princeton University historian, in *The New York Times.* (Should the poor girl fail to show up at her regular time, the campus police are presumably to tie her up and deliver her into one's bed.) Some women argue that to allow Mrs. Whitehead to back out of her pledge would be to stigmatize all women as irrational and incapable of adulthood under the law. You'd think she had signed a contract to trade sow bellies at $5 and then gave premenstrual syndrome as her reason for canceling.

But is a deal a deal? Not always. Not, for instance, when it involves something illegal: prostitution (sorry, Professor Stone), gambling debts, slavery, polygyny, sweatshop labor, division of stolen goods and, oh yes, baby selling. Nor does it matter how voluntary such a contract is. So if your ambition in life is to be an indentured servant or a co-wife, you will have to fulfill this desire in a country where what Michael Kinsley calls "the moral logic of capitalism" has advanced so far that the untrained eye might mistake it for the sort of patriarchal semifeudalism practiced in small towns in Iran.

Well, you say, suppose we decided that contract motherhood wasn't prostitution or baby selling but some other, not flatly illegal, transaction: sale of parental rights to the father or some such. Then a deal would be a deal, right? Wrong. As anyone who has ever shopped for a co-op apartment in New York City knows, in the world of commerce, legal agreements are abrogated, modified, renegotiated and bought out all the time. What happens when contracts aren't fulfilled is what most of contract law is about.

Consider the comparatively civilized world of publishing. A writer signs up with one publisher, gets a better offer from another, pays back his advance—maybe—and moves on. Or a writer signs up to produce a novel but finds she'd rather die than see it printed, although her editor thinks it's a sure-fire best seller. Does the publisher forcibly take possession of the manuscript and print 100,000 copies because it's his property and a deal's a deal? No. The writer gives back the advance or submits another idea or persuades her editor she's such a genius she ought to be given even more money to write a really good book. And, somehow, Western civilization continues.

The closer we get to the murky realm of human intimacy the more reluctant we are to enforce contracts in anything like their potential severity. Marriage, after all, is a contract. Yet we permit divorce. Child-support agreements are contracts. Yet a woman cannot bar the father of her children from leaving investment banking for the less lucrative profession of subway musician. Engagement is, if not usually a formal contract, a public pledge of great seriousness. Yet the bride or groom abandoned at the altar has not been able to file a breach of promise suit for almost a hundred years. What have we learned since desperate spouses lit out for the territory and jilted maidens jammed the courts? That in areas of profound human feeling, you cannot promise because you cannot know, and pretending otherwise would result in far more misery than allowing people to cut their losses.

When Mary Beth Whitehead signed her contract, she was promising something it is not in anyone's power to promise: not to fall in love with her baby. To say, as some do, that she "should have known" because she'd had two children already is like saying a man should have known how he'd feel about his third wife because he'd already been married twice before. Why should mothers be held to a higher standard of self-knowledge than spouses? Or, more to the point, than fathers? In a recent California case a man who provided a woman friend with sperm, no strings attached, changed his mind when the child was born and sued for visitation rights. He won. Curiously, no one suggested that the decision stigmatized all his sex as hyperemotional dirty-dealers.

Fatherhood and motherhood are identical.

It is at this point that one begins to feel people have resigned their common sense entirely. True, a man and a woman contribute equally to the genetic makeup of a baby. But twenty-three pairs of chromosomes do not a baby make. In the usual course of events the woman is then pregnant for nine months and goes through childbirth, a detail overlooked by those who compare maternity contracts to sperm donation. The proper parallel to sperm donation is egg donation.

Feminists who argue that respecting Mrs. Whitehead's maternal feelings will make women prisoners of the "biology is destiny" arguments should think again. The Baby M decision did not disclaim the power of biology at all; it exalted male biology at the expense of female. Judge Sorkow paid tribute to Mr. Stern's drive to procreate; it was only Mrs. Whitehead's longing to nurture that he scorned. That Baby M had Mr. Stern's genes was judged a fact of supreme importance—more important than Mrs. Whitehead's genes, pregnancy and childbirth put together. We might as well be back in the days when a woman was seen merely as a kind of human potting soil for a man's seed.

Speaking as a pregnant person, I find the view of maternity inherent in maternity contracts profoundly demeaning. Pregnancy and delivery are not "services" performed for the baby's father. The unborn child is not riding about inside a woman like a passenger in a car. A pregnant woman is not, as one contract mother put it, "a human incubator"; she is engaged in a constructive task, in taxing physical work. Some of this work is automatic, and no less deserving of respect for that, but much of it is not—an increasing amount, it would appear, to judge by doctors' ever-lengthening list of dos and don'ts.

Now, why do I follow my doctor's advice: swill milk, take vitamins, eschew alcohol, cigarettes, caffeine, dental X-rays and even the innocent aspirin? And why, if I had to, would I do a lot more to help my baby be born healthy, including things that are uncomfortable and wearisome (like staying in bed for months, as a friend of mine had to) or even detrimental to my own body (like fetal surgery)? It's not because I want to turn out a top-of-the-line product, or feel a sense of duty to the baby's dad, or have invested the baby with all the rights and privileges of an American citizen whose address just happens to be my uterus. I do it because I love the baby. Even before it's born, I'm already forming a relationship with it. You can call that biology or social conditioning or a purely emotional fantasy. Perhaps, like romantic love, it is all three at once. But it's part of what pregnancy is—just ask the millions of pregnant women who feel this way, often to their own astonishment, sometimes under much less auspicious circumstances than Mrs. Whitehead's. It makes my blood boil when it is suggested that if contract mothers delivered under anesthesia and never saw their babies they wouldn't get a chance to "bond" and would feel no loss. I suppose the doctor could just tell them that they gave birth to a watermelon.

And so we arrive at the central emotional paradox of the Baby M case. We accept a notion that a man can have intense fatherly emotion for a child he's never seen, whose mother he's never slept with, let alone rubbed her back, or put his hand on her belly to feel the baby kick, or even taken her to the hospital. But a woman who violates her promise and loves the child she's had inside her for nine months, risked her health for, given birth to. . . She must be some kind of nut.

Women need more options, not fewer.

To suggest that female poverty can be ameliorated by poor mothers selling their children to wealthy fathers is a rather Swiftian concept. But why stop at contract motherhood when there's still a flourishing market for adoptive babies? Let enterprising poor women take up childbearing as a cottage industry and conceive expressly for the purpose of selling the baby to the highest bidder. And since the law permits parents to give up older children for adoption, why shouldn't they be allowed to sell them as well? Ever on the reproductive forefront, New Jersey recently gave the world the sensational case of a father who tried to sell his 4-year-old daughter to her dead mother's relatives for $100,000. Why he was arrested for doing what Mary Beth Whitehead was forced to do is anybody's guess.

Even leaving aside the fact that maternity contracts involve the sale of a human being, do women need another incredibly low-paying (around $1.50 an hour) service job that could damage their health and possibly even kill them, that opens up the most private areas of life to interference by a pair of total strangers, that they cannot get unless they first sign an ironclad contract forgoing a panoply of elementary human rights? By that logic, working in a sweatshop is an option, too—which is exactly what sweatshop employers have always maintained.

But people are going to do it anyway. Shouldn't they be protected?

There are some practices (drinking, abortion, infidelity) so entrenched in mass behavior and regarded as acceptable by so many that to make them illegal would be both undemocratic and futile. Contract motherhood is not one of them. In ten years only about 500 women have signed up. So the argument that we should legitimize it because it's just human nature in its infinite variety is not valid—yet.

Now, it's probably true that some women will bear children for money no matter what the law says. In the privacy of domestic life all sorts of strange arrangements are made. But why should the state enforce such bargains? Feminists who think regulation would protect the mother miss the whole point of the maternity contract, which is precisely to deprive her of protections she would have if she had signed nothing. If the contracts were unenforceable, the risk would be where it belongs, on the biological father and his wife, whose disappointment if the mother reneges, though real, can hardly be compared with a mother's unwilling loss of her just-born child. The real loser, of course, would be the baby-broker. (Noel Keane, the lawyer who arranged for Baby M, made about $300,000 last year in fees for such services.) And that would be a very good thing.

But most surrogates have been pleased with their experience.
Perhaps the Baby M trial is just a hard case making a bad law.

It's possible to be horrified by what happened to Mary Beth Whitehead and still think that contract motherhood can be a positive thing if carefully regulated. If there had been better screening at the clinic, if the contract had included a grace period, if actual infertility had been required of Elizabeth Stern, we would never have heard of Baby M. If, if, if.

Regulation might make contract motherhood less haphazard, but there is no way it can be made anything other than what it is: an inherently unequal relationship involving the sale of a woman's body and a child. The baby-broker's client is the father; his need is the one being satisfied; he pays the broker's fee. No matter how it is regulated, the business will have to reflect that priority. That's why the bill being considered in New York State specifically denies the mother a chance to change her mind, although the stringency of the Stern-Whitehead contract in this regard was the one thing pundits assured the public would not happen again. Better screening procedures would simply mean more accurately weeding out the trouble-makers and selecting for docility, naïveté, low self-esteem and lack of money for legal fees. Free psychological counseling for the mothers, touted by some brokers as evidence of their care and concern, would merely be manipulation by another name. True therapy seeks to increase a person's sense of self, not reconcile one to being treated as an instrument.

Even if the business could be managed so that all the adults involved were invariably pleased with the outcome, it would still be wrong, because they are not the only people involved. There are, for instance, the mother's other children. Prospective contract mothers, Mrs. Whitehead included, do not seem to consider for two seconds the message they are sending to their kids. But how can it not damage a child to watch Mom cheerfully produce and sell its half-sibling while Dad stands idly by? I'd love to be a fly on the wall as a mother reassures her kids that of course she loves them no matter what they do; it's just their baby sister who had a price tag.

And, of course, there is the contract baby. To be sure, there are worse ways of coming into the world, but not many, and none that are elaborately prearranged by sane people. Much is made of the so-called trauma of adoption, but adoption is a piece of cake compared with contracting. Adoptive parents can tell their child, Your mother loved you so much she gave you up, even though it made her sad, because that was best for you. What can the father and adoptive mother of a contract baby say? Your mother needed $10,000? Your mother wanted to do something nice for us, so she made you? The Sterns can't even say that. They'll have to make do with something like, Your mother loved you so much she wanted to keep you, but we took you anyway, because a deal's a deal, and anyway, she was a terrible person. Great.

Oh, lighten up. Surrogacy fills a need. There's a shortage of babies for adoption, and people have the right to a child.

What is the need that contract motherhood fills? It is not the need for a child, exactly. That need is met by adoption—although not very well, it's true, especially if parents have their hearts set on a "perfect baby," a healthy white newborn. The so-called baby shortage is really a shortage of those infants. (Shortage from the would-be adoptive parents' point of view; from the point of view of the birth mothers or Planned Parenthood, there's still a baby surplus.) What William Stern wanted, however, was not just a perfect baby; the Sterns did not, in fact, seriously investigate adoption. He wanted a perfect baby with his genes and a medically vetted mother who would get out of his life forever immediately after giving birth. That's a tall order, and one no other class of father—natural, step-, adoptive—even claims to be entitled to. Why should the law bend itself into a pretzel to gratify it?

The Vatican's recent document condemning all forms of conception but marital intercourse was marked by the church's usual political arrogance and cheeseparing approach to sexual intimacy, but it was right about one thing. You don't have a right to a child, any more than you have a right to a spouse. You only have the right to try to have one. Goods can be distributed according to ability to pay or need. People can't.

It's really that simple.

Incestuous Fathers and Their Families

Judith Lewis Herman

*These fathers . . . tend toward abuses of authority of every conceivable kind, and they not infre-
quently endeavor to secure their dominant position in the family by socially isolating the members of the family from the world outside. Swedish, American, and French surveys have pointed
time and again to the patriarchal position of such fathers, who set up a "primitive family
order."*

Herbert Maisch, *Incest*, 1972

Forty women who had had incestuous relationships with their fathers shared their stories with us. Most were young women in their twenties or early thirties. At the time we
met them, most had already married and some had already divorced; half had children.
They worked at common women's jobs; they were mothers and houseworkers, typists
and secretaries, waitresses and factory workers, teachers and nurses. About half came
from working-class and half from middle-class families.[1] Their ethnic and religious
backgrounds reflected the predominant Catholicism of the state of Massachusetts,
where most of them lived (see Tables 1 and 2). To all appearances, they were an ordinary group of women.

All of the informants were white. We made the decision to restrict the interviewing
to white women in order to avoid even the possibility that the information gathered
might be used to fuel idle speculation about racial differences. White people have in-
dulged for too long in discussion about the sexual capacities, behaviors, and misbe-
haviors of black people. There is no question, however, that incest is a problem in
black families, as it is in white families. Many of the first, most daring, and most honest contributions to the public discussion of incest were made by black women, and
much of our work has been inspired by theirs.[2]

All of the informants were outpatients in psychotherapy. Some allowed their therapists to discuss their histories with us; others agreed to be interviewed in person as
well; and a few, having heard of our study, carried on a correspondence with us. We
chose to restrict the study to women who had therapists because we believed that our
work could not be carried out without causing pain. Every interview we conducted
was stressful, both for the informants and for ourselves. As one woman commented,
"Every time I tell about it, I hurt in a new place." By limiting the study to patients in
therapy, we made certain that the informants had at least one safe place in which to
deal with their renewed memories. . . .

Though all the informants were patients in psychotherapy, they were not in any obvious manner a disturbed group of people. Most functioned quite well in their daily
lives, and some had achieved remarkable success, particularly in their work. They
were special, perhaps, only in that they had admitted to themselves that they had problems in their personal lives and were trying to do something about it. Our method of
locating the informants tended to select for a relatively healthy group of patients.

Our definition of incest reflected a predominantly psychological rather than a bio-

TABLE 1
DEMOGRAPHIC CHARACTERISTICS OF INCEST VICTIMS AND COMPARISON GROUP[a]

Demographic characteristic	Incest victims		Comparison group	
	No. = 40	%	No. = 20	%
Age				
18–25	23	57.5	11	55
26–30	7	17.5	6	30
31–35	5	12.5	2	10
36+	5	12.5	1	5
Mean	27.7		26.8	
Marital status				
Single	15	37.5	11	55
Married	14	35.	4	20
Separated or divorced	11	27.5	5	25
Children				
Yes	20	50	5	25
No	20	50	15	75
Religious background				
Catholic	17	42.5	8	40
Protestant	14	35	9	45
Jewish	5	12.5	3	15
n.a.	2	5		
Educational level				
Advanced degree	3	7.5	6	30
B.A.	12	30	7	35
Some college	11	27.5	7	35
High school graduate	10	25	0	0
<Twelfth grade	4	10	0	0

[a]Comparison group for tables 1–3 are daughters of seductive fathers.

logical or social concept of the taboo. Incest was defined to mean any sexual relationship between a child and an adult in a position of paternal authority. From the psychological point of view, it does not matter if the father and child are blood relatives. What matters is the relationship that exists by virtue of the adult's parental power and the child's dependency. In fact, most of the informants (thirty-one, or 78 percent) had been molested by their biologic fathers. Five had been molested by stepfathers, and four by adoptive fathers.

We further defined a sexual relationship to mean any physical contact that had to be kept a secret. From a biological or social point of view, only contact which might lead to defloration or pregnancy, that is vaginal intercourse, is dignified with the name of incest. This narrow definition is reflected both in the criminal codes of most states and in the popular thinking on the subject. From the point of view of the adult male, sexual activity that stops short of penile penetration is often described as "unconsummated," as though somehow it does not "count." But from a psychological point of view, espe-

TABLE 2
FAMILY BACKGROUND OF INCEST VICTIMS AND COMPARISON GROUP

Family background	Incest victims		Comparison group	
	No. = 40	%	No. = 20	%
Father's occupation				
Working class	19	47.5	11	55
Middle layers or				
self-employed	21	52.5	9	45
Mother employed outside home				
Yes	9	22.5	6	30
No	31	77.5	14	70
Parents separated or divorced				
Yes	9	22.5	5	25
No	31	77.5	15	75
Victim's place in family				
Only daughter	15	37.5	11	55
Oldest daughter	17	42.5	4	20
Other	8	20	5	25

cially from the child's point of view, the sexual motivation of the contact, and the fact that it must be kept secret, are far more significant than the exact nature of the act itself. From the moment that the father initiates the child into activities which serve the father's sexual needs, and which must be hidden from others, the bond between parent and child is corrupted.

The composite portrait of the incestuous family which emerged from the testimony of the informants is only one version of a complex reality. It is, first of all, a retrospective portrait, with all the simplification and distortion that inevitably degrades an adult's memory of childhood. Second, it is a portrait drawn from the perspective of the victim alone. Nevertheless, as the investigation progressed, we gained increasing confidence in the accuracy of the informants' accounts. Each individual's testimony had the vividness and integrity of well-preserved memory, and the accounts of many informants were so similar that they tended to validate each other. Finally, the general picture which emerged from the collective testimony of the informants has been corroborated in many respects by other researchers who have directly observed incestuous fathers, mothers, or entire families.

The families in which the informants grew up were conventional to a fault. Most were churchgoing and financially stable; they maintained a facade of respectability. They were for the most part unknown to mental health services, social agencies, or the police. Because they conformed to traditional family norms, their private disturbances were easily overlooked:

Marion: Yes, we were what you call an intact family. My mother lived at Church and Church functions. My father sang in the choir, and he molested me while my mother was at

Sunday School class parties. There was no drinking or smoking or anything the world could see. Only God knows.

The informants described their fathers as perfect patriarchs. They were, without question, the heads of their households. Their authority within the family was absolute, often asserted by force. They were also the arbiters of the family's social life and frequently succeeded in virtually secluding the women in the family. But while they were often feared within their families, they impressed outsiders as sympathetic, even admirable men.

The daughters themselves were often impressed, for their fathers did have many strengths. Most took their responsibility to provide for the family very seriously. Their daughters knew them to be hard-working, competent, and often very successful:

Yvonne: My father was a jack of all trades. Throughout his life he did many interesting things. He was manager of a state agency, foreman of a construction company, and even a politician; he ran for the State Senate. He was likable and could talk anyone into helping him out when he was in a jam. I remember him as a big man, about six feet tall, and very good-looking.

Christine: My sisters and I used to feel really proud to see our father dressed up in his uniform. Or when he was called away on flight duty we'd be very excited to hear him talk about bombs and how he was going to protect our country.

Thirty-one of the forty fathers were the sole support of their families. Two policemen, three military officers, two physicians, and two college professors were included in their number, as well as an assortment of businessmen, storekeepers, and skilled tradesmen. Many worked long hours and held more than one job. Their role as family breadwinner was honored with almost ritual solemnity:

Lily: No matter what had gone on that week, every Friday my father would bring home his paycheck. He'd take my mother's hand and put the check in it and close her hand over it without saying a word.

The competence in work and social life of incestuous fathers has also been documented in many previous studies. I. B. Weiner, in a clinical study of five fathers referred for outpatient treatment, observed that the fathers all had "successful work histories" and their families were not in "economic distress."[3] Herbert Maisch, in his study of 72 cases reported to the German courts, characterized the offenders as working-class men with average or above-average levels of skill.[4] Several investigators remarked as well on the fathers' above-average intelligence.[5] Noel Lustig, in his study of six military men who committed incest, described the fathers as "strongly motivated to maintain a facade of role competence as the family patriarch in the eyes of society." The men were well thought of outside their families.[6]

In addition, the families of our informants adhered rigidly to the traditional sexual division of labor. Most of the mothers were full-time houseworkers who depended entirely upon their husbands for their livelihood. Six mothers did some part-time work outside the home. Only three mothers had full-time jobs. None of the mothers had the working skills or experience which would have made independent survival a realistic option.

The mothers were considered inferior to the fathers, not only in their work achievements, but also simply in their status as women. These were families in which sex roles were rigidly defined, and male superiority was unquestioned:

Christine: My father just thought women were stupid. He had a very, very low opinion of women, and he never made my mother feel like she was worth anything. Nothing she could do was any good.

The preference for males was expressed in countless ways. Boys in the family were given more freedom and privileges than girls, or were excused from household chores. Some families paid for the education of their sons but not their daughters. One daughter recalled that with each of her mother's numerous pregnancies, her father proudly informed the relatives that his wife was expecting a boy.

In many families, it was considered a male prerogative to supervise and restrict the activities of the females. Fathers exercised minute control over the lives of their wives and daughters, often virtually confining them to the house. The boys in the family were sometimes enlisted as deputies in this policing role. Many daughters reported that their fathers discouraged their mothers from driving a car, visiting friends, or participating in activities outside the home:

Yvonne: My mother was a secretary when she met my father, and she became his secretary. After they were married, my parents moved away from my mother's birthplace, to Vermont. My father told my mother she should not work or drive there because it was too cold and too dangerous in the snow. She never drove or worked again.

Daughters were also deterred from establishing any independent social contacts. The fathers consolidated their power within the family by isolating their wives and children from the outside world:

Sheila: We had no visitors. My father was very exclusive, and my mother was afraid to let people in when he had been drinking. People just didn't come to our house. I remember my best friend who lived across the street from me: people would float in and out of her house like it was Grand Central Station. I used to think, wouldn't it be nice to be able to do that.

One of the most significant distinguishing characteristics of the incestuous fathers was their tendency to dominate their families by the use of force. Half of the informants reported that their fathers were habitually violent and that they themselves had seen their mothers beaten. Other children in the family were often beaten as well. The fathers were selective in their choice of targets: one child was often singled out as a scapegoat, while a more favored child was spared. This lesson was not lost on the daughters, who quickly recognized the advantages of being in their fathers' good graces:

Esther: My father is an extremely macho and egotistical person, an educated elitist who always felt that he married beneath him. In fact, he is extremely intelligent and artistically creative. I have always admired his superior intellect and his talent. But he is also a very willful and childishly demanding person who has always had his own way. He is and always was subject to fits of irrational violence, and the whole family is scared to death of him. Except for me, that is.

This violence, though terrifying to the mothers and children, did not exceed certain clear limits. No family member was injured seriously enough to require hospitalization, though there were some close calls, and no outside intervention was provoked. Although the fathers often appeared completely out of control in the privacy of their homes, they never made the mistake of attacking outsiders. They were not known as bullies or troublemakers; in the presence of superior authority, they were generally ingratiating, deferential, even meek. In this, as in many other aspects of family life, they seemed exquisitely sensitive to the bounds of the male prerogative, and did not exceed the socially condoned limits of violence.

Many previous studies have recognized the dictatorial role of fathers in incestuous families. One explained the father's "dominant position" as resulting from his "intimidation and control of the family."[7] Another described the father as "the authoritarian head of the house."[8] Still another observer indicated that "in an overwhelming majority of all cases, the family structure was formed by . . . the dominating influence of the husband and father."[9]

Other observers, however, have described the same fathers as "ineffectual and dependent," "inadequate," or "weak, insecure and vulnerable.[10] Far from appearing as tyrants, these fathers emerge as rather pitiful men, sometimes even as victims of a "domineering or managing wife."[11] The solution to this apparent contradiction lies in the fathers' ability to assess their relative power in any situation and to vary their behavior accordingly. In the presence of men much more powerful than themselves, such as police, prosecutors, therapists, and researchers, the fathers knew how to present themselves as pathetic, helpless, and confused. Only in the privacy of their homes, where they knew they would encounter no effective opposition, did they indulge their appetites for domination. Face to face with men of equal or superior authority, they became engaging and submissive.

Male professionals who are not themselves intimidated often find it hard to imagine how women and children might be. As one expert on child abuse admits: "Many sexually abusive fathers are described as tyrants in the home . . . Professionals who have worked with sexual abuse frequently encounter a father who has been described in these terms. When he enters the office for an interview, the professional is astonished to find this 'violent and unpredictable' man to be 5'7", 150 pounds and neatly dressed. He is of a calm disposition and appears to be a rather anxious, harassed and overburdened man, puzzled by recent events."[12] A 5'7", 150-pound man out in public and on good behavior may not seem at all frightening to a larger man in a position of authority. But the same man may be quite large enough to terrorize his wife and children behind closed doors.

Alcoholism was another common characteristic of the incestuous fathers of our informants, though not a distinguishing one. Over a third of the informants considered their fathers to be problem drinkers. Like the violence, however, the fathers' drinking was effectively concealed from outsiders. Family relationships were often severely disrupted by the father's excessive drinking, and in a few cases the father's health was seriously affected, but most fathers retained their ability to work and to conform to normal standards of public behavior. If the father's drinking problem was recognized at all, it usually fell into the category of "a good man's failing." Very few fathers received any medical or psychiatric treatment for alcoholism or, for that matter, for any other problem.

Alcoholism has frequently been associated with incestuous behavior. In one study of imprisoned sex offenders, for example, 46 percent of the incestuous fathers were diagnosed as alcoholic, a figure that approximates our own. But as that study points out, although sex offenders who are alcoholic often commit their crimes while drunk, it is naive to attribute the offense to demon alcohol. The sexual assault, more often than not, is planned in advance. On careful questioning, offenders often admit that they drink in order to gather courage for the approach.[13]

While the fathers of our informants preserved a facade of competent social functioning, the mothers were often unable to fulfill their traditional roles. Over half of the informants (55 percent) remembered that their mothers had had periods of disabling illness which resulted in frequent hospitalizations or in the mother's living as an invalid at home. Over a third (38 percent) of the daughters had been separated from their mothers for some period of time during childhood. The separations occurred because their mothers either were hospitalized or felt unable to cope with their child care duties and temporarily placed their daughters in the care of relatives. Three mothers died before their daughters were grown, one by suicide. Another mother committed suicide after her daughter left home.

Depression, alcoholism, and psychosis were among the most common causes of the mothers' disability. Many daughters remembered their mothers as suffering from mysterious ailments which made them seem withdrawn, peculiar, and unavailable. One daughter reported that when she was ten, her mother developed the delusion that she was dying of cancer and took to bed for a year. Many other daughters commented on their mothers' strange maladies which seemed to elude definition:

> *Janet:* She was almost like a recluse. She was very alone. It was obvious to me by the time I reached high school that my mother was really strange. My sisters and I used to joke about it.

As in the case of the fathers, the mothers' psychiatric and medical problems usually went undiagnosed and untreated.

If the cause of the mother's ailment sometimes seemed obscure, in other cases it was only too obvious: repeated enforced pregnancies. The average number of children for this group of mothers was 3.6, well above the national mean of 2.2. Seventeen mothers had four children or more, and five had eight or more children. Although some daughters reported that their mothers loved babies and had always wanted large families, in many cases the pregnancies were more or less imposed on women who felt helpless to prevent them:

> *Rita:* I blame my father for her death, to a certain degree. After the seventh child, they found out she had cancer, and they told her not to get pregnant again. But she couldn't control it, my father being the man he is. He felt, if you're going to have sex, you have to have the child. And he was the type of man who would say, if I can't get it from my wife, I'll go elsewhere. He's also the type of man where, if she didn't want to open her legs, he'd pinch her thighs.

Whether or not they wanted to have many children, the mothers of large families often suffered physically from their multiple pregnancies and became overwhelmed with the burden of caring for many small children:

Christine: Now I know she was only 98 pounds at the age of twenty-five. She was yellow, jaundiced; she had some kind of kidney infection; and she was sick with every one of her pregnancies. We were barely a year apart, and I think having kids in such rapid succession, my mother was really tired out.

Four of the mothers also had severely handicapped children, whose care absorbed virtually all their energies. . . .

Economically dependent, socially isolated, in poor health, and encumbered with the care of many small children, these mothers were in no position to challenge their husbands' domination or to resist their abuses. No matter how badly they were treated, most simply saw no option other than submission to their husbands. They conveyed to their daughters the belief that a woman is defenseless against a man, that marriage must be preserved at all costs, and that a wife's duty is to serve and endure.

Most of our informants remembered their mothers as weak and powerless, finding their only dignity in martyrdom. The few who described their mothers as strong meant by this that there was apparently no limit to their capacity for suffering:

Rita: She held on because that's all she had. Everything she did was self-sacrifice. She made sure there was food on everyone's plate—whatever we left behind, that's what she ate. She went around in the same housedress and a pair of loafers day after day—never any new clothing. She never wore makeup, never colored her hair, never spent money on herself. Her kids came first.

Anne-Marie: She always said, give with one hand and you'll get with the other, but she gave with two hands and always went down. She was nothing but a floor mat. She sold out herself and her self-respect. She was a love slave to my father.

None of the fathers adapted to their wives' disabilities by assuming a maternal role in the family. Rather, they reacted to their wives' illnesses as if they themselves were being deprived of mothering. As the family providers, they felt they had the right to be nurtured and served at home, if not by their wives, then by their daughters.

Thirty-two (80 percent) of the informants were the oldest or the only daughters in their families.[14] Before the age of ten, almost half (45 percent) had been pressed into service as "little mothers" within the family. They cared for their younger sisters and brothers and took on responsibility for major household tasks. Many became astonishingly competent in this role. Pride in their accomplishments as little adults became their compensation for loss of childhood:

Christine: I could see that my mother needed help, but she wouldn't ask for it; she'd nag and bitch, and that would turn my sisters off. My sisters were very unproductive. So I'd pitch in without being asked. I'd vacuum, I'd do the laundry, I'd wash the dishes, I'd do this, I'd do that. This was from the time I was, oh, nine. I still think I can do a lot of things better than my mother.

Whether or not they were obliged to take on household responsibilities, most of the daughters were assigned a special duty to "keep Daddy happy." They mediated parental quarrels and placated their fathers when their mothers dared not approach them. They became their fathers' confidantes and often shared their grievances and secrets.

In their special roles as little mother or as father's consort, the daughters believed that they bore the responsibility for holding the family together. None of the informants thought that her parents were happily married; many were well aware that their parents were miserable together. Though a few daughters wished devoutly that their parents would divorce, most dreaded this possibility, and did whatever they could to avert it. They lived in terror that their fathers would desert the family and that their mothers would fall apart completely.

Since it was their duty to provide a sympathetic audience for their fathers, many daughters heard about their parents' marital troubles in great detail. The fathers' complaints were monotonously simple. They considered themselves deprived of the care to which they felt entitled. In their estimation, their wives were not giving enough: they were cold; they were frigid; they refused sex; they withheld love.

These complaints seemed plausible enough to the daughters, who themselves often felt deprived of maternal affection. Some daughters were additionally aware that their mothers had highly negative sexual attitudes:

Janet: My mother is a terrible prude. I don't remember any of her sayings, but I remember the feeling behind them. It was so ugly, it made sex sound like the dirtiest thing around.

In retrospect, however, most daughters felt that their fathers' complaints wore a little thin and that their parents' problems must have been more complicated than their fathers' accounts had led them to believe. As adults, they puzzled over what went wrong and who was most at fault:

Marion: In my case I put most of the blame on my mother. She is a cold person—cannot show love to anyone except babies. She started a large family and ignored my father from the day she got pregnant. I have seen her many times shove Daddy away from her. I feel she drove my Dad to this thing. He was starved for affection. Still, he may have had a deeper problem; I'll never know. He couldn't seem to keep his hands to himself. I never brought a girlfriend home. He would squeeze all the neighbors' wives in the wrong places. He didn't seem to care if we saw him or not. He made me sick at my stomach.

Janet: He would just talk in very personal terms about how deprived he was. But then my mother says she always did have sex with him, so I don't know who was telling the truth.

At the time, most of the daughters took their fathers' side. It was easy enough to sympathize with the fathers' feeling of deprivation, for most of the daughters themselves felt slighted or neglected by their mothers. Though many could see that their mothers were ill or overwhelmed with their own problems, few, as children, could afford the luxury of compassion. They knew only that they bore the burden of their mothers' shortcomings and were obliged to nurture others while their own longings for nurture went unsatisfied. In these circumstances, the daughters could not escape feeling profoundly disappointed in their mothers.

At best, the daughters viewed their mothers ambivalently, excusing their weaknesses as best they could. The one daughter out of the forty who cherished a positive image of her mother did so on the basis of a fantasy which she created after her mother's death. Though her mother had endured savage beatings herself and had been helpless to prevent the abuse of her children, this daughter clung to the belief that her mother would have taken protective action, had she lived.

At worst, the relations between mother and daughter were marked by active hostility. Many of the daughters remembered their mothers only with bitterness and contempt. They described the women who had borne them as selfish, uncaring, and cruel. In their moments of despair, these daughters felt the absence of the most primary bonds of caring and trust. They believed they had been unwanted from the moment of their birth, and they cursed their mothers for bringing them into the world:

Esther: My mother was extraordinarily rejecting. I was born ten months after my brother, and I was clearly an "accident," greatly regretted.

Paula: She's an asshole. I really don't like my mom. I guess I am bitter. She's very selfish. She was seventeen when she had me, and her mother put her in a home. She blames me for ruining her life because she got pregnant with me. But I'm not the one who spread my legs.

Sandra: Why do people bother having kids? Why did my mother have me? I'm sure in those days people knew how to get rid of them. She seemed to know how. I wish she was dead so I could forget about her—or that I was dead so that she'd suffer. Why does God allow people like her to live?

Other authors have also remarked on the alienation between mothers and daughters which seems to prevail in incestuous families. Maisch found that 61 percent of the mothers and daughters in his study had a distant or hostile relationship which preceded the onset of overt incest.[15]

By contrast, most of our informants had some fond memories of their fathers. Although they feared their fathers, they also admired their competence and power. Many described their fathers as gifted, likable, and intelligent, terms that they rarely applied to their mothers. Some remembered that, as children, they had frankly adored their fathers:

Sheila: It was nice having a father who did things with you. He loved to take us on trips and show us around. He was fun to be with.

Lenore: We had long intellectual conversations. My father lectured me about history. I was a captive audience. I was so impressed. He was my idol.

Feelings of pity for the fathers were also common. With few exceptions, the daughters seemed more tolerant of their fathers' shortcomings and more forgiving of their failures than they were toward their mothers, or themselves:

Esther: I find that most of my anger is toward my mother rather than my father. I know that is not quite rational, but I can't help feeling that the bond between mother and child ought to be such that a child is assured protection. I somehow do not expect that fathers are as responsible for the welfare of offspring as mothers are.

All of the daughters received favored treatment from their fathers, in the form of gifts, privileges, or exemption from punishments. Many spent long hours in the exclusive company of their fathers, often on adventures which were kept secret from the rest of the family:

> *Christine:* He used to call me his mama-san, and I used to massage his feet. He used to take me to stag bars. I thought that was great. I used to really like him. I was definitely Daddy's girl.

In the special alliance with their fathers, many daughters found the sense of being cared for which they craved, and which they obtained from no other source. The attentions of their fathers offered some compensation for what was lacking in their relations with their mothers.

Mothers were often suspicious and resentful of this special relationship. They perceived, correctly, that what bound father and daughter together was in part a shared hostility toward themselves. The mothers' resentment made the daughters feel guilty, but could not entirely extinguish the pleasure they derived from their favored status. Some even exulted in their mothers' mortification:

> *Paula:* Face it, she was just jealous. The man she loved preferred me!

These daughters, in short, were alienated from their mothers, whom they saw as weak, helpless, and unable to nurture or protect them. They were elevated by their fathers to a special position in the family, in which many of the mothers' duties and privileges were assigned to them. They felt obligated to fulfill this role in order to keep their families together. Moreover, their special relationship with their fathers was often perceived as their only source of affection. Under these circumstances, when their fathers chose to demand sexual services, the daughters felt they had absolutely no option but to comply.

Most of the daughters (80 percent) were under thirteen years of age when their fathers first approached them sexually. The average age was nine. The sexual contact was limited at first to fondling and gradually proceeded to masturbation and oral-genital contact. Most fathers did not attempt vaginal intercourse, at least until their daughters had reached puberty. Force was rarely used. It was not necessary:

> *Yvonne:* The first time I remember any sexual advances, I was about four or five. I hadn't started school yet. My parents were having a party—that is, my mother was entertaining some women. My father took my brother and me to bed to be out of the way. My brother lay on one side of him, me on the other. I remember him curling up beside me, pressing me to him from behind and touching my vagina. I also remember him playing with my ass. I only remember lying there and him telling me that was what Adam and Eve did, so it was okay.

Those authors who restrict their definition of incest to intercourse find that the daughters are somewhat older, on the average, at the onset of the relationship. In Maisch's study, the average age of the daughter was 12¼ at the time intercourse began.[16] Other researchers who define incest, as we do, to mean any sexual contact find, as we do, that most relationships begin when the children are grade-schoolers. The girls in one study were five to fourteen years old; those in another were between the ages of six and fourteen.[17]

The father's explanations to our informants, if any were offered, always sounded silly in retrospect. Younger girls were told, "This is how we learn about the birds and the bees," "This is our special game," or "Don't you want to make Daddy feel good?" Older girls were told, "I'm getting you ready for your husband," "You should feel comfortable about sex," or "You need me to teach you the facts of life." Many of the fathers seemed to consider it their parental prerogative to introduce their daughters to sex.

Sometimes the sexual encounter took on the aspect of an initiation rite. By introducing their daughters into secret and forbidden knowledge, the fathers compelled their daughters to leave girlhood behind and taught them something about their place in the world as women:

Jackie: That was the year I grew up. I got my period, and I gave up my dolls and stopped being a tomboy.

Sara: As a child I thought, why would someone that I love and who loves me do anything wrong to me. There seemed to be no other answer but . . . this is natural, and this is the way it is. I thought maybe, just maybe, this was my personal indoctrination into womanhood.[18]

Seven of the daughters could remember only a single incident in which they were molested by their fathers. But the majority recalled that once begun, the sexual contact was repeated whenever the father could find an opportunity. On the average, the incestuous relationship went on for three years. Other studies agree that the majority of incestuous relationships are of long duration.[19]

Although many of our informants were too young to have a clear idea of the significance of the father's behavior, the father's furtive attitude usually indicated to the daughters that there was something wrong with what they were doing:

Lenore: When I was around seven, that's when the first sexual incident happened with my father. They used to have us kids in bed with them sometimes, and he continued this after mother was in the hospital. I got more favored attention. One time he called me in. He had a hard on and he had a rubber on. He told me to jerk him off. He told me to squeeze it and he came. I was a pretty innocent kid, pretty isolated. I didn't know what it was. I can't remember whether he told me not to tell, but it was intense and hurried and he was ashamed. He sent me away right after he came. I knew he would deny it, but I have a vivid memory of it.

Few of the daughters had anything positive to say about the sexual contact itself. Though many enjoyed other aspects of their special relationship with their fathers, most dreaded the sexual encounters and invented whatever pitiful strategies they could to avoid them:

Rita: I hated it all the time; it was like a nightmare. There was nothing I could do. I went along with the program. I don't know why he went along with it, because I never responded. Every time I'd say, "Daddy, I gotta go pee." You know, anything to get out of it.

Fear, disgust, and shame were the feelings most commonly remembered. Most of the daughters coped with the sexual episodes by mentally dissociating themselves from them. They "froze up" or pretended that "it wasn't really happening":

Sheila: My head just died then. It was an impossible thing for me to handle, so I just didn't handle it. It's like it never happened. Every time I try to talk about it, my mind goes blank. It's like everything explodes in my head.

A few informants remembered that they had experienced some pleasure in the sexual encounters, or that they had sometimes initiated the contact once the routine of the sexual relationship had become established. These memories only exacerbated their feelings of confusion and shame:

Paula: With my father, I was the aggressor. He'd come in my bed and cuddle me and eat me; then he'd threaten me not to tell. He loved me very much. He just had a sickness. He was a good man in every other way. He went to church and worked six days a week. Maybe I did go up to my father and cuddle him, but I was a child; you don't make anything of it.

In these few instances, the fathers might have been able to convince themselves that their daughters desired and enjoyed their sexual attentions. But in most cases, the fathers persisted in their sexual demands even in the face of their daughters' obvious reluctance. Why they chose to do so is a matter of speculation. Presumably, they experienced their own needs as so compelling that they chose to ignore their daughters' unhappiness.

Some researchers who have studied incestuous fathers directly emphasize the father's unfulfilled dependent wishes and fear of abandonment. In the father's fantasy life, the daughter becomes the source of all the father's infantile longings for nurturance and care. He thinks of her first as the idealized childhood bride or sweetheart, and finally as the all-good, all-giving mother. The reality, that she is the child and he the adult, becomes quite immaterial to him. In the compulsive sexual act he seeks repeated reassurance that she will never refuse or frustrate him.[20]

In addition, the father must experience the sexual act itself as powerfully rewarding. He can structure the sexual encounter exactly to his liking, with no fear that his performance will be judged or ridiculed. His excitement is heightened by the need for secrecy and the sense of indulging in the forbidden. The sexual contact becomes like an addiction, one which, unlike alcohol or other drugs, leaves no morning hangover other than possibly a guilty conscience. The incestuous father can indulge his habit repeatedly and suffer no bodily consequences; if there are any, it is the daughter who suffers them.

Finally, in some cases the daughter's unhappiness actually contributes to the father's enjoyment. Many researchers have noted that incest, like other sex crimes, fulfills the offender's hostile and aggressive wishes. Power and dominance, rather than sexual pleasure, may be the primary motivation. One researcher, who administered psychological tests to convicted incest offenders, concluded that the incest was an expression of hostility to all women, and that the daughter was selected as the victim because she was perceived as the woman least capable of retaliation.[21]

Most of our informants were warned not to tell anyone about the sexual episodes. They were threatened with the most dreadful consequences if they told: their mothers would have a nervous breakdown, their parents would divorce, their fathers would be put in jail, or they themselves would be punished and sent away from home. One way or another, the girls were given to understand that breaking secrecy would lead to separation from one or both of their parents. Those who remembered no warnings simply intuited that guarding the incest secret was part of their obligation to keep the family together:

> *Janet:* I just knew there would be dire consequences if I told. My mother would fall apart, or they would separate. I didn't even want to imagine what would happen.

In some cases, the fathers threatened severe bodily harm:

> *Maggie:* He told me if I told anyone he would have me shot. I believed him because he was a cop. I'm thirty years old and I'm still afraid of him.

The majority of the daughters (58 percent) never explicitly told their mothers, or anyone else, of the incest as long as they remained at home. Nevertheless, they longed for their mothers to come to their rescue. Often they tried, indirectly, to indicate to their mothers that something was wrong. Many had vague symptoms of distress: they complained of abdominal pains or pain while urinating; they became fearful or withdrawn; they had nightmares. Such "nonspecific" symptoms are typical of incestuously abused children, in the observations of many clinicians.[22] A few of our informants as children developed compulsive, ritualized sexual behaviors that would have alerted any knowledgeable observer to the fact that something was wrong. For instance, one girl, at the age of five, began approaching male acquaintances and unzipping their pants. Others "experimented" sexually with younger children, subjecting them to the same assaults to which they themselves had been subjected. These and numerous other indirect cries for help were ignored or misunderstood by the mothers. Many daughters believed that their mothers knew, or should have known, about the incest, and they bitterly resented the fact that their mothers did not intervene:

> *Sheila:* One day she was at work, and she was so worried that something really bad was happening at home that she actually left work and came home. When she got home, I was locked in the bathroom crying, and I remember her saying to my father, "What's the matter with her?" I guess I have a hard time reconciling the fact that that happened and she still didn't realize I was in trouble. How come she never asked *me* what was happening to me? How come she never tried to find out how *I* felt?

> *Christine:* My mother's philosophy is to ignore things and hope they'll go away. She's always a victim; even in little things she always finds stupid reasons why she can't do anything about the situation. She knew about the incest; there's no way she couldn't have known. But she's never acknowledged it. She just says men are that way and there's nothing she could do about it.

Those daughters who did confide in their mothers were uniformly disappointed in their mothers' responses. Most of the mothers, even when made aware of the situation, were unwilling or unable to defend their daughters. They were too frightened or too dependent upon their husbands to risk a confrontation. Either they refused to believe their daughters, or they believed them but took no action. They made it clear to their daughters that their fathers came first and that, if necessary, the daughters would have to be sacrificed:

> *Yvonne:* The last time my father made these advances I was about eight or nine. My mom caught us again and my dad promised he wouldn't do it again. Then he got very drunk, went

outside, and lay under a tree at night. My mom woke me up and told me my dad was drunk under the tree and wouldn't come in. She wanted me to ask him to come in before he got pneumonia. I got up, went out on the porch—it was damp and cool out—and did as my mother asked. I asked my dad to come in. He did. I decided after that that they were both pretty nuts.

Only three mothers, on learning about the incest, responded by separating from their husbands, and even in these few cases the separations were brief. The mothers found life without their husbands too hard to bear, and they took them back within a matter of months. Three other mothers, on discovering the incest secret, sent their daughters away from home:

Paula: She was afraid I'd become a lesbian or a whore. So she put me in a mental hospital. It was a good excuse to get rid of me.

In general, those daughters who told their mothers had reason to regret it. Sensing correctly that no protection would be forthcoming if they told, most of the daughters bore the incestuous relationship in silence, biding their time until they were old enough to leave home.

Some of the daughters developed close relationships with adult women outside the family, which partially compensated for their disappointment with their mothers. Though few dared to confide their secrets to these outsiders, the relationships helped the daughters to endure the misery of their family life:

Marion: My mother's sister was the only person in my childhood that I remember relating to at all. She lived on a farm with her three children, and I used to go there in the summer. I love the outdoors and that is where I would play most of the time. I never stayed at home if I could help it. I didn't tell her about my Dad, but we talked about Mom and how funny she acted sometimes. She said if I knew how they had been brought up, I would understand. She never explained it. I remember wishing she was my mother.

Sandra: My best friend's mother used to take me in when my mother threw me out. If it weren't for her, I'd be sleeping in hallways. Anyone with half a brain and half a heart would open their doors, but not too many really do it. I was well off there; I lived with them till I had my first labor pains. Marriage was a change for the worse. I wish I'd stayed with them.

The girls who found surrogate mothers were among the most fortunate. All of the women longed for a mother who could be strong, competent, and affectionate. Many desperately envied their friends and classmates who appeared to have normal mothers:

Lenore: When I hear other women complaining about their mothers, I feel like screaming, "You stupid idiot, don't you realize how lucky you are?"

Some of the daughters expressed their disappointment in both parents by elaborating the fantasy that they were adopted and that their true parents would one day find and rescue them. Others simply resigned themselves to the fact that, from an emotional point of view, they were orphans:

Janet: I remember very clearly at age nine I decided that if they did get divorced, I didn't want to live with either one of them.

As the daughters reached adolescence, they often became more assertive and rebellious. The fathers responded with intense jealousy, bordering on paranoia. They did whatever they could to seclude and isolate their daughters and to prevent them from developing normal relationships with peers. They saw the outside world as filled with sexual dangers and opportunities, and they often regarded their daughters as untrustworthy little bitches who needed to be closely guarded. Many daughters reported that their fathers would tear up their clothes, forbid lipstick or makeup, and refuse to allow parties or dates:

> *Sheila:* He would raise the roof because of the clothing that I wore or how I looked. I think I was the last kid in my whole group to start wearing lipstick. I didn't really understand what it was all about. All I knew was my father was telling me I was very bad for some reason and it all involved *that.*

Other fathers eventually accepted the inevitable and permitted their daughters to have some social life, but insisted on interrogating their daughters about their sexual activities:

> *Lenore:* He would tell me not to throw myself away on some boy and sacrifice my intellect. I got the message loud and clear that you can't be sexual and have your intellect too. Later I realized that he wanted to keep me for himself. I was Daddy's little girl. When I hit high school, around age fifteen, I started screwing around a lot. I had been so isolated I never made friends. This seemed like an easy way to make contact with people. As soon as my father found out, he would find an excuse to beat the crap out of me. It happened whenever I had a new boyfriend. Supposedly his attitude was very libertarian. He wanted to hear about what I was doing. He was kind of lecherous about it.

As the fathers' jealousy and sexual demands became more and more intolerable, the daughters began to try to escape from the family. Thirteen girls ran away from home at least once (see Table 3). Most of the attempts were short-lived, for the girls quickly realized that they were not equipped to survive in the street, and they reluctantly returned home. Only two girls managed to make good their escape. From mid-adolescence, they supported themselves as strippers or prostitutes:

> *Paula:* I ran away to New York. I was on my own at age sixteen. I never had a pimp; I wasn't that crazy. I knew a lot of women in the business and I did a lot of speed and downs. If I hadn't met up with my boyfriend, I'd be dead today.

Three girls who ran away were pursued, caught, and committed to hospitals on "stubborn child" complaints. Their incest history did not come to light during these hospitalizations. Three others tried to get away from home by requesting foster placements or admission to residential schools. They, too, were unsuccessful:

> *Esther:* The way I was able to get away from my father was by running away with an older man. Before that I had tried to get professional help with the aim of being placed in a girls' residence. I had several sessions with a social worker to whom I was unable to reveal the reason for my intense desire to leave home. She met with my father, and she was favorably impressed with his great love and concern for me. She refused to help me gain admittance at that girls' residence.

Just as the girls' childhood distress symptoms had been ignored, their adolescent escape attempts were misunderstood. None of the professionals with whom these girls

TABLE 3
DISTRESS SYMPTOMS IN INCEST VICTIMS AND COMPARISON GROUP

Distress symptom	Incest victims		Comparison
	No. = 40	%	No. = 20
Adolescent pregnancy[a]			
Yes	18	45	3
No	22	55	17
Runaway attempt			
Yes	13	32.5	1
No	27	67.5	19
Major depressive symptoms			
Yes	24	60	11
No	16	40	9
Suicide attempt			
Yes	15	37.5	1
No	25	62.5	19
Drug or alcohol abuse			
Yes	8	35	1
No	32	65	19
Sexual problems			
Yes	21	55	10
No	19	45	10
Promiscuity			
Yes	14	35	3
No	26	65	17
Victimization			
Yes (rape)	6	15	3
(beatings[a])	11	27.5	0
No	24	60	17
Self-image[b]			
Predominantly +	3	7.5	2
Dual or confused ±	13	32.5	16
Predominantly −	24	60	2

[a]Differences between the two groups were significant at the $p < .05$ level.
[b]Differences between the two groups were significant at the $p < .02$ level.

came into contact undertook to find out why they were so desperate to get away from their families.

Sooner or later, most of the daughters realized that the only way to escape from their fathers was to find another powerful male protector. A great many became pregnant or married prematurely. Eighteen of the forty women (45 percent) became pregnant during adolescence. In most cases, they had no particular desire for children, and the pregnancies were unintended. Planned or not, however, the pregnancies usually did put an end to the incest.[23]

For many of the daughters, marriage appeared to be the passport to freedom. Some confessed the incest secret for the first time to their husbands or fiances. A number of the men responded in a very caring and appropriate manner: they were angry at the fathers and concerned about the harm that had been done to the daughters. Women who were lucky enough to find men who responded in this way usually felt extremely grateful.

As the fathers felt their daughters slipping out of their control, they began to cast about for substitutes. If there were younger sisters in the family, the fathers often transferred their sexual attentions to them. In eleven families (28 percent), incest was repeated with younger sisters. In another ten families (25 percent), the daughters suspected that their sisters had been molested but could not be positive about it. In one third of the families, there was no repetition of the incest because there were no available sisters. The phenomenon of the father's "moving on" to a younger daughter has been observed by many authors, some of whom report even higher proportions of families in which this occurs.[24]

Brothers were not molested, according to our informants. However, a number of brothers were physically abused, and several developed assaultive and abusive behavior in identification with their fathers. One of the daughters was molested by her brother as well as her father; she felt that her father, in breaching the incest taboo, had given her brother tacit permission to do the same. Others suspected that their brothers were carrying on the family tradition in the next generation:

> *Marion:* In all your research do you think it's inherited? I hate to say this, but I think my brother has the problem. I remember we had a cottage at the ocean when his little girl was three or four. I caught them in bed one time when we were all supposed to be gone. I saw him fondling her and it made me sick. After that I saw very little of him until recently. He has two granddaughters now. I feel he's abnormally proud of the one; I can't explain it, but it's there. This I have never told anyone.

In several families, the fathers deserted once the daughters had left home. This outcome confirmed the daughters' belief that they had been responsible for keeping the family together, and that the parents' marriage depended upon the incestuous relationship for its survival.

In no case was the incestuous relationship ended by the father. The daughters put a stop to the sexual contact as soon as they could, by whatever means they could. But most felt that in their fathers' minds, the incestuous affair never ended, and that their fathers would gladly resume the sexual relationship if they were ever given an opportunity. Though all the daughters eventually succeeded in escaping from their families, they felt, even at the time of the interview, that they would never be safe with their fathers, and that they would have to defend themselves as long as their fathers lived.

NOTES

1 Class backgrounds were determined in accordance with criteria in Harry Braverman, *Labor and Monopoly Capital* (New York: Monthly Review Press, 1974). "Middle class" is shorthand for the combined categories of "middle layers of employment" and "self-employed."

2 Maya Angelou, *I Know Why the Caged Bird Sings* (New York: Random House, 1970);

Anne Moody, *Coming of Age in Mississippi* (New York: Dial Press, 1968); Toni Morrison, *The Bluest Eye* (New York: Holt, Rinehart & Winston, 1970); Gayl Jones, *Corregidora* (New York: Random House, 1975).

3 I. B. Weiner, "Father-Daughter Incest: A Clinical Report," *Psychiatric Quarterly* 36 (1962): 607–632.

4 Herbert Maisch, *Incest* (New York: Stein & Day, 1972).

5 Weiner, "Father-Daughter Incest"; Hector Cavallin, "Incestuous Fathers: A Clinical Report," *American Journal of Psychiatry* 122 (1966): 1132–1138.

6 Noel Lustig, John Dresser, Seth Spellman and Thomas Murray, "Incest: A Family Group Survival Pattern," *Archives of General Psychiatry* 14 (1966): 31–40.

7 S. Kirson Weinberg, *Incest Behavior* (New York: Citadel, 1955), p. 63.

8 Bruno Cormier, Miriam Kennedy, and Jadwiga Sangowicz, "Psychodynamics of Father-Daughter Incest," *Canadian Psychiatric Association Journal* 7 (1962): 206.

9 Maisch, *Incest,* p. 139.

10 David Raphling, Bob Carpenter, and Allan Davis, "Incest: A Genealogical Study," *Archives of General Psychiatry* 16 (1967): 505–511; Lukianowicz, "Incest," p. 304; Werner Tuteur, "Further Observations on Incestuous Fathers," *Psychiatric Annals* 2 (1972): 77.

11 Joseph Peters, "Children Who Are Victims of Sexual Assault and the Psychology of Offenders," *American Journal of Psychotherapy* 30 (1976): 411.

12 David Walters, *Physical and Sexual Abuse of Children* (Bloomington: Indiana University Press, 1975), p. 122.

13 Richard Rada, Robert Kellner, D. R. Laws, and Walter Winslow, "Drinking, Alcoholism, and the Mentally Disordered Sex Offender," *Bulletin of the American Academy of Psychiatry and Law* 6 (1978): 296–300.

14 Several other authors have commented on the oldest daughter's particular vulnerability to incestuous abuse. See e.g. Tormes, *Child Victims of Incest;* Browning and Boatman, "Children at Risk"; Weinberg, *Incest Behavior;* Karin Meiselman, *Incest* (San Francisco: Jossey-Bass, 1978).

15 Maisch, *Incest.*

16 Maisch, *Incest.*

17 Lukianowicz, "Incest"; Irving Kaufman, Alice Peck, and Consuelo Tagiuri, "The Family Constellation and Overt Incestuous Relations Between Father and Daughter," *American Journal of Orthopsychiatry* 24 (1954): 266–277.

18 Anonymous letter, May 1979, in *Reaching Out,* newsletter of RESPOND, an organization working with women and domestic violence in Somerville, Mass.

19 Weinberg, *Incest Behavior;* Maisch, *Incest;* Kaufman et al., "Family Constellation"; Lukianowicz, "Incest"; Tormes, *Child Victims of Incest.*

20 Cormier et al., "Psychodynamics"; Lustig et al., "Family Group Survival Pattern."

21 Cavallin, "Incestuous Fathers."

22 Christine Adams-Tucker, "Sex-Abused Children: Pathology and Clinical Traits," paper presented at Annual Meeting of the American Psychiatric Association, May 1980; Vincent De Francis, *Protecting the Child Victim of Sex Crimes Committed by Adults* (Denver: American Humane Association, 1969), pp. 152–180.

23 Virginia Abernethy and her colleagues describe a family constellation which they associate with a high risk for unwanted pregnancy in young women. Though overt incest is not mentioned, the family dynamics that these authors describe are similar to those observed in incestuous families. They note the presence of a powerful father, a devalued mother, an exclusive relationship between father and daughter, and the reassignment of some maternal functions to the daughter. They interpret the pregnancy as a flight from the "threateningly incestuous" situation. Virginia Abernethy, Donna Robbins, George Abernethy, Henry Grunebaum, and Justin Weiss, "Identification of Women at Risk for Unwanted Pregnancy," *American Journal of Psychiatry* 132 (1975): 1027–1031.

24 Cavallin, "Incestuous Fathers"; Lukianowicz, "Incest"; Paul Sloane and Eva Karpinski, "Effects of Incest on the Participants," *American Journal of Orthopsychiatry* 12 (1942): 666–673; A. M. Gligor, "Incest and Sexual Delinquency: A Comparative Analysis of Two Forms of Sexual Behavior in Minor Females" (Ph.D. diss., Case Western Reserve University, 1966).

Gender Personality and the Sexual Sociology of Adult Life

Nancy Chodorow

Hence, there is a typically asymmetrical relation of the marriage pair to the occupational structure.

This asymmetrical relation apparently both has exceedingly important positive functional significance and is at the same time an important source of strain in relation to the patterning of sex roles.

Talcott Parsons
"The Kinship System of the Contemporary United States"

Girls and boys develop different relational capacities and senses of self as a result of growing up in a family in which women mother. These gender personalities are reinforced by differences in the identification processes of boys and girls that also result from women's mothering. Differing relational capacities and forms of identification prepare women and men to assume the adult gender roles which situate women primarily within the sphere of reproduction in a sexually-unequal society.

GENDER IDENTIFICATION AND GENDER ROLE LEARNING

All social scientists who have examined processes of gender role learning and the development of a sense of identification in boys and girls have argued that the asymmetrical organization of parenting in which women mother is the basic cause of significant contrasts between feminine and masculine identification processes.[1] Their discussions range from concern with the learning of appropriate gender role behavior—through imitation, explicit training and admonitions, and cognitive learning processes—to concern with the development of basic gender identity. The processes these people discuss seem to be universal, to the extent that all societies are constituted around a structural split, growing out of women's mothering, between the private, domestic world of women and the public, social world of men.[2] Because the first identification for children of both genders has always been with their mother, they argue, and because children are first around women, women's family roles and being feminine are more available and often more intelligible to growing children than masculine roles and being masculine. Hence, male development is more complicated than female because of the difficult shifts of identification which a boy must make to attain his expected gender identification and gender role assumption. Their view contrasts sharply to the psychoanalytic stress on the difficulties inherent in feminine development as girls make their convoluted way to heterosexual object choice.[3]

Because all children identify first with their mother, a girl's gender and gender role identification processes are continuous with her earliest identifications and a boy's are not. A girl's oedipal identification with her mother, for instance, is continuous with her earliest primary identification (and also in the context of her early dependence and attachment). The boy's oedipal crisis, however, is supposed to enable him to shift in favor of an identification with his father. He gives up, in addition to his oedipal and preoedipal attachment to his mother, his primary identification with her.

What is true specifically for oedipal identification is equally true for more general gender identification and gender role learning. A boy, in order to feel himself adequately masculine, must distinguish and differentiate himself from others in a way that a girl need not—must categorize himself as someone apart. Moreover, he defines masculinity negatively as that which is not feminine and/or connected to women, rather than positively.[4] This is another way boys come to deny and repress relation and connection in the process of growing up.

These distinctions remain even where much of a girl's and boy's socialization is the same, and where both go to school and can participate in adulthood in the labor force and other nonfamilial institutions. Because girls at the same time grow up in a family where mothers are the salient parent and caretaker, they also can begin to identify more directly and immediately with their mothers and their mothers' familial roles than can boys with their fathers and men. Insofar as a woman's identity remains primarily as a wife/mother, moreover, there is greater generational continuity in role and life-activity from mother to daughter than there can be from father to son. This identity may be less than totally appropriate, as girls must realistically expect to spend much of their life in the labor force, whereas their mothers were less likely to do so. Nevertheless, family organization and ideology still produce these gender differences, and generate expectations that women much more than men will find a primary identity in the family.

Permanent father-absence, and the "father absence" that is normal in our society, do not mean that boys do not learn masculine roles or proper masculine behavior, just as there is no evidence that homosexuality in women correlates with father absence.[5] What matters is the extent to which a child of either gender can form a personal relationship with their object of identification, and the differences in modes of identification that result from this. Mitscherlich, Slater, Winch, and Lynn all speak to these differences.[6] They suggest that girls in contemporary society develop a personal identification with their mother, and that a tie between affective processes and role learning—between libidinal and ego development—characterizes feminine development. By contrast, boys develop a positional identification with aspects of the masculine role. For them, the tie between affective processes and role learning is broken.

Personal identification, according to Slater and Winch, consists in diffuse identification with someone else's general personality, behavioral traits, values, and attitudes. Positional identification consists, by contrast, in identification with specific aspects of another's role and does not necessarily lead to the internalization of the values or attitudes of the person identified with. According to Slater, children preferentially choose personal identification because this grows out of a positive affective relationship to a person who is there. They resort to positional identification residually and reactively, and identify with the perceived role or situation of another when possibilities for personal identification are not available.

In our society, a girl's mother is present in a way that a boy's father, and other adult men, are not. A girl, then, can develop a personal identification with her mother, because she has a real relationship with her that grows out of their early primary tie. She learns what it is to be womanlike in the context of this personal identification with her mother and often with other female models (kin, teachers, mother's friends, mothers of friends). Feminine identification, then, can be based on the gradual learning of a way of being familiar in everyday life, exemplified by the relationship with the person with whom a girl has been most involved.

A boy must attempt to develop a masculine gender identification and learn the masculine role in the absence of a continuous and ongoing personal relationship to his father (and in the absence of a continuously available masculine role model). This positional identification occurs both psychologically and sociologically. Psychologically, as is clear from descriptions of the masculine oedipus complex, boys appropriate those specific components of the masculinity of their father that they fear will be otherwise used against them, but do not as much identify diffusely with him as a person. Sociologically, boys in father-absent and normally father-remote families develop a sense of what it is to be masculine through identification with cultural images of masculinity and men chosen as masculine models.

Boys are taught to be masculine more consciously than girls are taught to be feminine. When fathers or men are not present much, girls are taught the heterosexual components of their role, whereas boys are assumed to learn their heterosexual role without teaching, through interaction with their mother.[7] By contrast, other components of masculinity must be more consciously imposed. Masculine identification, then, is predominantly a gender role identification. By contrast, feminine identification is predominantly *parental:* "Males tend to identify with a cultural stereotype of the masculine role; whereas females tend to identify with aspects of their own mother's role specifically."[8]

Girls' identification processes, then, are more continuously embedded in and mediated by their ongoing relationship with their mother. They develop through and stress particularistic and affective relationships to others. A boy's identification processes are not likely to be so embedded in or mediated by a real affective relation to his father. At the same time, he tends to deny identification with and relationship to his mother and reject what he takes to be the feminine world; masculinity is defined as much negatively as positively. Masculine identification processes stress differentiation from others, the denial of affective relation, and categorical universalistic components of the masculine role. Feminine identification processes are relational, whereas masculine identification processes tend to deny relationship.

These distinctions do not mean that the development of femininity is all sugar and spice for a girl, but that it poses different *kinds* of problems for her than the development of masculinity does for a boy. The feminine identification that a girl attains and the masculine identification about which a boy remains uncertain are valued differently. In their unattainability, masculinity and the masculine role are fantasized and idealized by boys (and often by girls), whereas femininity and the feminine role remain for a girl all too real and concrete. . . .

FAMILY AND ECONOMY

Women's relatedness and men's denial of relation and categorical self-definition are appropriate to women's and men's differential participation in nonfamilial production and familial reproduction. Women's roles are basically familial, and concerned with personal, affective ties. Ideology about women and treatment of them in this society, particularly in the labor force, tend to derive from this familial location and the assumptions that it is or should be both exclusive and primary for women, and that this exclusivity and primacy come from biological sex differences. By contrast, men's roles as they are defined in our society are basically not familial. Though men are interested in being husbands and fathers, and most men do occupy these roles during their lifetime, ideology about men and definitions of what is masculine come predominantly from men's nonfamilial roles. Women are located first in the sex-gender system, men first in the organization of production.

We can reformulate these insights to emphasize that women's lives, and beliefs about women, define them as embedded in social interaction and personal relationships in a way that men are not. Though men and women participate in both the family and the nonfamilial world, the sexual division of labor is such that women's first association is within the family, a relational institution, and men's is not. Women in our society are primarily defined as wives and mothers, thus in particularistic relation to someone else, whereas men are defined primarily in universalistic occupational terms. These feminine roles and women's family functions, moreover, stress especially affective relationship and the affective aspects of family life. As I discuss in Chapter I, being a mother and wife is increasingly centered on emotional and psychological functions—women's work is "emotional work."[9] By contrast, men's occupational roles, and the occupational world in general, are increasingly without room for affect and particularistic commitments. Women's two interconnected roles, their dual relatedness to men and children, replicate women's internalized relational triangle of childhood—preoccupied alternately with male-female and mother-child issues.

The definitional relatedness of being a wife and mother, and women's intrafamilial responsibility for affectively defined functions, receive further support from the way the family is related socially to the extrafamilial world. Parsons and many feminist theorists point out that it is the husband/father whose occupational role is mainly determinant of the class position and status of the whole family, and sociologists who measure socioeconomic status by *paternal* occupation and education seem to concur. The husband/father thus formally articulates the family in the larger society and gives it its place. And although families increasingly depend on income from both spouses, class position derives ideologically from what the male spouse does. The wife, accordingly, is viewed as deriving her status and class position mainly from her husband, even if she also is in the labor force and contributes to the maintenance of the family's life style. She is seen as a representative of her family, whereas her husband is seen as an independent individual.

The wife/mother role draws on women's personality in another way, as a result of the fundamentally different modes of organization of the contemporary sex-gender system and contemporary capitalism. The activities of a wife/mother have a nonbounded quality. They consist, as countless housewives can attest and as women poets, novelists, and feminist theorists have described, of diffuse obligations. Women's activities in the home involve continuous connection to and concern about children and attunement to adult masculine needs, both of which require connection to, rather than separateness from, others. The work of maintenance and reproduction is characterized by its repetitive and routine continuity, and does not involve specified sequence or progression. By contrast, work in the labor force—"men's work"—is likely to be contractual, to be more specifically delimited, and to contain a notion of defined progression and product.

Even when men and women cross into the other's sphere, their roles remain different. Within the family, being a husband and father is different from being a wife and mother; as women have become more involved in the family, men have become less so. Parsons's characterization of men's instrumental role in the family may be too extreme, but points us in the right direction. A father's first responsibility is to "provide" for his family monetarily. His emotional contribution is rarely seen as of equal importance. Men's work in the home, in all but a few households, is defined in gender-stereotyped ways. When men do "women's" chores—the dishes, shopping, putting children to bed—this activity is often organized and delegated by the wife/mother, who retains residual responsibility (men "babysit" their own children; women do not). Fathers, though they relate to their children, do so in order to create "independence."[10] This is facilitated by a father's own previous socialization for repression and denial of relation, and his current participation in the public nonrelational world. Just as children know their fathers "under the sway of the reality principle,"[11,12] so also do fathers know their children more as separate people than mothers do.

Outside the family, women's roles and ideology about women are more relational than nonfamilial male roles and ideology about men. Women's work in the labor force tends to extend their housewife, wife, or mother roles and their concern with personal, affective ties (as secretaries, service workers, private household workers, nurses, teachers). Men's work is less likely to have affective overtones—men are craft workers, operatives, and professional and technical workers. . . .

Women's role in the home and primary definition in social reproductive, sex-gender terms are characterized by particularism, concern with affective goals and ties, and a diffuse, unbounded quality. Masculine occupational roles and men's primary definition in the sphere of production are universalistically defined and recruited, and are less likely to involve affective considerations. This nonrelational, economic and political definition informs the rest of their lives. The production of feminine personalities oriented toward relational issues and masculine personalities defined in terms of categorical ties and the repression of relation fits these roles and contributes to their reproduction.

MOTHERING MASCULINITY, AND CAPITALISM

Women's mothering in the isolated nuclear family of contemporary capitalist society creates specific personality characteristics in men that reproduce both an ideology and psychodynamic of male superiority and submission to the requirements of production. It prepares men for participation in a male-dominant family and society, for their lesser emotional participation in family life, and for their participation in the capitalist world of work.

Masculine development takes place in a family in which women mother and fathers are relatively uninvolved in child care and family life, and in a society characterized by sexual inequality and an ideology of masculine superiority. This duality expresses itself in the family. In family ideology, fathers are usually important and considered the head of the household. Wives focus energy and concern on their husbands, or at least think and say that they do. They usually consider, or at least claim, that they love these husbands. Mothers may present fathers to children as someone important, someone whom the mother loves, and may even build up their husbands to their children to make up for the fact that these children cannot get to know their father as well as their mother. They may at the same time undercut their husband in response to the position he assumes of social superiority or authority in the family.

Masculinity is presented to a boy as less available and accessible than femininity, as represented by his mother. A boy's mother is his primary caretaker. At the same time, masculinity is idealized or accorded superiority, and thereby becomes even more desirable. Although fathers are not as salient as mothers in daily interaction, mothers and children often idealize them and give them ideological primacy, precisely because of their absence and seeming inaccessibility, and because of the organization and ideology of male dominance in the larger society.

Masculinity becomes an issue in a way that femininity does not. Masculinity does not become an issue because of some intrinsic male biology, nor because masculine roles are inherently more difficult than feminine roles, however. Masculinity becomes an issue as a direct result of a boy's experience of himself in his family—as a result of his being parented by a woman. For children of both genders, mothers represent regression and lack of autonomy. A boy associates these issues with his gender identification as well. Dependence on his mother, attachment to her, and identification with her represent that which is not masculine: a boy must reject dependence and deny attachment and identification. Masculine gender role training becomes much more rigid than feminine. A boy represses those qualities he takes to be feminine inside himself, and rejects and devalues women and whatever he considers to be feminine in the social world.

Thus, boys define and attempt to construct their sense of masculinity largely in negative terms. Given that masculinity is so elusive, it becomes important for masculine identity that certain social activities are defined as masculine and superior, and that women are believed unable to do many of the things defined as socially important.

It becomes important to think that women's economic and social contribution cannot equal men's. The secure possession of certain realms, and the insistence that these realms are superior to the maternal world of youth, become crucial both to the definition of masculinity and to a particular boy's own masculine gender identification.[13] . . .

Women's mothering produces a psychological and ideological complex in men concerning women's secondary valuation and sexual inequality. Because women are responsible for early child care and for most later socialization as well, because fathers are more absent from the home, and because men's activities generally have been removed from the home while women's have remained within it, boys have difficulty in attaining a stable masculine gender role identification. Boys fantasize about and idealize the masculine role and their fathers, and society defines it as desirable.

Given that men control not only major social institutions but the very definition and constitution of society and culture, they have the power and ideological means to enforce these perceptions as more general norms, and to hold each other accountable for their enforcement. (This is not solely a matter of force. Since these norms define men as superior, men gain something by maintaining them.)[14] The structure of parenting creates ideological and psychological modes which reproduce orientations to and structures of male dominance in individual men, and builds an assertion of male superiority into the definition of masculinity itself.

The same repressions, denials of affect and attachment, rejection of the world of women and things feminine, appropriation of the world of men and identification with the father that create a psychology of masculine superiority also condition men for participation in the capitalist work world. Both capitalist accumulation and proper work habits in workers have never been purely a matter of economics. Particular personality characteristics and behavioral codes facilitated the transition to capitalism. Capitalists developed inner direction, rational planning, and organization, and workers developed a willingness to come to work at certain hours and work steadily, whether or not they needed money that day.

Psychological qualities become perhaps even more important with the expansion of bureaucracy and hierarchy: In modern capitalism different personality traits are required at different levels of the bureaucratic hierarchy.[15,16] Lower level jobs are often directly and continuously supervised, and are best performed by someone willing to obey rules and conform to external authority. Moving up the hierarchy, jobs require greater dependability and predictability, the ability to act without direct and continuous supervision. In technical, professional, and managerial positions, workers must on their own initiative carry out the goals and values of the organization for which they work, making those goals and values their own. Often they must be able to draw on their interpersonal capacities as a skill. Parental child-rearing values and practices (insofar as these latter reflect parental values) reflect these differences. Working class parents are more likely to value obedience, conformity to external authority, neatness, and other "behavioral" characteristics in their children; middle-class parents emphasize more "internal" and interpersonal characteristics like responsibility, curiosity, self-motivation, self-control, and consideration.[17]

These behavioral and personality qualities differentiate appropriately according to the requirements of work in the different strata. But they share an important common-

ality. Conformity to behavioral rules and external authority, predictability and dependability, the ability to take on others' values and goals as one's own, all reflect an orientation external to oneself and one's own standards, a lack of autonomous and creative
self-direction. The nuclear, isolated, neolocal family in which women mother is suited
to the production in children of these cross-class personality commitments and capacities. . . .

Contemporary family structure produces not only malleability and lack of internalized standards, but often a search for manipulation. These character traits lend themselves to the manipulations of modern capitalism—to media and product consumerism, to the attempt to legitimate a polity that serves people unequally, and finally
to work performance. The decline of the oedipal father creates an orientation to external authority and behavioral obedience. Exclusive maternal involvement and the extension of dependence create a generalized need to please and to "succeed," and a
seeming independence. This need to succeed can help to make someone dependable
and reliable. Because it is divorced from specific goals and real inner standards but has
involved the maintenance of an internal dependent relationship, it can also facilitate
the taking of others' goals as one's own, producing the pseudo-independent organization man.

An increasingly father-absent, mother-involved family produces in men a personality that both corresponds to masculinity and male dominance as these are currently
constituted in the sex-gender system, and fits appropriately with participation in capitalist relations of production. Men continue to enforce the sexual division of spheres as
a defense against powerlessness in the labor market. Male denial of dependence and of
attachment to women helps to guarantee both masculinity and performance in the
world of work. The relative unavailability of the father and overavailability of the
mother create negative definitions of masculinity and men's fear and resentment of
women, as well as the lack of inner autonomy in men that enables, depending on particular family constellation and class origin, either rule-following or the easy internalization of the values of the organization.

Thus, women's and men's personality traits and orientations mesh with the sexual
and familial division of labor and unequal ideology of gender and shape their asym-
metric location in a structure of production and reproduction in which women are in
the first instance mothers and wives and men are workers. This structure of production
and reproduction requires and presupposes those specific relational modes, between
husband and wife, and mother and children, which form the center of the family in
contemporary society. An examination of the way that gender personality is expressed
in adulthood reveals how women and men create, and are often committed to creating,
the interpersonal relationships which underlie and reproduce the family structure that
produced them.

NOTES

1 For a review of the literature which argues this, see Biller, 1971, *Father, Child.* See also
Stoller, 1965, "The Sense of Maleness." For a useful recent formulation, see Johnson, 1975,
"Fathers, Mothers."

2 See Mead, 1949, *Male and Female;* Michelle Z. Rosaldo, 1974, "Women, Culture, and Society"; Nancy Chodorow, 1971, "Being and Doing," and 1974, "Family Structure and Feminine Personality," in Rosaldo and Lamphere, eds., *Women, Culture and Society,* pp. 43–66; Beatrice B. Whiting and John W. M. Whiting, 1975, *Children of Six Cultures;* John Whiting, 1959, "Sorcery, Sin"; Burton and Whiting, 1961, "The Absent Father."

3 The extent of masculine difficulty varies, as does the extent to which identification processes for boys and girls differ. This variance depends on the extent of the public-domestic split in a subculture of society—the extent to which men, men's work, and masculine activities are removed from the home, and therefore masculinity and personal relations with adult men are hard to come by for a child.

4 See Richard T. Roessler, 1971, "Masculine Differentiation and Feminine Constancy," *Adolescence,* 6, #22, pp. 187–196; E. M. Bennett and L. R. Cohen, 1959, "Men and Women, Personality Patterns and Contrasts," *Genetic Psychology Monographs,* 59, pp. 101–155; Johnson, 1963, "Sex Role Learning," and 1975, "Fathers, Mothers"; Stoller, 1964, "A Contribution to the Study," 1965, "The Sense of Maleness," and 1968, "The Sense of Femaleness," *Psychoanalytic Quarterly,* 37, #1, pp. 42–55.

5 See Biller, 1971, *Father, Child.*

6 Mitscherlich, 1963, *Society Without the Father;* Philip E. Slater, 1961, "Toward a Dualistic Theory of Identification," *Merrill-Palmer Quarterly of Behavior and Development,* 7, #2, pp. 113–126; Robert F. Winch, 1962, *Identification and Its Familial Determinants;* David B. Lynn, 1959, "A Note on Sex Differences," and 1962, "Sex Role and Parent."

7 Johnson, 1975, "Fathers, Mothers," and Maccoby and Jacklin, 1974, *The Psychology of Sex Differences,* point this out.

8 D. B. Lynn, 1959, "A Note on Sex Differences," p. 130.

9 This phrase is Arlie Hochschild's. (See Arlie Russell Hochschild, 1975, "The Sociology of Feeling and Emotion: Selected Possibilities," in Marcia Millman and Rosabeth Moss Kanter, eds., *Another Voice,* pp. 280–307.) She uses it to refer to the internal work women do to make their feelings accord with how they think they ought to feel. My usage here extends also to work for and upon other people's emotions.

10 See, for example, Johnson, 1975, "Fathers, Mothers"; Parsons and Bales, 1955, *Family, Socialization;* Deutsch, 1944, *Psychology of Women.*

11 Conscious of him as a separate person, verbally rather than preverbally.

12 Alice Balint, 1939, "Love for the Mother."

13 On these issues, see Lynn, 1959, "A Note on Sex Differences," and 1962, "Sex Role and Parent"; Parsons, 1942, "Age and Sex"; Mitscherlich, 1963, *Society Without the Father;* Slater, 1968, *The Glory of Hera;* Mead, 1949, *Male and Female.*

14 But for discussions of ways that this accountability is actively maintained, see Joseph H. Pleck and Jack Sawyer, 1974, *Men and Masculinity,* and Marc F. Fasteau, 1974, *The Male Machine.*

15 It is certainly possible that these same characteristics apply in all extensively bureaucratic and hierarchical settings (in the U.S.S.R., and Eastern Europe, for instance); however, the work I am drawing on has investigated only the capitalist West, and especially the United States.

16 My formulation of the personality requirements of the hierarchical firm follows Edwards, 1975, "The Social Relations of Production."

17 See Melvin L. Kohn, 1969, *Class and Conformity.*

BIBLIOGRAPHY

Balint, Alice, 1939, "Love for the Mother and Mother-Love," pp. 91–108 in Michael Balint, ed., *Primary Love and Psycho-Analytic Technique.* New York, Liveright Publishing, 1965.

Bennett, E. M., and L. R. Cohen, 1959, "Men and Women, Personality Patterns and Contrasts," *Genetic Psychology Monographs,* 59, pp. 101–155.

Biller, Henry B., 1971, *Father, Child, and Sex Role.* Lexington, Mass., D. C. Heath.

Burton, Roger V., and John W. M. Whiting, 1961, "The Absent Father and Cross-Sex Identity," *Merrill-Palmer Quarterly of Behavior and Development,* 7, #2, 1961, pp. 85–95.

Chodorow, Nancy, 1971, "Being and Doing: A Cross-Cultural Examination of the Socialization of Males and Females," pp. 173–197 in Vivian Gornick and Barbara K. Moran, eds., *Woman in Sexist Society: Studies in Power and Powerlessness.* New York, Basic Books.

———, 1974, "Family Structure and Feminine Personality," pp. 43–66 in Michelle Z. Rosaldo and Louise Lamphere, eds., *Woman, Culture and Society.* Stanford, Stanford University Press.

Deutsch, Helene, 1944 and 1945, *Psychology of Women,* vols. 1 and 2. New York, Grune & Stratton.

Edwards, Richard C., 1975, "The Social Relations of Production in the Firm and Labor Market Structure," in Richard C. Edwards, Michael Reich, and David M. Gordon, eds., *Labor Market Segmentation.* Lexington, Mass., D. C. Heath.

Fasteau, Marc F., 1974, *The Male Machine.* New York, McGraw-Hill.

Hochschild, Arlie Russell, 1975, "The Sociology of Feeling and Emotion: Selected Possibilities," pp. 280–307 in Marcia Millman and Rosabeth Moss Kanter, eds., *Another Voice.* New York, Anchor Books.

Johnson, Miriam, 1963, "Sex Role Learning in the Nuclear Family," *Child Development,* 34, pp. 319–334.

———, 1975, "Fathers, Mothers, and Sex-Typing," *Sociological Inquiry,* 45, #1, pp. 15–26.

Kohn, Melvin L., 1969, "A Note on Sex Differences in the Development of Masculine and Feminine Identification," *Psychological Review,* 66, pp. 126–135.

Lynn, David B., 1959, "A Note on Sex Differences in the Development of Masculine and Feminine Identification," *Psychological Review,* 66, pp. 126–135.

———, 1962, "Sex Role and Parent Identification," *Child Development,* 33, pp. 555–564.

Maccoby, Eleanor, and Carol Jacklin, 1974, *The Psychology of Sex Differences.* Stanford, Stanford University Press.

Mead, Margaret, 1949, *Male and Female.* New York, Dell Publishing, 1968.

Mitscherlich, Alexander, 1963, *Society Without the Father: A Contribution to Social Psychology.* New York, Schocken Books, 1970.

Parsons, Talcott, 1942, "Age and Sex in the Social Structure of the United States," in 1964, *Essays in Sociological Theory.* New York, Free Press.

Parsons, Talcott, and Robert F. Bales, 1955, *Family, Socialization and Interaction Process.* New York, Free Press.

Pleck, Joseph H., and Jack Sawyer, 1974, *Men and Masculinity.* New Jersey, Prentice-Hall.

Roessler, Richard T., 1971, "Masculine Differentiation and Feminine Constancy," *Adolescence,* 6, #22, pp. 187–196.

Rosaldo, Michelle Z., 1974, "Woman, Culture, and Society: A Theoretical Overview," in M. Z. Rosaldo and Louise Lamphere, eds., 1974, *Woman, Culture and Society.*

Slater, Philip E., 1961, "Toward a Dualistic Theory of Identification," *Merrill-Palmer Quarterly of Behavior and Development,* 7, #2, pp. 113–126.

———, 1968, *The Glory of Hera: Greek Mythology and the Greek Family.* Boston, Beacon Press.

Stoller, Robert J., 1964, "A Contribution to the Study of Gender Identity," *International Journal of Psycho-Analysis,* 45, pp. 220–226.

———, 1965, "The Sense of Maleness," *Psychoanalytic Quarterly,* 34, pp. 207–218.

———, 1968, "The Sense of Femaleness," *Psychoanalytic Quarterly,* 37, #1, pp. 42–55.
Whiting, Beatrice B., and John W. M. Whiting, 1975, *Children of Six Cultures.* Cambridge, Harvard University Press.
Whiting, John W. M., 1959, "Sorcery, Sin and the Superego: A Cross-Cultural Study of Some Mechanisms of Social Control," pp. 147–168 in Clellan S. Ford, ed., 1967, *Cross-Cultural Approaches: Readings in Comparative Research.* New Haven, Human Relations Area Files.
Winch, Robert F., 1962, *Identification and Its Familial Determinants.* New York, Bobbs-Merrill.

A Womb of One's Own

Betsy Hartmann

There isn't much understanding in some marriages. My sister has six, and another one has eight. And I said to one of them that she shouldn't have any more. And she said, "What can I do? When my husband comes home drunk, he forces me to sleep with him." And that is what happens to a lot of women. And if the women don't do it, the men hit them, or treat them badly. Or the men get jealous and think their wives must be with other men. And the women have to do whatever they say. I think it is changing a little, because the young women are more aware.

Rene, a twenty-nine-year-old Peruvian woman, unmarried mother of one son

It took place in the room of a gentleman whose name I did not know . . . it was fairly dark and the only light for the operation was an electric torch. Only the desire to get rid of the child I was carrying gave me the courage to stay. It was unthinkable that I should be expelled from college, and I couldn't bear my parents to find out that I was pregnant.

He began the operation. I felt a sharp and intense pain, worse than I had ever felt before. I wanted to cry out and scream. I felt as though part of my flesh was being ripped out by his metal instruments. . . . Gradually the pain lessened. I lay stretched out on the wooden table, almost unconscious, but only for a few moments. Then the man wrote a prescription and gave it to me, and showed me out. . . .

This operation traumatized me and made me think that I might not be able to have children. . . . So when I did become pregnant, I felt so happy and liberated, as though I was being reborn. . . .

Several years after we were married, my husband and I discussed my abortions. It turned out that my husband had known of the existence of contraceptives, but hadn't wanted to talk to me about it because he thought I was too young, and because he thought it could have gone to my head and led me to go off with someone else.

Alima, a thirty-year-old Senegalese woman who works as a secretary
with a private firm in Dakar

I am Indrani from Sri Lanka. I was living and working in the tea estate area. . . . The only birth control method we know is sterilization. . . .

All medical and social welfare staff, including foreign aid people, are forcing us to be sterilized. . . . The tea plantation community is given 500 rupees for a female sterilization, and in the rest of the country half of this amount is given. When there is a serious illness, the factory management are supposed to provide transport to the hospital. But even if someone is uncon-

scious, they are not given transport. But when a woman decides to say yes for a sterilization, immediately the lorry is ready to go to the hospital.

During or soon after childbirth, women are asked if they want sterilization. When a woman does not agree, she can be refused work in the fields and she may be refused Thriposha (a protein-enriched flour, provided free by CARE). During the work in the fields, the supervisors are also encouraging women to be sterilized. If you do not agree to a sterilization after your second child, you are not admitted to hospital for your next delivery.

After sterilization, women feel very weak, and after years many still have complaints. Some women did not know that the operation is permanent and stops fertility forever.

Indrani, a member of the Tamil minority in Sri Lanka, who is now living as a refugee in India

On 1st March 1982, Mrs. K. gave birth by caesarian section to a second daughter. In the days following delivery, a young woman doctor put a great deal of pressure on Mrs. K. and her husband to sign forms of consent for what it appears were injections for rubella vaccination and Depo-Provera contraceptive cover. It seems no attempt was made to explain why the injections might be beneficial or the future effects or side effects of Depo-Provera. They were repeatedly told that the injections were a "good thing" and, as Mr. K. put it, "push, push, pushed" to have them. Mrs. K. was in fact readmitted to the Accident and Emergency ward twice and once for a longer stay to the hospital with massive bleeding in the two months that followed the birth. The Ks seemed to think that this had something to do with these injections.

Although the Ks are native Bengali speakers, Mr. K. speaks reasonable English and understands more. I certainly found it perfectly possible to explain to him that Depo-Provera is a contraceptive—a fact which came as an obvious surprise to him.

Letter dated July 1982, from Bloomsbury Community Health Council, Great Britain[1]

Although Rene, Alima, Indrani, and "Mrs. K." come from different societies and different walks of life, their experiences reflect a common plight: women's lack of control over their own reproduction. Today what should be a woman's birthright—the right to decide when to have a child and to practice safe birth control—is denied millions of women around the world. Pitted against them are a number of obstacles: economic discrimination, subordination within the family, religious and cultural restrictions, the nature of health care systems, and the distortion of family planning programs to serve the end of population control. Woman's biology need not be her destiny, but today her reproductive fate is largely shaped by forces beyond her control.

BARRIERS TO REPRODUCTIVE CONTROL

Although poverty and patriarchy serve as inducements to high fertility, it does not necessarily follow that women want to bear as many children as is biologically possible—eight, ten, even more. Many women would like to practice birth control, to space their pregnancies or to end them altogether once their need for children is met. What then is standing in their way?

A number of surveys have tried to provide a precise measurement of how many women would like either to limit or to space births. The recent World Fertility Survey, conducted in twenty-seven Third World countries, found that almost half the married women questioned wanted no more children, and that younger women especially tended to desire a smaller family size. In general, the number of women who wanted no more children exceeded the number of those using contraceptives, and this was interpreted as indicating a large "unmet need" for birth control.[2]

More compelling—though perhaps less "scientific"—evidence of women's unmet need for birth control comes from women talking to women. For when women, even of different class and cultures, sit down and speak seriously to each other, one thing that they share in common is both the blessing and curse of fertility.

In 1978, author Perdita Huston broke ground with her classic *Message from the Village,* based on in-depth interviews with village women from Kenya, Egypt, Sri Lanka, Tunisia, and Mexico. In almost every society she visited she found women eager to learn about birth control, although there were many obstacles in their way.[3]

Similarly, Audrey Bronstein, in her study of Latin American peasant women, reports:

> Every woman I spoke to, with one exception, wanted reliable information about how to control her own fertility. The fact that most women had been forced to have more children than they wanted was the most damning evidence of the suffering and loss of human rights experienced by peasant women under the rule of both their husbands and the political factors controlling their lives.[4]

Similar findings have emerged from studies in Bangladesh, from a recent Oxfam survey of rural women in Kenya, from the reports of Third World women's organizations.[5]

Why women want to space or limit births is not difficult to fathom. The physical hardship of repeated pregnancies can exact a terrible toll on a woman's health. Between the ages of fifteen and forty-five, a woman in rural Bangladesh can now expect to have an average of eight pregnancies and to spend nearly seventeen years either pregnant or breast-feeding. This would be hard for any woman, but for already undernourished women the difficulty is greatly magnified. An estimated two-thirds of all pregnant women in the Third World are anemic.[6]

Childbirth literally kills hundreds of thousands of poor women every year. Maternal mortality rates in excess of 500 per 100,000 live births are not uncommon in many Third World countries, compared to 5 to 30 in the industrialized world.

Put another way, the complications of pregnancy account for between 10 and 30 percent of *all* deaths of women of reproductive age in areas of Asia, Africa, and Latin America, but less than 2 percent in the United States and Europe.[7] The risk is greater for women under twenty or over thirty-four, and for women who have borne three or more children and suffer from the nutritional maternal depletion syndrome.[8] Many women do not have access even to rudimentary medical care during childbirth, much less sophisticated emergency equipment, so that even minor problems can lead to death.

For desperately poor women, having many children can be a heavy economic and emotional burden. A Mexican woman told Perdita Huston: "If I am going to have more children, who is going to feed them? When my children are crying, is it God who comes to comfort them?"[9]

The large number of induced abortions that occur worldwide every year—an estimated 30 to 50 million—also reflects the desire of women to limit births. Half of these are illegal. The medical complications of improperly performed illegal abortions are now reaching epidemic proportions in many parts of the Third World, and represent a leading cause of death among women of childbearing age.[10]

In Latin America, where abortion is outlawed in most countries because of opposition from the Catholic Church, one fifth to one half of all maternal deaths are due to illegal abortion, and scarce hospital beds are filled with victims. In Bolivia, complications from illegal abortions account for over 60 percent of the country's obstetrical and gynecological expenses.[11]

Seeking to limit their pregnancies, women, then, are also risking their lives.

Even in countries with liberal abortion laws, poor women often resort to illegal abortions because they lack access to legal abortion facilities or cannot afford to pay for the legal operation. In 1978, six years after the enactment of India's relatively liberal abortion law, for example, there were only 1 million legal abortions in the country compared to an estimated 5 million illegal ones.[12]

Recourse to dangerous illegal abortion not only underlines the need for widespread, cheap, legal abortion facilities, but the need for access to safe contraceptive alternatives. The problem is not simply supply—in many Third World countries the per capita availability of contraceptives is quite high—but more fundamental social barriers blocking women from contraceptives.

Male dominance is one of the strongest obstacles. In most cultures wives must have their husband's consent before they can decide to limit their fertility. And many men are reluctant to agree: They fear the possibility of their wife's infidelity or the loss of their control over her. As a doctor in a rural Mexican clinic explained to Perdita Huston,

> When a wife wants to do something on her own, such as trying to limit the number of mouths to feed in the family, the husband will become angry and even beat her. He thinks it is unacceptable that she is making a decision on her own. She is challenging his authority, his power over her—and thus the very nature of his virility.[13]

Not surprising, in the households where men and women share power more equally, acceptance of family planning is much higher.[14] Including men in discussions with family planning workers also seems to make a difference. But more often than not, family planning programs are geared exclusively toward women, ignoring the basic reality of male dominance.

Male control of the medical profession also discourages many women from visiting family planning clinics. As a Mexican anthropologist explains:

> A woman is supposed to be the property of one man: her husband. If she goes to a clinic another man, the doctor, is going to see her and touch her. Her husband won't let her go . . . and she, too, is reluctant. This is a great barrier to the acceptance of family planning in Mexico.[15]

In many Muslim cultures the problem is intensified by the practice of female seclusion. If no men other than a woman's husband and close male relations are allowed to see her, much less touch her, how likely is it that she will be able to consult a male doctor about family planning?

More female doctors and health workers are only part of the answer, however, for the problem lies more fundamentally in the very nature of health services. In most Third World countries, the scant resources devoted to health are usually spent in urban areas, on modern hospitals which serve a small elite. In rural areas, where people lack access to even rudimentary health care, they also usually lack access to decent family planning services. In Kenya, 58 percent of married women between the ages of fifteen and forty-nine who are exposed to the risk of pregnancy do not even know where they can obtain modern methods of contraception; in Mexico, the figure is 47 percent.[16]

Even when people do know where to get contraceptives, the time it takes to travel to a clinic, wait there, and return serves to discourage them—in Kenya, such a journey typically takes six hours. And once at the clinic, Kenyan women are sometimes refused birth control, especially if they are young and unmarried.[17] For people who can hardly afford basic medicines, the cost of contraceptives can also be prohibitive.

Many Third World health systems prefer modern Western-style medicine, undervaluing traditional forms. For family planning, this means that birth control methods in use for generations, whether they be herbal pessaries, withdrawal, abstinence, or prolonged breast-feeding, are passed over in favor of modern contraceptives, which are often less culturally acceptable and more disruptive of traditional practices. A Nigerian doctor warns of the implications for Africa: "The impact of a carelessly designed family planning program that may interfere with local beliefs and constraints can only serve to increase fertility levels."[18]

In order for women to feel confident about contraception and to use it effectively, they need to understand how the reproductive system works. Basic health education, however, is seldom emphasized in most health care systems or family planning programs. Even in an industrialized country like the United States, sex education is a source of endless controversy, for keeping women in the dark about their bodies is another powerful way of keeping them "in their place."

In many countries organized religion also presents a barrier to women's use of contraception. This is most obvious in the case of the Catholic Church's condemnation of all "artificial" forms of birth control. In the Church's view, using contraceptives or having an abortion is a sin.

In the case of Islam, according to Egyptian feminist Nawal El Saadawi, nothing in the *Koran* either explicitly supports or opposes contraception. Thus among Islamic religious authorities, some "maintain that Islam approves of family planning and even abortion; yet others hold firmly to the position that Islam not only opposes abortion, but even the utilization of contraception." In the Arab world, she maintains, it is not religion per se that is the issue, but the way religion is used "by those who rule to keep down those who are ruled."[19]

Many governments also follow pronatalist policies in the belief that an expanding population is vital to national development, prestige, and security. In sub-Saharan Africa, for example, five countries—Chad, Ivory Coast, Gabon, Guinea-Bissau, and Mauritania—do not support family planning, and until recently the number was much higher.[20] To facilitate economic growth (and some speculate to increase the proportion of the Malay ethnic group in the population), the Malaysian government wants to achieve a fivefold increase in the population over the next 115 years. The Prime Minister is telling families to "go for five" children.[21]

In Latin America the Catholic Church has prevented many governments from establishing national family planning programs. In Peru, for example, the Church helped to block the implementation of the government's 1977 Population Policy, which called for voluntary family planning services, and recently succeeded in pressuring the government to eliminate voluntary surgical sterilization as a birth control method. As a result, only the most privileged Peruvian women have access to modern forms of contraception, and thousands of women are forced each year to resort to dangerous illegal abortions.[22] Left-wing movements in Latin America have also tended to oppose family planning, failing to distinguish between population control interventions from abroad and women's real need for birth control. However, this opposition is beginning to fade under the influence of feminism.

Unfortunately, many governments that have implemented national family planning programs have done so not for reasons of women's health or reproductive freedom, but because of pressure from international donors to control population growth. Ironically, population control itself often blocks women's access to safe birth control.

The issue goes far beyond the simple question of contraception to involve power relationships at almost every social level, from the family on up to the national government. Recognizing this basic reality, many feminists today are defining reproductive rights much more broadly. Their demands include the following:

- The right to economic security through the opportunity to work for equal pay for equal work, so that women can adequately care for themselves and their families.
- The right to a safe workplace and environment for all, so that women are not exposed to hazards that threaten their ability to bear healthy children, or forced to choose between sterilization and jobs.
- The right of quality child care, so that women can enter the work force secure in the knowledge that their children will be looked after.
- The right to abortion and contraceptive choice.
- The right to reproductive education, so that women and men of all ages are better able to understand and control their own bodies.
- The right to decent medical care, necessary not only to ensure contraceptive safety, but a basic human right.
- The right to choose how to give birth, and to have control over the development and use of new reproductive technologies.
- The right of lesbian women and women with disabilities to be mothers.
- The need for men to participate as equal partners in childbearing, housework, and birth control, so women no longer have to shoulder the "double burden."
- An end to discrimination so that all people—regardless of race, sex, or class—can lead productive lives, and exercise real control over their own reproduction.[23]

Clearly, reproductive rights are predicated on achieving basic rights in almost every sphere of life. For while reproduction may be an intensely personal experience, it is also a fundamentally social one, at the center of a web of human relations. It is important never to lose sight of the whole while focusing on the center. Indeed, it is the failure to see the whole that lies behind the narrow conception and single-minded pursuit of population control.

NOTES

1 Peruvian quotation from Audrey Bronstein's interview notes for *The Triple Struggle: Latin American Peasant Women* (London: War on Want Campaigns Ltd., 1982); Senegalese quotation from Mariama Kamara, "Bearing the Brunt," *People* (IPPF), vol. 10, no. 4 (1983), pp. 17–18; Sri Lankan quotation from "Population Control Practices on the Tea Plantations of Sri Lanka," statement delivered at Women's International Tribunal and Meeting on Reproductive Rights, held at Amsterdam, 22–28 July 1984; U.K. letter from Marge Berer, *Who Needs Depo-Provera?* (London: Community Rights Project, July 1981), p. 25.

2 Robert Lighthouse Jr. and Susheela Singh, "The World Fertility Survey: Charting Global Childbearing," *Population Bulletin,* vol. 37, no. 1 (March 1982), pp. 42–43. See also ibid., p. 130.

3 Perdita Huston, *Message from the Village* (New York: Epoch B Foundation, 1978).

4 Bronstein, *The Triple Struggle,* p. 260.

5 On Bangladesh, see Betsy Hartmann and James K. Boyce, *A Quiet Violence: View from a Bangladesh Village* (London: Zed Press; San Francisco: Institute for Food and Development Policy; India: Oxford University Press, 1983), and Jenneke Arens and Jos van Beurden, *Jhagrapur: Poor Peasants and Women in a Village in Bangladesh* (Bombay: Orient Longman, 1979), and Loes Keysers, *Does Family Planning Liberate Women?,* Master of Development Studies thesis (The Hague: Institute of Social Studies, May 1982). On Kenya see Gill Shepherd, *Responding to the Contraceptive Needs of Rural People, A Report to OXFAM on Kenya in 1984* (Oxford: OXFAM, 1984). There are serious limitations to Shepherd's interview methods, however, since she frequently began her discussions with women by stating that Kenya had an urgent need for population control. For statements by Third World women's organizations, see *Divided in Culture, United in Struggle,* Report of the International Tribunal and Meeting on Reproductive Rights, Amsterdam, 22–28 July 1984 (Amsterdam: Women's Global Network on Reproductive Rights, 1986).

6 Bangladesh statistics from Zafrullah Chowdhury, "A Double Oppression in Bangladesh," in Bair, ed., *Health Needs,* p. 5. Anemia statistic from Debbie Taylor, "Women: An Analysis," in *Women: A World Report* (London: Methuen Ltd., 1985), p. 43.

7 World Health Organization, Division of Family Health, *Health and the Status of Women* (Geneva: 1980), and "Healthier Mothers and Children Through Family Planning," *Population Reports,* Series J, No. 27 (May-June 1984), p. J661.

8 Kathleen Newland, *The Sisterhood of Man* (New York: W.W. Norton and Co., 1979), p. 52.

9 Huston, *Message from the Village,* p. 131.

10 *World Development Report 1984,* p. 130, and Population Crisis Committee, "World Abortion Trends," *Population,* no. 9 (April 1979).

11 World Health Organization, "Health and the Status of Women." Bolivian figures from Newland, *The Sisterhood of Man,* p. 61.

12 Population Crisis Committee, "World Abortion Trends."

13 Huston, *Message from the Village,* p. 119.

14 See Christine Oppong and Elina Haavio-Mannila, "Women, Population and Development," in Philip M. Hauser, ed., *World Population and Development* (Syracuse, N.Y.: Syracuse University Press, 1979), p. 480.

15 Huston, *Message from the Village,* p. 109.

16 *World Development Report 1984,* p. 135.

17 On travel time, see Shepherd, *Responding to the Contraceptive Needs,* p. 8. Refusal of birth control, personal communication with Paula Park.

18 Dr. S. Okun Ayangade, *International Journal of Obstetrics and Gynecology,* vol. 15, no. 6 (1978), p. 499, quoted in Waife, *Traditional Methods of Birth Control.*

19 Nawal El Saadawi, "On Women's Shoulders," *People* (IPPF), vol. 6, no. 4 (1979). This article is an excerpt from her book *The Hidden Face of Eve: Women in the Arab World* (London: Zed Press, 1979).

20 See World Bank, *Population Growth and Policies in Sub-Saharan Africa,* p. 60.

21 Gavin Jones, "Towards an Optimum Population: The Malaysian Case," *People* (IPPF), vol. 12, no. 4 (1985).

22 Peru information from Rosa Domingo Trapasso of the Peruvian women's group Promocion Cultural "Creatividad y Cambio." A coalition of Peruvian women's groups has now mounted a campaign for public family planning services.

23 Thanks to Adele Clark for drafts of articles on this subject. List is also drawn from literature of various reproductive rights organizations. Also see Adele Clark and Alice Wolfson, "Socialist-Feminism and Reproductive Rights: Movement Work and Its Contradictions," *Socialist Review,* vol. 14, no. 6 (November-December 1984).

Here Come the Brides

John Krich

The condominiums come in mirror images, but not the occupants. On the front door of one stucco chalet hangs a Chinese character made of brass. Call it cross-cultural mistletoe for the couple living inside, another product of a growing American phenomenon. The husband turns out to be a small-town white kid come to the big city, prematurely middle-aged, middlebrow in his conspicuous collections of carvings and trophies, middle management, though never quite as managerial as he'd like, flashing a salesman's charm that readily gives way to anger. The wife is young, comely, and Asian; wearing house sandals but groomed for a party, a good listener whose skills have been severely taxed, uncomfortable with her new language but comforted by her new surroundings, covering her suspicion with drowsiness, a bit sunken along with the living room. As she offers tea and the homemade egg rolls called *lumpia,* nurses her newborn, and beams at the wedding album, it is hard to imagine that she was plucked from a row of snapshots in a mail-order catalog. Or that this marriage wasn't arranged in heaven, but in Hawaii—by an introduction service called Cherry Blossoms.

Then come the corrections in one another's version of events, made most gingerly; the nervous jokes about age difference; the curious blanks drawn when trying to remember the names of close in-laws; the references to unspecified conflicts and secret diaries where "he write that he travel looking for other girls to marry after me"; the questions that the wife pretends she can't grasp until she retreats into the "no comment" of a nap, causing the whispered confessions—which come whenever she "lets me out of her sight"—about how "it's been no picnic," about the bitching, the sulking, the misunderstandings.

And there's that troublesome word *love,* which is either actively disdained—in favor of talk about "trade-offs" or "liabilities and assets"—or flashed continually, like an expensive Javanese mask. Love is blind, as they say—especially in this context, where there's so much to be blind about. The longer they tell their story, the more this couple reveals the forces rending them apart, and the fears that made them cleave together. Cozy as it all seems, the world beyond keeps swirling through this condo. Settled on their white ottoman, they remain a man and a woman in flight—like so many who have chosen the path of these postal courtships.

The men: *"The woman I yearn to spend my life with does not seem to reside in North America."*

The women: *"I believe the god will let us to be together one day. Is that a dream? I love only American music."*

That world is not only getting smaller; it's getting lonelier. Never has it been easier for nations to mingle, and never have expectations been greater for one culture to provide what the other lacks. Economic interdependencies give way to psychic ones: those with power seek those with beauty, those with money seek those with heart. It's not surprising then that the delivery of Asian brides to mostly white American grooms has, within the last five years, become a multimillion-dollar-a-year industry. Since there's a perceived shortage of U.S. homemakers willing to shoulder traditional matrimonial tasks, some entrepreneurs are going abroad—where the labor can be bought cheaper and the quality control kept more rigid. Imperialists of the heart, these men strike out for poorer lands in search of the raw materials necessary to the manufacture of their fantasies. If emotional fulfillment is as vital to U.S. national security as South African chrome, then it must be secured in regular shipments. Love itself has become the ultimate consumer good, and as with so many others, an increasing number of shoppers are no longer buying American.

The catalogs: *"Congratulations! You have taken the first step towards discovering an eternal treasure!" "For many discerning men, there can be no other choice than a Lady of the Orient." "These women possess wit, charm and grace unmatched anywhere in the world." "[They] are faithful and devoted to their husbands. . . . When it comes to sex, they are not demonstrative; however, they are uninhibited [and] believe sex is healthy." "She wakes up in the morning with a smile on her face and she does wake up in the morning!" "You have heard the phrase 'A Woman of the 80s.' We recommend a Woman for all time . . . An Asian Woman!"*

There are now over a thousand organizations in the United States, Canada, Western Europe, and Australia peddling introductions to those women. They can be found in the classifieds of upstanding journals, including this one, innocently offering "international friendship" and "pen pals." Once their brochures arrive, the pitch is hard sell and carefully aimed—emphasizing the "soft, feminine, and cooperative" over the "crude, rude, and overbearing." Despite ostentatious logos like "Jewels of the Orient," "Asian Sweethearts," and "East Meets West Club," most are struggling, small-time operations, run out of a post office box. Many have been started by couples who met through some other agency and decided to put their own coupling to work: "My adorable little Asian princess . . . and I are so deliriously happy with one another," bubbles one typical operator, "that we wish to share our experience with others like yourself." Nowhere in this sharing is there any guarantee of sexual favors, or marriage, or even that the men's letters will be answered. So long as there's no actual or implied promise of specific services, these businesses remain legally invulnerable.

Although no one has kept exact figures, it's a safe bet that 10,000 marriages have resulted from these air-mail relationships over the past 12 years. Most of the pen pal businesses are crude copies of the formula established by Cherry Blossoms, which, under the direction of Harvard Ph.D. and ex-hippie John Broussard, has become the highest-volume matchmaking shop. Begun at the whimsical request of a single male in 1974, Cherry Blossoms has now expanded to publishing three separate, bimonthly directories, running up to 48 pages, featuring Philippine "Island Blossoms," Asian women in general, and miscellaneous hopefuls from Peru to Yugoslavia. The services' fees run from $5 to $10 for an introductory batch of a few sample addresses to $300 for all current and back issues—depending upon a variety of plans in which the subscriber may be offered "first crack" at a designated number of women. The clients also get their predilections listed in the services' register and their names placed in newspaper ads throughout the Far East.

Cherry Blossoms sends along a chatty newsletter describing women deemed less photogenic, offered at discount rates. This mimeographed sheet also alerts the men to "rotten apples": women who use their letters to solicit "samples of foreign currency" for their private collection or ask for donations to "typhoon relief."

The subscribers' package is bulked out with a handbook, *How to Write to Oriental Ladies.* Rewritten elsewhere as *From "Dear Lady" to "I Do,"* the booklet includes rudimentary tips on how to get the correspondence ball rolling, advice on travel and immigration procedures, and a glossary of handy phrases in Thai or Tagalog. While these outfits insist at every turn that Asian women aren't fussy about trivial matters like age or race, their booklets feature lengthy advice on how to soften or conceal potential blemishes—such as being black, disabled, or divorced. Dedicated "to gentle people and faithful lovers everywhere," the Cherry Blossoms guide nonetheless advances the basic rule: "When in doubt, leave it out." This genteel discretion is not extended to potential brides: they are typically subjected to questionnaires urging them to reveal everything from stints of prostitution to membership in communist organizations, their attitudes on premarital sex to abortion. The inequity of power is heightened by an inequity of knowledge.

The men: *"There are a lot of desperate men out there. Attractive men, successful men, microbiologists. They're not losers. They're just not attracted to American women anymore—because these women have become impossible."*

The women: *"Due to a hurting experience before, I want to meet someone who's total stranger to me." "I look a man even he's above 70 years old or he's driver or welder or any."*

There is no mystery to commerce—even when it deals in bodies. The credits and debits are balanced like yin and yang. On one side of the Pacific, there's a limitless supply of desperately poor females who'll do anything to become U.S. citizens. On the other, there's an increasing demand for their services from men who'll do anything to retain their power advantage within family life. At first glance, the moral to this story seems obvious, the vicious villains and helpless heroines easily identifiable. Unfortunately, as in the world's larger geopolitical drama, the rich often need more from the poor than the other way around. Too bad the world, in getting smaller, is not getting simpler. There are subplots galore in this tale of two continents—and two sexes.

The men: *"It's a great relationship—her life's me and that's it."*

The women: *"I'm OK now. I'm great, with someone who takes care and is so understanding to me."*

The tale begins with the men doing most of the telling—and all of the buying. As one of the mail-order operators jokes, in a retort aimed at the feminist critics ever at his heels, "It's not helpless Asian ladies we exploit for money. It's horny Western men." There's been a surplus of distressed females throughout the ages, but there would be no trade in Asian brides without the frustrations created by this particular age. It doesn't matter whether he's a cocky Texas lawyer, a fastidious high school teacher, a former All-American athlete, or a chipper electronic whiz; each husband prefaces his remarks with a portrait of the women he's lost, rather than the ones he's found. Our narrators do not so much share some fetish for the exotic, as a disillusionment—bordering on revulsion—with what is around the corner.

The men: *"American girls left me really disappointed." "They look like tubs of lard stuffed into Levi's." "They're pushy, spoiled rotten, and they talk like sailors." "They're not cooperative, but combative—and they never appreciate what you do for them." "In the morning, you wonder how many guys before me? Was it the football team?" "Maybe it's our fault, the fault of men for repressing them for so long." "But they're not psychologically together. They just don't seem to know what they want."*

Haven't we heard this somewhere before? In a curious role reversal, these last of the supermachos offer the classic complaints women have long made about men: they're confused, immature, promiscuous; they're also opinionated and materialistic. They fear commitments and neglect personal satisfactions in favor of careers. They let themselves go to seed: one disgruntled husband even suggested that all women want is "to watch TV and booze it up." Worst of all, they tend to be smarter or more successful than the men, who are left exhausted by the jostling for position entailed by the recent redefining of sexual roles.

The men: *"It's not easy when everything is up for discussion. Why don't you do this? Why don't you do that? Even my mother gives me a hard time. She wants to know why I don't cook once in a while. Now I just smile and tell her, 'I'm retired from all that.' My wife smiles too."*

Few of these men are trailer park misfits or the sort of gents who paper their bedrooms in aluminum foil. In one of the many surveys that the introduction services trot out as proof of their mainstream appeal, the statistics indicate that those who seek Asian brides are above average in education, income, and status.

These same samplings tell us that the average age at marriage for the husbands is 52; for the wives, 32. The Asian bride trade is tailor-made for those men driven to sustain youth beyond its normal bounds. For divorced men and elderly widowers with more modest goals, it can simply be a quick means of re-acquiring a sock-sorter or a live-in nurse.

But the surveys cannot test the would-be husbands for insecurity. The more the men rail against the women's movement, the more they show themselves to be its unwanted offspring. They want a refuge from chaos: all of them speak of wanting someone "who'll be there every night," as one put it, "who won't cheat, and who I can trust to do right by me—even down to how she takes care of the dog." Responding to the lure of far-off places, these men seek the girl-next-door. Through no fault of their own, she's become the girl-next-continent.

The men: "All this mail-order jazz is a lot of bull. If you met someone at a dance, you wouldn't call her a dance-hall girl. It's not like the Wild West where brides came out in a stagecoach. After the introduction's made, it's up to you."

For now, most couples find out all they want to know through old-fashioned letter writing—and they seem to like it that way. As a holdover from less hurried, more reasoned times, the slow pace of the mail befits those who wish to be holdovers too. Some men prove to be inveterate correspondents—with alphabetized file cabinets of pen pals from Anabella to Zhou Ying. Oh, the thrills of romance from across the Pacific! The exotic East delivered to the doorstep, in harmless half-ounce packets! The men emphasize that their moves toward matrimony are considered, often agonizing. But why hurry to reduce their postal harem? Suddenly, each of them's the most popular guy on the block. And they've done it without having to splash on cologne, haunt cocktail lounges, dust off dubious charms, reveal a bald spot or a paunch. Shopping by mail can even be justified as a money-saving measure. Think of how much it costs to date in this country! Or to hang out in bars! The silk route turns out to be a path of least resistance—where procedures are clear, risks minimal.

The men: "It's very safe. There are no messy endings. And it's slow enough that you really get to know someone—not like dating here, when suddenly you get in way over your head."

Once they get to know someone, the men venture out to meet their pen pal—or pals. For some of them, their travels in search of Miss Right constitute their sole and fleeting opportunity to feel like swashbucklers. They recount their "shopping trips," as they call them, in a tone usually reserved for discoverers of the North Pole: "We didn't know each other. We're from two different cultures; and here, in the middle of Taipei, we were gonna meet up for a blind date, which was, when you think about it, unbelievable." Lo and behold, the sales clerks from Peoria cross the international date line to become the emperors of Quezon City! Their pen pals serve as a parade of willing tour guides, and the two-week vacation takes on the power of a hallucination. In such heady moments, they may forget that they came for a mate and instead sate a variety of appetites—especially since, as one pointed out, "a lot of the girls, even if they're virgins, will spend the night with you if they think that will do the trick." Others concentrate dutifully on their chosen lady—presuming her charms match up to her penmanship—savoring a courtship whose Victorian pace is enforced by watchful relatives.

The men: "I couldn't believe it once I got over there. The choices were mindboggling." "All the girls called me 'Superman.'" "It was like I was a white god. You walk around here, you're just another schmuck. In Cebu City, the heads were turning. You'd think Robert Redford or Paul Newman hit town."

The women: *"I tell him, if you make love to me, you must marry me. I thought him sincere because he travel to see my mother. Thirty hours to Mindanao. Even after he propose, he keeps looking. He go to Hong Kong, Malaysia, traveling around for long time to see pen pals there. He had other girlfriend in Philippines. I go up to his hotel room instead of waiting in the lobby. I find them together. Then the game was up."*

The men: *"They got this system of chaperones in the Philippines. In my case, it seems like the whole family tagged along. We always had 15 people on our dates because everyone wanted a meal. When I asked permission from her father, I said, 'Sir, I'd like to marry your daughter.' He answered, 'Can I have another sandwich?'"*

The choice made, the blessed event follows apace. It is usually staged in the bride's home country, because a U.S. visa is far easier to obtain for a spouse than for a fiancée and because the women tend to place more value on the ceremony itself. Often there are two consecrations: one civic, the other Buddhist or Shinto or Catholic or Moslem. The Kodachrome record shows one pale, nervous face surrounded in the warm circle of a hundred new relatives. It is the first perk of the traditional family life he's been seeking.

The men: *"She is spoiling me, though, with all the attention I get, all of my nails manicured, gives me a shower daily, body massage nightly, shines my shoes and no sooner take a garment off till she has hung it up. She is well worth the price of your catalog."*

But why do these men journey eastward in the first place? Similar mail-order agencies now tout the semi-Asian virtues of Latin American *"chiquitas,"* who would seem to share the same "traditional" values and financial need.

Alas, when it comes to being stereotyped, Asian women have a 5,000-year head start. From yesterday's geishas to today's Singapore Girl, the pampered courtesans of the mandarins to the pick-by-number masseuses of Bangkok, the world's largest pool of females has long been tagged with a single occupation and preoccupation. The dependent, man-pleasing image remains easy to put over—even though Asian women have long labored in the rice paddies or on the looms, just as they are now filling the ranks of the most modern occupations in some of the most urbanized spots on the planet.

Since the Second World War, this myth of the Kama Sutra goddess has taken on the weight of historic inevitability. Because of the widespread American military presence in the Far East, jet-age prostitution has developed as a major component in the financial stability of such puppet states as the Philippines, Thailand, and Taiwan. Catering first to the needs of U.S. servicemen, and now aimed at the wholesale, assembly line satisfaction of Japanese and European executives, "sex tourism" is not merely condoned throughout Asia; it is encouraged as an important source of foreign currency. Without a ready supply of poor and uneducated peasant girls, most Asian governments would be in debt up to their epaulets. Without the mystique that casts Asian women as sexual toys, such a massive industry could not exist—and neither could its legally sanctioned adjunct, the mail-order trade.

The men: *"Of course, lots of them have to become prostitutes, because the only thing that they have to negotiate with is their body. But I'd rather marry a Philippine prostitute than an American woman any day. They're good girls looking for one man."*

The women: *"My husband, he always say that I am foxy. I don't know what he means by that."*

The mystique works so well because it is two sided. While the sinful reputation of her fallen sisters attests to considerable bedroom skills, the Asian woman is all the more desirable when viewed as the world's last unsullied creature, one whose spiritual and moral purity has been safeguarded by tradition. The potential whore is reconstituted as the uncorrupted virgin; the destitute waif bears her lot with the dignity of a princess. It makes for powerful rescue fantasies.

The men: *"My wife was a simple, barefoot girl. She lived in a house with no electricity and no TV. She was 21 years old and she'd never been on a date. Never. She wouldn't even hold my hand. She was very, very pure. With her, what I saw was what I got. I wasn't going to pay for someone else's mistakes." "They come out of these hovels—these shacks you or I wouldn't put a pig or a chicken in—and they're wearing these perfectly clean, white, starched dresses. Everyone of them comes out looking like Miss Universe."*

There are certainly enough Asian misses willing to enter this ultimate of beauty contests. That's because the prize is no mere tiara, but includes among other dividends the more highly valued green card offered to permanent residents by the U.S. Immigration and Naturalization Service. Marriage to an American, unless determined to be a sham by the INS, not only guarantees that green card; it also makes a woman's relatives eligible to immigrate and reduces her wait for full citizenship from five years to three. A few small ads placed in Asian newspapers combine with word of mouth to lure a torrent of interest—especially since the women are listed in the catalogs for free. So the aspirants come forward, in most cases from the Philippines—that perfect hothouse for pro-American, anti-divorce wives—but also from tranquil Javanese villages, Malaysian rubber plantations, palm-fringed Thai atolls, the ever-enlarging industrial smudges along the coasts of Taiwan, and even the work brigades of Beijing. They apply in a wobbly hand.

The women: *"With this short letter, I will lay my hands to your staff for the personal assistance and possible success in the near future! I have sincere wish you join your club. I only have honest and good intention. I am, after all, a human being and not an android or something, and I have feelings, compassion, and sorrow just like you."*

Human beings, after all, they become anonymous merchandise stacked in neat catalog rows. The snapshots are often blurred, but the women's terrifying innocence is sharply in focus. Clutching Snoopy dolls or their kids, they lounge in tiny bedchambers inundated with American trash and American hopes, cluttered with cheap souvenirs of lives waiting to be led, the journey yet to be undertaken. With their Calvin Klein jeans and Robby Benson T-shirts, most look up-to-date, but the catalog layouts display the cultural leaps being attempted: Javanese dancers in embroidered sarongs are juxtaposed with miniskirted secretaries. The women's fractured English—left purposefully uncorrected, as if to further emphasize their vulnerability—attests to distinctly un-American outlooks.

The women: *"Interests: the tandem bicycle, sweet potato, Chinese sit crosslegged. Hobbies: badminton, reading the books, hearing the songs, and clean a house compound. Favorite actor: Clint Eastwood. Favorite actress: Brooke Shields. Favorite dish: Chinese dish."*

In this lineup of spouses where everything seems out in the open, nothing really is. The dutiful lists of hobbies and interests never include job hunting or making ends meet. From these catalogs, you get the impression that these women while away their time "strumming guitar," dancing, waterskiing. "He [my husband] must have great courage, for I am a poor singer, interested in singing loudly." There is not a hint anywhere about financial hardship. Only yearning, motiveless hearts! They work hard to create the impression of looking solely for intellectual companions from afar: "I'm quite confident that the difference between our two countries would make an extremely captivating topic." The approved look is virginal, the talk calculated coy: "My name mean yellow fruit, which tastes very sweet. It's hard to explain; you got to try for yourself."

That fruit grows best in the Philippines. Take horrendous underemployment, add a working familiarity of American culture, widespread schooling in English, a dash of the colonial mentality, just enough prosperity to elicit a craving for more, Catholicism, family oriented mores breaking down in the face of economic chaos—and *voilà! Mabuhay!* "On every corner, in every candy store," one husband remembers, "the girls want to know, 'You married, mister?' " The urgency of the question is further fueled by the impending threat of civil war. "Some of the Filipinas are writing to 60, 70 guys—in Norway, Switzerland, Japan," one husband says. "Answering letters becomes their job for the day." And enough of a full-time obsession for many that a member of the Philippine opposition recently introduced a bill in parliament making it a crime punishable by up to eight years imprisonment "to publish or broadcast any advertisement recruiting or selling Filipino women as wives to foreigners." Yet where prostitution and underemployment loom, marriage to some febrile foreign gent can be a means of remaining relatively unbought.

The men: *"Hey, some of them would marry the most obnoxious slobs, 20-karat assholes—when they're starving and there's a steak dinner on the other side of the plate. On the other hand, a lot of girls are choosing amongst hundreds of letters. They wouldn't sell themselves off for anything that wasn't good value in return."*

While they're aware of the women's economic distress, the husbands manage to find ways to exempt their choices from such motivation. The brides have ways too. They cling to a discretion whose origins may be tactical and cultural. Many won't even admit that they were looking to escape their countries in the first place. "A friend, she get my picture and send it without asking," went one standard refrain. "After I get so many letters. . . , I think maybe this a chance to improve my English." Surely, there's an easier way to learn another language. And are these women really willing to yield up their lifetime's fealty just to have a roof over their heads? Such an assumption shows more disregard for the dignity of these women than even the worst sexist could muster—and the women's letters and ads suggest that those who take the leap have other motives as well.

The women: *"The men I have known in my country are not gentlemen. Philippine men, they beat their wives. American men treat their wives better."*

Green cards aside, interest in Western men may be prompted by the search for a more sensitive, less autocratic mate. The irony here is that their search must be conducted amid the group of American men least likely to fit that description. Many of the women are victims of "our old traditions. I got married without love between us. I must obey my parents." Irony upon irony: the mail-order trade that appears the highest expression of coercion can be the first opportunity for some Asian women to use their own feelings in choosing a mate.

Many of the women seeking foreign husbands are unwed or abandoned mothers, unacceptable to the men of their own countries because they carry the stigma of failure or bring with them the financial burden of another man's offspring. For them, a foreigner may represent their last chance. Others are simply "still looking for the right guy that make my heart beat quickly." That search, never easy, has been made more problematic by the vast social displacements that have come with economic development in Asia. With the influx into the cities, the old family networks that eased matchmaking are breaking down. With American-style progress has come American-style atomization.

"The funny thing about men these days," writes one woman from Kuala Lumpur, "is that they want to do everything with women except to have commitment."

The men: "I don't think the transition was too rough on her. She cried every day for two years."

The women: "I don't cry anymore. I used to write every day. Now I write only at Christmas. A neighbor teach me to play bingo. Now I have bingo; I don't miss my family so much."

For the mail-order bride, commitment is the easy part. Once married and ensconced in the United States, the women find that persistent homesickness is only the first hurdle. The standard refugee traumas are bad enough, but these imported brides have to grapple in isolation with two equally challenging adjustments. They must learn the customs of a new country and a new husband all at once. Often, they become acquainted with the hindrances of the latter before they've been exposed to the opportunities of the former. If becoming an American is their main aim, they are at the complete mercy of their spouse for the three years until citizenship is granted—and the husband holds the power to deport her if she doesn't play by his rules. It is in this sense that every mail-order bride, no matter how willing, is a captive.

The women: "That first year, I cannot go out by myself. I would get lost. I know how to drive. I got my license. I just don't know the area too well, and I'm afraid to talk to other people. . . . I rather stay in Taiwan. Speak my own language. I feel more useful there."

The men: "Most girls think they know what to expect, but they don't." "Most of the guys lie and bullshit to them." "They make them think this is the land of milk and honey." "They assume that as soon as you get off the boat, there's a job waiting for you."

A surprising number of these "traditionalist" couples want, or need, the women to seek employment. But lacking the language skills, or finding that their education counts for little, those who expect to work for a living quickly learn that those vaunted opportunities are not quite open at all.

And strangely enough, the common complaint that the husbands seem to voice is that they have gotten too much "loyal wife" for the money. These men who claim to abhor the assertiveness of their own countrywomen report that they can't communicate with their new partners until they've become a bit more like themselves. To a man, they speak of having to teach their wives to express their feelings, even anger. Americanization begins at home.

The women: *"It's true. I don't want to write check without his permission. I take a long time to learn to say it is not his money, but* our *money."*

The men: *"She won't go anywhere without me or do anything without me—not even go to sleep." "She practically asks for permission to go to the toilet." "She always says it's the Filipino way. And finally, sometimes, I have to just say, honey, this is not the goddamn Philippines. And this is my way."*

"My way" can be enforced with fists, although actual instances of wife battering among mail-order couples are difficult to trace. Many of the women are not aware of shelters and social services or are reluctant to use them for fear of deportation. For every rare one who does come forward, there are surely many more who must cope by themselves with some gradient of coercion. Challenged with evidence of abuse cases, the mail-order husbands like to cite the rumors they've heard of brides who take their American men for all the money they're worth, then disappear once they've got their citizenship papers. To the husband, one crime is no more justifiable than the other. In this bargain, the terror cuts both ways—and the keeper is often as fearful and watchful as the captive.

The men: *"My wife keeps saying she's going to walk out one of these days—I can't tell if she's kidding or not."*

The women: *"Here, I got more freedom. But mostly I don't look out window. My husband not like me talking. He's not bad man, just a nasty guy, with temper."*

Just as the situation breeds betrayal, sudden or gradual, so it provides incentives for success. It will take many years before we know whether these marriages prove any more durable than those of American marriages in general—although, statistically speaking, that wouldn't take much. Yet unlike their American counterparts, these newlyweds show an uncommon determination to bridge their differences. Few of the wives are going to casually give up on their effort: most have been schooled in making the best of it on the home front and do not accept divorce as an alternative. These women have cast too much aside—and the men have invested an equal amount in effort, cash, and the idealization of their quest.

The men: *"The first year was very tough. With the conflicts we had, if we hadn't already been married, we probably never would have gotten married."*

The women: *"Your mate is picked by God. You have only to be patient and get along."*

If Asian women seem more willing than their American sisters to make compromises, that is because some bring with them a different model of what marriage is supposed to provide. Where wedlock is seen primarily as a pragmatic partnership, it ceases to carry the burden as an emotional cure-all. This view of marriage, based in its most idealized form on mutual aid and on the slow unearthing of feeling, has certainly proven useful to the continuation of the species throughout the centuries—and it is one these 20th-century husbands strain to emulate.

The men: "*When I married her, I didn't love her. I admired her and I respected her, and I decided to take a chance. In the Asian tradition, one learns to love someone. And I feel it's growing every day. It's not the same thing as in the States. It comes slowly; it's healthier this way.*"

The replacement of American homemakers with Asian stand-ins confirms the old axiom that "none are free until all are free." Still, taken as a whole, the phenomenon hardly represents a serious inroad into the gains made by women. These are gains that appear irreversible worldwide, and it will take a great deal more than a few thousand rather fragile "old-fashioned" marriages to reverse the tide. The march toward a workable equality of the sexes is not what's threatened by the growing attraction of white American males to Asian women and the ideal they are imagined to embody; the only thing threatened is the relatively new concept of marrying for passion and separating for lack of same. It is one more joust—this time from the male side—over our contemporary prescriptions for happiness.

The men: "*We believe in traditional roles—like the man washes the car, the woman sweeps. It's so easy to get along that way, where everything's clear.*"

The women: "*It's not true that Asian men and American men different. Men are men everywhere—some help the women out, and some don't.*"

Some American feminists and Asian American organizations have condemned the mail-order trade as legalized prostitution and pen pal marriage as inherently abusive, but such rhetoric serves to obscure reality rather than transform it. If the Asian trade leads to a kind of slavery, then it is a volunteered servitude that is but a single link of chain apart from the unwritten contract that binds any man to any woman. Judging these brides by Western standards often means trying to convince the oppressed of just how unhappy they would feel if they could only see their true condition. Unfortunately, the path of human want is rarely politically correct, and history does not move by morally approved acts. Listening to the voices rising from these catalogs of need, what emerges is that those needs are not there to be labeled false or backward. They are there to be met.

The women: "*I am here in this stranger place, with no one can share my loneliness.*" "*Do you think you can maybe like me, love me? Need someone for loving. Isn't a joke.*"

There are bound to be more and more stories of intercultural courtship—where happy endings are unlikely, but surprise endings can do the same job. For often as not, the reprieve that's granted is that neither party ends up getting anything that resembles the order they've placed. "If it was really mail order," one husband joked, "I'd have made my wife a bit younger. And a lot richer!" Where a human heart is the cargo, the customer can never be sure of exactly what he's ordering or whether he ever gets it delivered intact. The no-fault bride turns out to know very well how to point a finger. The bullying husband ends up in an arm wrestle with his own stereotypes.

The men: "*Asian women are not the subservient types that the media make us believe.*" "*They can be very strong willed. I'll tell you, my wife won't take no shit off nobody.*"

The women: "*In America, it's not easy like I think. You can't pick money off the streets. It's hard work, enjoying my life.*"

In the Posturepedic nuptial bed, over morning bowls of Raisin Bran, on proverbial weekend outings, it turns out that, most of the time, there's no Suzy Wong present, no Simon Legree. He is no John Wayne and she is no geisha. Instead of "inborn submissiveness," she demonstrates, with exposure to new possibilities, a pesky tendency toward human enlargement. Confronted with the silence that comes with slavish assent, reinforcing his solitude, he discovers rather enlightened cravings for a loud and living mate. Behind the triple locks of matrimony, the sprinkler systems and the electric eyes, they are not master and servant, but two people grappling with the long odds against durable understanding. Trapped in the most daunting circumstances, impelled by the most muddled intentions, all they can do is carry on the grim work of making the world one—with an ancient talisman hung outside for good luck.

Imperialism, the Family, and Cultures of Resistance

Mina Davis Caulfield

The contemporary women's movement has insisted on describing women's oppression in terms of women's concrete experience, and on discarding abstract ideologies that prevent honest description. In order to assert the crucial importance of the family and personal life and to develop a critique of women's oppression in the family, we have had to go beyond the idea that only commodity production and public political relations are significant. Unfortunately, we have not used the same honesty in examining the experiences of women in other cultures, especially women in colonial situations. Our emphasis on "sisterhood," on the common oppression of all women by male domination, has contributed to ethnocentrism in our movement. The strength and excitement generated by the concept and practice of sisterhood have caused us to look first or exclusively at those aspects of daily life shared by all females (sex stereotyped roles, devaluation of domestic labor, etc.), without considering the contrasts between our situation as women, and the situation of women in colonial or neocolonial societies.

The family must be examined in relation to imperialism as a system, or we are likely to continue the ethnocentrism that has been important in keeping the movement largely white and culturally Anglo middle class. We have made the small, isolated nuclear household and the non-collective nature of domestic labor—both characteristic of American capitalism—central to our analysis of women's oppression; we cannot assume that our conclusions apply to other societies.

Imperialism does not simply reproduce the capitalist mode of production, either industrial or domestic. Rosa Luxemburg has argued that capitalism "depends in all respects on noncapitalist strata and social organizations existing side by side with it," not only as markets but also as sources of labor power and resources.[1] At the same time, capitalist imperialism seeks to stamp out other modes of economy. Without necessarily accepting her argument as to the necessity of these noncapitalist systems for the continued existence of capitalism, it seems clear that she is pointing out an important contradiction. This tendency of imperialist systems to eradicate other economic and social systems, but at the same time to preserve and exploit them in distorted forms that remain outside the sphere of commodity production, is crucial to an understanding of the relation between imperialism and family structures. In colonial societies family-based economic and social systems are thus simultaneously assaulted and exploited. At the same time such systems are central to the physical survival, cultural identity, and anti-imperialist struggles of the people.

Imperialism assaults the total culture: it does not simply impose foreign domination, introduce new productive forces, or make available new market commodities to a "backward" area. Imperial intrusion deeply affects social structures, economic relations, and cultural traditions; it imposes powerful alien institutions and represents them as inherently—racially and culturally—superior. In response, many colonized peoples have developed resistance strategies centering around new forms of cultural affirmation directly or subtly opposed to the massive imperial affirmation of Western European cultural superiority. . . .

Imperialist assaults on families take many forms. In the first place, families as sources of power frequently constitute real threats to the authority of the invader. Just as imperialists are concerned to dominate and exploit the preexisting state apparatus, economic system, and religious institutions, so also they seek to eliminate the corporate power of kin groups, especially in those societies which are organized around lineages. Various colonial strategies, such as the forcible introduction of private property in land to replace communal ownership and control, are mechanisms for breaking down the organizational strength of families, as well as for facilitating the appropriation of land for the commercial uses of the "export sector." The Western preference for small, father-headed families does not simply reflect an ethnocentric bias toward the "Christian" norm, but is part of a larger strategy of "divide and rule."

Within the family, the power of men is increased. Insofar as colonial authority is extended to portions of the dominated population, these portions will tend to be male, not female. The Western practice of educating boys rather than girls, the introduction of private property rights to men even in areas of traditional female inheritance, and the religious ideology of male dominance in the Holy Family all reinforce whatever elements of male chauvinism may exist in the traditional culture, and threaten traditions of female independence or equality. At the same time men as well as women are coming under the overall domination of the colonizers: traditional socializing roles are taken out of the family into mission schools, land is expropriated, customs are outlawed, etc. The family as a whole, whatever its structure, loses power in society, and the increased power of men in relation to women is not accompanied by a net increase in men's power.

The assault on the power of the family and the intensification of male dominance are not the only effects of imperialism on families. Imperialism introduces economic enterprises—plantation agriculture, mining, industry—that typically use colonial labor on an individual basis, regardless of the preexisting productive units (extended families, kin-based cooperative groups, etc.). Slave labor systems are perhaps the ultimate in this individuating pattern, where each worker is bought and sold separately, regardless of family ties; only the very young, below the age of any possible productive output, are recognized as belonging to a collectivity that the master need take into account.

In the slave societies of the West Indies and the Southern United States, despite the planters' indifference or hostility to family bonds, slaves *in their own productive relations* resisted the pressures toward individuation. Through minimal and extended family networks slave women and men devised organizational forms for the survival of the young, and maintained cultural patterns of resistance to and rebellion against the colonizer. In these societies slaves could not depend for survival on the handouts of the masters; autonomous productive systems were clearly present.[2]

Survival strategies included cultivating "provision grounds" after hours in many Caribbean societies, and sharing stolen or illegally hunted and cultivated food in the quarters of North American slaves. In all such strategies, kin or pseudo-kin networks organized primarily by women but including fathers, brothers, and sons provided the organizational framework.[3]

In the Caribbean, such minimal productive systems based on family labor were in many cases extended into society-wide marketing systems. Surpluses were actually generated by these groups, working at night after their long hours in the sugar fields, and women traveled about with them, often illegally, cementing social bonds of many kinds in the process and facilitating the creation of new cultural patterns and organizational communications, leading in many cases to active revolts. In this example, it is clear that we must look not only at the ways in which the colonizer acts to *break down* family solidarity, but also the ways in which the colonized—women, men, and children—act to *maintain, consolidate, and build anew* the basic units in which children can grow and be encultured in the values and relationships that are independent of and in opposition to the imperial culture. There may be many institutions involved in a culture of resistance—religions, educational systems, or the marketing organization described above; but the family is basic, with its forms of economic organization and socializing functions. And it is in the family networks that we see most clearly the rejection of imperialist attempts to isolate each individual worker in his or her productive relations.

This process of isolation is not limited to systems of slave labor. The introduction by imperialism of wage labor cuts workers off from kin groups, and drives a further wedge between men and women. In most colonial situations men are the preferred target for recruitment into wage labor, while women must take on various kinds of double work loads. Generally, women remain responsible for traditional subsistence and nurturing activities, and in addition they take on one or both of two new jobs: wage work at lower rates of pay than men, and the former subsistence jobs of men who are absent from the domestic labor force. In both cases, survival of the family as a group and the biological survival of children become the primary tasks of women. These activities constitute forms of production and reproduction which are *alternative* to complete dependence on the economic systems introduced by the colonizers; by the same token, women and families become the focal points for the perpetuation of alternative systems of values, customs, and culture which are so important in building resistance movements. . . .

Carol Stack, Joyce Ladner, and Nancy Tanner, in their writings on the black family in the United States, have stressed the importance of kin-based networks with women as the key figures in maintaining survival strategies. Carol Stack says of these networks:

> The basis of familial structure and cooperation is not the nuclear family of the middle class, but an extended cluster of kinsmen related chiefly through children but also through marriage and friendship, who align to provide domestic functions. This cluster, or domestic network, is diffused over several kin-based households, and fluctuations in individual household composition do not significantly affect cooperative arrangements.[4]

Putting the point in a more historical framework, Nancy Tanner says:

> The Black American kinship system, as it developed in the United States, has put a premium on flexibility. This has meant maintaining a wide range of bilateral kin ties that can be activated as need arises. Kin often reside together or care for one another's children. Extended kin networks may reach from the rural South to northern cities. These flexible kin ties are an important and historically persistent part of the Black American kinship system.[5]

The migration to urban centers has not destroyed the basic family structure that American blacks have developed to deal with the pressures of colonial existence. Black women have been central to the perpetuation of autonomous value systems of the group. These women are far from the "domestic wards" Karen Sacks poses as the fate of women in class societies. As Joyce Ladner says, "One of the chief characteristics defining the Black woman is her realistic approach to her own resources. Instead of becoming resigned to her fate, she has always sought creative solutions to her problems. The ability to utilize her existing resources and yet maintain a forthright determination to struggle against the racist society in whatever overt and subtle ways necessary is one of her major attributes."[6]

The emphasis on resourcefulness, flexibility, and creativity rather than fatalism, passivity, and dependence (qualities usually attributed to women—and to peasants) is crucial: the family forms developed to deal with imperialism cannot be interpreted as foot-dragging, conservative attempts to return to a pre-imperialist "golden age." As Fanon has pointed out,[7] elements of traditional culture are transformed in the process of struggle against oppression; the transformation of families is an example of this process. In looking to future transformations of colonial and neocolonial societies, this long history of the struggles of women and families points to the possible development of new family forms, building on the past but surely not returning to it. I have not meant to imply that precolonial family structures were models of non-oppressive relations; imperialism has tended to reinforce pre-existing forms of male dominance and ideologies of male supremacy. The oppressive aspects of colonized families must be recognized, not minimized; but future transformations of the family will need analysis which goes beyond the assumption that families can only be agents of patriarchal oppression.

Ending imperialism will not necessarily end all forms of oppression of women in these societies, just as building socialism does not guarantee liberation from male domination. To the extent, however, that the struggle against imperialism takes place with the active participation of women and men who are consciously striving for an end to the special forms of exploitation relating to families, that struggle can make use of the creative forces so apparent in the history of colonial peoples. Cultures of resistance are not simply adaptive mechanisms; they embody important alternative ways of organizing production and reproduction and value systems critical of those of the oppressor. Recognition of the special position of families in these cultures and social structures can lead to new forms of struggle, new goals.

The resourcefulness and creativity of women in their domestic strategies of survival have made the family forms characteristic of colonized groups a source of strength for anti-colonial resistance which has been far too little recognized. Furthermore, the importance of these family systems suggests a reason for the relative lack of success of feminist appeals to third-world women. Colonized women are not interested so much in combating the domestic dominance of their husbands (though this may indeed be a problem for them) as in insuring the *inclusion* of men in domestic networks of mutual support. Female solidarity or "sisterhood" does not have the same meaning for women engaged in creating and maintaining extensive female-centered networks for gaining strength in the domestic subsistence and child-rearing areas of production as it has for the isolated housewife in advanced capitalist societies. The idea of social and economic resourcefulness and self-reliance is not new for women in colonial situations. The primary form of oppression experienced by these women is not the intimate dependency that feminists are combating. On the contrary, the direction of female strategies under colonial exploitation has been toward strengthening kin bonds with both women *and* men, and toward resisting the dichotomization of role and responsibility which colonialism fosters.

We know very little about female and family-oriented survival strategies under the wide variety of colonial systems of domination; male bias in anthropology has obscured both the exploitation and the sources of power of women, as many of my sisters in the field are now pointing out. What I have presented here is not a general theory of working and peasant families in the entire colonial and neocolonial world. At the least, there are important contrasts in the degree of intensity of the trends I have noted between societies with highly articulated precolonial class and caste systems such as India, China, and the Islamic countries on the one hand, and the plantation societies I have discussed. More information is needed before a general theory can be advanced; what I am suggesting here is a partial theoretical framework.[8]

We need to listen more to women who are living under neocolonialism and colonialism. Much of American feminism does not speak to their needs or experience. If we are interested in discovering the kinds of social and economic changes necessary for doing away with sexist *and* imperialist domination, we cannot assume that our own experience will tell us how much women everywhere suffer under the oppression of their husbands and fathers, or that our role is to explain to all women who their exploiters really are. Further, we must avoid seeing people who exist under conditions of severe oppression simply as *victims.* Sufferers everywhere don't simply suffer; they fight back, and that very definitely includes the women who live with the types of super-exploitation that I have discussed. To recognize the active resistance of the victims of imperialism is crucial to a consciousness of the common sources of oppression, as well as its diverse forms, a consciousness free of guilt, which will help us fight back against our own suffering.

NOTES

1 Rosa Luxemburg, *The Accumulation of Capital* (London, 1963), p. 365.
2 See my discussion on the data on slavery in Mina Caulfield, "Slavery and the Origins of Black Culture: Elkins Revisited," in Peter Rose, ed., *Slavery and Its Aftermath* (New York, 1970).
3 See Angela Davis on the central role of women in slave communities.
4 "Sex Roles and Survival Strategies in an Urban Black Community," in Michelle Zimbalist Rosaldo and Louise Lamphere, eds., *Woman, Culture, and Society* (California: Stanford University Press), 1974, p. 114. See also Carol Stack, *All Our Kin: Strategies for Survival in a Black Community* (New York: Harper & Row), 1974.
5 "Matrifocality in Indonesia and Africa and among Black Americans," in Rosaldo and Lamphere, p. 154.
6 *Tomorrow's Tomorrow: the Black Woman* (Garden City, N.Y., 1971), pp. 276–77.
7 Frantz Fanon, *The Wretched of the Earth* (New York, 1963), pp. 223–25.
8 I do not want to leave the impression, however, that what we need is a multitude of North American bourgeois anthropologists descending on colonized populations to seek out and write up such strategies for scholarly journals. The usefulness of such studies to the populations in question is at the very least doubtful. I am reminded of the aftermath of the 1929 revolt of Ibo women, when the British sent two women anthropologists to "study the causes of the riot and to uncover the organizational base that permitted such spontaneity and solidarity among the women" (Nancy Leis, "Women in Groups: Ijaw Women's Associations," in Rosaldo and Lamphere, p. 223). More counterinsurgency research we don't need.

Sexuality

The Culture of Romance

Shulamith Firestone

So far we have not distinguished "romance" from love. For there are not two kinds of love, one healthy (dull) and one not (painful) ("My dear, what you need is a mature love relationship. Get over this romantic nonsense."), but only less-than-love or daily agony. When love takes place in a power context, everyone's "love life" must be affected. Because power and love don't make it together.

So when we talk about romantic love we mean love corrupted by its power context—the sex class system—into a diseased form of love that then in turn reinforces this sex class system. We have seen that the psychological dependence of women upon men is created by continuing real economic and social oppression. However, in the modern world the economic and social bases of the oppression are no longer *alone* enough to maintain it. So the apparatus of romanticism is hauled in. (Looks like we'll have to help her out, Boys!)

Romanticism develops in proportion to the liberation of women from their biology. As civilization advances and the biological bases of sex class crumble, male supremacy must shore itself up with artificial institutions, or exaggerations of previous institutions, e.g., where previously the family had a loose, permeable form, it now tightens and rigidifies into the patriarchal nuclear family. Or, where formerly women had been held openly in contempt, now they are elevated to states of mock worship.[1] Romanticism is a cultural tool of male power to keep women from knowing their condition. It is especially needed—and therefore strongest—in Western countries with the highest rate of industrialization. Today, with technology enabling women to break out of their roles for good—it was a near miss in the early twentieth century—romanticism is at an all-time high.

How does romanticism work as a cultural tool to reinforce sex class? Let us examine its components, refined over centuries, and the modern methods of its diffusion—cultural techniques so sophisticated and penetrating that even men are damaged by them.

1) *Eroticism.* A prime component of romanticism is eroticism. All animal needs (the affection of a kitten that has never seen heat) for love and warmth are channeled into genital sex: people must never touch others of the same sex, and may touch those of the opposite sex only when preparing for a genital sexual encounter ("a pass"). Isolation from others makes people starved for physical affection; and if the only kind they can get is genital sex, that's soon all they crave. In this state of hypersensitivity the least sensual stimulus produces an exaggerated effect, enough to inspire everything from schools of master painting to rock and roll. Thus *eroticism is the concentration of sexuality—often into highly-charged objects ("Chantilly Lace")—signifying the displacement of other social/affection needs onto sex.* To be plain old needy-for-affection makes one a "drip," to need a kiss is embarrassing, unless it is an erotic kiss; only "sex" is O.K., in fact it proves one's mettle. Virility and sexual performance become confused with social worth.[2]

Constant erotic stimulation of male sexuality coupled with its forbidden release through most normal channels are designed to encourage men to look at women as only things whose resistance to entrance must be overcome. For notice that this eroticism operates in only one direction. Women are the only "love" objects in our society, so much so that women regard *themselves* as erotic.[3] This functions to preserve direct sex pleasure for the male, reinforcing female dependence: women can be fulfilled sexually only by vicarious identification with the man who enjoys them. Thus eroticism preserves the sex class system.

The only exception to this concentration of all emotional needs into erotic relationships is the (sometimes) affection within the family. But here, too, unless they are *his* children, a man can no more express affection for children than he can for women. Thus his affection for the young is also a trap to saddle him into the marriage structure, reinforcing the patriarchal system.

2) *The Sex Privatization of Women.* Eroticism is only the topmost layer of the romanticism that reinforces female inferiority. As with any lower class, group awareness must be deadened to keep them from rebelling. In this case, because the distinguishing characteristic of women's exploitation as a class is sexual, a special means must be found to make them unaware that they are considered all alike sexually ("cunts"). Perhaps when a man marries he chooses from this undistinguishable lot with care, for as we have seen, he holds a special high place in his mental reserve for "The One," by virtue of her close association with himself; but in general he can't tell the difference between chicks (Blondes, Brunettes, Redheads).[4] And he likes it that way. ("A wiggle in your walk, a giggle in your talk, THAT'S WHAT I LIKE!") When a man believes all women are alike, but wants to keep women from guessing, what does he do? He keeps his beliefs to himself, and pretends, to allay her suspicions, that what she has in common with other women is precisely what makes her different. Thus her sexuality eventually becomes synonymous with her individuality. *The sex privatization of women is the process whereby women are blinded to their generality as a class which renders them invisible as individuals to the male eye.* Is not that strange Mrs. Lady next to the President in his entourage reminiscent of the discreet black servant at White House functions?

The process is insidious: When a man exclaims, "I love Blondes!" all the secretaries in the vicinity sit up; they take it personally because they have been sex-privatized. The blonde one feels personally complimented because she has come to measure her worth through the physical attributes that differentiate her from other women. She no longer recalls that any physical attribute you could name is shared by many others, that these are accidental attributes not of her own creation, that her sexuality is shared by half of humanity. But in an authentic recognition of her individuality, her blondeness would be loved, but in a different way: She would be loved first as an irreplaceable totality, and then her blondeness would be loved as one of the characteristics of that totality.

The apparatus of sex privatization is so sophisticated that it may take years to detect—if detectable at all. It explains many puzzling traits of female psychology that take such form as:

Women who are personally complimented by compliments to their sex, i.e., "Hats off to the Little Woman!"

Women who are not insulted when addressed regularly and impersonally as Dear, Honey, Sweetie, Sugar, Kitten, Darling, Angel, Queen, Princess, Doll, Woman.

Women who are secretly flattered to have their asses pinched in Rome. (Much wiser to count the number of times other girls' asses are pinched!)

The joys of "prickteasing" (generalized male horniness taken as a sign of personal value and desirability).

The "clotheshorse" phenomenon. (Women, denied legitimate outlets for expression of their individuality, "express" themselves physically, as in "I want to see something 'different.'")

These are only some of the reactions to the sex privatization process, the confusion of one's sexuality with one's individuality. The process is so effective that most women have come to believe seriously that the world needs their particular sexual contributions to go on. ("She thinks her pussy is made of gold.") But the love songs would still be written without them.

Women may be duped, but men are quite conscious of this as a valuable manipulative technique. That is why they go to great pains to avoid talking about women in front of them ("not in front of a lady")—it would give their game away. To overhear a bull session is traumatic to a woman: So all this time she has been considered only "ass," "meat," "twat," or "stuff," to be gotten a "piece of," "that bitch," or "this broad" to be tricked out of money or sex or love! To understand finally that she is no better than other women but completely indistinguishable comes not just as a blow but as a total annihilation. But perhaps the time that women more often have to confront their own sex privatization is in a lover's quarrel, when the truth spills out: then a man might get careless and admit that the only thing he ever *really* liked her for was her bust ("Built like a brick shithouse") or legs anyway ("Hey, Legs!"), and he can find that somewhere else if he has to.

Thus sex privatization stereotypes women: it encourages men to see women as "dolls" differentiated only by superficial attributes—not of the same species as themselves—and it blinds women to their sexploitation as a class, keeping them from uniting against it, thus effectively segregating the two classes. A side-effect is the converse: if women are differentiated only by superficial physical attributes, men appear more individual and irreplaceable than they really are.

Women, because social recognition is granted only for a *false* individuality, are kept from developing the tough individuality that would enable breaking through such a ruse. If one's existence in its generality is the only thing acknowledged, why go to the trouble to develop real character? It is much less hassle to "light up the room with a smile"—until that day when the "chick" graduates to "old bag," to find that her smile is no longer "inimitable."

3) *The Beauty Ideal.* Every society has promoted a certain ideal of beauty over all others. What that ideal is is unimportant, for any ideal leaves the majority out; ideals, by definition, are modeled on *rare* qualities. For example, in America, the present fashion vogue of French models, or the erotic ideal Voluptuous Blonde are modeled on qualities rare indeed: few Americans are of French birth, most don't look French and never will (and besides they eat too much); voluptuous brunettes can bleach their hair (as did Marilyn Monroe, the sex queen herself), but blondes can't develop curves at will—and most of them, being Anglo-Saxon, simply aren't built like that. If and when, by artificial methods, the majority can squeeze into the ideal, the ideal changes. If it were attainable, what good would it be?

For the exclusivity of the beauty ideal serves a clear political function. Someone—most women—will be left out. And left scrambling, because as we have seen, women have been allowed to achieve individuality only through their appearance—looks being defined as "good" not out of love for the bearer, but because of her more or less successful approximation to an external standard. This image, defined by men (and currently by homosexual men, often misogynists of the worst order), becomes the ideal. What happens? Women everywhere rush to squeeze into the glass slipper, forcing and mutilating their bodies with diets and beauty programs, clothes and makeup, anything to become the punk prince's dream girl. But they have no choice. If they don't the penalties are enormous: their social legitimacy is at stake.

Thus women become more and more look-alike. But at the same time they are expected to express their individuality through their physical appearance. Thus they are kept coming and going, at one and the same time trying to express their similarity and their uniqueness. The demands of Sex Privatization contradict the demands of the Beauty Ideal, causing the severe feminine neurosis about personal appearance.

But this conflict itself has an important political function. When women begin to look more and more alike, distinguished only by the degree to which they differ from a paper ideal, they can be more easily stereotyped as a class: They look alike, they think alike, and even worse, they are so stupid they believe they are not alike.

These are some of the major components of the cultural apparatus, romanticism, which, with the weakening of "natural" limitations on women, keep sex oppression going strong. The political uses of romanticism over the centuries became increasingly complex. Operating subtly or blatantly, on every cultural level, romanticism is now—

in this time of greatest threat to the male power role—amplified by new techniques of communication so all-pervasive that men get entangled in their own line. How does this amplification work?

With the cultural portrayal of the smallest details of existence (e.g., deodorizing one's underarms), the distance between one's experience and one's perceptions of it becomes enlarged by a vast interpretive network. If our direct experience contradicts its interpretation by this ubiquitous cultural network, the experience must be denied. This process, of course, does not apply only to women. The pervasion of image has so deeply altered our very relationships to ourselves that even men have become objects—if never *erotic* objects. Images become extensions of oneself; it gets hard to distinguish the real person from his latest image, if indeed, the Person Underneath hasn't evaporated altogether. Arnie, the kid who sat in back of you in the sixth grade, picking his nose and cracking jokes, the one who had a crook in his left shoulder, is lost under successive layers of adopted images: the High School Comedian, the Campus Rebel, James Bond, the Salem Springtime Lover, and so on, each image hitting new highs of sophistication until the person himself doesn't know who he is. Moreover, he deals with others through this image-extension (Boy-Image meets Girl-Image and consummates Image-Romance). Even if a woman could get beneath this intricate image facade—and it would take months, even years, of a painful, almost therapeutic relationship—she would be met not with gratitude that she had (painfully) loved the man for his real self, but with shocked repulsion and terror that she had found him out. What he wants instead is The Pepsi-Cola Girl, to smile pleasantly to his Johnny Walker Red in front of a ski-lodge fire.

But, while this reification affects both men and women alike, in the case of women it is profoundly complicated by the forms of sexploitation I have described. Woman is not only an Image, she is the Image of Sex Appeal. The stereotyping of women expands: now there is no longer the excuse of ignorance. Every woman is constantly and explicitly informed on how to "improve" what nature gave her, where to buy the products to do it with, and how to count the calories she should never have eaten—indeed, the "ugly" woman is now so nearly extinct even she is fast becoming "exotic." The competition becomes frantic, because everyone is now plugged into the same circuit. The current beauty ideal becomes all-pervasive ("Blondes have more fun . . .").

And eroticism becomes erotomania. Stimulated to the limit, it has reached an epidemic level unequalled in history. From every magazine cover, film screen, TV tube, subway sign, jump breasts, legs, shoulders, thighs. Men walk about in a state of constant sexual excitement. Even with the best of intentions, it is difficult to focus on anything else. This bombardment of the senses, in turn, escalates sexual provocation still further: ordinary means of arousal have lost all effect. Clothing becomes more provocative: hemlines climb, bras are shed. See-through materials become ordinary. But in all this barrage of erotic stimuli, men themselves are seldom portrayed as erotic objects. Women's eroticism, as well as men's, becomes increasingly directed toward women.

One of the internal contradictions of this highly effective propaganda system is to expose to men as well as women the stereotyping process women undergo. Though the idea was to better acquaint women with their feminine role, men who turn on the TV are also treated to the latest in tummy-control, false eyelashes, and floor waxes (Does she . . . or doesn't she?). Such a crosscurrent of sexual tease and exposé would be enough to make any man hate women, if he didn't already.

Thus the extension of romanticism through modern media enormously magnified its effects. If before culture maintained male supremacy through Eroticism, Sex Privatization, and the Beauty Ideal, these cultural processes are now almost too effectively carried out: the media are guilty of "overkill." The regeneration of the women's movement at this moment in history may be due to a backfiring, an internal contradiction of our modern cultural indoctrination system. For in its amplification of sex indoctrination, the media have unconsciously exposed the degradation of "femininity."

In conclusion, I want to add a note about the special difficulties of attacking the sex class system through its means of cultural indoctrination. Sex objects *are* beautiful. An attack on them can be confused with an attack on beauty itself. Feminists need not get so pious in their efforts that they feel they must flatly deny the beauty of the face on the cover of *Vogue*. For this is not the point. The real question is: is the face beautiful in a *human* way—does it allow for growth and flux and decay, does it express negative as well as positive emotions, does it fall apart without artificial props—or does it falsely imitate the very different beauty of an *inanimate* object, like wood trying to be metal?

To attack eroticism creates similar problems. Eroticism is *exciting*. No one wants to get rid of it. Life would be a drab and routine affair without at least that spark. That's just the point. Why has all joy and excitement been concentrated, driven into one narrow, difficult-to-find alley of human experience, and all the rest laid waste? When we demand the elimination of eroticism, we mean not the elimination of sexual joy and excitement but its rediffusion over—there's plenty to go around, it increases with use—the spectrum of our lives.

NOTES

1 Gallantry has been commonly defined as "excessive attention to women without serious purpose," but the purpose is very serious: through a false flattery, to keep women from awareness of their lower-class condition.

2 But as every woman has discovered, a man who seems to be pressuring for sex is often greatly relieved to be excused from the literal performance: His ego has been made dependent on his continuously proving himself through sexual conquest; but all he may have really wanted was the excuse to indulge in affection without the loss of manly self-respect. That men are more restrained than are women about exhibiting emotion is because, in addition to the results of the Oedipus Complex, to express tenderness to a woman is to acknowledge her equality. Unless, of course, one tempers one's tenderness—takes it back—with some evidence of domination.

3 Homosexuals are so ridiculed because in viewing the male as sex object they go doubly against the norm: even women don't read Pretty Boy magazines.

4 "As for his other sports," says a recent blurb about football hero Joe Namath, "he prefers Blondes."

The Feminine Body

Sandra Lee Bartky

I

In a striking critique of modern society, Michel Foucault has argued that the rise of parliamentary institutions and of new conceptions of political liberty was accompanied by a darker counter-movement, by the emergence of a new and unprecedented discipline directed against the body. More is required of the body now than mere political allegiance or the appropriation of the products of its labor: The new discipline invades the body and seeks to regulate its very forces and operations, the economy and efficiency of its movements.

The disciplinary practices Foucault describes are tied to peculiarly modern forms of the army, the school, the hospital, the prison, and the manufactory; the aim of these disciplines is to increase the utility of the body, to augment its forces:

> What was then being formed was a policy of coercions that act upon the body, a calculated manipulation of its elements, its gestures, its behaviour. The human body was entering a machinery of power that explores it, breaks it down and rearranges it. A 'political anatomy', which was also a 'mechanics of power', was being born; it defined how one may have a hold over others' bodies, not only so that they may do what one wishes, but so that they may operate as one wishes, with the techniques, the speed and the efficiency that one determines. Thus, discipline produces subjected and practiced bodies, 'docile' bodies.[1]

The production of "docile bodies" requires that an uninterrupted coercion be directed to the very processes of bodily activity, not just their result; this "micro-physics of power" fragments and partitions the body's time, its space, and its movements.[2]

Foucault's account in *Discipline and Punish* of the disciplinary practices that produce the "docile bodies" of modernity is a genuine *tour de force,* incorporating a rich theoretical account of the ways in which instrumental reason takes hold of the body with a mass of historical detail. But Foucault treats the body throughout as if it were one, as if the bodily experiences of men and women did not differ and as if men and women bore the same relationship to the characteristic institutions of modern life. Where is the account of the disciplinary practices that engender the "docile bodies" of women, bodies more docile than the bodies of men? Women, like men, are subject to many of the same disciplinary practices Foucault describes. But he is blind to those disciplines that produce a modality of embodiment that is peculiarly feminine. To overlook the forms of subjection that engender the feminine body is to perpetuate the silence and powerlessness of those upon whom these disciplines have been imposed. Hence, even though a liberatory note is sounded in Foucault's critique of power, his analysis as a whole reproduces that sexism which is endemic throughout Western political theory.

We are born male or female, but not masculine or feminine. Femininity is an artifice, an achievement, "a mode of enacting and reenacting received gender norms which surface as so many styles of the flesh."[3] In what follows, I shall examine those disciplinary practices that produce a body which in gesture and appearance is recognizably feminine. I consider three categories of such practices: those that aim to produce a body of a certain size and general configuration; those that bring forth from this body a specific repertoire of gestures, postures, and movements; and those directed toward the display of this body as an ornamented surface. I shall examine the nature of these disciplines, how they are imposed and by whom. I shall probe the effects of the imposition of such discipline on female identity and subjectivity. In the final section I shall argue that these disciplinary practices must be understood in the light of the modernization of patriarchal domination, a modernization that unfolds historically according to the general pattern described by Foucault.

II

Styles of the female figure vary over time and across cultures: they reflect cultural obsessions and preoccupations in ways that are still poorly understood. Today, massiveness, power, or abundance in a woman's body is met with distaste. The current body of fashion is taut, small breasted, narrow-hipped, and of a slimness bordering on emaciation; it is a silhouette that seems more appropriate to an adolescent boy or a newly pubescent girl than to an adult woman. Since ordinary women have normally quite different dimensions, they must of course diet.

Mass-circulation women's magazines run articles on dieting in virtually every issue. The *Ladies' Home Journal* of February 1986 carries a "Fat-Burning Exercise Guide," while *Mademoiselle* offers to "Help Stamp Out Cellulite" with "Six Sleek-Down Strategies." After the diet-busting Christmas holidays and later, before summer bikini season, the titles of these features become shriller and more arresting. The reader is now addressed in the imperative mode: Jump into shape for summer! Shed ugly winter fat with the all-new Grapefruit Diet! More women than men visit diet doctors, while women greatly outnumber men in self-help groups such as Weight Watchers and Overeaters Anonymous—in the case of the latter, by well over 90 percent.[4]

Dieting disciplines the body's hungers: Appetite must be monitored at all times and governed by an iron will. Since the innocent need of the organism for food will not be denied, the body becomes one's enemy, an alien being bent on thwarting the disciplinary project. Anorexia nervosa, which has now assumed epidemic proportions, is to women of the late twentieth century what hysteria was to women of an earlier day: the crystallization in a pathological mode of a widespread cultural obsession.[5] A survey taken recently at UCLA is astounding: Of 260 students interviewed, 27.3 percent of the women but only 5.8 percent of men said they were "terrified" of getting fat: 28.7 percent of women and only 7.5 percent of men said they were obsessed or "totally preoccupied" with food. The body images of women and men are strikingly different as well: 35 percent of women but only 12.5 percent of men said they felt fat though other people told them they were thin. Women in the survey wanted to weigh ten pounds less than their average weight; men felt they were within a pound of their ideal weight. A total of 5.9 percent of women and no men met the psychiatric criteria for anorexia or bulimia.[6]

Dieting is one discipline imposed upon a body subject to the "tyranny of slenderness"; exercise is another.[7] Since men as well as women exercise, it is not always easy in the case of women to distinguish what is done for the sake of physical fitness from what is done in obedience to the requirements of femininity. Men as well as women lift weights, do yoga, calisthenics, and aerobics, though "jazzercise" is a largely female pursuit. Men and women alike engage themselves with a variety of machines, each designed to call forth from the body a different exertion: There are Nautilus machines, rowing machines, ordinary and motorized exercycles, portable hip and leg cycles, belt massagers, trampolines, treadmills, arm and leg pulleys. However, given the widespread female obsession with weight, one suspects that many women are working out with these apparatuses in the health club or at the gym with a different aim in mind and in quite a different spirit than the men.

But there are classes of exercises meant for women alone, these designed not to firm or to reduce the body's size overall, but to resculpture its various parts on the current model. M. J. Saffon, "international beauty expert," assures us that his twelve basic facial exercises can erase frown lines, smooth the forehead, raise hollow cheeks, banish crow's feet, and tighten the muscles under the chin.[8] There are exercises to build the breasts and exercises to banish "cellulite," said by "figure consultants" to be a special type of female fat. There is "spot-reducing," an umbrella term that covers dozens of punishing exercises designed to reduce "problem areas" like thick ankles or "saddlebag" thighs. The very idea of "spot-reducing" is both scientifically unsound and cruel, for it raises expectations in women that can never be realized: The pattern in which fat is deposited or removed is known to be genetically determined.

It is not only her natural appetite or unreconstructed contours that pose a danger to women: The very expressions of her face can subvert the disciplinary project of bodily perfection. An expressive face lines and creases more readily than an inexpressive one. Hence, if women are unable to suppress strong emotions, they can at least learn to inhibit the tendency of the face to register them. Sophia Loren recommends a unique solution to this problem: A piece of tape applied to the forehead or between the brows will tug at the skin when one frowns and act as a reminder to relax the face.[9] The tape is to be worn whenever a woman is home alone.

III

There are significant gender differences in gesture, posture, movement, and general bodily comportment: Women are far more restricted than men in their manner of movement and in their lived spatiality. In her classic paper on the subject, Iris Young observes that a space seems to surround women in imagination which they are hesitant to move beyond: This manifests itself both in a reluctance to reach, stretch, and extend the body to meet resistances of matter in motion—as in sport or in the performance of physical tasks—and in a typically constricted posture and general style of movement. Woman's space is not a field in which her bodily intentionality can be freely realized but an enclosure in which she feels herself positioned and by which she is confined.[10] The "loose woman" violates these norms: Her looseness is manifest not only in her morals, but in her manner of speech, and quite literally in the free and easy way she moves.

In an extraordinary series of over two thousand photographs, many candid shots taken in the street, the German photographer Marianne Wex has documented differences in typical masculine and feminine body posture. Women sit waiting for trains with arms close to the body, hands folded together in their laps, toes pointing straight ahead or turned inward, and legs pressed together.[11] The women in these photographs make themselves small and narrow, harmless; they seem tense; they take up little space. Men, on the other hand, expand into the available space; they sit with legs far apart and arms flung out at some distance from the body. Most common in these sitting male figures is what Wex calls the "proferring position": the men sit with legs thrown wide apart, crotch visible, feet pointing outward, often with an arm and casually dangling hand resting comfortably on an open, spread thigh.

In proportion to total body size, a man's stride is longer than a woman's. The man has more spring and rhythm to his step; he walks with toes pointed outward, holds his arms at a greater distance from his body, and swings them farther; he tends to point the whole hand in the direction he is moving. The woman holds her arms closer to her body, palms against her sides; her walk is circumspect. If she has subjected herself to the additional constraint of high-heeled shoes, her body is thrown forward and off-balance: The struggle to walk under these conditions shortens her stride still more.[12]

But women's movement is subjected to a still finer discipline. Feminine faces, as well as bodies, are trained to the expression of deference. Under male scrutiny, women will avert their eyes or cast them downward; the female gaze is trained to abandon its claim to the sovereign status of seer. The "nice" girl learns to avoid the bold and unfettered staring of the "loose" woman who looks at whatever and whomever she pleases. Women are trained to smile more than men, too. In the economy of smiles, as elsewhere, there is evidence that women are exploited, for they give more than they receive in return; in a smile elicitation study, one researcher found that the rate of smile return by women was 93 percent, by men only 67 percent.[13] In many typical women's jobs, graciousness, deference, and the readiness to serve are part of the work; this requires the worker to fix a smile on her face for a good part of the working day, whatever her inner state.[14] The economy of touching is out of balance, too: men touch women more often and on more parts of the body than women touch men: female secretaries, factory workers, and waitresses report that such liberties are taken routinely with their bodies.[15]

Feminine movement, gesture, and posture must exhibit not only constriction, but grace as well, and a certain eroticism restrained by modesty: all three. Here is field for the operation for a whole new training: A woman must stand with stomach pulled in, shoulders thrown slightly back, and chest out, this to display her bosom to maximum advantage. While she must walk in the confined fashion appropriate to women, her movements must, at the same time, be combined with a subtle but provocative hip-roll. But too much display is taboo: Women in short, low-cut dresses are told to avoid bending over at all, but if they must, great care must be taken to avoid an unseemly display of breast or rump. From time to time, fashion magazines offer quite precise instructions on the proper way of getting in and out of cars. These instructions combine all three imperatives of women's movement: A woman must not allow her arms and legs to flail about in all directions; she must try to manage her movements with the appearance of grace—no small accomplishment when one is climbing out of the back seat of a Fiat—and she is well advised to use the opportunity for a certain display of leg.

All the movements we have described so far are self-movements; they arise from within the woman's own body. But in a way that normally goes unnoticed, males in couples may literally steer a woman everywhere she goes: down the street, around corners, into elevators, through doorways, into her chair at the dinner table, around the dance-floor. The man's movement "is not necessarily heavy and pushy or physical in an ugly way; it is light and gentle but firm in the way of the most confident equestrians with the best trained horses."[16]

IV

Are we dealing in all this merely with sexual *difference?* Scarcely. The disciplinary practices I have described are part of the process by which the ideal body of femininity—and hence the feminine body-subject—is constructed; in doing this, they produce a "practiced and subjected" body, i.e., a body on which an inferior status has been inscribed. A woman's face must be made up, that is to say, made over, and so must her body: she is ten pounds overweight; her lips must be made more kissable; her complexion dewier; her eyes more mysterious. The "art" of make-up is the art of disguise, but this presupposes that a woman's face, unpainted, is defective. Soap and water, a shave, and routine attention to hygiene may be enough for *him;* for *her* they are not. The strategy of much beauty-related advertising is to suggest to women that their bodies are deficient, but even without such more or less explicit teaching, the media images of perfect female beauty which bombard us daily leave no doubt in the minds of most women that they fail to measure up. The technologies of femininity are taken up and practiced by women against the background of a pervasive sense of bodily deficiency: This accounts for what is often their compulsive or even ritualistic character.

The disciplinary project of femininity is a "set-up": It requires such radical and extensive measures of bodily transformation that virtually every woman who gives herself to it is destined in some degree to fail. Thus, a measure of shame is added to a woman's sense that the body she inhabits is deficient: she ought to take better care of herself; she might after all have jogged that last mile. Many women are without the time or resources to provide themselves with even the minimum of what such a regimen requires, e.g., a decent diet. Here is an additional source of shame for poor women who must bear what our society regards as the more general shame of poverty. The burdens poor women bear in this regard are not merely psychological, since conformity to the prevailing standards of bodily acceptability is a known factor in economic mobility.

The larger disciplines that construct a "feminine" body out of a female one are by no means race- or class-specific. There is little evidence that women of color or working-class women are in general less committed to the incarnation of an ideal femininity than their more privileged sisters. This is not to deny the many ways in which factors of race, class, locality, ethnicity, or personal taste can be expressed within the kinds of practices I have described. The rising young corporate executive may buy her cosmetics at Bergdorf-Goodman while the counter-server at McDonald's gets hers at the K-Mart; the one may join an expensive "upscale" health club, while the other may have to make do with the $9.49 GFX Body-Flex II Home-Gym advertised in the *National Enquirer:* Both are aiming at the same general result.[17]

In the regime of institutionalized heterosexuality woman must make herself "object and prey" for the man: It is for him that these eyes are limpid pools, this cheek baby-smooth.[18] In contemporary patriarchal culture, a panoptical male connoisseur resides within the consciousness of most women: They stand perpetually before his gaze and under his judgment. Woman lives her body as seen by another, by an anonymous patriarchal Other. We are often told that "women dress for other women." There is some truth in this: Who but someone engaged in a project similar to my own can appreciate the panache with which I bring it off? But women know for whom this game is played: They know that a pretty young woman is likelier to become a flight attendant than a plain one and that a well-preserved older woman has a better chance of holding onto her husband than one who has "let herself go.". . .

To succeed in the provision of a beautiful or sexy body gains a woman attention and some admiration but little real respect and rarely any social power. A woman's effort to master feminine body discipline will lack importance just because she does it: Her activity partakes of the general depreciation of everything female. In spite of unrelenting pressure to "make the most of what they have," women are ridiculed and dismissed for the triviality of their interest in such "trivial" things as clothes and make-up. Further, the narrow identification of woman with sexuality and the body in a society that has for centuries displayed profound suspicion toward both does little to raise her status. Even the most adored female bodies complain routinely of their situation in ways that reveal an implicit understanding that there is something demeaning in the kind of attention they receive. Marilyn Monroe, Elizabeth Taylor, and Farrah Fawcett have all wanted passionately to become actresses-artists and not just "sex objects."

But it is perhaps in their more restricted motility and comportment that the inferiorization of women's bodies is most evident: Women's typical body language, a language of relative tension and constriction, is understood to be a language of subordination when it is enacted by men in male status hierarchies. In groups of men, those with higher status typically assume looser and more relaxed postures: The boss lounges comfortably behind the desk while the applicant sits tense and rigid on the edge of his seat. Higher-status individuals may touch their subordinates more than they themselves get touched; they initiate more eye contact and are smiled at by their inferiors more than they are observed to smile in return.[19] What is announced in the comportment of superiors is confidence and ease, especially ease of access to the Other. Female constraint in posture and movement is no doubt over-determined: The fact that women tend to sit and stand with legs, feet, and knees close or touching may well be a coded declaration of sexual circumspection in a society that still maintains a double standard, or an effort, albeit unconscious, to guard the genital area. In the latter case, a woman's tight and constricted posture must be seen as the expression of her need to ward off real or symbolic sexual attack. Whatever proportions must be assigned in the final display to fear or deference, one thing is clear: Woman's body language speaks eloquently, though silently, of her subordinate status in a hierarchy of gender. . . .

NOTES

1 Michel Foucault, *Discipline and Punish: The Birth of the Prison,* trans. Alan Sheridan (New York: Vintage Books, 1979), p. 138.

2 Ibid., p. 28.

3 Judith Butler, "Embodied Identity in de Beauvoir's *The Second Sex*" (unpublished manuscript presented to American Philosophical Association, Pacific Division, March 22, 1985), p. 11.

4 Marcia Millman, *Such a Pretty Face: Being Fat in America* (New York: W. W. Norton, 1980), p. 46.

5 Susan Bordo, "Anorexia Nervosa: Psychopathology as the Crystallization of Culture," *Philosophical Forum* 17, no. 2 (Winter 1985–86): 73–104 (reprinted in this volume).

6 *USA Today* (Thursday, May 30, 1985).

7 Phrase taken from the title of Kim Chernin, *The Obsession: Reflections on the Tyranny of Slenderness* (New York: Harper and Row, 1981), an examination from a feminist perspective of women's eating disorders and of the current female preoccupation with body size.

8 M. J. Saffon, *The 15-Minute-A-Day Natural Face Lift* (New York: Warner Books, 1981).

9 Sophia Loren, *Women and Beauty* (New York: William Morrow, 1984), p. 57.

10 Iris Young, "Throwing Like a Girl: A Phenomenology of Feminine Body Comportment, Motility and Spatiality," *Human Studies* 3 (1980): 137–56.

11 Marianne Wex, *Let's Take Back Our Space: "Female" and "Male" Body Language as a Result of Patriarchal Structures* (Berlin: Frauenliteraturverlag Hermine Fees, 1979). Wex claims (p. 23) that Japanese women are still taught to position their feet so that the toes point inward, a traditional sign of submissiveness.

12 In heels, the "female foot and leg are turned into ornamental objects and the impractical shoe, which offers little protection against dust, rain and snow, induces helplessness and dependence. . . . The extra wiggle in the hips, exaggerating a slight natural tendency, is seen as sexually flirtatious while the small steps and tentative, insecure tread suggest daintiness, modesty and refinement. Finally, the overall hobbling effect with its sadomasochistic tinge is suggestive of the restraining leg irons and ankle chains endured by captive animals, prisoners and slaves who were also festooned with decorative symbols of their bondage." Susan Brownmiller, *Femininity* (New York: Simon and Schuster, 1984), p. 184.

13 Nancy Henley, *Body Politics* (Englewood Cliffs, N.J.: Prentice-Hall, 1977), p. 176.

14 For an account of the sometimes devastating effects on workers, like flight attendants, whose conditions of employment require the display of a perpetual friendliness, see Arlie Hochschild, *The Managed Heart: The Commercialization of Human Feeling* (Berkeley: University of California Press, 1983).

15 Henley, *Body Politics,* p. 108.

16 Ibid., p. 149.

17 In light of this, one is surprised to see a 2-ounce jar of "Skin Regeneration Formula," a "Proteolytic Enzyme Cream with Bromelain and Papain," selling for $23.95 in the tabloid *Globe* (April 8, 1986, p. 29) and an unidentified amount of Tova Borgnine's "amazing new formula Beverly Hills" (otherwise unnamed) going for $41.75 in the *National Enquirer* (April 8, 1986, p. 15).

18 ". . . it is required of woman that in order to realize her femininity she must make herself object and prey, which is to say that she must renounce her claims as sovereign subject." Simone de Beauvoir, *The Second Sex* (New York: Bantam Books, 1968), p. 642.
19 Henley, *Body Politics,* pp. 101, 153, and passim.

The Sexual Dilemma

Lillian B. Rubin

WIFE: *I say that foreplay begins in the morning.*
HUSBAND: *It seems to me being sexual would make us closer, but she says it works the other way—if she felt closer, there'd be more sex.*

It's a common complaint in marriages—wives and husbands all too often divided as these two are. We wonder about it, ask each other questions, try to persuade the other with reason, and, when that fails, we argue. Sooner or later we make up, telling each other that we'll change. And, in the moment the words are said, we mean them. We try, but somehow the promises aren't fulfilled; somehow, without thought or intention, we slip back into the old ways. The cycle starts again; the struggle is resumed.

We're told by the experts that the problem exists because we don't communicate properly. We must talk to each other, they insist—explain what we need and want, what feels good, what bad. So "communication" has become a household word, the buzzword of the age. We think about it, talk about it, read books, take courses, see therapists to learn how to do it. We come away from these endeavors with resolutions that promise we'll change our ways, that we'll work with our partner on being more open and more expressive about what we're thinking and feeling. But too often our good intentions come to naught, especially when it comes to reconciling our sexual differences.

These are difficult issues, not easily amenable to intervention by talk, no matter how earnest, how compelling our efforts at honesty may be. One couple, aged thirty-three and thirty-five, married eight years and the parents of two children, told of these differences. Speaking quickly and agitatedly, the wife said:

Talk, talk, talk! He tries to convince me; I try to convince him. What's the use? It's not the words that are missing. I don't even know if the problem is that we don't understand each other. We understand, all right. But we don't like what we know; that's the problem.

Her husband's words came more slowly, tinged as they were with resignation and frustration.

I understand what she wants. She wants us to be loving and close, then we can have sex. But it's not always possible that way. We're both busy; there are the kids. It can't be like a love affair all the time, and if we have to wait for that, well [his words trailing off] . . . what the hell, it'll be a long wait.

The wife, speaking more calmly but with her emotional turmoil still evident just below the surface of her words:

> He complains that I want it to be like a love affair, but that's not it. I want to feel some emotion from him; I want an emotional contact, not just a sexual one.

The husband, vexed and bewildered:

> When she starts talking about how I'm sexual but not emotional, that's it; that's where I get lost. Isn't sex emotional, for Christ's sake?

From both husband and wife, an angry yet plaintive cry. It's not words that divide them, however. They tell each other quite openly what they think, how they feel. It just doesn't seem to help in the ways they would wish. But, if it's not a simple matter of communication, then what is it that makes these issues seem so intransigent, so resistant to resolution even with the best intentions we can muster?

Some analysts of society point to the culture, to the ideologies that have defined the limits of male and female sexuality. Certainly there's truth in that. There's no gainsaying that, through the ages of Western society, women's sexuality has come under attack, that there have been sometimes extreme pressures to control and confine it—even to deny its existence. There's no doubt either that we have dealt with male sexuality with much more ambivalence. On the one hand, it too has been the object of efforts at containment; on the other, we have acknowledged its force and power—indeed, built myth and monument in homage to what we have taken to be its inherently uncontrollable nature.

Such social attitudes about male and female sexuality, and the behavioral ideals that have accompanied them, not only shape our sexual behavior but affect our experience of our own sexuality as well. For culture both clarifies and mystifies. A set of beliefs is at once a way of seeing the world more clearly while, at the same time, foreclosing an alternative vision. When it comes to sex—precisely because it's such a primitive, elemental force—all societies seek some control over it and, therefore, the mystification is greater than the clarification. Thus, for example, Victorian women often convinced themselves that they had no sexual feelings even when the messages their bodies sent would have told them otherwise if they had been able to listen. And, even now, men often engage in compulsive sexual behavior that brings them little, if any, pleasure without allowing themselves to notice the joylessness of it. Both behaviors a response to cultural mandates, both creating dissonance, if not outright conflict, when inner experience is at odds with behavioral expectations.

The blueprint to which our sexuality conforms, then, is drawn by the culture. But that's not yet the whole story. The dictates of any society are reinforced by its institutional arrangements and mediated by the personal experience of the people who must live within them. And it's in that confluence of social arrangement and psychological response that we'll come to understand the basis of the sexual differences that so often divide us from each other.

For a woman, there's no satisfactory sex without an emotional connection; for a man, the two are more easily separable. For her, the connection generally must precede the sexual encounter:

> For me to be excited about making love, I have to feel close to him—like we're sharing something, not just living together.

For him, emotional closeness can be born of the sexual contact.

> It's the one subject we never get anywhere on. It's a lot easier for me to tell her what she wants to hear when I feel close, and that's when I get closest—when we're making love. It's kind of hard to explain it, but [trying to find the words] . . . well, it's when the emotions come roaring up.

The issues that divide them around intimacy in the relationship are nowhere to be seen more clearly than here. When she speaks of connection, she usually means intimacy that's born of some verbal expression, some sharing of thought and feeling:

> I want to know what he's thinking—you know, what's going on inside him—before we jump into bed.

For him, it's enough that they're in the same room.

> To me, it feels like there's a nice bond when we're together—just reading the paper or watching the tube or something like that. Then, when we go to bed, that's not enough for her.

The problem, then, is not *how* we talk to each other but *whether* we do so. And it's connected to what words and the verbal expression of emotion mean to us, how sex and emotion come together for each of us, and the fact that we experience the balance between the two so differently—all of which takes us again to the separation and individuation experiences of childhood.

For both boys and girls, the earliest attachment and the identification that grows from it are much larger, deeper, and more all-embracing than anything we, who have successfully buried that primitive past in our unconscious, can easily grasp. Their root is pure eros—that vital, life-giving force with which all attachment begins. The infant bathes in it. But we are a society of people who have learned to look on eros with apprehension, if not outright fear. For us, it is associated with passion, with sex, with forces that threaten to be out of control. And we teach our young very early, and in ways too numerous to count, about the need to limit the erotic, about our fears that eros imperils civilization.

In the beginning, it's the same for children of either sex. As the child grows past the early symbiotic union with mother, as the boundaries of self begin to develop, the social norms about sexuality begin to make themselves felt. In conformity with those norms, the erotic and emotional are split one from the other, and the erotic takes on a more specifically sexual meaning.

But here the developmental similarities end. For a boy at this stage, it's the emotional component of the attachment to mother that comes under attack as he seeks to repress his identification with her. The erotic—or sexualized—aspect of the attachment is left undisturbed, at least in heterosexual men. To be sure, the incest taboo assures that future sexual *behavior* will take place with a woman other than mother. But the issue here is not behavior but the emotional structure that underlies it.

For a girl, the developmental requirement is exactly the opposite. For her, it's the erotic component of the attachment to a woman that must be denied and shifted later to a man; the larger emotional involvement and the identification remain intact.

This split between the emotional and the erotic components of attachment in childhood has deep and lasting significance for the ways in which we respond to relationships—sexual and otherwise—in adulthood. For it means that, for men, the erotic aspect of any relationship remains forever the most compelling, while, for women, the emotional component will always be the more salient. It's here that we can come to understand the depth of women's emotional connection to each other—the reasons why nonsexual friendships between women remain so central in their lives, so important to their sense of themselves and to their well-being. And it's here also that we can see why nonsexual relationships hold such little emotional charge for men.

It's not as folklore has held, that a woman's sexual response is more muted than a man's, or that she doesn't need or desire sexual release the way a man does. But, because it's the erotic aspect of her earliest attachment that has to be repressed in childhood if a girl is later to form a sexual bond with a man, the explicitly sexual retains little *independent* status in her inner life. A man may lust after *women,* but a woman lusts after a *man.* For a woman, sex usually has meaning only in a relational context—perhaps a clue to why so many girls never or rarely masturbate in adolescence or early adulthood.

We might argue that the social proscriptions against masturbation alone could account for its insignificance in girls and young women. But boys, too, hear exhortations against masturbation—indeed, even today, many still are told tales of the horrors that will befall them. Yet, except to encourage guilt and secrecy, such injunctions haven't made much difference in its incidence among them.

It would be reasonable to assume that this is a response to the mixed message this society sends to men about their sexuality. On the one hand, they're expected to exercise restraint; on the other, there's an implicit understanding that we can't really count on them to do so—that, at base, male sexuality cannot be controlled, that, after all, boys will be boys.

Surely such differences in the ways in which male and female sexuality are viewed could account for some of the differences between the sexes in their patterns and incidence of masturbation. But I believe there's something else that makes the social prohibitions take so well with women. For with them, an emotional connection in a relationship generally is a stimulus, if not a precondition, for the erotic.

If women depend on the emotional attachment to call up the sexual, men rely on the sexual to spark the emotional, as these words from a forty-one-year-old man, married fourteen years, show:

> Having sex with her makes me feel much closer so it makes it easier to bridge the emotional gap, so to speak. It's like the physical sex opens up another door, and things and feelings can get expressed that I couldn't before.

For women, emotional attachments without sex are maintained with little difficulty or discomfort; for men, they're much more problematic. It's not that they don't exist at all, but that they're less common and fraught with many more difficulties and reservations.

This is the split that may help to explain why men tend to be fearful of homosexuality in a way that women are not. I don't mean by this that women welcome homosexual stirrings any more than men do. But, for women, the emotional and the erotic are separated in such a way that they can be intensely connected emotionally without fear that this will lead to a sexual connection. For men, where the emotional connection so often depends on a sexual one, a close emotional relationship with another man usually is experienced as a threat.

We can see most clearly how deep these differences run when we compare the sexual behaviors of lesbians and homosexual men. Here, the relationships are not muddied by traditional gender differences, suspicions, and antagonisms, and the differences between men and women are stark—there for anyone to see.

In a series of intensive interviews with gay women and men, I was struck repeatedly by the men's ability to take pleasure in a kind of anonymous sex that I rarely, if ever, saw in the lesbian world. For gay women, sex generally is in the context of a relationship—transient perhaps but, for however long it lasts, with genuine elements of relatedness. There are no "fucking buddies" whose names are irrelevant or unknown among lesbians—a common phenomenon with homosexual men. The public bathhouses so popular with many gay men are practically nonexistent for the women because the kind of impersonal, fleeting sexual encounters such places specialize in hold no attraction for most of them.

Among gay men, a friendship that doesn't include sex is rare. With gay women, it's different. Like their straight sisters, lesbians can have intensely intimate and satisfying relationships with each other without any sexual involvement. Certainly a nonsexual friendship will sometimes slide over into a sexual relationship. But, when it does, it's the emotional aspect of the entire relationship, not just the sexual, that's at center stage for the women.

Whether a person is straight or gay, the character of the split between sex and emotion is the same. But the way it's experienced generally is quite different depending upon whether the sexual partner is a woman or a man. Among straight men, because the sexual involvement is with a woman, it calls up the memory of the infantile attachment to mother along with the old ambivalence about separation and unity, about emotional connection and separateness. It's likely, therefore, that it will elicit an intense emotional response—a response that's threatening even while it's gratifying. It's what men look for in their sexual relations with a woman, as these words from a thirty-four-year-old husband tell:

> It's the one time when I can really let go. I guess that's why sex is so important to me. It's the ultimate release; it's the one place where I can get free of the chains inside me.

And it's also what they fear. For it threatens their defenses against the return of those long-repressed feelings for that other woman—that first connection in their lives. So they hold on to the separation between the sexual and emotional, and thereby keep the repression safe. Thus, moments after speaking of sex as the "one place" where he could feel free, the same man spoke of his apprehensions:

> Much as I look for it, sex can also be a problem for me sometimes. I can get awfully anxious and tense about it. If I don't watch it, so much begins to happen that I get scared, like I don't

know where I'm at. So that puts a damper on things. I'm a little ashamed to say it, but I can do a whole lot better sexually with someone else—you know, someone I don't care about—than I can with her. With someone like that, it doesn't mess up my insides and get all that stuff boiling around.

"What is this 'stuff' that upsets you so?" I wondered aloud. Discomfited, he lowered his head and muttered, "I don't really know." "Could you try to figure it out for me?" I prodded gently.

Well, it's really hard to put it into words, but let's see. The closest I can get is to say it feels like something I don't want to know about—maybe something I'm not supposed to know about. [A thoughtful pause] Jesus, I said that, but I'm not even sure what it means. Let's see! It's something like this. If I let it all happen—I mean, let all those feelings just happen—I don't know where it'll end. It's like a person could get caught in them, trapped, so that you could never get out. Hell, I don't know. I've heard people say sex is like going back to the womb. Maybe that's it. Only you came out of the womb, and here it feels like you might never get out again. Does that make any sense to you?

Without doubt the sex act evokes a set of complex and contradictory emotional responses for both women and men—responses that leave them each feeling at once powerful and vulnerable, albeit in different ways. For a man, there's power in claiming a woman's body—a connection with his maleness that makes him feel alive, masterful, strong. A thirty-three-year-old man, married eight years, said wistfully:

When things are quiet between us sexually, as they are now, it's not just the sex I miss, it's the contact.

"Do you mean the contact with Marianne?" I asked.

Yeah, but it's what it stands for; it's not just her. I mean, it's the contact with her, sure, but it's how it makes me feel. I guess the best word for that is "alive"; it makes me feel alive and [searching for the word] I guess you could say, potent.

At the same time, there's anxiety about the intense, out-of-control feelings that are moving inside him—feelings that leave him vulnerable again to the will and whim of a woman.

I'm not always comfortable with my own sexuality because I can feel very vulnerable when I'm making love. It's a bit crazy, I suppose, because in sex is when I'm experiencing the essence of my manhood and also when I can feel the most frightened about it—like I'm not my own man, or I could lose myself, or something like that.

It deserves a slight detour to comment on the phrase "the essence of my manhood," used by this man to describe his sexual potency and feelings. It makes intuitive sense to us; we know just what he means. Yet it set me to wondering: What is the essence of womanhood?

Some women, I suppose, might say it lies in nurturance, some might speak about mothering, most probably would be puzzled because there would be no single, simple answer that would satisfy. But one thing is sure: For most women, the "essence of womanhood" would not lie in their genitals or in their experience of their sexual powers. That it's such a common experience among men is, perhaps, an effect of their early difficulties in establishing a male identity. Nothing, after all, more clearly separates a boy from his mother than this tangible evidence of his maleness.

This aside now done, let's return to the complex of feelings a man experiences around a sexual connection with a woman. There's comfort in being in a woman's arms—the comfort of surrender to the feelings of safety and security that once were felt so deeply, the warming sense of being nurtured and nourished there once again. And there are enchantment and ecstasy to be found there as well—the thrill of experiencing the "essence of manhood," the delight of recapturing the unity with another that had to be forsworn so long ago. But it's also those same feelings that can be felt as a threat. For they constitute an assault on the boundaries between self and other he erected so long ago. And they threaten his manliness, as this culture defines it, when he experiences once again his own dependent needs and wishes.

Thus delight and fear play catch with each other—both evident in the words men use to describe the feelings and fantasies that sex elicits. They speak sometimes of "falling into a dark cavern," and at other times of "being taken into a warm, safe place." They say they're afraid of "being drawn into an abyss," and also that it feels like "wandering in a soft, warm valley." They talk about feeling as if they're drowning, and say also that it's like "swimming in warmth and sunshine." They worry about "being trapped," and exult about feeling "free enough to fly."

Sometimes the same man will describe his feelings with such contradictory words:

> It depends. Sometimes I can get scared. I don't even know exactly why, but I feel very vulnerable, like I'm too wide open. Then it feels dangerous. Other times, no sweat, it's just all pure pleasure.

Sometimes it's different men who speak such widely disparate thoughts. No matter. All together they tell us much about the intensity of the experience, of the pleasure and the pain that are part of the sexual connection.

For a woman, there's a similar mix of feelings of power, vulnerability, and pleasure. There's a power in her ability to turn this man who usually is so controlled, so in charge, into what one woman called "a great big explosion" and another characterized as "a soft jellyfish." A thirty-four-year-old woman, married eleven years, put it this way:

> There's that moment in sex when I know I'm in control, that he really couldn't stop anymore because his drive is so great, that I feel wonderful. I feel like the most powerful person in that instant. It's hard to explain in words what that feels like—I mean, the knowledge I have at that second of my own sexual power.

And, alongside this sense of her own power, there's vulnerability also. Thus, sighing in bemusement at the intricacies of her own feelings, she continued:

> But it's funny because there's also that instant when he's about to enter me when I get this tiny flash of fear. It comes and goes in a second, but it's almost always there. It's a kind of inner tensing up. There's a second when instead of opening up my body, I want to close it tight. I guess it's like being invaded, and I want to protect myself against it for that instant. Then he's in and it's gone, and I can get lost in the sexual excitement.

The fear that each of them experiences is an archaic one—the remnants of the separation-unity conflict of childhood that's brought to the surface again at the moment of sexual union. The response is patterned and predictable. He fears engulfment; she fears invasion. Their emotional history combines with cultural mandates about femininity and masculinity to prepare them each for their own side; their physiology does the rest. . . .

Rape, Racism, and the Myth of the Black Rapist

Angela Davis

Some of the most flagrant symptoms of social deterioration are acknowledged as serious problems only when they have assumed such epidemic proportions that they appear to defy solution. Rape is a case in point. In the United States today, it is one of the fastest-growing violent crimes.[1] After ages of silence, suffering and misplaced guilt, sexual assault is explosively emerging as one of the telling dysfunctions of present-day capitalist society. The rising public concern about rape in the United States has inspired countless numbers of women to divulge their past encounters with actual or would-be assailants. As a result, an awesome fact has come to light: appallingly few women can claim that they have not been victims, at one time in their lives, of either attempted or accomplished sexual attacks.

In the United States and other capitalist countries, rape laws as a rule were framed originally for the protection of men of the upper classes, whose daughters and wives might be assaulted. What happens to working-class women has usually been of little concern to the courts; as a result, remarkably few white men have been prosecuted for the sexual violence they have inflicted on these women. While the rapists have seldom been brought to justice, the rape charge has been indiscriminately aimed at Black men, the guilty and innocent alike. Thus, of the 455 men executed between 1930 and 1967 on the basis of rape convictions, 405 of them were Black.[2]

In the history of the United States, the fraudulent rape charge stands out as one of the most formidable artifices invented by racism. The myth of the Black rapist has been methodically conjured up whenever recurrent waves of violence and terror against the Black community have required convincing justifications. If Black women have been conspicuously absent from the ranks of the contemporary anti-rape movement, it may be due, in part, to that movement's indifferent posture toward the frame-up rape charge as an incitement to racist aggression. Too many innocents have been offered sacrificially to gas chambers and lifer's cells for Black women to join those who often seek relief from policemen and judges. Moreover, as rape victims themselves, they have found little if any sympathy from these men in uniforms and robes. And stories about police assaults on Black women—rape victims sometimes suffering a second rape—are heard too frequently to be dismissed as aberrations. "Even at the strongest time of the civil rights movement in Birmingham," for example,

Young activists often stated that nothing could protect Black women from being raped by Birmingham police. As recently as December, 1974, in Chicago, a 17-year old Black woman reported that she was gang-raped by 10 policemen. Some of the men were suspended, but ultimately the whole thing was swept under the rug.[3]

During the early stages of the contemporary anti-rape movement, few feminist theorists seriously analyzed the special circumstances surrounding the Black woman as rape victim. The historical knot binding Black women—systematically abused and violated by white men—to Black men—maimed and murdered because of the racist manipulation of the rape charge—has just begun to be acknowledged to any significant extent. Whenever Black women have challenged rape, they usually and simultaneously expose the use of the frame-up rape charge as a deadly racist weapon against their men. As one extremely perceptive writer put it:

> The myth of the black rapist of white women is the twin of the myth of the bad black woman—both designed to apologize for and facilitate the continued exploitation of black men and women. Black women perceived this connection very clearly and were early in the forefront of the fight against lynching.[4]

. . . Racism has always drawn strength from its ability to encourage sexual coercion. While Black women and their sisters of color have been the main targets of these racist-inspired attacks, white women have suffered as well. For once white men were persuaded that they could commit sexual assaults against Black women with impunity, their conduct toward women of their own race could not have remained unmarred. Racism has always served as a provocation to rape, and white women in the United States have necessarily suffered the ricochet fire of these attacks. This is one of the many ways in which racism nourishes sexism, causing white women to be indirectly victimized by the special oppression aimed at their sisters of color.

The experience of the Vietnam War furnished a further example of the extent to which racism could function as a provocation to rape. Because it was drummed into the heads of U.S. soldiers that they were fighting an inferior race, they could be taught that raping Vietnamese women was a necessary military duty. They could even be instructed to "search" the women with their penises.[5] It was the unwritten policy of the U.S. Military Command to systematically encourage rape, since it was an extremely effective weapon of mass terrorism. Where are the thousands upon thousands of Vietnam veterans who witnessed and participated in these horrors? To what extent did those brutal experiences affect their attitudes toward women in general? While it would be quite erroneous to single out Vietnam veterans as the main perpetrators of sexual crimes, there can be little doubt that the horrendous repercussions of the Vietnam experience are still being felt by all women in the United States today.

It is a painful irony that some anti-rape theorists, who ignore the part played by racism in instigating rape, do not hesitate to argue that men of color are especially prone to commit sexual violence against women. . . .

The myth of the Black rapist continues to carry out the insidious work of racist ideology. It must bear a good portion of the responsibility for the failure of most anti-rape theorists to seek the identity of the enormous numbers of anonymous rapists who remain unreported, untried and unconvicted. As long as their analyses focus on accused rapists who are reported and arrested, thus on only a fraction of the rapes actually committed, Black men—and other men of color—will inevitably be viewed as the villains responsible for the current epidemic of sexual violence. The anonymity surrounding the vast majority of rapes is consequently treated as a statistical detail—or else as a mystery whose meaning is inaccessible.

But why are there so many anonymous rapists in the first place? Might not this anonymity be a privilege enjoyed by men whose status protects them from prosecution? Although white men who are employers, executives, politicians, doctors, professors, etc., have been known to "take advantage" of women they consider their social inferiors, their sexual misdeeds seldom come to light in court. Is it not therefore quite probable that these men of the capitalist and middle classes account for a significant proportion of the unreported rapes? Many of these unreported rapes undoubtedly involve Black women as victims: their historical experience proves that racist ideology implies an open invitation to rape. As the basis of the license to rape Black women during slavery was the slaveholders' economic power, so the class structure of capitalist society also harbors an incentive to rape. It seems, in fact, that men of the capitalist class and their middle-class partners are immune to prosecution because they commit their sexual assaults with the same unchallenged authority that legitimizes their daily assaults on the labor and dignity of working people.

The existence of widespread sexual harassment on the job has never been much of a secret. It is precisely on the job, indeed, that women—especially when they are not unionized—are most vulnerable. Having already established their economic domination over their female subordinates, employers, managers and foremen may attempt to assert this authority in sexual terms. That working-class women are more intensely exploited than their men adds to their vulnerability to sexual abuse, while sexual coercion simultaneously reinforces their vulnerability to economic exploitation.

Working-class men, whatever their color, can be motivated to rape by the belief that their maleness accords them the privilege to dominate women. Yet since they do not possess the social or economic authority—unless it is a white man raping a woman of color—guaranteeing them immunity from prosecution, the incentive is not nearly as powerful as it is for the men of the capitalist class. When working-class men accept the invitation to rape extended by the ideology of male supremacy, they are accepting a bribe, an illusory compensation for their powerlessness.

The class structure of capitalism encourages men who wield power in the economic and political realm to become routine agents of sexual exploitation. The present rape epidemic occurs at a time when the capitalist class is furiously reasserting its authority in face of global and internal challenges. Both racism and sexism, central to its domestic strategy of increased economic exploitation, are receiving unprecedented encouragement. It is not a mere coincidence that as the incidence of rape has arisen, the position of women workers has visibly worsened. So severe are women's economic losses that their wages in relationship to men are lower than they were a decade ago. The proliferation of sexual violence is the brutal face of a generalized intensification of the sexism which necessarily accompanies this economic assault.

Following a pattern established by racism, the attack on women mirrors the deteriorating situation of workers of color and the rising influence of racism in the judicial system, the educational institutions and in the government's posture of studied neglect toward Black people and other people of color. The most dramatic sign of the dangerous resurgence of racism is the new visibility of the Ku Klux Klan and the related epidemic of violent assaults on Blacks, Chicanos, Puerto Ricans and Native Americans. The present rape epidemic bears an extraordinary likeness to this violence kindled by racism.

Given the complexity of the social context of rape today, any attempt to treat it as an isolated phenomenon is bound to founder. An effective strategy against rape must aim for more than the eradication of rape—or even of sexism—alone. The struggle against racism must be an ongoing theme of the anti-rape movement, which must not only defend women of color, but the many victims of the racist manipulation of the rape charge as well. The crisis dimensions of sexual violence constitute one of the facets of a deep and ongoing crisis of capitalism. As the violent fact of sexism, the threat of rape will continue to exist as long as the overall oppression of women remains an essential crutch for capitalism. The anti-rape movement and its important current activities—ranging from emotional and legal aid to self-defense and educational campaigns—must be situated in a strategic context which envisages the ultimate defeat of monopoly capitalism.

NOTES

1 Nancy Gager and Cathleen Schurr, *Sexual Assault: Confronting Rape in America* (New York: Grosset & Dunlap, 1976), p. 1.
2 Michael Meltsner, *Cruel and Unusual: The Supreme Court and Capital Punishment* (New York: Random House, 1973), p. 75.
3 "The Racist Use of Rape and the Rape Charge." A Statement to the Women's Movement From a Group of Socialist Women (Louisville, Ky.: Socialist Women's Caucus, 1974), pp. 5–6.
4 Gerda Lerner, editor, *Black Women in White America: A Documentary History,* New York, Pantheon Books, 1972, p. 193.
5 Arlene Eisen-Bergman, *Women in Vietnam,* San Francisco, People's Press, 1975, Part I, Chapter 5.

Letter from a War Zone

Andrea Dworkin

Sisters: I don't know who you are, or how many, but I will tell you what happened to us. We were brave and we were fools; some of us collaborated; I don't know the outcome. It is late 1986 now, and we are losing. The war is men against women; the country is the United States. Here, a woman is beaten every eighteen seconds: by her husband or the man she lives with, not by a psychotic stranger in an alley. Understand:

women are also beaten by strangers in alleys but that is counted in a different category—gender-neutral assault, crime in the streets, big-city violence. Woman-beating, the
intimate kind, is the most commonly committed violent crime in the country, according to the FBI, not feminists. A woman is raped every three minutes, nearly half the
rapes committed by someone the woman knows. Forty-four percent of the adult
women in the United States have been raped at least once. Forty-one percent (in some
studies seventy-one percent) of all rapes are committed by two or more men; so the
question is not how many rapes there are, but how many rapists. There are an estimated 16000 new cases of father-daughter incest each year; and in the current generation
of children, thirty-eight percent of girls are sexually molested. Here, now, less than
eight percent of women have not had some form of unwanted sex (from assault to obscene harassment) forced on them.

We keep calling this war normal life. Everyone's ignorant; no one knows; the men
don't mean it. In this war, the pimps who make pornography are the SS, an élite,
sadistic, military, organized vanguard. They run an efficient and expanding system of
exploitation and abuse in which women and children, as lower life forms, are brutalized. This year they will gross $10 billion.

We have been slow to understand. For fun they gag us and tie us up as if we are
dead meat and hang us from trees and ceilings and door frames and meat hooks; but
many say the lynched women probably like it and we don't have any right to interfere
with them (the women) having a good time. For fun they rape us or have other men, or
sometimes animals, rape us and film the rapes and show the rapes in movie theatres or
publish them in magazines, and the normal men who are not pimps (who don't know,
don't mean it) pay money to watch; and we are told that the pimps and the normal men
are free citizens in a free society exercising rights and that we are prudes because this
is sex and real women don't mind a little force and the women get paid anyway so
what's the big deal? The pimps and the normal men have a constitution that says the
filmed rapes are "protected speech" or "free speech." Well, it doesn't actually *say*
that—cameras, after all, hadn't been invented yet; but they interpret their constitution
to protect their fun. They have laws and judges that call the women hanging from the
trees "free speech." There are films in which women are urinated on, defecated on,
cut, maimed, and scholars and politicians call them "free speech." The politicians, of
course, deplore them. There are photographs in which women's breasts are slammed
in sprung rat traps—in which things (including knives, guns, glass) are stuffed in our
vaginas—in which we are gang-banged, beaten, tortured—and journalists and intellectuals say: Well, there is a lot of violence against women *but* . . . But what, prick? But
we run this country, cunt.

If you are going to hurt a woman in the United States, be sure to take a photograph.
This will confirm that the injury you did to her expressed a point-of-view, sacrosanct
in a free society. Hey, you have a right not to like women in a democracy, man. In the
very unlikely event that the victim can nail you for committing a crime of violence
against her, your photograph is still constitutionally protected, since it communicates
so eloquently. The woman, her brutalization, the pain, the humiliation, her smile—because you did force her to smile, didn't you?—can be sold forever to millions of nor-

mal men (them again) who—so the happy theory goes—are having a "cathartic" experience all over her. It's the same with snuff films, by the way. You can torture and disembowel a woman, ejaculate on her dismembered uterus, and even if they do put you away someday for murder (a rather simple-minded euphemism), the film is legally *speech. Speech.*

In the early days, feminism was primitive. If something hurt women, feminists were against it, not for it. In 1970, radical feminists forcibly occupied the offices of the ostensibly radical Grove Press because Grove published pornography marketed as sexual liberation and exploited its female employees. Grove's publisher, an eminent boy-revolutionary, considered the hostile demonstration CIA-inspired. His pristine radicalism did not stop him from calling the very brutal New York City police and having the women physically dragged out and locked up for trespassing on his private property. Also in 1970, radical feminists seized *Rat,* an underground rag that devoted itself, in the name of revolution, to pornography and male chauvinism equally, the only attention gender got on the radical left. The pornographers, who think strategically and actually do know what they are doing, were quick to react. "These chicks are our natural enemy," wrote Hugh Hefner in a secret memo leaked to feminists by secretaries at *Playboy.* "It is time we do battle with them. . . What I want is a devastating piece that takes the militant feminists apart." What he got were huge, raucous demonstrations at Playboy Clubs in big cities.

Activism against pornography continued, organized locally, ignored by the media but an intrinsic part of the feminist resistance to rape. Groups called Women Against Violence Against Women formed independently in many cities. Pornography was understood by feminists (without any known exception) as woman-hating, violent, rapist. Robin Morgan pinpointed pornography as the theory, rape as the practice. Susan Brownmiller, later a founder of the immensely influential Women Against Pornography, saw pornography as woman-hating propaganda that promoted rape. These insights were not banal to feminists who were beginning to comprehend the gynocidal and terrorist implications of rape for all women. These were *emerging* political insights, not learned-by-rote slogans.

Sometime in 1975, newspapers in Chicago and New York City revealed the existence of snuff films. Police detectives, trying to track down distribution networks, said that prostitutes, probably in Central America, were being tortured, slowly dismembered, then killed, for the camera. Prints of the films were being sold by organized crime to private pornography collectors in the United States.

In February 1976, a day or two before Susan B. Anthony's birthday, a snazzy, first-run movie house in Times Square showed what purported to be a real snuff film. The marquee towered above the vast Times Square area, the word *Snuff* several feet high in neon, next to the title the words "made in South America where life is cheap." In the ads that blanketed the subways, a woman's body was cut in half.

We felt despair, rage, pain, grief. We picketed every night. It rained every night. We marched round and round in small circles. We watched men take women in on dates. We watched the women come out, physically sick, and still go home with the men. We leafletted. We screamed out of control on street corners. There was some vandalism: not enough to close it down. We tried to get the police to close it down. We tried to get the District Attorney to close it down. You have no idea what respect those guys have for free speech.

The pimp who distributed the film would come to watch the picket line and laugh at us. Men who went in laughed at us. Men who walked by laughed at us. Columnists in newspapers laughed at us. The American Civil Liberties Union ridiculed us through various spokesmen (in those days, they used men). The police did more than laugh at us. They formed a barricade with their bodies, guns, and nightsticks—to protect the film from women. One threw me in front of an oncoming car. Three protestors were arrested and *locked up* for using obscene language to the theatre manager. Under the United States Constitution, obscene language is not speech. Understand: it is not that obscene language is unprotected speech; it is not considered speech at all. The protestors, talking, used obscene language that was not speech; the maiming in the snuff film, the knife eviscerating the woman, was speech. All this we had to learn.

We learned a lot, of course. Life may be cheap, but knowledge never is. We learned that the police protect property and that pornography is property. We learned that the civil liberties people didn't give a damn, my dear: a woman's murder, filmed to bring on orgasm, was speech, and they didn't even *mind* (these were the days before they learned that they had to say it was bad to hurt women). The ACLU did not have a crisis of conscience. The District Attorney went so far as to find a woman he claimed was "the actress" in the film to show she was alive. He held a press conference. He said that the only law the film broke was the law against fraud. He virtually challenged us to try to get the pimps on fraud, while making clear that if the film had been real, no United States law would have been broken because the murder would have occurred elsewhere. So we learned that. During the time *Snuff* showed in New York City, the bodies of several women, hacked to pieces, were found in the East River and several prostitutes were decapitated. We also learned that.

When we started protesting *Snuff,* so-called feminist lawyers, many still leftists at heart, were on our side: no woman could sit this one out. We watched the radical boy lawyers pressure, threaten, ridicule, insult, and intimidate them; and they did abandon us. They went home. They never came back. We saw them learn to love free speech above women. Having hardened their radical little hearts to *Snuff,* what could ever make them put women first again?

There were great events. In November 1978, the first feminist conference on pornography was held in San Francisco. It culminated in the country's first Take Back the Night March: well over 3000 women shut down San Francisco's pornography district for one night. In October 1979, over 5000 women and men marched on Times Square. One documentary of the march shows a man who had come to Times Square to buy sex looking at the sea of women extending twenty city blocks and saying, bewildered and dismayed: "I can't find one fucking woman." In 1980, Linda Marchiano published *Ordeal.* World-famous as Linda Lovelace, the porn-queen extraordinaire of *Deep Throat,* Marchiano revealed that she had been forced into prostitution and pornography by brute terrorism. Gang-raped, beaten, kept in sexual slavery by her pimp/husband (who had legal rights over her as her husband), forced to have intercourse with a dog for a film, subjected to a sustained sadism rarely found by Amnesty

International with regard to political prisoners, she dared to survive, escape, and expose the men who had sexually used her (including *Playboy*'s Hugh Hefner and *Screw*'s Al Goldstein). The world of normal men (the consumers) did not believe her; they believed *Deep Throat.* Feminists did believe her. Today Marchiano is a strong feminist fighting pornography.

In 1980, when I read *Ordeal,* I understood from it that every civil right protected by law in this country had been broken on Linda's prostituted body. I began to see gang rape, marital rape and battery, prostitution, and other forms of sexual abuse as civil rights violations which, in pornography, were systematic and intrinsic (the pornography could not exist without them). The pornographers, it was clear, violated the civil rights of women much as the Ku Klux Klan in this country had violated the civil rights of blacks. The pornographers were domestic terrorists determined to enforce, through violence, an inferior status on people born female. The second-class status of women itself was constructed through sexual abuse; and the name of the whole system of female subordination was *pornography*—men's orgasm and sexual pleasure synonymous with women's sexually explicit inequality. Either we were human, equal, citizens, in which case the pornographers could not do to us what they did with impunity and, frankly, constitutional protection; or we were inferior, not protected as equal persons by law, and so the pimps could brutalize us, the normal men could have a good time, the pimps and their lawyers and the normal men could call it free speech, and we could live in hell. Either the pornographers and the pornography did violate the civil rights of women, or women had no rights of equality.

I asked Catharine A. MacKinnon, who had pioneered sexual harassment litigation, if we could mount a civil rights suit in Linda's behalf. Kitty worked with me, Gloria Steinem (an early and brave champion of Linda), and several lawyers for well over a year to construct a civil rights suit. It could not, finally, be brought, because the statute of limitations on every atrocity committed against Linda had expired; and there was no law against showing or profiting from the films she was coerced into making. Kitty and I were despondent; Gloria said our day would come. It did—in Minneapolis on December 30, 1983, when the City Council passed the first human rights legislation ever to recognize pornography as a violation of the civil rights of all women. In Minneapolis, a politically progressive city, pornography had been attacked as a *class* issue for many years. Politicians cynically zoned adult bookstores into poor and black areas of the city. Violence against the already disenfranchised women and children increased massively; and the neighborhoods experienced economic devastation as legitimate businesses moved elsewhere. The civil rights legislation was passed in Minneapolis because poor people, people of color (especially Native Americans and blacks), and feminists demanded justice.

But first, understand this. Since 1970, but especially after *Snuff,* feminist confrontations with pornographers had been head-on: militant, aggressive, dangerous, defiant. We had thousands of demonstrations. Some were inside theatres where, for instance, feminists in the audience would scream like hell when a woman was being hurt on the screen. Feminists were physically dragged from the theatres by police who found the celluloid screams to be *speech* and the feminist screams to be *disturbing the peace.* Banners were unfurled in front of ongoing films. Blood was poured on magazines and sex paraphernalia designed to hurt women. Civil disobedience, sit-ins, destruction of magazines and property, photographing consumers, as well as picketing, leafletting, letter-writing, and debating in public forums, have all been engaged in over all these years without respite. Women have been arrested repeatedly: the police protecting, always, the pornographers. In one jury trial, three women, charged with two felonies and one misdemeanor for pouring blood over pornography, said that they were acting to prevent a greater harm—rape; they also said that the blood was already there, they were just making it visible. They were acquitted when the jury heard testimony about the actual use of pornography in rape and incest *from the victims:* a raped woman; an incestuously abused teenager.

So understand this too: *feminism works;* at least primitive feminism works. We used militant activism to defy and to try to destroy the men who exist to hurt women, that is, the pimps who make pornography. We wanted to destroy—not just put some polite limits on but *destroy*—their power to hurt us; and millions of women, each alone at first, one at a time, began to remember, or understand, or find words for how she herself had been hurt by pornography, what had happened to her because of it. Before feminists took on the pornographers, each woman, as always, had thought that only she had been abused in, with, or because of pornography. Each woman lived in isolation, fear, shame. Terror creates silence. Each woman had lived in unbreachable silence. Each woman had been deeply hurt by the rape, the incest, the battery; but something more had happened too, and there was no name for it and no description of it. Once the role of pornography in *creating* sexual abuse was exposed—rape by rape, beating by beating, victim by victim—our understanding of the nature of sexual abuse itself changed. To talk about rape alone, or battery alone, or incest alone, was not to talk about the totality of how the women had been violated. Rape or wife-beating or prostitution or incest were not discrete or free-standing phenomena. We had thought: some men rape; some men batter; some men fuck little girls. We had accepted an inert model of male sexuality: men have fetishes; the women must always be blond, for instance; the act that brings on orgasm must always be the same. But abuse created by pornography was different: the abuse was multifaceted, complex; the violations of each individual woman were many and interconnected; the sadism was exceptionally dynamic. We found that when pornography created sexual abuse, men learned any new tricks the pornographers had to teach. We learned that anything that hurt or humiliated women could be sex for men who used pornography; and male sexual practice would change dramatically to accommodate violations and degradations promoted by the pornography. We found that sexual abuses in a woman's life were intricately and complexly connected when pornography was a factor: pornography was used to accomplish incest and then the child would be used to make pornography; the pornography-consuming husband would not just beat his wife but would tie her, hang her, torture her, force her into prostitution, and film her for pornography; pornography used in gang rape meant that the gang rape was enacted according to an already existing script, the sadism of the gang rape enhanced by the contributions of the pornographers. The forced filming of forced sex became a new sexual violation of women. In sexual terms, pornography created for women and children concentration camp conditions. This is not hyperbole.

One psychologist told the Minneapolis City Council about three cases involving pornography used as "recipe books": "Presently or recently I have worked with clients who have been sodomized by broom handles, forced to have sex with over 20 dogs in the back seat of their car, tied up and then electrocuted on their genitals. These are children [all] in the ages of 14 to 18. . . . where the perpetrator has read the manuals and manuscripts at night and used these as recipe books by day or had the pornography present at the time of the sexual violence."

A social worker who works exclusively with adolescent female prostitutes testified: "I can say almost categorically never have I had a client who has not been exposed to prostitution through pornography. . . . For some young women that means that they are shown pornography, either films, videotapes, or pictures as this is how you do it, almost as a training manual in how to perform acts of prostitution. . . . In addition, out on the street when a young woman is [working], many of her tricks or customers will come up to her with little pieces of paper, pictures that were torn from a magazine and say, I want this. . . . it is like a mail order catalogue of sex acts, and that is what she is expected to perform. . . . Another aspect that plays a big part in my work . . . is that on many occasions my clients are multi, many rape victims. These rapes are often either taped or have photographs taken of the event. The young woman when she tries to escape [is blackmailed]."

A former prostitute, testifying on behalf of a group of former prostitutes afraid of exposure, confirmed: "[W]e were all introduced to prostitution through pornography, there were no exceptions in our group, and we were all under 18." Everything done to women in pornography was done to these young prostitutes by the normal men. To them the prostitutes were synonymous with the pornography but so were all women, including wives and daughters. The abuses of prostitutes were not qualitatively different from the abuses of other women. Out of a compendium of pain, this is one incident: "[A] woman met a man in a hotel room in the 5th Ward. When she got there she was tied up while sitting on a chair nude. She was gagged and left alone in the dark for what she believed to be an hour. The man returned with two other men. They burned her with cigarettes and attached nipple clips to her breasts. They had many S and M magazines with them and showed her many pictures of women appearing to consent, enjoy, and encourage this abuse. She was held for 12 hours, continuously raped and beaten. She was paid $50 or about $2.33 per hour."

Racist violation is actively promoted in pornography; and the abuse has pornography's distinctive dynamic—an annihilating sadism, the brutality and contempt taken wholesale from the pornography itself. The pornographic video game "Custer's Revenge" generated many gang rapes of Native American women. In the game, men try to capture a "squaw," tie her to a tree, and rape her. In the sexually explicit game, the penis goes in and out, in and out. One victim of the "game" said: "When I was first asked to testify I resisted some because the memories are so painful and so recent. I am here because of my four-year-old daughter and other Indian children. . . . I was attacked by two white men and from the beginning they let me know they hated my people. . . . And they let me know that the rape of a 'squaw' by white men was practically honored by white society. In fact, it had been made into a video game called 'Custer's Last Stand' [sic]. They held me down and as one was running the tip of his knife across my face and throat he said, 'Do you want to play Custer's Last Stand? It's great, you lose but you don't care, do you? You like a little pain, don't you, squaw?' They both laughed and then he said, 'There is a lot of cock in Custer's Last Stand. You should be grateful, squaw, that All-American boys like us want you. Maybe we will tie you to a tree and start a fire around you.' "

The same sadistic intensity and arrogance is evident in this pornography-generated gang rape of a thirteen-year-old girl. Three deer hunters, in the woods, looking at pornography magazines, looked up and saw the blond child. "There's a live one," one said. The three hunters chased the child, gang-raped her, pistol-whipped her breasts, all the while calling her names from the pornography magazines scattered at their campsite—Golden Girl, Little Godiva, and so on. "All three of them had hunting rifles. They, two men held their guns at my head and the first man hit my breast with his rifle and they continued to laugh. And then the first man raped me and when he was finished they started making jokes about how I was a virgin . . . The second man then raped me . . . The third man forced his penis into my mouth and told me to do it and I didn't know how to do it. I did not know what I was supposed to be doing . . . one of the men pulled the trigger on his gun so I tried harder. Then when he had an erection, he raped me. They continued to make jokes about how lucky they were to have found me when they did and they made jokes about being a virgin. They started . . . kicking me and told me that if I wanted more, I could come back the next day . . . I didn't tell anyone that I was raped until I was 20 years old." These men, like the men who gang-raped the Native American woman, had fun; they were playing a game.

I am quoting from some representative but still relatively *simple* cases. Once the role of pornography in the abuse is exposed, we no longer have just rape or gang rape or child abuse or prostitution. We have, instead, sustained and intricate sadism with no inherent or predictable limits on the kinds or degrees of brutality that will be used on women or girls. We have torture; we have killer-hostility.

Pornography-saturated abuse is specific and recognizable because it is Nazism on women's bodies: the hostility and sadism it generates are carnivorous. Interviewing 200 working prostitutes in San Francisco, Mimi H. Silbert and Ayala M. Pines discovered astonishing patterns of hostility related to pornography. No questions were asked about pornography. But so much information was given casually by the women about the role of pornography in assaults on them that Silbert and Pines published the data they had stumbled on. Of the 200 women, 193 had been raped as adults and 178 had been sexually assaulted as children. That is 371 cases of sexual assault on a population of 200 women. Twenty-four percent of those who had been raped mentioned that the rapist made specific references to pornography during the rape: "the assailant referred to pornographic materials he had seen or read and then insisted that the victims not only enjoyed the rape but also the extreme violence." When a victim, in some cases, told the rapist that she was a prostitute and would perform whatever sex act he wanted (to dissuade him from using violence), *in all cases* the rapists responded in these ways: "(1) their language became more abusive, (2) they became significantly more violent, beating and punching the women excessively, often using weapons they had shown the women, (3) they mentioned having seen prostitutes in pornographic films, the majority of them mentioning specific pornographic literature, and (4) after completing the forced vaginal penetration, they continued to assault the women sexually in ways they claimed they had seen prostitutes enjoy in the pornographic literature they cited." Examples include forced anal penetration with a gun, beatings all over the body with a gun, breaking bones, holding a loaded pistol at the woman's vagina "insisting this was the way she had died in the film he had seen."

Studies show that between sixty-five and seventy-five percent of women in pornography were sexually abused as children, often incestuously, many put into pornography as children. One woman, for instance, endured this: "I'm an incest survivor, ex-pornography model and ex-prostitute. My incest story begins before pre-school and ends many years later—this was with my father. I was also molested by an uncle and a minister . . . my father forced me to perform sexual acts with men at a stag party when I was a teenager. I am from a 'nice' middle-class family . . . My father is an $80000 a year corporate executive, lay minister, and alcoholic . . . My father was my pimp in pornography. There were 3 occasions from ages 9–16 when he forced me to be a pornography model . . . in Nebraska, so, yes, it does happen here." This woman is now a feminist fighting pornography. She listens to men mostly debate whether or not there is any social harm connected to pornography. People want experts. We have experts. Society says we have to prove harm. We have proved harm. What we have to prove is that women are human enough for harm to matter. As one liberal so-called feminist said recently: "What's the harm of pornography? A paper cut?" This woman was a Commissioner on the so-called Meese Commission.* She had spent a year of her life looking at the brutalization of women in pornography and hearing the life-stories of pornography-abused women. Women were not very human to her.

In pain and in privacy, women began to face, then to tell, the truth, first to themselves, then to others. Now, women have testified before governmental bodies, in public meetings, on radio, on television, in workshops at conventions of liberal feminists who find all this so messy, so declassé, *so unfortunate.* Especially, the liberal feminists hate it that this mess of pornography—having to do something about these abuses of women—might interfere with their quite comfortable political alliances with all those normal men, the consumers—who also happen to be, well, friends. They don't want the stink of this kind of sexual abuse—the down-and-dirty kind for fun and profit—to rub off on them. Feminism to them means getting success, not fighting oppression.

Here we are: weep for us. Society, with the acquiescence of too many liberal-left feminists, says that pornographers must *not* be stopped because the freedom of everyone depends on the freedom of the pornographers to exercise speech. The woman gagged and hanging remains the speech they exercise. In liberal-left lingo, stopping them is called *censorship.*

The civil rights law—a modest approach, since it is not the barrel of a gun—was passed twice in Minneapolis, vetoed twice there by the mayor. In Indianapolis, a more conservative city (where even liberal feminists are registered Republicans), a narrower

---

*Named by the pornographers and their friends after the very right-wing Edwin Meese, the Commission was actually set up by the moderate former Attorney General, William French Smith.

version was adopted: *narrower* means that only very violent pornography was covered by the law. In Indianapolis, pornography was defined as the graphic, sexually explicit subordination of women in pictures and/or words that also included rape, pain, humiliation, penetration by objects or animals, or dismemberment. Men, children, and transsexuals used in these ways could also use this law. The law made pornographers legally and economically responsible for the harm they did to women. Makers of pornography, exhibitors, sellers, and distributors could be sued for trafficking in pornography. Anyone coerced into pornography could hold the makers, sellers, distributors, or exhibitors liable for profiting from the coercion and could have the coerced product removed from the marketplace. Anyone forced to watch pornography in their home, place of work or education, or in public, could sue whoever forces them and any institution that sanctions the force (for instance, a university or an employer). Anyone physically assaulted or injured because of a specific piece of pornography could sue the pornographer for money damages and get the pornography off the shelves. Under this law, pornography is correctly understood and recognized as a practice of sex discrimination. Pornography's impact on the status of women is to keep all women second-class: targets of aggression and civilly inferior.

The United States courts have declared the Indianapolis civil rights law unconstitutional. A Federal Appeals Court said that pornography did all the harm to women we said it did—causing us both physical injury and civil inferiority—but its success in hurting us only proved its power as speech. Therefore, it is protected speech. Compared with the pimps, women have no rights.

The good news is that the pornographers are in real trouble, and that we made the trouble. *Playboy* and *Penthouse* are both in deep financial trouble. *Playboy* has been losing subscribers, and thus its advertising base, for years; both *Playboy* and *Penthouse* have lost thousands of retail outlets for their wares in the last few years. We have cost them their legitimacy.

The bad news is that we are in trouble. There is much violence against us, pornography-inspired. They make us, our bodies, pornography in their magazines, and tell the normal men to get us good. We are followed, attacked, threatened. Bullets were shot into one feminist antipornography center. Feminists have been harassed out of their homes, forced to move. And the pornographers have found a bunch of girls (as the women call themselves) to work for them: not the chickenshit liberals, but real collaborators who have organized specifically to oppose the civil rights legislation and to protect the pornographers from our political activism—pornography should not be a feminist issue, these so-called feminists say. They say: Pornography is misogynist *but* . . . The *but* in this case is that it derepresses us. The victims of pornography can testify, and have, that when men get derepressed, women get hurt. These women say they are feminists. Some have worked for the defeated Equal Rights Amendment or for abortion rights or for equal pay or for lesbian and gay rights. But these days, they organize to stop us from stopping the pornographers.

Most of the women who say they are feminists but work to protect pornography are lawyers or academics: lawyers like the ones who walked away from *Snuff;* academics who think prostitution is romantic, an unrepressed female sexuality. But whoever they are, whatever they think they are doing, the outstanding fact about them is that they are ignoring the women who have been hurt in order to help the pimps who do the hurting. They are collaborators, not feminists.

The pornographers may well destroy us. The violence against us—in the pornography, in the general media, among men—is escalating rapidly and dangerously. Sometimes our despair is horrible. We haven't given in yet. There is a resistance here, a real one. I can't tell you how brave and brilliant the resisters are. Or how powerless and hurt. Surely it is clear: the most powerless women, the most exploited women, are the women fighting the pornographers. Our more privileged sisters prefer not to take sides. It's a nasty fight, all right. Feminism is dying here because so many women who say they are feminists are collaborators or cowards. Feminism is magnificent and militant here because the most powerless women are putting their lives on the line to confront the most powerful men for the sake of all women. Be proud of us for fighting. Be proud of us for getting so far. Help us if you can. The pornographers will have to stop us. We will not give in. They know that and now so do you.

Love,
Andrea Dworkin

A Letter of the Times, or Should This Sado-masochism Be Saved?

Alice Walker

Dear Lucy,

You ask why I snubbed you at the Women for Elected Officials Ball. I don't blame you for feeling surprised and hurt. After all, we planned the ball together, expecting to raise our usual pisspot full of money for a good cause. Such a fine idea, our ball: Come as the feminist you most admire! But I did not know you most admired Scarlett O'Hara and so I was, for a moment, taken aback.

I don't know; maybe I should see that picture again. Sometimes when I see movies that hurt me as a child, the pain is minor; I can laugh at the things that made me sad. My trouble with Scarlett was always the forced buffoonery of Prissy, whose strained, slavish voice, as Miz Scarlett pushed her so masterfully up the stairs, I could never get out of my head.

But there is another reason I could not speak to you at the ball that had nothing to do with what is happening just now between us: this heavy bruised silence, this anger and distrust. The day of the ball was my last class day at the University, and it was a very heavy and discouraging day.

Do you remember the things I told you about the class? Its subject was God. That is, the inner spirit, the inner voice; the human compulsion when deeply distressed to seek healing counsel within ourselves, and the capacity within ourselves both to create this counsel and to receive it.

(It had always amused me that the God who spoke to Harriet Tubman and Sojourn-er Truth told them exactly what they needed to hear, no less than the God of the Old Testament constantly reassured the ancient Jews.)

Indeed, as I read the narratives of black people who were captured and set to slav-ing away their lives in America, I saw that this inner spirit, this inner capacity for self-comforting, this ability to locate God within that they expressed, demonstrated some-thing marvelous about human beings. Nature has created us with the capacity to know God, to experience God, just as it has created us with the capacity to know speech. The experience of God, or in any case the possibility of experiencing God, *is innate!*

I suppose this has all been thought before; but it came to me as a revelation after reading how the fifth or sixth black woman, finding herself captured, enslaved, sexual-ly abused, starved, whipped, the mother of children she could not want, lover of chil-dren she could not have, crept into the corners of the fields, among the haystacks and the animals, and found within her own heart the only solace and love she was ever to know.

It was as if these women found a twin self who saved them from their abused con-sciousness and chronic physical loneliness; and that twin self is in all of us, waiting only to be summoned.

To prepare my class to comprehend God in this way, I requested they read narra-tives of these captured black women and also write narratives themselves, as if they *were* those women, or women like them. At the same time, I asked them to write out their own understanding of what the inner voice, "God," is.

It was an extraordinary class, Lucy! With women of all colors, all ages, all shapes and sizes and all conditions. There were lesbians, straights, curveds, celibates, prosti-tutes, mothers, confuseds, and sundry brilliants of all persuasions! A wonderful class! And almost all of them, though hesitant to admit it at first—who dares talk seriously of "religious" matters these days?—immediately sensed what I meant when I spoke of the inner, companion spirit, of "God."

But what does my class on God have to do with why I snubbed you at the ball? I can hear you wondering. And I will get on to the point.

Lucy, I wanted to teach my students what it felt like to be captured and enslaved. I wanted them to be unable, when they left my class, to think of enslaved women as ex-otic, picturesque, removed from themselves, deserving of enslavement. I wanted them to be able to repudiate all the racist stereotypes about black women who were en-slaved: that they were content, that they somehow "chose" their servitude, that they did not resist.

And so we struggled through an entire semester, during each week of which a stu-dent was required to imagine herself a "slave," a mistress or a master, and to come to terms, in imagination and feeling, with what that meant.

Some black women found it extremely difficult to write as captured and enslaved women. (I do not use the word "slaves" casually, because I see enslavement from the enslaved's point of view: there is a world of difference between being a slave and being enslaved.) They chose to write as mistress or master. Some white women found it nearly impossible to write as mistress or master, and presumptuous to write as enslaved. Still, there were many fine papers written, Lucy, though there was also much hair tugging and gnashing of teeth.

Black and white and mixed women wrote of captivity, of rape, of forced breeding to restock the master's slave pens. They wrote of attempts to escape, of the sale of their children, of dreams of Africa, of efforts at suicide. No one wrote of acquiescence or of happiness, though one or two, mindful of the religious spirit often infusing the narratives studied, described spiritual ecstasy and joy.

Does anyone want to be a slave? we pondered.

As a class, we thought not.

Imagine our surprise, therefore, when many of us watched a television special on sado-masochism that aired the night before our class ended, and the only interracial couple in it, lesbians, presented themselves as mistress and slave. The white woman, who did all the talking, was mistress (wearing a ring in the shape of a key that she said fit the lock on the chain around the black woman's neck), and the black woman, who stood smiling and silent, was—the white woman said—her slave.

And this is why, though we have been friends for over a decade, Lucy, I snubbed you at the ball.

All I had been teaching was subverted by that one image, and I was incensed to think of the hard struggle of my students to rid themselves of stereotype, to combat prejudice, to put themselves into enslaved women's skins, and then to see their struggle mocked, and the actual enslaved *condition* of literally millions of our mothers trivialized—because two ignorant women insisted on their right to act out publicly a "fantasy" that still strikes terror in black women's hearts. And embarrassment and disgust, at least in the hearts of most of the white women in my class.

One white woman student, apparently with close ties to our local lesbian S&M group, said she could see nothing wrong with what we'd seen on TV. (Incidentally, there were several white men on this program who owned white women as "slaves," and even claimed to hold legal documents to this effect. Indeed, one man paraded his slave around town with a horse's bit between her teeth, and "lent" her out to other sado-masochists to be whipped.) It is all fantasy, she said. No harm done. Slavery, real slavery, is over, after all.

But it isn't over, Lucy, and Kathleen Barry's book on female sexual slavery and Linda Lovelace's book on *being* such a slave are not the only recent indications that this is true. There are places in this world, Lucy, where human beings are still being bought and sold! And so, for that reason, when I saw you at the ball, all I could think was that you were insultingly dressed. No, that is not all I thought: once seeing you dressed as Scarlett, I could not see you. I did not *dare* see you. When you accuse me of looking through you, you are correct. For if I had seen you, Lucy, I'm sure I would have struck you, and with your love of fighting this would surely have meant the end of our ball. And so it was better *not* to see you, to look instead at the woman next to you who had kinked her hair to look like Colette.

A black student said to the S&M sympathizer: I feel abused. I feel my privacy as a black woman has been invaded. Whoever saw that television program can now look at me standing on the corner waiting for a bus and not see *me* at all, but see instead a slave, a creature who *would* wear a chain and lock around my neck for a white person—in 1980!—and accept it. *Enjoy* it.

Her voice shook with anger and hurt.

And so, Lucy, you and I will be friends again because I will talk you out of caring about heroines whose real source of power, as well as the literal shape and condition of their bodies, comes from the people they oppress. But what of the future? What of the women who will never come together because of what they saw in the relationship between "mistress" and "slave" on TV? Many black women fear it is as slaves white women want them; no doubt many white women think some amount of servitude from black women is their due.

But, Lucy, regardless of the "slave" on television, black women do not want to be slaves. They never wanted to be slaves. We will be ourselves and free, or die in the attempt. Harriet Tubman was not our great-grandmother for nothing; which I would advise all black and white women aggressing against us as "mistress" and "slave" to remember. We understand when an attempt is being made to lead us into captivity, though television is a lot more subtle than slave ships. We will simply resist, as we have always done, with ever more accurate weapons of defense.

As a matter of fact, Lucy, it occurs to me that we might plan another ball in the spring as a benefit for this new resistance. What do you think? Do let us get together to discuss it, during the week.

Your friend,
Susan Marie

Second Thoughts

Myrna Kostash

Once upon a time I thought I had pornography all figured out. Its meaning and signification. Its purpose. How it could be combatted. The alternatives to it. On rereading my first analyses and critiques of the phenomenon, I am struck by the self-confidence of my theoretical assertions, my conviction that I had confined this many-headed beast neatly within the frame of my feminist understanding. Specifically, I wrote confidently of the difference between erotica and pornography and of the possibility that we could produce the erotic in our subterranean feminist cells. I entered assuredly into the debate around sexuality that the antiporn campaign enjoined; that porn is about this and that aspect of hetero-sex. I spoke of the perfect victimization, the categorical objectification of women in the pornographic image, that we are imaged *out there* outside our consciousness, our subjectivity. And I called, unproblematically, for the banning of that image.

Nowadays I am not so sure. As the antipornography debate and campaign have matured, broadened, become more complex, *I* have become more confused. Now, I cannot present anything definitive or conclusive or *correct;* I can only offer my tentativeness, my doubts, my second thoughts, so as to, I hope, encourage other women to express all the contradictoriness of our collective thinking and feeling about pornography, as painful as it is to acknowledge. Of course, in doing so we make ourselves vulnerable to those with more doctrinaire views who would see us as irresolute, but that is the price we pay for intellectual and political growth. And we owe it to the women's movement to do so publicly and not yield the terrain of debate to polarized argument.

"In the best of possible worlds, how would we represent sex? With tenderness, affection, respect, with humour, playfulness. We would take delight in the sensuous detail, we would caress, we would be open, psychically, to the 'lunar,' to that part of our nervous system which is intuitional, which apprehends patterns, which is artistic. The 'erotica' which corresponds to this ideal would represent freely chosen sexual behavior in which the partners would serve each other's (and Eros'!) pleasure equally and in which the 'I love you' is made flesh." I wrote that in 1981. You can see that I attempted a definition of the erotic in what I hope are feminist terms, but the trouble with this is that it is, of course, a utopian vision: necessarily vague, evasive, dreamy, because we are not much used to contemplating a condition of sexual happiness. What we are used to is sexual terror and guilt and disappointment. What we are used to is our silence on the subject.

When we attempt such definitions, therefore, we are talking about what is *possible,* not what is already realized. And if our sexual happiness is *not* a realized thing—socially, culturally, psychologically—in the real world, then who are we trying to fool when we say we can draw the line, *in the real world,* between the erotic and the pornographic? The erotic, in feminist terms, does not exist. The erotic will be the project of a postpatriarchal, postcapitalist culture of lovers. What does exist at this point is the difference between the more and the less pornographic: at one end, "snuff" films, at the other, *Cosmopolitan* magazine covers, and, somewhere between, crotch shots from *Penthouse.* By trying to draw lines among these phenomena—by saying that scenes of sexual torture are what we're worried about, not soft-focus "pussy," or that the explicitly sexual, not the soft-core suggestive, is problematic—we are being naive.

I know that we have attempted to draw these lines because we do not want to march under the same banner with the antismut brigades, nor do we want to seem like poor sports, and we especially don't want to be drawn into a position where to be antipornography is just a smokescreen for disgust with female sexuality. And we have focused on violence as the quintessential component of porn and have said of an image that is "just" a crotch shot, "Well, *that's* not pornographic." *That,* I suppose, is erotic?

What has in part happened here, I think, is what American feminist sociologist Kathleen Barry calls the "erosion of sensibility and sensitivity": to attack *Playboy* is now seen, even by feminists, as somehow excessive, somehow not the point. (As the pornography subcommittee of the Metropolitan Toronto Task Force on Violence against Women discovered, 89.6 percent of the pornography available in 1983 was unavailable or sold under the counter in 1970. In 13 years much of what we used to call pornography became normal.) Compared to images of torture, I suppose crotch shots *are* relatively harmless—and I have heard decent men argue that they are beautiful because "pussy is beautiful"—but somewhere along the line we have lost our original insight into the misogynist nature of *all* exploitative images of women and have diluted our critique of the objectification inherent in almost any representation of our sexuality in the culture of a male-dominated society. We have lost or forgotten what we originally knew to be true: that, for our purposes as feminists, the iconography of heterosexuality is, by definition, a representation of dominance/submission, activity/passivity, power/powerlessness. Is, by definition, pornographic. To try to separate the "pornographic" from the everyday is an exercise requiring some imagination.

Here, for instance, is a definition of pornography used by Vancouver sociologist Jillian Ridington in a discussion paper she presented to the Association of Women and the Law in 1983: "Pornography is a presentation, whether live, simulated, verbal, pictorial, filmed or videotaped, or otherwise represented, of sexual behaviour in which one or more participants are coerced, overtly or *implicitly,* into participation; or are injured or abused physically or *psychologically;* or in which an *imbalance of power* is obvious, or *implied* by virtue of the immature age of any participant or by contextual aspects of the presentation, and in which such behaviour can be taken to be advocated or endorsed" [emphasis added]. Now this is one of the stricter definitions I have come across, but I have to ask: By this definition, *what* in popular culture, in elite culture, in advertising, in best sellers, in movies, in all those places where heterosexual coupling is portrayed or implied, where the turn-on is psychological, where an imbalance of power is of the essence in the message, what is *not* pornographic?

I can't believe I just wrote that. Do I mean it? If, by the logic of definitions and, let's face it, by the logic of our own feelings as we make our way through the streets, our culture is profoundly and pervasively pornographic, then what does it mean to say, "We are going to examine pornography," as though we could pick it up where the erotic—whatever that is—leaves off?

It seems to me that we've laid another sort of trap for ourselves as well in this attempt to distinguish erotica and pornography: we continue to talk about all this as though it were only about sex; as though the one is to be distinguished from the other by the way it depicts sex. What we need, we say to one another, is another way of making love, other sorts of turn-ons, new routes of sensuality, and so on. Are we not at the same point of our understanding here as we were of rape just before we made the analytical breakthrough that rape is not about sick male sexuality but about *power*? We argue that pornography can somehow be cleaned up, its worst aspects deleted so as not to offend feminist sensibilities. We talk about deprogramming the male sexual imagination by offering masturbatory fantasies from the women's movement, as though pornography were only about sexual immaturity. Even if we can create small spaces of sexual alternatives, we would still be left with the source of our malaise (of which pornography is only a symptom): social and cultural powerlessness.

We are also evading our own complicity in the reproduction of the pornographic. And this brings me to the second of my confusions: fantasy. Kathleen Barry has said of pornography that in its imagery woman is the "naturally masochistic sexual object" who exists only for men's sexual use and satisfaction. That it is organized entirely around erection and ejaculation. That women are simply consumed. But here's a curious thing: I have noticed that in this imagery, by and large, in spite of the ropes and chains, the leather accoutrements, the gloved fists, the boots, and so on, we do not look as if we have been beaten up. Where are the bruises, the wounds and welts of *real* violence? It may be, as Kathleen Barry suggests, that this is due to the "reality distortion" of porn, the make-believe that sadism is the other half of the duality that women complete with masochism; the make-believe that "it doesn't really hurt." Or that the pain has been transformed, in the very moment of its experience, into pleasure. And that that moment, by yet another reality distortion, is therefore something we participate in of our free will because it feels good after all. I would go further. What this paradigm also seems to say is that our consent is necessary in order for the image to have its orgasmic effect, in much the same way that a rapist requires his victim to say she "likes it" or "loves him."

What is going on here? Why must we be seen to like and want such treatment? Here are a couple of ideas. Suppose that somewhere deeply hidden is the primal male desire to make a connection with the female, to unite, to mate. You do not devour your mate; you lie down with her, and she with you. Is it possible that even in pornography, in spite of its distortion and its viciousness, in spite of the systematic organization of male desire in paradigms of power, men want to be close to women? Of course, given their social and economic superiority in the real world, men find it difficult, if not impossible, to desire this intimacy and connection without simultaneously needing to reconfirm their power in fantasies of sexual dominance. Given their fear of bewilderment at autonomous female sexuality, men likewise find it difficult to seek knowledge of their mate without first rendering her manageable through fantasies of her quiescent availability. But the possibility remains: the pornographic image contains a projection of the male need for sexual partnership.

Suppose also that the pornographic image includes our consent and our pleasure because, at the level of fantasy, we *do* consent, we *do* take our pleasure? There is evidence from consciousness-raising-group discussions, at least, that the orgasms of a lot of women are orchestrated around fantasies of submission to the penis (or penises, in the case of more elaborate fantasies). We've all been made to feel guilty about this and various feminist therapies have offered to purge us of such atavism, but the fact is that, even outside masturbatory fantasies, there is a lot of very sexual, not to say pornographic, suggestion aimed at us and that it works: we become aroused. A lingerie ad playing on the fantasy of the older woman and her boyish lover (she is cool as a cucumber in black silk; he, dishevelled, is offering her her morning coffee). The famous scene of sexual consummation between the heroine and the priest in the novel *The Thornbirds*. Richard Gere in any of his movies where he takes off his shirt. Television cable porn programs—60 percent of whose urban viewers are women, according to one source. I'm not arguing that our arousal extenuates such calculated imagery. But I do want to suggest that it is far too simple to see pornography just as something "done" to us. We women have our own pornographic imagination and I wonder if these fantasies aren't necessary in some way. In them we can be really sexy without suffering the social consequences; we can experiment with all the different ways of "getting off"; we can *enjoy* ourselves, where in real life our guilt about our own sexuality is so easily turned into hostility to men's desire. Of course, just as with men's fantasies, the materials of such arousal are very limited and crude, but until there is a revolution in the institutions that regulate sexual relations—the family, the school, the workplace—perhaps the pornographic fantasy is one of the few ways that women and men, captives together of those institutions, victims alike of their alienating procedures, are permitted connection.

Finally I come to my confusion around censorship. There was a time I felt clear about this: pornography is dangerous to women and should be banned, like a toxic substance polluting our environment. That was my feminist position. However, I am also a writer. And as a result of debates within the Writers' Union of Canada concerning freedom of expression and the freedom to read, I found myself arguing from another position altogether. To paraphrase Albert Camus, freedom to publish and read does not necessarily assure a society of justice and peace, but without these freedoms it has no assurance at all. Since these two positions are irreconcilable (and calling pornography a "commodity" is no help at all: an image, a word, is not a can of soup), I have flipped and flopped.

While I am deeply sympathetic to the impulse to, say, burn pornography in a big bonfire downtown, trash the video shops, string up the publishers and distributors, put my boyfriend in a political reeducation camp whenever he buys *Penthouse* (and send my own fantasies there too), I can't act on it.

Some feminists argue that the issue is to, as the feminist newspaper *Broadside* has expressed it, "regain control of the State's power by redefining and refining the definition of obscenity so that it meets our standards and needs." But like other contributors to this book, I argue that the state is hardly a neutral, let alone prowoman, institution that can be captured and directed toward our projects; it is specific to the development of capitalist patriarchy; its capture and transformation require a revolution. In any case, obscenity is not the issue. The Criminal Code, in reference to obscenity, talks about the "undue exploitation of sex," as though there were some we could put up with. Is explicit sex obscene? Are suntan lotion ads okay? It seems that, in practice, it is only the police who are sure of the difference between the tolerable and intolerable. And that censor boards tend to find noncommercial explicit sex unacceptable and the commercial variety quite tolerable. And that the courts find prosecution of obscenity costly and difficult. And that, in the case of Victoria-based Red Hot Video, three tapes were found to be obscene and the shop fined $100 for each one. At the time of writing, the decision was still under appeal. That's liberal democracy for you. The authorities aren't just being coy. They really aren't sure what is hateful and what isn't, what is offensive to women and why. A perfect example of this, and for me a very persuasive argument against giving the authorities any jurisdiction in this matter, is what happened to the May, 1983, issue of *Penthouse*.

It gained attention when, because of a feature entitled "Wonders of the Eastern World"—reproductions of sexual art from India, China and Japan—it was seized by customs officers in Ontario and sent back to the U.S. The offending (obscene?) parts were the great number of erect and penetrating penises, but, when these were blacked out with big dots, the magazine was allowed to be sold in Canada. The customs officers, needless to say, did not find offensive or obscene the usual pages of "split beaver" shots. Nor were they offended—and this is the crux of the story—by a cartoon near the front of the magazine. It shows a man and woman on a bed, making love doggie-style. The man is holding a pistol to the back of the woman's head and the caption reads: "Oh, you don't have to worry about getting pregnant. I've taken all of the precautions." To me this is the ultimate pornographic fantasy: the masculine wish for our death. And yet no state authority found it obscene. So much for strategic alliances with the state. So much for hoping that in the application of censorship the state will be sensitive to the distinctions between erotica and porn, between porn and explicit sexuality, between desire and hate.

By way of conclusion let me try this out on you. I have argued that pornography is not about sex. What is it about? Given the fact that sexual repression in the family together with prostitution and pornography (which originally meant "writing about prostitutes" and what can be done to them and, these days, also to wives, daughters, lovers) are one highly interdependent system, at the heart of which is the "exchange of women"; and given the fact that this exchange of women (in which a man gives another man a woman as a gift in order to establish kinship between them) means that women are for men to dispose of and we are in no position to give ourselves away (which describes our situation in pornography as well); and given that the exchange of women is otherwise known as marriage, may I suggest that pornography is about marriage? Smash monogamy! Remember that one? Maybe we were onto something. . . .

Compulsory Heterosexuality and Lesbian Existence

Adrienne Rich

. . . Whatever its origins, when we look hard and clearly at the extent and elaboration of measures designed to keep women within a male sexual purlieu, it becomes an inescapable question whether the issue we have to address as feminists is, not simple "gender inequality," nor the domination of culture by males, nor mere "taboos against homosexuality," but the enforcement of heterosexuality for women as a means of assuring male right of physical, economical, and emotional access.[1] One of many means of enforcement is, of course, the rendering invisible of the lesbian possibility, an engulfed continent which rises fragmentedly to view from time to time only to become submerged again. Feminist research and theory that contributes to lesbian invisibility or marginality is actually working against the liberation and empowerment of woman as a group.[2]

The assumption that "most women are innately heterosexual" stands as a theoretical and political stumbling block for many women. It remains a tenable assumption, partly because lesbian existence has been written out of history or catalogued under disease; partly because it has been treated as exceptional rather than intrinsic; partly because to acknowledge that for women heterosexuality may not be a "preference" at all but something that has had to be imposed, managed, organized, propagandized, and maintained by force, is an immense step to take if you consider yourself freely and "innately" heterosexual. Yet the failure to examine heterosexuality as an institution is like failing to admit that the economic system called capitalism or the caste system of racism is maintained by a variety of forces, including both physical violence and false consciousness. To take the step of questioning heterosexuality as a "preference" or "choice" for women—and to do the intellectual and emotional work that follows—will call for a special quality of courage in heterosexually identified feminists but I think the rewards will be great: a freeing-up of thinking, the exploring of new paths, the shattering of another great silence, new clarity in personal relationships. . . .

I have chosen to use the terms *lesbian existence* and *lesbian continuum* because the word *lesbianism* has a clinical and limiting ring. *Lesbian existence* suggests both the fact of the historical presence of lesbians and our continuing creation of the meaning of that existence. I mean the term *lesbian continuum* to include a range—through each woman's life and throughout history—of woman-identified experience; not simply the fact that a woman has had or consciously desired genital sexual experience with another woman. If we expand it to embrace many more forms of primary intensity between and among women, including the sharing of a rich inner life, the bonding against male tyranny, the giving and receiving of practical and political support; if we can also hear in it such associations as *marriage resistance* and the "haggard" behavior identified by Mary Daly (obsolete meanings: "intractable," "willful," "wanton," and "unchaste". . . "a woman reluctant to yield to wooing")[3]—we begin to grasp breadths of female history and psychology which have lain out of reach as a consequence of limited, mostly clinical, definitions of "lesbianism."

Lesbian existence comprises both the breaking of a taboo and the rejection of a compulsory way of life. It is also a direct or indirect attack on male right of access to women. But it is more than these, although we may first begin to perceive it as a form of nay-saying to patriarchy, an act of resistance. It has of course included role playing, self-hatred, breakdown, alcoholism, suicide, and intrawoman violence; we romanticize at our peril what it means to love and act against the grain, and under heavy penalties; and lesbian existence has been lived (unlike, say, Jewish or Catholic existence) without access to any knowledge of a tradition, a continuity, a social underpinning. The destruction of records and memorabilia and letters documenting the realities of lesbian existence must be taken very seriously as a means of keeping heterosexuality compulsory for women, since what has been kept from our knowledge is joy, sensuality, courage, and community, as well as guilt, self-betrayal, and pain.[4]

Lesbians have historically been deprived of a political existence through "inclusion" as female versions of male homosexuality. To equate lesbian existence with male homosexuality because each is stigmatized is to deny and erase female reality once again. To separate those women stigmatized as "homosexual" or "gay" from the complex continuum of female resistance to enslavement, and attach them to a male pattern, is to falsify our history. Part of the history of lesbian existence is, obviously, to be found where lesbians, lacking a coherent female community, have shared a kind of social life and common cause with homosexual men. But this has to be seen against the differences: women's lack of economic and cultural privilege relative to men; qualitative differences in female and male relationships, for example, the prevalence of anonymous sex and the justification of pederasty among male homosexuals, the pronounced ageism in male homosexual standards of sexual attractiveness, etc. In defining and describing lesbian existence I would hope to move toward a dissociation of lesbian from male homosexual values and allegiances. I perceive the lesbian experience as being, like motherhood, a profoundly *female* experience, with particular oppressions, meanings, and potentialities we cannot comprehend as long as we simply bracket it with other sexually stigmatized existences. Just as the term "parenting" serves to conceal the particular and significant reality of being a parent who is actually a mother, the term "gay" serves the purpose of blurring the very outlines we need to discern, which are of crucial value for feminism and for the freedom of women as a group.

—As the term "lesbian" has been held to limiting, clinical associations in its patriarchal definition, female friendship and comradeship have been set apart from the erotic, thus limiting the erotic itself. But as we deepen and broaden the range of what we define as lesbian existence, as we delineate a lesbian continuum, we begin to discover the erotic in female terms: as that which is unconfined to any single part of the body or solely to the body itself, as an energy not only diffuse but, as Audre Lorde has described it, omnipresent in "the sharing of joy, whether physical, emotional, psychic," and in the sharing of work; as the empowering joy which "makes us less willing to accept powerlessness, or those other supplied states of being which are not native to me, such as resignation, despair, self-effacement, depression, self-denial." . . .

NOTES

1 For my perception of heterosexuality as an economic institution I am indebted to Lisa Leghorn and Katherine Parker, who allowed me to read their unpublished manuscript, "Redefining Economics" (1980). See their article: "Towards a Feminist Economics: A Global View," *Second Wave* 5, no. 3 (1979): 23–30.

2 I would suggest that lesbian existence has been most recognized and tolerated where it has resembled a "deviant" version of heterosexuality; e.g., where lesbians have, like Stein and Toklas, played heterosexual roles (or seemed to in public) and have been chiefly identified with male culture. See also Claude E. Schaeffer, "The Kuterai Female Berdache: Courier, Guide, Prophetess and Warrior," *Ethnohistory* 12, no. 3 (Summer 1965): 193–236. (Berdache: "an individual of a definite physiological sex [m. or f.] who assumes the role and status of the opposite sex and who is viewed by the community as being of one sex physiologically but as having assumed the role and status of the opposite sex" [Schaeffer, p. 231].) Lesbian existence has also been relegated to an upper-class phenomenon, an elite decadence (as in the fascination with Paris salon lesbians such as Renée Vivien and Natalie Clifford Barney), to the obscuring of such "common women" as Judy Grahn depicts in her *The Work of a Common Woman* (Oakland, Calif.: Diana Press, 1978) and *True to Life Stories* (Oakland, Calif.: Diana Press, 1978).

3 Mary Daly, *Gyn/Ecology,* Boston: Beacon Press, 1978.

4 "In a hostile world in which women are not supposed to survive except in relation with and in service to men, entire communities of women were simply erased. History tends to bury what it seeks to reject" (Blanche W. Cook, "'Women Alone Stir My Imagination': Lesbianism and the Cultural Tradition," *Signs: Journal of Women in Culture and Society* 4, no. 4 [Summer 1979]: 719–20). The Lesbian Herstory Archives in New York City is one attempt to preserve contemporary documents on lesbian existence—a project of enormous value and meaning, still pitted against the continuing censorship and obliteration of relationships, networks, communities, in other archives and elsewhere in culture.

Virgin Women

Marilyn Frye

. . . Every term in my feminism classes, a time comes when heterosexual women students articulate the question: Do you have to be a lesbian to be a feminist? I don't know how much other teachers of Women's Studies hear this question. My classroom is a situation which brings the connection between feminism and lesbianism to one's attention. I am a lesbian, I am "out" to my Women's Studies students, and I expose them to a great deal of wonderful and strong feminist thinking by feminists of many cultures and locales who are lesbians. In the classroom, this question signals our arrival at a point where newcomers to feminism are beginning to grasp that sexual acts, sexual desire, and sexual dread and taboo are profoundly political and that feminist politics is as much about the disposition of bodies, the manipulation of desire and arousal, and the bonds of intimacy and loyalty as it is about gender stereotypes, economic opportunity and legal rights. . . . But what goes on in my class is clearly not the only thing that gives rise to this question.

One thing that leads students to ask this question is that they very commonly run into people who apparently believe that if you are a feminist you must be a lesbian.

I usually ask women in my Women's Studies classes if they have been called lesbians or dykes or been accused of being lesbian, and almost always a majority of them say they have. One woman was called a lesbian when she rejected the attentions of a man in a bar; another was called "butch" when she opened and held a door for a male friend; another was asked if she was a lesbian when she challenged a man's sexist description of another woman. A woman told a man that she did not want to have sex with him and he called her a lesbian. A young woman told her mother that she was going to Washington for the big pro-choice march; her mother, disapproving and fearing for her daughter's safety, said "Oh, so now you're going to go off and become a lesbian." A woman who divorced her husband and lives on her own is gossiped about in a way that spreads the suggestion that she is a lesbian. A woman says she is frequently assumed to be a lesbian because of her athletic build and refusal to wear skirts. A woman who does not experience sexual arousal or orgasm with her husband is quizzed about her lesbian tendencies by her doctor and her therapist. A woman reports that her friends refer to her Women's Studies class as her "lesbian class"; several other women say some of their friends do that too.

The message of these exchanges is clearly that a woman who is feminist or does anything or betrays any attitude or desire which expresses her autonomy or deviance from conventional femininity is a lesbian. . . .

I want to suggest that this notion of a connection between feminism and lesbianism is *not* merely an *ad hoc* fiction invented by patriarchal loyalists to vilify feminism and intimidate feminists. . . . An intrinsic connection between feminism and lesbianism in a contemporary Euroamerican setting is just a historically specific manifestation of an ancient and intrinsic connection between patriarchal/fraternal social order and female heterosexuality. For females to be subordinated and subjugated to males on a global scale, and for males to organize themselves and each other as they do, billions of female individuals, virtually all who see life on this planet, must be reduced to a more-or-less willing toleration of subordination and servitude to men. The primary sites of this reduction are the sites of heterosexual relation and encounter—courtship and mar-riage-arrangement, romance, sexual liaisons, fucking, marriage, prostitution, the nor-mative family, incest and child sexual assault. . . . The secondary sites of the forced fe-male embodiment of subordination are the sites of the ritual preparations of girls and women for heterosexual intercourse, relations or attachments. I refer to training in proper deportment and attire and decoration, all of which is training in and habituation to bodily restriction and distortion; I refer to diets and exercise and beauty regimens which habituate the individual to deprivation and punishment and to fear and suspi-cion of her body and its wisdom; I refer to the abduction and seasoning of female sex-ual slaves; to clitoridectomy and other forms and sorts of physical and spiritual mutila-tion; all of which have no cultural or economic purpose or function if girls and women do not have to be ready for husbands and male lovers, pimps, johns, bosses and slavers. . . .

Lesbian feminists have noted that if the institution of female heterosexuality is what makes girls into women and is central to the continuous replication of patriarchy, then women's abandonment of that institution recommends itself as one strategy (perhaps among others) in the project of dismantling patriarchal structures. And if heterosexual encounters, relations and connections are the sites of the inscription of the patriarchal imperatives on the bodies of women, it makes sense to abandon those sites. And if fe-male heterosexuality is central to the way sexism and racism are knit together in strange paradoxical symbiosis, it makes sense that non-participation in that institution could be part of a strategy for weakening both racism and patriarchy.

Women speaking in other-than-lesbian feminist voices have responded by saying that withdrawal from participation in the institution of female heterosexuality is only a personal solution and only available to a few; it is not a political, not a systemic strate-gy. I think, on the contrary, that it can be a systemic strategy, because female hetero-sexuality is constructed. If women take the construction of ourselves and the institu-tions and practices which determine and govern us into our own hands, we can construct something else. . . .

Commitment to the naturalness or inevitability of female heterosexuality is com-mitment to the power relations which are expressed and maintained by the institutions of female heterosexuality in patriarchal cultures around the world. . . .

Female heterosexuality is not a biological drive or an individual woman's erotic at-traction or attachment to another human animal which happens to be male. Female heterosexuality is a concrete historical reality—a set of social institutions and practices defined and regulated by patriarchal kinship systems, by both civil and religious law, and by strenuously enforced mores and deeply entrenched values and taboos. Those definitions, regulations, values and taboos are about male fraternity and the oppression and exploitation of women. They are not about human warmth, fun, pleasure, deep knowledge between people. If any of the latter arise within the boundaries of these in-stitutions and practices, it is because warmth, fun, pleasure and acknowledgement are among the things humans are naturally capable of, not because heterosexuality is natu-ral or is naturally a site of such benefits.

So, is it possible to be a feminist without being a lesbian? My inclination is to say that feminism, which is thoroughly anti-patriarchal, is not compatible with female heterosexuality, which is thoroughly patriarchal. But I anticipate the following reply:

"To suppose that all relation, connection, or encounter of any passionate or erotic or genital sort or involving any sort of personal commitment between a woman and a man must belong to this patriarchal institution called 'female heterosexuality,' that it must be suffocated by this rubric, . . . to suppose that is to suppose we are all totally formed by history, social institutions and language. That is a kind of hopeless determinism which is politically fatal and is contradicted by your own presence here as a lesbian."

I agree that I cannot embrace any absolute historical, social determinism. The feminist lesbians' permanent project of defining ourselves and our passions and our communities is a living willful refusal of such determinism. But the free space of creation exists only when it is actively, aggressively, courageously, persistently occupied. Patriarchal histories and cultures mitigate against such space constantly, by coercion, by bribery, by punishment, and by shaping the imagination. What I am saying is that if you would have committed or occasional female/male connections—erotic, reproductive, home-making, partnership, friendship—which are not defined by your culture's patriarchal institutions of female heterosexuality, then you have to create the possibility of that. I am saying that as I see it that possibility *does not exist in patriarchal history and culture.* If it did, it would not be patriarchal.

Following up on a tip from Sarah Hoagland many years ago, I argued in my essay "To Be and Be Seen" that there are no lesbians in the universes of patriarchy. A similar and more generic point is useful here.

The word "virgin" did not originally mean a woman whose vagina was untouched by any penis, but a free woman, one not betrothed, not married, not bound to, not possessed by any man. It meant a female who is sexually and hence socially her own person. In any universe of patriarchy, there are no Virgins in this sense, and hence Virgins must be unspeakable outlaws, outcasts, thinkable only as negations, their existence impossible. Radically feminist lesbians have claimed, and have been inventing ways of living out, positive Virginity, in creative defiance of patriarchal definitions of the real, the meaningful. The question at hand may be herstorical: Will anyone, can anyone manage to, invent and construct modes of living Virginity which include women's maintaining erotic, economic, home-making, partnering connections with men? What must be imagined here is females who are willing to engage in chosen connections with males, who are wild females, undomesticated females, thoroughly defiant of patriarchal female heterosexuality. Such females will be living lives as sexually, socially and politically deviant and impossible as the lives undertaken by radically feminist lesbians. What must be imagined here is females who are willing to engage in chosen connections with males, who are wild, undomesticated females, creating themselves here and now.

In a way, it is not my place to imagine these wild females who have occasional and/or committed erotic, reproductive, home-making, partnered or friendship relations with males. The work and the pleasure of that imagining belong to those who undertake to invent themselves thus. But I do have a vivid, though partial, image of them. It derives both from my own experience as an impossible being and from my intense desire for alliance and sisterhoood with women of my acquaintance who engage in relations with men in the patriarchal context but who also seem to me to have a certain aptitude for Virginity. . . . So I offer for your consideration a sketch of my image of these wild women: (This is not a recipe for political correctness, and I am not legislating: this is a report from my Imagination.)

These Virgins do not attire and decorate themselves in the gear which in their cultures signal female compliance with male-defined femininity and which would form their bodies to such compliance. They do not make themselves "attractive" in the conventional feminine modes of their cultures and so people who can ignore their animal beauty say they are ugly. They maintain as much economic flexibility as they possibly can to ensure that they can revert to independence any time economic partnership is binding them to an alliance less than fully chosen. They would no more have sex when they don't expect to enjoy it than they would run naked in the rain when they don't expect to enjoy it. Their sexual interactions are not sites where people with penises make themselves men and people with vaginas are made women.*

These Virgins who connect with men don't try to maintain the fictions that the men they favor are better men than other men. When they are threatened by people who feel threatened by them, they do not point to their connections with men as soothing proof that they really aren't manhaters. They don't avail themselves of male protection. They do not pressure their daughters or their mothers, sisters, friends, or students to relate to men the ways they do so they can feel validated by the other women's choices. They never consider bringing any man with them to any feminist gathering that is not specifically meant to include men, and they help to create and to defend (and they enjoy) women-only spaces.

These Virgins who connect with men are not manipulable by orchestrations of male approval and disapproval, orchestrations of men's and children's needs, real or fake. They are not capable of being reduced to conformity by dread or anxiety about things lesbian, and are unafraid of their own passions for other Virgins, including those who are lesbians. They do not need to be respectable.

These Virgins refuse to enter the institution of marriage, and do not support or witness the weddings of others, including the weddings of their favorite brothers. They are die-hard marriage-resisters. They come under enormous pressure to marry, but they do not give in to it. They do not consider marriage a privilege. Not even the bribe of spousal health insurance benefits lures them into marriage, not even as they and their partners get older and become more anxious about their health and their economic situations.

These Virgins have strong, reliable, creative, enduring, sustaining, ardent friendships with women. Their imagination and their politics are shaped more fundamentally by a desire to empower women and create friendship and solidarity among women than by a commitment to appease, comfort or change men.

---

*These felicitons phrases are due to John Stoltenberg, *Refusing to Be a Man: Essays on Sex and Justice* (Portland, Ore.: Breitenbush, 1989), *passim.*

These Virgins who connect with men do not feel that they could be themselves and be in closets; they are "out" as loose and noncompliant females, a very noticeable phenomenon on the social and political scene. They make themselves visible, audible, and tangible to each other, they make community and sisterhood with each other and with lesbian Virgins, and they support each other in their wildness. They frolic and make trouble together. They create ways to have homes and warmth and companionship and intensity with or without a man included. They create value and they create meaning, so when the pressures to conform to patriarchal female heterosexuality are great, they have a context and community of resistance to sustain them and to engage their creative energies in devising new solutions to the problems conformity pretends to solve. They create music, novels, poetry, art, magazines and newspapers, knowledge, skills and tools, political actions and programs. And in their magazines and newspapers, they articulate their imagination, their cultural and political differences, their various values; they berate each other, they support each other, they pay attention to each other.

Are these beings I imagine possible? Can you fuck without losing your virginity? I think everything is against it, but *it's not my call*. I can hopefully image, but the counter-possible creation of such a reality is up to those who want to live it, if anyone does.

Some women have hoped that you *do* have to be a lesbian to be a real, extreme, to-the-root, troublemaking feminist, because then, since they are not lesbians and would never in the world became lesbians, they have an excuse for not thinking or acting radically feminist and not alienating men. Much of what passes for women's fear of lesbianism is really fear of men—fear of what men might do to non-compliant females. But I do not want to provide such an excuse for moderate or safe feminism.

"Do you have to be a lesbian to be a feminist?" is not quite the right question. The question should be "Can a woman be heterosexual and be radically feminist?" My picture is this: you do not have to be a lesbian to uncompromisingly embody and enact a radical feminism, but you also cannot be heterosexual in any standard patriarchal meaning of that word—you cannot be any version of patriarchal wife. Lesbian or not, to embody and enact a consistent and all-the-way feminism you have to be a heretic, a deviant, an undomesticated female, an impossible being. You have to be a Virgin.

A Transitional Feminist Sexual Morality

Ann Ferguson

[Earlier] it was argued that our contemporary American society is sexually alienated because of its gender dualism and the conflict between the ideology of romantic individualism and the reality of eroticised gender subordination. An ideal vision of sexuality that would remove these inconsistencies could occur only by a socialist-feminist transformation of our political economy which espoused the elimination of gender dualism as a principle of erotic life.

But our contemporary society is far from such a socialist-feminist transformation. Thus it would be utopian to demand that such an ideal be adopted by feminists in their present sexual practices. Acknowledging this, many feminist theorists who first suggested androgyny as a feminist ideal for human development have abandoned it (e.g. Daly, 1973, 1978; Dworkin, 1974, 1987; Rubin, 1975, 1984). Although I too first advocated androgyny, I now suggest an alternative tack. We can still hold to the vision of an ideal human development suggested by androgyny (cf. Ferguson, 1977) if we make two distinctions. First, we should not describe the vision as "androgyny" but "gynandry." The reversal of the two roots referring to masculine and feminine is not just word play, but points to the need for a feminist transformation of values that involves more than simply patching together the traditional qualities associated with masculinity and femininity.

Second, we must distinguish the vision question from the practical political question of what should be our feminist transitional ideal sexuality. Since feminism is a political social movement which challenges the values of contemporary male dominance, we must have some contrary values of our own that we stand for. We need an interim sexual morality to deal with contemporary questions of how to "draw the line" between sexual practices which should be forbidden and those which are permissible from a feminist point of view.

Contrary to the extreme relativists in the feminist sex debate, feminists do need to be moralists in order to advocate a public policy of what activities are so exploitative of women and children as to require legal prohibition. We also require a transitional feminist sexual morality for moral guidance when we are engaged in creating counter-cultural values with feminist friends, creating sex education programmes for youth, or in advising our own children and those who see us as role models.

A key question for framing a transitional feminist sexual morality is this: how can we both support a consensual sexual ethics that promotes sexual experimentation for pleasure, and yet take account of the social domination structured into certain sorts of sexual practices in capitalist patriarchy? On the one hand, we must reject the moralistic idea supported by many radical feminists that every personal interaction must be subject to the judgement of the feminist community for its political correctness. On the other hand, we need to suppose, unlike some pluralist feminists, that there is a political import to many personal interactions which cannot help but be relevant to feminists since structures of domination may be present whether or not they are acknowledged by consenting partners.

One way to create a cushion of space for personal diversity that will allow for fringe practices to be acceptable areas for sexual experimentation by feminists is to use a three-part distinction between forbidden, basic and risky feminist sexual practices (Ferguson, 1983, 1984).

The difference between a forbidden and a risky practice is that the latter involves taking risks from a feminist perspective because the practices are suspected of leading to dominance/subordination relationships. To say that they are risky implies that there is no final proof that they in fact must involve dominance/subordination relationships—rather, in fact they are contested precisely because there is conflicting evidence at present. Basic feminist practices, on the other hand, are those where there is nothing about the general features of the act or the social structures in which it is undertaken which suggests that it is risky in the above sense.

One effect of making a distinction between forbidden, risky and basic feminist practices is to provide for an area of disagreement between feminists on personal value choices that, though contested, is not a condition for excluding someone as a sister in the feminist community. Feminists should permit other feminists the right to take risks in many of their personal value choices without censuring them for being non-feminist if they disagree with their choices. Feminists will often disagree about which feminist sex/affective practices are basic and which risky. For example, a lesbian-feminist may perceive her straight friend's heterosexuality to be risky while this woman in turn may perceive the class or racial differences in her lesbian friend's relationship to be more risky! But having a three-way distinction allows us the space to disagree on where to draw the line without writing each other out of the feminist community, as long as we can agree on what practices are forbidden from a feminist perspective.

Forbidden sexual practices are ones which the majority of feminists think should be illegal. These would include rape and domestic battering. Included in the forbidden category of sexual practices should be those difficult cases where there is strong reason to think that consensual permission is not present given the extreme social inequalities of the partners; for instance, generational incest and adult/child sexuality. Since not all feminists agree on where to draw the line between risky and forbidden practices, we should look at these contested cases more carefully.

INCEST

In the case of both incest and adult/child sex there are feminists who have defended the idea of dropping the sanctions against these practices.[1] While I agree that some forms of incest, for example, those involving adults, or children of comparable ages, should be acceptable to feminists, the sticky cases are those which involve major differences in age, power and status between the participants. Thus the incest cases that remain contested turn out to be special cases of adult/child sexuality.

Since Firestone's and Dworkin's early work, many feminists have done detailed studies of father/daughter incest which document the systematic way that male dominant society allows fathers to use their patriarchal power in the family to play off mothers against daughters, thus strengthening their own power (Herman, 1982; Rush, 1980). Furthermore, the near absence of mother/child incest suggests that the forms of sex/affective energy that tie mothers to children, though they are erotic, are not genitally sexualised, nor is this likely given the gender split between emotion and pleasure in capitalist patriarchal forms of sex/affective energy. Thus, the call to "off the incest taboo" must be seen for what it is: a utopian and dangerous slogan that is likely merely to lead to the legitimation of male sexual abuse of children.

ADULT/CHILD SEXUALITY

Adult/child sex should be forbidden in a transitional feminist morality. This is not because it is inconceivable that human adults and children should have reciprocal sex but because it is nearly impossible to achieve in our society as presently structured.

Some pluralist feminists have disagreed with the policy implications of such a stand on the grounds of the "slippery slope"—that is, how can age of consent laws be formulated fairly so as to protect the very young from predatory adults yet not forbid sex between those very close in age but on different sides of an arbitrarily agreed line for adulthood, eighteen and sixteen year olds, for example?

Obviously it is not easy to draw the line between child and adult. In part this depends on the way a society institutionalises this line by when it permits economic independence of children from parents. Our society creates conflicting consciousness in teenagers by infantilising them through economic dependence and authoritarian prison-like schools at the same time as the media and market forces of sexual consumerism encourage them to think of themselves as sexual commodities. Such a situation creates youth who may want to consent to sex with an adult yet do not have the minimum economic independence to give them bargaining power. Thus, our transitional sexual morality must defend age of consent laws between adults and teenagers or children, even though the enforcement of these may be arbitrary in some cases.

One policy initiative that feminists could take with respect to age of consent laws is to frame laws which ban sexual relations between children under eighteen and anyone eighteen or older who is more than six years older than they. This would allow teenagers to be sexual with their peers and with young adults. At the same time it would protect them from potentially exploitative sexual relationships until they reach a minimal maturity level.

FORBIDDEN *VS* RISKY SEX

Our feminist transitional sexual morality should be pluralist with respect to most adult consensual sex. We should not condemn as non-feminist those practices which may seem extremely risky to us in terms of suspected dominance/subordination dynamics, as long as they are engaged in in private. Thus, such practices as consensual S/M, male breadwinner/female housewife sex, and prostitution have been critiqued as practices that may involve dominance and subordination. But there is no final proof that roled sex can never be reciprocal even if it is patterned after the gender dualism of compulsory heterosexuality. And though, for example, economic dependence and the psychological role of server strongly suggest that housewives will not be in a position to have equal sexual bargaining power, there well may be mitigating circumstances which allow a woman in such a position emotional parity with a particular husband. Thus, though we may want to advise of the risks of such practices to our friends and young people under our care, we should not claim these practices to be morally forbidden.

UNSAFE SEX: THE PROBLEM OF AIDS AND OTHER SEXUALLY TRANSMITTED DISEASES

The AIDS epidemic has created a serious moral and political problem for feminists. On the one hand, the fact that AIDS is a fatal disease communicated through blood and sperm suggests that feminists ought to urge the adoption of safe sex practices (e.g. using condoms, etc.) which minimise the health risks of such practices. But, on the other hand, it would be dangerous to put physically unsafe sex practices on our list of legally forbidden practices, for this would suggest that the state should pass coercive legislation such as mandatory testing for AIDS for marriage licences and even coercive legislation forbidding certain kinds of sexual practice, for example, laws against sodomy.

Feminists need to balance the defence of the rights of sexual minorities against state intervention in their sexual practices with the right of individuals not to be exposed to fatal sexual diseases without their knowledge. In the case of AIDS and other sexually transmitted diseases, feminists might make a distinction between what is morally forbidden and what is legally forbidden: not everything that we may want to forbid morally is something we may want the state legally empowered to coerce. Thus, feminists ought to morally forbid unsafe sex practices but yet oppose legislation which would make such practices illegal because of the danger that the state could encroach on civil rights in their enforcement of the law. Vigorous sex education with respect to safe and unsafe sex practices is a better means to creating situations where people practise safe sex than making the practices illegal.

Feminists are coming to realise that the fight against AIDS is a crucial one, for if we do not become involved in demanding money for research and public education about AIDS, the New Right will continue to use the existence of AIDS in racist, sexist and heterosexist ways to encourage the public to react in moral panic which will scapegoat minorities and gay men and create the danger of restrictive anti-sex legislation which will restrict the sexual freedoms of all of us.

CONSENSUAL S/M AMONG ADULTS

Many radical feminists maintain that S/M relationships ought to be morally forbidden from a feminist perspective, both because they involve the infliction of physical pain (hence violence) against women and because they perpetuate the eroticising of dominance/subordination roles so as to perpetuate male dominance. To defend the view that feminists should judge consensual S/M sex risky rather than morally forbidden, we need to consider both aspects of these practices: their potentially physically unsafe aspect and their eroticisation of dominance aspect.

Feminist sex manuals like Pat Califia's *Sapphistry* (1980) attempt to delineate safe sex practices for those engaging in consensual S/M. But aside from the physical dangers of a sexual practice that uses physical pain as an inducement to physical pleasure, there is the more difficult question of the suspected eroticisation of domination that S/M involves. Though its feminist defenders argue that the roles and fantasies enacted by the role of sadist and masochist are pure theatre, there is no escaping the fact that much of such theatre involves the enactment of roles that are explicitly degrading: e.g. master and slave or servant or dog, a parent punishing a child, or other clearly hierarchical positions. Should we accept the view of the pluralists that "anything goes" in fantasy life, and that individuals have the right to private choices in this area (cf. Samois, 1981)? Or are the radical feminists correct that there is no clear line between fantasy and reality *vis-à-vis* a person's ultimate values (Linden *et al* (eds), 1982)? Is it true that persons who get off on masochism in bed are by that practice perpetuating a vulnerable ego in other areas of their social life? Or is that person merely venting an unconscious (and possibly unchangeable) aspect of her emotional life thus expurgating its influence from the rest of her life? And might many of those engaged in so-called consensual S/M practices, especially those who are the masochists, actually be constrained into maintaining these practices (Jonel, 1982)?

Despite the heated claims by both proponents and opponents of S/M that it is empowering *vs* disempowering to the women who engage in it, there is no clear proof either way and therefore consensual S/M should be considered a risky but not a forbidden practice for feminists.[2] Since it is risky, I would not want to advise anyone to experiment with it, but if someone is determined to try it, they ought not to be morally censured from engaging in it, though they should perhaps be advised against physically unsafe practices that they might otherwise try.

There is one further difficult aspect of S/M which a feminist sexual morality must deal with, and this is the public display of S/M fantasy objects, e.g. chains, handcuffs, Nazi insignia and the like. Must feminist political coalitions, women's centres and other public organisations support the right of S/M practitioners to create a public S/M sexual identity with the appropriate paraphernalia in the same way that feminists have defended the right of homosexuals to wear public symbols which express their sexual preference?

There is surely a disanalogy between the support of public gayness and the support of public S/M insignia. In the case of the latter but not the former, feminists have a right to withhold such support. Consensual lesbian or gay relations do not carry the same danger of general negative effects to others as does the public display of S/M symbols or the adoption of S/M as a public sexual identity.

The danger in the full justification of consensual S/M with the right to all its public trappings is as follows. Consensual S/M is justified (if at all) by being a theatre of private meanings. But S/M feminists have no right to insist on being supported to wear symbols of their sexual fantasies in public. This is because feminists must make a strong public stand against non-consensual violence and hierarchical coercion. As Alice Walker argues (Walker, 1982b) there is no clear way for the general public to understand the distinction between feminists supporting consensual and non-consensual violence when self-avowed lesbian feminists (e.g. a white woman with a whip and a black woman wearing a collar and handcuffs) present themselves publicly as S/M lovers.

A second reason why public display of S/M in a feminist context is problematic is its effect on women who have suffered non-consensual violence: rape survivors and victims of domestic battering. Whips, chains, collars and handcuffs cannot help but have a negative emotional meaning to those who have suffered the non-consensual use of these instruments. Thus, it is not surprising that many who have suffered such violence or whose political work involves working with survivors of such violence may want to avoid the emotional upset to themselves or these women that public displays of explicit S/M symbols would involve.

In sum, public display of S/M symbols is problematic for two reasons: first, because the standard meaning of these symbols implies the negation of the equal and consensual relations that feminism stands for, and second, because such symbols (in their standard meaning) violate the ground rules (a feeling of safety and security) that victims of non-consensual violence have a right to expect from spaces controlled by feminists. For these reasons, feminists ought not to support the public display of S/M graphic sex roles, even though we should support the right of an adult feminist to practise consensual S/M in private if she wishes.[3]

In arguing that private S/M should be categorised as risky and graphic public symbols of S/M forbidden, a moral distinction has been made between public and private which feminists who believe that the personal is the political may question. The need for feminists to re-appropriate this distinction for certain uses will be defended further below.

HOUSEWIFERY, MARRIAGE AND PROSTITUTION

Putting housewifery and prostitution in the same camp, not as morally forbidden but morally risky from a feminist point of view, allows us to highlight the structural features of these practices which have been targetted by radical feminists in both waves of the American and European women's movements—the fact that women who are economically dependent on men are expected to trade economic support for sexual favours, and that this makes for an unequal negotiating relationship.

At the same time as feminists need to have a way to advise against housewife/marriage and prostitution as risky practices in many circumstances, we need to acknowledge that many working-class women may have no better alternatives to choose. Many women choose to be housewives because they wish to raise children with a man and cannot afford child care. And others become prostitutes because of economic and personal coercion.

Since housewifery and prostitution have the same structure, it is hypocritical to outlaw one and not the other. While our ideal socialist-feminist society hopefully would eliminate both, this is not a realistic possibility within capitalist patriarchy. Thus, feminist public policy in our society today should advocate the elimination of legal sanctions against prostitution. Such a move would spare the women involved the stigma of outlaws (Delacoste and Alexander (eds), 1987). However, this does not mean that feminists need to approve of prostitution, any more than socialist-feminists approve of capitalism! But just as our disapproval of capitalism does not imply that we want to outlaw feminist businesses under capitalist patriarchy, so it doesn't follow that we should outlaw prostitution even though in an ideal socialist-feminist society prostitution would not exist.

Our moral disapproval of prostitution should not be used to stigmatise prostitutes. Marriage, like prostitution, should be classified as risky but not forbidden for feminists. We should press for specific laws against procurement (pimping) and the various sorts of violence and economic coercion through which women are constrained into prostitution (cf. Barry, 1979). Such activities should be rigorously prosecuted in a way that is not now happening.

Another example of a problematic decision for feminists is heterosexual marriage. The legal institution of heterosexual marriage still creates legal structural inequalities between men and women: rape in marriage is still permissible in many American states and homemakers are not eligible for their spouses' social security benefits. It also legitimises economic and social privileges for heterosexual couples that are not possible for homosexual couples. Feminists ought, therefore, to eschew standard marriage ceremonies in order not to perpetuate the public symbolic meaning of heterosexism and women as legal possessions of men.

Private "ceremonies of commitment" or legal contracts which are not explicitly marriage contracts are permissible since they don't carry the same patriarchal and heterosexist interpretation. They also allow straight feminists, lesbian feminists and our male allies the opportunity to create a counterculture of sex/affective resistance to the sexual symbolic code of patriarchal heterosexual marriage. Couple commitment is an important feature of counter-cultural communities. Public alternative ceremonies of commitment allow a social expression to a community that does not carry the capitalist patriarchal meaning of legal marriage ceremonies. . . .

NOTES

1 For example, Shulamith Firestone in *The Dialectic of Sex* and Andrea Dworkin in *Womanhating* suggest that feminists smash the incest taboo as a way to undercut the Oedipus complex and thus the power of patriarchy based on the sex/affective relations in the nuclear family. Gayle Rubin has argued that some forms of incest (e.g. brother/sister incest) be removed from stigmatised status and be accepted by feminists (Rubin, talk, Fall, 1986). Others have argued that consensual adult/child sex should be permissible in order to support children's right to be sexually active (cf. Tsang, 1981).
2 For more on the pro-S/M point of view, see Califia, 1981, Rubin and the other authors in Samois, 1981, and Rubin, 1984. For the anti-S/M argument see the authors in Barry, 1979, 1981; Linden *et al*, 1982; Raymond, 1986.
3 Pro-S/M defenders may criticise this conclusion by the argument that a refusal by feminists to support public use of certain kinds of S/M symbols, e.g. in Lesbian/Gay Pride marches, or in other feminist-controlled spaces, has the danger of marginalising consensual S/Ms and rendering them more vulnerable to police attacks. The response to this is a balancing-of-harms argument: that when the risks of contributing to the emotional terrorising of previously traumatised women and of presenting symbols that may lead the public to misunderstand the goals of the Women's Movement are weighed against the possible gains to S/Ms of public legitimacy by the use of public symbols, the dangers of the former outweigh the benefits of the latter.

Strategies for Organizing Against Female Sexual Slavery

Charlotte Bunch

One of the major tasks of this international workshop focused on strategies for action against female sexual slavery and the functions of an international feminist network. We began this by listing and discussing the major themes, problems, and strategies that had emerged during individual presentations from each region and from resource people. The resource presentations provided participants with a basic level of information in such areas as trafficking in children, sexual torture of prisoners, prostitute organizations, the human rights community, and the workings of the UN.

Our discussion of strategies initially centered on what is a feminist approach to countering the exploitation of women in prostitution and of violence against women (rape, incest, sexual mutilation, battery, pornography, and torture) in the context of patriarchal society. We looked at the various ways in which these issues are connected to the treatment of women in all areas, to cultural attitudes toward female sexuality, and to oppression by class, race, militarism, and neocolonialism.

After some general discussion, we identified three major areas where we wanted to do more work in depth: 1) Legislation and Prostitution; 2) Violence and Sexuality; and 3) Institutionalization of Female Sexual Slavery. We chose this division of the topic because it provided the working groups assigned to each area with both the theoretical problems involved in the issue and with practical questions of strategies for action. Further, each topic included both national and international concerns and each related to an area where there are existing groups or constituencies with related concerns that we might work with. Each group then considered strategies for combating female sexual slavery in their area generally, and strategies for developing an effective international network in that area as well. A fourth working group, formed to begin outlining the basic platform and structures for an international network, will be discussed later in this chapter.

In the following pages, I outline the issues taken up by the three topical working groups. These groups each consisted of between five and nine people who deliberated together for one to one and a half days and then presented a short, written report to the larger group. The reports were amended and agreed to in principle by the workshop groups as a whole, which then adopted them as part of the network. Following the groups' instructions, I have edited them and provided some additional commentary based on my notes and the tapes of the discussion.

LEGISLATION AND PROSTITUTION

This working group was concerned with our position on national legislation relating to prostitution and to the oppression of women in other areas, such as marriage laws, which contribute to forcing women into prostitution. In this regard, it sought to develop strategies that would oppose the institution of prostitution, but not penalize the individual women in prostitution. When we distinguish between the institution of prostitution and the individuals within it, it becomes clear that legal action should focus on prosecuting the sex industry—procurers, pimps, travel agencies, and other exploiters of women—rather than on the victims of this exploitation. This group also discussed how the network could relate to international agencies, UN conventions and resolutions, and international human rights groups concerned with aspects of female sexual slavery.

The group's report begins with a statement regarding our concept of law. The following is a summary of the group's work: laws are instruments that control the lives of people; laws are formed according to the understanding and beliefs of legislators (primarily men) and the dominant economic system. In a patriarchal society, laws are always favorable to men, maintain the subordination of women, conserve the status quo, and legitimize the existing economic, political, and racial systems.

Laws, however, can also be instruments that facilitate the process of change and advance the situation of women. This is true, particularly when women committed to women's rights participate in the formulation of laws, and when they recognize the strengths and weaknesses of legislation and how it can be utilized to promote human rights. In some instances, laws can serve as a means of protection for women, although so-called protective legislation has also been used to limit women's activities.

In many countries, in addition to the recognized legal systems, there exist customs and customary law, patriarchal in nature, that are used by the dominating groups to control the lives of women and other oppressed people. Such customary laws and civil and penal codes constitute another legal system that suppresses women and their basic right to self-determination. In this regard, we make special reference to the oppressive character of marriage and divorce laws, dowry, bride price, child marriages, racial discrimination, immigration laws, abortion laws, and employment legislation. The situations for women that are created by these laws often contribute to pushing women into prostitution. Customary laws and civil and penal codes thus reinforce and perpetuate the double standard of morality established by religious beliefs.

Prostitution is often a logical form of survival in a patriarchal society in which women are considered as private and public property and are reduced to sexual objects. Patriarchal ideology divides women into "madonnas" and "whores" in order to control the lives of women at all levels of society. This is the fundamental coercion that objectifies women's bodies and reduces sex to a commodity. Whether women are forced into prostitution or choose it, they are under the control of the system. This control encompasses every aspect of women's lives.

Laws relating to prostitution reinforce the patriarchal system and its control over women. These laws become part of the institutional apparatus that maintains control over all women. By condemning women who do what a male society demands as "necessary," prostitution laws force women to stay within the institution of prostitution, even when they want or attempt to leave it.

The legal system of prohibition of prostitution treats women as criminals and puts the onus of blame or punishment on them, while not penalizing pimps or customers. The legalization of prostitution, however, still focuses on the women who are controlled and manipulated by regulation; legalization also legitimizes the male society's contention that prostitution is inevitable and that men have the right to women's bodies. Both prohibition and legalization further the dependency of women in prostitution on pimps—individual or the state—and on the police who have power over their lives.

The only adequate solution in terms of legislation that concerns the women in prostitution themselves is decriminalization of prostitution per se. Decriminalization makes the act of prostitution itself neither legal nor illegal, thus removing the focus and punishment from the individual women in prostitution, while still not legitimizing the institution of prostitution. While working for the decriminalization of the act of prostitution itself, we must also call for the strengthening and application of laws against the exploitation of prostitution by procurers and pimps, against the trafficking of women and children, and against all forms of sexual violence. All existing laws regarding prostitution, soliciting, vagrancy, and so on need to be reexamined and amended from this perspective. Decriminalization of prostitution and prosecution of the exploiters of the prostitution of others are both called for in the 1949 United Nations Convention for the Suppression of the Traffic in Persons and of the Exploitation of the Prostitution of Others, and in the 1981 United Nations Convention for the Elimination of All Forms of Discrimination against Women.

Strategies

1 Study the existing legal system regarding prostitution, in particular, and women in general, in each country, in order to compile a complete picture of the legal situation of prostitution and female sexual slavery on a national and global level.

2 Seek the abolition of discrimination against women in all laws dealing with employment, education, and other areas of public life.

3 Work toward legislation that guarantees women equal rights in marriage and divorce laws.

4 Work for the decriminalization of prostitution per se and the strengthening of laws that oppose the enslavement of women by pimps and prosecute those involved in all forms of trafficking of women.

5 Initiate and support efforts to combat police harassment of women in prostitution and efforts that promote the prosecution of violent crimes against women in prostitution. Seek an end to all discriminatory measures against women in prostitution.

6 Work to provide refuge centers and supportive services aimed at assisting women to escape or leave prostitution.

7 Cooperate with organizations which are committed to addressing these issues from a perspective that is compatible with our feminist network.

8 Establish permanent relationships with international governmental organizations and nongovernmental organizations dealing with the problems of prostitution, trafficking in women and children, and female sexual slavery.

9 Provide necessary information and consulting services to nations requesting such services who seek to make improvements in their legislation and services related to prostitution and violence against women.

10 Promote investigation into international trafficking of women, sex tourism, etc.

VIOLENCE AND SEXUALITY

This working group considered violence against women—rape, battery, incest, pornography, sexual mutilation—and how these relate to prostitution and trafficking in women. It also looked at issues of female sexuality, how this is manipulated and controlled in patriarchal society, and how to assure women's rights to sexual self-determination without condoning the exploitation of female sexuality. Related concerns included how female dependency, particularly economic dependency, and traditional customs often contribute to the vulnerability of women to sexual abuse.

The following are the group's conclusions: violence against women is intimately connected to the power relationships that exist between men and women in a patriarchal society. The power that men exercise over women engenders violence, and fear exists as the basis of all forms of violence against women.

In discussing the issue of violence against women, an understanding of the concept of sexuality is essential. Two questions must be raised: 1) how has sexuality been defined in a patriarchal society? and 2) what is the definition of sexuality that we must adopt as the basis of our network against female sexual slavery?

Patriarchal definitions of sexuality have resulted in the objectification of women as either sex objects or reproductive units. In our view, a redefinition of sexuality must reject this notion of sex as a commodity, and understand sexuality as a means through which people can relate to each other as human beings and not as beings of a specific sex. We uphold women's freedom of sexual choice. We feel that an acceptance of sexuality from only the perspectives of reproduction or of women as sex objects for men to use is an expression of patriarchal ideology that has mutilated female sexuality.

Women are victims of many forms of domination by men that are exercised through the structures of sexism, racism, and classism. Therefore, attempts to address the situation of violence against women must incorporate strategies that look at specific problems within the larger context of creating structural changes in society in all these areas.

We understand that there exists *one* universal patriarchal oppression of women which takes different forms in different cultures and different regions. However, all these diverse expressions of patriarchal oppression like sexual mutilation, rape, pornography, torture, forced marriages, etc. mutilate women. Economic dependency generates psychological and emotional dependency in women, and all such forms of dependency reinforce each other, making women more vulnerable. The creation of dependency on all levels results in violence against women occurring in a variety of forms, that is, through the body, through the mind, in the workplace, in education, etc.

We must understand and recognize the commonality of patriarchal oppression experienced by all women if we are to devise a common strategy to eradicate female sexual slavery. We feel that it is necessary to devise strategies at two levels: strategies to create and maintain an international network; and, strategies to begin communication among regional and local groups regarding the issues raised by the network.

In relation to strategy-building at the international level, we recommend that our network be built upon existing structures such as CAMS (International Commission for the Abolition of Sexual Mutilations). We point out that organizations based in the so-called First World are viewed with a great deal of hostility and suspicion by Third World women, and this factor should be taken into consideration when deciding on the location of the network's base of operation.

The second level of strategy-building in the regions must take into consideration specific regional needs. After a review of the major problems that need to be addressed in various regions, and the difficulties involved in addressing these issues due to political, cultural, and religious factors, we have come up with the following strategy recommendations.

Strategies

1 To make the different forms of violence against women and their relationship to female sexual slavery more visible in all our countries, since they are frequently kept hidden.

2 To make these issues visible by using different tactics to raise what are often suppressed as "undiscussible" issues in certain countries. For example, if it is particularly difficult to discuss a certain form of female sexual slavery in one country, a woman in that country might disseminate information about what is happening in that area in a neighboring country. This might have the effect of helping to open up avenues for discussion about that issue in her own country.

3 To communicate with and utilize the resources of other regional and local groups and organizations in order to reach people with information about female sexual slavery and what can be done to combat it.

4 To work with immigrant women who could provide information about the situations of women in their own countries that they had to leave. These women could also be channels through which information about the exploitation and violence against women could be sent back into the countries of their origin.

5 To establish training centers for women (prostitute and pre-prostitute) in nontraditional fields and to create intermediate shelters for prostitutes that provide them with practical services and protection from pimps. In addition, we need to pressure other groups, including governments where appropriate, to support these centers and to help ensure that these women will find employment after they receive job training.

6 To insist on nonsexist, coeducational education from primary school level for all, and to change the content of text books especially with regard to their attitudes towards women and girls. Whenever possible, women's groups should establish communication with school teachers and parent associations about these issues.

7 To make contact with women in the media, and through them, develop ways to use the media to expose violence against women and how it can be prevented.

8 To start campaigns on specific issues of violence and female sexual slavery on an international level which would be coordinated by the network but organized according to the specific conditions of each region and country.

9 To adopt International or National Days Against All Forms of Violence Against Women. This would create a greater sense of solidarity among women globally and allow the organization of national and international campaigns each year. This strategy has been used successfully in Latin America, where for several years, groups have organized such a day on November 25. This date commemorates the death of three sisters from the Dominican Republic who were raped, tortured, and killed during the Trujillo regime. The group invited others to consider this date or to adopt another, appropriate to their region.

INSTITUTIONALIZATION OF FEMALE SEXUAL SLAVERY

This working group was concerned with strategies to combat specific forms of female sexual slavery and prostitution that are institutionalized as parts of other patriarchal interests. It considered the effects of militarism, military bases, and war conditions on sexual violence against women; it looked at the sexual torture of women prisoners; and it discussed the growing phenomena of organized sex tours and mail order brides as current examples of how women's bodies are being systematically sold.

These are the group's conclusions: in looking at how female sexual slavery is institutionalized throughout society from the local to the international levels, it is clear that domination and violence against women is linked to the domination of people generally through militarism, racism, and economic exploitation. All of these are manifestations of a patriarchal ideology that legitimizes the right of one group to dominate another, usually by means of coercion and physical violence—beginning in the family and escalating to global warfare. Throughout all of these forms of domination, the sexual exploitation of women persists.

This report focuses on the particular forms of female sexual slavery that have arisen as part of the present economic world order and the military power that sustains it. These practices are, however, simply the latest manifestations of female sexual slavery, which has had many different forms in other cultural and economic conditions. Further, the structures that oppress women today are often based on remnants of feudalism or of traditional customs that have become even more oppressive when combined with the prevailing economic conditions, which are manipulated for the benefit of a powerful few.

The internationalization of capital and the international division of labor have further exploited women through various kinds of sexual enslavement, not only locally, but also on a transnational level. The national security ideology, a patriarchal ideology that sees the state as fatherland, absolute and supreme, with the right to unquestioning obedience of its citizens, is the justification for much of this exploitation. A blatant expression of this ideology is the use of military power to protect the interests of transnational corporations through military bases and intervention in strategic places. Local dictatorships assure political stability to foreign investments through military repression and so-called democratic states exert control through police and intelligence networks.

A more subtle form of exploitation occurs through "development" schemes imposed on the Third World by financial institutions such as the World Bank. Many countries have gone into enormous debt through national policies geared toward the industrialized world's interests such as tourism, transnational corporations, and the export of human labor. In this world economic order, women are more than ever exploited as cheap labor in agriculture and industry, as prostitutes for the military and in the "service" sector, and as migrant workers in foreign countries, many of whom are forced into prostitution. In a patriarchal culture, this political economic thrust has intensified the control and abuse of women in an organized way by business, governments, and the military.

A particularly hideous example of how these oppressions combine is the torture of women by the modern military state. Since the military is based on the masculinist values of power, physical domination, and public authority, it sees women who oppose it as threatening to its masculine defined hierarchy. There is, therefore, a distinctive pattern of sexual torture for a female political prisoner, aimed at violating her personal worth and sense of human dignity as a woman. This torture involves sexual enslavement in a situation from which she cannot escape and in which she suffers sexual attacks upon her body and her psyche.[1]

Militarism is symptomatic of a male-dominated society that uses violence and power to control others. One form of its enslavement of women is the demand for bodies to cater to men's "rest and recreational" needs. Prostitution has proliferated around military bases and ports for many years, and with it comes violence against these women. Women forced into military prostitution become dependent on the base and their relations to the rest of the culture are often destroyed. Military prostitution and violence against women is exacerbated during war situations such as that in Lebanon. In Asia, mobile field brothels were funded by American dollars during the Indochina war where there was practically a prostitute for every GI.

Many victims of military brothels have been transferred to duty as prostitutes for tourists. Sex tourism is the "buy-and-sell" of women's bodies for sexual service to men as part of tourist activities. It is one of the growing institutions of female sexual exploitation which governments use to obtain foreign currency and which airlines, hotels, travel agencies, and local pimps use to make profits. It is international both in trafficking women's bodies from one country to another and in receiving support from governments in both receiving and sending countries. It combines sexual oppression with class and race discrimination since it primarily involves the selling of Third World women.[2]

Marriage by catalog where brides are ordered by photos is another example of economic and sexual exploitation of poor women. "Happiness without Barriers" and promises of fidelity and docility are some of the slogans used by commercial matchmakers who profit from such marriages. Pictures of women from the Third World with their vital statistics are presented as commodities to male clients. Many of these women are later forced into prostitution.

Strategies

This group began with a general principle underlining all its strategies: the focus of our work on these issues must be on exposing and bringing an end to the sex industry and exploiters of women, not on limiting the rights of women. Our approach respects the rights of movement of women and guards against a growing tendency to harass and restrict women (especially Third World women) traveling alone or in groups.

1 Seek international recognition of the right of a woman to determine the nature and extent of her sexual activity as a political right. Any woman seeking to escape from sexual violence or enslavement should be recognized as a political refugee and afforded protection and asylum as such. This status must include a woman's right to self-defense when under physical attack.

2 Investigate and expose the international trafficking of women in the sex industry, the procurement practices—such as deceptive advertising for employment and phony marriages, and the exploitation of women in particularly vulnerable situations such as migrants, displaced persons, and refugees. Enlist human rights and church groups to assist in this exposure and in confronting the transnational institutions which are investing in trafficking directly and which control development options in Third World countries which contribute to women's vulnerability.

3 Demand the creation of alternative plans for the development of national economies that do not exploit women's bodies in the sex industry or in production. Challenge the national interests which profit off the sexual exploitation of women.

4 Conduct public education campaigns about these practices through utilizing the media and through dialogue with groups that have common concerns. Develop lists of sympathetic media and of those who exploit sexual topics and share this information with women through the network. Develop media guidelines about who to debate and in what circumstances.

5 Create awareness—particularly among peace, labor, political groups—of the connections between sexual enslavement, violence, militarism, and torture of women in such situations as: in jails—whether incarcerated as political or regular prisoners; by police or terrorist forces in society; as prostitutes controlled by pimps or brothel keepers; in refugee camps or hamlets; in military or war settings; on the job as workers and as union organizers.

6 Bring international attention and pressure to bear on individual cases of female sexual slavery. Local groups must give feminist interpretations to cases and determine what outside support is useful. The network can then be used to mobilize petitions and telegrams of support or to send media observers to trials or to expose crimes against women in other areas.

7 Take direct action at the points of contact with the sex industry such as demonstrations at airports where tours leave or at travel agencies; picket and harass agencies or individuals involved in these practices; campaign against and remove racist and sexist advertisements, posters, publications, etc.

8 Provide humanitarian services to women in exploitative situations and challenge local agencies and governments to provide for these.

9 Work toward a long-term end to militarism, economic, racial, and sexual exploitation and the patriarchy that sustains all forms of domination.

THE NETWORK

The fourth working group outlined points that formed the basis for discussion and decisions about the focus of the network, how it would function, and what its relationship would be to existing organizations and groups. This was approached with the understanding that this network is part of a global movement of women who seek to abolish patriarchy and all forms of domination, whether by sex, race, class, religion, or nationality. As such, our network does not see itself as working in isolation but rather as taking on particular tasks within this larger feminist struggle.

The International Feminist Network Against Female Sexual Slavery and Traffic in Women will focus on the issues of violence and exploitation of women through the use of female sexuality. The primary manifestations that this network will address are prostitution, trafficking in women, sex tourism, and their relationship to violence against women in rape, sex mutilation, incest, battery, forced marriages, dowry and bride wealth, pornography and the torture of political prisoners. We recognize further that, particularly in certain regions, some of these issues must be approached in relation to other concerns, such as sexual harassment, the exploitation of women's work, female poverty, racism, and the denial of women's right to choice in matters of sexuality and reproduction. It was agreed, therefore, that while it is important to narrow our focus enough so that we are not attempting to take on everything at once, we also recognize that female sexual slavery is integrally related to so many issues that we cannot separate our work against it from a consideration of these as well.

The network will be based on the directions set out in the reports and strategies of the three working groups on: Legislation and Prostitution; Violence and Sexuality; and the Institutionalization of Female Sexual Slavery. In considering our concept of feminism, we see it primarily reflected in the analysis and strategies of these reports. Beyond the reports and such general statements about the goals of feminism as stated in the document "Developing Strategies for the Future: Feminist Perspectives," we recognize that feminism needs to be expressed in different ways in different cultural contexts.[3]

In considering how individuals would relate to the network, it was felt that there must be general agreement with our political approach as outlined by the working groups and with the central focus of the network on female sexual slavery. Beyond this core of agreement, we seek to approach the meaning of feminism without forcing consensus on every issue, particularly given the different conditions and development of feminism in various countries. However, it was also stated that, while everyone might not agree on all issues, no one publicly identified with the network could be working actively against feminist issues that are of great importance to many in the network, such as abortion and lesbian rights. These two controversial issues were discussed as examples precisely because they were not major themes of our network, but they do highlight the difficulty of working globally when the consciousness about, and sense of priority around, certain feminist concerns, differs from region to region as well as among different individuals, often depending on cultural or religious assumptions.

Another dilemma discussed was the importance of acknowledging cultural differences while not adopting double standards based on them. The specific conditions in each country make it necessary to work in different ways and often on different priorities, but we cannot say that certain oppressive practices are okay in some places but not in others. While traditional customs or current imperialism sometimes make the conditions of exploitation of women in prostitution different in Third World countries than in industrialized ones, we cannot say that such exploitation is tolerable in one place and not in another. For example, just because many women in developing countries are in poverty, with few job options, does not excuse the violence against and coercion of them by sex tourism. Nor, on the other hand, do we accept the notion that Third World women in prostitution need our assistance while European and North American women trapped by pimps are not worthy of our concern.

Another area in which we reject a double standard is in relation to heterosexual and homosexual prostitution. While our network is focused on the abuse of women and therefore deals primarily with heterosexual crimes against women, we do not condone homosexual exploitation of prostitution. But we also do not, as many imply, see homosexual abuse as worse than heterosexual abuse. For example, the sexual violation of children by adults is neither worse nor less onerous if it is done by men against boys than if it is done by men against girls.

This network is not a hierarchical organization with an international headquarters at the top and local chapters, but rather a means of assisting, linking, and coordinating work done by many organizations, individuals, and grass-roots groups. It will be centered in the regions. It is hoped that groups and individuals will use the network to help circulate information nationally and internationally and thus assist us all in finding out what others are doing. The network can also be used by regional groups to help coordinate actions from region to region or internationally to facilitate days of protest or meeting around particular concerns. Further, the network can provide linkages for local or regional groups to international agencies and/or to other regional groups.

In discussing how the network would function, we were concerned with the problem of how to have a viable network with access to resources and major lines of communication without centering it in the Western industrialized countries. Given that this network is just beginning and has few centralized resources, our decision for now was to work primarily through the regions and by utilizing existing regional and international groups. The hope was expressed that each region would devise a structure appropriate to its situation and that, eventually, there would be a documentation and coordination center in each region.

Finally, the participants agreed that in the next two years, the emphasis of the network will be on organizing groups and actions in local communities and in the regions. We will seek to develop global strategies primarily through the evolution of regional activity and/or from interaction among the regions. This approach to organizing the network will be evaluated in 1985 at the time of the United Nations End of the Decade Conference on Women scheduled for Nairobi, Kenya. At that meeting, some participants from Rotterdam and other contacts who work with the network in the ensuing years will gather to review the progress of the network and to organize for further action against female sexual slavery.[4]

NOTES

1 For a fuller discussion of this form of sexual slavery see Ximena Bunster, "The Torture of Women Political Prisoners: A Case Study in Female Sexual Slavery," in *International Feminism: Networking Against Female Sexual Slavery,* Barry, Bunch, and Castley, eds. (New York: IWTC, 1984), pp. 94–102.

2 For more on sex tourism and military prostitution, see Yayori Matsui, "Why I Oppose Kisaeng Tours," ibid., pp. 64–72.

3 See "Developing Strategies for the United Nations Decade for Women," pp. 283–300.

4 Several meetings of the network were held in 1985 in Nairobi. It was decided to continue working primarily at the regional and local levels, while maintaining some international communication through these groups and via existing international organizations such as ISIS and the International Women's Tribune Centre.

Suggestions for Further Reading: Part 4

The literature on various aspects of feminism is now so extensive that we have made
no attempt to provide exhaustive bibliographies. Instead, we have suggested just a few
books that provide accessible introductions to various topics or have become classics
in the field.

STAYING ALIVE

Amott, Teresa L., and Julie A. Matthaei: *Race, Gender and Work: A Multicultural Economic
    History of Women in the United States,* South End, Boston, 1991.
Andolsen, Barbara Hilkert: *Good Work at the Video Display Terminal: A Feminist Ethical Anal-
    ysis of Changes in Clerical Work,* University of Tennessee Press, Knoxville, 1989.
Baehr, Ninia: *Abortion Without Apology: A Radical History for the 1990's,* South End, Boston,
    1990.
Baxendall, Rosalyn, Linda Gordon, and Susan Reverby (eds.): *America's Working Women: A
    Documentary History—1600 to the Present,* Vintage, New York, 1976.
Bulkin, Ely, Minnie Bruce Pratt, and Barbara Smith: *Yours in Struggle,* Long Haul Press,
    Brooklyn, 1984.
Crosny, Faye J.: *Juggling: The Unexpected Advantages of Balancing Career and Home for
    Women and Their Families,* Free Press, New York, 1991
Gilman, Charlotte Perkins: *Women and Economics: The Economic Factor Between Men and
    Women as a Factor in Social Evolution,* Harper & Row, New York, 1966. Originally pub-
    lished in 1898.
Guy, Donna J.: *Sex and Danger in Buenos Aires: Prostitution, Family, and Nation in Argentina,*
    University of Nebraska Press, Lincoln, 1992.
ISIS Women's International Information and Communication Service: *Women in Development:
    A Resource Guide for Organization and Action,* New Society, Philadelphia, 1984.
Leghorn, Lisa, and Katherine Parker: *Women's Worth: Sexual Economics and the World of
    Women,* Routledge & Kegan Paul, Boston, London, and Henley, 1981.
Luxton, Meg: *More Than a Labour of Love: Three Generations of Women's Work in the Home,*
    Women's Educational Press, Toronto, 1980.
MacKinnon, Catharine A.: *Sexual Harassment of Working Women: A Case of Sex Discrimina-
    tion,* Yale University Press, New Haven, 1979.
Paludi, Michelle: *Ivory Power: Sexual Harassment on Campus,* State University Press, Albany,
    1990.
Reardon, Betty: *Sexism and the War System,* Teachers College Press, New York, 1985.
Schechter, Susan: *Women and Male Violence,* South End, Boston, 1982.
Shiva, Vandana: *Staying Alive: Women, Ecology and Development,* Zed, London, 1989.
Sokoloff, Natalie J.: *Between Money and Love: The Dialectics of Women's Home and Market
    Work,* Praeger, New York, 1980.
Stallard, Karen, Barbara Ehrenreich, and Holly Sklar: *Poverty in the American Dream: Women
    and Children First,* South End, Boston, 1983.
Ward, Kathryn (ed.): *Women Workers and Global Restructuring,* ILR, Ithaca, N.Y., 1990.

FAMILY

Chodorow, Nancy: *The Reproduction of Mothering: Psychoanalysis and the Sociology of Gen-
    der,* University of California Press, Berkeley, Los Angeles, London, 1978.

Dinnerstein, Dorothy: *The Mermaid and the Minotaur: Sexual Arrangements and Human Malaise,* Harper Colophon, New York, 1977.

O'Brien, Mary: *The Politics of Reproduction,* Routledge & Kegan Paul, Boston, London, and Henley, 1981.

Overall, Christine: *Ethics and Human Reproduction: A Feminist Analysis,* Unwin Hyman, Boston, 1987.

Rich, Adrienne: *Of Woman Born: Motherhood as Experience and Institution,* Norton, New York, 1976.

Rubin, Lillian Breslow: *Worlds of Pain: Life in the Working-Class Family,* Basic Books, New York, 1976.

Ruddick, Sara: *Maternal Thinking: Toward a Politics of Peace,* Beacon, Boston, 1989.

Skolnick, Arlene: *Embattled Paradise: The American Family in an Age of Uncertainty,* Basic Books, New York, 1991.

Stack, Carol B.: *All Our Kin: Strategies for Survival in a Black Community,* Harper & Row, New York, 1974.

Strasser, Susan: *Never Done: A History of American Housework,* Pantheon, New York, 1982.

Swerdlow, Amy, Renate Bridenthal, Joan Kelly, and Phyllis Vine: *Household and Kin: Families in Flux,* Feminist Press, Old Westbury, N.Y., 1981

Trebilcot, Joyce (ed.): *Mothering: Essays in Feminist Theory,* Rowman and Allanheld, Totowa, N.J., 1984.

Walker, Scott (ed.): *The New Family,* Graywolf, St. Paul, 1991.

SEXUALITY

Barry, Kathleen: *Female Sexual Slavery,* Prentice-Hall, Englewood Cliffs, N.J., 1979.

Barry, Kathleen, Charlotte Bunch, and Shirley Castley (eds.): *International Feminism: Networkings Against Female Sexual Slavery: Report of the Global Feminist Workshop to Organize Against Traffic in Women, Rotterdam, the Netherlands, April 6–15, 1983,* International Women's Tribune Centre, Inc., New York, 1984.

Bartkey, Sandra Lee: *Femininity and Domination: Studies in the Phenomenology of Oppression,* Routledge, New York and London, 1990.

The Boston Women's Health Book Collective, *Our Bodies, Ourselves,* Simon and Schuster, current edition.

Brownmiller, Susan: *Against Our Will: Men, Women and Rape,* Simon and Schuster, New York, 1975.

Burstyn, Varda (ed.): *Women Against Censorship,* Douglas and MacIntyre, Vancouver and Toronto, 1985.

Gordon, Linda: *Women's Body, Women's Rights: A Social History of Birth Control in America,* Penguin, New York, 1977.

Hite, Shere: *The Hite Report: A Nationwide Survey of Female Sexuality,* Dell, New York, 1976.

Hite, Shere: *The Hite Report on Male Sexuality: How Men Feel About Love, Sex and Relationships,* Knopf, New York, 1981.

Kimmel, Michael: *Men Confront Pornography,* Crown, New York, 1990.

Lederer, Laura: *Take Back the Night: Women on Pornography,* Morrow, New York, 1980.

Leidholdt, Dorchen, and Janice G. Raymond: *The Sexual Liberals and the Attack on Feminism,* Pergamon, New York, 1987.

Snitow, Ann, Christine Stansell, and Sharon Thompson: *Powers of Desire: The Politics of Sexuality,* Monthly Review Press, New York, 1983.

Vance, Carol S.: *Pleasure and Gender: Exploring Female Sexuality,* Routledge & Kegan Paul, Boston, 1984.

Acknowledgments

Abortion Proclamation (of the New York Pro-Choice Coalition at St. Patrick's Cathedral, April 2, 1989): "Abortion—Every Woman's Right." Reprinted by permission. The New York Pro Choice Coalition was first umbrella group of providers and activists in New York, founded in 1985 by Merle Hoffman.

Albelda, Randy. Reprinted by permission from Randy Albelda, "Aborting Choice," *Dollars & Sense,* September 1990, pp. 16–17. *Dollars & Sense* is a progressive monthly economics magazine. First-year subscriptions are available for $14.95 from the office at One Summer Street, Somerville, MA 02143.

Allen, Jeffner. "Motherhood: The Annihilation of Women," from *Mothering: Essays in Feminist Theory,* ed. Joyce Trebilcot (Savage, Md.: Rowman & Littlefield Publisher, Inc., 1984), pp. 315–330. Reprinted by permission of the publisher.

Aptheker, Bettina. Reprinted by permission from *Tapestries of Life: Women's Work, Women's Consciousness, and the Meaning of Daily Experience,* by Bettina Aptheker (Amherst: University of Massachusetts Press, 1989), copyright © 1989 by the University of Massachusetts Press. Passage from *The Tribe of Dina: A Jewish Women's Anthology,* edited by Melanie Kay Kantrowicz and Irene Klepfisz. Copyright © 1986 by Bernice Mennis. Used by permission. Excerpts from Leslie Marmon Silko, *Storyteller* (New York: Seaver Books, 1981), pp. 3–4, used by permission of the author.

Bartky, Sandra Lee. "The Feminine Body," reprinted from Sandra Lee Bartky, "Foucault, Femininity, and the Modernization of Patriarchal Power," from *Feminism and Foucault: Reflections on Resistance,* edited by Irene Diamond and Lee Quinby. Copyright © 1988 by Irene Diamond and Lee Quinby. Reprinted with the permission of Northeastern University Press.

Beck, Melinda, et al. Excerpted from Melinda Beck et al., "Trading Places," *Newsweek,* July 16, 1990, pp. 48–54. © 1990 Newsweek Inc. All rights reserved. Reprinted by permission.

Becker, William H. "Years of Tears: Feminism's Personal Questions—for Men," reprinted by permission from *Bucknell World,* the magazine of Bucknell University, January 1990, p. 36

Blakely, Mary Kay. "Calling All Working Fathers," Ms., December 1986, pp. 33–34. Reprinted with permission, Ms. Magazine, © 1986.

Brewer, Rose M. "Black Women in Poverty: Some Comments on Female-Headed Families," from *Signs: Journal of Women in Culture and Society,* vol. 13, no. 2 (Winter 1988): 331–339. © 1988 by The University of Chicago. All rights reserved. Reprinted by permission.

Bunch, Charlotte. "Lesbians in Revolt," reprinted by permission from *Lesbianism and the Women's Movement,* Diana Press, Oakland, Calif., 1975, pp. 29–37.

Bunch, Charlotte. Reprinted from "Strategies for Organizing Against Female Sexual Slavery," from the book *Passionate Politics: Feminist Theory in Action, Essays 1968–88,* pp. 306–320, with permission from St. Martin's Press, New York, NY. Copyright © 1987 by Charlotte Bunch.

Bunch, Charlotte. Reprinted from "Prospects for Global Feminism," from the book *Passionate Politics: Feminist Theory in Action, Essays 1968–1988* pp. 301–305, with permission from St. Martin's Press, New York, NY. Copyright © 1987 by Charlotte Bunch.

Bunster-Bunalto, Ximena. "Surviving Beyond Fear: Women and Torture in Latin America," reprinted by permission of Greenwood Publishing Group, Westport, CT, from *Women and Change in Latin America,* edited by June Nash and Helena Safa, pp. 297–324. Copyright © 1986 by Bergin & Garvey.

Caulfield, Mina Davis. "Imperialism, the Family and Cultures of Resistance," reprinted by permission from *Socialist Revolution,* 20, vol. 4., no. 2., pp. 67–85.

Charlotte Perkins Gilman Chapter of the New American Movement. Reprinted by permission from "A View of Socialist Feminism," from Charlotte Perkins Gilman Chapter of the New American Movement, *A View of Socialist Feminism.*

Chodorow, Nancy. "Gender Personality and the Sexual Sociology of Adult Life," reprinted by permission from "The Sexual Sociology of Adult Life" in *The Reproduction of Mothering: Psychoanalysis and the Sociology of Gender.* Berkeley, Los Angeles, London: University of California Press, 1978, pp. 173–190. Copyright © 1978 The Regents of the University of California.

Chow, Esther Ngan-Ling. Excerpted from Esther Ngan-Long Chow, "The Feminist Movement: Where Are All the Asian American Women?" from *Making Waves: An Anthology of Writings by and about Asian American Women,* by Asian Women United of California, pp. 362–377. Copyright © 1989 by Asian Women United of California. Reprinted by permission of Beacon Press.

Collins, Patricia Hill. "Toward an Afrocentric Feminist Epistemology," *Black Feminist Thought: Knowledge, Consciousness and the Politics of Empowerment* (Boston: Unwin Hyman, 1990), chap. 10, pp. 201–220. Reprinted by permission of Routledge, Chapman and Hall.

Daniels, Cynthia R. Reprinted by permission from Cynthia R. Daniels, "There's No Place Like Home," from *Dollars & Sense,* December 1986, pp. 16–18, 22. *Dollars & Sense* is a progressive monthly economics magazine. First-year subscriptions are available for $14.95 from the office at One Summer Street, Somerville, MA 02143.

Davis, Angela. "Rape, Racism, and the Myth of the Black Rapist," from *Women, Race and Class,* by Angela Davis. Pp. 172–201. Copyright © 1981 by Angela Davis. Reprinted by permission of Random House, Inc.

Dworkin, Andrea. "Letter from a War Zone," From *Letters from a War Zone* by Andrea Dworkin, pp. 308–322. Copyright © 1988 by Andrea Dworkin. Used by permission of the publisher, Dutton, an imprint of New American Library, a division of Penguin Books USA Inc.

Dziech, Billie Wright, and Linda Weiner. "The Lecherous Professor: A Portrait of the Artist," from *The Lecherous Professor* by Billie Wright Dziech and Linda Weiner. Copyright © 1984 by Billie Wright Dziech and Linda Weiner. Reprinted by permission of Beacon Press.

Eason, Yla. Excerpted by permission from Yla Eason, "When the Boss Wants Sex," *Essence,* March 1981. Copyright Essence Communications, Inc.

Ehrenreich, Barabara. Reprinted by permission of the author from Barbara Ehrenreich, "The Politics of Talking in Couples: Conversus Interruptus and Other Disorders," *Ms.,* May 1981, pp. 46–48.

Ehrenreich, Barbara, and Annette Fuentes. Reprinted by permission from "Life on the Global Assembly Line," from *Ms.,* January 1981, pp. 53–59, 71. Annette Fuentes is co-author with Barbara Ehrenreich of *Women in the Global Factory* (Boston: South End Press, 1984).

Engels, Friedrich. Reprinted by permission from Friedrich Engels, "Origin of the Family, Private Property, and the State," from *Origin of the Family, Private Property, and the State,* International Publishers Company, Inc., New York, 1942, 1970, pp. 87–138, 138–145.

Enloe, Cynthia. Reprinted by permission from Cynthia Enloe, "Bananas, Bases, and Patriarchy," *Radical America,* vol. 19, no. 4, pp. 7–23.

Ferguson, Ann. "A Transitional Feminist Sexual Morality," reprinted by permission of Unwin Hyman, part of HarperCollins Publishers Ltd., from Ann Ferguson, *Blood at the Root* (London: Pandora Press, Unwin Hyman, 1989), pp. 209–218, 265–266.

Firestone, Shulamith. "The Culture of Romance," from *The Dialectic of Sex* (New York: Bantam Books, 1972), pp. 146–155. Reprinted by permission of William Morrow and Company, Inc., Publishers, New York.

Flax, Jane. Reprinted by permission of the author from "Women Do Theory," *Quest,* vol. 5, no. 1 (Summer 1979): 20–26.

Freud, Sigmund. Selection ("Femininity") is reprinted from *New Introductory Lectures on Psychoanalysis* by Sigmund Freud, translated from the German and edited by James Strachey, by permission of W. W. Norton & Company, Inc. Copyright © 1965, 1964 by James Strachey. Copyright 1933 by Sigmund Freud. Copyright renewed 1961 by W. J. H. Sprott.

Frye, Marilyn. "Virgin Women," reprinted by permission of the author and the publisher from "Willful Virgin *or* Do You Have to Be a Lesbian to Be a Feminist?" from *Willful Virgin: Essays in Feminism, 1976–1992,* pp. 124–137, copyright © 1992 by Marilyn Frye; published by the Crossing Press, Freedom, CA 95019.

Frye, Marilyn. Excerpted by permission from Marilyn Frye, "The Possibility of Feminist Theory," from *Theoretical Perspectives on Sex Difference*, ed. Deborah L. Rhode, pp. 174–184, 293. Copyright 1990 by Yale University Press.

Gutis, Philip S. From Philip S. Gutis, "Family Redefines Itself, and Now the Law Follows," *New York Times,* May 28, 1989, sec. 6E. Copyright © 1989 by The New York Times Company. Reprinted by permission.

Hartmann, Betsy. Excerpts from *Reproductive Rights and Wrongs* by Betsy Hartmann. Copyright © 1987 by Betsy Hartmann. Reprinted by permission of HarperCollins Publisher.

Hartmann, Heidi I. Excerpted from Heidi I. Hartmann, "The Unhappy Marriage of Marxism and Feminism: Towards a More Progressive Union," from *Women and Revolution*, edited by Linda Sargent. Boston: South End Press. Copyright © by Heidi I. Hartmann. Reprinted by permission of South End Press and the author. pp. 1–41.

Heise, Lori. Reprinted by permission from Lori Heise, "The Global War Against Women," as excerpted by the *Utne Reader* from *World Watch*, March/April 1989.

Herman, Judith Lewis. "Incestuous Fathers and Their Families," reprinted by permission of the publisher from *Father-Daughter Incest* by Judith Lewis Herman, pp. 67–95. Cambridge, Mass.: Harvard University Press. Copyright © 1981 by the President and Fellows of Harvard College. For permission to photocopy this selection, please contact Harvard University Press.

Hochschild, Arlie Russell. "The Managed Heart" reprinted with permission from Arlie Russell Hochschild, "Smile Wars," *Mother Jones*, December 1983, pp. 35–42. © 1983, Foundation for National Progress.

Hossfeld, Karen J. Reprinted by permission from Karen J. Hossfeld, "'Their Logic Against Them': Contradictions in Sex, Race, and Class in Silicon Valley," from *Women Workers and Global Restructuring*, ed. Kathryn Ward (Ithaca, N.Y.: ILR Press, Cornell University, 1990), pp. 149–178.

Hubbard, Ruth. Reprinted by permission from Ruth Hubbard, "The Political Nature of 'Human Nature,'" from *Theoretical Perspectives on Sex Difference*, ed. Deborah L. Rhode, pp. 63–73, 271–272. Copyright 1990 by Yale University Press.

Keppel, Bo. "The Impact of Sexism, Racism and Classism on HIV Infected Women: An Overview." Copyright © 1991 Bo Keppel. Reprinted by permission of the author, East Stroudsberg University, East Stroudsberg, PA 18301.

King, Deborah. Excerpted from Deborah King, "Multiple Jeopardy: The Context of a Black Feminist Ideology," from *Signs: Journal of Women in Culture and Society*, vol. 14, no. 1 (Autumn 1988): 42–72. © 1988 by the University of Chicago. All rights reserved. Reprinted by permission.

Kostash, Myrna. "Second Thoughts," reprinted by permission from *Women Against Censorship*, ed. Varda Burstyn, pp. 32–39. Copyright 1985 Douglas & McIntyre, Toronto, Ontario, Canada.

Krich, John. "Here Come the Brides," reprinted with permission from *Mother Jones*, February/March 1986, pp. 34–37, 43–46. © 1986, Foundation for National Progress.

Lerner, Gerda. Reprinted by permission from Gerda Lerner, "Reconceptualizing Differences Among Women," from *Journal of Women's History*, vol. 1, no. 3 (Winter 1990): 106–122. Copyright: Gerda Lerner, 1990.

Lester, Julius. Reprinted by permission of the author from "Being a Boy," *Ms.*, June 1973, pp. 112–113.

MacKinnon, Catharine A. "Sex Equality: On Difference and Dominance." Reprinted by permission of the publishers from *Toward a Feminist Theory of the State* by Catharine A. MacKinnon. Cambridge, Mass.: Harvard University Press. Copyright © 1989 by Catharine A. Mac Kinnon. For permission to photocopy this selection, please contact Harvard University Press.

Mainardi, Pat. Reprinted by permission of the author from Pat Mainardi, "The Politics of Housework," in *Sisterhood Is Powerful* (New York: Vintage Books, 1970), pp. 447–454.

McLaughlin, Andrée Nicola. From "Black Women, Identity, and the Quest for Humanhood and Wholeness: Wild Women in the Whirlwind." Copyright © 1990 by Andrée Nicola McLaughlin from *Wild Women in the Whirlwind: Afra-American Culture and the Contemporary Literary Renaissance*, edited by Joanne M. Braxton and Andrée Nicola McLaughlin, pp. 147–180. Copyright © 1989 by Rutgers, The State University. Reprinted by permission of Rutgers University Press.

Mill, John Stuart. Excerpted from John Stuart Mill, "The Subjection of Women," from *Essays on Sex Equality* by John Stuart Mill and Harriet Taylor Mill, edited and with an introductory essay by Alice S. Rossi. Chicago and London: University of Chicago Press, 1970, pp. 125–156. Copyright © 1990 by the University of Chicago. Reprinted by permission.

Mitchell, Juliet. From *Woman's Estate* by Juliet Mitchell. Copyright © 1966, 1970, 1971 by Juliet Mitchell. Reprinted by permission of Pantheon Books, a division of Random House, Inc.

Moraga, Cherríe. "From a Long Line of Vendidas: Chicanas and Feminism," excerpted and reprinted from *Loving in the War Years* by Cherríe Moraga, with permission from the author and from the publisher, South End Press, 116 Saint Botolph Street, Boston, MA 02115.

National Organization for Women, "Bill of Rights." © 1967 National Organization for Women.

Newman, Katherine S. Reprinted with permission of The Free Press, a division of Macmillan, Inc., from "Middle Class Women in Trouble," in *Falling from Grace: The Experience of Downward Mobility in the American Middle Class* by Katherine S. Newman, pp. 202–204, 285–286. Copyright © 1988 by Katherine S. Newman.

Pearce, Diana M. Reprinted with permission from the Institute for Women's Policy Research from "The Feminization of Poverty: Update," from *First Annual Women's Policy Research Conference Proceedings* (Washington, D.C.: Institute for Women's Policy Research, May 19, 1989), pp. 147–152.

Pharr, Suzanne. "Homophobia: A Weapon of Sexism," reprinted by permission of the author from "Homophobia and Sexism," in Pharr, *Homophobia as a Weapon of Sexism* (Inverness, Calif.: Chardon Press, 1988), pp. 8–43. Available from The Women's Project, 2224 S. Main, Little Rock, AR 72206.

Pharr, Suzanne. Reprinted by permission from "Hate Violence Against Women," *Transformation*, vol. 5, no. 1 (January 1990): 1–3. Subscriptions are available from the Women's Project, 2224 S. Main, Little Rock, AR 72206.

Pollitt, Katha. "The Strange Case of Baby M," reprinted by permission from *The Nation*, May 23, 1987, pp. 681–686, 688. Copyright © 1987 The Nation Co., Inc.

Reed, Evelyn. "Women: Caste, Class, or Oppressed Sex?" from *Problems of Women's Liberation* by Evelyn Reed. New York: Pathfinder Press, Inc., 1970, pp. 64–76. Copyright © 1970 by International Socialist Review. Reprinted by permission of Pathfinder Press, Inc.

Rich, Adrienne. "Compulsory Heterosexuality and Lesbian Existence," reprinted by permission from *Signs: Journal of Women in Culture and Society*, vol. 5, no. 4 (1980): 647–650. Copyright © 1980 by Adrienne Rich. The complete text of this essay, with a new foreword, is available from Antelope Press, 1612 St. Paul, Denver, CO 80206

Rollins, Judith. "Deference and Maternalism," from Judith Rollins, *Between Women: Domestics and Their Employers* (Philadelphia: Temple University Press, 1985), pp. 155–203, 248–253. © 1985 by Temple University. Reprinted by permission of Temple University Press.

Rubin, Lillian B. "The Sexual Dilemma," from *Intimate Strangers* by Lillian B. Rubin, pp. 98–119. Copyright © 1983 by Lillian B. Rubin. Reprinted by permission of HarperCollins Publishers.

Shulman, Alix Kates. "A Marriage Contract," from "A Marriage Agreement," *Up from Under*, vol. 1, no. 2 (Fall 1970): 5, 6, 8. © 1970 by Alix Shulman.

Sidel, Ruth. From *On Her Own*, by Ruth Sidel. Copyright © 1990 by Ruth Sidel. Used by permission of Viking Penguin, a division of Penguin Books USA Inc.

Spiller, Katherine. Reprinted by permission of the author from Katherine Spiller, "Corporate Women and the Mommy Track." The article first appeared in *The Feminist Majority Report*, vol. 2, no. 1 (July 1989): 4–5

Steinberg, Jon. "At Debt's Door," *Ms.*, November 1989, pp. 74–79. Reprinted with permission, *Ms.* Magazine, © 1989.

Walker, Alice. "A Letter of the Times, or Should This Sado-masochism Be Saved?" from *You Can't Keep a Good Woman Down*, pp. 118–123. Copyright © 1973 by Alice Walker; reprinted by permission of Harcourt Brace Jovanovich, Inc.

Wilkerson, Margaret B., and Jewell Handy Gresham. "The Racialization of Poverty," from *The Nation*, July 24/31, 1989, pp. 126–132. Copyright © 1989 The Nation Co., Inc.

Wilson, Edward O. "Sex" is reprinted by permission of the publishers from *On Human Nature* by Edward O. Wilson. Cambridge, Mass.: Harvard University Press, chap. 6. Copyright © 1978 by the President and Fellows of Harvard College. For permission to photocopy this selection, please contact Harvard University Press.

Witt, Shirley Hill. Reprinted by permission from Shirley Hill Witt, "Native Women Today: Sexism and the Indian Woman," *Civil Rights Digest*, 1974.

Wittig, Monique. "One Is Not Born a Woman," from a paper delivered at the Second Sex Conference by Monique Wittig, New York Institute for the Humanities, 1979. Reprinted by permission of the author, c/o Sanford J. Greenburger Associates, N.Y.

Women Count—Count Women's Work (Wages for Housework Resolution). Reprinted by permission of the Wages for Housework Campaign.

Index of Authors and Titles